The Path Forward

The Path Forward

Psychological Services in the Community with Justice-Involved Individuals and to Forensic Systems

Edited by

Kirk Heilbrun
David DeMatteo

OXFORD
UNIVERSITY PRESS

OXFORD
UNIVERSITY PRESS

Oxford University Press is a department of the University of Oxford.
It furthers the University's objective of excellence in research, scholarship,
and education by publishing worldwide. Oxford is a registered trade mark of
Oxford University Press in the UK and in certain other countries.

Published in the United States of America by Oxford University Press
198 Madison Avenue, New York, NY 10016, United States of America.

CIP data is on file at the Library of Congress.

ISBN 9780197773000

DOI: 10.1093/9780197773031.001.0001

Printed by Marquis Book Printing, Canada

The manufacturer's authorized representative in the EU for product safety is
Oxford University Press España S.A. of Parque Empresarial San Fernando de Henares,
Avenida de Castilla, 2 – 28830 Madrid (www.oup.es/en or product.safety@oup.com).
OUP España S.A. also acts as importer into Spain of products made by the manufacturer.

MIX
Paper | Supporting responsible forestry
FSC® C103567
FSC www.fsc.org

List of Figures

List of Tables

List of Contributors

Elisha R. Agee PsyD is Assistant Professor, Department of Psychiatry & Neurobehavioral Sciences, University of Virginia, Charlottesville, VA, USA.

Apryl Alexander PsyD is Metrolina Distinguished Professor of Health and Policy, University of North Carolina at Charlotte, Charlotte, NC, USA.

Natalie Anumba PhD is Associate Professor of Psychiatry and Behavioral Sciences, University of Massachusetts Chan Medical School, Worcester, MA, USA.

Shelby Arnold PhD, Staff Psychologist, Center for Recovery-Oriented Cognitive Therapy, Beck Institute, Philadelphia, PA, USA.

Shannon M. Bader PhD, ABPP is Senior Project Associate, Policy Research Associates, Troy, NY, USA.

Carly Lyn Baetz JD, PhD is Associate Professor, Department of Psychology, Purdue University Northwest, Hammond, IN, USA.

Stanley L. Brodsky PhD is Professor Emeritus, The University of Alabama, Tuscaloosa, AL, USA.

Jeffrey Burl PhD is Assistant Professor, Department of Psychiatry, UMass Chan Medical School, Worcester, MA, USA.

Emma Cenzon MA, LMHCA is a Psychology Graduate Assistant, Purdue University Northwest, IN, USA.

Avery J. Chard MS is a Clinical Psychology Ph.D. Student, Drexel University, Philadelphia, PA, USA.

Dewey Cornell PhD is Virgil Ward Professor of Education, University of Virginia, Charlottesville, VA, USA.

Savannah Cuellar is Research Assistant, Montclair State University, NJ, USA.

Holley E.N. Davis is Communications Director, Administration, Policy Research Associates, Troy, NY, USA.

David DeMatteo JD, PhD is Professor of Psychology in the Department of Psychological and Brain Sciences and Professor of Law at the Thomas R. Kline School of Law, Drexel University, Philadelphia, USA.

Sarah L. Desmarais PhD is President & CEO, Policy Research Associates, Inc., Troy, NY, USA.

Joel Dvoskin PhD, ABPP is Clinical Assistant Professor of Psychiatry, University of Arizona College of Medicine, Tucson, AZ, USA.

Hailey Fasone MA, Psychology Graduate Student, Department of Psychological and Brain Sciences, Drexel University, Philadelphia, PA, USA.

Christy L. Giallella PhD is Owner, Christy Giallella, LLC, NJ, USA.

Naomi Sevin Goldstein PhD, Professor, Department of Psychological and Brain Sciences, Drexel University, Philadelphia, PA, USA.

Jay Gonzales, M.S., Esq., Philadelphia District Attorney's Office

Paul Grant PhD, Director of Research, Innovation, and Practice, Center for Recovery-Oriented Cognitive Therapy, Beck Institute, Philadelphia, PA, USA.

Patricia Griffin PhD, Wyndmoor, PA, USA.

Simone P. Grisamore MS is a Clinical Psychology PhD Student, Drexel University, Philadelphia, PA, USA.

Thomas Grisso PhD is Emeritus Professor, Department of Psychiatry and Behavioral Sciences, University of Massachusetts Chan Medical School, Worcester, MA, USA.

Stephen D. Hart PhD is Professor of Psychology, Simon Fraser University, Canada, and Director and Threat Assessment Specialist, Protect International, Vancouver, Canada.

Kirk Heilbrun PhD is Professor, Department of Psychological and Brain Sciences, Drexel University, Philadelphia, USA.

Elan C. Hope PhD is Vice President, Research & Evaluation, Policy Research Associates, Inc., Troy, NY, USA.

Tierney Huppert MS is Clinical Psychology Ph.D. Student in the Department of Psychology, Montclair State University, Montclair, NJ, USA.

Chelsea Jackson MS, JD, JD/PhD student, Department of Psychological and Brain Sciences, Drexel University, Philadelphia, PA, USA.

Haleh Kanani MS is a JD/PhD Student, Department of Psychological and Brain Sciences, Drexel University, Philadelphia, PA, USA.

Sharon Kelley, J.D., PhD., Institute of Law, Psychiatry, and Public Policy, University of Virginia, and Assistant Professor of Psychiatry and Neurobehavioral Sciences, University of Virginia School of Medicine, Charlottesville, VA, USA.

Kathleen Kemp PhD is Associate Professor, Department of Psychiatry and Human Behavior, Brown University Warren Alpert Medical School, Providence, RI, USA.

Jordan Kerere MEd is a PhD Candidate, Clinical & School Psychology, University of Virginia, Charlottesville, VA, USA.

Christopher M. King JD, PhD is Associate Professor of Psychology, Psychology Department, Montclair State University, Montclair, NJ, USA.

Rena Kreimer MSW is Director of Training & Technical Assistance, Juvenile Justice Research & Reform Lab, Drexel University, Philadelphia, PA, USA.

Darryl Kroner PhD, Professor, Department of Criminology and Criminal Justice, Southern Illinois University, Carbondale, IL, USA.

Ivan Kruh PhD is Partner, National Youth Screening & Assessment Partners, MA, USA.

Douglas B. Marlowe JD, PhD is Senior Scientific Consultant, All Rise, the National Association of Drug Court Professionals, and Senior Scientific Consultant, All Rise, the National Association of Drug Court Professionals, Chadds Ford, PA, USA.

Jeanne McPhee PhD is Assistant Professor, Department of Psychiatry and Behavioral Sciences, University of California San Francisco, San Francisco, CA, USA.

Robert Morgan PhD, Dean of the College of Health and Human Services and Professor, Southern Illinois University Carbondale, IL, USA.

Ashley Murray PhD is Assistant Professor, Department of Psychiatry and Behavioral Sciences, University of Massachusetts Chan Medical School, MA, USA.

Daniel C. Murrie PhD is Director of the Institute of Law, Psychiatry, and Public Policy, University of Virginia, and Professor of Psychiatry and Neurobehavioral Sciences, University of Virginia School of Medicine, Charlottesville, VA, USA.

Amanda NeMoyer JD, PhD is Assistant Research Professor, Department of Psychological and Brain Sciences, Drexel University, Philadelphia, PA, USA.

Ilsa Papunen BA is Research Coordinator, Department of Psychological and Brain Sciences, Drexel University, Philadelphia, PA, USA.

Lindsey Pinto LSW, Licensed Social Worker, Center for Recovery-Oriented Cognitive Therapy, Beck Institute, Philadelphia, PA, USA.

Heidi Putney PhD is Assistant Professor of Psychiatry, Training Director of Comprehensive Psychology Training Program, University of Massachusetts Chan Medical School, Worcester, MA, USA.

Mina Ratkalkar PhD, LCSW, Durham, NC, USA.

Karen Collins Rice MS is Co-Founder, Heroes Active Bystandership Training, WA, USA.

Emma Roberts is a Psychology Graduate Assistant in the Department of Psychology, Purdue University Northwest, Hammond, IN, USA.

Barry Rosenfeld PhD is Professor of Psychology, Fordham University, New York, NY, USA.

Kayla Thompson Graduate Research Assistant, Department of Psychology, Purdue University Northwest, Hammond, IN, USA.

Robin Timme PsyD, ABPP (Forensic), CCHP-A is Principal, Falcon Correctional and Community Services, Inc., Chicago, IL, USA.

Abigail Tucker PhD, Chief Strategy Officer, Polara Health, Prescott, AZ, USA.

Gina Vincent PhD is President, National Youth Screening and Assessment Partners, Worcester, MA, USA.

Sana Vora MA is a Doctoral Student, Psychology, Montclair State University, Montclair, NJ, USA.

Tracy Moran Vozar PhD, Director of Perinatal Depression Program, Endeavor Health, Washington, DC, USA.

Kellie Wiltsie PhD, JD is a staff psychologist, Department of Corrections, WI, USA.

Heidi Zapotocky PhD, Staff Psychologist, Ancora Psychiatric Hospital, Ancora, NJ, USA.

Amanda Zelechoski JD, PhD is Clinical Professor of Psychology, Notre Dame University, Notre Dame, IN, USA.

1

Introduction

Kirk Heilbrun and David DeMatteo

Psychologists provide a number of services to individuals in the juvenile and criminal justice systems, and to the larger forensic systems of which they are a part. This book will attempt to capture some of these services that are among the most distinctive, needed, and relevant. We have divided these into four domains: (1) forensic mental health assessment; (2) interventions; (3) consultation and program development; and (4) education. In this introductory chapter, we describe these domains in more detail, explain our choice of topics, and provide the questions that each of the chapter contributors addressed regarding their respective services. In the book's final chapter, we analyze, discuss, and integrate the services that have been described by the various contributors.

This book is not intended to be comprehensive. Rather, it illustrates how some particularly promising or valuable services can be provided in a specialized and expert fashion. We seek to be creative and forward thinking, identifying projects and providers that demonstrate the best of what our field offers, or services with the most potential for growth and future utility. We spend less time on areas that have received a great deal of attention and are most "established." For example, this book will provide some useful information regarding psychological evaluations for the courts, although a great deal has been written on that topic (see, e.g., Melton et al., 2018). It will also encompass work in the areas of intervention, consultation, program development, and education—areas that have received less attention as part of psychological services with justice-involved individuals in the community. These chapters may be useful for students, advanced trainees, practitioners, clinical administrators, and policymakers, and may also be of interest to researchers by illustrating specialized practice with a distinctive focus or in emerging areas.

We considered how best to convey our focus through the book's title. When services are delivered directly to individuals involved with the criminal or juvenile justice system, does the service "to justice-involved individuals" best capture it? Perhaps not; it has long been recognized that such services may have multiple clients (APA, 1978; Monahan, 1980), so "services to" could be misleading. Services "for" such individuals might work better. But that implies a certain detachment and a primary focus on relevant third parties such as courts, attorneys, and probation/parole departments that no longer seems fully justified based on our professional ethics (APA, 2013, 2017), or by the increasing focus on a partnership in services to justice-involved individuals.

Kirk Heilbrun and David DeMatteo, *Introduction.* In: *The Path Forward.* Edited by: Kirk Heilbrun and David DeMatteo, Oxford University Press. © Oxford University Press (2026). DOI: 10.1093/9780197773031.003.0001

For two reasons, we decided that "services with" best captures what we are trying to convey. The first acknowledges that respect for human rights and dignity is now seen as more consistent with a partnership in service delivery between psychologist and client—applying even when the services delivered are required or strongly encouraged (see, e.g., Dennis & Monahan, 1996, regarding mandated community treatment) as part of a criminal or juvenile justice disposition. The second reason is that while the justice-involved individual is an important ultimate client, we also include professional activities such as consultation, program development, and education. "Services with" acknowledges that these activities mediate between client need and ultimate service delivery.

Not all the services described in this book are with individuals, however. Some are primarily delivered to the various systems and subsystems associated with the overlap of criminal/juvenile justice and mental health. Providing systems mapping so that such systems can function more effectively at the intersection is one example. Helping to modify an approach to juvenile probation involving graduated sanctions is another. Each example is discussed in detail in one of the chapters that follow. Since there is a mixture of projects with individual- and system-level orientations, we decided to have that reflected in our title. "The Path Forward" conveys our hope that much of the conceptualization and operationalization associated with this exceptional work will be continued and expanded.

Relevant Context

The projects and services described in these chapters are not specific to psychology, nor unique to any specialty area within psychology. They do contain elements of *forensic psychology, correctional psychology, and police psychology,* so it is helpful to provide a working definition of each. The *Specialty Guidelines for Forensic Psychology* indicates that forensic psychology is the professional practice of psychology within any subdisciplines that applies scientific, technical, or specialized knowledge of psychology to law to assist in addressing legal, contractual, and administrative matters (APA, 2013). Correctional psychology may be defined as a subfield of psychology in which psychological science or scientifically oriented professional practice is applied to the justice system to inform the classification, treatment, and management of offenders to reduce risk and improve public safety (Neal, 2018). Police and public safety psychology involves assisting law enforcement and other public safety personnel and agencies, using assessment, clinical intervention, operational support, and organizational consultation, in carrying out their missions (APA, 2023).

Individuals may be justice involved in the community following arrest and before conviction, or following criminal conviction and sentencing (most often on probation, or under community supervision following release from incarceration). They are among those encountered by police and other public safety personnel.

Traditional professional boundaries would apply forensic psychology to legal decisions made prior to conviction, correctional psychology to post-conviction classification and rehabilitation, and police and public safety psychology to officer selection and promotion of effective performance.

Inevitably, however, these specialty areas overlap. The various projects described in the following chapters would not consistently be considered entirely forensic or correctional in nature. Problem-solving courts offer a good example. Such courts function as an alternative to the traditional process of prosecution, conviction, sentencing, and incarceration (DeMatteo et al., 2019). Depending on whether the selection of participants was pre-adjudication, used selection criteria such as reoffending risk and treatment amenability, and was subject to judicial approval, one could readily see components of both correctional and forensic specialties. A second example of overlap might involve any legal question addressing the resentencing of an incarcerated individual. Those who received mandatory life sentences following convictions for offenses committed when they were younger than eighteen were entitled, under two U.S. Supreme Court decisions (*Miller v. Alabama*, 2012; *Montgomery v. Louisiana*, 2016) to be considered for a new sentence. When such a sentence might result in releasing that individual from incarceration in the near future, there are components of both forensic psychology (informing the court regarding sentencing considerations such as reoffense risk and reentry needs) and correctional psychology (rehabilitation planning addressing relevant unmet needs and release planning for community transitioning).

We observe three influences in the decades since 1990[1] that appear to have moved psychological services with justice-involved individuals in the community in a more rehabilitative direction: therapeutic jurisprudence, risk assessment, and the Sequential Intercept Model. Therapeutic jurisprudence was first proposed in 1987 as a legal theory by David Wexler and Bruce Winick. It considered the properties of law, policy, and decisions and the extent to which such decisions are associated with human dignity and personal well-being. It has expanded from its early emphasis on criminal, mental health, and mental disability law to become considerably broader—but much of its influence was (and remains) on how the legal process could be more rehabilitative (Yamada, 2021).

The question of an individual's likelihood of future antisocial conduct of different kinds is relevant to a variety of pretrial and presentencing matters (e.g., juvenile transfer, capital sentencing, bail). It is also important in correctional classification, the process of rehabilitation planning, and as a measure of intervention effectiveness. The evolution from a primary emphasis in risk assessment on the *prediction* of such

[1] This date coincides with the unexpected and tragic death of Saleem Shah in 1991. His work at NIMH, leading the Center for Studies of Crime and Delinquency, was responsible for substantially enhancing the scientific support of the practice of both forensic psychology and correctional psychology. It seems likely that much of the movement toward relevant and empirically supported interventions with justice-involved individuals in the community would have occurred sooner if he had not died more than three decades ago.

conduct (Monahan, 1981) to both the *appraisal* and *reduction* of such risk (Andrews et al., 1990) provided a stronger justification for planning, delivering, and evaluating the effectiveness of interventions to reduce risk.

The Sequential Intercept Model (Munetz & Griffin, 2006) offers a basis for decriminalizing the legal response to the conduct of individuals with severe mental illness. It also provides a means of shaping and integrating policy across behavioral health and criminal justice systems through the use of cross-system mapping (Griffin et al., 2015), an approach to coordinated planning that promotes informed decision-making and facilitates effective communication.

Description of the Book

We sought the contributors of each of the chapters in this book in several ways. Through our familiarity with psychology in the criminal and juvenile justice systems—a specialty area for both of us—and in consideration of the context discussed in the previous section, we chose the domains of assessment, intervention, consultation, and education. Within each domain, we identified contributors based on reputation, publications, prominence in the field, and provision of important services relevant to justice-involved individuals.

Structure

Four domains were identified. In this section, we describe each in more detail.

Assessment

This section focuses on a longstanding contribution by psychology to the juvenile and criminal justice systems: providing psychological evaluations for courts and attorneys. This has been termed "forensic mental health assessment" (FMHA; see Heilbrun, 2001) and can be distinguished from other forms of psychological assessment that are designed to identify treatment targets and assist in planning for behavioral health interventions. One way to consider the nature and range of such evaluations is through identifying the legal question each is intended to inform. Examples include criminal questions such as *Miranda* waiver capacity (Goldstein & Goldstein, 2010), competence to stand trial (Zapf & Roesch, 2008), criminal responsibility (Packer, 2009), sentencing (Melton et al., 2018), and capital sentencing (Cunningham, 2010).[2] FMHA also includes questions pertaining to juveniles, such

[2] There are also a number of civil law questions that are informed by FMHA. These include guardianship (Drogin & Barrett, 2010), child custody (Fuhrmann & Zibbell, 2012; Gould & Mulchay, 2023), civil commitment (Pinals & Mossman, 2011), workplace discrimination and harassment (Goodman-Delahunty

as competence to stand trial (Kruh, 2008), adjudication and transfer (Heilbrun et al., 2017), and sentencing in criminal court (Kavanaugh & Grisso, 2020). In addition to such FMHA, there are related evaluations conducted at the request of public and private organizations, such as police selection and fitness for duty (Corey & Zelig, 2020) and workplace disability (Piechowski, 2011, 2023) or threat assessment (Cornell, 2018).

There has been a great deal of theoretical, empirical, and applied attention to this area over the last four decades. Our view is that FMHA and these related evaluations have developed into a specialty area that is well supported by the foundational research, appropriately recognized by the law, and professionally guided by standards such as the *Ethical Principles of Psychologists and Code of Conduct (EPPCC*; APA, 2017) and the *Specialty Guidelines for Forensic Psychology* (APA, 2013). But there are particular developments and contexts that add substantially to the maturation of the field in these areas. One involves the incorporation of social justice and cultural competence into the nature of the assessment, which is particularly important since many of those evaluated in the criminal and juvenile justice systems are of minority racial and ethnic status. This is addressed in one chapter in this section focusing on the use of racial identity as a means of better informing FMHA (Ratkalkar, this volume). Another involves the role of trauma, and its impact on FMHA (Zelechoski, this volume). Another kind of evaluation—threat assessment for school violence (Cornell, this volume)—reflects areas of significant progress that are quite important and should be continued, and are also included in this section. Finally, there are different contexts from which psychologists may conduct this kind of assessment. One of the more promising for the provision of both service and training involves the university-based clinic (Conroy, 2021; Heilbrun et al., 2017). Such a clinic, based at the University of Virginia, is described in another chapter in this section (Murrie, this volume).

Intervention

One of the important developments in forensic psychology within the last two decades involves increasing attention to questions involving rehabilitation. This has been influenced by the development of community-based mechanisms such as problem-solving courts (DeMatteo et al., 2019), with developments in risk assessment (Monahan & Steadman, 1994) and its subsequent attention to reducing risk (Douglas & Otto, 2020) providing the opportunity for greater collaboration between the areas of forensic, correctional, and clinical psychology.

One excellent example of a crime risk-reducing program with justice-involved individuals in the community is *Changing Lives and Changing Outcomes* (Morgan et al., 2018). This program was designed to reduce the risk of future

& Foote, 2011), and psychological damages (Kane & Dvoskin, 2011). These are not discussed further, however, because the focus of this book is on criminal and juvenile proceedings.

offending by participants, allowing the psychologist to use an approach such as Risk-Need-Responsivity (Bonta & Andrews, 2017) to identify intervention targets, duration, and individualized learning style. (Morgan and Kroner discuss program development in community corrections in the next section of this book.)

Several promising interventions are described in the chapters in this section. The application of Cognitive Therapy—Rehabilitation (CT-R; Beck et al., 2020), an adaptation of Beck's original cognitive therapy modified for delivery to individuals with serious mental illness, and for others involved in the criminal justice system, is discussed by Arnold, Grant, and Pinto (this volume). Modifications of cognitive behavioral therapy and dialectical behavior therapy, as applied to justice-involved individuals in the community, are discussed by Heilbrun and colleagues (this volume) and by Rosenfeld and King (this volume), respectively. The treatment of trauma in girls is the subject of a chapter by Alexander (this volume).

Consultation and Program Development

Psychologists are useful in a third area with justice-involved individuals in the community: consultation and program development. In this section, the chapters describe six such important contributions. Morgan and Kroner address the process of program development for interventions with adults on probation, using their own work (Morgan et al., 2018) in the development of *Changing Lives and Changing Outcomes*. The process of providing consultation to other professionals and organizations engaged in work with justice-involved individuals is discussed by Dvoskin, who is recognized widely for the usefulness of his consultation. System mapping using the Sequential Intercept Model (Munetz & Griffin, 2006) is addressed by the co-developer of this model (Griffin) and two of her colleagues who are experienced in conducting system mappings (Kemp and Giallella). Such mappings allow jurisdictions and organizations to identify overarching needs in serving justice-involved individuals, and integrate the contributions of legal and behavioral health systems in providing these services in a more effective and informed fashion (Griffin et al., 2015). Consultation with police departments using a recently developed model, Active Bystandership for Law Enforcement (ABLE) provides an alternative to the social pressure on serving police officers to avoid reporting misconduct by fellow officers—by giving them both skills and support for doing so in a constructive fashion. This is addressed in a chapter in this section (Tucker & Collins, this volume) as well. The remaining two chapters focus on consultation in the development of problem-solving courts (an important innovation in diversion and community corrections; Marlowe, this volume) and on the use of a graduated approach to using sanctions with justice-involved youth on probation (Goldstein et al., this volume).

Education

The fourth section provides descriptions of various innovative aspects of education/training for those who work with justice-involved individuals. To some extent, this means doctoral-level training in applied psychology with a forensic or correctional "major area of emphasis." We recognize that other disciplines (e.g., psychiatry, social work) also provide important contributions to this work; we focus on psychology training to be consistent with the larger theme of this book. Nor would an individual necessarily need a doctoral degree with a clinical internship to do this work—but we anticipate that doctoral-level psychologists will continue to provide a significant part of the leadership and supervision of community-based services with justice-involved individuals.

Accordingly, this section begins with a chapter describing doctoral training in forensic and correctional psychology in the United States. This chapter (DeMatteo et al., this volume) does not include predoctoral internship training (required as part of doctoral programs in clinical and counseling psychology), nor does it address post-doctoral training in this area. These are discussed in the second chapter (Anumba et al., this volume).

The remaining chapters are devoted to the training of various groups in areas that are important to community-based services to justice-involved individuals. Continuing education and consultation related to broader policy are discussed by Sarah Desmarais, the president of Policy Research Associates. Working with correctional staff on the topic of trauma-informed interactions, the topic of another chapter, is particularly important in light of the growing evidence of high rates of trauma and adversity experienced by those involved with the criminal and juvenile justice systems (see Timme, this volume). The effective delivery of expert witness services will probably remain a high priority for many forensic psychologists; in his chapter, Stan Brodsky describes the evolution and status of his program of research and training in expert witness testimony. Finally, the provision of risk assessment and risk management services has been through several iterations during the last three decades. One example of its current status and the training and delivery of such services by individuals of different disciplines is discussed by Steve Hart (this volume) in describing Protect International.

Chapter Content

These chapters have been designed to describe particular topics *and* certain approaches to addressing these topics. The provider of the particular service varies across different contexts. These include public organizations, private companies, universities, and individual or group practices. We have invited individuals who offer varied contributions, some of which are foundational (e.g., predoctoral training) and others highly specialized (e.g., ABLE training); some of which are established (e.g., risk assessment) and others newer (e.g., CT-R-based interventions for justice-involved individuals); some of which serve individual clients (e.g., treating trauma in justice-involved girls) while others focus on systems (e.g., SIM mapping). Their commonality pertains to the relevance and importance of their contributions, and their place among the contributions of forensic, correctional, and police psychology in the future.

Chapter Sections

Chapter contributors have been asked to discuss their respective topics in seven areas. These are as follows: project description; foundations and support for project services; the beginning and subsequent development of these services; the generalizability of their work (could others provide it?); considerations of diversity, equity, and inclusiveness; their advice to others seeking to do similar work; and any other relevant and meaningful conclusions.

Project Description

Each chapter begins with a fairly detailed description of the nature of the project and the services provided. (Some of these descriptions will refer to a specific, discrete project while others, such as "predoctoral training," may encompass multiple organizations and services.) This description includes the following areas:

- Nature of services
- Clients
- Providers
- Size and scope
- Time spent
- How prospective clients become aware of these services
- Role of training (if any)
  - For junior colleagues joining the project
  - For trainees still involved in predoctoral, internship, or postdoctoral training
- Keys to effective service provision.

Foundations of and Support for Project Services

Some of these projects have been developed in recent years and feature important innovations. All of them, however, rely on some combination of theory and scientific evidence that is so important in the delivery of services in psychology. What is the nature of such support? To what extent have accepted theory and peer-reviewed scientific evidence been incorporated into the design and implementation of the services described in the previous section? This may be akin to the field's efforts to operationalize "best practice," but we deliberately avoid using that term because some of these projects are too recent to have developed the very substantial research base needed to support a "best practice" designation. Nonetheless, the information requested in this section is similar to what would ultimately be applied to considering such a designation.

Beginning and Development of Project Services

This section is relevant to the specific projects, some of which might be replicated by others in the field. But it also provides important information for those who might implement their own projects in other areas, as it offers examples of how such projects begin and grow. Chapter contributors are asked to reflect on how the original idea was conceived, and subsequently implemented through modification and planning. How long did it take until the project was fully operational? (This is different from the question of whether it has grown as much as it might, or will. It refers to when the project moved from a beginning or pilot stage to a more established status.) A related question involves the resources needed to develop the project in this way. In the earlier project description, the contributor provides an account of the size and scope of the project once it has been established. Here, the focus involves the time and resources needed to get it started.

Generalizability

These projects were selected because we consider them to be important, and anticipate that their services will be expanded in the coming years. The views of the respective contributors are particularly important on this point, as they have a detailed awareness of this aspect of psychological services in the community to justice-involved individuals. Accordingly, they are asked for their view on whether the field needs others doing similar work. Since public funding is variable, insurance is often not available, and many justice-involved clients do not have the financial means to pay for such services, how should they be funded? Contributors provide their perspective on whether providers should expect to offer substantially reduced or *pro bono* rates.

Some of these projects rely on the distinctive skills of those providing the services. Such distinctive skills may be essential for success. But can they be identified and taught? Are some services being delivered by individuals using skills that are very hard to replicate, even with appropriate training, supervision, and modeling? The answer to this question is important, as the generalizability of a specific project may be limited if its successful implementation depends too much on the presence of very unusual skills that are also hard to teach.

Diversity, Equity, and Inclusiveness

The importance of Diversity, Equity, and Inclusiveness (DEI) in identifying and planning services for justice-involved individuals in the community is clear (APA, 2013, 2017), particularly given the disproportionate representation of BIPOC individuals in the juvenile and criminal justice systems. The meaningful incorporation of DEI into these services can be complex and nuanced, however. Contributors are asked to identify how their projects have incorporated DEI into planning, implementation, and operation. Has the urgency of this priority increased during the last decade, as reflected in their particular project? Some services are designed to avoid barriers to access by BIPOC individuals—but others may not be, and such barriers may be significant. Finally, contributors are asked to identify important priorities in this area to be addressed during the coming decade.

Advice to Other Service Providers

If these chapters do offer examples of projects and services that can be usefully replicated, then advice from those actually involved might be very useful. Contributors are asked how they gauged the market, considering the need for services and how they might obtain referrals. In addition, there is the question regarding the duration of start-up: gradual or more quickly? Some projects might deliver services as part of a larger practice or clinic. Others might be better described as a niche contribution offered on an as-needed basis (particularly when the service is educational or consultative). The process of making this service availability known to those who might request it could depend on the balancing of website availability and social media involvement with more traditional professional involvement (conferences, presentations, publications, professional organizations). There may be particularly effective steps to be taken, just as there may be others to be avoided. Contributors are asked for their best advice based on the success they have experienced in building a reputation that yields referrals and other requests for services.

Conclusions

Finally, contributors have the opportunity to discuss any other aspects of this work that were not elicited by the questions described in this section. They draw upon their experience with the project, their answers to these questions, and their vision about the future of this work to reach conclusions about what has worked for them—and how it might work for others in the field.

References

American Psychological Association (APA) Task Force on the Role of Psychology in the Criminal Justice System. (1978). Report of the task force on the role of psychology in the criminal justice system. *American Psychologist, 33*, 1099–1113. http://dx.doi.org/10.1037/0003-066X.33.12.1099

American Psychological Association (APA). (2013). Specialty guidelines for forensic psychology. *American Psychologist, 68*(1), 7–19. http://dx.doi.org/10.1037/a0029889

American Psychological Association (APA) (2017). *Ethical principles of psychologists and code of conduct.* Retrieved July 25, 2023 from https://www.apa.org/ethics/code

American Psychological Association (APA) (2023). *Specialties and subspecialties: Police and public safety psychology.* Retrieved July 24, 2023 from https://www.apa.org/ed/graduate/specialize/police

Andrews, D. A., Bonta, J., & Hoge, R. D. (1990). Classification for effective rehabilitation: Rediscovering psychology. *Criminal Justice and Behavior, 17*(1), 19–52. http://dx.doi.org/10.1177/0093854890017001004

Andrews, D. A., Zinger, I., Hoge, R. D., Bonta, J., Gendreau, P., & Cullen, F. T. (1990). Does correctional treatment work? A clinically relevant and psychologically informed meta-analysis. *Criminology, 28*(3), 369–404. http://dx.doi.org/10.1111/j.1745-9125.1990.tb01330.x

Beck, A., Grant, P., Inverso, E., Brinen, A., & Perivoliotis, D. (2020). *Recovery-oriented cognitive therapy for serious mental health conditions.* Guilford.

Bonta, J., & Andrews, D. (2017). *The psychology of criminal conduct* (6th ed.). Routledge.

Conroy, M. A. (2021). Establishing a forensic training clinic. In K. Heilbrun, H. J. Wright II, C. Giallella, & D. DeMatteo (Eds.), *University and public behavioral health organization collaboration: Models for success in justice contexts* (pp. 45–65). Oxford University Press. https://doi.org/10.1093/med-psych/9780190052850.003.0004

Corey, D., & Zelig, M. (2020). *Evaluations of police suitability and fitness for duty.* Oxford.

Cornell, D. (2018). *Comprehensive School Threat Assessment Guidelines.* School Threat Assessment Consultants LLC.

Cunningham, M. (2010). *Evaluation for capital sentencing.* Oxford.

DeMatteo, D., Heilbrun, K., Thornewill, A., & Arnold, S. (2019). *Problem-solving courts and the criminal justice system.* Oxford.

Dennis, D., & Monahan, J. *Coercion and aggressive community treatment: A new frontier in mental health law.* Plenum.

Douglas, K. S., & Otto, R. K. (Eds.). (2020). *Handbook of violence risk assessment* (2nd ed.). Routledge. https://doi.org/10.4324/9781315518374

Drogin, E. Y., & Barrett, C. L. (2010). *Evaluation for guardianship.* Oxford.

Fuhrmann, G. S. W., & Zibbell, R. A. (2012). *Evaluation for child custody.* Oxford.

Goldstein, A., & Sevin Goldstein, N. (2010). *Evaluating capacity to waive Miranda rights.* Oxford.

Goodman-Delahunty, J., & Foote, W. E. (2011). *Evaluation for workplace discrimination and harassment.* Oxford.

Gould, J. W., & Mulchay, C. (2023). Child custody evaluations. In D. DeMatteo & K. C. Scherr (Eds.), *The Oxford handbook of psychology and law* (pp. 237–257). Oxford.

Griffin, P., Heilbrun, K., Mulvey, E., DeMatteo, D., & Schubert, C. (Eds.) (2015). *Criminal justice and the Sequential Intercept Model: Promoting community alternatives for people with severe mental illness.* Oxford.

Heilbrun, K., DeMatteo, D., King, C., & Filone, S. (2017). *Evaluating juvenile transfer and disposition: Law, science, and practice.* Taylor & Francis.

Heilbrun, K. (2001). *Principles of forensic mental health assessment.* Kluwer Academic/Plenum Press.

Kane, A. W., & Dvoskin, J. A. (2011). *Evaluation for personal injury claims.* Oxford.

Kavanaugh, A., & Grisso, T. (2020). *Evaluations for sentencing of juveniles in criminal court.* Oxford.

Kruh, I. (2008). *Evaluation of juveniles' competence to stand trial.* Oxford.

Melton, G., Petrila, J., Poythress, N., Slobogin, C., Otto, R., Mossman, D., & Oberlander, L. (2018). *Psychological evaluations for the courts: A handbook for mental health professionals and lawyers* (4th ed.). Guilford.

Miller v. Alabama, 132 S.Ct. 2455 (2012).

Montgomery v. Louisiana, 136 S.Ct. 718 (2016).

Monahan, J. E. (Ed.) (1980). *Who is the client? The ethics of psychological intervention in the criminal justice system.* American Psychological Association. http://dx.doi.org/10.1037/10051-000

Monahan, J. (1981). *The clinical prediction of violent behavior.* National Institute of Mental Health. U.S. Government Printing Office.

Monahan, J., & Steadman, H. J. (Eds.). (1994). *Violence and mental disorder: Developments in risk assessment.* The University of Chicago Press.

Morgan, R., Kroner, D., & Mills, J. (2018). *A treatment manual for justice involved persons with mental illness: Changing Lives and Changing Outcomes.* Routledge.

Munetz, M., & Griffin, P. (2006). Use of the Sequential Intercept Model as an approach to decriminalization of people with serious mental illness. *Psychiatric Services, 57*(4), 544–549.

Neal, T. (2018). Forensic psychology and correctional psychology: Distinct but related subfields of psychological science and practice. *American Psychologist, 73*(5), 651–662. http://dx.doi.org/10.1037/amp0000227

Packer, I. (2009). *Evaluation of criminal responsibility.* Oxford.

Piechowski, L. D. (2011). *Evaluation of workplace disability.* Oxford.

Piechowski, L. D. (2023). Evaluating workplace disability. In D. DeMatteo & K. C. Scherr (Eds.), *The Oxford handbook of psychology and law* (pp. 223–236). Oxford.

Pinals, D. A., & Mossman, D. (2011). *Evaluation for civil commitment.* Oxford.

Yamada, D. (2021). Therapeutic jurisprudence: Foundations, expansion, and assessment. *University of Miami Law Review, 75*(3), 660–750. https://repository.law.miami.edu/umlr/vol75/iss3/3

Zapf, P., & Roesch, R. (2008). *Evaluation of competence to stand trial.* Oxford.

2

University Clinic-Based Forensic Mental Health Assessment

Daniel C. Murrie, Elisha Agee, and Sharon Kelley

We describe a university-based clinic that trains forensic evaluators, and provides high-quality forensic assessments locally, regionally, and nationally. The University of Virginia (UVA) Forensic Clinic is based within the Institute of Law, Psychiatry, and Public Policy (ILPPP), a multi-disciplinary academic institute situated in the UVA School of Medicine and affiliated with the UVA School of Law (see Bonnie et al., 2021). The clinic began roughly fifty years ago as a small pilot project at the start of a national shift toward performing forensic mental health assessments in the community, rather than in state psychiatric hospitals (Melton et al., 1985, 2018). We describe the historical and professional foundations of the clinic, and forensic mental health assessments generally. We discuss the recent growth of this clinic, and ways this model may be adapted at other universities. Finally, we offer concrete suggestions for others interested in providing similar services, along with a frank discussion of strengths and weaknesses of our model.

Although the UVA Forensic Clinic is now a large clinic that employs many mental health professionals, as well as staff and trainees, it began as a much smaller service with a very narrow training mission. Because its context and history have been so influential in shaping the clinic, we begin by explaining these origins.

Clinic Origins

The UVA Forensic Clinic was an afterthought to the broader Institute of Law, Psychiatry, and Public Policy (ILPPP). As detailed elsewhere (Bonnie et al., 2021), the ILPPP began in the 1970s, just as mental health law was emerging as a distinct field of legal and scientific study. Three key judicial decisions in 1972 (*Jackson v. Indiana; Lessard v. Schmidt; Wyatt v. Stickney*) addressed the rights of psychiatric patients in various ways, making that year a convenient marker as the starting point for the field of mental health law generally and for the ILPPP specifically. In the first decade of collaboration between the ILPPP and the Commonwealth of Virginia, psychiatrist P. Browning Hoffman and legal scholar Richard Bonnie addressed the challenges these

Daniel C. Murrie, Elisha Agee, and Sharon Kelley, *University Clinic-Based Forensic Mental Health Assessment*. In: *The Path Forward*. Edited by: Kirk Heilbrun and David DeMatteo, Oxford University Press. © Oxford University Press (2026).
DOI: 10.1093/9780197773031.003.0002

landmark decisions raised, such as legal reform of the civil commitment system, protecting the rights of institutionalized psychiatric patients, and developing specialized professional education in mental health law (Bonnie et al., 2021). One of the first collaborative efforts—designing a strategy to "de-institutionalize" forensic mental health assessments—ultimately led to a university-based training clinic for forensic mental health assessment.

Through the 1970s, forensic mental health assessments addressing competence, sanity, and other psycho-legal questions were conducted almost exclusively in state psychiatric hospitals. Melton and colleagues (2018) describe this as the traditional model, or the "institution-based, inpatient model" (p.102). Even a straightforward assessment of adjudicative competence might require the defendant to be transported several hours across the state to a psychiatric hospital with a forensic unit, spend a month in observation and assessment, and then be transported back to jail as hospital-based clinicians submit a report to the court. Such procedures were then (and even for decades later) typical across the nation; but in retrospect, there were many drawbacks. The model required great time and expense to transport defendants to distant locations, removing them from community ties and resources, requiring tremendous expense for inpatient hospitalization—all for an assessment that (in most cases) did not require using inpatient services.

Virginia was the first state to explore a more local, "community-based" approach to forensic assessments (Melton et al., 2018, p. 103). The Virginia General Assembly initiated a pilot project with a House Joint Resolution passed in 1980. Immediate statewide implementation was not feasible, so the ILPPP developed a pilot study involving several jurisdictions, which allowed for a quasi-experimental design that compared the pilot jurisdictions with those that operated using the traditional inpatient hospital-based model. The pilot project—detailed in the book *Community Mental Health Centers and the Courts: An Assessment of Community-Based Forensic Services* (Melton et al., 1985)—was a clear success.

The pilot project revealed that community clinicians could be trained to a high level of forensic expertise and that community-based services could reduce costly hospital admissions for forensic assessments. Indeed, the project revealed "strong support for the notion that a community-based system of forensic services results in substantial fiscal savings while reducing unnecessary intrusions into the defendant's interests in bail and a speedy trial" (Melton et al., 1985, p. 43). Research documented numerous positive outcomes in the work products produced (forensic assessment reports), the state funds saved, and even the expertise developed among state clinicians, who testing showed were performing similarly to a national sample of board-certified forensic experts (Melton et al., 1985). The curriculum and training materials developed for this pilot project became the first manual to guide forensic assessment, which has evolved into the leading textbook for forensic assessments, *Psychological Assessments for the Courts,* now in its fourth edition (Melton et al., 2018).

Ultimately, Virginia expanded the pilot project throughout the state and made related changes to statute and policy (see Bonnie et al., 2021 for more on ILPPP collaborations with Virginia government to develop statute and policy). For example, the statutes governing competence, sanity, and other questions related to forensic mental health (e.g., sentencing of capital offenders and sexual offenders) were all revised to indicate that any evaluator court-appointed to address these questions must have appropriate training. The ILPPP provided these trainings and maintained records of who completed them. These specialized trainings have since been available through the ILPPP at low cost to state employees, but are also open to others (many attendees are clinicians from states without formal forensic training programs). Annual courses include Forensic Assessment of Adults (5 days addressing competence, sanity, ethics, malingering, expert testimony, etc.), Violence Risk Assessment of Adults, Evaluating People Charged with Sexual Offenses, Forensic Assessment of Juveniles, Violence Risk Assessment of Young People, and Assessments at Capital Sentencing (until Virginia abolished the death penalty in 2021). Each of these routine training sessions is directed by ILPPP faculty, but features various speakers, including ILPPP faculty and other regional or national experts. The ILPPP offers additional "special topic" training sessions (usually with national experts) addressing any further, or advanced, training needs each year. Thus, the ILPPP training collaboration with the state typically provides at least twenty days of training to forensic mental health professionals annually.

Forensic Training Required a Clinic

As these forensic trainings were emerging in the 1980s, and developing into an annual routine, the ILPPP established a small forensic clinic for the sole purpose of conducting forensic assessments that could be used for teaching purposes. Historically, clinical faculty (psychologists and psychiatrists) led the assessments, often with law students or psychiatry residents observing. The interdisciplinary faculty discussed cases at case conferences or similar clinic meetings, and the grainy video recordings of the interviews became aids for the annual training sessions. Original faculty report that in these early years, the clinic accepted only a dozen or so cases per year, solely for instructional purposes (Fitch, personal communication, 2024).

Not until the 1990s did it become clear that the clinic could expand beyond a limited function of generating a few teaching examples and serve Virginia by conducting court-ordered or even privately-retained assessments more often. Psychologist Gary Hawk oversaw the clinic and the training program through the 1990s and increasingly accepted court orders for forensic assessments. These court-ordered assessments eventually became a source of revenue to support clinic faculty, particularly as state funding decreased. Because the clinic had the benefit of a multidisciplinary team (with access to a forensic psychologist, psychiatrist, social worker, and legal scholars), it became a niche practice addressing more complex, challenging, or high-profile cases. Beyond simply welcoming law students and psychiatry students to observe cases, the clinic began to provide formal clinical training programs. Dr. Hawk and psychiatrist Eileen Ryan supervised clinical psychology practicum students, clinical psychology interns, and psychiatry residents. After the UVA Medical School ended psychology internships and began postdoctoral fellowships around 2001, the clinic trained the first UVA postdoctoral fellows in forensic psychology. Sadly, Dr. Hawk died in 2002, a tremendous loss to the UVA clinic and training programs, as well as the broader field and community.

From 2008 until the present, the clinic has been directed by clinical psychologist Daniel Murrie and expanded from a few dozen assessments each year to several hundred each year; revenue increased by over ten-fold. Whereas the clinic had comprised only one psychologist and postdoctoral fellow circa 2008, full-time clinic faculty have expanded to five forensic psychologists (all former ILPPP postdoctoral fellows) and one forensic neuropsychologist. Trainees include two postdoctoral fellows and sometimes a psychiatry fellow and psychology practicum student(s). This expansion allowed faculty to further specialize their forensic practice niches, enhancing clinical services and bringing further expertise to ILPPP training sessions. The increasing case volume and expansion of the clinic have provided a substantial increase in revenue, allowing added positions for trainees (i.e., an additional postdoctoral fellowship in forensic psychology) and expanding the training mission of the ILPPP.

Training

The training mission of the UVA Forensic Clinic has evolved to focus on two primary goals, consistent with broader movements to provide training in law and psychology at various educational stages, from undergraduate students to practicing professionals (Bersoff et al., 1997; DeMatteo et al., 2009). A primary focus remains the state-sponsored training programs, a form of continuing education that provides the statutorily-required training for practicing psychologists and psychiatrists to become eligible to conduct court-appointed assessments in Virginia. High-quality forensic training requires not only teaching general principles, but also sharing detailed case examples, redacted sample reports, resource materials, and practical suggestions. This requires that faculty are routinely engaged in the types of assessments they are teaching.

A second training focus of the clinic is students or fellows in formal UVA training programs. Primarily, these include the postdoctoral fellows in forensic psychology and forensic psychiatry through the UVA School of Medicine. Postdoctoral fellows in neuropsychology participate as well. These postdoctoral fellows learn in an apprenticeship model, joining faculty in forensic assessments and report-writing. Over the course of a training year, they may shift from more observational or limited roles (leading only portions of the assessment or report) to more active and expanded roles (leading the interview and report, with faculty playing only a supportive and supervisory role), a common instructional approach for specialized tasks. For certain types of assessments (e.g., capital sentencing, emotional injury), fellows are always limited to an assisting role, but for other types of assessment (e.g., pre-employment assessments of police candidates, simple competence to stand trial assessments) fellows may progress to a lead role. UVA trainees also include practicum students from UVA's two doctoral programs in clinical psychology. The clinic also serves law students; some clinic faculty teach a law school course addressing forensic assessments and students observe cases as part of this course. Finally, the clinic sometimes hosts undergraduate students, and even serves as a resource or teaching site for one faculty who teaches an undergraduate course in forensic psychology. In our view, a key strength of the clinic is the diversity of training functions it provides, in that it offers opportunities to trainees at every level of training in law and psychology (see, e.g., Bersoff et al., 1997; DeMatteo et al., 2009), as well as those in psychiatry and in law. These trainees—even though they are from different disciplines and at different stages—often benefit from interacting with one another as well as with supervising faculty from other disciplines.

Project Description: UVA Forensic Clinic

As detailed above, the UVA Forensic Clinic—like the ILPPP in which it is based—has evolved dramatically over nearly fifty years of history. The current version of the clinic can be described as follows.

Services

As the name implies, the UVA Forensic Clinic provides forensic mental health assessments, that is, assessments performed specifically to assist the court in reaching a decision about a criminal defendant or civil litigant. One of the most common forms of assessment in the clinic is assessments of adjudicative competence (also known as competence to stand trial, or fitness to proceed), because these are the most common form of forensic mental health assessment across the United States (Melton et al., 2018; Zapf & Roesch, 2009). The clinic also performs many other common forms of forensic assessments: i.e., those addressing legal sanity (criminal responsibility), risk of violence, risk of sexual re-offending, and pre-sentencing mitigation. Other types of assessments that may be less common nationally—that is, assessments addressing capital sentencing, re-sentencing of those sentenced as juveniles (*Miller* assessments), disputed confessions, or waiver of rights—are more common in the clinic due to the interest, expertise, or focus of some clinic faculty.

Though most assessments in the clinic address criminal proceedings, some address civil litigation, particularly psychological injury. Most of these tend to address potential psychological injuries from underlying criminal behavior (e.g., sexual assaults, violence, police misconduct), though the clinic's forensic neuropsychologist addresses personal injury cases that warrant neuropsychological assessment of potential traumatic brain injury or cognitive damage.

A portion of clinic services do not address any form of litigation. These include pre-employment and fitness for duty assessments, primarily addressing those in law enforcement, emergency services, and other government or public services positions. Indeed, the UVA Forensic Clinic includes a "public safety" service focused on fitness for duty assessments as well as pre-employment assessments of emergency and public safety workers. Some clinic faculty conduct formal threat assessments (see Meloy et al., 2021) of individuals who (typically) have no pending criminal charges, but have nevertheless evoked concerns about their potential for violence, particularly in universities, businesses, or other public settings. Despite the variety in the assessments conducted through the clinic, the common theme is a rigorous and empirically-supported mental health assessment, performed to inform some sort of legal or administrative decision.

Unlike most mental health clinics, the UVA Forensic Clinic provides *no* treatment services of any sort. Even for those involved in the legal system, the clinic provides no group or individual therapy, medication management, or any other type of treatment (e.g., competence restoration). Though certain assessments may ultimately recommend or *inform* treatment, supervision, or other interventions, none of the clinic faculty are treatment providers. This may be a limitation, or at least a cost, of an exclusive focus on forensic assessment and consultation.

Finally, some clinic services are entirely consultative, with no direct clinical contact. These may include private consultation to attorneys, for example, or "teaching testimony" addressing psychological research or best practices for forensic assessments. Some clinic faculty also consult nationally on forensic services and broader public mental health services. They provide teaching or training to state mental health systems, attorney groups, federal law enforcement, or large systems that rely on forensic mental health expertise in some way. In short, the focus of the clinic is always forensic mental health assessments, but the clinic services may range from individual assessments to broad consulting on training, practice, and delivery of forensic services.

Clients

In forensic assessment, the client is rarely the defendant or litigant undergoing assessment, but rather the courts ordering assessments or the attorneys retaining the evaluator (Melton et al., 2018; Monahan, 1980). Thus, the clinic's clients are primarily courts and attorneys. Many of the assessments are court ordered, often (but not always) upon motion of the defense or prosecution. Other assessments are requested directly by counsel. A smaller portion reflects other arrangements such as a consensus appointment upon agreement by opposing parties. By this point, the UVA Forensic Clinic has provided services in state, federal, and military courts. Clinic faculty have provided services, in some capacity, in a majority of U.S. states.

Other clinic clients include police or other public safety departments, or government agencies seeking pre-employment or fitness for duty assessments. Finally, there are occasions in which the client is a university or a business requesting a threat assessment, which is a form of consultation that explores the degree to which a person is moving toward targeted violence, and then suggests strategies to manage that risk of violence.

Regarding marketing, the UVA Forensic Clinic has no formal advertising and no formal marketing presence beyond a website. We have never formally examined how courts and attorneys initially become aware of our services, but our impression is that most of our new referrals result from informal "word of mouth." Other referrals may result from scholarship, such as professional publications or lectures to professional groups, which may have a secondary benefit of outreach and informal "marketing" (a potential benefit of university-based services). Historically, there were periods in which the clinic was small and specialized enough that courts and attorneys primarily referred unusual or particularly complex cases, perhaps based on the assumption that a clinic in a medical school had greater resources or expertise for complicated cases. As the clinic expanded, they have increasingly referred more typical or routine assessment requests as well.

Providers, Size, and Scope

As described in the historical sections, the clinic began as an afterthought: a small service to perform occasional forensic assessments—usually one dozen or less per year—primarily for training purposes. But over the past dozen years, the clinic has expanded from one faculty psychologist and one postdoctoral fellow to several faculty and fellows, performing a few hundred assessments each year. This expansion allowed for greater specialization among the faculty—each performs some common forensic assessments (competence, sanity, violence risk assessment), but each has also developed specialized forensic practice niches. This enhances clinical services and provides further specialized expertise for the ILPPP trainings described earlier. The increasing case volume and substantial growth of the clinic has shifted the clinic from a small component of the ILPPP to its largest function, and the ILPPP's primary funding source.

All six clinic faculty psychologists are based *primarily* in the UVA Forensic Clinic, though most perform other roles like teaching and research within the ILPPP and in other parts of the university. At times, psychiatrists who perform forensic assessments have been based in the clinic part-time, amid other duties in the School of Medicine. Clinic trainees typically include two postdoctoral fellows in forensic psychology and one in forensic psychiatry. Doctoral students in clinical psychology may work in the clinic as practicum students, psychiatry residents may complete a forensic rotation, and undergraduate students occasionally intern or work as clinic assistants. Full-time staff include a business manager and a clinic coordinator, who each serve other roles in the ILPPP as well.

In recent history, the team of clinic faculty has grown from one (Murrie) in 2008 to hiring others (e.g., Kelley, Agee, Gardner, Guarnera) over the next fifteen years. All faculty were hired from among those who completed the UVA Postdoctoral Fellowship in Forensic Psychology, except a forensic neuropsychologist who shifted his assignment from another part of the medical school (Bender). The clinic has occasionally relied on postdoctoral fellowship graduates as contractors to handle cases on behalf of the clinic, while they continue their primary role at a different university or a private practice.

Hiring and contracting solely with graduates of the postdoctoral fellowship has many benefits. One strength of this model is that the new faculty (or contract evaluators) are already familiar with the clinic; they are well-vetted and well-trained in the clinic ethos, standard practices, and even style of report-writing. Clinic leadership is very familiar with, and confident in, our graduates' work. The team is close and cohesive, producing similar work-products much like a clinic "brand." Of course, the homogeneity of the clinic team is also a potential weakness; though faculty reflect a variety of education and training from varied programs, all of them have spent most of their careers in the UVA Forensic Clinic, so the clinic does not generally feature faculty who bring years of experience working as clinicians in other settings. The clinic has never recruited external clinicians who may bring new areas of expertise (e.g., child custody assessments), although such recruiting may be one strategic way to expand services or capacity.

Keys to Effective Services

As we discuss later, there are certainly other models for university-based forensic clinics, and we are not convinced the UVA Forensic Clinic is the *optimal* model. There are certainly better, or more strategic, arrangements for certain purposes. But we are grateful for several strengths of the model, most of which involve symbiotic relationships with other ILPPP functions and faculty roles.

A key strength of the clinic is the way in which its functions are intertwined with other academic functions. Universities are ideal for synergistic activities, so a university-based clinic both enhances and benefits from adjacent activities and scholarship. Although all faculty are *primarily* clinicians, most have some teaching duties. So, the clinic provides endless case examples (sometimes with live or video observation) for classroom teaching in the law school or in psychology courses (as well as the professional trainings the ILPPP provides, described earlier). Clinic duties also inform and provide teaching examples for our training we provide to attorneys and judges. Providing good training requires immersion in the relevant science and practice guidelines, correcting common misunderstandings, and routinely researching answers to thoughtful student questions. As a result, routine teaching—particularly in the state-sponsored training programs—is a "non-clinical" activity that we find brings great benefit to the clinical services we provide.

All clinic faculty are scholars, or at least aim to produce good scholarship amid the competing clinic demands such as court deadlines. Fortunately, practice in the clinic sometimes enhances (rather than just delays) scholarship. For example, many empirical studies or reviews by faculty have been directly prompted by practical questions that emerge from conducting forensic assessments in the clinic (e.g., Agee et al., 2020; Gardner et al., 2022, 2023; Guarnera et al., 2017; Murrie et al., 2013; Zelle et al., 2021, 2023). Other scholarship aims to present best practices for certain types of assessments (e.g., DeMatteo et al., 2011; Kelley & Foster, 2023; Murrie & Zelle, 2015, in press), and thus—we hope and believe—helps to ensure that faculty are further attuned and accountable to best professional practices.

Foundations for Project Services

As detailed earlier, the foundations for the UVA Forensic Clinic are closely intertwined with the foundations of the field of forensic mental health assessment generally. The clinic was established to support one of the first training programs for forensic assessment; these trainings required creating a curriculum (because no such training programs existed at the time). But that curriculum has evolved to serve the broader field (Melton et al., 2018). Thus, the clinic has always been tightly tied to instructional efforts, and efforts to disseminate best practices.

The clinic has also benefited from proximity to other foundational research and scholarship in forensic mental health. Certain key research programs that have informed and shaped the field of forensic mental health assessment have been based at UVA. One example is the MacArthur Foundation's study of legal competencies (Bonnie et al., 1997; Hoge et al., 1997; Poythress et al., 2002), led by ILPPP founder and long-term director Richard Bonnie. Likewise, the MacArthur study of violence and mental disorder (Monahan et al., 1994, 2001) was led by John Monahan, faculty at UVA School of Law and long-term affiliate of ILPPP. These research programs influenced forensic training and practice far beyond UVA. But their proximity inevitably shaped ILPPP trainings and practice within the ILPPP's clinic.

Of course, it is crucial for any forensic clinic to be steeped in all the relevant science and practice guidelines, not only those in their proximity. So, the clinic relies heavily on best-practice guidance and scholarship (e.g., Heilbrun, 2009; Melton et al., 2018; Packer, 2009; Zapf & Roesch, 2009), assigning these key texts to trainees. Clinic faculty also tend to study wide-scale forensic practice to identify common weaknesses and opportunities for improvement. Through close ties with Virginia's Office of Forensic Services, particularly their forensic assessment oversight system, clinic faculty study Virginia forensic reports (e.g., Gardner et al., 2018, 2022; Murrie et al., 2008, 2020) to inform ILPPP trainings, but also to inform and improve practice within the clinic.

Generalizability

Generally, we perceive there is much room to develop other university-based forensic clinics across the United States, and beyond. Even years ago, authorities lamented that the need for forensic mental health services has "outstripped the capacity of the field to train practitioners to provide these services in a competent and ethical manner" (Packer, 2008, p. 245). This was in the context of a workforce shortage of mental health professionals (Thomas et al., 2009). Since then, the demand for many forms of forensic mental health assessment—particularly assessments of competence to stand trial—has increased steadily in the United States (Kois et al., 2024; Murrie et al., 2023). Likewise, the workforce shortage of psychologists (American Psychological Association, 2022) and other mental health professionals persists.

Thus, universities have had a critical role to play in meeting the workforce needs for well-trained forensic mental health professionals. Universities can meet these needs more directly, through developing forensic clinics (Heilbrun et al., 2013). But they can also do so less directly, through training future forensic evaluators: Training may prioritize earlier stages, such as doctoral psychology programs with a forensic emphasis (e.g., Drexel University, Sam Houston State University), postdoctoral fellowships in forensic psychology (e.g., University of Denver, University of Massachusetts Chan Medical School) or forensic psychiatry (e.g., Yale University). Training may also prioritize practicing psychologists and psychiatrists, much like UVA's ILPPP training program. Although more state-supported forensic training programs have emerged in the past several decades, still only a minority of states have formal training programs, and many of these programs are quite brief or limited (Gowensmith et al., 2015). In short, there are forms of formal forensic training appropriate to almost every educational stage from undergraduate training onward (Bersoff et al., 1997; DeMatteo et al., 2009; Poythress, 1979). This training is certainly not *exclusive* to universities—forensic psychiatric hospitals are a crucial training context, for example,—but much forensic training is in the university context.

Our impression on the matter—which is certainly biased—is that *all* university-based forensic training programs can benefit from a university-based forensic clinic. Forensic assessment cannot be trained in the abstract. Even introductory training requires case materials and case examples; more advanced training requires supervised practice. Furthermore, there is potential for synergy and further benefit when multiple training programs are connected to the same clinic (as in ours), such as a state-supported training program for practicing professionals, a forensic psychology fellowship, and a forensic psychiatry fellowship. Trainees benefit from interaction with trainees at other stages, and in other disciplines.

Similar Services and Contexts

The UVA Forensic Clinic is one of at least one dozen university-based forensic clinics operating in the United States. Over one decade ago, a thorough internet search revealed fourteen forensic clinics based in universities (Heilbrun et al., 2013). More have emerged since then (e.g., University of Denver). Most tend to prioritize forensic assessment, though some provide treatment to those involved in the criminal legal system. Some were primarily sites for formal fellowships in forensic psychiatry (Indiana University School of Medicine)[1] while others were training clinics for clinical psychology doctoral programs that had a forensic emphasis (e.g., Sam Houston State University). Certainly, these examples underscore the plausibility of university-based forensic clinics, and illustrate the potential for these clinics to vary in many important ways. The UVA Forensic Clinic may be among the oldest university-based forensic clinics, but it is certainly not the only such clinic, or the only viable model for university-based forensic services, as we emphasize later.

We encounter many attorneys who assume a university-based clinic must be state-funded (or university-funded) and thus have a financial security that allows for free or low-cost services. Much to our disappointment, this is a significant misunderstanding. Most state universities receive only a small part of their funding from the state, and most medical-school clinics are essentially for-profit businesses, operating in a large, profit-focused system. Thus, the UVA Forensic Clinic must be entirely self-sustaining, even paying building rent and utilities much like any private clinic or group private practice. Like other faculty in medical schools, our clinic faculty must generate enough revenue to cover not only their salaries, but also fringe benefits and other overhead. Ours do so through a combination of forensic assessments and other grants or contracts. The few other forensic clinics based in medical schools—such as the forensic psychiatry clinic in the Vanderbilt University Medical Center—function similarly (personal communication (10-10-25), Kimberly Brown).

To be clear, this medical-school model is certainly *not* the only feasible model for a university-based clinic. For example, a few psychology clinics in universities with forensic training programs rely on space provided by the university. The University of Denver offers a Master's program in forensic psychology, and their Forensic Institute for Research, Service, and Training (FIRST) features a clinic that shares physical space with the Psychology Department. Likewise, Sam Houston State University's doctoral program in clinical psychology hosts a clinical psychology training clinic on university property (like many doctoral psychology programs) that also performs forensic assessments (unlike most doctoral psychology programs). Obviously, this kind of university support—providing physical space, office staff, and other core resources—is ideal in many ways. Furthermore, faculty in these programs may receive much of their funding from other university-based duties, such as teaching; in some, providing supervision in the clinic is considered part of teaching duties. If the goal of an academic program is forensic training, it is certainly optimal for the program to provide the infrastructure (e.g., clinic space) necessary for that training, and such support often allows the university-based clinic to offer services to clients at a reduced

[1] To be clear, there are dozens of formal fellowships in forensic psychiatry that are based in medical schools within large universities (for a listing, see https://aapl.org/fellowship). However, few of these specifically feature a university-based forensic assessment clinic. Most forensic psychiatry fellowships include rotations in prisons and jails, court clinics, and/or forensic psychiatric facilities.

rate, much like other (non-forensic) university-based psychology training clinics. For example, the Sam Houston State University Psychological Services Center offers a range of psychological services (including forensic services), often provided by graduate students in psychology and supervised by university faculty or staff, at prices well below typical market rates. In many similar psychology department training clinics, the trainees outnumber supervising faculty, because the primary goal is training students.

Funding and *Pro Bono* Work

As detailed earlier, a significant constraint for the UVA Forensic Clinic (and the few other clinics situated in medical schools) is the need to remain financially profitable. Though maximizing profit is not a *primary* goal, profit is necessary for the ongoing viability and stability of any clinic in any medical school. Clinics that operate at a deficit rarely last long. At the same time, the UVA Forensic Clinic is devoted to providing high-quality services in *all* cases, including those involving the population often described as "indigent defendants." Virginia has a state-wide, flat fee schedule for all court-ordered competence ($700) and sanity ($800) assessments; though these figures doubled in recent years, they remain *much* lower than rates in most states. Other types of assessments that we consider important for equitable justice also tend to pay little (e.g., assessments addressing immigration or asylum matters). Because thorough assessments may take many hours, these routine, flat-fee court-ordered cases always carry financial loss for the clinic, and we consider them much like *pro bono* work.[2] We also take a limited number of truly *pro bono* referrals, usually from attorneys working on a *pro bono* basis. These often include cases involving appeals, immigration matters, or other situations in which little funding is available, but high-quality work is important. Providing low-cost or no-cost services can be more feasible in university clinics that feature university support: e.g., through faculty salary support, office space, office staff, or other contributions. But generally, clinicians in medical schools must generate their own funding (as well as funding for overhead support) through clinic revenue, much like a private business, and this is true of clinicians in the UVA Forensic Clinic.

So, at least in our clinic, performing the low-fee court-ordered work (or similar *pro bono* work) also requires performing higher-fee work, which typically comes in the form of (a) more specialized assessments for Virginia courts; (b) assessments for states other than Virginia; (c) assessments in federal court; (d) assessments retained privately, whether civil or criminal; or (e) other consulting services. This financial

[2] Even the simplest competence assessment—which usually requires a few hours of interview, a few hours of report review, and hours of report writing—amounts to well under $100 per hour. We have conducted court-ordered sanity assessments in lengthy, complicated, high-profile homicide cases that ultimately net far less than $10 per hour.

model has been feasible thus far, but clinic faculty—who must meet their "cost center" like any medical school faculty—have consistently struggled to titrate their load of *pro bono* or low-fee court-ordered cases. These are often interesting and engaging cases, ideal for many training purposes. For clinic faculty, performing these types of assessments is also central to our goals of equitable justice. We generally believe all cases—not only those featuring strong funding mechanisms or litigants with resources—require thorough assessments that follow best professional practices. But the payment structure limits the number of routines, court-ordered cases our clinicians can accept, at least if a concurrent goal is to maintain a profitable clinic that can continue performing high-quality assessments for decades more.

Therefore, in terms of *funding*, we suspect our medical-school context is among the more challenging for a university-based training clinic. In most ways, it is preferable to have greater university resources in a university-based clinic. But perhaps our experiences bode well for other clinics (or potential clinics). If we have sustained a profitable, expanding clinic with little financial support from a university, the path may be smoother for contexts in which a university provides physical space, salary support for faculty, or other resources. Of course, any clinic must remain financially solvent to carry out its mission, so finances will inevitably influence the referrals a clinic accepts, the fees the clinic charges, and (to some degree) the workload and morale of faculty and staff.

Finally, we offer one more caveat regarding generalizability, or the feasibility of other university-based clinics like ours. Generally, and perhaps because misunderstandings are common, we have emphasized the ways in which a medical-school-based clinic is much like a private practice: faculty must generate enough revenue to cover salaries and overhead, they must balance any *pro bono* work with revenue-generating work, and scholarship may come at the expense of paid work. However, we should also emphasize that working in a medical-school-based forensic clinic is *not identical to* working in a private practice. First, the negatives: whereas private practices are generally autonomous and nimble (like other small businesses), universities are neither. The university context—even if a clinic is largely independent—often requires layers of bureaucracy or administrative review for certain business or employment matters that might be handled much more simply in a private practice setting. Second, although a university rarely attempts to micro-manage any clinical services, we have sometimes declined forensic assessments we might otherwise accept because the case is in some way connected to the university context or because of potential complications that could come from media attention to faculty work on highly-publicized proceedings. In these ways, a university-based forensic clinic experiences some complications and constraints that a private clinic may not.

On the other hand, a university-based clinic may differ from some private practices in ways that we appreciate. Our model leaves us likely to adopt a team (multi-evaluator) approach to assessments that we rarely see in traditional private practice. For example, we sometimes include two senior psychologists (even without trainees) on particularly complex or sensitive cases; we routinely involve a neuropsychologist alongside psychologists, or we integrate consultation with psychiatrists or physicians. We often adopt a team approach even when there is no funding for an additional evaluator and the practice appears financially unwise (essentially dividing one hourly rate between two evaluators). In short, we suspect the academic context fosters greater collaboration, even at the level of individual assessments. We often find the close collaboration more engaging, and conducive to excellent work, even if it is less lucrative.

Additionally, a university setting offers an environment helpful for recruiting excellent trainees and faculty. The setting also tends to attract trainees and faculty who are interested in positions with multiple components (e.g., clinical work and research), and who—in particular—value applied scholarship. Relatedly, the university context has benefits over a private practice model for seeking grants and contracts to further such research, which diversifies the clinic's income stream and allows faculty to have the types of "blended" positions that attracted them to the clinic in the first place.

We are also particularly grateful for the university-based clinic model when we consider ways to address the risks of adversarial allegiance (Murrie et al., 2013; Murrie & Boccaccini, 2015), the pressure for forensic experts to drift toward findings that support the party who retained them. Of course, *no* forensic expert is immune to such pressures, but the stability of a long-term university-based clinic makes it easier to decline cases, and to convey "unhelpful" opinions to attorneys, even if doing so means there will be no future referrals from those attorneys. All of us faculty have benefited from the clinic's reputation—which began before any of us were involved—so we remain motivated to protect and cultivate a reputation for thorough and *objective* work products, rather than simply persuasive work products. Of course, these factors may also be true for well-established private clinics or private practitioners; they are certainly *not* unique to university clinics. But we have found the university context helpful for buffering certain pressures, and for certain types of credibility.[3]

We have also been able to experiment with specific services to minimize adversarial allegiance. For example, we have encouraged and performed assessments under "joint referral" arrangements, i.e., when opposing parties agree to solicit one assessment from the UVA Forensic Clinic, rather than each opposing party retaining separate assessments. We have also offered assessments in which our clinicians are "blinded" to the referral source (https://www.ilppp.org/innovative-

[3] In general, our impression is that our university context and our faculty roles enhance the credibility of our work (e.g., reports, testimony, and consultation). Of course, we hope this is "earned" credibility—based on the expertise that our faculty have developed and shared in our university setting—not simply a superficial credibility based on a university name or affiliation. But we should also acknowledge some instances in which others have suggested the university base gives us *less* credibility. Generally, these perspectives come during cross-examination, or in comments from other evaluators who suggest that our academic context leaves our evaluators politically motivated, politically liberal, or "ivory tower" academics who are distant from the practicalities of criminal proceedings or work in facilities, and thus committed to practice standards that are not realistic for others in the field. In short, the university setting has sometimes prompted criticism that faculty are not "real" clinicians familiar with "real world" practicalities.

referral-strategies), but much to our disappointment, few attorneys have requested these arrangements.

Diversity, Equity, and Inclusiveness

For several decades, cultural responsivity[4] has been an increasing priority in psychology and psychiatry, as have been efforts to enhance diversity, equity, and inclusiveness (DEI) in educational pathways and the workforce. Forensic psychology and psychiatry have seemed slower to address the importance of race, ethnicity, and culture, perhaps lagging behind other disciplines within psychology (Bergkamp et al., 2023). However, more recent work has begun to guide forensic clinicians in better considering the relevance of race, ethnicity, and other identities in the broader legal context in which they work, and in their daily duties, such as interviewing and report writing (e.g., Fanniff et al., 2023; Heilbrun et al., 2021; Ratkalkar et al., 2023; Riggs Romaine & Kavanaugh, 2018). Indeed, there appears to be emerging consensus that certain practices are important for culturally informed forensic mental health assessment (e.g., Fanniff et al., 2023) and that a defendant or litigant's racial identity is a potentially important consideration in forensic assessment (e.g., Heilbrun et al., 2021).

Like the broader field of which we are a part, our efforts to address race, ethnicity, and culture—and to implement these emerging practices—have been imperfect and evolving. Our clinic team features far less racial diversity than the populations with whom we work. Though this lack of diversity is a general problem in our field, we notice that even just a few hours away in Washington D.C., the workforce of forensic mental health professionals reflects more ethnic and racial diversity than in our smaller university town and university clinic. Most of our faculty and trainees are women—consistent with broader shifts in the field of forensic psychology (see Neal & Line, 2022)—though most of the criminal defendants we see are men.

Differences between examiner and examinee create multiple challenges to building rapport and adequately understanding an examinee's history and experience. Again, we are grateful that emerging best practices have begun to address these challenges. A review of such resources (e.g., Barber-Rioja & Rosenfeld, 2018; Fanniff et al., 2023; Heilbrun et al., 2021) is important, but beyond the scope of this chapter. Even aided by these emerging resources, we are struck by the ways that forensic assessment

[4] There have been many terms to refer to addressing and considering the role of culture in the field of psychology. In earlier years, this practice was referred to as cross-cultural or multiculturalism and in more recent decades was referred to as cultural competence. As clinicians and scholars came to see that cultural competence might wrongly suggest that a clinician could be entirely "competent" in cultural considerations (rather than engaging an ongoing process), terms such as cultural responsivity (self-reflection and adaptation to the cultural norms and needs of others) and cultural humility (ongoing self-reflection and self-critique of one's own culture and the cultures of others and approaching situations with an openness to learning and growth) have emerged (Bergkamp et al., 2023; Hook et al., 2013; Tervalon, & Murray-Garcia, 1998).

requires curiosity and cultural awareness across a wide variety of identities and experiences even beyond the more common considerations of race and ethnicity, gender, and sexual orientation. For example, some cases in Washington, D.C. have required that we consider the cultural norms and experiences of those who have recently immigrated to the United States and settled in a community of those with similar ethnic and cultural identities. Other cases in Washington, D.C. have required considering very different cultural norms, values, and perspectives, such as those of people charged with crimes in the U.S. Capital on January 6, 2021, or other politically motivated crimes. Cases elsewhere in our region have required considering aspects of remote, rural culture in the Appalachian region; unique religious communities; or narrow subcultures devoted to niche interests or ideologies. We attempt to ask examinees about their various identities and explore relevant research where available (see e.g., Heilbrun et al., 2021 for discussion of each). At times, the university context has allowed for more convenient consultation with scholars or experts who are familiar with a particular culture, language, or ideological movement. But the necessity of becoming culturally informed—common to forensic evaluators in any context—feels no less challenging.

Linguistic differences may pose a challenge to accurate and culturally sensitive forensic assessment. We are routinely ordered to evaluate defendants whose primary language is not English. Whenever possible, we refer to an evaluator who is fluent in the examinee's primary language; but this is feasible only for those speaking a few more common languages (e.g., Spanish). In many cases, we cannot identify an evaluator fluent in the necessary language, and thus we require an interpreter. Though the university hospital with which we are affiliated has access to "language lines" and uses them often, we consider in-person interpretation far preferable, and we seek formally court-certified interpreters. Even experienced court-certified interpreters, however, often require further guidance on interpreting for forensic assessments (e.g., interpreting words precisely, without summary or paraphrasing for clarity).

Trainees and Diversity

As a university training clinic, we recognize instances when examinees have been wary of trainees observing and participating (much the same way medical patients may be reasonably wary of medical trainees observing or participating). This has sometimes required additional care to explain trainee participation and build rapport. In more instances, however, aspects of trainees' identities—whether related to race, ethnicity, language, regional background, life stage, or other experiences—have greatly contributed to improved rapport, thoughtful questions, and insight.

The presence of trainees is a further reason to try to foster a culture that supports and encourages reflection and conversations about DEI and sociocultural identities. Fostering such a culture requires frank conversations about the strengths and weaknesses of our clinic's culture and the broader fields of which we are a part.

The former includes acknowledging the weakness of a relatively homogenous faculty or clinic team, referring cases to evaluators with greater case-specific cultural expertise when feasible, and pursuing greater diversity (of all sorts) among our clinic team. The latter—addressing limits in our broader field—requires acknowledging just how little our field understands about how our own social positions and identities shape our work. Forensic clinicians—like all professionals—seem to be vulnerable to a variety of biases and idiosyncrasies (Murrie & Boccaccini, 2023), and we work within a criminal legal system marked by racial and ethnic biases at almost every stage (e.g., Kovera, 2019; The Sentencing Project, 2022). There is no reason to believe that forensic clinicians are somehow invulnerable to the variety of biases that plague the rest of the criminal legal system and the professionals within it. Yet there has been little research to shed light on potential racial bias among professionals like us, although this may be changing (see, e.g., Guarnera et al., 2024). University-based training clinics have a unique opportunity to promote this type of research and foster conversations that nudge the field toward greater self-examination.

More broadly, university-based clinics have unique opportunities to contribute to greater diversity in the forensic mental health workforce. Ideally, clinics like ours prioritize diversity (of all sorts) in recruitment, selection, and training decisions. But as we do so, we recognize ways in which certain forms of training in our field—such as postdoctoral fellowships—are structured in ways that are not particularly welcoming. For many postdoctoral fellowships, salaries are low, and training requires an expensive relocation process for only one year of training. Our clinic, for example, is based in a university town with modest diversity (it is less homogenous than some regions) but far less racial and ethnic diversity than large urban centers. University-based training clinics are often well-suited to provide high-quality training, but we likely need to do more to foster highly *accessible* training. One simple potential strategy is welcoming diverse trainees at earlier and earlier stages—such as welcoming undergraduate students to observe assessments or "shadow" clinic work—rather than only seeking the most diverse applicants from the much-narrowed, selective sample that is seeking training at later stages (e.g., postdoctoral fellowships).

Advice to Others Seeking to Provide Similar Services

In our view, establishing a university-based training clinic is certainly worthwhile, but not simple. First, doing so requires specialized expertise. Most clinics of this sort emerge not simply from one forensic expert, but a critical mass of professionals with relevant expertise. The UVA Forensic Clinic has always been interdisciplinary, initially featuring faculty from law and psychiatry. Likewise, the similar clinic at Vanderbilt University features both psychologists and psychiatrists. Even forensic psychology clinics in psychology departments, which may rely on a primary leader, still tend to rely on multiple faculty or staff with varied expertise necessary to supervise a range of cases, as well as many students who are highly motivated to learn forensic assessments.

Second, university-based forensic clinics with a training emphasis will require *tremendous* supervisory time and resources. Forensic assessment is a highly-specialized discipline that typically requires individualized, live supervision and in-vivo training. In some non-forensic clinical contexts, it may be typical for a supervisor to oversee many trainees who provide a clinical service (e.g., therapy) to several clients, and then meet with supervisees for weekly supervision. But such arrangements are inadequate for training forensic assessment, which requires something more like an apprenticeship model. For example, supervisors complete each stage of an assessment *with* a trainee, discussing impressions and decisions at every stage; they then conduct forensic interviews together, and ultimately exchange drafts until a written report is finalized. Though trainees typically take more active and advanced roles over the course of training, they continue to "co-conduct" many assessments before they may, for example, conduct a forensic interview *without* a supervisor present and observing. This supervision model requires much more supervisor time and attention than the supervision models common in other types of clinical training.

Indeed, in many clinical contexts, trainees may function as "service extenders"—providing billable services more affordably than more senior clinicians—in ways that allow a clinic to serve more clients (often with greater profit or at lower costs). But in forensic assessment, trainees are rarely "service extenders" in this sense.[5] Forensic clinics can rarely charge for trainee services. We do not recommend trainees as a "revenue-generating" strategy, and we do not recommend a training emphasis if a *primary* clinic goal is profit. Supervisors must remain deeply involved, even in late stages of training for many reasons: the stakes of a forensic assessment are significant, and the work products (assessment reports, or even expert testimony) are often highly scrutinized. In our clinic, supervisors are typically the ones to testify when testimony is required (usually based on agreement with the attorney at the outset of the case), though there are exceptions. When trainees do testify, supervisors are heavily involved in preparation and usually observe trainee testimony. All this to say: a university-based clinic with any training functions will require *extensive* supervision and oversight. Clinics should expect to both "scale up" supervision and "scale down" caseloads relative to private forensic practices that do not feature a training program.

Like any forensic clinician starting a private practice, those considering a university-based forensic clinic should consider the market, the gaps in needed services, but particularly the strengths that clinic faculty and trainees may contribute

[5] There are exceptions of course, such as programs in which psychiatry fellows conduct routine assessments of trial competence, or (in our clinic) when psychology fellows eventually conduct pre-employment assessments without live supervision. But even in these scenarios, the trainees are typically post-doctoral, and fully-licensed mental health professionals. That is, they are at the point in education and credentialing when non-forensic clinicians would be performing clinical services independently.

to the surrounding legal system. For some university clinics, a tremendous contribution might be simply providing reliable, timely, and higher-quality assessments to systems experiencing high demand. An obvious example is the "competence crisis" most U.S. states are experiencing, wherein they are seeking more evaluators to fulfill the demand for court-ordered assessments of adjudicative competence (see Kois et al., 2024; Murrie et al., 2023). A university-based clinic might be a critical help to their locality or state (and serve a unique training function) simply by providing excellent, timely competence assessments, even if they provide few other services. Other potential clinics may fulfill needs by providing highly-specialized services that are less likely to be available among general private practitioners. University-based clinics—perhaps especially those in medical schools—may employ more specialists in forensic mental health (e.g., our forensic neuropsychologist). They may also benefit from relationships with those in nearby medical school departments (e.g., we consult with a toxicologist to address the effects of medications and illicit substances). As in our experience, a clinic that grows (adding more clinicians) allows those clinicians to increasingly specialize in areas of interest, developing greater expertise to respond to specialized referrals, though the overall clinic may still be responsive to a wide variety of routine referrals and system needs.

Conversely, smaller clinics—or those just beginning—should resist the temptation to offer a wide variety of services, especially if some of those services lie at the edges of clinician/faculty expertise, or if they will not be able to offer those specialized services often enough to maintain and improve proficiency in them. Indeed, even our moderately-sized clinic consistently declines certain types of assessments (e.g., those prompted by divorce or child custody litigation, or sexually violent predator proceedings) for which our faculty have not developed adequate interest and/or experience to perform them well and consistently. Different forms of forensic mental health assessment require different expertise, and there is certainly no need for any clinic to attempt all forms of forensic mental health assessment. Indeed, we doubt that any clinic could competently do so.

Conclusions

We have described our university-based training clinic, which emerged from a state training program for forensic assessments. Clinics like ours may be an excellent resource for trainees across many stages and disciplines, and they may be a key strategy to improve the forensic mental health workforce. Key benefits of these clinics include the opportunity for synergistic activities—conducting forensic assessments alongside research, teaching, and consultation—in ways that each type of activity can enrich the other. But these clinics also require a sustainable business structure; even if profits are not the primary goal, the clinic must remain profitable. Finally, such clinics require a firm commitment to training, understanding that trainees are not "service-extenders" or "revenue generators," but rather apprentices in whom we invest, over longer periods, and ultimately enjoy as colleagues and contributors to the field.

Acknowledgements

We thank Becca Bergquist, Larry Fitch, Brett Gardner, and Mia Ricardo for their input and contributions to this chapter.

References

Agee, E. R., Zelle, H., Kelley, S., Moore, S. J. (2020). Marshaling administrative data to study the prevalence of mental illness in assault on law enforcement cases. *Behavioral Sciences & the Law, 37*(6), 636–649. https://doi.org/10.1002/bsl.2437

American Psychological Association. (2022). *Potential health service psychologist workforce capacity decrease* [Fact sheet]. https://www.apa.org/workforce/publications/health-service-psychologists-survey/workforce-capacity-factsheet.pdf

Barber-Rioja, V., & Rosenfeld, B. (2018). Addressing linguistic and cultural differences in the forensic interview. *International Journal of Forensic Mental Health, 17*(4), 377–386. https://doi.org/10.1080/14999013.2018.1495280

Bergkamp, J., McIntyre, K. A., & Hauser, M. (2023). An uncomfortable tension: Reconciling the principles of forensic psychology and cultural competency. *Law and Human Behavior, 47*(1), 233–248. https://doi.org/10.1037/lhb0000507

Bersoff, D. N., Goodman-Delahunty, J., Grisso, J. T., Hans, V. P., Poythress, N, G., & Roesch, R. G. (1997). Training in law and psychology. Models from the Villanova Conference, *American Psychologist, 52*(12), 1301–1310. https://psycnet.apa.org/doi/10.1037/0003-066X.52.12.1301

Bonnie, R. J., Hoge, S. K., Monahan, J., Poythress, N., Eisenberg, M., & Feucht-Haviar, T. (1997). The MacArthur adjudicative competence study: A comparison of criteria for assessing the competence of criminal defendants. *Journal of the American Academy of Psychiatry and the Law Online, 25*(3), 249–259.

Bonnie, R. J., Murrie, D. C., Zelle, H. (2021). The Institute of Law, Psychiatry, and Public Policy at the University of Virginia. In K. Heilbrun, H. J. Wright, C. Giallella, & D. DeMatteo (Eds.), *University and public behavioral health organization collaboration in justice contexts: Models for success* (pp. 14–29). Oxford University Press.

DeMatteo, D., Marczyk, G., Krauss, D. A., & Burl, J. (2009). Educational and training models in forensic psychology. *Training and Education in Professional Psychology*, 3(3), 184–191. DOI: 10.1037/a0014582. https://psycnet.apa.org/doi/10.1037/a0014582

DeMatteo, D., Murrie, D. C., Anumba, N. M., & Keesler, M. E. (2011). *Forensic mental health assessments in death penalty cases.* Oxford University Press. https://doi.org/10.1093/acprof:oso/9780195385809.001.0001

Fanniff, A. M., York, T., & Gutierrez, R. (2023). Developing consensus for culturally informed forensic mental health assessment: Experts' opinions on best practices. *Law and Human Behavior, 47*(3), 385–402. https://doi.org/10.1037/lhb0000531

Gardner, B. O., Murrie, D. C., Guarnera, L. A., & Torres, A. N. (2023). Reporting potentially irrelevant information—defendant race/ethnicity, criminal history, and substance use—in competence to stand trial reports: A state-wide study. *Psychology, Public Policy, and Law. 29*(3), 349–363. https://psycnet.apa.org/doi/10.1037/law0000393

Gardner, B. O., Murrie, D. C., & Torres, A. N. (2022). To proceed or not to proceed: Conducting insanity assessments of incompetent defendants. *Psychology, Public Policy, and Law, 28*(1), 67–77. https://psycnet.apa.org/doi/10.1037/law0000304

Gardner, B. O., Murrie, D. C., & Torres, A. (2018). Insanity findings and assessment practices: A state-wide review of court-ordered reports. *Behavioral Sciences & the Law, 36*(3), 303–316. https://psycnet.apa.org/doi/10.1002/bsl.2344

Guarnera, L., Murrie, D. C., & Boccaccini, M. T. (2017). Why do forensic experts disagree? Sources of unreliability and bias in forensic psychology assessments. *Translational Issues in Psychological Science, 3*(2), 143–152. https://psycnet.apa.org/doi/10.1037/tps0000114

Guarnera, L. A., Murrie, D. C., Gardner, B., & Bender, S. (2024). Are forensic evaluators more likely to conclude that black or white defendants are malingering? *Law and Human Behavior, 48*(5–6), 545–563. https://doi.org/10.1037/lhb0000589.

Gowensmith, W. N., Pinals, D. A., & Karas, A. C. (2015). States' standards for training and certifying evaluators of competency to stand trial. *Journal of Forensic Psychology Practice, 15*(4), 295–317. https://psycnet.apa.org/doi/10.1080/15228932.2015.1046798

Heilbrun, K. (2009). *Assessment for risk of violence in adults.* Oxford University Press.

Heilbrun, K., Kavanaugh, A., Grisso, T., Anumba, N., Dvoskin, J., & Golding, S. (2021). The importance of racial identity in forensic mental health assessment. *The Journal of the American Academy of Psychiatry and the Law, 49*(4), 478–487. https://doi.org/10.29158/JAAPL.210099-21

Heilbrun, K., Kelley, S. M., Koller, J. P., Giallella, C., & Peterson, L. (2013). The role of university-based forensic clinics. *International Journal of Law and Psychiatry, 36*(3–4), 195–200. https://psycnet.apa.org/doi/10.1016/j.ijlp.2013.04.019

Hoge, S. K., Bonnie, R. J., Poythress, N., Monahan, J., Eisenberg, M., & Feucht-Haviar, T. (1997). The MacArthur adjudicative competence study: Development and validation of a research instrument. *Law and Human Behavior, 21*(2), 141–179.

Hook, J. N., Davis, D. E., Owen, J., Worthington, E. L., Jr., & Utsey, S. O. (2013). Cultural humility: Measuring openness to culturally diverse clients. *Journal of Counseling Psychology, 60*(3), 269–277. https://doi.org/10.1037/a0032595

Jackson v. Indiana, 406 U.S. 715 (1972).

Kelley, S., & Foster, E. E. (2023). A guide to feedback in forensic mental health assessment. *Professional Psychology: Research and Practice, 54*(6), 403–412. https://psycnet.apa.org/doi/10.1037/pro0000530

Kois, L. E., Potts, H., Cox, J., & Zapf, P. (2024). Court-reported competence to proceed data across the United States. *Law and Human Behavior, 48*(3), 182–202. https://psycnet.apa.org/doi/10.1037/lhb0000565

Kovera, M. B. (2019). Racial disparities in the criminal justice system: Prevalence, causes, and a search for solutions. *Journal of Social Issues, 75*(4), 1139–1164. https://doi.org/10.1111/josi.12355

Lessard v. Schmidt, 349 F. Supp. 1078 (E.D. Wis. 1972).

Melton, G. B., Petrila, J., Poythress, N. G., Slobogin, C., Otto, R. K., Mossman D., & Condie, L. O. (2018). *Psychological assessments for the courts: A handbook for mental health professionals and lawyers* (4th ed.). Guilford.

Melton, G. B., Weithorn, L. A., & Slobogin, C. (1985). *Community mental health centers and the courts: An assessment of community-based forensic services.* University of Nebraska Press.

Meloy, J. R., Hoffmann, J., Deisenger, E. R. D., & Hart, S. (2021). Threat assessment and threat management. In Meloy, J. R., & Hoffmann, J. (Eds.), *International handbook of threat assessment* (2nd ed., pp. 3–21). Oxford University Press.

Monahan, J. E. (Ed.) (1980). *Who is the client? The ethics of psychological intervention in the criminal justice system.* American Psychological Association. http://dx.doi.org/10.1037/10051-000

Monahan, J., & Steadman, H. J. (Eds.). (1994). *Violence and mental disorder: Developments in risk assessment.* The University of Chicago Press.

Monahan, J., Steadman, H. J., Silver, E., Appelbaum, P. S., Robbins, P. C., Mulvey, E. P.,... & Banks, S. (2001). *Rethinking risk assessment: The MacArthur study of mental disorder and violence.* Oxford University Press.

Murrie, D. C., & Boccaccini, M. T. (2023). How reliable and objective are forensic mental health evaluators? In D. DeMatteo & K. C. Scherr (Eds.), *The Oxford handbook of psychology and law.* (pp. 343–364). Oxford University Press.

Murrie, D. C., & Boccaccini, M. T., (2015). Adversarial allegiance among forensic experts. *Annual Review of Law and Social Science, 11*, 37–55. doi: 10.1146/annurev-lawsocsci-120814-121714

Murrie, D. C., Boccaccini, M. T., Guarnera, L. A., & Rufino, K. A. (2013). Are forensic experts biased by the side that retained them? *Psychological Science, 24*(10) 1889–1897. https://doi.org/10.1177/0956797613481812

Murrie, D. C., Boccaccini, M. T., Zapf, P. A., Warren, J. I., & Henderson, C. E. (2008). Clinician variation in findings of competence to stand trial. *Psychology, Public Policy, and Law, 14*(3), 177–193. https://awspntest.apa.org/doi/10.1037/a0013578

Murrie, D. C., Gardner, B. O., & Torres, A. N. (2020). Competency to stand trial assessments: A state-wide review of court-ordered reports. *Behavioral Sciences and the Law, 38*(1), 32–50.

Murrie, D. C., Gowensmith, W. N., Kois, L., & Packer, I. (2023). Assessments of competence to stand trial are evolving amid a national "competency crisis." *Behavioral Sciences and the Law, 41*(5), 310–325.

Murrie, D. C., & Zelle, H. (2015). Criminal competencies. In B. L. Cutler & P. A. Zapf (Eds.), *APA handbook of forensic psychology, Vol. 1. Individual and situational influences in criminal and civil contexts* (pp. 115–157). American Psychological Association. https://doi.org/10.1037/14461-005

Murrie, D. C., & Zelle, H. (in press). Criminal competencies. In P. A. Zapf (Ed.-in-Chief), A. Alexander, T. Daftary-Kapur, A. Fanniff, & D. Sivasubramaniam (Assoc. Eds.), *APA handbook of forensic psychology (2nd ed.): Vol. 1: Individual and Situational Influences in Criminal and Civil Contexts.* American Psychological Association.

Neal, T. M. S., & Line, E. N. (2022). Income, demographics, and life experiences of clinical-forensic psychologists in the United States. *Frontiers in Psychology, 13*, 910672. doi: 10.3389/fpsyg.2022.910672. PMID: 35874388; PMCID: PMC9302360

Packer, I. K. (2009). *Assessment of criminal responsibility.* Oxford University Press.

Packer, I. K. (2008). Specialized practice in forensic psychology: Opportunities and obstacles. *Professional Psychology: Research and Practice, 39*(2), 245–249. https://doi.org/10.1037/0735-7028.39.2.245

Poythress, N. G. (2002). *Adjudicative competence: The MacArthur studies* (Vol. 15). Springer Science & Business Media.

Poythress, N. G. (1979). A proposal for training in forensic psychology. *American Psychologist, 34*(7), 612–621. https://doi.org/10.1037/0003-066X.34.7.612

Ratkalkar, M., Jackson, C., & Heilbrun, K. (2023). Race-informed forensic mental health assessment: A principle-based analysis. *International Journal of Forensic Mental Health, 22*(4), 314–325. https://doi.org/10.1080/14999013.2023.2178556

Riggs Romaine, C. L., & Kavanaugh, A. (2018). Risks, benefits, and complexities: Reporting race and ethnicity in forensic mental health reports. *International Journal of Forensic Mental Health, 18*(2), 138–152. https://doi.org/10.1080/14999013.2018.1531094

Tervalon, M., & Murray-Garcia, J. (1998). Cultural humility versus cultural competence: A critical distinction in defining physician training outcomes in multicultural education. *Journal of Health Care for the Poor and Underserved, 9*(2), 117–125. https://doi.org/10.1353/hpu.2010.0233

The Sentencing Project. (July 14, 2022). *Shadow report to the United Nations on Racial Disparities in the United States Criminal Justice System.* The Sentencing Project. https://www.sentencingproject.org/policy-brief/shadow-report-to-the-united-nations-on-racial-disparities-in-sentencing-in-the-united-states/

Thomas, K. C., Ellis, A. R., Konrad, T. R., Holzer, C. E., & Morrisey, J. P. (2009). County-level estimates of mental health professional shortage in the United States. *Psychiatric Services, 60*(10), 1323–1328. https://doi.org/10.1176/ps.2009.60.10.1323

Wyatt v. Stickney, 344 F. Supp. 373 (M.D. Ala. 1972).

Zapf, P. A., & Roesch, R. (2009). *Assessment of competence to stand trial.* Oxford University Press.

Zelle, H., Kelley, S. M., Agee, E. R. (2023). Police interactions with persons with mental illness. In R. Roesch (Ed.), *Routledge encyclopedia of psychology in the real world: Vol. Psychology and law.* (Available online only, no pagination). Routledge. https://doi.org/10.4324/9780367198459-REPRW249-1

Zelle, H., Kelley, S., Agee, E. R., & Seibert, W. L. (2021). Police use of force standards and mental health crises in the United States: Identifying research and policymaking. *International Journal of Law and Psychiatry, 80*, 101750. https://doi.org/10.1016/j.ijlp.2021.101750

3

Considering Intersectional Identity in Forensic Mental Health Assessment

Mina Ratkalkar

Forensic psychologists perform the critical function of conducting forensic mental health assessment (FMHA) for courts and attorneys. FMHA bridges mental health and legal domains and provides legal decision makers with information on specific legal questions (e.g., whether someone is competent to stand trial). Forensic evaluators can have a significant influence on legal proceedings. The *Specialty Guidelines for Forensic Psychology* (SGFP; American Psychological Association [APA], 2013) indicate that evaluators should be impartial, fair, and objective. However, much of the information forensic evaluators routinely consider is subjective or open to interpretation. The SGFP provides aspirational guidelines[1] and promotes ethical, accurate, and culturally informed forensic psychological assessment.

If and *how* evaluators obtain and interpret crucial information related to race, ethnicity, and culture (REC) varies greatly despite the SGFP (APA, 2013) urging evaluators to

- Recognize that their own cultural influences, beliefs, and biases may affect their ability to practice competently and impartially (SGFP 2.07—Considering the Impact of Personal Beliefs and Experience);
- Appreciate individual and group differences in culture and identity and their influence on the FMHA process (SGFP 2.08 Appreciation of Individual and Group Differences); and
- Consider personal, linguistic, and cultural differences that might affect judgments, test selection, or reduce the accuracy of interpretations of data (SGFP 10.03—Appreciation of Individual Differences).

There is little explicit guidance on how to conduct FMHA that is consistent with the SGFP, however. The field of forensic psychology has yet to develop best practices on systematically considering and incorporating REC in FMHA. This chapter describes strategies for doing so and their rationale. First, I define and outline key

[1] This is true for most states. If the state has incorporated SGFP guidelines into state law, however—as in Pennsylvania, for example—then these guidelines are legally enforceable.

Mina Ratkalkar, *Considering Intersectional Identity in Forensic Mental Health Assessment*. In: *The Path Forward*.
Edited by: Kirk Heilbrun and David DeMatteo, Oxford University Press. © Oxford University Press (2026).
DOI: 10.1093/9780197773031.003.0003

terms relevant to diversity, equity, and inclusiveness (DEI) and identity in the context of FMHA. Next, I describe the rationale for developing and using approaches requiring the exploration of evaluees' and evaluators' identities. I include a review of evolving professional literature related to assessing the influence of intersectional identity in FMHA to ground subsequent practice and training recommendations. A practical list of *Do's* and *Don'ts* is included to help evaluators systematically consider the influence of identity during data collection, report writing, and testimony. This chapter concludes with practice and training suggestions to flexibly accommodate trainees and evaluators at all stages of education and professional development.

Centering Diversity, Equity, and Inclusiveness (DEI) in FMHA

Broadly, the field of psychology promotes a diversity, equity, and inclusion framework (American Psychological Association, 2021). Forensic psychology journals increasingly (albeit inconsistently) report on diversity constructs (Nijdam-Jones et al., 2023). Research is evolving on social justice, cultural competence, and responsiveness, and their role in psychology (e.g., Barber Rioja & Rosenfeld, 2018; Fanniff et al., 2023; Shepherd & Lewis-Fernandez, 2016).

Forensic evaluators are tasked with providing objective expert opinions by gathering and interpreting data from various sources (e.g., interviews, records, psychological assessments). Though evaluees' identities are central to forensic data collection and interpretation, efforts to acknowledge DEI have not historically been a part of FMHA. In the field of forensic psychology, *REC-neutral* evaluations—evaluations assuming race, ethnicity, or culture do not exert a meaningful influence on FMHA unless there are explicit reasons to think otherwise—have been the accepted norm. For example, a 2014 casebook with fifty sample FMHA reports (Heilbrun et al., 2014) included only one report that addressed race or ethnicity in the analysis. Over a decade after the publishing of the SGFP (American Psychological Association, 2013), there is little published literature describing good practice in considering the influence of multiple facets of identity in FMHA. REC-neutral evaluations are often an accepted aspect of training in forensic psychology. Training is often conducted in settings that are historically white, with limited diversity in racial perspectives, collective memory, and history (Feagin, 2013). However, there is growing recognition that considering REC and other aspects of identity in FMHA can *enhance* evaluators' accuracy (Heilbrun et al., 2021). This can hold true *even in cases in which there is no specific or explicit evidence* that REC will be integral to legal referral questions (Ratkalkar et al., 2023).

Still, approaches to FMHA rarely consider historical and current structural context despite well-documented, longstanding racial disparities in the legal and healthcare systems (Metzl & Hansen, 2014). In 2021, both the American Psychiatric Association and the American Psychological Association issued public apologies for their participation and support of systemic racism and inequality. Both announcements highlighted the importance of recognizing the depth and pervasiveness of past harms to promote fairness and justice to citizens of minoritized races (Heilbrun et al., 2021). The goal of incorporating DEI considerations into FMHA is not to advocate for a specific examinee or for social values or social justice. However, in FMHA, recognizing and assessing the influence of historic and systemic inequality may contribute to social justice. It is critical for forensic evaluators to strive for fairness and objectivity. However, phenomena such as public apologies and shifting attitudes among forensic professionals suggest that social justice should have a more meaningful place in FMHA (Hunt & Shepherd, 2023). Acknowledging the modern-day impact of historical harms (e.g., disparities in arrests and sentencing; fear of mistreatment by courts or police; discrimination based on appearance, disability, or nationality) helps evaluators better understand their potential effects on examinees' contexts.

This chapter begins with DEI to highlight how considering DEI-related factors (e.g., race, sexual orientation, gender) can be integral to the FMHA process for *all* evaluees and referral questions, with more detailed consideration when they appear more relevant and influential. In this chapter, the following terms and definitions are used to offer inclusive and more specific language to discuss identity (Atkin et al., 2022) and to offer guidance in how evaluators consider identity in FMHA:

- *Racial identity:* The significance and qualitative meaning that people attribute to their race in their self-conceptualization.
- *BIPOC:* Black, Indigenous, and People of Color.
- *Cultural competence:* Knowledge and skills that include cultural awareness, beliefs, knowledge as well as familiarity with clients' (or evaluees') culture, worldview, and expectations (Sue & Sue, 2022).
- *Cultural responsiveness:* The continual development of knowledge, awareness, reflective practice, and skills needed to promote health, well-being, and equity for diverse individuals and communities (American Psychological Association Task Force on Race and Ethnicity Guidelines in Psychology, 2019).
- *Ethnicity:* A descriptor of a social group with shared culture, language, and/or place of origin (Golash-Boza, 2018).
- *Intersectionality:* The complex and cumulative way that multiple facets of identity (e.g., race, gender) affect how people are perceived and how they experience combined or overlapping effects of discrimination (Crenshaw, 1991).
- *Race:* A socially constructed system that categorizes people into different groups based on perceived physical differences and/or recent ancestry to create and maintain a power hierarchy (Smedley & Smedley, 2005).
- *Racism:* Organized systems within societies that cause avoidable and unfair inequalities in power, resources, capacities, and opportunities across racial groups that privilege whiteness (Paradies et al., 2015; Smedley & Smedley, 2005).

Foundations and Support for Assessing the Impact of Intersectionality in FMHA

The most recent edition of the *Diagnostic and Statistical Manual of Mental Disorders* (5th ed., text rev.; DSM-5-TR; American Psychiatric Association, 2022) includes diagnostic considerations regarding discrimination, gender differences, and their impact on mental health. Each facet of someone's identity—and their overlapping effects—shapes how people are perceived and move through the world. Clinicians should be aware that greater intersectionality is more likely to signal cumulative trauma (Williams et al., 2023). For forensic evaluators to critically consider intersectionality, we must do the following:

1) Be open and adequately prepared to explore the possibility of discrimination based on identity.
2) Recognize that some identities are visible (e.g., assumed gender) while others are invisible (e.g., religious beliefs; Hays, 2016). Some are fluid depending on the individual and their context (e.g., neurodiversity is most impairing and apparent at school or work, someone's sexual orientation is only visible when they are with their partner). The visibility of an identity is not necessarily correlated with its significance to the individual or its salience to legally relevant behavior.
3) Be mindful that identities may be mistaken or incorrectly interpreted by others (e.g., associating race with nationality). Others' perceptions can be as or more significant than someone's own description of their identity (Williams et al., 2023), and its effect on legally-relevant behavior can be context-dependent and change over time.
4) Ask open-ended questions and assess associated experiences, thoughts, and behaviors.
5) Acknowledge the impact of structural (e.g., past and present discriminatory housing policies) and personal bias, including blind spot bias (Neal & Brodsky, 2016).

Bias contributes to inequities in decision-making, discrimination, and racial trauma (Eberhardt, 2019). Forms of cognitive bias perpetuating discrimination include moral licensing (deriving confidence from past moral behavior). Evaluators who believe they have already addressed bias and cultural blind spots may be less likely to acknowledge stereotypes or assumptions (Monin & Miller, 2001). Confirmation bias involves the tendency to seek, favor, and use information consistent with our conclusions while discounting information inconsistent with them. In FMHA, confirmation bias may contribute to evaluators favoring information relevant to their perceptions or stereotypes. Racial bias can affect forensic evaluators' diagnoses (Mikton & Grounds, 2007) and hinder appraisals of identity influences in FMHA.

Heilbrun and colleagues (2021) explored the importance of racial identity in FMHA. They asserted that conducting FMHA without adequately considering race can result in bias in some cases despite intentions to be objective. Such a biased assessment may perpetuate existing disparities and contribute to structural racism by leaving out critical information relevant to the forensic question. Forensic mental health evaluators are susceptible to cultural, racial, and gender bias (e.g., Sreenivasan et al., 2022) and other cognitive biases (Neal et al., 2022). Heuristics, also called Type 1 or rapid autonomous processing (Evans & Stanovich, 2013; see generally Kahneman, 2011), can make evaluators prone to judgment errors. Type 2 processing is more effortful and intentional and can override implicit biases. Yet even Type 2 processing may exacerbate bias, particularly in experts, if unchecked (Neal et al., 2022). Thus, addressing and mitigating bias—including unexplored cultural or racial bias—in FMHA requires direct and critical examination of one's own beliefs and of case-specific, potentially biasing information.

Guarnera and colleagues (2017) cited multiple potential influences as sources of bias and inaccuracy in forensic psychology: the inherent difficulty of conducting FMHA; limited training and certification among evaluators; unstandardized assessment methods; individual evaluator differences; and adversarial allegiance, or bias in favor of the retaining side (Murrie et al., 2013). Even seemingly objective measures and evidence-based assessments (e.g., risk assessment tools) allow evaluators discretion in interpretation. In addition, forensic evaluators use multiple data sources to inform their conclusions. Each of these complexities can affect evaluators' ability to assess and consider intersectional identity meaningfully in FMHA. Further, each data source and type of information an evaluator considers, and the order in which they consider them, can impact hypotheses and findings. Taken together, developing a systematic yet flexible approach seems important to consider how evaluators' and evaluees' identities may be relevant to specific FMHA. People may have privilege in one area of their life (e.g., high education level) but lack it in another (e.g., female gender). Evaluators should be aware of the overlapping effects of socialization. The following examples use gender to illustrate these effects (Hays, 2013):

- Nonprivileged (minoritized) people are socialized to be aware of the lines separating those with privilege from those without privilege (e.g., women learn that men are awarded more social latitude to be assertive in the workplace; Babcock ct al., 2022)
- Privileged members of systems are socialized to ignore these lines and differences (e.g., male employees believe they respond the same way to their male and female bosses' assertive behavior); and
- Privilege separates privileged and nonprivileged people from important information about one another (e.g., a male employee being unaware that his female boss times her commute to reduce her risk of sexual assault).

Accordingly, two people from the same community or workplace may have drastically different life experiences depending on their respective identities. In FMHA, learning more about these identities can give a fuller and more accurate picture of a person's life and relevant capacities and behavior.

Development of Approaches to Assessing the Impact of Intersectional Identities in FMHA

Foundational literature in forensic psychology, such as the principles of forensic mental health assessment (Heilbrun et al., 2009), has helped to promote good practice in FMHA. Ratkalkar and colleagues (2023) examined these thirty-eight established principles of FMHA and explained how twelve of these foundational principles of FMHA (Heilbrun et al., 2009) can be applied in conducting culturally responsive evaluations. Culturally responsive FMHA emphasizes evaluators' and evaluees' intersectional identities in a field in which most forensic mental health evaluators are White (Neal & Line, 2022) though racial and ethnic diversity has increased among psychology graduate students (Assefa et al., 2023). Black, Indigenous, and other People of Color (BIPOC) are overrepresented among justice-involved people (Carson, 2021). Cultural responsiveness also considers intersectional influences in data collection and interpretation in forensic evaluation—including clinical interviews—and in the legal system generally (Ratkalkar et al., 2023). To assess perceptions of best practices, Fanniff and colleagues (2023) examined experts' opinions on culturally informed FMHA. A total of twenty-eight practices (of 81 possibilities) were deemed "very important" for each phase of the forensic evaluation process, from preparation to report writing. The practices most of the psychologists in the sample identified as "very important" included questions evaluators should ask (e.g., how evaluees identify their race and ethnicity) and multiple factors to consider in the formulation of an opinion (e.g., experiences with racism). This study provides important information toward good practice in culturally responsive FMHA, but their sample of experts was small and nearly all white. While the field focuses on developing more rigorous and systematic approaches, Fanniff and colleagues (2023) suggested that forensic evaluators consider the twenty-eight practices, particularly regarding their importance in culturally responsive FMHA.

Mitigating Bias in FMHA

As forensic psychology increasingly considers the importance of racial and social justice (Hunt & Shepherd, 2023), I recommend certain tools for systematically gathering relevant information related to intersectional identity. Considering one's potential biases, social power and privilege is an important part of cultural responsiveness in FMHA. The field may face potential tensions between objectivity and cultural responsiveness in FMHA. Forensic psychologists must be aware of different types of biasing information (e.g., an evaluee's appearance), but behavioral observations cannot (and should not) be eliminated from reports. Most debiasing strategies—including self-reflection (Neal & Brodsky, 2016)—do not appear to mitigate the effects of implicit bias or meaningfully improve decision-making (Forscher et al., 2019). Neal and colleagues (2022) reviewed some promising debiasing methods including experiential teaching about cognitive bias (e.g., Sellier et al., 2019), increasing accountability and the expectation of justifying one's argument later (Lerner & Tetlock, 1999), and "considering-the-opposite" of one's argument and exploring alternative hypotheses. While the field develops evidence-based strategies to examine the impact of intersectional identities, existing tools and paradigms can help evaluators more systematically examine and weigh sources of identity-related information.

Frameworks for Examining the Impact of Intersectionality in FMHA

This section first discusses the application of specific frameworks that can assist in systematically examining intersectionality for trainees and experienced practitioners alike. Next, I discuss a flexible information management tool based on one of these frameworks to (a) include information specific to the identities and cultures of evaluators and examinees, (b) consider the relevance of all case-specific information to the legal question, and (c) consider multiple hypotheses and employ debiasing techniques (e.g., "consider the opposite").

Systematically Considering Case Information: Linear Sequential Unmasking—Expanded

Linear Sequential Unmasking (LSU; Dror et al., 2015) and *LSU-Expanded* (LSU-E; Dror & Kukucka, 2021) are evidence-based procedural frameworks to guide the consideration and evaluation of case information. Though LSU-E was initially intended for forensic analysts, it can be incorporated into any forensic discipline including FMHA (Quigley-McBride et al., 2022). Some of the potential benefits of LSU-E in FMHA include increased awareness of potential bias in data sources, including sources that appear "neutral" regarding identity (e.g., legal documents). LSU-E involves considering sources individually and sequentially, with opportunities to consider and document alternative hypotheses at different points in the evaluation process. This process can help with clarity in communicating findings in reports or in testimony. Moreover, evaluators and trainees will have a paradigm to better choose the order in which they consider data (or decline to consider it if they deem it irrelevant). Each of these potential benefits can improve the overall quality of training, supervision, and practice of FMHA (Kukor & Miller, 2024). Specific to assessing the influence of intersectional identities, LSU-E provides a way to systematically document processes intended to increase cultural responsiveness (e.g., hypotheses about intersectional and cultural influences on behavior).

Training in and exposure to assessing intersectional identity's impact on FMHA would ideally be done early in one's training or career. Establishing the habit of systematically slowing down, monitoring data collection and interpretation, and generally keeping personal data on cases and outcomes are all potential benefits of learning and implementing LSU-E. With some practice, evaluators can learn how to do this efficiently and as a standard part of their work. Trainees may have to use training cases and/or hypothetical cases. Supervisors should exercise flexibility in acknowledging different approaches to considering identity and cultural information. However, supervisors can encourage trainees to effectively seek such information and create multiple hypotheses (e.g., the relevance of race-based mistrust between evaluee and attorney in a competency to stand trial evaluation).

Learning about culturally responsive FMHA is an evolving process. More advanced practitioners can benefit from using this framework after mastering it. For evaluators who have experience in conducting independent forensic evaluations, I recommend reviewing a past case and challenging themselves to consider hypotheses, particularly those related to REC identity and culture, that they may not have considered at the time. I also encourage experienced evaluators to consider the order effects of seeking and reviewing certain types of information. For example, if evaluators had not reviewed previous evaluations before seeing an examinee, might they have asked different questions? Did seeing someone's race on a case file yield images and assumptions (e.g., assuming a white man arrested in a rural area in a Southern state is Christian and politically conservative)?

Assessing Intersectional Identity in Context: Structural Competence and Bioecological Systems Models

Assessment of an evaluee's larger environment provides important context for understanding behavior relevant to legal questions in FMHA. The model for Structural Competence (Metzl & Hansen, 2014) builds on the concept of cultural competence. Structural competence is a framework initially developed to enhance providers' abilities to recognize and address the social, economic, and political factors that influence health outcomes. But the core tenets of this model apply to FMHA as well. Structural competence is the ability to discern how symptoms, clinical problems, diseases, and attitudes toward patients (or evaluees) are influenced by "upstream" social determinants (Metzl & Hansen, 2014). It shifts the focus from individual-level cultural factors to larger structural issues that, in FMHA, influence mental health, health, and behavior. The key aspects of structural competency include:

- Recognizing structures that shape clinical interactions (e.g., broader sociopolitical, economic contexts influencing mental health and behavior);
- Developing extra-clinical language to discuss the impact of social structures on health (e.g., incorporating terminology from diverse disciplines to better describe how structural factors influence outcomes);

- Rearticulating "cultural" formulations in structural terms by connecting cultural competency practices with a structural understanding of stigma and health disparities.
- Observing and imagining structural interventions to consider changing the structures influencing health; and
- Developing structural humility to embrace continuous learning and recognize the limits of knowledge.

Structural competency aims to address limitations in cultural competency by focusing on forces that affect health and mental health outcomes at levels beyond individual interactions and providing a framework for practitioners to engage with social determinants of health. This model equips providers with skills to identify social and political factors that influence systemic inequalities (Metzl & Hansen, 2014). By incorporating structural competency into forensic training and practice, future and current providers can better understand and address the complex structural factors that impact legally relevant behavior. Not asking about evaluees' identities or assessing how these identities interact with key structures to influence opportunities, expectations, and behavior might mean that evaluators are overlooking important aspects of evaluees' experiences.

Another helpful framework is the Bioecological Model (Bronfenbrenner, 2005). It is a comprehensive theory of human development that emphasizes the interaction between an individual and their environment. The model has four key components: Process, Person, Context, and Time.

- *Process* refers to the progressively complex reciprocal interactions between an individual and their environment.
- *Person* acknowledges the role of personal characteristics, such as genetic factors, personality traits, and physical attributes, in shaping development.
- *Context* encompasses the environmental systems that influence development, divided into five interconnected levels:
  - Microsystem: The immediate environment (e.g., family, school);
  - Mesosystem: Interactions between microsystems;
  - Exosystem: Indirect influences (e.g., parents' workplace);
  - Macrosystem: Broader cultural and societal factors; and
  - Chronosystem: Changes over time.
- *Time* considers how developmental processes and outcomes may vary based on the specific time period in which they occur, as well as the duration and frequency.

The Bioecological Model emphasizes that development is a result of complex, bidirectional interactions between an individual and their environment. In FMHA, this perspective can be especially helpful in understanding how people think, behave, and make decisions across different contexts (e.g., as a child in their religious community and later as an adult with undiagnosed AD/HD whose friends used drugs regularly).

The ADDRESSING Model

Clinicians can use Hays' ADDRESSING model (2016) as a valuable tool for recognizing their own power and privilege—and the effects of how their identities intersect compared to individual examinees—in forensic assessment contexts. In adaptations of the ADDRESSING model, "targeted identities" refer to social identity groups that have historically had less power, fewer privileges, and reduced access to resources within society (Winer et al., 2018). These groups often face systemic barriers, discrimination, and oppression, in contrast to "dominant identities" which are societally privileged (Hays, 2016).

By systematically examining each component of the model, clinicians more comprehensively understand their own background and how it may influence their perceptions and judgments. This self-reflection process allows forensic evaluators to identify areas where they may hold privileged positions or unconscious biases that could impact assessment. For example, an evaluator might recognize that their age, race, ethnicity, or socioeconomic status differs significantly from those of the evaluee, potentially leading to misunderstandings or misinterpretations of behavior or symptoms. The evaluator can then take steps to mitigate these potential problems, such as seeking additional cultural context, consulting with colleagues from diverse backgrounds, or using culturally appropriate assessment tools. This awareness can lead to more nuanced and culturally responsive forensic assessments.

Exploring Intersectional Factors in FMHA Using Hays' ADDRESSING Model

In this section, I provide questions that may assist evaluators in using the ADDRESSING Model (Hays, 2016). These example questions can assist evaluators in self-reflection. Though self-reflection alone may not mitigate bias (Neal & Brodsky, 2016), it is a helpful practice in thinking and writing about intersectional identity. Evaluators can use these questions as a guide to conduct comprehensive interviews in FMHA. The dominant and targeted identities are from the social context of the United States and may be applicable to other Western countries. Evaluators should consider which identities are dominant in their respective places of practice.

Age & Generational Influences

- *Dominant Identity*: Adult
- *Targeted Identities:* Child, Adolescent, Older Adult

Individual and Family Level Questions:

- Who was most involved in raising you? What were their relationships to you?
- Have you ever been a caregiver (e.g., to a child or family member)? What are/were some of your responsibilities?
- How do you think your age affects your quality of life—positively or negatively?

Community and Structural Level Question:

- Which assumptions do you think people make about you and others your age?

Developmental Disability

- *Dominant Identity:* Non-disabled
- *Targeted Identities:* People with intellectual disabilities, autism, AD/HD, etc.

Individual and Family Level Questions:

- When did you first learn about your disability? Which words did you use at the time to describe it? Which names or words do you use now?
- What were some challenges you faced in social situations, at school, or at work while growing up (especially if undiagnosed)?
- Are there any special skills or abilities you may have because of your disability?

Community and Structural Level Questions:

- Are there places you couldn't go or things you couldn't do because of your disability?
- Tell me about any opportunities you were denied because of your disability, if any. How clear was it to others that the denial was because of your disability?

Disability Acquired Later in Life

- *Dominant Identities:* Non-disabled people without mental health conditions
- *Targeted Identities:* People with mental health conditions, limited mobility, or physical limitations, etc.

Individual and Family Level Questions:

- What is your understanding of the diagnosis you were given?
- How visible or invisible is your condition to others? Does the visibility ever change? If so, how (e.g., less visible with treatment, more visible while speaking)?
- How have you felt throughout your life about telling people about your disability or diagnosis? How has that changed as you've gotten older, if at all?

Community and Structural Level Questions:

- What does getting treatment look like where you live?
- How accessible or affordable is treatment for your condition? Is telehealth an option?
- What do you wish others knew about living with your condition? What are some things you wish you didn't have to explain about your disability?

Religion and Spirituality

- *Dominant Identities:* Christian, secular
- *Targeted Identities:* Muslim, Jewish, Hindu, Buddhist, etc.

Individual and Family Level Questions:

- What were some of the most important religious or spiritual traditions to you while growing up? How about now?

Community and Structural Level Questions:

- How connected do you feel to a community because of your faith?
- What do you think other people's opinions are of your religion? How much do others' opinions about your faith affect you?
- Did you celebrate any holidays that weren't recognized on official calendars? If so, did you have to take off from work or school, or celebrate on weekends?

Ethnicity and Racial Identity

- *Dominant Identity (Ethnicity):* European heritage
- *Targeted Identities (Ethnicity):* Ethnicity from (or descendants of people from) non-European nations

- *Dominant Identity (Race):* White
- *Targeted Identities (Race):* BIPOC (e.g., multiracial people, Black people)

Individual and Family Level Questions:

- How do you describe your racial or ethnic identity? How does it compare to how others in your family describe their race or ethnicity?

Community and Structural Level Questions:

- What are some expectations people may have of you because of your race or ethnicity? How do you feel about those expectations?
- How visible or invisible (or safe) do you feel because of your race or ethnicity in public? How does that differ depending on where you are?

Sexuality

- *Dominant Identities:* Straight, heterosexual
- *Targeted Identities:* Gay, lesbian, bisexual, queer, asexual, etc.

Individual and Family Level Questions:

- How would you describe your sexual orientation? How has that shifted over time, if at all?
- What was it like when you first came out? To whom?

Community and Structural Level Questions:

- How does your orientation affect how others view your relationships? How do you feel about this?

Socioeconomic Status (SES)

- *Dominant identities:* Wealthy or upper middle class, highly educated.
- *Targeted identities:* Low income, people living in under-resourced communities, people who did not graduate high school.

Individual and Family Level Questions:

- As a child, how often were lights shut off or other bills unpaid?

- How did you spend time when you weren't in school? How accessible were parks, neighborhood spaces, or after-school programs?

Community and Structural Level Questions:

- How did you typically get around—public transit or car? How accessible or affordable was gas or transportation?
- What were some of the biggest threats to people's safety where you lived?
- How was security handled at school? Were there police or metal detectors on site?

Indigenous Heritage

- *Dominant Identities:* Historically and/or current colonizing culture
- *Targeted Identities:* Indigenous people, First Peoples

Individual and Family Level Questions:

- How connected do you feel to your culture and heritage? What does that look like in your daily life?
- What are some questions people have asked you about your heritage? Which questions—if any—are you okay with answering? Which ones feel invasive or upsetting?

Community and Structural Level Questions:

- Describe anything you wish others knew about the experiences of people of your heritage.
- How does a lack of knowledge about these experiences affect you and people in your community?

National Origin

- *Dominant Identities:* Citizens born in the United States (or current country)
- *Targeted Identities:* Refugees, immigrants, undocumented people, international students, etc.

Individual and Family Level Question:

- How many generations of your family have been in the United States (or current country)?

Community and Structural Level Questions:

- What are some of the legal processes you and/or your family have been through since immigrating? How clear or confusing were these processes? Why?
- What is one custom or social rule from your nation (or culture) of origin that you wish people followed in the United States?

Gender

- *Dominant Identities:* Men, cisgender
- *Targeted Identities:* Women, transgender, queer, nonbinary, etc.

Individual and Family Level Questions:

- How would you describe your gender identity?
- Are you more comfortable with people of your own gender or of other genders? Why?

Community and Structural Level Question:

- Who or what influenced you most in teaching you what it means to be the person of your gender?

Promising Tools for Assessing Intersectionality and Relevance to the Legal Question

The LSU-E Worksheet for FMHA

A practical information management tool, the Linear Sequential Unmasking—Expanded Worksheet for FMHA (Quigley-McBride et al., 2022; see Appendix), shows promise in supporting systematic examination of the impact of intersectional identities and culture on FMHA. The worksheet was intended to be flexible across forensic disciplines but was written with forensic analysts in mind. It was adapted in 2024 for forensic mental health evaluators by adding sections to consider the opposite hypotheses, sections for cultural and identity-related information and hypotheses, and a Likert scale to rate the perceived credibility of each data source. The LSU-E Worksheet for FMHA gives practitioners a framework to methodically organize and assess information sources throughout the evaluation process. The LSU-E Worksheet for FMHA is subject to change and will have future empirical data regarding its use and outcomes.

The LSU-E prompts forensic professionals to consider the subjectivity, relevance, biasing power, and perceived credibility of each data source. Forensic evaluators can include information about intersectional identities in this guide. The LSU-E Worksheet for FMHA supports evaluators in prioritizing and optimizing case-relevant information, including information about REC and other identities. In training settings, this methodical process of reasoning and documentation can open the door to appraising and considering intersectional identity in FMHA, including when both supervisors and supervisees are from privileged groups (Kukor & Miller, 2024). Though it is not yet clear whether LSU-E mitigates bias in FMHA, the systematic nature of the process can increase evaluators' awareness and intentionality in data collection and interpretation. Anecdotal feedback from forensic evaluators who have used the LSU-E Worksheet for FMHA indicated it can help forensic evaluators by providing rationale and testimony on their forensic opinions. Empirical data collection about this approach should elucidate how evaluators' and evaluees' identities may be systematically factored into hypotheses and conclusions.

University of Connecticut Racial/Ethnic Stress and Trauma Scale (UnRESTS)

Many assessment tools are standardized using samples that do not provide ecological validity for populations with which they are often used (Council of National Psychological Associations for the Advancement of Ethnic Minority Interests, 2016). Identifying and/or developing additional assessment tools that do not introduce additional bias against diverse populations is an important step to better serve courts and justice-involved people (Shepherd & Spivak, 2021). Jackson and colleagues (in press) identified the University of Connecticut Racial/Ethnic Stress & Trauma Scale (UnRESTS; Williams et al., 2018) as a tool that appears appropriate for present use in FMHA to assess racial trauma in people from minoritized racial and ethnic groups. UnRESTS begins by asking respondents to identify their racial or ethnic group and then explores their racial and ethnic identity development. It covers experiences of direct racism, racism from loved ones, indirect racism (like publicized hate crimes), and subtle racism (such as microaggressions). If any experiences meet the criteria for Post Traumatic Stress Disorder (PTSD), the interview includes additional questions to clarify symptoms related to traumatic racialized events. UnRESTS covers racial trauma that can result from both overt racist events and cumulative discriminatory experiences. It is important to note that learning about racist events affecting others can contribute to racial trauma, even if not personally experienced. BIPOC may not always connect their mental health and behavioral symptoms to racial trauma, and some may be uncomfortable with the term "racial trauma." Instead, ask evaluees to describe their identities and experiences in their own words and in their preferred language, using a qualified interpreter if applicable.

Advice to Trainees and Practitioners Seeking to Assess the Impact of Racial and Cultural Identity in FMHA

In this section, I offer practice-oriented recommendations for culturally responsive FMHA. These recommendations are drawn from a recent principles-based analysis (Ratkalkar et al., 2023) and Fanniff and colleagues' (2023) consensus practices, or expert-endorsed steps for culturally informed FMHA. Using the current version of the SGFP (APA, 2013) and established principles of FMHA (Heilbrun et al., 2009) as sources of authority, practice recommendations are organized as follows:

- General principles—broadly applicable and less relevant to specific stages of FMHA.
- Preparation—discussed in the sequence they would occur in evaluations.
- Data collection—gathering and reviewing information; determining relevance to the legal question.
- Written communication and testimony—the basis for courts' consideration when there is no expert testimony and provides a foundation if testimony is presented.

Evaluators should directly ask evaluees which aspects of their identity they believe are most impactful (e.g., "Of all your identities—like your race, gender, [or other identities relevant to the evaluee]—which ones do you think most affect how other people treat you? Why? What are some examples from childhood? From adulthood?"). These open-ended questions can help ascertain which identities contribute to vulnerabilities or discrimination and which ones are points of strength or pride. Notably, areas of strength and vulnerability are not mutually exclusive. Evaluators can gain clarity on which factors most influence examinees' decision-making, behavioral, and emotional responses relevant to FMHA. Currently, FMHA lacks validated and accepted structured tools to assess the impact of intersectional identity. Until specialized measures are developed, evaluators may benefit from considering the following Do's and Don'ts.

Do

- *Clarify the forensic question and its scope.* For example, assessing competency to stand trial is much narrower in scope than assessing someone for mitigating factors in a capital case.
- *Consider how, rather than if, intersectional identities of both evaluators and evaluees could affect FMHA.* Rather than considering these factors secondary to "standard" interview questions, such as asking about mental health history, evaluators can prioritize identity-related considerations when indicated. This may include a thorough assessment of bioecological or structural factors. For example, an evaluator could ask about access to safe spaces to play or live during

childhood, police presence at public schools, or if any places seem "off limits" to live because of fear of discrimination or violence (see Table 3.1 for more examples).

- *Consult with colleagues and seek training outside your expertise or experience.* Exposure to diverse people, evaluation opportunities, or referral questions may not be available in your direct training, practice area, or geographical location. Intentionally seek training to improve fluency with talking about race, culture, and intersectional identity—one's own and those of others. This is especially relevant for evaluators who may not have as much lived experience speaking about their backgrounds as compared to evaluators with more minoritized identities.
- *Practice explaining the rationale for a culturally responsive approach to FMHA that explores the impact of intersectional identity.* Open discussion of culture and identity is not always welcomed, and speaking openly about these topics may be viewed as a politicized or social agenda. Evaluators should practice explaining how culturally responsive approaches can increase objectivity and fairness rather than diminish them. The SGFP explicitly includes considering culture, identity, and potential bias as part of FMHA.
- *Ask open-ended questions directly.* Do not assume that an evaluee with minoritized identities has experienced discrimination that is relevant to the legal question. Similarly, be open to the possibility that people may have experienced harms outside of an evaluator's experience or understanding. Ask for examples or hypotheticals that illustrate how someone navigates their relationships, environments, and community (see Table 3.1 for examples). Ascertain whether specific identities are generally invisible, visible, fluid, and/or context-dependent.
- *Consider using the LSU-E Worksheet or other methods to document data collection and interpretation—particularly data related to evaluators' and evaluees' identities—as a standard part of practice.* This need not be time intensive. But considering multiple hypotheses about how identity can apply to FMHA and having records of the order in which you examined *any* case information can assist in (1) case conceptualization, (2) identifying and mitigating potential bias, (3) forming conclusions, and (4) supporting future testimony.
- *Stay informed about the evolving understanding of cultural factors and their impact on forensic assessments.* Update practices as new research and case law develop. Stay up to date on preferred terms, such as using person-centered language and words to describe race, gender, and identity.
- *Advocate for greater diversity in forensic psychology to ensure that a broader range of perspectives and experiences are represented in the field.* Diverse evaluators may approach FMHA from the context of lifelong experience speaking about their identities.

Table 3.1 Revised Principles of FMHA and Consensus Practices: Implications for Considering and Assessing the Impact of Intersectional Identities

FMHA Principle	Implications for FMHA Examining the Impact of Intersectional Identities
GENERALLY	
1. Control potential evaluator bias in general through monitoring case selection, continuing education, and consultation with knowledgeable colleagues (SGFP 2.01–2.09).	– Review evaluees' demographics and referral questions routinely to identify areas for training and professional development (SGFP 2.02). – Consult with colleagues about intersectional influences in FMHA; note gaps in quality and availability of consultation (SGFP 2.02). – *Attend trainings that address how cultural identities impact the assessment process (SGFP 2.02). – *Read new peer-reviewed articles and books on culturally informed practices in forensic assessment (SGFP 2.02). – *Reflect on ways your own cultural identities and privilege impact the evaluation process (SGFP 2.07). – *Consider your limits of competence before accepting a referral for an evaluation of an examinee on the basis of their cultural identities (SGFP 2.01).
2. Be familiar with specific aspects of the legal system, particularly communication, discovery, deposition, and testimony (SGFP 2.04).	– Be familiar with the role of race and other aspects of identity in legal proceedings (e.g., jury selection; SGFP 2.08). – Acknowledge historical systemic racism and discrimination, particularly in the U.S. legal system. – Acknowledge points in the legal process with potential for racial trauma (e.g., upon arrest, with corrections officers or case workers, attorneys). – Recognize potential for implicit or explicit bias (e.g., BIPOC being perceived differently or more negatively, than white evaluees during similar legal interactions; SGFP 2.08). – *Review ethics codes; the SGFP; and relevant state, federal, and international law and policy regarding the incorporation of cultural identities relevant to your discipline and the type of evaluation.

continued

Table 3.1 *continued*

FMHA Principle	Implications for FMHA Examining the Impact of Intersectional Identities
3. Do not become adversarial, but present and defend your opinions effectively (SGFPs 1.01–1.02).	– Be familiar with literature supporting cultural responsivity and humility (SGFP 2.08). – Recognize culturally responsive FMHA may be unfamiliar to legal professionals. Be prepared to describe the process fairly and accurately, including rationale for using it instead of REC-neutral approaches (SGFP 6.02). – Understand the possibility of cultural and racial mistrust and acknowledge the impact of historical harms that may affect present relationships between: • Judge and evaluator; • Evaluator and evaluee; • Attorney and evaluee (SGFP 2.06).
IN SPECIFIC CASES	
Preparation	
1. Identify relevant forensic issues (SGFP 2.08).	– The narrower the issue, the more limited the implications for substantial influence of race-related factors. – The broader the issue, the more potential for substantial racial influence. – Example: Competency to Stand Trial • Rational and factual knowledge impairments—fewer considerations related to intersectional identities; • Capacity to assist counsel—may be affected by identity-related mistrust and misunderstanding in some cases (e.g., how will this discussion be received by the law?) – Example: Capital Sentencing • Developmental and intersectional influences; • Violence risk including expectations related to identity (e.g., men must fight to stand up for themselves) • Structural factors in risk assessment (e.g., previous contact with the justice system—requires nomothetic data about disparities in the justice system); • Consider the structural role of bias, systemic or discriminatory policies, or privilege in shaping family and social history; • *All* relevant factors may be influenced by identities.
2. Select the most appropriate model to guide data gathering, interpretation, and communication.	– Existing models do not explicitly address culturally responsive approaches; may need to modify or at least approach them through a culturally responsive lens (SGFP 1.02).

Data Collection	
3. Use multiple sources of information for each area being assessed. Review the available background information and actively seek important missing elements (SGFP 9.02).	– Seek idiographic and nomothetic data about an evaluee's intersectional identities (e.g., importance of religious identity; cultural practices of racial and ethnic group; violence in evaluee's community affecting actual and perceived safety). – *Ask examinees directly how they identify their race and ethnicity. – *Assess acculturation. – *Show awareness of and respect, interest, and concern for the examinee's social and cultural background.
4. Obtain relevant historical information.	– Expand historical information to include questions regarding: • Discrimination; • Trauma and adverse experience, especially due to REC and identity; • Mistrust of those of other identities (whether majoritized or minoritized) and factors exacerbating or ameliorating mistrust; • Demographics and cultural expectations of communities of origin, including protective factors and privilege.
5. Assess clinical characteristics in relevant, reliable, and valid ways (SGFPs 1.01 & 1.02).	– *Consider how examinee's linguistic backgrounds might impact evaluation process (SGFP 10.02). – Recognize how differences in communication styles can contribute to misunderstanding (SGFP 10.03). – Examples: • Use of African American Language [AAL] as a potential barrier and source of bias for white evaluators to fully capture Black evaluees' statements; • Evaluees from non-Western cultures exhibiting somatic signs of distress. Evaluators should ask about physical symptoms or bodily experiences of psychological distress. – On the basis of examinee's cultural identities: • *Consider the appropriateness of each test regarding evaluees' identities when selecting assessment measures (SGFP 10.02); • *Consider whether any adjustments to test administration are needed (SGFP 10.02).

continued

Table 3.1 *continued*

FMHA Principle	Implications for FMHA Examining the Impact of Intersectional Identities
6. Assess legally relevant behavior (SGFP 10.01).	– Pay attention to psycholegal capacities involving trust, attribution of motive, decision-making, and communication (SGFP 10.03). – *Consider the role of racial trauma, adverse experience, and functional/adaptive identity-related suspicion in these capacities, including during the evaluation. – BIPOC may relate criminal offending to perceived racial injustice that exacerbates hopelessness. – Different worldviews: internal vs. external locus of control and responsibility vary across cultures and racial groups. – Worldview differences between evaluator and evaluee can affect appraisal of evaluee's accountability, agency, and potential treatment response (SGFP 10.03). – *Consider cultural factors in interpreting behavior and examinee's level of insight into their behaviors or mental health. – *Consider cultural context and culturally normative behaviors when formulating diagnoses (SGFP 10.01).
7. Provide appropriate notification of purpose and/or obtain appropriate authorization before beginning (SGFP 6.03).	– *Consider cultural factors when scheduling assessments (SGFP 10.04). – This involves communicating and seeking understanding and decision-making, communication, and attribution of motive of the evaluator and the legal system (SGFP 6.03). – For evaluees who decline to participate, ask why—and include considerations regarding identity (SGFP 6.03). – Possible direct questioning about what, if anything, evaluators might do to establish a sufficient working relationship to obtain good information (e.g., clarifying procedures, seeking observations versus judgments from collaterals, describing hearing of others' experiences with the justice system). – *Assess language fluency for examinees who did not speak English as their first language (SGFP 10.02). – *Select neutral and well-trained interpreters. – *Adjust language (e.g., avoid overly lengthy questions, jargon) when using interpreters. – *Discuss procedures and need for exact, uninterpreted interpretation with interpreters. – *Discuss concepts that will likely arise with the interpreter prior to the interview.

Written Communication	
8. Use plain language; avoid technical jargon.	– Still applies, but language regarding race and identity is technical in a different way. To practice cultural humility, include plain language including a description of evaluee's perception of their race and intersectional identities. May also include scientific or theoretical language (with citations), particularly if speaking about an evaluee outside one's own race or ethnicity (SGFP 11.02).
9. Write report in sections, according to model and procedures.	– Might need to broaden existing sections (e.g., Social History). – Consider adding specific sections (e.g., "Cultural Influences" or "Identity Context" sections to discuss each evaluee within the context of their cultural and intersectional identities). – *Consider the impact of stressors associated with structural inequality, racism, and discrimination in formulations (SGFP 10.03). – *In the report, explain the following based on the examinee's cultural and racial identities (SGFP 10.06 & 11.01): • *Relevant adjustments to data-collection strategies; • *The appropriateness of each test used; • *Psychometric strengths and/or limitations when conveying assessment results; • *If validated measures are not available, address the limitations of each test used and their impact on test interpretation. • *Any adjustments necessary during test administration.

**All items with an asterisk are consensus practices identified in Fanniff et al. (2023).*
Specific SGFPs from the Specialty Guidelines in Forensic Psychology (SGFP) relevant to items are in parentheses (see American Psychological Association, 2013).
Source: Adapted from *Heilbrun et al., 2009*., Reproduced with permission of the Licensor through PLSclear.

Don't

- *Assume that evaluees identify with the word "trauma."* For many people with minoritized identities, trauma based on race, gender, disability, or religion is simply a part of their lived experience. Instead, consider using UnRESTS or open-ended questions to gauge the history and frequency of potentially traumatic experiences related to intersectional identity.
- *Default to conducting REC-neutral evaluations.* By doing so, evaluators miss opportunities to gather information relevant to FMHA and to better understand how their own identities influence the evaluator-evaluee dyad.
- *Inflate or minimize experiences of discriminatory adverse experiences.* Asking open-ended questions can help in this respect, particularly toward exploring one's feelings, frequency, and expectations surrounding such events.
- *Use or interpret tests without considering their norm reference groups.* Diverse evaluees may not be adequately represented in the derivation or validation groups for specific tests. It is important to note these limitations in test selection, or when relevant, in the body of a report. In some cases, it is preferable to avoid using the test entirely for this reason and to document why.

Conclusion

The approaches to culturally responsive FMHA emphasizing intersectional identity described in this chapter are intended for early trainees to advanced practitioners. While each evaluator cannot be an expert on every identity, forensic psychologists can improve how systematically and readily they assess the effects of intersectional identity and structural factors on FMHA. Individual evaluators can begin by asking *how* they consider identity (their own and others'), how they asked about individual evaluees' experience, and if they obtained a clearer understanding of someone's social and historical experience of inclusion and exclusion (structurally and bioecologically). All evaluators can improve fluency in speaking about culturally responsive topics and using information management tools regardless of past experience. I approach this current work from the perspective of a neurodiverse South Asian American woman raised in a multigenerational, culturally Hindu household by parents and family members who were immigrants to the United States. I completed social work training and licensure and worked as a forensic social worker prior to becoming a forensic psychologist. Social work training has cultural perspectives and social justice embedded in standard curricula and takes a distinct clinical approach prioritizing a bioecological model. I also completed post-master's certification in sex therapy, a subfield that requires training and willingness to intentionally discuss sensitive or uncomfortable topics. However, I firmly believe the approaches presented here are feasible for all forensic evaluators. These approaches can add critical context and understanding about intersectionality toward the goals of conducting fair and informed FMHA.

References

American Psychiatric Association. (2013). *Diagnostic and statistical manual of mental disorders* (5th ed.). Author. https://doi.org/10.1176/appi.books.9780890425596

American Psychiatric Association. (2022). *Diagnostic and statistical manual of mental disorders* (5th ed.; text rev.). Author.

American Psychological Association. (2013). Specialty guidelines for forensic psychology. *American Psychologist, 68*(1), 7–19. doi: 10.1037/a0029889

American Psychological Association. (2021). *Equity, diversity, and inclusion framework*. Author. https://www.apa.org/about/apa/equity-diversity-inclusion/framework.pdf

Assefa, M., Williams, W. R., & Stamm, K. (2023). Today's graduate students are racially and ethnically diverse. *Monitor on Psychology, 54*(5), 23. https://www.apa.org/monitor/2023/07/racial-ethnic-diversity-grad-students

Atkin, A. L., Christophe, N. K., Stein, G. L., Gabriel, A. K., & Lee, R. M. (2022). Race terminology in the field of psychology: Acknowledging the growing multiracial population in the U.S. *American Psychologist, 77*(3), 381–393. https://doi.org/10.1037/amp0000975

Babcock, L., Peyser, B., Vesterlund, L., & Weingart, L. (2022). *The No Club: Putting a stop to women's dead-end work*. Simon and Schuster.

Barber Rioja, V., & Rosenfeld, B. (2018). Addressing linguistic and cultural differences in the forensic interview. *International Journal of Forensic Mental Health, 17*(4), 377–386. https://doi.org/10.1080/14999013.2018.1495280

Bronfenbrenner, U. (2005). *Making human beings human: Bioecological perspectives on human development*. Sage Publications.

Carson, E. A. (2021). *Prisoners in 2020—Statistical tables* (NCJ 302776). U.S. Department of Justice, Bureau of Justice Statistics. https://bjs.ojp.gov/content/pub/pdf/p20st.pdf

Crenshaw, K. (1991). Mapping the margins: Intersectionality, identity politics, and violence against women of color. *Stanford Law Review, 43*(6), 1241–1299. https://doi.org/10.2307/1229039

Dror, I. E., & Kukucka, J. (2021). Linear sequential unmasking–expanded (LSU-E): A general approach for improving decision making as well as minimizing noise and bias. *Forensic Science International: Synergy, 3*, 100161. https://doi.org/10.1016/j.fsisyn.2021.100161

Dror, I. E., Thompson, W. C., Meissner, C. A., Kornfield, I., Krane, D., Saks, M., & Risinger, M. (2015). Context management toolbox: A linear sequential unmasking (LSU) approach for minimizing cognitive bias in forensic decision making. *Journal of Forensic Sciences, 60*(4), 1111–1112. https://doi.org/10.1111/1556-4029.12805

Eberhardt, J. L. (2019). *Biased: Uncovering the hidden prejudice that shapes what we see, think, and do*. Penguin Press.

Evans, J. S. B., & Stanovich, K. E. (2013). Dual-process theories of higher cognition: Advancing the debate. *Perspectives on Psychological Science, 8*(3), 223–241. https://doi.org/10.1177/1745691612460685

Fanniff, A. M., York, T., & Gutierrez, R. (2023). Developing consensus for culturally informed forensic mental health assessment: Experts' opinions on best practices. *Law and Human Behavior, 47*(3), 385–402. https://doi.org/10.1037/lhb0000531

Feagin, J. R. (2013). *The white racial frame: Centuries of racial framing and counter-framing* (2nd ed.). Routledge. https://doi.org/10.4324/9780203076828

Forscher, P. S., Lai, C. K., Axt, J. R., Ebersole, C. R., Herman, M., Devine, P. G., & Nosek, B. A. (2019). A meta-analysis of procedures to change implicit measures. *Journal of Personality and Social Psychology, 117*(3), 522–559. https://doi.org/10.1037/pspa0000160

Golash-Boza, T. (2018). *Race and racisms: A critical approach.* Oxford University Press.

Guarnera, L. A., Murrie, D. C., & Boccaccini, M. T. (2017). Why do forensic experts disagree? Sources of unreliability and bias in forensic psychology evaluations. *Translational Issues in Psychological Science, 3*(2), 143–152. https://doi.org/10.1037/tps0000114

Harro, B. (2000). The cycle of socialization. In M. Adams, W. J. Blumenfeld, R. Castañeda, H.W. Hackman, M. L. Peters, & X. Zúñiga (Eds.), *Readings for diversity and social justice: An anthology on racism, antisemitism, sexism, heterosexism, ableism, and classism* (pp. 45–51). Routledge.

Hays, P. A. (2013). *Connecting across cultures: The helper's toolkit.* Sage Publications.

Hays, P. A. (2016). The new reality: Diversity and complexity. In P. A. Hays (Ed.), *Addressing cultural complexities in practice: Assessment, diagnosis, and therapy* (pp. 3–18). American Psychological Association. https://doi.org/10.1037/14801-001

Heilbrun, K., DeMatteo, D., Brooks-Holliday, S., & LaDuke, C. (Eds.) (2014). *Forensic mental health assessment: A casebook* (2nd ed.). Oxford University Press.

Heilbrun, K., Grisso, T., & Goldstein, A. (2009). *Foundations of forensic mental health assessment.* Oxford University Press.

Heilbrun, K., Kavanaugh, A., Grisso, T., Anumba, N., Dvoskin, J., & Golding, S. (2021). The importance of racial identity in forensic mental health assessment. *Journal of the American Academy of Psychiatry and the Law Online, 49*(4), 478–487. https://jaapl.org/content/early/2021/10/12/JAAPL.210099-21

Hunt, J. S., & Shepherd, S. M. (2023). Racial justice in psycholegal research and forensic psychology practice: Current advances and a framework for future progress. *Law and Human Behavior, 47*(1), 1–11. https://doi.org/10.1037/lhb0000526

Jackson, C., Zapotocky, H., Fasone, H., Huppert, T., & Heilbrun, H. (in press). *A review of measures of racial and ethnic identity: Possible application in forensic mental health assessment. Journal of Forensic Practice.*

Kahneman, D. (2011). *Thinking, fast and slow.* Farrar, Straus and Giroux.

Kukor, T., & Miller, S. (2024). *Teaching decision-making and reasoning in forensic supervision* [Webinar]. Palo Alto University. https://www.paloaltou.edu/events/live-teaching-decision-making-and-reasoning-forensic-supervision

Lerner, J. S., & Tetlock, P. E. (1999). Accounting for the effects of accountability. *Psychological Bulletin, 125*(2), 255–275. https://doi.org/10.1037/0033-2909.125.2.255

Metzl, J. M., & Hansen, H. (2014). Structural competency: Theorizing a new medical engagement with stigma and inequality. *Social Science & Medicine, 103*, 126–133.

Mikton, C., & Grounds, A. (2007). Cross-cultural clinical judgment bias in personality disorder diagnosis by forensic psychiatrists in the UK: A case-vignette study. *Journal of Personality Disorders, 21*(4), 400–417. https://doi.org/10.1521/pedi.2007.21.4.400

Monin, B., & Miller, D. T. (2001). Moral credentials and the expression of prejudice. *Journal of Personality and Social Psychology, 81*(1), 33–43. https://doi.org/10.1037/0022-3514.81.1.33

Murrie, D. C., Boccaccini, M. T., Guarnera, L. A., & Rufino, K. A. (2013). Are forensic experts biased by the side that retained them? *Psychological Science, 24*(10), 1889–1897. https://doi.org/10.1177/0956797613481812

Neal, T., & Brodsky, S. L. (2016). Forensic psychologists' perceptions of bias and potential correction strategies in forensic mental health evaluations. *Psychology, Public Policy, and Law, 22*(1), 58–76. https://doi.org/10.1037/law0000077

Neal, T., Lienert, P., Denne, E., & Singh, J. P. (2022). A general model of cognitive bias in human judgment and systematic review specific to forensic mental health. *Law and Human Behavior, 46*(2), 99–120. https://doi.org/10.1037/lhb0000482

Neal, T., & Line, E. N. (2022). Income, demographics, and life experiences of clinical-forensic psychologists in the United States. *Frontiers in Psychology*, 06 July 2022, 910672. https://doi.org/10.3389/fpsyg.2022.910672

Nijdam-Jones, A., Cortvriendt, J., & Daffern, M. (2023). Diversity in the *International Journal of Forensic Mental Health. International Journal of Forensic Mental Health, 22*(4), 354–365. https://doi.org/10.1080/14999013.2023.2243853

Paradies, Y., Ben, J., Denson, N., Elias, A., Priest, N., Pieterse, A., Gupta, A., Kelaher, M., & Gee, G. (2015). Racism as a determinant of health: A systematic review and meta-analysis. *PloS one, 10*(9), e0138511. https://doi.org/10.1371/journal.pone.0138511

Quigley-McBride, A., Dror, I. E., Roy, T., Garrett, B. L., & Kukucka, J. (2022). A practical tool for information management in forensic decisions: Using Linear Sequential Unmasking-Expanded (LSU-E) in casework. *Forensic Science International: Synergy, 4*, 100216. https://doi.org/10.1016/j.fsisyn.2022.100216

Ratkalkar, M., Jackson, C., & Heilbrun, K. (2023). Race-informed forensic mental health assessment: A principles-based analysis. *International Journal of Forensic Mental Health, 22*(4), 314–325. https://doi.org/10.1080/14999013.2023.2178556

Sellier, A. L., Scopelliti, I., & Morewedge, C. K. (2019). Debiasing training improves decision making in the field. *Psychological Science, 30*(9), 1371–1379. https://doi.org/10.1177/0956797619861429

Shepherd, S. M., & Lewis-Fernandez, R. (2016). Forensic risk assessment and cultural diversity: Contemporary challenges and future directions. *Psychology, Public Policy, and Law, 22*(4), 427–438. https://doi.org/10.1037/law0000102

Shepherd, S. M., & Spivak, B. L. (2021). Finding colour in conformity part II—Reflections on structured professional judgement and cross-cultural risk assessment. *International Journal of Offender Therapy and Comparative Criminology, 65*(1), 92–99. https://doi.org/10.1177/0306624X20928025

Smedley, A., & Smedley, B. D. (2005). Race as biology is fiction, racism as a social problem is real: Anthropological and historical perspectives on the social construction of race. *American Psychologist, 60*(1), 16–26. https://doi.org/10.1037/0003-066X.60.1.16

Sreenivasan, S., DiCiro, M., Rokop, J., & Weinberger, L. E. (2022). Addressing systemic bias in violence risk assessment. *The Journal of the American Academy of Psychiatry and the Law, 50*(4), 626–635. doi: 10.29158/JAAPL.220031-21. Epub 2022 Oct 12

Sue, D. W., & Sue, D. (2022). *Counseling the culturally diverse: Theory and practice* (9th ed.). Wiley.

Williams, M. T., Metzger, I. W., Leins, C., & DeLapp, C. (2018). Assessing racial trauma within a DSM–5 framework: The UConn Racial/Ethnic Stress & Trauma Survey. *Practice Innovations, 3*(4), 242–260. https://doi.org/10.1037/pri0000076

Williams, M. T., Osman, M., & Hyon, C. (2023). Understanding the psychological impact of oppression using the Trauma Symptoms of Discrimination Scale (TSDS). *Chronic Stress, 7*, 1–12. https://doi.org/10.1177/24705470221149511

Winer, J. P., Wadsworth, L. P., Forgeard, M., Pinder-Amaker, S., Bjorgvinsson, T., & Beard, C. (2018). Development and implementation of a single-session diversity and multicultural psychology group intervention within an academic psychiatric hospital. *The Behavior Therapist, 41*(7), 327–334.

4

Conducting Forensic Mental Health Assessments with Youth

A Trauma-Informed Approach

Amanda D. Zelechoski, Carly L. Baetz, Kayla Thompson, Emma Roberts, and Emma Cenzon

> *"I just wish that the system would have more of our backstory...like, I didn't ask for this. I didn't ask to get abused. I didn't ask to get adopted. I didn't ask to be in this place. Don't get me wrong, everybody knows the consequences of stealing a car or going and smoking or taking pills or whatever, but nobody thinks about that it's because it's that fight or flight response. And that's what I don't think any of our probation officers or judges understand. We're still juveniles. We're developing and our traumas are a big thing that they don't understand."*
>
> *—Carla, age 17*[1]

Introduction

Carla's story is not uncommon. She is one of countless youth we have encountered in the legal system with stories to tell about their experiences with trauma, often in multiple forms across several stages of development. In fact, the research is now unequivocal that legally-involved youth have rates of trauma exposure that far exceed those found among non-legally involved youth in community samples (Duron et al., 2022). We also know that trauma exposure, particularly chronic or complex trauma, can profoundly shape individuals' behavior, thought processes, and ability to regulate emotions, which, in turn, may influence how they interact with others and the world. Many of the symptoms associated with trauma exposure, such as hypervigilance, dysregulation, and avoidance, can also bring individuals to the attention of the justice system.

[1] All names and other identifying information have been changed to protect the privacy of those in this chapter for whom quotations and case material are cited.

Amanda D. Zelechoski et al., *Conducting Forensic Mental Health Assessments with Youth.* In: *The Path Forward.*
Edited by: Kirk Heilbrun and David DeMatteo, Oxford University Press. © Oxford University Press (2026).
DOI: 10.1093/9780197773031.003.0004

Though forensic mental health assessments (hereinafter FMHA) often involve psycholegal questions in which trauma exposure and impact may be directly or indirectly relevant, little focus has been given to trauma as a particular or necessary domain in forensic evaluation contexts. By using a trauma-informed lens, we are likely to gain information that could fundamentally change our understanding and perspective on a variety of factors that may be central to the psycholegal question, such as the etiology of offending behavior, the risk for future offending, a youth's amenability to treatment, and the weighing of treatment options to recommend those with the highest likelihood of success.

The prevalence of trauma exposure is disproportionately high among both adults and youth involved in the criminal justice system, particularly with respect to adverse childhood experiences or ACEs (Graf et al., 2021; Testa et al., 2022). However, given that more of the extant literature has focused on forensic assessment of trauma with adults (see, e.g., Bailey & Brown, 2020; Javier et al., 2020), this chapter will focus primarily on trauma-informed FMHA for youth. However, much of what will be discussed and recommended is also applicable and transferable to adult forensic assessment contexts.

This chapter will highlight the prevalence of trauma exposure and traumatic stress symptoms among legally-involved youth, as well as the need for trauma-focused FMHA that identifies and contextualizes youths' ongoing experiences of trauma, both prior to and throughout their juvenile justice system involvement. In addition to demonstrating practical considerations and guidelines for trauma-focused FMHA through a case example, the impact of conducting these types of evaluations on both evaluators and trainees will also be discussed. The chapter will conclude with two key insights: (1) all juvenile FMHA are inherently trauma evaluations in some capacity; and (2) the construct of "*post*traumatic stress symptoms" falls short, given that most legally-involved youth continue to experience trauma, both during and far beyond their justice system involvement.

Consider the following illustrative case example to anchor and frame our discussion.

Caleb is a 16-year-old male who was arrested and charged with gun possession and attempted murder approximately 3 months ago. He has been residing in juvenile detention since his arrest. The prosecutor is seeking to waive Caleb's case from juvenile to adult court and Caleb's attorney is objecting to the transfer. A waiver hearing has now been scheduled. In anticipation of the hearing, Caleb's attorney has referred him for a forensic evaluation. In the community, Caleb resides with his mother and younger sister. He is in 9th grade, with a history of one grade retention and multiple suspensions for fighting in his community school. His school attendance has been inconsistent since he began high school at age 14. He has a history of frequent marijuana use, beginning at age 13, and he currently smokes marijuana three to four times per day. He has no known history of using alcohol or other substances. Per his attorney, he has a history of two prior arrests for assaulting peers in school and in the community. But this is his first time in detention, where he has been struggling interpersonally and academically and he has been in several fights with peers since his admission. Caleb's attorney has also indicated that he has no prior history of outpatient or inpatient mental health treatment, or any known mental health diagnoses. His attorney believes that he was referred to the school counselor in 9th grade when his attendance dropped, but he was reportedly "noncompliant" and refused to participate after the first session.

Given the referral question, a typical FMHA for a case like Caleb's would likely include a battery of measures to evaluate his history of offending behaviors, his risk for future offending, his level of sophistication and maturity, and his amenability to treatment. Specific measures might include an intelligence test, an achievement test, a behavioral and/or symptom inventory, a personality assessment, and a risk assessment measure. An evaluator would also likely review Caleb's school records, prior court records, and medical and mental health records, as well as obtain collateral information from his caregivers and teachers. Differential diagnoses would be considered, including substance use disorder; a disruptive, impulse control or conduct disorder; or perhaps Attention-Deficit/Hyperactivity Disorder. When making recommendations for treatment, the evaluator would likely emphasize the need for substance use treatment, as well as treatment that addresses Caleb's impulsivity and underlying anger issues. Although all of these components are important, they are likely to miss a crucial part of Caleb's experience that could profoundly change our conceptualization of his behavior, our understanding of his risk to society, and our ability to provide effective treatment recommendations.

Why a Trauma-Informed Lens is Needed in Juvenile FMHA

Based upon the information we currently have about Caleb, we do not necessarily have a reason to suspect a history of trauma exposure or traumatic stress symptoms. In fact, his presentation is similar to that of many youths with legal involvement (e.g., substance use, aggressive behavior, truancy). So why would we stop to consider the role that trauma might be playing in his case? The answer lies in decades of research revealing alarmingly high rates of trauma exposure and traumatic stress symptoms among legally-involved youth, with 90 percent or more reporting exposure to at least one form of trauma (in their lifetime) (Abram et al., 2004; Astridge et al., 2023; Baglivio et al., 2014). Comparatively, approximately 25 percent of youth under age 16 in the United States report experiencing at least one traumatic event (NCTSN, 2018).

For the large majority of trauma-exposed youth in legal settings, their first exposure to a traumatic event occurred within the first five years of life, with almost one-third of youth reporting exposure to several or co-occurring types of traumatic experiences annually throughout adolescence (Dierkhising et al., 2013). The types of traumatic experiences reported by legally-involved youth are often severe and include physical abuse, sexual abuse, neglect, domestic violence, community violence, and traumatic loss (Ford et al., 2007). Given what we know about rates of trauma exposure in this population, it is not surprising that 70 percent of legally involved youth also meet the criteria for a mental health disorder, with Posttraumatic Stress Disorder (PTSD) accounting for approximately 30 percent of those cases (Dierkhising et al., 2013). As a point of comparison, the national average for a PTSD diagnosis in youth aged 13–18 is approximately 5 percent (Hamblen & Barnett, 2022).

There are many influences that may contribute to the elevated rates of trauma exposure and PTSD among youth in the legal system, including socioeconomic and systemic factors. For example, youth in lower socioeconomic communities are at greater risk of exposure to violence chronic stress, and intergenerational trauma, with more limited access to mental health resources (Harms & Garrett-Ruffin, 2023; Mock & Arai, 2010). Furthermore, legally-involved youth with PTSD are at significant risk for additional challenges, including depression, suicidality, oppositional defiant and conduct disorders, substance abuse, and increased risk-taking behaviors (Ford, 2012). Exposure to trauma and offending also has a bidirectional relationship: trauma exposure can increase the risk of offending behaviors which, in turn, can lead to more trauma exposure (Kerig & Becker, 2010).

It is also important to note that system-involvement itself, especially detention and/or incarceration during adolescence and early adulthood, can also lead to trauma exposure, exacerbation of existing traumatic stress symptoms, and poor physical and mental health outcomes in adulthood (Barnert et al., 2017). For example, many detention centers have high rates of maltreatment, including youth-on-youth violence, sexual abuse, excessive use of physical restraints, and isolation/solitary incarceration (Annie E. Casey Foundation, 2015), and youth may be subjected to unnecessary use of force and/or physical abuse while incarcerated. In 2018, 7.1 percent of adolescents in juvenile justice facilities across the country reported being sexually assaulted in their current facility (Smith & Stroop, 2019). Access to consistent and quality mental health services may also be lacking in some juvenile placements (Sedlak & McPherson, 2010).

Incorporating a Trauma-Informed Lens into Juvenile FMHA

The significant prevalence of trauma exposure among legally-involved youth exemplifies the need for evaluators to approach all types of juvenile FMHA with a trauma-informed lens to ensure the consideration of history and impact of past trauma, provide a safe and empathic setting for youth to share their experiences, and avoid retraumatization (Goldenson et al., 2022). There are a number of ways to approach FMHA with juveniles through a trauma-informed lens, and numerous reasons why it is necessary and important.

At its core, adopting a trauma-informed approach to FMHA shifts the common systemic paradigm from "What is wrong with you?" to "What happened to you?" (Bloom, 2013; Sweeney et al., 2018). When implementing a trauma-informed approach to juvenile FMHA, a critical starting point is identifying and acknowledging the presence and effects of past trauma on current functioning and behavioral presentations of the youth (Goldenson et al., 2022). An in-depth developmental assessment could provide information on past diagnoses, previous involvement in the juvenile justice system, potential history of abuse and neglect, and a diverse array of adverse childhood experiences. This foundational assessment component may reveal potentially traumatic experiences that contribute to or account for the youth's delinquent behavior, as well as contextualize psychiatric symptoms (Simjouw et al., 2024). Ideally, this should be done in a way that helps the youth feel heard and normalizes their experiences.

Nothing in Caleb's known history suggests that he has experienced trauma. And if asked a simple question, such as "Have you ever experienced trauma?," he might still answer "no." Some youth may not know what the word "trauma" means, whereas others may consider their life experiences to be "normal" and do not think of them as "traumatic" (Zelechoski et al., 2021). Some may not have disclosed their experiences to anyone before and may be reluctant to do so in this context. We would also consider utilizing a validated, trauma-specific measure, such as the UCLA PTSD-Reaction Index (Steinberg et al., 2004) or the Child PTSD Symptom Scale for DSM-5 (CPSS-5; Foa et al., 2017), to ask structured and specific questions that explore Caleb's trauma ***history***.

Suppose we discover that Caleb has, in fact, experienced several distressing events in his life. Specifically, he has a history of being bullied by his peers beginning at age 5, and he was sexually abused by his uncle at age 10. His uncle is now in prison but is due to be released to the community in a few months. Let us also imagine that Caleb says that he lives in a community where he has witnessed multiple shootings and has lost good friends to gun violence. He reports that he carries a weapon at all times because he is concerned for his safety. When asked about his biological father, he might reluctantly acknowledge that his father died by suicide in front of him at age 14, but decline to provide any more details about that experience. Some of the pieces now start to fit together in terms of the patterns, timelines, and potential antecedents for Caleb's increasing delinquent behavior and encounters with the legal system.

Using a trauma-informed FMHA with Caleb would incorporate a variety of additional questions and domains into the assessment, and might change the conceptualization of Caleb's past and present functioning and future risk. Examples of using this approach to appraising trauma-related patterns through additional inquiries and considerations are provided in footnotes that follow.

Caleb is a 16-year-old male[2] *who was arrested and charged with gun possession*[3] *and attempted murder approximately 3 months ago. He has been residing in juvenile detention*[4] *since his arrest. The prosecutor is seeking to waive Caleb's case from juvenile to adult court and Caleb's attorney is objecting to the transfer. A waiver hearing has now been scheduled. In anticipation of the hearing, Caleb's attorney has referred him for a forensic evaluation. In the community.*[5] *Caleb resides with his mother and younger sister.*[6] *He is in 9th grade, with a history of one grade retention*[7] *and multiple suspensions for fighting*[8] *in his community school. His school attendance has been inconsistent since he began high school at age 14.*[9] *He has a history of frequent marijuana use, beginning at age 13, and he currently smokes marijuana three to four times per day.*[10] *He has no known history of using alcohol or other substances.*[11] *Per his attorney, he has a history of two prior arrests for assaulting peers in school and*

[2] Additional demographic information, such as race, ethnicity, and gender identity, may provide context for potential exposure to areas such as historical trauma, racial trauma, and identity and intersectionality considerations (see, e.g., Belisle et al., 2024; Riggs Romaine & Kavanaugh, 2019).

[3] Though it may not be relevant, appropriate, or even permissible in some jurisdictions to inquire about the circumstances of the alleged offense in a juvenile waiver/decertification evaluation, there are numerous trauma-related factors and contexts to consider regarding when and why youth carry weapons (see e.g., Ross et al., 2023; Bancalari et al., 2022).

[4] What has his environment been like while in detention? What, if any, consistent relationships does he have both inside and outside of the facility? How is he getting along with peers and staff? What seem to be his triggers? How has he adapted to his environment over time?

[5] What is his community like? What was it like growing up in his neighborhood? What were the risk factors and protective factors inherent in that environment? What, if any, community support was available to Caleb as he grew up? Was he involved with any extracurricular sports, clubs, organizations, churches, or other prosocial activities? Were those opportunities available and accessible to him? What additional environmental exposures or deficiencies might have posed additional risk, such as lead exposure, lack of access to safe outdoor green spaces, food insecurity, and community violence.

[6] What are Caleb's relationships with his mother and younger sister? How have those relationships changed over time? What is Caleb's history of and capacity for attachment? Has his biological father ever been involved in his life? Have there been other caregivers or adults who lived in the home or played a caregiving role throughout his childhood?

[7] What were the circumstances surrounding the grade retention? Was it due to disruptive behavior, potential learning disorder, failing grades, truancy, or other reasons? Caleb's grade level and developmental stage at the time may also play a role.

[8] What is the context for these fights and are there patterns? What seem to be the precursors? Is Caleb initiating these fights? Defending others? What seems to trigger him? What does the sequence and timing look like; e.g., is the conflict brewing over several days or are they more impulsive or spur of the moment? How severe are the resulting injuries to him and others? Is he getting into fights anywhere other than school?

[9] Did the attendance problems not start until high school? If so, what about that transition from middle school to high school caused such a shift in school attendance (e.g., peers, logistics of getting to/from school, increased academic difficulty, other reasons)? Additional contextual information could further elucidate this issue. For example, does he walk to school? Take the bus? Feel safe at school?

[10] What additional contextual information can we gather about Caleb's marijuana use patterns? How did he first get introduced to marijuana? When and how much does he typically use? In what environments and with whom? What times of day? How does it make him feel? What is his perspective on why he uses? For many trauma-exposed youth, substance use (marijuana, in particular) is a means of self-regulation when alternative strategies are unknown or not accessible (Scheidell et al., 2018).

[11] It is notable that Caleb has reportedly not experimented with alcohol or other substances besides marijuana. This could indicate that he has used one substance as an effective method of self-regulation, rather than experimenting with substances for any number of other reasons. This has implications for both treatment and level of risk considerations.

in the community but this is his first time in detention.[12] *While in detention, Caleb has been struggling interpersonally*[13] *and academically*[14] *and he has been in several fights with peers since his admission.*[15] *Caleb's attorney has also indicated that he has no prior history of outpatient or inpatient mental health treatment or any known mental health diagnoses.*[16] *His attorney believes that he was referred to the school counselor*[17] *in 9th grade when his attendance dropped, but he was reportedly "noncompliant" and refused to participate after the first session.*[18]

As we learn more about Caleb's history of trauma, we also learn that he is experiencing repeated threats of violence in detention and is struggling with being away from his mother and sister for the first time in his life. Further exploring his symptoms and current functioning, we also begin to suspect that at least some of the emotional and behavioral dysregulation reported by his attorney and other collateral sources is actually related to traumatic stress. To appraise this possibility, we could administer a trauma-specific measure to better capture and understand his ***symptoms*** (e.g., UCLA PTSD-RI). Through this more comprehensive and specific assessment, we learn that Caleb is experiencing clinically significant symptoms of hypervigilance, hyperreactivity, negative cognitions about himself and others, and avoidance of thoughts and feelings related to his traumatic experiences. Adding this information to our knowledge about his history of being bullied and his chronic exposure to community violence and loss, we have added context to explain his hypervigilance and hyperactivity, and the catalytic role these may be playing in his maladaptive behaviors, such as fighting and carrying a weapon. When we further explore his use of substances through a trauma lens, we learn from Caleb that he has been experiencing nightmares about his mother dying every night since his father passed away, and using marijuana is the only thing that reduces these bad dreams. He also indicates that because of these nightmares, he is unable to go to sleep if he does not smoke marijuana before going to bed each night.

[12] What were the circumstances surrounding those prior altercations and arrests? Are there patterns that emerge related to his fighting behavior, as well as antecedents and consequences? What might have been environmental or interpersonal triggers that led to the physical altercations?

[13] What do Caleb's current interpersonal struggles look like? What does his interpersonal and social history look like? Has he had periods of strong relational health and consistent, stable connections to others, including peers and mentors? Does he have the capacity to form interpersonal connections and, if so, what conditions are conducive to form such connections?

[14] Is Caleb struggling in similar or different ways as when he was previously held back? What does his "struggling" look like (e.g., missed assignments, failing tests, spacing out)?

[15] Have the fighting situations been similar to prior fighting patterns in school or in the community for Caleb? Or are there different circumstances or catalysts that seem to have emerged in the detention setting?

[16] Has Caleb ever been evaluated or are these assumptions based on lack of contact with the mental health system? Have there been any signs of mental health issues or symptoms?

[17] What was the basis of that referral?

[18] There are numerous avenues to explore related to Caleb's participation, or lack thereof, in meeting with his school counselor. For many trauma-exposed youth, the level of immediate intimacy required in such contexts, without having built a trusting and safe therapeutic relationship, can trigger fight-flight-freeze responses that may look like treatment resistance or noncompliance, but are actually innate and protective survival instincts taking over. For more information, discussion, and recommendations on this specific issue, see Zelechoski et al. (2024).

In addition to using a trauma-informed approach to understanding Caleb's current challenges and risk factors, we can also employ a trauma-informed framework to identify and incorporate Caleb's strengths and protective factors into our overall conceptualization. Protective factors play a critical role in mitigating the impact of trauma on legally involved youth, fostering resilience and promoting positive outcomes despite adverse experiences (Aazami et al., 2023). There are a variety of ways to assess protective factors and resilience in youth, including through interview questions of the youth and collateral sources, as well as by administering specific assessment tools. For more information on incorporating assessment of protective factors, see, e.g., Shaw et al. (2020), Aazami et al. (2023), and Lensch et al. (2021).

How to Conduct a Trauma-Informed Juvenile FMHA

For FMHA to be trauma-informed, the process and manner in which the assessment is conducted are as important as the content and overall conceptualization. Knowledge of both past developmental trauma and current mental health functioning necessitate a focus on providing sensitivity, empathy, and capacity for choice and empowerment for the youth throughout the assessment process (Goldenson et al., 2022). This is especially important for youth residing in juvenile detention settings, where they may not feel safe. It is therefore essential to focus on building trust, establishing rapport, and attempting to provide a safe and comfortable space when conducting FMHAs. It is important for the evaluator to clearly explain their role in a transparent, developmentally-appropriate, and trauma-sensitive manner. Building rapport and establishing trust for trauma-exposed youth will also likely yield more accurate and thorough responses to assessment questions (Dianiska et al., 2024).

In its guide to conducting trauma-informed mental health assessments, the Substance Abuse and Mental Health Services Administration (SAMHSA, 2014), gave several examples of actionable trauma-informed components: (1) providing youth with as much information as possible about the measures used in the evaluation; (2) allowing youth to choose the order in which they complete measures; (3) offering to conduct the evaluation over the course of several sessions; and (4) being as transparent as possible about the nature and purpose of the evaluation, including how their responses will be used and next steps. Similarly, the National Child Traumatic Stress Network (NCTSN; 2015) published a set of essential elements related to trauma-informed juvenile justice, which included assessment guidelines. Specifically, NCTSN recommended that trauma-informed assessments: (1) include instruments that are reliable and valid for legally-involved youth; (2) identify current trauma-

and behavioral health-related symptoms causing impairment; (3) determine the relationship between traumatic stress and behavioral health symptoms and criminogenic factors; and (4) identify the youth's strengths that can positively impact treatment and legal processes.

Approaching FMHA through the lens of trauma can also decrease the likelihood of retraumatizing the youth being assessed (Goldenson et al., 2022). Knowing how to recognize when a youth is being potentially retraumatized and how to appropriately intervene is important when conducting FMHA (Center on Child Trauma and Well-being, n.d.). Additionally, it is important to carefully observe the youth's behavioral changes and patterns to recognize if they are in a state of retraumatization (Center for Substance Abuse Treatment, 2014). With detention settings already perpetuating feelings of unsafety and violence for youth, the sensitive nature of questions that are asked during an FMHA could be retraumatizing. It is important to avoid language that implies judgment about youths' traumatic exposures, use age-appropriate language when speaking with youth about their traumatic experiences, answer questions, and react in a transparent and compassionate manner. It is also critical to be cognizant of youths' triggers (if known) and to avoid exacerbating feelings and traumatic stress symptoms (Center for Substance Abuse and Treatment, 2014).

Returning to Caleb, we would begin our assessment with a focus on building rapport and providing a thorough explanation of the purpose of our evaluation. We would also make sure that he is aware of the differences between this type of assessment versus those conducted within the context of therapy. We would also make sure that Caleb is aware of our plan for the evaluation session, including the types of assessment measures used and the topics explored. Questions related to past experiences of trauma and/or trauma-related symptoms would be prefaced with an explanation about those questions (e.g., we intend to ask him some questions about difficult things he may have experienced in his life and we ask these questions of every youth we evaluate). The timing of these questions is also important; we would intentionally ask trauma-related questions somewhere in the middle of the evaluation rather than at the beginning or end. This ensures that we've established sufficient rapport with Caleb before delving into more sensitive topics, but we are not concluding the evaluation with a discussion of his difficult experiences. We would also try to provide Caleb with as much choice throughout the evaluation process as possible, within the parameters of facility policies and prioritizing safety. This might include describing the components of the evaluation process or the different types of psychological tests we need to administer and allowing him to collaborate with us in structuring the order of these activities, when we take breaks, and (when appropriate and in accordance with test administration protocols) whether we read assessment questions to him or he reads them to himself.

Additional Considerations

Considering the Potential Impact of Trauma-Informed FMHA on the Evaluator

Given the high prevalence of trauma in forensic populations, mental health professionals who conduct FMHA should be cognizant of their increased risk for developing PTSD symptoms as a result of repeated exposure to others' traumatic experiences. This is sometimes referred to as Secondary Traumatic Stress (STS) (Hensel et al., 2015). Related symptoms may include increased anxiety, dissociation, intrusive thoughts, withdrawal/avoidance, and difficulties with sleep (Levin et al., 2021). Signs of STS may also include irritability, mood swings, anger or guilt, difficulty concentrating, anhedonia, changes in appetite, increased hypervigilance, fatigue, decreased empathy, and changes in self-esteem. These symptoms can resemble those of PTSD and can have negative consequences for one's general health, relationships, and work performance. STS can have a detrimental effect on work performance by increasing the risk of bias, impairing judgment, producing lower-quality work, and decreasing productivity. STS can also lead to cognitive distortions, emotional numbing, and impaired cognitive functioning, all of which may interfere with an evaluator's ability to reach an unbiased opinion.

Evaluators have an ethical duty to recognize how they might be internalizing trauma exposure and actively work to minimize these effects (see e.g., APA, 2017, Section 2.06; Goldenson & Gutheil, 2023). As a clinician, an overall healthy well-being is crucial to effectively conducting forensic mental health assessments. One can reduce vulnerability to secondary trauma and its effects in a variety of ways across a multitude of domains. First, one must ensure they are maintaining their physical health by getting enough exercise, eating well-balanced meals, and prioritizing sleep to feel relaxed. Maintaining mental and emotional well-being is equally important and can be done by practicing mindfulness and engaging in hobbies. Just as they are essential for youth, support systems also play a vital role. In the workplace, one must establish clear boundaries, learn to say "no," and divide responsibilities to reduce constant exposure to trauma. Being proactive by recognizing the signs of secondary trauma and engaging in coping strategies will better prepare an evaluator to handle the effects of secondary trauma. Maintaining healthy boundaries can also be protective and is more feasible with supervision and support from other professionals (Davies & Jones, 2024). Training on recognizing the signs and symptoms of STS, as well as individual and organizational strategies for mitigating the impacts of STS, is also imperative.

Is it Really "Post" Traumatic?

Lastly, for many legally-involved youth, trauma exposure is chronic, ongoing, and often exacerbated within the communities and/or settings where they may be residing (i.e., detention or youth placement; Novak & De Francisco Lopes, 2022). As a result, it is important to consider our diagnostic nomenclature's use of the prefix "post" when we diagnose youth with PTSD. For many of these youth, "post" is simply a misnomer that fails to capture the true nature of the experiences they are currently facing and will continue to face upon release back into the community (Burrell, 2013). Accordingly, though a formal PTSD diagnosis may still be appropriate and necessary, providing additional context that trauma exposure is likely to be ongoing and its impact manifesting in evolving ways for particular youth could be critical for overall case conceptualization and legal and clinical decision-making.

Conclusion

Given the high prevalence rates of trauma exposure and trauma-related mental health symptoms among youth in the legal system, every juvenile FMHA should incorporate a trauma-informed approach. This approach prioritizes recognizing the widespread impact of trauma, integrating knowledge about trauma into assessment practices, and actively working to avoid re-traumatization during evaluations. Employing a trauma-informed lens ensures that evaluators consider the complex interplay between trauma and behavior, providing a more accurate and compassionate understanding of the youth's circumstances. Furthermore, this work underscores the importance of self-care and systemic support for evaluators, who are at risk of experiencing secondary traumatic stress. By adopting a trauma-informed framework, forensic mental health evaluators can better conceptualize juvenile cases, promote effective rehabilitation, contribute to fairer outcomes in the justice system, and sustain their own well-being, thereby advancing the broader goals of equity, healing, and resilience among trauma-impacted populations.

References

Aazami, A., Valek, R., Ponce, A. N., & Zare, H. (2023). Risk and protective factors and interventions for reducing juvenile delinquency: A systematic review. *Social Sciences, 12*(9), 474. https://doi.org/10.3390/socsci12090474

Abram, K. M., Teplin, L. A., Charles, D. R., Longworth, S. L., McClelland, G. M., & Dulcan, M. K. (2004). Posttraumatic stress disorder and trauma in youth in juvenile detention. *Archives of General Psychiatry, 61*(4), 403–410.

American Psychological Association. (2017). *Ethical principles of psychologists and code of conduct.* American Psychiatric Publishing.

Annie E. Casey Foundation. (2015). *Maltreatment of youth in U.S. juvenile corrections facilities - An update.* https://assets.aecf.org/m/resourcedoc/aecf-maltreatmentyouthus corrections-2015.pdf

Astridge, B., Li, W. W., McDermott, B., & Longhitano, C. (2023). A systematic review and meta-analysis on adverse childhood experiences: Prevalence in youth offenders and their effects on youth recidivism. *Child Abuse & Neglect, 140*, 106055.

Baglivio, M. T., Epps, N., Swartz, K., Huq, M. S., Sheer, A., & Hardt, N. S. (2014). The prevalence of adverse childhood experiences (ACE) in the lives of juvenile offenders. *Journal of Juvenile Justice*, *3*(2), 1–17.

Bailey, T. D., & Brown, L. S. (2020). Complex trauma: Missed and misdiagnosis in forensic evaluations. *Psychological Injury and Law*, *13*(2), 109–123.

Bancalari, P., Sommer, M., & Rajan, S. (2022). Youth exposure to endemic community gun violence: A systematic review. *Adolescent Research Review*, *7*(3), 383–417. https://doi.org/10.1007/s40894-022-00178-5

Barnert, E. S., Dudovitz, R., Nelson, B. B., Coker, T. R., Biely, C., Li, N., & Chung, P. J. (2017). How does incarcerating young people affect their adult health outcomes? *Pediatrics*, *139*(2), e20162624. https://doi.org/10.1542/peds.2016-2624

Belisle, L. A., Pinchevsky, G., & Ortega, G. (2024). Examining the prevalence of adverse childhood experiences (ACEs) among justice-involved youth in the US: The importance of accounting for race/ethnicity, gender, and gendered racial/ethnic groups. *Child Abuse & Neglect*, *149*, 106514.

Bloom, S. L. (2013). *Creating sanctuary: Toward the evolution of sane societies*. Routledge.

Burrell, S. (2013). *Trauma and the environment of care in juvenile institutions*. National Center for Child Traumatic Stress.

Center for Substance Abuse Treatment. (2014). *Understanding the impact of trauma*. National Library of Medicine, Substance Abuse and Mental Health Services Administration. www.ncbi.nlm.nih.gov/books/NBK207191/

Davies, J., & Jones, L. (2024). Trauma informed organisational consultancy and staff supervision in forensic services. *International Journal of Forensic Mental Health*, *23*(4), 403–414. https://doi.org/10.1080/14999013.2024.2337635

Dianiska, R. E., Quas, J. A., & Lyon, T. D. (2024). Using rapport building to improve information yield when interviewing adolescents: A systematic review and call for research. *Child Abuse & Neglect*, *154*, 106898. https://doi.org/10.1016/j.chiabu.2024.106898

Dierkhising, C. B., Ko, S. J., Woods-Jaeger, B., Briggs, E. C., Lee, R., & Pynoos, R. S. (2013). Trauma histories among justice-involved youth: Findings from the National Child Traumatic Stress Network. *European Journal of Psychotraumatology*, *4*, 10.3402/ejpt.v4i0.20274. https://doi.org/10.3402/ejpt.v4i0.20274

Foa, E. B., Asnaani, A., Zang, Y., & Capaldi, S. (2017). Psychometrics of the Child PTSD Symptom Scale for DSM-5 for trauma-exposed children and adolescents. *Journal of Clinical Child and Adolescent Psychology*, *47*(1), 38–46. https://doi.org/10.1080/15374416.2017.1350962

Ford, J. D. (2012). Posttraumatic stress disorder among youth involved in juvenile justice. In E. L. Grigorenko (Ed.), *Handbook of juvenile forensic psychology and psychiatry* (pp. 485–501). Springer US. https://doi.org/10.1007/978-1-4614-0905-2_31

Ford, J., Chapman, F., Hawke, J., & Albert, D. (2007). *Trauma among youth in the juvenile justice system: Critical issues and new directions*. https://www.courts.ca.gov/documents/BTB25-1G-02.pdf

Goldenson, J., Brodsky, S. L., & Perlin, M. L. (2022). Trauma-informed forensic mental health assessment: Practical implications, ethical tensions, and alignment with therapeutic jurisprudence principles. *Psychology, Public Policy, and Law*, *28*(2), 226–239. https://doi.org/10.1037/law0000339

Goldenson, J., & Gutheil, T. (2023). Forensic mental health evaluators' unprocessed emotions as an often-overlooked form of bias. *Journal of the American Academy of Psychiatry and the Law. 51*(4), 551–557. https://jaapl.org/content/51/4/551

Graf, G. H. J., Chihuri, S., Blow, M., & Li, G. (2021). Adverse childhood experiences and justice system contact: A systematic review. *Pediatrics*, *147*(1). e2020021030. https://doi.org/10.1542/peds.2020-021030

Hamblen, J., & Barnett, E. (2022). *PTSD in children and adolescents – PTSD*. National Center for PTSD. Va.gov. https://www.ptsd.va.gov/professional/treat/specific/ptsd_child_teens.asp

Harms, M. B., & Garrett-Ruffin, S. D. (2023). Disrupting links between poverty, chronic stress, and educational inequality. *NJP Science of Learning*, *8*(1), 50. https://doi.org/10.1038/s41539-023-00199-2

Hensel, J. M., Ruiz, C., Finney, C. & Dewa, C. S. (2015). Meta-analysis of risk factors for secondary traumatic stress in therapeutic work with trauma victims. *Journal of Traumatic Stress*, *28*: 83–91. https://doi.org/10.1002/jts.21998

Javier, R. A., Owen, E. A., & Maddux, J. A. (Eds.). (2020). *Assessing trauma in forensic contexts.* Springer Nature.

Kerig, P. K., & Becker, S. P. (2010). Trauma and girls' delinquency: Critical issues and new directions. *Journal of Child & Adolescent Trauma*, *3*(1), 51–59. https://link.springer.com/article/10.1080/19361521.2012.697023

Lensch, T., Clements-Nolle, K., Oman, R. F., Evans, W. P., Lu, M., & Yang, W. (2021). Adverse childhood experiences and co-occurring psychological distress and substance abuse among juvenile offenders: The role of protective factors. *Public Health*, *194*, 42–47.

Levin, A. P., Putney, H., Crimmins, D., & McGrath, J. G. (2021). Secondary traumatic stress, Burnout, compassion satisfaction, and perceived organizational trauma readiness in forensic science professionals. *Journal of Forensic Sciences*, *66*(5), 1758–1769. https://doi.org/10.1111/1556-4029.14747

Mock, S. E., & Arai, S. M. (2010). Childhood trauma and chronic illness in adulthood: Mental health and socioeconomic status as explanatory factors and buffers. *Frontiers in Psychology. 1*, 246. doi: 10.3389/fpsyg.2010.00246

National Child Traumatic Stress Network. (2015). *Essential elements of a trauma-informed juvenile justice system.* The National Child Traumatic Stress Network. https://www.nctsn.org/resources/essential-elements-trauma-informed-juvenile-justice-system

Novak, A., & De Francisco Lopes, V. (2022). Child delinquency, ACEs, and the juvenile justice system: Does exposure to ACEs affect justice system experiences for children?. *Youth Violence and Juvenile Justice*, *20*(2), 113–138.

Riggs Romaine, C. L., & Kavanaugh, A. (2019). Risks, benefits, and complexities: Reporting race and ethnicity in forensic mental health reports. *International Journal of Forensic Mental Health, 18*(2), 138–152.

Ross, K. M., Walsh, C. S., O'Connor, K. E., & Sullivan, T. N. (2023). Ecological promotive and protective factors deterring gun carriage for young adults living in communities with high rates of community violence. *Journal of Community Psychology, 51*(3), 1164–1180.

Scheidell, J. D., Quinn, K., McGorray, S. P., Frueh, B. C., Beharie, N. N., Cottler, L. B., & Khan, M. R. (2018). Childhood traumatic experiences and the association with marijuana and cocaine use in adolescence through adulthood. *Addiction, 113*(1), 44–56.

Sedlak, A. J., & McPherson, K. S. (2010). Youth's needs and services: Findings from the Survey of Youth in Residential Placement. *Juvenile Justice Bulletin*, Office of Juvenile Justice and Delinquency Prevention. https://www.ojp.gov

Shaw, M., Rogers, G., & Geffner, R. (2020). Trauma and resiliency in forensically involved youth: Applications, evaluations, and recommendations. In R. A. Javier, E. A. Owen, & J. A. Maddux (Eds.), *Assessing trauma in forensic contexts* (pp. 443–461). Springer Nature.

Simjouw, A., Vogel, V., & De Ruiter, C. (2024). Trauma-informed care training in forensic mental health services: A scoping review. *International Journal of Forensic Mental Health, 23*(4), 375–389. https://doi.org/10.1080/14999013.2024.2323934

Smith, E., & Stroop, J. (December, 2019). *Sexual victimization reported by youth in juvenile facilities, 2018.*| Bureau of Justice Statistics, U.S. Department of Justice. https://bjs.ojp.gov/library/publications/sexual-victimization-reported-youth-juvenile-facilities-2018

Steinberg, A. M., Brymer, M. J., Decker, K. B., & Pynoos, R. S. (2004). The University of California at Los Angeles Post-Traumatic Stress Disorder Reaction Index. *Current Psychiatry Reports.*, 6(2), 96–100. doi: 10.1007/s11920-004-0048-2. PMID: 15038911.

Substance Abuse and Mental Health Services Administration. (2014). *Trauma-informed care in behavioral health services* (Treatment Improvement Protocol (TIP) Series 57).

Sweeney, A., Filson, B., Kennedy, A., Collinson, L., & Gillard, S. (2018). A paradigm shift: Relationships in trauma-informed mental health services. *British Journal of Psychiatry Advances, 24*(5), 319–333. https://doi.org/10.1192/bja.2018.29

Testa, A., Jackson, D. B., Ganson, K. T., & Nagata, J. M. (2022). Adverse childhood experiences and criminal justice contact in adulthood. *Academic Pediatrics, 22*(6), 972–980.

Zelechoski, A. D., Bohner, J., & Perry, B. D. (2024). Beyond recidivism: Reconceptualizing success through relational health for trauma-exposed youth experiencing juvenile justice involvement. *Frontiers in Psychology, 15*, 1263451. https://doi.org/10.3389/fpsyg.2024.1263451

Zelechoski, A. D., Cross, H. L., Luehrs, R., Freedle, A., Bruick, S., Harrison, K., . . . Will, K. (2021). Trauma assessment in juvenile justice: Are we asking the right questions in the right ways? *Journal of Aggression, Maltreatment & Trauma, 30*(3), 324–346.

Additional Resources

Baetz, C. L., Branson, C. E., Weinberger, E., Rose, R. E., Petkova, E., Horwitz, S. M., & Hoagwood, K. E. (2022). The effectiveness of PTSD treatment for adolescents in the juvenile justice system: A systematic review. *Psychological Trauma: Theory, Research, Practice, and Policy, 14*(4), 642–652. https://doi.org/10.1037/tra0001073

Branson, C. E., Baetz, C. L., Horwitz, S. M., & Hoagwood, K. E. (2017). Trauma-informed juvenile justice systems: A systematic review of definitions and core components. *Psychological Trauma: Theory, Research, Practice, and Policy, 9*(6), 635–646. https://doi.org/10.1037/tra0000255

Dargis, M., Sitney, M., Caldwell, B., Caldwell, M., Edwards, B. G., Harenski, C., Anderson, N. E., Van Rybroek, G., Koenigs, M., & Kiehl, K. A. (2019). Development of an expert-rater assessment of trauma history in a high-risk youth forensic sample. *Psychological Trauma: Theory, Research, Practice and Policy, 11*(7), 713–721. https://doi.org/10.1037/tra0000423

Duron, J. F., Williams-Butler, A., Mattson, P., & Boxer, P. (2022). Trauma exposure and mental health needs among adolescents involved with the juvenile justice system. *Journal of Interpersonal Violence, 37*(17–18), NP15700–NP15725.

Edner, B. J., Glaser, B. A., Calhoun, G. B., Dukes-Murray, H., Khan, Z., & Donaldson, K. (2020). Efficacy of the MMPI-A in detecting trauma among delinquent youth: Cross-validation of the Trauma Scale for Juvenile Offenders (TSJO). *Journal of Forensic Psychiatry & Psychology, 31*(1), 1–16.

Jahic, I., Trulson, C. R., Caudill, J. W., Bonner, T., Slemaker, A., & DeLisi, M. (2021). Adverse childhood experiences and forensic typologies: Getting specific about trauma among institutionalized youth. *International Journal of Environmental Research and Public Health, 18*(21), 11307. https://doi.org/10.3390/ijerph182111307

Keels, M. (2024). Responding to the trauma that is endemic to the criminal legal system: Many opportunities for juvenile prevention, intervention, and rehabilitation. *Annual Review of Criminology, 7*(1), 329–355.

Kerig, P. K., Ford, J. D., Alexander, A. R., & Modrowski, C. A. (2024). Interventions for trauma-affected youth in the juvenile justice system: An overview of diagnostic, ethical, and clinical challenges and evidence-based treatments. *Psychological Injury and Law, 17*(3), 199–220. https://doi.org/10.1007/s12207-024-09497-5

McNair, F. D., Havens, J., Surko, M., Weinberger, E., Baetz, C., Moaveni, M., Bart, A., Marr, M., Quinlan, C., & Horwitz, S. M. (2019). Post-traumatic stress and related symptoms among juvenile detention residents: Results from intake screening. *Child Abuse & Neglect*, *92*, 22–31. https://doi.org/10.1016/j.chiabu.2019.03.011

Riggs-Romaine, C. L., Goldstein, N. E. S., Hunt, E., & DeMatteo, D. (2011). Traumatic experiences and juvenile amenability: The role of trauma in forensic evaluations and judicial decision making. *Child & Youth Care Forum*, *40*(5), 363–380. https://doi.org/10.1007/s10566-010-9132-4

5
Behavioral Threat Assessment in Schools

Dewey Cornell and Jordan Kerere

Behavioral threat assessment and management (BTAM, often shortened to "threat assessment") is a relatively new field of forensic practice that originated with the U.S. Secret Service as a means to identify individuals whose behavior indicated that they posed a serious threat to attack the president (Fein & Vossekuil, 1998). However, BTAM rapidly expanded to become a violence prevention strategy for threats in the workplace, schools, and other settings (Meloy & Hoffman, 2021).

BTAM differs from other forms of violence risk assessment in several important ways. BTAM is not intended to prevent all forms of violence but is concerned with targeted violence, meaning that there is an identifiable target, usually an individual, but sometimes multiple parties in a particular setting or group. A threat assessment is initiated in response to a report that someone has made a threat or engaged in threatening behavior that suggests they are planning or preparing to attack their target.

BTAM is typically conducted by multidisciplinary teams that bring together mental health professionals, law enforcement, and other professionals, such as administrative leaders, legal counsel, and human resources depending on the setting. Such a team can provide diverse perspectives to analyze the threat and a wide scope of action to manage risk.

The BTAM team collects information to distinguish between individuals who made a threat without serious intent or ability to carry it out from those who *pose* a threat, meaning that they have both serious intent and the capability to carry out an attack. When a person who poses a threat has been identified, the BTAM process shifts from assessment to management. Management refers to preventive interventions designed to reduce the risk of violence, which can range from protective actions and security measures to efforts to address a grievance, conflict, or other problem motivating the individual.

After a series of school shootings in the 1990s, both the FBI (O'Toole, 2000) and U.S. Secret Service (Fein et al., 2002) recommended that schools use a threat assessment approach. The U.S. Secret Service's National Threat Assessment Center (NTAC) has provided general guidance (NTAC, 2019) for schools to develop their

Dewey Cornell and Jordan Kerere, *Behavioral Threat Assessment in Schools*. In: *The Path Forward*.
Edited by: Kirk Heilbrun and David DeMatteo, Oxford University Press. © Oxford University Press (2026).
DOI: 10.1093/9780197773031.003.0005

own threat assessment programs. Other groups built upon this guidance to construct more specific models for schools to follow, most notably the Salem-Keizer Cascade Model (Van Dreal, 2016), the Violence Threat Risk Assessment (VTRA) model (Cameron, 2018), and the Comprehensive School Threat Assessment Guidelines[1] (CSTAG; Cornell, 2024). This chapter uses research and practice with the CSTAG model (developed by chapter author Cornell) to examine the psychological services that school threat assessment provides to students, and its potential value in preventing their involvement in the criminal justice system.

Psychological Services in Schools

Most public schools report delivering psychological services to their students, including individual (84 percent), group (56 percent), and family (38 percent) interventions (NCES, 2024). Public schools receiving federal funding are required to provide specialized services to students identified as having some form of disability. In 2023, 7.5 million students received special education services or accommodations under the Individuals with Disabilities Act (IDEA), representing 15 percent of the total public school population (NCES, 2024).

Schools do not typically use DSM diagnoses, but rather classify students based on their need for learning support. Although categories and criteria vary across states, students are often designated as in need of services based on a pattern of strengths and weaknesses of skills necessary for learning (e.g., behavioral and emotional control, reading, writing, math). In brief, when a student is identified as eligible for services, the school follows standard guidelines to establish an Individualized Education Program (IEP) or a 504 Plan (Lemons et al., 2019).

Many students are not eligible for special education services, but still have mental health needs. Suicidality, for example, is prevalent among adolescents, with 20 percent of high school students reporting suicidal ideation and 9 percent reporting at least one suicide attempt (Centers for Disease Control and Prevention [CDC], 2023). These students might be supported through short-term counseling. Students experiencing a loss or trauma (such as the death of a family member) might be served by a bereavement support group.

Schools use a multi-tiered model of service delivery similar to the public health prevention model. At tier one, interventions are provided for all students, such as schoolwide anti-bullying (Limber, 2011) or social-emotional learning programs (Ross & Tolan, 2017). At tier two, interventions are targeted for at-risk groups, such as mediation sessions between students having a dispute or conflict. At tier three, students can receive ongoing, intensive interventions, such as special education services.

[1] CSTAG was originally named the Virginia Student Threat Assessment Guidelines (VSTAG).

Psychological services are delivered by a variety of different professionals, primarily school psychologists, school counselors, and school social workers. In addition, schools may contract with community-based clinical psychologists, child psychiatrists, and social workers (Rappaport, 2001). More than 50,000 school psychologists are employed in elementary and secondary schools (U.S. Bureau of Labor Statistics, 2023). The responsibilities of school psychologists are diverse, but they are most often engaged in testing to determine eligibility for special education services, and depending on the district, also provide counseling and intervention services, collaborate with teachers and families, and participate in school-wide prevention programs. The National Association of School Psychologists (NASP) recommends 1 school psychologist for every 500 students, but the national ratio is 1:1,119 (NASP, 2024).

School counselors can also provide mental health services to students, as well as academic support and career preparation. Approximately 112,000 school counselors work across the United States to meet the needs of 50,000,000 students (American Civil Liberties Union [ACLU], 2019). The American School Counselor Association (ASCA) recommends 1 counselor for every 250 students, but the national average is 1:385 (ASCA, 2023).

School social workers play a critical role in helping families connect with community systems to support student needs. The School Social Work Association of America recommends 1 social worker for every 250 students, but the national average is 1:2,106 (ACLU, 2019).

The advent of BTAM teams has added to the responsibilities of school mental health professionals. One consequence of this nationwide understaffing of school mental health professionals is a huge gap between needs and available services. According to the National Center for Education Statistics (2024), 58 percent of students report seeking school-based mental health services, but only 19 percent received any treatment. Further, less than half of public schools agree they can effectively provide services to meet all student needs (NCES, 2024).

Effective and well-implemented interventions not only help individual students succeed in school, but also prevent future delinquency and involvement in the criminal justice system (Farrington et al., 2017; Mielke & Farrington, 2021). Students with mental health needs who are not receiving services are more likely to struggle academically, engage in disruptive behaviors, and receive more punitive consequences like exclusionary discipline or law enforcement referrals (Gerlinger et al., 2021; Mielke & Farrington, 2021). One meta-analysis found that many types of services (e.g., cognitive-behavioral therapy, multisystemic therapy, parent and foster care training) can be effective at reducing school-based violence and criminal behavior (Farrington et al., 2017). Students who do become involved in the legal system at an early age are at increased risk for antisocial behavior, mental illness, substance abuse, and recidivism (Fisher & Fisher, 2023; Mowen et al., 2018; Wiley & Esbensen, 2016).

The U.S. Department of Education Office for Civil Rights Data Collection (CRDC) reported that 61,900 students were referred to law enforcement, leading to 8,900 school-based arrests in the 2020–2021 school year (2023). The U.S. Department of Justice (DOJ) estimates that approximately half of school-based arrests were for drug possession, disorderly conduct, and fighting (Davis, 2023). About 21 percent of school-based arrests involved threats against school faculty, 28 percent threats against the school facility, and 36 percent threats against students (Davis, 2023).

Scope of Violence in Schools

School shootings have had a devastating impact on many communities and created nationwide concern that schools are dangerous places (Cornell, 2015). As a result, school security has grown into a multi-billion-dollar industry with products ranging from metal detectors and video cameras to bullet-resistant glass and school shooter drills (Jennings et al., 2011; Tanner-Smith & Fisher, 2015). Although the traumatic impact of any school shooting is enormous, the 130,000 K-12 schools in the United States are, statistically, much safer locations than the public perceives. Shootings and homicides are much more common in residences, and in public buildings such as stores and restaurants, than in schools (Nekvasil & Cornell, 2012). Despite continuing perceptions that schools are not safe, only about 2 percent of homicides of school-age children occur at school (CDC, 2024). Annual FBI crime statistics show comparatively low rates of serious violent crime (homicide, rape, robbery, and aggravated assault) in schools (NIBRS, 2024). These statistics are important to consider because many teachers believe that their workplace is a dangerous setting and parents are afraid to send their child to school (Brenan, 2022). This affects the credibility of threat assessment teams when they conclude that a student's threat is not as serious as it is perceived to be by others.

Although schools are relatively safe from serious violent crime, there are substantial problems with less severe forms of aggression. About 19 percent of middle and high school students report being bullied in the past school year and 6 percent of high school students participated in a fight (Irwin et al., 2024). Further, 6 percent of teachers have been threatened by students and 4 percent have been attacked (Irwin et al., 2024).

Comprehensive School Threat Assessment Guidelines

The Comprehensive School Threat Assessment Guidelines (CSTAG; Cornell, 2024) is a BTAM model developed at the University of Virginia in 2001.[2] BTAM must be adapted for K-12 schools to recognize the unique needs and challenges of the educational setting. First, the model must consider the developmental immaturity of young

[2] One of this chapter's authors (DC) discloses that he has a financial interest as the developer of the Comprehensive School Threat Assessment Guidelines.

people that affects their judgment, self-control, and response to frustration. Verbal threats and minor physical altercations are relatively common among children, and often can be managed with supervision, education, and counseling. Teams must be careful not to overreact to misbehavior that warrants correction and discipline, but rarely poses a serious threat of physical injury or death. The likelihood of severe or life-threatening acts of violence is much lower in children and begins to rise in adolescence, peaking in late adolescence and early adulthood. Thus, a central task of the CSTAG team is to distinguish the small number of serious threats from the much larger number of non-serious threats. Threat assessment is often construed as a hunt for a mass shooter, but in practice, the vast majority of threats involve students who have behaved inappropriately and raised concern, but do not pose a serious threat of violence.

Second, schools have an educational mission that is qualitatively different from a workplace or government agency. Schools have an overarching responsibility to help all students learn, grow, and be successful. Many of the students referred for a threat assessment are experiencing challenges in school and have educational and support needs. In contrast, an employer has a markedly different obligation to employees or customers who threaten violence, and often seeks a strategy of de-escalation leading to permanent separation. CSTAG teams instead take a problem-solving approach that aims to help the student resolve whatever conflict or concern underlies the threat with the goal, in most cases, of keeping them in school.

Third, schools have direct access to their students and a variety of services that are not available in other settings. Schools can both assess and manage most threatening situations, and need only call upon community resources in the most challenging cases. It is especially important that the school has a multidisciplinary team that can draw upon a multi-tiered menu of services, from short-term counseling and parent consultation to intensive special education.

The threat assessment process works similarly to court diversion programs (Wilson & Hoge, 2012). In schools, CSTAG teams can divert students from law enforcement actions and exclusionary school discipline (e.g., out-of-school suspension, expulsion) onto more supportive pathways. School exclusion has been identified as an ineffective and frequently harmful practice that does not improve student behavior and increases the risk of school failure and dropout (Morgan et al., 2014). Students removed from their schools face many difficulties upon re-entry. One systematic review found that systematic barriers in the education system, such as inflexible enrollment policy and strict credit requirements, inadequate follow-up with community services, and delays in stable housing and finances caused significant stress for juveniles trying to reintegrate into their school communities and led to re-engagement in criminal behavior (O'Neill et al., 2017). The cycle between exclusionary discipline, criminal behavior, and legal system involvement, known as the school-to-prison pipeline, has affected millions of juveniles (Mallett, 2016). The ability of CSTAG teams to divert students who make threats from exclusionary discipline or law enforcement consequences (elaborated below) diverts them from this pipeline.

The CSTAG model takes a flexible, context-dependent, and problem-solving approach to threat assessment that is based on the idea that students typically make threats when they are unable to independently solve a problem; therefore, the threat assessment team aims to help the student resolve this problem in a prosocial, nonviolent manner. CSTAG teams use a five-step decision tree (see Appendix) and a 184-page manual (Cornell, 2024) to triage threats and focus attention on the most serious cases. When a threat is reported, the CSTAG team follows a protocol to collect data from multiple sources in order to make a threat classification and take appropriate action. Typically, the team will analyze the threat report, interview the student of concern as well as witnesses or targets of the threat, consult with relevant school staff (such as the student's teacher or counselor), and review relevant records. The data collection process is flexible and can be adjusted to the seriousness and complexity of the case. There are four threat classification conclusions: (1) not a threat, (2) transient threat, (3) serious substantive threat, and (4) very serious substantive threat.

In about 10 percent of cases, the threat is just a rumor or misunderstanding and the case is resolved as *not a threat* (Cornell & Maeng, 2024; Maeng et al., 2024). For instance, a group of students might start a false rumor that another student is planning to attack the school. While this rumor might be intended as nothing more than a prank, others might believe the rumor, become alarmed, and report it. For example, a student was arrested and placed in a juvenile detention center for threats that turned out to be a fabrication by others (Yancey-Bragg, 2022). Reported threats that spread across the school can raise great concern that the school administration must try to assuage.

If a student has made a threatening statement or engaged in some other form of threatening behavior (such as attempting to acquire a firearm from a peer), the team will consider whether the threat is transient or substantive. A transient threat is an expression of emotion without serious intent to harm someone, whereas a substantive threat involves serious intent. This distinction is crucial because it determines the actions of the team in response to the threat. Transient threats are often ill-advised attempts at humor or rhetorical statements that express frustration or anger. Teams classify a threat as transient if they are confident that the student does not have the intent to carry out the threat. In such cases, the student usually offers an explanation for the statement or behavior of concern and there is sufficient corroborating evidence that is convincing to the team. For example, a student who has been teased by a peer might become angry and threaten to "kill you" if he does not stop. Based on interviews with the participants and witnesses, and consideration of the student's history as well as his response to questions on a standard interview, the team might decide that the student does not seriously intend to kill his classmate. The team would classify such a threat as transient, but follow up with interventions to deal with the peer conflict. Approximately 70 percent of cases are classified as transient (Burnette et al., 2018; Cornell & Maeng, 2024; Maeng et al., 2024). Students who make transient threats might benefit from social skills training or conflict resolution, but typically do not require exclusionary discipline or law enforcement consequences.

However, if the team cannot confidently classify the threat as transient, they will treat it as a *substantive* threat. When a threat is classified as substantive, the team takes immediate protective action to prevent the threat from being carried out, usually by increasing their supervision of the student, warning threatened individuals, and notifying parents of all involved students. The team also considers what interventions are needed to further reduce the risk of violence depending on the seriousness of the threat.

There are two types of substantive threats: *serious substantive* threats to assault or fight someone (similar to a simple assault) and *very serious substantive* threats to kill, rape, or injure someone with a weapon (similar to a felonious assault). The distinction between serious and very serious substantive threats refers to the type of harm and not the level of appraised risk. Once there is concern that there is any non-trivial degree of risk that the student will carry out a threat to harm someone, the team must undertake protective actions designed to reduce the risk of violence. Thus, the focus is on risk reduction and not efforts to quantify an elusive (and likely unstable) level of risk. The team's primary concern for students who make serious or very serious substantive threats is to manage the threat by identifying actions and interventions that can reduce the risk of violence. Approximately 15 percent of threat assessment cases are classified as serious substantive (Burnette et al., 2018; Maeng et al., 2024). Arguments that lead to threats to fight are common in middle grades and often lead to some form of counseling to resolve the dispute (Burnette et al., 2020).

Very serious substantive threats comprise about 5 percent of threat assessment cases (Cornell & Maeng, 2024; Maeng et al., 2024). In response to a very serious substantive threat, teams will undertake a more extensive safety evaluation, reviewing all available information from relevant sources and conducting detailed interviews with the student, parents, and other relevant individuals. The safety interview of the student is usually conducted by a mental health professional, either a member of the school team or, in some districts, someone from a community-based agency.

During the safety evaluation, the student who made the threat should be carefully supervised by school personnel, parents, or other responsible adults. The goal of the safety evaluation is to identify what problem(s) the student who made the threat is experiencing and to determine what kinds of services or support are needed to reduce the risk of violence. The safety evaluation should assess the student's motives for making the threat and their perception of the potential consequences for carrying out a violent action. The evaluation should also cover other sources of distress, conflict, or trauma in the student's life that may have contributed to their threat. The CSTAG manual includes a detailed outline of questions and topics for the safety interviews with the student, parents, and other parties (Cornell, 2024).

As part of the safety evaluation, the school resource officer often will conduct a law enforcement investigation to determine whether a crime has been committed, whether the offense justifies arrest or legal charges, and whether there is evidence of planning and/or preparation for an attack. The officer will recommend any changes in school security measures.

The safety evaluation is used to construct a safety plan. This plan differs from more traditional risk assessments because it does not label the student as dangerous or make a prediction of whether the student will be violent. This model recognizes that assigning a risk level or score to a student is likely to be unreliable and potentially misleading. If the team is unable to resolve the threat as transient, they will focus on reducing risk with protective actions (like warning victims, notifying parents, and increasing supervision) and interventions to address any identified problems or needs (such as peer conflicts, bullying, or emerging mental illness). The safety plan is concerned with identifying risk and protective factors, and practical interventions that will reduce the risk of violence, consistent with evolving models of risk assessment (Heilbrun et al., 2020, 2024). One difference, however, is that the safety plan has a more immediate timeframe and narrow scope because it is concerned with a particular threat toward identified targets, and aims to resolve the conflict or problem underlying that threat.

This safety plan usually outlines how a student can return to school and under what conditions. The plan also considers the impact of the threat on others in the school community and what support services and information-sharing is appropriate. The implementation and effectiveness of the safety plan is monitored by the threat assessment team to make sure the school community remains safe and the students and others involved in the threat are appropriately supported. The CSTAG manual provides a series of case studies including behavior intervention plans (Cornell, 2024).

CSTAG Research

The first CSTAG field test was conducted in 2002 and found that school teams could safely resolve student threats of violence with little reliance on exclusionary discipline or law enforcement consequences (Cornell et al., 2004). To date, the University of Virginia research team has conducted six controlled studies on CSTAG outcomes (Cornell et al., 2009, 2011, 2012; JustChildren & Cornell, 2013; Maeng et al., 2020a; Nekvasil & Cornell, 2012), as well as statewide assessments of CSTAG use in Virginia (Cornell & Maeng, 2020) and Florida (Maeng et al., 2024). These studies have concentrated primarily on the prevalence and characteristics of student threats, threat assessment classifications made by teams, and case outcomes, including disciplinary actions and services provided. A series of studies examined the fairness and equity of threat assessment outcomes across student groups defined by race and ethnicity, family income, and disability status (Cornell et al., 2024b, 2024c; Maeng et al., 2024).

Threat Characteristics

Threats occur in all grade levels and are made by students from all demographic groups, but disproportionately by males, students in middle grades (upper elementary and middle school), and students receiving special education services (Burnette et al., 2020; Maeng et al., 2024). Florida schools using the CSTAG model conducted a threat assessment on 1.5 percent of their student body, with slightly higher rates in middle (1.8 percent) and high (1.6 percent) schools and lower rates in elementary schools (0.9 percent; Cornell et al., 2024a).

Threats by Adults

Many states and districts limit their threat assessment teams to threats made by students, but states like Virginia require threat assessments for threats by any individual. According to an annual state survey, Virginia public schools reported that about 98 percent of 5064 threat assessment cases involved currently enrolled students during the 2021–2022 school year (Virginia Department of Criminal Justice Services, 2022). The remaining cases involved students from other schools, former students, parents, current or former staff, and a spouse or relative of someone associated with the school.

The CSTAG manual (Cornell, 2024) provides guidance on adapting the model for adult cases, with examples involving threats by a parent, the intimate partner of a staff member, and an employee. Threats by adults often raise greater concern than threats by children because adults have a greater capability to carry out a threat and schools have fewer options in responding to an adult threat. Threats by adults that arouse fear can constitute criminal acts. However, many threats by an adult could be transient expressions of anger or frustration without serious intent. In cases in which an adult has made an angry, threatening statement, they should be given an opportunity to calm down and reflect on what they have said, and in many cases, the threat can be resolved as transient.

When a threat by an adult is not readily resolved as transient, school authorities must turn to the risk reduction strategies and resources available to them. Teams should always look for ways to de-escalate and resolve conflicts, but in some circumstances, school authorities might restrict someone from coming onto school property and targeted individuals might seek protective orders. A serious threat that rises to the level of a criminal act might lead to arrest or legal charges.

Violent Outcomes

There has been limited research on violent attacks or injuries following a threat assessment. Because school shootings are extraordinarily rare, and none of the thousands of schools in CSTAG studies have experienced a school shooting, it has not been possible to make scientifically rigorous claims about the effects of threat assessment on shootings. It can be observed that CSTAG teams have responded to tens of thousands of student threats, many involving threats to kill or shoot someone, with no fatalities reported.

Some research has examined the frequency of student attempts to carry out a threat and whether anyone was injured by an attack. In Virginia, about 3 percent of student threats were attempted, with substantive threats being 36 times more likely to be attempted than transient threats (Burnette et al., 2018). Attempt rates in Florida have been somewhat higher. In the largest sample to date of violent outcomes following a threat assessment ($N = 14{,}048$), approximately 11 percent of threats involved an attack and less than 1 percent resulted in injuries requiring hospital treatment (Kerere et al., 2024).

There is some correlational evidence that threat assessment can reduce more common types of student aggression such as fighting and bullying. Threat assessment teams often identify peer conflicts and bullying as the underlying problem leading to a student threat and their interventions could have a wider impact on school climate. In a quasi-experimental controlled study of 280 high schools, state-administered school climate surveys showed that students in schools using CSTAG reported less bullying and greater willingness to seek help than students in control group schools (Cornell et al., 2009). School records also showed fewer long-term suspensions when using the CSTAG model. A second controlled study of forty-nine high schools found that using CSTAG was associated with reductions in long-term suspensions and bullying compared to control group schools (Cornell et al., 2011). A study of 332 middle schools found students in schools using CSTAG reported less peer victimization, teachers reported feeling safer, and school records again showed a decline in long-term suspensions (Nekvasil & Cornell, 2015).

Law Enforcement Actions

School resource officers (SROs) and other school-based law enforcement personnel have become increasingly prevalent in U.S. schools. In the 2019–2020 year, there were about 23,000 active SROs (Davis, 2023). There are mixed findings about the role of SROs in schools. Most research has found that students, teachers, and parents have a positive view of their school's SRO (Crichlow-Ball et al., 2022; Jancaric et al., 2024; Wood & Hampton, 2021), but there are concerns that the presence of SROs is correlated with increased rates of school exclusion and arrests (Tocci et al., 2023). Several studies reported that schools that received federal funding to bring SROs into their schools had a subsequent increase in both law enforcement actions and disciplinary actions.

It is not surprising that arrests and suspensions would increase in schools with high levels of student behavior problems that successfully obtained grant funding to combat them, but such schools might not represent the larger population of schools that do not necessarily have the same conditions and needs. Schools in which the leadership is concerned about student misbehavior and crime might be expected to take a stricter approach to school discipline independent of whether there are SROs. Moreover, other studies find that the level of disciplinary and law enforcement actions in a school are associated with the role of the SROs in the school, with some schools emphasizing a strict enforcement approach and others using officers in a more preventive role (Debnam et al., 2022; Fisher & Devlin, 2020). More rigorous studies are needed to demonstrate a causal effect of SRO presence independent of the actual levels of crime and misbehavior in the school and independent of other school leadership actions. Concerns about SROs could be ameliorated by more carefully selecting officers, clearly defining their role, and integrating them with school functions (Canady, 2018).

Research has consistently shown that students who receive a threat assessment rarely face law enforcement action. A Virginia study of 1836 students found that 5 percent of students who received a threat assessment also received formal law enforcement action (Cornell et al., 2018). In Florida, more than 21,000 students received a threat assessment, but only 150 (0.7 percent) were arrested, 77 (0.4 percent) charged, and 33 (0.2 percent) incarcerated (Cornell et al., 2024c). There were no significant racial differences in either sample. Instead, older grade level and substantive classification were significantly related to higher odds of legal action.

Fairness and Equity

There is a longstanding concern about the fairness and equity of school discipline, especially the use of exclusionary practices (e.g., suspension, expulsion, transfer) that are disproportionately applied to students of color, students from low-income families, and students with disabilities (Morgan et al., 2014). Zero-tolerance policies were adopted as a school safety measure in the 1990s and apply harsh disciplinary consequences in the form of automatic removal from school for any violation of a school safety rule, regardless of the circumstances or the severity of the infraction (Johnson & Johnson, 2023). Although zero tolerance continues to be a popular educational practice, multiple studies have found that suspension does not achieve its goals of improving student behavior and deterring other students from similar misbehavior (Huang & Cornell, 2021) and is instead associated with lower academic achievement and higher risk of school dropout and juvenile court involvement (Fabelo et al., 2011; Noltemeyer et al., 2015).

From the outset, school threat assessment was conceived as an alternative to zero tolerance (O'Toole, 2000). Whereas the hallmark of zero tolerance is the uniform application of strict punishment regardless of the circumstances, BTAM takes the opposite approach: each case receives an assessment that considers the circumstances and context of a student's behavior, followed by management actions proportional to the seriousness of the threat and the risk of violence. Research has consistently found that schools using CSTAG make comparatively little use of school exclusion and show reductions over time (Cornell et al., 2018, 2024b). Notably, a cluster randomized controlled trial of forty schools found that students in schools following the CSTAG model were significantly more likely to receive counseling and a parent conference, and less likely to receive a suspension or alternative school placement than students in schools following a traditional discipline approach (Cornell et al., 2012).

In the largest sample to date (*N* = 18,776 students in 1700 Florida schools), 4985 (26.5 percent) students were suspended from school and 291 (1.5 percent) were expelled following their threat assessment (Cornell et al., 2024b; Maeng et al., 2024). Consistent with previous findings in Virginia (Cornell et al., 2018), rates of expulsion and placement change did not significantly differ by student race (Cornell et al., 2024b). These results contrast markedly with disparities observed for other discipline cases in the same schools.

Practitioner Advice

As behavioral threat assessment becomes an increasingly recognized standard of practice in schools, mental health professionals can be a valuable resource for both assessment and intervention phases of the process. Schools often seek external consultation for challenging cases from community agencies, mental health facilities, and independent practitioners.

Unlike risk assessments, which evaluate general potential for harm at any time, threat assessments focus specifically on evaluating and managing identified threats of violence toward specific targets. This distinction is crucial because it often requires the evaluator to gather information from multiple sources about a particular incident, grievance, or interpersonal conflict. The practitioner must obtain access to school records and other information available to the threat assessment team, as well as permission to interview key sources, most often the student of concern and the student's parents.

There are two primary goals of the safety planning interview with a student of concern. First, the evaluator wants to examine the student's mental status and overall psychological functioning. The evaluator might identify any urgent mental health problems that require hospitalization or immediate treatment, such as psychotic symptoms or suicidal intent. Beyond acute needs, there may be chronic mental health concerns, such as anxiety, anger, or impulsivity that warrant intervention. There may also be distress due to trauma, abuse, neglect, or other difficulties in the student's family or social environment. There may be underlying conditions, such as autism spectrum disorder, that limit the student's ability to navigate social situations, communicate effectively, and resolve interpersonal conflicts. Depending on the student's presentation, the evaluator might consider psychological testing relevant to a particular diagnosis or condition.

The second primary goal of the safety interview is to understand the student's motives and intentions regarding the target of the threat and what kind of grievance or conflict underlies the threat. What steps has the student taken to plan or prepare to carry out the threat? Has the student acquired weapons, practiced using them, sought accomplices, or made other preparations for an attack? Threat assessment practitioners try to determine where the student falls on a "pathway to violence" (Calhoun & Weston, 2021). As much as reasonably possible, the evaluator will look for corroboration from other sources of information, recognizing that students might not be forthcoming or entirely accurate in their report.

The threat assessment practitioner understands that violence does not result from a particular set of factors, and there is no number of factors that reaches the threshold for violence. There are many different patterns of factors that can lead to violence and for this reason, checklists of warning signs have limited value. The context and circumstances of the behavior can be more important than the number of factors. A malignant combination of two or three factors could be more dangerous than a lengthy list of factors that do not cohere around a motive and plan for violence.

Students with disabilities that affect emotional and behavioral adjustment are disproportionately referred for a threat assessment (Cornell et al., 2024a). In such cases, any recommendations for mental health services or changes to the student's educational program must be considered by the student's special education team and follow special education procedures. In some cases, a threat assessment might identify a student who is not currently recognized as having a disability, but might need an evaluation for special education services. Again, the school must follow its special education procedures to evaluate the student's learning needs and determine eligibility. This can be a complicated process, and threat assessment should be conducted in close coordination with special education services.

For further guidance, the National Center for School Safety published a *School Threat Assessment Toolkit* (Cornell & Maeng, 2024) that outlines recommended practices across different threat assessment models. It identifies relevant aspects of the Family Educational Rights and Privacy Act (FERPA) as well as special education considerations involving IEP and 504 Plans. There is a list of state-level contacts for information about state threat assessment requirements. The *International Handbook of Threat Assessment* (Meloy & Hoffman, 2021) provides an extensive overview of foundational knowledge and fields of practice.

To ensure the effectiveness of threat assessment programs like the CSTAG model, schools must provide robust support to achieve and maintain high fidelity of implementation, adequate staffing, and sufficient funding. Implementation fidelity requires schools to adhere closely to established threat assessment procedures and continuously evaluate their effectiveness (Cornell, 2024). Adequate staffing involves recruiting professionals who have been trained in threat assessment. Sufficient funding is necessary to support these staffing needs, as well as provide necessary resources, like additional training, reference manuals, and consultation services.

Threat assessment cannot be conducted if students, teachers, parents, and others in the school community are not willing to report threats or similar concerning behavior. Studies by the U.S. Department of Justice (Peterson, 2021) and the U.S. Secret Service (Alathari et al., 2021) found that a significant number of mass shooters and individuals planning school attacks had previously shared their intentions, often leading to the prevention of these attacks.

Schools should provide multiple methods for students and others in the school community to report threats through both confidential and anonymous methods (U.S. Secret Service, 2023). Students may be reluctant to report threats because they regard it as snitching and fear retaliation. An educational program on threat assessment that stressed the importance of preventing a shooting and distinguished seeking help from snitching was able to increase student willingness to report threats (Stohlman & Cornell, 2019). Students are more willing to report threats when they perceive school discipline to be fair and the school climate to be supportive (Payne et al., 2024).

Conclusion

Behavioral threat assessment and management is a growing practice in U.S. schools and other settings. Research has shown school threat assessment to be a safe and effective alternative to zero-tolerance approaches. The threat assessment process can divert students from exclusionary school discipline and criminal justice involvement that have been described as a school-to-prison pipeline (Brown et al., 2020). The school or community-based mental health professional plays a key role in the threat assessment process by identifying the problems or concerns underlying the threat and providing students with counseling and mental health services to reduce the risk of violence.

For trainees or practitioners early in their careers, there are many workshops, conferences, and related training opportunities in the field of behavioral threat assessment and management. The Association of Threat Assessment Professionals (ATAP; https://www.atapworldwide.org/) is a resource for professional development and offers a certification in threat management. The National Threat Assessment Center of the U.S. Secret Service (https://www.secretservice.gov/protection/ntac) provides training and consultation on threat assessment, as does the FBI through its National Center for the Analysis of Violent Crime (https://www2.fbi.gov/hq/isd/cirg/ncavc.htm#bau). The federal Cybersecurity and Infrastructure Security Agency (CISA; https://www.youtube.com/watch?v=Ddc6j4w6naA) offers a wide range of training in security topics, including school safety and behavioral threat assessment. Finally, the Department of Homeland Security's National Threat Evaluation and Reporting (NTER) Office provides a Master Training Program (https://www.dhs.gov/btai).

Appendix School Threat Assessment Decision Tree

School Threat Assessment Decision Tree

Step 1. **Evaluate the threat.**
Obtain a detailed account of the threat, usually by interviewing the person who made the threat, the intended victim, and other witnesses. Write the exact content of the threat and key observations by each party. Consider the circumstances in which the threat was made and the student's intentions. Is there communication of intent to harm someone or behavior suggesting intent to harm?

→ **No** → Not a threat. Might be an expression of anger that merits attention.

↓ Yes

Step 2. **Attempt to resolve the threat as transient.**
Is the threat an expression of humor, rhetoric, anger, or frustration that can be easily resolved so that there is no intent to harm? Does the person retract the threat or offer an explanation and/or apology that indicates no future intent to harm anyone?

→ **Yes** → Case resolved as transient; add services as needed.

↓ No

Step 3. **Respond to a substantive threat.**
For all substantive threats:

a. Take precautions to protect potential victims.
b. Warn intended victim and parents.
c. Look for ways to resolve conflict.
d. Discipline student, when appropriate.

Serious means a threat to hit, fight, or beat up whereas very serious means a threat to kill, rape, or cause very serious injury with a weapon.

→ **Serious** → Case resolved as serious substantive threat; add services as needed.

↓ Very serious

Step 4. **Conduct a safety evaluation for a very serious substantive threat.**
In addition to a–d above, the student may be briefly placed elsewhere or suspended pending completion of the following:

e. Screen student for mental health services and counseling; refer as needed.
f. Law enforcement investigation of evidence of planning and preparation, and criminal activity.
g. Develop safety plan that reduces risk and addresses student needs. Plan should include review of Individual Education Plan if already receiving special education services and further assessment if possible disability.

↓

Step 5. **Implement and monitor the safety plan.**
Document the plan.
Maintain contact with the student.
Monitor whether plan is working and revise as needed.

References

Alathari, L., Drysdale, D., Driscoll, S., Blair, A., Mauldin, D., Carlock, A., McGarry, J., Cotkin, A., Nemet, J., Johnston, B., & Vineyard, N. (2021). *Averting targeted school violence: A U.S. Secret Service analysis of plots against schools.* National Threat Assessment Center, United States Secret Service, U.S. Department of Homeland Security.

American Civil Liberties Union (ACLU). (2019). *Cops and no counselors: How the lack of school mental health staff is harming students.* https://www.aclu.org/wp-content/uploads/legal-documents/030419-acluschooldisciplinereport.pdf

American School Counselor Association (ASCA). (2023). *Student-to-school-counselor ratio 2022–2023.* https://www.schoolcounselor.org/getmedia/a988972b-1faa-4b5f-8b9e-a73b5ac44476/ratios-22-23-alpha.pdf

Brenan, M. (2022). *Ten years after the Sandy Hook School massacre: A look back. Gallup.* https://news.gallup.com/opinion/gallup/406394/ten-years-sandy-hook-school-massacre-look-back.aspx

Brown, S. J., Mears, D. P., Collier, N. L., Montes, A. N., Pesta, G. B., & Siennick, S. E. (2020). Education versus punishment? Silo effects and the school-to-prison pipeline. *Journal of Research in Crime and Delinquency*, *57*(4), 403–443. https://doi.org/10.1177/0022427819897932

Burnette, A. G., Datta, P., & Cornell, D. (2018). The distinction between transient and substantive student threats. *Journal of Threat Assessment and Management*, *5*(1), 4–20. https://doi.org/10.1037/tam0000092

Burnette, A. G., Konold, T., & Cornell, D. (2020). Grade-level distinctions in student threats of violence. *Journal of School Violence*, *19*(3), 323–335. https://doi.org/10.1080/15388220.2019.1694031

Calhoun, F. S., & Weston, S. W. (2021). Rethinking the path to intended violence. In J. R. Meloy & J. Hoffman (Eds.), *International handbook of threat assessment* (2nd ed., pp 392–406). Oxford University Press.

Cameron, J. K. (2018). *Violence Threat Risk Assessment (VTRA) Protocol.* North American Center for Crisis Response, Inc.

Canady, M. (2018). *Best practices for school resource officer programs.* National Association of School Resource Officers. https://www.nasro.org/clientuploads/About-Mission/NASRO-Standards-and-Best-Practices.pdf

Centers for Disease Control and Prevention (CDC). (2023). *Youth risk behavior survey: Data summary and trends report.* https://www.cdc.gov/yrbs/dstr/index.html

Centers for Disease Control and Prevention (CDC). (2024). *Key findings: School-associated violent death study.* https://www.cdc.gov/youth-violence/data-research/school-associatedviolentdeathstudy/index.html#:~:text=Homicide%20is%20the%20second%20leading,from%20a%20school%2Dsponsored%20event

Civil Rights Data Collection (CRDC). (2023). *Referrals to law enforcement and school-related arrests in U.S. public schools.* https://www2.ed.gov/about/offices/list/ocr/docs/referrals-and-arrests-part-5.pdf

Cornell, D. (2024). *Comprehensive School Threat Assessment Guidelines.* School Threat Assessment Consultants LLC.

Cornell, D. (2015). Our schools are safe: Challenging the misperception that schools are dangerous places. *American Journal of Orthopsychiatry*, *85*, 217–220. http://dx.doi.org/10.1037/ort0000064

Cornell, D. G., Allen, K., & Fan, X. (2012). A randomized controlled study of the Virginia Student Threat Assessment Guidelines in kindergarten through grade 12. *School Psychology Review*, *41*(1), 100–115. https://doi.org/10.1080/02796015.2012.12087378

Cornell, D., Gregory, A., & Fan, X. (2011). Reductions in long-term suspensions following adoption of the Virginia Threat Assessment Guidelines. *Bulletin of the National Association of Secondary School Principals*, *95*, 175–194. https://doi.org/10.1177/0192636511415255

Cornell, D., Kerere, J., Konold, T., Maeng, J., Afolabi, K., Huang, F., & Cowley, D. (2024a). *Referral rates for school threat assessment.* [Unpublished manuscript]. School of Education and Human Development, University of Virginia.

Cornell, D., & Maeng, J. (2020). *Student threat assessment as a safe and supportive prevention strategy: Final technical report.*. Curry School of Education, University of Virginia.

Cornell, D., & Maeng, J. (2024). *School Threat Assessment Toolkit.* National Center for School Safety.

Cornell, D., Maeng, J., Huang, F., Shukla, K., Konold, T. (2018). Racial/ethnic parity in disciplinary consequences using student threat assessment. *School Psychology Review*, *47*(2), 183–195. https://doi.org/10.17105/SPR-2017-0030.V47-2

Cornell, D., Maeng, J., Winter, S., Huang, F., Konold, T., Kerere, J., Afolabi, K., & Cowley, D. (2024b). *Behavioral threat assessment and equity in exclusionary school discipline.* [Unpublished manuscript]. School of Education and Human Development, University of Virginia.

Cornell, D., Maeng, J., Winter, S., Huang, F., Konold, T., Kerere, J., Afolabi, K., & Cowley, D. (2024c). *Equity in law enforcement actions following a school threat assessment.* [Unpublished manuscript]. School of Education and Human Development, University of Virginia.

Cornell, D., Sheras, P., Gregory, A., & Fan, X. (2009). A retrospective study of school safety conditions in high schools using the Virginia Threat Assessment Guidelines versus alternative approaches. *School Psychology Quarterly*, *24*(2), 119–129. https://dx.doi.org/10.1037/a0016182

Cornell, D., Sheras, P., Kaplan, S., McConville, D., Douglass, J., Elkon, A., McKnight, L., Branson, C., & Cole, J. (2004). Guidelines for student threat assessment: Field-test findings. *School Psychology Review*, *33*(4), 527–546. https://doi.org/10.1080/02796015.2004.12086266

Crichlow-Ball, C., Cornell, D., & Huang, F. (2022). Student perceptions of school resource officers and threat reporting. *Journal of School Violence, 21*(2), 222–236. https://doi.org/10.1080/15388220.2022.2054423

Davis, E. J. (2023). *School resource officers, 2019–2020.* Bureau of Justice Statistics, Office of Justice Programs, U.S. Department of Justice.

Debnam, K., Camacho, D., Henderson, L., & Bottiani, J. (2022). "A social worker... teacher... principal—we're everybody": The school police officer role in schools. *Journal of School Violence, 21*(4), 459–474. https://www.google.com/search?client=safari&rls=en&q=Debnam%2C+K.%2C+Camacho%2C+D.%2C+Henderson%2C+L.%2C+%26+Bottiani%2C+J.+(2022).+"A+social+worker...+teacher...+principal—we're+everybody"%3A+The+school+police+officer+role+in+schools.+Journal+of+School+Violence%2C+21(4)%2C+459–474&ie=UTF-8&oe=UTF-8

Fabelo, T., Thompson, M. D., Plotkin, M., Carmichael, D., Marchbanks, M. P., & Booth, E. A. (2011). *Breaking schools' rules: A statewide study of how school discipline relates to students' success and juvenile justice involvement.* Justice Center, The Council of State Governments. https://csgjusticecenter.org/wp-content/uploads/2020/01/Breaking_Schools_Rules_Report_Final.pdf.

Farrington, D. P., Gaffney, H., Losel, F., & Ttofi, M. M. (2017). Systematic reviews of the effectiveness of developmental prevention programs in reducing delinquency, aggression, and bullying. *Aggression and Violent Behavior, 33*, 91–106. https://www.ojp.gov/pdffiles1/nij/179981.pdf.

Fein, R. A., & Vossekuil, B. (1998). *Protective intelligence and threat assessment investigations: A guide for state and local law enforcement officials* (NIJ/OJP/DOJ Publication No. 170612). U.S. Department of Justice. https://www.secretservice.gov/ntac.htm.

Fein, R., Vossekuil, B., Pollack, W., Borum, R., Modzeleski, W., & Reddy, M. (2002). *Threat assessment in schools: A guide to managing threatening situations and to creating safe school climates.* U.S. Secret Service and Department of Education.

Fisher, B. W., & Devlin, D. N. (2020). School crime and the patterns of roles of school resource officers: Evidence from a national longitudinal study. *Crime & Delinquency, 66*(11), 1606–1629. https://doi.org/10.1177/0011128719875702

Fisher, B. W., & Fisher, A. E. (2023). Criminal justice system contact of students with disabilities by race and ethnicity: Examining the role of school practice. *Children and Youth Services Review, 149.* https://doi.org/10.1016/j.childyouth.2023.106953

Gerlinger, J., Viano, S., Gardella, J. H., Fisher, B. W., Curran, F. C., & Higgins, E. (2021). Exclusionary school discipline and delinquent outcomes: A meta-analysis. *Journal of Youth and Adolescence, 50*(2), 1493–1509. https://doi.org/10.1007/s10964-021-01459-3

Heilbrun, K., Slobogin, C., & Dvoskin, J. (2024). Reimagining risk assessment: Comment on Viljoen and Vincent (2020). *Clinical Psychology: Science and Practice, 31*(2), 132–135. https://doi.org/10.1037/cps0000208

Heilbrun, K., Yasuhara, K., Shah, S., & Locklair, B. (2020). Approaches to violence risk assessment: Overview, critical analysis, and future directions. In K. S. Douglas & R. K. Otto (Eds.), *Handbook of violence risk assessment* (2nd ed., pp. 3–27). Routledge.

Huang, F. L., & Cornell, D. G. (2021). Teacher support for zero tolerance is associated with higher suspension rates and lower feelings of safety. *School Psychology Review*, *50*(2), 388–405. https://doi.org/10.1080/2372966X.2020.1832865

Irwin, V., Wang, K., Cui, J., & Thompson, A. (2024). *Reports on indicators of school crime and safety: 2023*. Institute of Education Sciences, U.S. Department of Education, Office of Justice Programs, U.S. Department of Justice.

Jancaric, M., Jewett, P., & Borowsky, I. W. (2024). Students' perspectives and utilization of school resource officers after experiences with school discipline or law enforcement. *Psychology in the Schools*, *61*(11), 4273–4285. https://doi.org/10.1002/pits.23280

Jennings, W. G., Khey, D. N., Maskaly, J., & Donner, C. M. (2011). Evaluating the relationship between law enforcement and school security measures and violent crime in schools. *Journal of Police Crisis Negotiations*, *11*(2), 109–124. https://doi.org/10.1080/15332586.2011.581511

Johnson, N. N., & Johnson, T. L. (2023). *Zero tolerance policy analysis: A look at 30 years of school-based ZT policies in practice in the United States of America*. Cogent Education. https://doi.org/10.1080/2331186X.2023.2179863

JustChildren, & Cornell, D. (2013). *Prevention v. punishment: Threat assessment, school suspensions, and racial disparities*. https://education.virginia.edu/documents/yvpthreat-assessment-reduces-school-suspension-and-racial-disproportionality2018-09-26pdf

Kerere, J., Cornell, D., Huang, F., & Maeng, J. (2024). *Attacks following a school threat assessment*. [Unpublished manuscript]. School of Education and Human Development, University of Virginia.

Lemons, C. J., Sinclair, A. C., Gesel, S., Gandhi, A. G., & Danielson, L. (2019). Integrating intensive interventions into special education services: Guidance for special education administrators. *Journal of Special Education Leadership*, *32*(1), 29–38.

Limber, S. P. (2011). The Olweus Bullying Prevention Program: An overview of its implementation and school safety. In S. Jimerson, A. Nickerson, M. J., Mayer, & M. J., Furlong (Eds.), *Handbook of school violence and school safety: International research and practice* (pp. 369–382). Routledge.

Maeng, J. L., Cornell, D. G., & Edwards, K. D. (2023). Threat assessment and disparities in school discipline. *Journal of Threat Assessment and Management*, *11*(3), 186–196. https://doi.org/10.1037/tam0000213

Maeng, J. L., Cornell, D., & Huang, F. (2020a). Student threat assessment as an alternative to exclusionary discipline. *Journal of School Violence*, *19*(3), 377–388. https://doi.org/10.1080/15388220.2019.1707682

Maeng, J., Cornell, D., Kerere, J., Huang, F., Konold, T., Afolabi, A., & Cowley, D. (2024). *Statewide implementation of school threat assessment in Florida: Final technical report.* School of Education and Human Development, University of Virginia.

Mallett, C. A. (2016). The school-to-prison pipeline: A critical review of the punitive paradigm shift. *Child and Adolescent Social Work Journal, 33*, 15–24.

Meloy, J. R., & Hoffman, J. (2021). *International handbook of threat assessment* (2nd ed.). Oxford University Press.

Mielke, M., & Farrington, D. P. (2021). School-based interventions to reduce suspension and arrest: A meta-analysis. *Aggression and Violent Behavior, 56.* https://doi.org/10.1016/j.avb.2020.101518

Morgan, E., Salomen, N., Plotkin, M., & Cohen, R. (2014). *The school discipline consensus report: Strategies from the field to keep students engaged in school and out of the juvenile justice system.* The Council of State Governments Justice Center. https://www.ojp.gov/library/publications/school-discipline-consensus-report-strategies-field-keep-students-engaged.

Mowen, T. J., Brent, J. J., & Bares, K. J. (2018). How arrest impacts delinquency over time between and within individuals. *Youth Violence and Juvenile Justice, 16*(4), 358–377. https://doi.org/10.1177/1541204017712560

National Association of School Psychologists (NASP). (2024). *State shortages data dashboard.* https://www.nasponline.org/about-school-psychology/state-shortages-data-dashboard

National Center for Education Statistics (NCES). (2024). *Mental health and well-being.* https://nces.ed.gov/surveys/spp/results.asp#sc-safety-apr24-chart-5

National Incident-Based Reporting System (NIBRS). (2024). *National-Incident-Based Reporting System.* Bureau of Justice Statistics, Federal Bureau of Investigation, US Department of Justice. https://bjs.ojp.gov/national-incident-based-reporting-system-nibrs#0-0

National Threat Assessment Center (NTAC). (2019). *Protecting America's schools: A U.S. Secret Service analysis of targeted school violence.* National Threat Assessment Center, United States Secret Service, U.S. Department of Homeland Security.

Nekvasil, E. K., & Cornell, D. G. (2012). Student reports of peer threats of violence: Prevalence and outcomes. *Journal of School Violence, 11*, 357–375. https://doi.org/10.1080/15388220.2012.706764

Nekvasil, E. K., & Cornell, D. G. (2015). Student threat assessment associated with safety in middle schools. *Journal of Threat Assessment and Management, 2*(2), 98–113. https://doi.org/10.1037/tam0000038

Noltemeyer, A. L., Ward, R. M., & Mcloughlin, C. (2015). Relationship between school suspension and student outcomes: A meta-analysis. *School Psychology Review, 44*(2), 224–240.

O'Neill, S. C., Strnadova, I., & Cumming, T. M. (2017). Systems barriers to community re-entry for incarcerated youths: A review. *Children and Youth Services Review*, *79*, 29–36. https://doi.org/10.1016/j.childyouth.2017.05.025

O'Toole, M. E. (2000). *The school shooter: A threat assessment perspective.* Critical Incident Response Group, National Center for the Analysis of Violence Crime, Quantico, VA: FBI Academy.

Payne, C., Cornell, D., & Konold, T. (2024). Anonymous reporting systems, school climate, and student threat reporting. *Journal of Threat Assessment, 11*(3). 113–148 https://doi.org/10.1037/tam0000228

Peterson, J. (2021). A multi-level, multi-method investigation of the psycho-social life histories of mass shooters. National Institute of Justice, U.S. Department of Justice.

Rappaport, N. (2001). Psychiatric consultation to school-based health centers: Lessons learned in an emerging field. *Journal of the American Academy of Child and Adolescent Psychiatry*, *40*(12), 1473–1475.

Ross, K. M., & Tolan, P. (2017). Social and emotional learning in adolescence: Testing the CASEL model in a normative sample. *The Journal of Early Adolescence*, *38*(8), 1170–1199. https://doi.org/10.1177/0272431617725198

Stohlman, S., & Cornell, D. (2019). An online educational program to increase student understanding of threat assessment. *Journal of School Health*, *89*(11), 899–906. https://pubmed.ncbi.nlm.nih.gov/31478217/.

Tanner-Smith, E. E., & Fisher, B. W. (2015). Visible school security measures and student academic performance, attendance, and postsecondary aspirations. *Journal of Youth and Adolescence*, *45*(1), 195–210.

Tocci, C., Stacy, S. T., Siegal, R., Renick, J., LoCurto, J., Lakind, D., Gruber, J., & Fisher, B. W. (2023). Statement on the effects of law enforcement in school settings. *American Journal of Community Psychology*, 1–18. https://doi.org/10.1002/ajcp.12723

U.S. Bureau of Labor Statistics. (2023). *Occupational employment and wage statistics: 19–3034 school psychologists.* https://www.bls.gov/oes/current/oes193034.htm

U.S. Secret Service. (2023). *Improving school safety through bystander reporting: A toolkit for strengthening K-12 reporting programs.* United States Secret Service, Cybersecurity and Infrastructure Security Agency, U.S. Department of Homeland Security.

Van Dreal, J. (2016). *Salem-Keizer Cascade Model.* https://behavioralthreatassessments.com/methodologies/salem-keizer-cascade-model/.

Virginia Department of Criminal Justice Services. (2022). *2022 Virginia School Safety Audit highlights.* https://www.dcjs.virginia.gov/virginia-center-school-and-campus-safety/virginia-school-safety-audit-program

Wiley, S. A., & Esbensen, F. A. (2016). The effect of police contact: Does official intervention result in deviance amplification? *Crime & Delinquency*, *62*(3), 283–307. https://doi.org/10.1177/0011128713492496

Wilson, H. A., & Hoge, R. D. (2012). The effects of youth diversion programs on recidivism: A meta-analytic review. *Criminal Justice and Behavior*, *40*(5), 497–518. https://doi.org/10.1177/0093854812451089

Wood, B. J., & Hampton, E. (2021). The influence of school resource officer presence on teacher perceptions of school safety and security. *School Psychology Review*, *50*(2–3), 360–370. https://doi.org/10.1080/2372966X.2020.1844547

Yancey-Bragg, N. (2022). *Family of 'heartbroken' teen sues Instagram, Florida school after wrongful arrest over fake threats.* https://www.usatoday.com/story/news/nation/2022/02/17/florida-teen-sues-instagram-nia-whims/6828800001/.

6

NYSAP, LLC

Implementing Evidence-Based Screening and Assessment in Juvenile Justice

Thomas Grisso, Gina Vincent, and Ivan Kruh

During the past twenty-five years, risk and mental health screening and assessment have proliferated in juvenile justice settings, becoming standard policy and practice in many states. This was not so until the twenty-first century. The need for evidence-based psychological tools for this purpose arose in part from the increase in zero-tolerance justice policies in the 1990s, resulting in excessive incarceration of youthful offenders (Grisso, 1996). Rising incarceration rates swept up many youth with mental disorders (Teplin et al., 2002), as well as many for whom the risk of future offending might be better managed in the community. This led to calls for methods to identify and respond to youth with mental health problems upon entry into juvenile justice settings (Skowyra & Cocozza, 2007b), as well as ways to help juvenile justice decision-makers better identify youths' risk levels for more effective risk management decisions (Vincent et al., 2012).

This chapter's description of *National Youth Screening and Assessment Partners* (NYSAP), LLC, grew in that historical context. NYSAP's objective is to reform juvenile justice policy and practice nationwide through implementation of valid screening and assessment tools, focused especially on mental health and risk screening and assessment, and proper use of these tools (e.g., case planning, diversion). NYSAP, LLC employs the growing research in implementation science identifying strategies essential for fidelity to and sustainability of evidence-based practices.

NYSAP, LLC grew out of a former university-based, grant-funded organization the authors had developed, called the *National Youth Screening Assistance Project.* A major focus of this chapter is our description of this evolution that transformed a university-based psychological service into a private enterprise. Throughout the chapter, we refer to the current for-profit NYSAP as "NYSAP Partners" and to the former university-based NYSAP as "NYSAP Project."

We first describe NYSAP Partners, including its services, clients, organization, and personnel. Then we discuss NYSAP Partners' theoretical, scientific, and professional practice foundations. This is followed by a history of the original university-based NYSAP Project, its grant-funded research and services, and how NYSAP Project

Thomas Grisso, Gina Vincent, and Ivan Kruh, *NYSAP, LLC*. In: *The Path Forward*. Edited by: Kirk Heilbrun and David DeMatteo, Oxford University Press. © Oxford University Press (2026). DOI: 10.1093/9780197773031.003.0006 evolved to become the private NYSAP Partners, LLC. Finally, we discuss benefits and limits encountered during transition from a university-based to a proprietary service. Our comments offer both caution and encouragement for those considering similar efforts.

NYSAP Partners

NYSAP Partners provides technical assistance (consultation and training) to juvenile justice agencies and programs for screening and assessment practices that will improve the lives of youth and enhance juvenile justice objectives. System reforms during the past two decades have encouraged juvenile justice settings to employ evidence-based methods to identify youths' characteristics that are important for justice system decisions about interventions and services to youth. NYSAP Partners assists juvenile justice systems in meeting those objectives.

Services and Clients

NYSAP Partners provides juvenile justice settings consultation and training for three types of screening and assessment services: (a) risk screening, risk/needs assessment, and risk-need-responsivity-based case planning (e.g., Andrews & Bonta, 2010); (b) behavioral (mental) health and trauma symptom screening; and (c) forensic clinical evaluations of juveniles' competence to stand trial. Consultation and training provided by NYSAP Partners vary within its three primary areas of assistance as described below. Client agencies are sometimes adopting these practices for the first time, while others are seeking modification of existing practices. Often, the clients are county-based juvenile justice programs or agencies, and sometimes they are state agencies seeking to establish a standard and method of practice statewide, often in response to newly legislated or court-ordered requirements.

Risk Screening and Risk-Needs Assessment

Many decisions in juvenile justice processing require judgments about the degree of risk a youth might pose in optional temporary placements and dispositions. In addition, the risk-need-responsivity model has become a best practice in juvenile justice, requiring that probation or court clinic staff use evidence-based methods for case planning (Andrews & Bonta, 2010; Vincent et al., 2012). NYSAP Partners assists various types of juvenile justice agencies (the client) to implement those practices, including youth diversion programs, pretrial detention, probation departments (for intake and predisposition planning), youth corrections, and youth forensic settings (e.g., court clinics).

Consultation services focus initially on assisting the client to select risk screening or risk/needs assessment instruments that meet their specific needs, have evidence of validity in the client's settings, and have been validated across race/ethnicity groups. Various validated risk/needs instruments are available, for example, the *Youth Level of Services/Case Management Inventory* (Hoge & Andrews, 2011) and the *Structured Assessment of Violence Risk in Youth* (Borum et al., 2006). The clients' collaborators (e.g., judges, attorneys, service providers) are provided education about the purpose and importance of these instruments and are engaged in the implementation plan, and sometimes in the selection of the tool. Once a plan is formed, we assist with development of the client's formal policies and procedures, including how information will be shared with decision-makers (e.g., judges), how to use the instruments for placement decisions and case planning, and how to design data systems and use data for continual improvement of practice.

NYSAP Partners provides intensive training for staff who will be administering, scoring, and interpreting the results of risk screening or assessment, as well as education for agency managers and court personnel. Training is typically provided on-site, but some remote options are available. NYSAP training is always followed by follow-up practice cases with every staff person to evaluate their consistency and proficiency in rating the instrument. If the client selects a risk/needs instrument for which NYSAP Partners does not provide training, NYSAP Partners connects them with the proper trainers on the tool, while still conducting the other implementation steps with the agency. After implementation, NYSAP engages with clients to gather data for examining whether instruments are appropriately used in decisions, to evaluate quality of case plans, and other similar activities. Finally, client agencies are assisted in developing longer-term quality assurance practices that maintain the integrity of their risk screening and assessment procedures. Often, after the system has used the risk assessment for a period of time, NYSAP Partners trains agency master trainers so they can sustain fidelity to the instrument and train new staff internally.

Behavioral Health and Trauma Screening

Screening for behavioral or mental health needs at intake in juvenile justice settings has become a best practice nationwide, often being required by law or regulations at the federal or state level. Such screening has two major purposes, depending on the setting. A primary purpose, especially at intake, is to identify youth who might have emergent psychological symptoms requiring immediate clinical attention and then to respond accordingly in the youth's interest. A second use is to signal the system that longer-range case plans might require attention to a youth's mental health needs. The agencies and programs that NYSAP Partners assists in meeting these needs are most often juvenile diversion programs and juvenile detention centers, but also includes intake probation and juvenile correction settings.

Types of consultation are much the same as described above for risk screening, including tool selection, strategic planning for implementation, developing formal policies and procedures, training of staff, and development of methods for continued quality assurance. The tools most often chosen for implementation are the *Massachusetts Youth Screening Instrument-Second Version* (MAYSI-2; Grisso & Barnum,

2003, 2006) and various screening tools for trauma symptoms. Often, training focuses not only on tool administration and use, but also basic information about youths' mental health and trauma symptoms and their implications for youth behavior and development. When a client is implementing both behavioral health screening and risk assessment, training includes ways to use mental health screening results in risk-based case planning to improve youths' responsiveness to other targeted interventions.

Assessment of Juveniles' Competence to Stand Trial (CST)

NYSAP Partners provides several services focused on improving forensic psychologists' and psychiatrists' evaluations of juveniles' capacities to meet legal criteria for CST. Clients typically are juvenile court clinics or agencies responsible for providing juvenile CST evaluations for a state or county. Services are of two types: systemic consultation and forensic examiner training.

Systemically, many jurisdictions are still in the process of developing systems for organizing, providing, and monitoring forensic evaluations for juveniles CST (Kruh & Grisso, 2017). In addition, many states have only rudimentary or unsystematic programs for the remediation of youth found incompetent to stand trial. NYSAP Partners' consultations in these cases examine the client jurisdiction's situation, offer a variety of models for them to consider, and assist in designing a system that meets the jurisdiction's needs. Regarding forensic examiner training, NYSAP Partners offers intensive training (e.g., 16-hour curricula) to psychologists and psychiatrists qualified to perform forensic evaluations with adolescents. All training is based on state-of-the-science developmental information, legal definitions, data collection methods, and evidence-based interpretation (e.g., Kruh & Grisso, 2009).

Other Services

After ten years in operation, NYSAP Partners' services have not only evolved with the needs of clients and new research in implementation, screening, and assessment, but also have added other services to address clients' needs. One of these services is Critical Intervention Mapping (CIM). CIM is a juvenile justice system version of Sequential Intercept Mapping (SIM) (Heilbrun et al., 2017), which has been employed in the adult system for almost twenty years (Griffin et al., 2015). It is an evidence-informed approach to systems planning that guides cross-systems collaborators through a process to improve the ability of a community to more effectively serve youth with behavioral health needs involved in the juvenile legal system (Skowyra & Cocozza, 2007a). The focus is on creating more efficient, effective, and equitable community-based systems of care for youth with behavioral health concerns. The CIM process yields a locally-developed *map representing current practice* across the juvenile legal continuum, including identification of local resources and gaps, priorities for change, and a preliminary action plan for ongoing practice improvement work. NYSAP Partners also offers a less comprehensive version of CIM, called "assets mapping," to help communities improve the service continuum around one particular decision point, such as case planning for youth on community supervision, or improving response to youth competence evaluations.

Organization and Operations

NYSAP Partners was registered as an LLC in Massachusetts in 2012. The first two authors of this chapter served as Managers (owners of the LLC), one serving as President (GV), and they were joined by the third author in later years. Each of the three service areas has a director. Initially, the original two managers also served as service area directors, but other directors were brought on as the business grew. Directors are responsible for overseeing and fulfilling client contracts for NYSAP Partner consultation and training in their service area. To fulfill contracted services, directors call upon experts who affiliate with NYSAP Partners, called associates, depending on their specific expertise and availability. Five associates have joined NYSAP Partners over the years as service needs have grown. Our associates include youth forensic psychologists and individuals who have worked in and managed juvenile probation services for years.

Managers, directors, and associates are all primarily employed by other organizations (e.g., universities, clinics, or private practice) or retired from previous employment. They are paid by NYSAP Partners for their hours of service related to client contracts, with directors receiving additional "overhead" compensation for their management of contracts. Overhead revenue beyond what is provided to directors is retained by the LLC to cover business costs, including a part-time employee for staff support; training coordinators; accounting, CPA, and payroll services; and LLC profit-sharing among the managers. Mission unity, identity, and operations are enhanced by frequent remote meetings throughout the year.

Since it began, NYSAP Partners has provided mental health screening, risk screening/assessment, and/or juvenile CST consultations to clients in over one-half of the states, as well as several sites outside the United States. Services are provided through fee-for-service contracts largely from county or state juvenile justice agencies. NYSAP Partners has a website but otherwise does not currently advertise its services formally. Clients typically find NYSAP Partners by reputation, word of mouth, or contact with national networks of juvenile justice advocacy organizations. We also obtain contracts by responding to postings of requests for bids by states or counties nationwide.

Theoretical and Scientific Foundations

NYSAP Partners' services have one overarching objective: to improve justice-system professionals' decisions affecting youth, society, and the justice system's objectives. In effect, our aim is to help juvenile justice decision-makers to improve the fairness of their decisions—that is, to increase their accuracy and reduce the influence of biases or assumptions absent sound evidence (Neal & Grisso, 2014).

There is a juvenile advocacy quality to our services. Juvenile justice policy and practice has a checkered history regarding its management of youths. Sometimes, its policies and decision-making have ignored the developmental capacities and needs of adolescents, focusing primarily on punishment and deterrence. We provide the juvenile justice system with various ways to make decisions that are more sensitive to the individual needs of youth, while also helping the system meet its public interest objectives. In this sense, we use science to change systems in ways that create fairer and more effective conditions for youth.

Theoretical Assumptions

Underlying NYSAP Partners' efforts to accomplish this are three broad theoretical assumptions. First, we assume that decision-making by professionals is improved by using instruments, tools, or tests that have scientifically demonstrated a valid, measurable relationship to the condition or prediction about which the decision is being made. Compared to unstructured professional judgment, the predictive superiority of decisions assisted by scientifically valid strategies has been demonstrated frequently in psychological science (Grove et al., 2000).

Second, general social psychology provides much evidence that changing the environment can be an effective way to change individual behavior. We assume that changing professionals' decision-making practices is often best accomplished by adoption of practices and standards by organizations or systems that provide the sociolegal context for the professional's decision-making. Adoption of a valid decision-making tool by a professional's employer (e.g., probation department) or client (e.g., a court clinic or agency that manages forensic examiners) sanctions and requires the use of the tool. Ultimately, the tool's use also is reinforcing to the professional because it provides structure and measurable positive outcomes. Systems, therefore, are the clients of NYSAP Partners.

Third, we see our services not only as putting tools in place but also as a way to change a system's culture. Successful implementation of risk assessment or mental health screening requires teaching staff the concepts and presumptions on which the tools are built. Typically, this requires educating them about science-based perspectives on adolescent development, adolescents' behavioral health problems, and differences between adolescents and adults in causes of offending. Such understanding theoretically improves staff performance with the screening and assessment tools, but also might change their general approach to youth under their supervision.

Scientific Foundation

The field of translational science identifies three steps for translating basic and applied scientific findings so that they can be used in real-world contexts: (a) creating practical and evidence-based methods for application; (b) developing best ways to implement those methods in real-world practice; and (c) evaluating outcomes when the methods are implemented (Grisso et al., 2019; Khoury et al., 2007).

Measurement to Support Evidence-Based Practice

Our consultation promotes only risk and behavioral health screening and assessment measures that have been designed and fully validated for our clients' purposes. Past research must have established the measure's validity specifically when used with justice-involved adolescents within the types of settings similar to the client's setting. Also, instruments must have scientific evidence that they are valid for use across the primary racial/ethnic groups served by a client before NYSAP Partners will recommend them. No standardized, evidence-based measures are available for evaluations of juveniles' CST, so our consultation in that area focuses on a structured interview guide that currently represents best practices (*Juvenile Adjudicative Competence Interview*: Grisso, 2005). NYSAP Partners also has worked with juvenile justice agencies to develop and validate risk instruments where no strong, generalizable instrument exists, such as youth pretrial detention tools for predicting recidivism and Prison Rape Elimination Act (PREA) screening.

Implementation Science

Our consultation follows lessons from implementation science, which is one of the cornerstones of NYSAP's work that sets us apart from many of the agencies that provide training on assessments. Implementation strategies are the methods used to enhance adoption, full integration, and sustainability of new approaches (e.g., RNR, assessment strategies, new interventions) in practice settings (Proctor et al., 2013; Viljoen & Vincent, 2024). To achieve improved outcomes, new approaches need to be paired with effective implementation strategies. In the context of implementing screening or assessment, implementation strategies include, at a minimum, (a) brief training for all relevant juvenile justice agency collaborators to engage them in decisions about the approach, (b) revising written procedures and policies, and (c) designing decision-support tools. Examples include templates for communication of screening or assessment results to the courts, case plans that follow RNR principles, or a decision tree for responses to mental health needs. The whole system needs to be set up in a manner that supports the new screening or assessment practice (Fixsen et al., 2019). Additionally, agencies should always pilot test the approach and gather data to ensure it is feasible and working as intended before rolling it out to the whole agency or state.

Outcome Research

Our consultation services are driven and supported by research demonstrating whether the methods and measures have achieved their purpose when properly implemented in real-world practice. For example, we have conducted much of the research evidence indicating risk-needs assessment, when implemented well and used properly, leads to a reduction in high-risk judgments, out-of-home placements, and/or formal processing (Vincent et al., 2016), is sustainable (Vincent et al., 2024) and cost-effective (Vincent et al., 2019). Similarly, research with the MAYSI-2 has been shown to increase referrals that provide youths with needed clinical attention (Williams & Grisso, 2011). Our consultation services also assist clients to collect data on their own outcomes that will offer evidence of their performance across time or the need for further refinement.

Racial and Ethnic Equity

All psychological services must attend to matters of racial and ethnic equity. This requires attention to questions of potential differences in who is served, how they are served, and with what effectiveness. Psychological services like NYSAP Partners serve juvenile justice agencies in which, in many jurisdictions, youth of color form the near majority or greater of the setting's youths. It is crucial, therefore, that any screening and assessment methods we employ must be scrutinized and selected based on evidence that they do not perform with different degrees of validity for youth of various races and ethnicities. This must be addressed at two levels: whether the method of measurement produces unbiased scores on the basis of race/ethnicity alone (American Educational Research Association et al., 2014) and whether the tools are implemented in a way that produces benefits equitably (Skeem & Lowenkamp, 2016; Vincent & Viljoen, 2020).

During NYSAP Partners' years, considerable controversy has arisen regarding the potential for racial bias in risk screening and assessment tools. The most recent evidence suggests very few risk instruments contain measurement bias by race or ethnicity (Ahmed et al., 2023; Ashford et al., 2022; Campbell & Miller, 2018; Desmarais et al., 2021). A recent systematic review indicated there is more evidence that implementation of risk assessment instruments leads to reductions in existing racial disparities in the system, or has no impact on disparities, than there is evidence for the reverse (Lawson et al., 2024). Nevertheless, NYSAP Partners remains vigilant concerning this issue, contributing to the scientific literature and adjusting our practices when advisable with new evidence-based information.

How NYSAP Partners Was Developed

NYSAP Partners was formed at the conclusion of a twenty-year, university-based, grant-funded initiative, the *National Youth Screening Assistance Project* (NYSAP Project). NYSAP Partners was later formed by the same psychologists who had built the NYSAP Project, borrowing on its research and experience to create an organization independent of the university. How the NYSAP Project evolved and eventually became NYSAP Partners is worth describing to demonstrate how a for-profit psychological service can evolve from a university base. The evolution is described in three phases from 1993 to 2013.

Development of a Mental Health Screening Tool

As noted earlier, punitive reforms in juvenile justice in the 1980s and 1990s greatly increased the incarceration of youthful offenders, often including those who were at low risk of re-offending and often with mental health needs (Grisso, 1996). Two groups began to react to these consequences (Cocozza & Skowyra, 2000). One was juvenile corrections directors, who said that they were being overwhelmed by youth with mental health problems who were being swept up by law enforcement's zero-tolerance net. The other group was youth advocate organizations calling for attention to identifying and responding to youths' mental health needs as they entered juvenile justice settings.

At that time, there was no way for juvenile justice staff to know about a youth's potentially serious mental health condition at intake in detention or correctional settings. If youth in such settings were ever to receive necessary services, the first step was for frontline staff to be able to identify them at intake. No such method existed. Responding to this concern, one of the authors (TG), a professor at UMass Chan Medical School's Law and Psychiatry Program, teamed up with a child psychiatrist directing the Boston Juvenile Court Clinic. They begin to envision a mental health screening tool capable of being administered by non-mental-health staff at intake in juvenile justice settings.

The university provided a seed grant to draft a proposed prototype, and the Massachusetts Department of Youth Services (MDYS) agreed to collaborate in the tool's development. With funding from the William T. Grant Foundation, the tool was developed and validated during a 3-year study involving data collection with over 1000 youth at intake in MDYS detention centers. The result was the *Massachusetts Youth Screening Instrument* (MAYSI), with its first published manual (Grisso & Barnum, 1998) followed by a second version, MAYSI-2 (Grisso & Barnum, 2003, 2006). The MAYSI-2 reflected further research-based refinements in the measure, and a

2006 edition included adjusted norms based on a national sample of over 79,000 justice-involved youth.

Creation of the NYSAP Project

The NYSAP Project was initiated as a university-based center to provide technical assistance nationwide for implementation of MAYSI-2 in juvenile detention and corrections setting. This was not a solo effort. In the early 2000s, the John D. and Catherine T. MacArthur Foundation launched a tremendous initiative, called *Models for Change: Systems Reform in Juvenile Justice* (John D. and Catherine T. MacArthur Foundation, n.d., a, b). Models for Change collaborated with four states (and 16 in later years) that were willing to accept assistance to reform their juvenile justice systems in ways that would be less retributive and more sensitive to developmental characteristics of adolescents. To assist these states, the MacArthur Foundation contracted with centers and juvenile justice experts, which it called its "National Resource Bank." Their role was to engage collaboratively to provide on-site technical assistance to the model states to create a wide range of reform policies and practices.

In this context, the Foundation contracted with our university-based MAYSI-2 project to implement mental health screening in Models for Change states. We then called our center the *National Youth Screening Assistance Project*, located within the Law and Psychiatry Program at our university. MacArthur Foundation support allowed us to develop strategies for implementing MAYSI-2 mental health screening in juvenile justice (Grisso et al., 2005) and to research its effectiveness.

Models for Change was a ten-year initiative. It had provided us the resources to develop methods and implementation strategies in two other important areas of juvenile justice reform: risk assessment and evaluations for juveniles' competence to stand trial. The promotion of valid risk assessment tools at various decision points in juvenile justice was especially important to help reduce overestimates of risk that produced unnecessary incarceration of youth (Vincent et al., 2012). The MacArthur Foundation funding allowed us to work with several states to develop implementation strategies for risk assessment in different settings, then to test the effectiveness of that implementation (Vincent et al., 2016), and use what we learned to develop a "how-to" guide (Vincent et al., 2012) for implementation of risk/needs assessment. The MacArthur Foundation then went on to blend funding with the Office of Juvenile Justice and Delinquency Prevention to carry this work to other states across the nation.

An earlier MacArthur initiative (Research Network on Adolescent Development and Juvenile Justice n.d., b), had produced research demonstrating the lesser developmental capacities of youth to meet legal criteria for competence to stand trial (CST) (Grisso et al., 2003). During Models for Change, the MacArthur Foundation funded the NYSAP Project to develop the first guidelines and tools for forensic clinicians' evaluations of juveniles' CST (Grisso, 2005; Kruh & Grisso, 2009). We disseminated these assessment strategies in four national regional workshops. This provided invaluable experiential understanding of the complexities when implementing forensic evaluation practices related to juveniles' CST. Finally, the MacArthur Foundation also provided funding for our development of a guide for state legislatures seeking to create developmentally sensitive juvenile CST laws (Larson & Grisso, 2012).

Transitioning from NYSAP Project to NYSAP Partners

The MacArthur Foundation concluded its Models for Change initiative in 2014. Great progress had been made toward a developmental reform in juvenile justice policies and practices in many states. But it was yet a fledgling movement, and there was reason for concern about sustaining it without the Foundation's continued funding to the states and the technical assistance centers that had been creating the reform's successes (Cavanagh et al., 2022). Was the movement's momentum sufficient to lead states to fund further technical assistance for reform? And could the centers that had been providing MacArthur-funded assistance manage to continue to do so under those conditions?

To continue the NYSAP Project within the university's structure would have been difficult. As in many medical schools, employment of our research and technical assistance professionals was based on coverage of their salaries by grants and contracts. This was feasible during the years of MacArthur Foundation funding. But revenue based on juvenile justice clients might be insufficient especially in start-up years while building a client base. In addition, high university overhead rates would substantially increase the cost to potential juvenile justice clients, possibly inhibiting their ability to obtain our services that they were essentially used to receiving without cost.

Therefore, we decided to develop an independent LLC carrying the NYSAP brand. We terminated the university-based NYSAP Project and developed NYSAP Partners LLC while retaining our faculty positions. Our efforts have been largely successful although not without challenges and compromises described in the following discussion.

University-Based to Private: Advantages and Challenges

When we made the move, we had no models to guide us in the process or to foresee the potential legal and ethical issues that arose. Having succeeded, we hope that our description of the benefits and challenges we have encountered might be of benefit to others who contemplate a similar effort.

Advantages

Perhaps the greatest benefits are flexibility and efficiency. Many universities have substantial overhead rates on grants and contracts that would challenge the resources of potential juvenile justice clients. University processing of contracts sometimes creates delays in working with outside agencies, as well as restrictions associated with university liability policies. All these matters are understandable and often necessary. But an independently-operated service offers one the ability to make adjustments quickly and easily depending on changing circumstances. This is especially important early in the development of an LLC, when a client base is not yet established. Our process allowed us to add associates to our NYSAP Partners with the increase in our client base and our knowledge of their specific needs.

If the developers of the LLC are retaining their university positions, the model can also have benefits for one's university-based work. Providing technical assistance nationwide to juvenile justice programs builds opportunities and potential partners for research grants on issues related to implementation. Sometimes this can stimulate proposals for grants to one's university-based research center. It may even be possible for an owner/manager of an LLC to direct some profits to the university to benefit maintenance of one's research laboratory.

Challenges and Limits

Managing a business poses challenges when one retains their full-time university position. An LLC requires the personal development and monitoring of financial contracts, as well as maintaining liability insurance that may vary in different client states. Typically, one must contract accounting services, file business licenses annually (sometimes in multiple states), and maintain a registry in the federal government's System for Award Management (SAM) so the LLC can acquire federal funding.

In addition, the evolution of an independent business out of a university-based program placed certain limitations on NYSAP Partners, especially given that its owners/managers continued to be university employees. Those limitations were of several kinds.

First, our university's regulations allowed full-time faculty to engage in outside private practice for a certain number of hours per week. However, to the extent that those activities would produce no revenue for the university, outside employment could not use university space, information technology, or accounting support. These reasonable conditions needed careful attention, requiring a sort of technological and financial firewall between our LLC efforts and our university work.

Second, our dual employment (private and university) offered the potential for conflicts of interest. With limited exceptions, employees of an agency of the Commonwealth of Massachusetts may not accept private financial benefits from another government branch of the Commonwealth, thus preventing state employees from potential use of their state position for private gain. Since NYSAP Partners were also university faculty, this prohibited the LLC from ever accepting contracts from branches of Massachusetts government: for example, the Department of Youth Services, Department of Mental Health, and the courts, public defenders, and Department of Probation. Across the years, our Law and Psychiatry Program (our university base) had fulfilled many such contracts for research and technical assistance. Therefore, when NYSAP Partners was formed, we resolved to maintain the performance of such Commonwealth contracts within the Law and Psychiatry Program, with NYSAP Partners accepting government agency contracts only from other states.

Finally, the MAYSI-2 had become quite profitable financially over the years. The instrument was used in thousands of juvenile justice programs nationwide, and the manual and screening materials had been translated for use in Europe in ten languages. Significant royalties had been generated by the NYSAP Project (university-based) agreements with the instrument's publisher and with a commercial online assessment company, providing it exclusive rights to offer MAYSI-2 for web-based administration by subscription. But we could not transport that asset to NYSAP Partners. As in most universities, products invented and developed with the university's resources are the property of the university. Fortunately, our university had always agreed to direct all its MAYSI-2 royalties to our Law and Psychiatry Program. This supported continuation of MAYSI-2 research and maintenance of our MAYSI-2 Helpdesk operations providing nationwide informational support to MAYSI-2 users. Therefore, while we continued to benefit from MAYSI-2 royalties in our roles in the university's Law and Psychiatry Program, MAYSI-2 "headquarters" was not transferred to NYSAP Partners.

Conclusions

We offer two observations about the prospects for others who may contemplate developing for-profit psychological services based on our experience. First, our focus on screening and assessment in juvenile justice settings is but one category of policy and practice for which juvenile justice is in need of assistance. There is much need, and therefore much room, for other psychological services addressing evidence-based practices to improve the system's attention to developmentally sensitive interventions for justice-involved youths.

Second, the story of NYSAP LLC's evolution from a university-based research project offers an example that might be worth considering by other university faculty. Our circumstances, however, were unique in some ways. The NYSAP Project that preceded NYSAP Partners had the good fortune to be developed in the context of MacArthur Foundation funding exceeding $5 million over fifteen years. In principle, though, such elaborate support is not necessary for others to employ this university-to-private service model. We welcome inquiries concerning details of the process, as well as collaboration with others in the field of psychology and juvenile justice.

References

Ahmed, S., Lee, S. C., & Helmus, L. M. (2023). Predictive accuracy of Static-99R across different racial/ethnic groups: A meta-analysis. *Law and Human Behavior, 47*(1), 275–291.

American Educational Research Association, American Psychological Association, and the National Council on Measurement in Education. (2014). *Standards for educational and psychological testing.* American Educational Research Association.

Andrews, D. A., & Bonta, J. (2010). *The psychology of criminal conduct* (5th ed.). Anderson.

Ashford, L. J., Spivak, B. L., & Shepherd, S. M. (2022). Racial fairness in violence risk instruments: A review of the literature. *Psychology, Crime & Law, 28*(9), 911–941.

Borum, R., Bartel, P., & Forth, A. (2006). *Structured assessment of violence risk in youth.* Psychological Assessment Resources.

Campbell, C., & Miller, W. (2018). A review of the validity of juvenile risk assessment across race/ethnicity. In *Oxford research encyclopedia of criminology and criminal justice.* https://oxfordre.com/criminology/display/10.1093/acrefore/9780190264079.001.0001/acrefore-9780190264079-e-345

Cavanagh, C., Paruk, J., & Grisso, T. (2022). The developmental reform in juvenile justice: Its progress and vulnerability. *Psychology, Public Policy, and Law, 28*(2), 151–166.

Cocozza, J., & Skowyra, K. (2000). Youth with mental health disorders: Issues and emerging responses. *Juvenile Justice, 7*(1), 3–13.

Desmarais, S. L., Zottola, S. A., Duhart Clarke, S. E., & Lowder, E. M. (2021). Predictive validity of pretrial risk assessments: A systematic review of the literature. *Criminal Justice and Behavior, 48*(4), 398–420.

Fixsen, D. L., Blase, K. A., & Van Dyke, M. K. (2019). *Implementation practice & science.* Active Implementation Research Network.

Griffin, P., LaDuke, C., Abreu, D., Winckworth-Prejsnar, K., Filone, S., Dorrell, S., & Finello, C. (2015). Using the Sequential Intercept Model in cross-system mapping. In P. Griffin, K. Heilbrun, E. Mulvey, D. DeMatteo, & C. Schubert (Eds.), *The Sequential Intercept Model and criminal justice: Promoting community alternatives for individuals with serious mental illness* (pp. 239–256). Oxford University Press.

Grisso, T. (1996). Society's retributive response to juvenile violence: A developmental perspective. *Law and Human Behavior, 20*(3), 229–247.

Grisso, T. (2005). *Evaluating juveniles' adjudicative competence: A guide for clinical practice.* Professional Resource Exchange.

Grisso, T., & Barnum, R. (1998). *Massachusetts Youth Screening Instrument*. University of Massachusetts Medical School.

Grisso, T., & Barnum, R. (2003, 2006). *Massachusetts Youth Screening Instrument—Second Version*. Professional Resource Press.

Grisso, T., Fountain, E., NeMoyer, A., & Thornton, L. (2019). The role of translational psychological science in juvenile justice reform. *Translational Issues in Psychological Science*, *5*(2), 13–20.

Grisso, T., Steinberg, L., Woolard, J., Cauffman, E., Scott, E., Graham, S., Lexcen, F., Reppucci, N., & Schwartz, R. (2003). Juveniles' competence to stand trial: A comparison of adolescents' and adults' capacities as trial defendants. *Law and Human Behavior*, *27*(4), 333–363.

Grisso, T., Vincent, G., & Seagrave, D. (2005). *Mental health screening and assessment in juvenile justice*. Guilford Press.

Grove, W., Zald, D., Lebow, B., Snitz, B., & Nelson, C. (2000). Clinical versus mechanical prediction: A meta-analysis. *Psychological Assessment*, *12*(1), 19–30.

Heilbrun, K., Goldstein, N. E., DeMatteo, D., Newsham, R., Gale-Bentz, E., Cole, L., & Arnold, S. (2017). The Sequential Intercept Model and juvenile justice: Review and prospectus. *Behavioral Sciences & the Law*, *35*(4), 319–336.

Hoge, R. D., & Andrews, D. A. (2011). *Youth Level of Service/Case Management Inventory 2.0* (YLS/CMI 2.0): User's manual. Multi-Health System.

John, D. and Catherine T. MacArthur Foundation. (n.d., a) *Models for Change: Systems Reform in Juvenile Justice*. https://www.modelsforchange.net

John, D., and Catherine T. MacArthur Foundation. (n.d., b). *Research Network on Adolescent Development and Juvenile Justice*. https://www.macfound.org/programs/pastwork/research-networks/research-network-on-adolescent-development-juvenil

Khoury, M. J., Gwinn, M., Yoon, P. W., Dowling, N., Moore, C. A., & Bradley, L. (2007). The continuum of translation research in genomic medicine: How can we accelerate the appropriate interpretation of human genome discoveries into health care and disease prevention? *General Medicine*, *9*(10), 665–674. http://dx.doi.org/10.1097/GIM.0b013e31815699d0

Kruh, I., & Grisso, T. (2009). *Evaluation of juveniles' competence to stand trial*. Oxford University Press.

Kruh, I., & Grisso, T. (2017). *Developing service delivery systems for evaluations of juveniles' competence to stand trial: A guide for states and counties*. National Center for Mental Health and Juvenile Justice. https://jjie.org/wp-content/uploads/2018/02/Juvenile_Competency_to_Stand_Trial_FINAL_508.pdf

Larson, K., & Grisso, T. (2012). *Developing statutes for competence to stand trial in juvenile delinquency proceedings: A guide for lawmakers*. National Youth Screening and Assessment Project and the John D. and Catherine T. MacArthur Foundation. https://modelsforchange.net/publications/330/

Lawson, S. G., Narkewicz, E. L., & Vincent, G. M. (2024). Disparate impact of risk assessment instruments: A systematic review. *Law and Human Behavior, 48*(5–6), 427–440. https://doi.org/10.1037/lhb0000582

Neal, T., & Grisso, T. (2014). The cognitive underpinnings of bias in forensic mental health evaluations. *Psychology, Public Policy and Law, 20*(2), 200–211.

Proctor, E. K., Powell, B. J., & McMillen, J. C. (2013). Implementation strategies: Recommendations for specifying and reporting. *Implementation Science, 8*(1), 1–11.

Skeem, J., & Lowenkamp, C. (2016). Risk, race, and recidivism: Predictive bias and disparate impact. *Criminology, 54*(4), 680–712.

Skowyra, K., & Cocozza, J. (2007a). *Blueprint for change: A comprehensive model for the identification and treatment of youth with mental health needs in contact with the juvenile justice system.* John D. and Catherine T. MacArthur Foundation. https://modelsforchange.net/publications/148/

Skowyra, K., & Cocozza, J. (2007b). *Mental health screening within juvenile justice: The next frontier.* National Center for Mental Health and Juvenile Justice. https://www.modelsforchange.net/publications/198/Mental_Health_Screening_within_Juvenile_Justice_The_Next_Frontier

Teplin, L., Abrams, K., McClelland, G., Dulcan, M., & Mericle, A. (2002). Psychiatric disorders in youth in juvenile detention. *Archives of General Psychiatry, 59*(*12*), 1133–1143.

Viljoen, J. L., & Vincent, G. M. (2024). Risk assessments for violence and reoffending: Implementation and impact on risk management. *Clinical Psychology: Science and Practice, 31*(2), 119–131.

Vincent, G. M., Drawbridge, D., Lawson, S. G., Todorovic, K., & Perrault, R. (2024). Sustainability of evidence-based practices: Risk-need-responsivity in probation7-years later. *Criminal Justice and Behavior, 51*(5), 643–666.

Vincent, G. M., Drawbridge, D., & Perrault, R. (2019). *Long-term cost effectiveness of risk-needs assessment and risk-need-responsivity (RNR) reforms in juvenile probation: The long-term RNR impact study.* Technical Report to the Office of Juvenile Justice and Delinquency Prevention. https://ojjdp.ojp.gov/library/publications/long-term-impact-and-cost-effectiveness-risk-needs-assessment-and-risk-need

Vincent, G. M., Guy, L. S., & Grisso, T. (2012). *Risk assessment in juvenile justice: A guidebook for implementation.* John D. & Catherine T. MacArthur Foundation. https://modelsforchange.net/publications/346/Risk_Assessment_in_Juvenile_Justice_A_Guidebook_for_Implementation.pdf

Vincent, G. M., Guy, L. S., Perrault, R. T., & Gershenson, B. G. (2016). Risk assessment matters, but only when implemented well: A multi-site study in juvenile probation. *Law and Human Behavior, 40*(6), 683–696.

Vincent, G. M., Paiva-Salisbury, M., Cook, N. E., Guy, L. S., & Perrault, R. (2012). Impact of risk/needs assessment on juvenile probation offers' decision-making: Importance of implementation. *Psychology, Public Policy, & the Law, 18*(4), 549–576.

Vincent, G., & Viljoen, J. (2020). Racial algorithms or systemic problems? Risk assessment s and risk disparities. *Criminal Justice and Behavior*, *47*(2), 1576–1584. https://www.ojp.gov/ncjrs/virtual-library/abstracts/knowledge-brief-does-mental-health-screening-fulfill-its-promise

Williams, V., & Grisso, T. (2011). *Does mental health screening fulfill its promise? Knowledge brief: Does mental health screening fulfill its promise?* https://modelsforchange.net/publications/316/#:~:text=In%20this%20study,%20researchers%20implemented%20a

7

Recovery-Oriented Cognitive Therapy for Justice-Involved Individuals

Shelby Arnold, Lindsey Pinto, and Paul M. Grant

Recovery-oriented cognitive therapy (CT-R; Beck et al., 2021) is a cognitive-behavioral approach for working with individuals involved with the criminal justice system. CT-R equips justice system and mental health providers with a powerful set of strategies that promote recovery, resiliency, and flourishing in the community, simultaneously and efficiently operationalizing both recovery principles (e.g., living one's desired life; Dorkins & Adshead, 2011; Mann et al., 2014) and risk mitigation (Arnold & Pinto, 2023). In this chapter, we describe a brief history of CT-R and its theoretical underpinnings, present CT-R's relevance to community-based justice services, and outline implementation practices, illustrating each point through a case study. The concluding section describes how CT-R applies at each stage of the criminal justice system, using the Sequential Intercept Model (SIM; Munetz & Griffin, 2006).

History of CT-R Development

CT-R was developed in the late 1990s by Paul Grant and Aaron T. Beck, working in neighborhoods (North Philadelphia, West Philadelphia) where the resources are limited, the impact of poverty and discrimination is profound, and the trust in the justice and mental health systems is low. Grant and Beck recognized the importance of modifying Beck's pioneering CBT protocols (Beck, 1963; Beck et al., 1979), especially for individuals who experience negative symptoms (e.g., withdrawal, isolation, limited access to energy and motivation, reduced verbal expressivity; Blanchard & Cohen, 2006). Involving interviews, basic scientific studies, the development of an initial protocol, and a clinical trial, this line of work led to the discovery that these individuals viewed themselves as incapable of connecting with others. Yet their desire was still present—most of them described wanting relationships, families, jobs, and a life in the community. CT-R became a psychosocial method to implement these goals: a way for providers to partner with often wary individuals in their

Shelby Arnold, Lindsey Pinto, and Paul M. Grant, *Recovery-Oriented Cognitive Therapy for Justice-Involved Individuals*. In: *The Path Forward*. Edited by: Kirk Heilbrun and David DeMatteo, Oxford University Press.
 DOI: 10.1093/9780197773031.003.0007

community, to help them feel less defeated and more connected, to pursue the life they had always wanted (for more on the development of CT-R, see Beck et al., 2021; Grant, 2019).

CT-R aligns with key principles of the Recovery Movement, a political effort by people with lived experience and by mental health advocates, demanding empowering community-based care as opposed to chronic institutionalization typical of the 1960s (Davidson et al., 2010). The term "recovery" captures both the process and the outcome of care sought by adherents (Davidson et al., 2009): individuals should have an active role in their treatment and goals should focus on their desired life. In CT-R, the concept of recovery means that people live meaningful lives of their choosing and build empowerment and resilience related to challenges that impede the pursuit of that life.

Grant and Beck's CT-R implementation efforts began in the early 2010s. Institutional and community-based staff in Pennsylvania and Georgia learned CT-R. These projects included justice-involved individuals in forensic state hospital units, within community forensic residences, and on community-based teams (assertive community, specialty care, mobile crisis). Over the ensuing decade, Grant and Beck's team has trained staff across the stages described by the Sequential Intercept Model (Munetz & Griffin, 2006), as outlined later in this chapter.

CT-R Theory and Empirical Support

At the core of CT-R's broad applicability—to both diverse persons and in a variety of settings—is a powerful theory that guides the approach. This theory contains three related mechanisms of action (Grant & Inverso, 2023). The *cognitive model* centers on the thinking that drives behavior and emotional reactions. The *theory of modes* describes systematic ways the organism relates to its internal and external environments. *Attentional narrowing* captures biases in mental focusing that can get a person stuck in their challenges, but also ways an intervention can help empower them.

The Cognitive Model

Beck's (1963) cognitive model describes behavior and emotion in terms of underlying beliefs: how a person views themselves, other people, the world more broadly, and their future. This model has accrued considerable empirical support over six decades for understanding many of the common challenges seen in forensic and mental health settings—depression, anxiety, anger, chronic pain, personality disorders, substance use, positive symptoms (e.g., hallucinations, delusions), negative symptoms (e.g., avolition, anhedonia), and criminality (Beck, 1999, 2019). Due to its application across a range of diagnoses and difficulties, the cognitive model is a person-centered template that helps providers better understand each person's unique set of challenges. Moving beyond challenge reduction, a major innovation of CT-R is to apply the cognitive model to flourishing. The same three categories of belief (self, other, and future) can apply to people's perceptions when they are thriving—or at least when their problems are less dominant. The primary mechanism of change in CT-R is intentionally strengthening these positive beliefs (Grant et al., in preparation).

Theory of Modes

Beck (1996) originally applied the idea of a mode—the interface between the organism and their environment—to personality disorders, ascribing the quick changing between states of emotion and behavior to different modes becoming active within the person. The theory is now transdiagnostic, describing psychopathology as a mismatch between the internal mode and the environment (Beck, Finkel, et al., 2021; Beck & Haigh, 2014). The idea of modes can also apply to everyday experiences, such as how we behave and feel differently when playing a sport, writing a paper, or reacting to a loud sound such as a car backfire. Beliefs or cognitive schemas—the cognitive model—are at the core of how the organism-environment interface is achieved, the shift between modes occurring when different sets of beliefs are activated.

CT-R emphasizes two specific types of modes a person can be in: the *disconnected* mode and the *adaptive* mode (Beck et al., 2021; Grant et al., in preparation). The disconnected mode is driven by negative beliefs about the self, others, and the future. In this mode, challenges are often at the forefront. The person in the disconnected mode has less access to energy, motivation, hope, or possibility. The behavioral response is either to retreat (e.g., negative symptoms) or to respond reactively (e.g., aggression, substance use, or self-harm). The adaptive mode, by contrast, is driven by positive beliefs. A person feels at their best or more like themselves. Challenges or symptoms fade to the background, the person has greater access to energy, motivation, and sees themselves more positively. In the adaptive mode, one is more likely to engage with others and to imagine a future. The primary aim of CT-R is to find each person's adaptive mode and to collaborate with the person to make this their dominant mode in life.

Attentional Narrowing

A hallmark finding from cognitive psychology is the bottleneck of attentional processes, the classic example being the difficulty people have in attending to two sources of information at the same time. For CT-R theory, it is variability (narrow vs. broad) of attention that helps to explain how the disconnected mode can become dominant, and how therapeutic interventions can break through to bring about the adaptive mode. Narrow attentional fixation—both conceptual and perceptual—can be useful for completing a task (e.g., writing a chapter, completing a workout routine), as the person focuses on the task at hand while screening out task-extraneous factors (e.g., what to make for dinner, the names of family members). Within CT-R theory (Grant et al., in preparation), the persistence of challenges (mental health, justice-involvement) is attributed to narrowing of attentional focus, limiting of cognitive flexibility, and the potential to respond differently in a stressful situation. For example, a person prone to aggressive behavior can experience attentional narrowing—individuals with lived experience call this "tunnel vision"—that heightens the impact of negative beliefs about the situation ("I am a bad person," "I have to act to stay safe," "others don't care about me"), with alternative beliefs ("I am a good person," "I have more important things to do," "there are people who care about me"). Consequently, courses of action do not jump to mind. Research supports this mechanism in aggressive behavior and substance use (Gable et al., 2015; Hicks et al., 2015). Empowerment in CT-R comes through strategies and interventions that broaden attentional scope in the moment, when the person is in the disconnected mode, thereby enabling transition to the adaptive mode, which helps them to act and feel differently. The person learns that they have more control in these situations and can use skills (relaxation, mindfulness, music, refocusing) to activate their adaptive mode, act differently, and refocus their energy.

Empirical Support for CT-R Model

Given the overrepresentation of mental health challenges in the justice system, coupled with the empirical support for cognitive-behavioral approaches as a gold standard for offender rehabilitation, innovative approaches that can achieve both needs are a priority (Casey & Rottman, 2005; Gottfried & Christopher, 2017; Honegger, 2015; James & Glaze, 2006; Landenberger & Lipsey, 2005). Accordingly, CT-R has been empirically validated—both the psychological (Grant & Beck, 2009, 2010; Campellone et al., 2016; Luther et al., 2024) and therapeutic models (Grant et al., 2012; Grant et al., 2017; Grant et al., in preparation)—and is expressly designed to advance an individual's pursuit of both forensic recovery (i.e., reduced risk, less frequent recidivism) and mental health conceptualizations of recovery (i.e., meaningful and desired life). Specific evaluation of CT-R on justice-related outcomes (e.g., recidivism, quality of life upon reentry) is ongoing.

CT-R has been implemented to some degree in at least sixteen U.S. states and territories (PA, NJ, NY, MA, VT, GA, MO, MT, CA, KY, FL, MS, NV, IL, WA, LA, Guam) across all levels of care. These range from highly restrictive institutional settings (civil units, forensic units, acute or crisis units, correctional institutions) to community residential settings (programmatic residences, group homes, supportive housing), community teams (assertive community, specialty care, mobile crisis, crisis call), and community programs (Certified Community Behavioral Health Centers, problem-solving courts). CT-R-trained providers come from different backgrounds, training, experience, and roles. They include psychiatrists, psychologists, social workers, peer specialists, recreation and rehabilitation professionals, nurses, court officers, probation officers, crisis line operators, and direct care staff. There is preliminary evidence that CT-R has promoted movement of long-institutionalized individuals into less restrictive environments (Grant, 2019), including, notably, reduced use of explicitly controlling interventions such as seclusion and physical and chemical restraints (Chang et al., 2014). CT-R-trained programs also report lower rates of hospitalization, a reduction in jail days, and increased engagement with community treatment teams for the individuals they serve (Beck et al., 2021; Grant, 2019).

CT-R for Community-Based Justice Services

CT-R meets both the needs of the justice-involved individuals and their providers. For individuals, the CT-R framework emphasizes each person's unique experience; anchors work in their strengths, interests, and passions; and empowers through highly collaborative approaches to care. For providers, CT-R includes flexible implementation options, streamlines continuity of care, and enhances intrinsic motivation to sustain community participation.

Flexible Practice

CT-R offers many options in terms of delivery, including who, where, how, and to whom it is delivered within community-based justice services. A range of provider types across multiple systems and disciplines can (and do) benefit from CT-R, each using it as a framework to understand the whole person (e.g., challenges, strengths, and goals) and adapt CT-R skills to meet the needs of their unique role, whether in traditional therapy or as a brief intervention in a court or case management meeting. In this way, CT-R can play a role in the many settings in which justice-involved persons find themselves, with all relevant players "speaking the same language" to promote empowerment. Whether in a formal treatment context, legal setting, or elsewhere in the community, CT-R strategies can foster connection and guide action plans that enable individuals to succeed.

Since CT-R provides both a framework for conceptualizing an individual, and specific strategies based on this conceptualization, it can be employed as a standalone therapeutic approach (in individual or group contexts), or it can deepen a provider's understanding of a person while they incorporate a multi-theoretical approach to care (e.g., using CT-R alongside Motivational Interviewing, DBT, or

Thinking for a Change groups). CT-R focuses on strengthening positive beliefs and building a meaningful life, which actualizes principles of the Good Lives Model (Ward & Brown, 2004), while also bolstering protective factors, indirectly reducing many of the RNR "Big Eight" criminogenic risk factors (e.g., antisocial cognitions, antisocial peers, education/vocation, and leisure time), and enhancing "responsivity" by centering action around individuals' stated desires for their future (Andrews et al., 1990). As many of the key elements of CT-R align with values of other clinical approaches (see Figure 7.1), CT-R fits within existing justice-related frameworks and can seamlessly integrate into other clinical evidence-based approaches.

Key
ACT: Acceptance and Commitment Therapy
CBT: Cognitive Behavioral Therapy
CBTP: Cognitive Behavioral Therapy for Psychosis
DBT: Dialectical Behavior Therapy

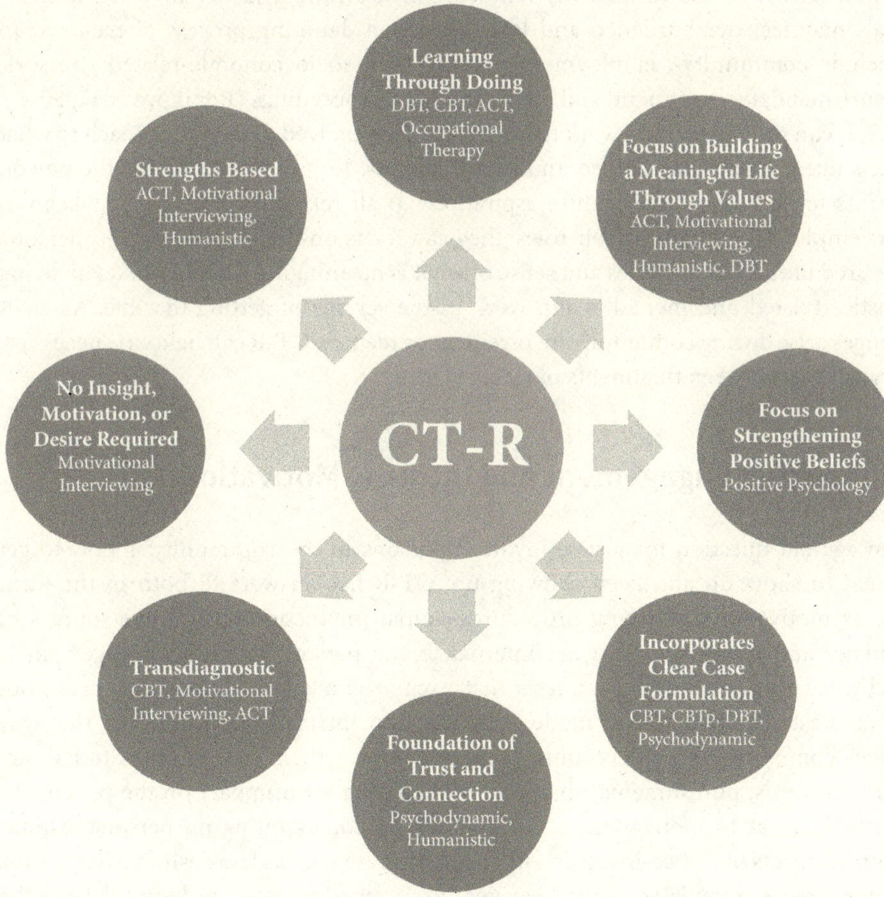

Figure 7.1 CT-R and Other Approaches to Community-Based Care

Another advantage of CT-R in the community is its applicability to comorbidities and intersecting challenges. For example, a person can experience a relapse in substance use, listen to distressing voices, and focus on being persecuted. CT-R emphasizes specific beliefs the person holds about themselves, others, or their future (e.g., "I am unsafe" or "others mean me harm," "I won't be able to handle it") as key to understanding these challenges. Interventions create opportunities to experience the positive version of these target beliefs (e.g., safety, sense of control, positive connection with others, future capability), with providers helping the person notice their own resiliency. In this way, there are no problems "too serious or difficult" to understand and develop successful strategies for empowerment.

Continuity of Care

Upon release to the community following incarceration, justice-involved individuals may feel overburdened and lost. The often daunting process of reentry can include community-, employment-, family- and socioeconomic-related stressors, court-mandated treatment, and continued legal proceedings (Borakove et al., 2015). CT-R can provide a framework to unify a justice-involved person's approach to what feels like a highly fragmented and siloed process. Key to this is the life the person wants to be living—their future aspirations. If all relevant community stakeholders employ CT-R within their roles, they can focus on the justice-involved person's desired life and their values and sense of what is meaningful, thereby contextualizing justice-related and mental health work in the service of getting that life. As challenges arise during community involvement or reentry, CT-R can help ease necessary transitions between treatments or levels of care.

Enhancing Engagement and Intrinsic Motivation

An age-old question for justice-involved persons in the community is how to get them to show up and keep showing up. CT-R has answers to both in the form of its motivation-enhancing procedures. Initial interactions search for sources of energy and motivation that are internal to the person. Typically, engagement is achieved through finding interests that excite them and activities that bring out their best self or adaptive mode. Tapping into intrinsic motivation in this way gives community providers more tools, and moves them away from external factors (rewards, punishments) that have limited long-term impact on the person. To sustain access to motivation, CT-R emphasizes collaborating on personal aspirations. Aspects of justice-involvement or care that are seen as less desirable (e.g., urine drug screens, mandated court hearings) are framed as steps to living the life the person wants to be living. CT-R also focuses on creating a balance of required activities (e.g., court appearances, treatment), and meaningful or goal-driven activities (e.g., attending a church service, cooking for family), which help the person thrive (Munetz et al., 2014).

CT-R Implementation

Implementation of CT-R is guided by a theory-driven, evidence-based protocol that addresses the implementation-level shortcomings seen in many other CBT interventions in forensic settings (Grant, 2019; Stirman et al., 2010). The components of this training model are comprehensive needs assessment, interactive workshop, expert-led consultation, and a workable sustainability plan. These procedures increase the likelihood of training success that enhances the skills of existing staff, while allowing each to bring their unique experiences within their respective roles to enhance the impact of CT-R.

Prior to formal training, CT-R experts conduct sessions with administrative stakeholders to develop a comprehensive training plan, identify staff across disciplines to participate, and establish desired outcomes and means of measurement. Focus groups build excitement for the training and help the experts better tailor training content to specific settings and staff. Workshops then provide theoretical foundation, strategies, and practical interventions that staff can use to empower the individuals they serve. Workshops vary in length and delivery method (i.e., self-paced online courses, live virtual trainings, or in-person training) and include opportunities for practicing and applying concepts.

Research shows that workshops are often not sufficient to get new skills into practice (Stirman et al., 2010). To ensure success, CT-R experts provide technical assistance in the form of ongoing consultation sessions after a workshop. This presents a continued opportunity to implement learning: through case conceptualization (the Recovery Map, see Table 7.1), targeted discussions of individuals on the service, milieu-based and group-based programming, or applying CT-R to paraprofessional or other unique roles (e.g., case management, peer support). Consultation sessions work best in a group format with multiple disciplines represented. The standard consultation period is six months but can be adjusted as needed.

To maximize sustainability beyond the technical assistance period, consultation can shift from external CT-R trainers leading the sessions to an internal CT-R champions leading while receiving feedback from the experts. Internal champions can also use a measure called the *CT-R Quality Scale* (Beck et al., 2021), a formalized self-assessment of programmatic CT-R strengths and areas for improvement. This measure can be administered at baseline, prior to any training occurring, and then routinely throughout implementation to identify needs and priorities, as well as to track progress. Emerging data suggest that full sustainability can often be achieved within one to two years following this gold-standard implementation protocol (Grant, 2019).

Table 7.1 CT-R Recovery Map

Recovery Map	
Accessing & Energizing the Adaptive Mode	
Interests/Ways to Engage:	Beliefs Activated while in Adaptive Mode:
Aspirations	
Goals:	Meaning of Accomplishing Identified Goals:
Challenges	
Current Behaviors/Challenges:	Beliefs Underlying Challenges:
Positive Action & Empowerment	
Current Strategies and Interventions:	Belief/Aspiration/Meaning/Challenge Targeted:

From the Beck Institute for Cognitive Behavior Therapy
Beckinstitute.org

How CT-R Works: A Case Example

In CT-R, treatment activities are designed so that individuals repeatedly experience their best selves (adaptive mode) and plan and take action toward a personally meaningful and desired life. They develop an identity that is larger and more valuable to them than ideas rooted in criminal charges, mental health challenges, diagnoses, or life circumstances. These recovery-oriented aims (best self, desired life) bolster protective factors linked to recidivism reduction (e.g., increased connection, meaningful ways to spend time), thereby reducing evidence-based criminogenic risk factors (e.g., antisocial cognitions, lack of educational/vocational activities). By seeing themselves more positively, and the future as more hopeful, individuals receiving CT-R can better sustain their desired life and way of living in the community long-term (Arnold et al., in press). The following case example illustrates the use of five core elements of CT-R—accessing, energizing, developing, actualizing, and strengthening (see Table 7.2)—with a justice-involved individual in the community.

"Michael"[1] has two children and lives at home with his mother. He is participating in treatment court after charges of simple assault and possession of a controlled

[1] This is a composite example for illustrative purpose, and as such, does not include any protected health information.

Table 7.2 Phases of CT-R & Justice Involvement

Phases	Misson
Initiating Connection Accessing the Adaptive Mode	– Build trust and connection. – Identify interests and passions to elicit a person's best self outside oftheir justice involvement. – Activate positive beliefs (i.e., "I am capable, "I belong, I can have fun.").
Expanding Connection Energizing the Adaptive Mode	– Extend connection and trust. – Make the experience ofthe adaptive mode more predictable and frequent while balancing forensic responsibility. – Generalize positive beliefs beyond "one time only."
Cultivating Hope Developing the Adaptive Mode	– Identify long-term targets ("aspirations") that embody a person's desired future. – Make these targets a powerful source of motivation and hope (enrich with imagery). – Understand the values underneath a person's desired future (i.e., why is it important to them?). – Set the course for intentional action toward what is important, meaningful, and hopeful.
Taking Action Actualizing the Adaptive Mode	– Plan and take action toward aspirations or underlying meaning. – Action provides context for navigating challenges and adhering to justice-related responsibilities. – Notice how current action gets them closer to their aspirations.
Capturing the Positive, Success, & Resiliency Strengthening the Adaptive Mode	– Collaboratively draw conclusions about experiences and what they mean about the self, others, and the future. – Strengthen key positive beliefs (related to themes like connection, capability, value, energy, and control). – Strengthen resilience beliefs as individuals take steps toward their future, experience success, and navigate challenges.

From the Beck Institute for Cognitive Behavior Therapy
Beckinstitute.org
©2024

substance. Staff in both his treatment court and outpatient substance use program are participating in a CT-R implementation with case consultation sessions (Grant, 2019). When initially presenting Michael for consultation, staff members remark that he has moved in and out of the justice system over the past twenty years, bouncing between correctional facilities, hospital units, and community supervision. They express feeling stuck with Michael, noting that he minimally engages with them, often gives one-word answers and becomes impatient to leave. He also turns down opportunities to take part in programming or to discuss his plans. Occasionally, they hear him sounding defeated about the future—saying, for example, "I'll just mess up anyway and end up back in jail, so why am I even here?" Per his mother, Michael spends most of his days isolating in his room and rejects her attempts at connection.

Accessing

The expert consultant begins with the first strategy of CT-R—establishing a connection and trust with Michael. In other words, *accessing his adaptive mode.* Interventions at this stage should elicit his interests, hobbies, areas of expertise, talents, and skills. Staff should talk with him about pursuits and, importantly, do the activities together. The team also seeks clues to his interests from his mother, who reports that he likes to cook for his family, play pick-up basketball in his neighborhood, and watch local sports games when he is living at home with her. She shares that he passed high school equivalency and developed skills in carpentry during an earlier incarceration. When asked when Michael is at his best, his mother says, "talking about cars," an area of considerable knowledge—his uncle is an auto mechanic and Michael spent time in his shop as a kid.

To address Michael's guardedness and mistrust, the CT-R consultant advises brief but frequent contacts featuring attempts at connection, and prioritizing approaches that help him experience control, such as seeking recommendations or watching short videos on cars, recipes, or sports. Success will be observable, as Michael will show both affective and behavioral shifts (e.g., smiling, laughing, increased verbal engagement) when in the adaptive mode. The consultant recommends that staff be prepared to help him notice these shifts and possible positive beliefs that may also become active at the time. For example, staff could ask, "It seems like you're smiling more when we talk about sports, do you notice that, too?" or "It seems like you really know a lot about cars, what do you think?"

Michael noticeably brightens during interactions with the staff member talking about recent sports games, watching highlights, and giving advice for barbecue recipes. Together they notice the meanings, such as "I am capable" and "I have something valuable to offer," though this quickly turns to hopelessness ("I'll never be able to do those things again"). To help the team generalize, the CT-R consultant emphasizes that anyone involved in Michael's care can access his adaptive mode, and that repeatedly doing so will help strengthen these key positive beliefs.

Energizing

In a subsequent consultation session, the CT-R expert recommends adjusting the strategy. Now that they know how to access Michael's adaptive mode, the focus is on *energizing* it to help him experience his best self more often. The team can do this by expanding the range of those with whom he engages in activities (other staff, members of the community, peers). It could also involve increasing the frequency of activities (multiple times per day, more days during the week) and finding new activities that could generate similar important beliefs (e.g., capability, control).

Different staff members begin to talk with Michael about sports. Some reflect with him on recent sports games, others ask for tips to shoot a three-pointer, and others talk to him about cars. Soon, he is giving advice about how to change the oil, how to select a mechanic, and what to look for when buying a car. His therapist encourages Michael to return to cooking at home, first by helping as his mother cooks, and over time considering taking on more responsibility as he did before. Each occasion creates an opportunity for him to see that he is worthwhile, has value, and is appreciated.

To get the most benefit from energizing, the CT-R consultant proposes that the team ask questions about doing enjoyable and meaningful activities more often, and to see that positive moments are not "one time only" but something he can take control of and repeatedly experience. She proposes that they ask Michael, "If you're able to connect with me, is it possible you can do it with others in the community too?" and "You've really been helping a lot lately at home, what does that say about you?" This ensures that he gets the relevant meaning from each experience and becomes gradually more comfortable considering possibilities for his future.

Developing

Summarizing their progress, the CT-R consultant observes that the team has connected with Michael, learned a lot about him, earned his trust, and helped him to begin to improve relations with his family. The next strategy is *developing* the adaptive mode. This involves identifying and enriching an individual's personally meaningful and values-based aspirations—desires for their future. For justice-involved individuals, aspirations are critical (Arnold et al., in press). These future targets serve as the "why" for navigating challenges (e.g., undesirable justice requirements, evaluations or court hearings, mental health, substance use). Aspirations also create a source of vital personal control, as the person can take daily steps toward a desired life regardless of their current legal status.

When a team member initially asks him about the future, Michael explains, "I want to get done with court and treatment and get clean for my kids." Over time, Michael feels more comfortable with staff, and describes wanting to repair his relationship with his kids, be more of a presence in his community like he used to (e.g., going to barbeques, playing basketball), and get a job as a mechanic. Following the advice of the CT-R consultant, a team member asks him what the "best part" of these aspirations would be. Michael explains that he values the sense of community, that he could bring people together, and that "people would see I'm still me." He also says that both his vocational aspirations and repairing his relationship with his kids would mean "others can rely on me," that "I am capable and have something to offer," and that "I have overcome a lot." These meanings become a guide for how a person with justice-involvement spends their time, experiences purpose, and actively works toward their dreams.

Actualizing

With this clear picture of Michael's aspirations, the CT-R expert proposes two new strategies: (1) collaborating on ways for him to take positive action steps toward these aspirations daily; and (2) helping him feel empowered when challenges arise. Positive action might include completing short-term steps toward the aspiration (e.g., job applications or a letter to his kids), or it might involve living the personal meaning realized by aspirations (e.g., finding ways each week to help others or contribute). Either would help Michael experience his best self increasingly often. Staff can also help Michael see that substance use treatment is a piece of the puzzle, which enhances intrinsic motivation to take part.

The CT-R consultant recommends that the team help Michael make the most of his activity at this stage. He can repeatedly notice his progress toward his aspirations and underlying values, that it is worth it to make difficult or sometimes unappealing steps to get closer to a desired future, and that he is contributing and making a difference. Questions include those such as: "What does it say about you that you planned a successful dinner with your family?" and "Is it worth [attending treatment, staying clean] if it gets you closer to being a mechanic and reconnecting with your kids?" Conclusions can also focus upon empowerment—successful use of skills for challenges or handling situations differently than the person might have in the past (e.g., "Did you notice that you did not use this time when stressed? What does that say about you?").

Strengthening

Throughout the consultation sessions, the CT-R expert emphasizes the importance of *strengthening* the adaptive mode by asking questions that target key conclusions, especially positive beliefs and resiliency beliefs. One key question is, "What does that say about you?" Any member of a team can pose these questions to catch successes and build positive beliefs that help the person sustain action. Particularly for justice-involved individuals, strengthening resiliency beliefs acts as a protective factor, cushioning against negative beliefs that could lead to setbacks. It also helps to strengthen an individual's identity as a good person or a person who can contribute meaningfully, rather than a person who has been involved with the justice system (Arnold et al., in press).

Generalizability and Expansion of CT-R Across the SIM

One of the key advantages of using CT-R with justice-involved individuals is its versatility, allowing varied formats and settings of implementation across a range of community-based services. In this section, we use the Sequential Intercept Model to illustrate how CT-R has been used at different points of contact across the justice system. We also describe future ideas and opportunities for expansion as CT-R dissemination broadens.

Intercept 0: Community Services

Intercept 0 (Abreu et al., 2017) is comprised of community-based crisis services with the goal of prevention or diversion from justice-system involvement at the outset (e.g., crisis teams or call lines, or linkage programs that connect individuals to treatment or other services *instead* of arresting them or otherwise involving them in the legal system).

CT-R has been used at this intercept to train and empower crisis call line staff and mobile intervention teams. In this context, CT-R is used as a framework for understanding the current crisis and using that understanding to quickly connect with the individual to de-escalate and develop a plan. CT-R has been particularly effective for supporting staff with frequent callers or users of crisis services; when the individual is known to staff, CT-R informs conceptualization of the crisis experience (using underlying beliefs as a guide), and outlines actionable strategies for de-escalation and redirection. Trained staff at Intercept 0 have also reported that CT-R helps with responding to challenging callers (e.g., callers who are hard to understand, or express provocative, sexual, or otherwise offensive statements) in a way that is strengths-based and invites a more comfortable connection. Expansion of CT-R at this intercept could include further training for call centers (e.g., 988), text-based services, and continued training of crisis responder providers (e.g., nursing, emergency services, case management).

Intercept 1 (Law Enforcement)

Intercept 1 consists of law enforcement or emergency service providers and allows for diversion to mental health or substance use treatment at the time of law enforcement involvement or arrest. As of 2024, CT-R has not been implemented at this intercept; however, given the success in adjacent crisis services at Intercept 0, CT-R shows promise. Since non-clinical stakeholders have readily used its principles, CT-R can be an effective approach for emergency personnel. It can provide a depth of understanding of clinical issues, as well as recovery-focused and strengths-based strategies for connection, de-escalation, and diversion. CT-R would be particularly useful to co-response teams to ensure that mental health providers and law enforcement have a common language and shared, effective toolbox.

Intercept 2 (Initial Court Hearings/Initial Detention)

Intercept 2 diverts individuals into community treatment at the time of jail intake/booking or during arraignments and initial court hearings. The length of contact with service providers at this stage varies widely; for some staff, they only spend enough time with individuals to get them linked to services, and for others they conduct longer-term community monitoring and support.

CT-R at Intercept 2 has taken the form of training staff at local jails, which includes discharge planning centers. Though contacts are brief, staff report that CT-R helps them to engage individuals quickly and effectively with services or monitoring providers. Access to, and intentional transmission of, strengths-based and person-centered information energizes new providers, who can more rapidly learn what is important to each person, improve engagement and trust, and create genuine connections between individuals and community providers to improve adherence and outcomes.

Continued expansion for CT-R at this stage would include training of court officials (e.g., judges, lawyers, court staff). Though some legal practitioners have been trained in CT-R (e.g., Intercept 3), more widespread training can continue to promote this person-centered approach, which may be particularly important for under-resourced or rural courts, where clinical providers and outreach teams may be less involved or non-existent.

Intercept 3 (Jails/Courts)

Intercept 3 diverts individuals to community-based treatment after being formally charged and booked in jail, with the goal of minimizing incarceration time and thus separation from the community and treatment. This intercept includes regular court dockets and specialty (problem-solving) courts which divert and link individuals to treatment needs that relate to their justice involvement.

CT-R has been implemented across a range of services at Intercept 3. For example, outpatient providers or monitors of community-based competency restoration have been trained in CT-R. Staff on these teams report that CT-R helps them stay connected to individuals during the restoration period and increases engagement and participation in restoration procedures, ongoing court appearances, and continued evaluation of competency. CT-R's focus on getting to know individuals' interests, and taking part in areas of strength and expertise together, has increased the number of service contacts, as well as the number of individuals who actively participate in restoration sessions. From a CT-R perspective, starting restoration treatment sessions with intentional, genuine connection through participation in an activity that demonstrates the individual's skill (e.g., teaching provider about a recipe they know, playing a certain card game, or sharing gardening tips) increases trust and openness to discussion of challenging topics, and also activates positive beliefs such as "I am capable" or "I am a good person." Intentional activation of positive beliefs prior to task performance can neutralize negative beliefs that may arise during legal education activities or discussing details about active legal cases, potentially increasing performance (Grant et al., 2018).

CT-R has also been implemented in problem-solving courts such as drug courts and mental health courts. These implementation projects provide opportunities for legal and clinical stakeholders to come together to discuss active court participants and fine-tune CT-R skills each team member can employ within their role to promote success of the justice-involved individuals. CT-R training also bridges between treatment courts and linked community programs that serve court participants. Staff describe CT-R as helping them get to know their participants better and understand their long-term aspirations to help build intrinsic motivation that sustains them during court participation and any setbacks that may occur.

CT-R has also been implemented at Intercept 3 within the jails themselves (on general population and specialized/alternative units). CT-R training has enhanced the existing work of jail clinicians, case managers, peer support, education services, chaplaincy services, and security staff. Staff in the jails have been able to use CT-R to connect with individuals, both with or without mental health and substance use histories, while also preparing for reentry. At this intercept, the priority for CT-R expansion is more widespread dissemination, particularly as a bridge between clinicians and non-clinicians who support participants during this stage.

Intercept 4 (Reentry)

Intercept 4 involves programs that support individuals through return to the community following incarceration. CT-R has been implemented in a range of reentry support services. For example, jail-based reentry teams have been trained in CT-R. Staff have reported that the concept of aspirations has potentiated a whole-person approach to planning a return to the community. Staff and individuals shared that specifically targeting community action toward aspirations or their underlying meaning provides balance to the day-to-day of reentry, refocusing conversations around what is important to the individual. Discussion of aspirations fosters a deeper connection between individuals and reentry coordinators, which can increase follow-through and continued engagement with services in the community.

CT-R has also been implemented on the community side of reentry on forensic community treatment teams and within forensic residential programs. CT-R has been used as a style of interaction for collaborative and multi-disciplinary teams, and to complement existing criminogenic risk reduction interventions. Future directions for CT-R at Intercept 4 involve expansion within all the diverse ways that reentry support manifests in the community. Continued training, particularly of non-clinical staff or peer providers, could prove especially useful at this intercept.

Intercept 5 (Community Corrections)

Intercept 5 includes community supervision (e.g., probation or parole) with a specific focus on individuals with mental health or substance-related challenges. This is an area with much potential for CT-R, but it has not yet been actualized by an implementation project. CT-R could look similar at Intercept 5 as it does at Intercept

4, supporting reentry services. The focus on connection and aspirations can help frame monitoring appointments with probation/parole officers, as well as case managers, and can tap into intrinsic motivation to stay connected and crime-free in the community.

Conclusion

CT-R is an evidence-supported, cognitive-behavioral approach that empowers individuals at the intersection of the mental health and justice systems. Using a strengths-based, person-centered framework, CT-R efficiently guides work toward personal recovery (e.g., individuals living desired lives) and forensic recovery (e.g., reduced recidivism). CT-R is an emerging, innovative practice supported by empirically-validated implementation strategies that can empower individuals and staff at all community-based stages of the criminal justice system.

References

Abreu, D., Parker, T. W., Noether, C. D., Steadman, H. J., & Case, B. (2017). Revising the paradigm for jail diversion for people with mental and substance use disorders: Intercept 0. *Behavioral Sciences & the Law*, *35*(5–6), 380–395. https://doi.org/10.1002/bsl.2300

Andrews, D. A., Bonta, J., & Hoge, R. D. (1990). Classification for effective rehabilitation: Rediscovering psychology. *Criminal Justice and Behavior*, *17*(1), 19–52.

Arnold, S., Lustig, N., Pinto, L., & Grant, P. M. (in press). Recovery-oriented cognitive therapy: A testable framework to promote successful long-term recovery from substance use for justice-involved individuals. *Journal for Advancing Justice*, V, 57–71.

Arnold, S., & Pinto, L. (2023). Recovery-Oriented Cognitive Therapy: A game changer for justice-involved individuals. *Psychiatric Times*, *40*(5), 32–33.

Beck, A. T. (1963). Thinking and depression: I. Idiosyncratic content and cognitive distortions. *Archives of General Psychiatry*, *9*(4), 324–333. https://doi.org/10.1001/archpsyc.1963.01720160014002

Beck, A. T. (1996). Beyond belief: A theory of modes, personality, and psychopathology. In P. M. Salkovskis (Ed.), *Frontiers of Cognitive Therapy* (pp. 1–25). Guilford Press.

Beck, A. T. (1999). *Prisoners of hate: The cognitive basis of anger, hostility, and violence.* HarperCollins.

Beck, A. T., (2019). A 60-year evolution of cognitive theory and therapy. *Perspectives on Psychological Science*, *14*(1), 16–20. https://doi.org/10.1177/1745691618804187

Beck, A. T., Finkel, M. R., & Beck, J. S. (2021). The theory of modes: Applications to schizophrenia and other psychological conditions. *Cognitive Therapy and Research*, *45*, 391–400. https://doi.org/10.1007/s10608-020-10098-0

Beck, A. T., Grant, P. M., Inverso, E., Brinen, A. P., & Perivoliotis, D. (2021). *Recovery-Oriented Cognitive Therapy for serious mental health conditions.* Guilford Press.

Beck, A. T., & Haigh, E. A. P. (2014). Advances in cognitive theory and therapy: The generic cognitive model. *Annual Review of Clinical Psychology, 10,* 1–24. https://doi.org/10.1146/annurev-clinpsy-032813-153734

Beck, A. T., Rush, A. J., Shaw, B. F., Emery, G. (1979). *Cognitive therapy of depression.* Guilford Press.

Blanchard, J. J., & Cohen, A. S. (2006). The structure of negative symptoms within schizophrenia: Implications for assessment. *Schizophrenia Bulletin, 32*(2), 238–245. https://doi.org/10.1093/schbul/sbj013

Borakove, M., Wosje, R.E., Cruz, F., Wickman, A., Dibble, T., & Harbus, C. (2015). *From silo to system: What makes a criminal justice system operate like a system?* Report prepared for The MacArthur Foundation. Accessed on May 9, 2024. https://safetyandjusticechallenge.org/wp-content/uploads/2021/06/From-Silo-to-System-30-APR-2015_FINAL.pdf

Campellone, T. R., Sanchez, A. H., & Kring, A. M. (2016). Defeatist performance beliefs, negative symptoms, and functional outcomes in schizophrenia: A meta-analytic review. *Schizophrenia Bulletin, 42*(6), 1343–1352. https://doi.org/10.1093/schbul/sbw026

Casey, P. M., & David B. Rottman, D. B. (2005). Problem-solving courts: Models and trends. *Justice System Journal, 26*(1), 35–56.

Chang, N. A., Grant, P. M., Luther, L., & Beck, A. T. (2014). Effects of a Recovery-Oriented Cognitive Therapy training program on inpatient staff attitudes and incidents of seclusion and restraint. *Community Mental Health Journal, 50*(4), 415–421. https://doi.org/10.1007/s10597-013-9675-6

Davidson, L., Rakfeldt, J., & Strauss, J. (2010). *The roots of the recovery movement in psychiatry: Lessons learned.* Wiley.

Davidson, L., Tondora, J., Lawless, M. S., O'Connell, M. J., & Rowe, M. (2009). *A practical guide to recovery-oriented practice: Tools for transforming mental health care.* Oxford University Press.

Dorkins, E., & Adshead, G. (2011). Working with offenders: Challenges to the recovery agenda. *Advances in Psychiatric Treatment, 17*(3), 178–187. https://doi.org/10.1192/apt.bp.109.007179

Gable, P. A., Poole, B. D., & Harmon-Jones, E. (2015). Anger perceptually and conceptually narrows cognitive scope. *Journal of Personality and Social Psychology, 109*(1), 163–174. https://doi.org/10.1037/a0039226

Gottfried, E. D., & Christopher, S. C. (2017). Mental disorders among criminal offenders: A review of the literature. *Journal of Correctional Health Care, 23*(3), 336–346. https://doi.org/10.1177/1078345817716180

Grant, P. M. (2019). *Recovery-Oriented Cognitive Therapy: A theory-driven, evidence-based, transformative practice to promote flourishing for individuals with serious mental health conditions that is applicable across mental health systems.* National Association of

State Mental Health Program Directors. https://www.nasmhpd.org/sites/default/files/TAC_Paper_7_508C.pdf

Grant, P. M., & Beck, A. T. (2009). Defeatist beliefs as a mediator of cognitive impairment, negative symptoms, and functioning in schizophrenia. *Schizophrenia Bulletin*, *35*(4), 798–806. https://doi.org/10.1093/schbul/sbn008

Grant, P. M., & Beck, A. T. (2010). Asocial beliefs as predictors of asocial behavior in schizophrenia. *Psychiatry Research*, *177*(1), 65–70. https://doi.org/10.1016/j.psychres.2010.01.005

Grant, P. M., Bredemeier, K., & Beck, A. T. (2017). Six-month follow-up of Recovery-Oriented Cognitive Therapy for low-functioning individuals with schizophrenia. *Psychiatric Services*, *68*(10), 997–1002. https://doi.org/10.1176/appi.ps.201600413

Grant, P. M., Huh, G. A., Perivoliotis, D., Stolar, N. M., & Beck, A. T. (2012). Randomized trial to evaluate the efficacy of cognitive therapy for low-functioning patients with schizophrenia. *Archives of General Psychiatry*, *69*(2), 121–127. https://doi.org/10.1001/archgenpsychiatry.2011.129

Grant, P. M., & Inverso, E. (2023). Recovery-Oriented Cognitive Therapy: Changing lives with a whole-person approach. *Psychiatric Times*, *40*(1), 29–31.

Grant, P. M., Perivoliotis, D., Luther, L., Bredemeier, K., & Beck, A. T. (2018). Rapid improvement in beliefs, mood, and performance following an experimental success experience in an analogue test of recovery-oriented cognitive therapy. *Psychological Medicine*, *48*(2), 261–268. https://doi.org/10.1017/S003329171700160X

Hicks, J. A., Fields, S., Davis, W. E., & Gable, P. A. (2015). Heavy drinking, impulsivity and attentional narrowing following alcohol cue exposure. *Psychopharmacology*, *232*(15), 2773–2779. https://doi.org/10.1007/s00213-015-3912-3

Honegger L. N. (2015). Does the evidence support the case for mental health courts? A review of the literature. *Law and Human Behavior*, *39*(5), 478–488. https://doi.org/10.1037/lhb0000141

James, D. J., & Glaze, L. E. (2006). *Mental health problems of prison and jail inmates*. Bureau of Justice Statistics Special Report NCJ 213600, U.S. Department of Justice.

Landenberger, N. A., & Lipsey, M. W. (2005). The positive effects of cognitive–behavioral programs for offenders: A meta-analysis of factors associated with effective treatment. *Journal of Experimental Criminology*, *1*(4), 451–476. https://doi.org/10.1007/s11292-005-3541-7

Luther, L., Rough, I. M., Grant, P. M., Beck, A. T., & Strauss, G. P. (2024). The role of defeatist performance beliefs in state fluctuations of negative symptoms in schizophrenia measured in daily life via Ecological Momentary Assessment. *Schizophrenia Bulletin*, 50(6),1427–1435, sbae128. Advance online publication. https://doi.org/10.1093/schbul/sbae128

Mann, B., Matias, E., & Allen, J. (2014). Recovery in forensic services: Facing the challenge. *Advances in Psychiatric Treatment*, *20*(2), 125–131. https://doi.org/10.1192/apt.bp.113.011403

Munetz, M. R., & Griffin, P. A. (2006). Use of the sequential intercept model as an approach to decriminalization of people with serious mental illness. *Psychiatric Services, 57*(4), 544–549.

Munetz, M. R., Ritter, C., Teller, J. L., & Bonfine, N. (2014). Mental health court and assisted outpatient treatment: Perceived coercion, procedural justice, and program impact. *Psychiatric Services, 65*(3), 352–358. https://doi.org/10.1176/appi.ps.002642012

Stirman, S. W., Bhar, S. S., Spokas, M., Brown, G. K., Creed, T. A., Perivoliotis, D., Farabaugh, D. T., Grant, P. M., & Beck, A. T. (2010). Training and consultation in evidence-based psychosocial treatments in public mental health settings: The ACCESS model. *Professional Psychology: Research and Practice, 41*(1), 48–56. https://doi.org/10.1037/a0018099

Ward, T., & Brown, M. (2004). The Good Lives Model and conceptual issues in offender rehabilitation. *Psychology, Crime & Law, 10*(3), 243–257. https://doi.org/10.1080/10683160410001662744

8

Cognitive Behavioral Therapy and Interventions with Justice-Involved Individuals

Kirk Heilbrun, Hailey Fasone, Kellie Wiltsie, Heidi Zapotocky, Chelsea Jackson, and Tierney Huppert

This chapter reviews Cognitive Behavioral Therapy (CBT) as it has been applied to justice-involved individuals. We begin by describing a specific project, a reentry clinic operated at Drexel University. In the second section, we turn to a broader review of the application of CBT services with justice-involved individuals, which provides the foundation on which the Drexel project is built. Questions of how this project began, how it has developed, and whether it might serve as a generalizable model for others are addressed in the subsequent sections. Issues related to diversity, equity, and inclusion are then discussed. Finally, we offer concrete suggestions for others interested in providing similar services, and provide brief concluding comments.

Project Description

The Drexel Reentry Project (DRP) provides cognitive behavioral therapy (CBT) services to justice-involved individuals. The DRP is housed within the Drexel University Psychological Services Center (PSC), a training clinic for clinical psychology doctoral students. It includes three different service tracks that reflect collaborations with two federal court programs, and with the Pennsylvania Innocence Project. Since 2015, the DRP has been accepting referrals from one of these programs, Supervision to Aid Reentry (STAR), a federal reentry court. Individuals referred for services at the DRP from STAR have been recently released from federal incarceration and have been identified as moderate to high risk of recidivism by the U.S. Probation Office. Participation in the DRP program is voluntary for STAR participants, although such participation is rewarded through the STAR court's incentives and can contribute to individuals receiving time off their required community supervision. Once referred to the DRP, individuals from STAR complete an intake that includes a risk-needs assessment and motivational interviewing. Beginning in 2023, the DRP has collaborated

Kirk Heilbrun et al., *Cognitive Behavioral Therapy and Interventions with Justice-Involved Individuals.* In: *The Path Forward.* Edited by: Kirk Heilbrun and David DeMatteo, Oxford University Press. © Oxford University Press (2026).
DOI: 10.1093/9780197773031.003.0008

with the Beck Institute to incorporate principles from recovery-oriented cognitive therapy (CT-R; Beck et al., 2020) into the treatment provided to STAR participants, with the goals of increasing motivation to participate in treatment, improving attendance and treatment engagement, and promoting treatment that is consistent with clients' personal goals as well as designed to reduce recidivism risk (See Arnold et al., this volume.).

In response to the need for psychological services with wrongfully-convicted individuals in the Philadelphia area, the DRP began accepting referrals from the Pennsylvania Innocence Project in 2019. Such exonerated individuals have a variety of treatment needs, including trauma symptoms, adjustment to reentry, and difficulty with interpersonal relationships. Participants pay for therapy services through the PSC's sliding fee scale based on income and number of dependents. To provide exonerated individuals with effective treatment, the DRP team reviewed the research on post-exoneration treatment needs and developed an evidence-based intervention toolkit in seven domains: (1) risk assessment, (2) intellectual functioning, (3) serious mental illness, (4) emotional patterns, (5) trauma, (6) adjustment, and (7) relationships (Heilbrun et al., 2023).

In early 2023, the DRP began accepting referrals from another federal problem-solving court: Strategies that Result in Developing Emotional Stability (STRIDES). The STRIDES court helps justice-involved individuals with severe and persistent mental illness achieve long-term behavioral health stability and reduce criminal recidivism risk. Those referred from STRIDES receive primary mental health services through other community providers, with DRP services focusing on wellness and risk reduction using a manualized CBT-based approach. These individuals often have co-occurring severe mental illness and substance use disorders.

The DRP provides a distinctive and specialized training opportunity for clinical psychology doctoral students at Drexel University. Student clinicians receive weekly group supervision and peer supervision that includes video and case note review. The primary treatment modality was in-person group therapy prior to the onset of the COVID-19 pandemic in 2020, but the DRP has since shifted to providing individual therapy services, primarily in person.

One significant barrier to treatment that has been consistently observed across all three tracks is inconsistent attendance. For STAR clients, data on treatment engagement suggest that the majority of past and current clients require substantial additional scheduled sessions due to appointments that are frequently missed, rescheduled, or canceled (Zapotocky et al., 2022). The DRP has taken various steps to address attendance and engagement difficulties, including the addition of a "patient navigator." This position involves providing daily reminders about session appointments, facilitating communication between clients, and completing initial consent forms and screening measures. The DRP's collaboration with the Beck Institute and incorporation of CT-R principles is designed to increase participant engagement in treatment by using an approach (the "adaptive mode") that incorporates more content that the client particularly enjoys.

Foundations and Support for Project Services

The impact of incarceration on justice-involved populations is associated with subsequent mood disorders and poorer health outcomes, and higher rates of suicide, violence, victimization, and reoffending (Schnittker et al., 2012). After reentry, many justice-involved individuals have difficulties adjusting to society, leading to deficits in occupational, social, and financial domains (Haney, 2003; Siennick et al., 2014). The Drexel DRP was created to address the identified needs of individuals reentering society following incarceration with two overarching goals: (a) to reduce the risk of reoffending, and (b) to improve overall adjustment during reentry. With these goals in mind, DRP service development has been informed by theoretical, empirical, and professional support and applications.

Research on justice-involved rehabilitation and intervention has long used the Risk-Need-Responsivity (RNR) model (Andrews et al., 1990). The RNR model is particularly important in correctional assessment and treatment. This approach to recidivism reduction and offender rehabilitation has three core principles (Dowden & Andrews, 2000). The "risk principle" indicates that interventions should be matched to offender risk level, positing that those with high-risk status would benefit from more intensive intervention. The "need principle" identifies criminogenic risk and need factors, including static (historical and unchangeable) and dynamic (those with the potential to change through planned intervention) factors, and their effect on offending behavior—underscoring the importance of targeting identified needs in rehabilitation. Examples of dynamic risk factors include antisocial attitudes, substance use, peers, and leisure time use. Finally, the "responsivity principle" refers to two characteristics of effective treatment—general responsivity (using empirically-supported treatment modalities) and specific responsivity (considering the characteristics of an individual influencing whether that person will respond favorably to the particular intervention provided). The RNR model suggests that effective programs should be tailored to individual risk assessment, address the biopsychosocial needs and risk factors common to justice-involved populations, and deliver empirically-supported treatment that is specific to client characteristics and strengths.

CBT is one of the most widely-used and empirically-supported therapeutic approaches to reducing recidivism and increasing quality of life among justice-involved populations (Barnes et al., 2017). CBT can address antisocial cognitive distortions and behaviors associated with criminal activity, such as dysfunctional expressions of anger and violence (Lipsey et al., 2007). Sessions are present-oriented and focus on skill building, equipping individuals to understand and regulate their emotions, build positive perspectives of themselves and others, and develop effective problem-solving skills to reduce impulsivity (Barnes et al., 2017; Hollin, 2019).

Considering a range of treatment orientations, CBT interventions have demonstrated the greatest impact on reducing criminal behavior in several meta-analyses (Hofmann et al., 2012; Landenberger & Lipsey, 2005; Wilson et al., 2005). There is considerable variability in specific program effectiveness, but research indicates that an important difference between successful versus less successful programs is the conceptualization of criminal behavior (Ross et al., 2021). Using the RNR model, effective CBT programs conceptualize offending behavior as a result of biopsychosocial and situational factors as opposed to primarily personal characteristics (Bonta & Andrews, 2024; Ross et al., 2021). By targeting how the individual thinks and identifying maladaptive patterns of behavior, successful programs aim to change the individual's perceptions of self, others, and situations (Ross et al., 2021). Programs are most effective when they outline specific goals for participants, deliver interventions using trained staff, and are constructively evaluated (Hollin, 2019). CBT-based interventions that also apply RNR concepts are successful in reducing sexual recidivism, violence recidivism, and general recidivism (Andrews et al., 1990; Dowden & Andrews, 2000; Hanson et al., 2009). CBT-based, RNR-informed interventions have been successfully employed by the DRP to address the varying treatment needs of individuals under federal supervision within the community (whether selected for behavioral health reasons or not), and individuals who have been wrongfully convicted and exonerated.

The DRP was informed by several criminal risk-reducing CBT programs that have been updated and revised over time. The incorporated programs include Reasoning and Rehabilitation (Ross & Fabiano, 1985), Aggression Replacement Training (Glick & Goldstein, 1987), the Cognitive Intervention Program (National Institute of Corrections, 1996), and Thinking for a Change (Bush et al., 1997). Programmatic objectives include introducing CBT principles (e.g., automatic thoughts; risky attitudes and beliefs; feelings), understanding risk and protective factors, and building skills. Identified skill areas include communication, self-care, identifying risky thinking, problem-solving, values-driven decision-making, and goal identification. Individuals work to apply CBT principles through problem-solving, new thinking, weighing choices and consequences, and making and evaluating plans (Heilbrun et al., 2017). The DRP utilizes the Level of Service/Case Management Inventory, which evaluates criminogenic risks and needs based on the RNR-model, to determine the appropriate duration and intensity of treatment. Those who are assessed and appraised to have medium, high, or very high risk of reoffending are designated as needing two treatment modules with an enhanced focus on applying effective problem-solving and decision-making skills (26 individual sessions in total), while those assessed as very low or low risk are provided with one 13-session treatment module.

In early 2023, the DRP expanded to include individuals under community supervision who also had co-occurring mental health and substance use challenges. The intervention used for such participants continues to prioritize understanding risk and protective factors and building reentry-relevant skills, while also incorporating sessions regarding psychotropic medication adherence, coping with medication side effects, monitoring mental health symptoms and signs of decompensation, and skills to cope with urges and cravings to use substances.

Given the limited empirical guidance on best practices for the treatment of individuals wrongfully convicted and exonerated, Heilbrun and colleagues (2023) created a domain-specific "toolkit" to address reentry-specific treatment needs. This toolkit was informed through subject matter expertise and consultation of literature, to identify relevant clinical domains including: (a) risk assessment; (b) intellectual functioning; (c) serious mental illness; (d) emotional patterns; (e) trauma; (f) adjustment; and (g) relationships. The interventions provided for those who have been wrongfully convicted are tailored to their distinctive needs, identified through a multicultural case conceptualization and treatment planning lens (Heilbrun et al., 2023).

Despite evidence for the success of RNR- and CBT-informed programs, there are commonly identified challenges in the literature. Within the RNR framework, there is growing attention to developing strategies to promote client engagement and motivation, as a lack of offender motivation has been a critical barrier to effective treatment (Olver et al., 2011). Recent research suggests continued difficulty with inconsistent attendance and engagement (Zapotocky et al., 2022) in such community-based programs. Additionally, risk assessment may complicate the process of determining appropriate treatment needs. Considering the criminal history of individuals who are returning to the community following lengthy incarceration, for example, may artificially inflate risk status and recommended treatment dosage (Zapotocky et al., 2023). The RNR model may be better utilized by targeting dynamic risk factors that are malleable, specific to individual needs, and more relevant to treatment amenability, but exercising caution in using decades-old criminal history to appraise dosage needs via the risk principle.

In contrast to the RNR model, the Good Lives Model (GLM; Ward & Stewart, 2003) shifts the focus from risk and criminogenic needs to personally meaningful goals, skills, and opportunities in pursuit of important personal goals and values. Some have proposed that a lack of motivation can be linked to programs that do not focus on personal values and aspirations (Barnao et al., 2016) and describe the GLM as a more appropriate rehabilitation approach. Others have argued that the differences between the RNR model and the GLM are not meaningful, and that many RNR programs with an integrated CBT framework effectively examine personal value-based goals through risk/need domains (Looman & Abracen, 2013). However, it does seem likely that the RNR model can be improved through attention to therapeutic alliance as part of the Responsivity principle.

In particular, several studies with justice-involved individuals highlight challenges with engagement in CBT programs. In one study of individuals identified as high risk for reoffending, only 35 percent completed treatment (Barnes et al., 2017). In a second study on a gender-responsive CBT program for women, 44 percent did not complete treatment (Zarling et al., 2022). A randomized controlled trial comparing CBT to standard drug counseling for substance and domestic violence offenses found no significant differences in session attendance, suggesting CBT does not necessarily enhance engagement (Easton et al., 2018). These findings underscore the challenge of general and CBT-specific treatment engagement across justice-involved populations. They also suggest potential limitations of the current CBT framework that may be contributing to lower engagement rates. It will be important to consider how CBT can enhance its current approach to responsivity, thus fostering more effective engagement and retention in treatment.

Using one such approach to treatment engagement difficulties, the DRP recently incorporated techniques from Recovery-Oriented Cognitive Therapy (CT-R; Beck et al., 2009). CT-R was developed for individuals with serious and persistent mental illness in inpatient settings who presented with diminished motivation; difficulty connecting and communicating with others; little hope for the future; disconnection from life goals, values, and aspirations; pessimistic beliefs about their abilities to overcome challenges; and low behavioral activation. The foundational perspective of CT-R is that recovery is possible for all people regardless of problem severity (Beck et al., 2009). CT-R has been shown to be effective for several mental health disorders across various populations at all levels of care (Beck, 2019; Beck Institute, n.d.; Grant, 2019). But there is limited research on using CT-R for justice-involved individuals *without* serious and persistent mental illness, although researchers suggest CT-R may be particularly applicable to those who experienced chronic institutionalization (Beck et al., 2020). Further, justice-involved populations often have distinctive needs and barriers that can make it difficult to enhance motivation, and present with similar treatment-interfering behaviors commonly encountered within inpatient facilities—or in treating individuals with severe and persistent mental illness in the community. Integrating alternative treatment approaches, such as CT-R, within current CBT frameworks may have the potential to increase treatment engagement and therapeutic alliance, thereby improving attendance, effectiveness, and efficiency.

Beginning and Development of Project Services

The original idea for this project did not succeed. It began with a contact from a local state-level judge to one of us (KH), who was known to the local courts because he had been providing forensic assessment services for years. The question was whether he could put together a project that would provide treatment services for justice-involved individuals on probation. Despite the interest from the judge, and the nominal involvement of a representative from the City Department of Parole and Probation and researchers from another local university, the working idea for the intervention seemed problematic. It involved the computer-assisted delivery of a weekly, 1-hour "CBT class" that would be taught to 25–30 individuals on probation who would come to a meeting room in the Department of Parole and Probation for

10 weeks. (In this pre-COVID, pre-Zoom era, the possibility of remote participation was not considered.) The problems with this working model, it seemed, were threefold: size, duration and modality, and training value. Considering the number of individuals that the judge wanted to receive services (hundreds per year), it was understandable that he also wanted the intervention to be brief in session length and overall duration, and delivered using computers so there was no need for the involvement of a psychologist in the delivery of the services. Nonetheless, I doubted that the nature and intensity of this proposed intervention would suffice to improve relevant skills in those who needed them. There was also no plan for pre-service screening, to screen out low-risk individuals, identify high-risk individuals for more intensive services, and select medium-risk individuals in a way that would be consistent with the risk and need principles (Bonta & Andrews, 2024). Finally, the potential training value appeared very limited. Doctoral trainees in clinical psychology interested in a forensic specialization find few opportunities for supervised intervention services with justice-involved individuals, in contrast with the more frequent opportunities for supervised forensic mental health assessment (DeMatteo et al., this volume). This proposal demonstrated need and interest, but it was unfortunately a poor fit for our work at Drexel, and discussions did not continue after a few meetings.

But shortly after it became clear that these discussions would not result in developing a project to deliver intervention services to justice-involved individuals, we became aware of another source of interest in this work. An attorney colleague knew several judges who had been heading up a federal reentry court in the Eastern District of Pennsylvania for about seven years. This problem-solving court and the associated program (Structure to Aid Reentry, or STAR) operated with the collaboration of the U.S. Office of Parole and Probation, the U.S. Attorney's office, and the Federal Defender's office. They had successfully obtained services for reentering clients in a number of areas (work, housing, finances, health), but were interested in a CBT-based, skills-oriented intervention that would both reduce the risk of reoffending for this population (selected for STAR participation in part because they were appraised at high risk for reoffending) and increase their prospects of more favorable adjustment during reentry.

This began a collaborative partnership that started in 2015. From the beginning, it was a much better fit for both Drexel's needs and those of our partner. We developed a structured set of two 13-session modules integrating elements of CBT-based interventions for justice-involved individuals emphasizing thinking, decision-making, emotional modulation, and skills with people and technology. The plan was to deliver one module—thirteen 1-hour sessions in group therapy modality—for medium-risk individuals, and both modules for high-risk individuals. We developed a 2–3 hour battery of front-end measures and devoted one subsequent hour to providing assessment feedback, obtaining clients' views about this feedback, and seeking to establish mutual goals.

It took about six months before the program was fully operational. We began accepting clients after spending two to three months developing the assessment battery and intervention modules, and another three months working out the details associated with having clinical trainees (from the Drexel PhD program) provide services. These services were supervised by one (later two) faculty members. Delivering services in groups of three to five clients, with two co-therapists, our first six months featured a variety of client-related and organizational challenges. Yet we were able to meet the requested service demand with about four trainees and one supervisor for the first year. There was actually greater interest among clinical trainees in participating in this project than we'd initially anticipated, underscoring the virtual dearth of available clinical intervention training and experience with justice-involved individuals that many encounter.

Generalizability

Does the field need similar projects to the one described in this chapter? The answer has several parts. The first is clinical need. It is likely that the need for interventions for individuals returning to the community following incarceration will continue to grow, just as such services will be useful for those who remain in the community following criminal conviction and a non-carceral sentence—or diversion to a problem-solving court. The nature of such services will also be important, as risk-reduction, skills-building interventions are combined with other treatments targeting trauma and other interventions designed to improve the quality of people's lives.

A second consideration is training. The delivery of such services should be performed by professionals who are skilled and available. This does not mean that it must be done exclusively by doctoral-level psychologists, but the supervision and program development provided by such individuals is important. Moreover, they can develop specialized skills and experience during their doctoral training—but there are limited opportunities at present for doctoral trainees in psychology to obtain this kind of experience.

Because the opportunity to obtain such trainee experience is valuable for specialized doctoral training programs, they can provide them at a lower cost—a third consideration. Trainees have less experience, but they are often highly motivated and eager to provide these services. Depending on the services needed, it may be feasible to establish a contract between a training program and a problem-solving court or department of parole and probation. This would allow a faculty member specializing in work with justice-involved individuals to lead the development of an intervention program, and supervisee trainees who provide the direct services. A financial and program-development model like this could mean a significantly lower cost (or even no cost) for services, as a faculty member could seek grant funding and conduct research on the effectiveness of a program that had been developed. This would mean that a high proportion of the services delivered in this way could be less expensive, as access to research and training could serve as alternative forms of compensation.

This kind of program can be replicated. Such replication would be assisted by several influences, including the presence of a doctoral training program with at least one faculty member willing to engage in program development and provide clinical supervision. It would be very useful if that faculty member were also engaged in effectiveness research, interested in seeking grant funding, and experienced in working with justice-involved individuals. In addition, the participation of about one doctoral trainee for every 5–10 referrals would suffice to provide the needed assessment and intervention services. If there is a psychology clinic already established in the training program, this can take care of many details related to the provision of direct services. Community contacts (e.g., judges, parole/probation directors, prosecutors, public defenders) are extremely valuable—particularly those who lead an already-existing program, or are willing to develop one.

Diversity, Equity, and Inclusiveness

The multicultural training of doctoral-level clinical psychology students is integral to delivering culturally competent and effective mental health care to diverse populations. This training provides students with the necessary knowledge, skills, and awareness to provide services that respect and respond to the distinctive needs and experiences of individuals from various racial, ethnic, and cultural backgrounds. Under the APA *Standards of Accreditation for Health Service Psychology and Accreditation Operation Procedures* (APA, 2018), doctoral-level clinical psychology programs are required to provide training that reflects respect for and understanding of cultural and individual characteristics, including but not limited to age, disability, ethnicity, gender, gender identity, language, national origin, race, religion, culture, sexual orientation, and socioeconomic status.

Drexel University's Clinical Psychology Ph.D. program requires that students enroll in a "Multicultural Perspectives in Psychology" course in their second year of training and prior to providing mental health services. This course offers a comprehensive overview of how cultural, ethnic, and racial factors influence the application of psychology, aiming to cultivate multicultural competence in clinical practice. The DRP extends this training in two ways. First, DRP trainees receive supervision in providing culturally-informed treatment services through enhanced awareness of their own attitudes, beliefs, biases, and assumptions. This promotes "cultural competence in practice" through sensitivity, humility, openness, and flexibility. Second, there are ongoing discussions of topics related to multicultural awareness and humility, further contributing to the development and strengthening of these skills. These discussions occur in weekly supervision meetings, which include (a) video review of clinical encounters, (b) consultation between faculty and DRP clinicians, (c) dissemination of scholarship related to diversity, equity, and inclusivity, and (d) presentations by guest speakers with expertise in these areas. Additionally, the DRP developed a "patient navigator" position in which one person is as a central point of contact for DRP clients, addressing questions, concerns, and potential barriers to treatment that may occur among justice-involved individuals of racial or ethnic minority status.

Over the past decade, there have been numerous calls to improve multicultural training for those in training to deliver health-related clinical services. Such recommendations include incorporating antiracist principles and intersectionality into research, education, policy, and clinical application (APA, 2021) and enhancing training ion culturally responsive care and responsible research practices (Gee et al., 2022). This is particularly important in light of the evidence demonstrating substantial disparities in the provision of mental health services to racial and ethnic minority populations (McGuire & Miranda, 2008). Barriers to treatment for such populations include systemic racism and inequalities (Fain, 2021), cultural stigma surrounding mental health (Gary, 2005), and implicit and ethnic bias among providers (Hall et al., 2015).

To address such disparities, several priorities related to DEI have been proposed. These include increasing the field's focus on multiculturalism (Nagy et al., 2019), identifying racism and other biases in order to alleviate their impact in research, training, policy, and practice, and considering the diversity of communities served to address social injustices, alleviate health disparities, and improve people's lives (Galán et al., 2021). These priorities can be applied to the goals of more effective services and enhanced social justice.

Advice to Others Seeking to Provide Similar Services

In this section, we describe the considerations for others thinking of establishing a CBT-based program providing assessment and treatment services to individuals reentering the community. We base these comments largely on our collective experience in establishing and operating such a program at Drexel University between 2015 and the present. Taking the early steps to establish these services allowed us to expand to other groups—we now provide services to those under the jurisdiction of a federal mental health court and to those who have been exonerated of criminal convictions. This discussion is provided in the larger context of forensic and correctional psychology; just as we used relevant data and published guidance in the program's establishment, we continue to consult empirical scientific evidence in its operation.

Gauging the Market

Those seeking to develop a program of services to justice-involved individuals in the community should begin by appraising the market for such services. Who will provide the referrals? The most obvious possibilities are the Department of Parole and Probation, which is likely to have a substantial caseload even in smaller communities. Other possibilities include problem-solving courts such as drug courts, mental health courts, or reentry courts. It is useful to meet with those responsible for making such referrals (and funding them, if such funding is coming from the referral source) to ensure that they are aware of the services being offered and are interested in using them. This will help the provider anticipate the frequency of such referrals—an important consideration in staffing and space decisions.

Will such services be fully voluntary? This is often not the case with justice-involved individuals, who may either be required or strongly encouraged to participate in treatment as a specified condition of their case. A clear and unequivocal requirement for treatment participation can create problems for the therapist, with the client convinced that s/he is only satisfying a requirement rather than having (or developing) motivation for change based on individualized goals and needs. However, having a referring agency or program that strongly recommends but does not actually require participation is less likely to result in a strongly reactive client stance. Clients may begin with the perception that therapy is not useful and they are present because they are encouraged (and perhaps rewarded) for their participation. But such a perception can change, particularly if the intervention combines a focus on skills that are useful for addressing problems that arise while living in the community, involves some shared decision-making about the focus, and incorporates an approach designed to enhance participation by focusing (at least in part) on topics of particular importance or interest to the client (see Arnold et al., this volume).

Some clients who are referred by programs that encourage but do not require participation will decline services. Our experience is that some of these decisions are made at the time of the initial contact, while others are effectively made through inconsistent attendance and limited participation. Decisions against participation made in the beginning are to be respected, although the therapist can encourage the prospective client to try the services and see if they are as useless/irrelevant/unpleasant/unnecessary as they seem in advance. One potentially useful comment involves the observation that a number of clients begin with this perception—but those who persist may end up concluding that therapy has addressed some important considerations, provided some useful skills, and actually has helped them in their lives.

The payment question is important when clients are expected to fund their own services but find it difficult because of financial challenges, which are frequent for justice-involved individuals in the community. Indeed, there is something unfair about requiring an individual to pay for a service they cannot afford. There are two potential solutions. First, the cost of therapy services should be calculated on a sliding scale based on ability to pay. Second, it is often the referring agency or program that provides the funding, perhaps through a contract for the delivery of a specified number of sessions. (If this is implemented, it is important to be able to deliver services that occur in set numbers. For example, in our program at Drexel we offer 13-session modules, with one module delivered to individuals appraised at medium risk or lower, and two modules provided to individuals appraised at high risk.)

Finally, there is the question of modality. Should the services be delivered in a group, or individually. We designed our program assuming that we would provide most services in groups, as there are a number of advantages (including peer influence and cost-effectiveness) associated with this modality. During 2020–2022, the

COVID-19 years, we pivoted to delivering services remotely—and quickly learned that it was not practical to provide remote group services with these individuals. We also learned that they could be delivered individually.

Starting Up: How Quickly?

Our view is that a certain infrastructure must be in place before services can be provided, even on a preliminary or trial basis. Questions involving content, modality, space (if applicable), communication, and support from the organization of which the provider is a part must all be addressed. Certainly, there will be many adjustments as the program develops—but providers should be prepared to deliver at all stages of the service process before beginning with anyone.

Matters involving the number of clients served and the pace of services cannot, however, be anticipated until the demand and rate of referrals are known. Our experience has been that referrals are irregular and tend to come in bursts, so a program might receive five referrals in a week and then none for the following two weeks. Acclimating to this pace is a part of program development. Working more directly with the individuals who are responsible for communicating the referrals might help; if referral sources are "holding on" to referrals in order to complete arrangements, it might be possible to persuade them to move toward a more uniform pace (or at least provide some advance notice as to when upcoming referrals might be expected).

The other question associated with start-up concerns the availability of clinicians to provide the services. If the service delivery model incorporates training and those actually delivering the services will be trainees, then the other start-up variable concerns their current level of training, their need for additional training prior to beginning, and the arrangement for ongoing supervision as they deliver services.

Degree of Specialization

It is helpful if those responsible for operating the program—supervisors and clinicians—have some degree of specialization in their orientation toward working with justice-involved individuals. Particularly when a training model is used, interest in and commitment to providing services to justice-involved individuals is even more important than experience. The distinctive challenges associated with working with individuals who are not necessarily interested in receiving services can be addressed and often overcome in a variety of ways. But without interest and commitment to these individuals, these challenges may be particularly discouraging.

Hence, we suggest specialization plays a twofold part in providing the services we are describing. It is valuable to have an organization (training program, clinic, or practice) that includes some degree of specialization, as this provides a foundation and a source of ideas that should make the delivery of services more effective. It is also important that the clinicians delivering the services have a specialized interest and commitment to a justice-involved population. Experience is less important, particularly at start-up, and certainly will be acquired as the program matures. But commitment enables the trainee to persist in the face of frustration and discouragement, with the added sense that they are learning skills they want to acquire.

Publicity

The extent to which publicity for these services is sought depends mostly on the program size one envisions. In our case, we had a sufficient number of clinical trainees to provide services to referrals from the Reentry Court. A few additional referrals came via word of mouth from a different source (Pennsylvania Innocence Project) to see individuals who had been exonerated—a sufficiently different population, so we could not provide the same services and had to prepare a somewhat different approach. We still had enough clinicians to cover both groups, and referrals from a third group (federal mental health court) in later years. Nonetheless, we did not take steps to publicize our services beyond the usual communication with these three referral sources.

Had we sought to grow our program more substantially, we would have taken several additional steps. Developing a more user-friendly website would have been the first step, enabling referral sources and even a few individuals to quickly access information and arrange for us to contact them. We would have made local presentations, including brief talks, CE workshops, and panels, that would have been more useful in generating referrals than the national presentations we did on this topic. We would have focused particularly on criminal defense attorneys, prosecutors, judges, and parole and probation offices, including those in surrounding counties. Finally, we would have considered a presence on social media.

Summary of Start-Up Steps

We would summarize the important steps in starting a program to deliver assessment and intervention services to justice-involved individuals in the community as follows:

1. Referrals: Who will provide them? Approximate number and rate?
2. Clinician availability: How many direct service providers will be needed? How many are currently available?
3. Financial arrangements: How will services be billed—to whom and at what rate? Will there be a contract?

4. Program development: Describe the substantive content of assessment and intervention services. What measures will be administered, and when? What topics will be addressed in therapy, and in what order? Level of structure of sessions? Duration?
5. Organizational approval: If the program is part of a larger organization, who needs to approve the development, implementation, and operation of this program?
6. Licensure: Who is licensed in the jurisdiction? Supervisors only? Clinicians delivering direct services?
7. Space: If services are delivered in person, where will they be provided? Is the space suitable in terms of privacy, staffing, access, and security?
8. Documentation
   a. Manual: Are assessment and treatment services described in a manual?
   b. Ongoing notes: Will progress notes be provided in the same fashion as other therapy notes?
   c. Communication: Who will be notified about what, and under what circumstances? Will referral sources (e.g., judges, probation officers) be notified about attendance? What are the limits to confidentiality (e.g., child abuse, threat to others, violation of conditions of parole)?
   d. Recording: Will sessions be recorded, either using audio or video? How long will these recordings be maintained?
9. Research role: Will information gathered during assessment and treatment be available for use as part of research, assuming deidentification? Will this be considered in advance of any particular study by an IRB finding of "exempt?"

Do's and Don'ts

There are particular recommendations we can make about program development and service delivery in this area. These include both steps to take, and others to avoid:

Do

- *Address multiple goals whenever possible (service, training, research).* The value of such programs is enhanced considerably when they are used to deliver specialized services, train clinicians in their use, and gather data to appraise the effectiveness of this work.
- *Collaborate with like-minded individuals across programs regionally and nationally.* Working together with others who have developed similar specialized programs is an excellent source of ideas and guidance.
- *Rely on the expertise of probation/parole officers to help.* Particularly when officers are oriented toward rehabilitation, they are extraordinarily helpful in their experience and their knowledge of their clients.

- *Communicate.* Specify in advance what information will be conveyed, and to whom, regarding the results of the assessment and treatment services. For example, our program indicates to prospective clients that the referring court will be notified about attendance, timeliness, the general focus of the session, and if there is a violation of the conditions of the client's parole. However, specific content of the sessions is not conveyed.
- *Prepare for problems.* Some problems are frequent (attendance and timeliness, for example) while others are rare (threats toward others, and child abuse, for instance).
- *Devote resources to promoting attendance.* Scheduling a meeting in the beginning that is attended by the PO, client, and therapist (which we call a "warm handoff") can help convey the importance and value of treatment. Devoting procedures to scheduling and reminding clients, some of whom are not well-organized or may be overwhelmed with other demands, can improve attendance and timeliness. In addition, using procedures that encourage the client to talk about areas important to them (in CT-R terms, the "adaptive mode"—see Arnold et al., this volume) can make other material more appealing.
- *Use peer supervisors.* It is difficult to obtain specialized supervision if therapists are trainees. While having a doctoral-level, licensed psychologist providing one level of supervision is essential, it is also useful to have more senior trainees providing peer supervision.
- *Consider client legal status.* There are important differences between treating clients who are pretrial and those who are already adjudicated. To the extent that treatment incorporates talking about thinking, feeling, and behavior associated with criminal offending, the most recent charge is often most salient. There is no problem, legally or ethically, with doing this with already-convicted clients. By contrast, there are significant Fifth Amendment problems and discovery risks if that is attempted with pretrial clients.
- *Use RNR model in guiding assessment and treatment interventions.* Important aspects of the RNR model include the risk principle (treat high-risk individuals more intensively) and the need principle (focus interventions particularly on areas of risk-relevant need). Using both helps maximize the risk-reducing impact of the intervention, which must be a high priority in providing such services.

Don't

- *Anticipate regular treatment attendance.* It has been our experience that many factors influence inconsistent attendance. These include multiple demands (job, family, PO meetings), reluctance to participate in therapy, difficulty with planning and organization, technical challenges (if therapy is remote), transportation difficulties (if therapy is in-person), and others. Such difficulties should be anticipated, and steps taken to minimize their impact.

- *Expect that most clients will understand basic aspects of therapy; use analogies from sports and entertainment.* Clients who are not selected by considering behavioral health will often have no experience with therapy. Other clients understand specific examples and analogies (e.g., sports, jobs) better than concepts. Tailoring the style of communicating and relating to the client's capacities and preferences is important.
- *Underestimate misperceptions of some regarding elevated risk of harm by clients.* Some in organizations will assume, when asked to approve a program involving treatment to justice-involved individuals, that such treatment would necessarily involve a greater risk of harm to therapists or others. While not necessarily accurate—we have operated such a program based in a university psychology clinic for eight years without a single incident involving threatened or actual harm to others—this perception is powerful, and likely will require built-in steps to address any problems that might arise.
- *Combine treatment role with any other (forensic assessment, advocacy).* Justice-involved individuals can have multiple needs. Sometimes they need advocacy, whether through legal representation or social support. Other times, an attorney representing them seeks a forensic assessment. Treatment programs should carefully avoid addressing any of these needs except treatment-related assessment and intervention to reduce risk and improve life quality.
- *Avoid legal reporting requirements (e.g., child abuse, risk of harm to third parties).* Legal reporting requirements apply to justice-involved individuals just as they do to other clients. Reports of child abuse or potential harm to a third party are mandated in somewhat different ways in different jurisdictions. Programs should know these requirements in their jurisdiction, and act accordingly.

Conclusions

The application of CBT with justice-involved individuals provides a strong empirical foundation for the delivery of relevant, meaningful services designed both to reduce the risk of an individual's criminal recidivism and to improve the quality of their life. The DRP is a replicable example of a program that offers such services to justice-involved individuals in the community. It has the potential to serve individuals, promote a safer society, and enhance the training of future clinical psychologists by providing them with intervention experience with a specialized population while prioritizing experience with diversity and applying their training in an unusual and important way.

References

American Psychological Association. (2015). *Standards of accreditation for health service psychology and accreditation operation procedures.* American Psychological Association.

American Psychological Association. (2021). *APA resolution on harnessing psychology to combat racism: Adopting a uniform definition and understanding.* https://www.apa.org/about/policy/resolution-combat-racism.pdf

Bonta, J., & Andrews, D. (2024). *The psychology of criminal conduct* (7th ed.). Routledge.

Andrews, D. A., Bonta, J., & Hoge, R. D. (1990). Classification for effective rehabilitation: Rediscovering psychology. *Criminal Justice and Behavior, 17*(1), 19–52. https://doi.org/10.1177/0093854890017001004

Barnao, M., Ward, T., Robertson, P. (2016). The good lives model: A new paradigm for forensic mental health. *Psychiatry, Psychology and Law., 23*(2), 288–301. doi: 10.1080/13218719.2015.1054923

Barnes, G. C., Hyatt, J. M., & Sherman, L. W. (2017). Even little bit helps: An implementation and experimental evaluation of cognitive-behavioral therapy for high-risk probationers. *Criminal Justice and Behavior, 44*(4), 611–630. https://doi.org/10.1177/0093854816673862

Beck Institute. (n.d.) *CT-R in justice-related settings.* https://beckinstitute.org/center-for-ct-r/ct-r-in-justice-related-settings/#:~:text=CT%2DR%20is%20transdiagnostic%20and,%2C%20and%20life%2Drelated%20challenges

Beck, A. T. (2019). *What is recovery-oriented cognitive therapy (CT-R)?* Beck Institute. https://beckinstitute.org/blog/what-is-recovery-oriented-cognitive-therapy-ct-r/

Beck, A. T., Grant, P., Inverso, E., Brinen, A. P., & Perivoliotis, D. (2020). *Recovery-oriented cognitive therapy for serious mental health conditions.* Guilford.

Beck, A. T., Rector, N. A., Stolar, N. M., & Grant, P. M. (2009). *Schizophrenia: Cognitive theory, research and therapy.* Guilford.

Bush, J., Glick, B., & Taymans, J. (1997). *Thinking for a Change.* National Institute of Corrections Academy, National Institute of Corrections.

Dowden, C., & Andrews, D. A. (2000). Effective correctional treatment and violent reoffending: A meta-analysis. Canadian *Journal of Criminology, 42*(4), 449–467.

Easton, C. J., Crane, C. A., & Mandel, D. (2018). A randomized controlled trial assessing the efficacy of cognitive behavioral therapy for substance-dependent domestic violence offenders: An integrated substance abuse-domestic violence treatment approach (SADV). *Journal of Marital and Family Therapy, 44*(3), 483–498. https://doi.org/10.1111/jmft.12260

Fain, C. (2021). Systemic racism and minority disparities in health care. *The Bridge: Interdisciplinary Perspectives on Legal & Social Policy, 6*(3), 1–35. https://digitalscholarship.tsu.edu/cgi/viewcontent.cgi?article=1033&context=thebridge

Galán, C. A., Bekele, B., Boness, C., Bowdring, M., Call, C., Hails, K., McPhee, J., Hawkins Mendes, S., Moses, J., Northrup, J., Rupert, P., Savell, S., Sequeira, S., Tervo-Clemmens, B., Tung, I., Vanwoerden, S., Womack, S., & Yilmaz, B. (2021). Editorial: A call to action for an antiracist clinical science. *Journal of Clinical Child & Adolescent Psychology, 50*(1), 12–57. https://doi.org/10.1080/15374416.2020.1860066

Gary, F. A. (2005). Stigma: Barrier to mental health care among ethnic minorities. *Issues in Mental Health Nursing, 26*(10), 979–999. https://doi.org/10.1080/01612840500280638

Glick, B., & Goldstein, A. P. (1987). Aggression replacement training. *Journal of Counseling & Development, 65*(7), 356–362. https://doi.org/10.1002/j.1556-6676.1987.tb00730.x

Grant, P. M. (2019). *Recovery-Oriented Cognitive Therapy: A theory-driven, evidence-based, transformative practice to promote flourishing for individuals with serious mental health conditions that is applicable across mental health systems.* National Association of State Mental Health Program Directors. https://www.nasmhpd.org/sites/default/files/TAC_Paper_7_508C_1.pdf

Hall, W. J., Chapman, M. V., Lee, K. M., Merino, Y. M., Thomas, T. W., Payne, B. K., Eng, E., Day, S. H., & Coyne-Beasley, T. (2015). Implicit racial/ethnic bias among health care professionals and its influence on health care outcomes: A systematic review. *American Journal of Public Health, 105*(12), e60–e76. https://doi.org/10.2105/AJPH.2015.302903

Haney, C. (2003, January). *The psychological impact of incarceration: Implications for post-prison adjustment.* Presented at the "From Prison to Home" Conference, Urban Institute.

Hanson, R. K., Bourgon, G., Helmus, L., & Hodgson, S. (2009). The principles of effective correctional treatment also apply to sexual offenders: A meta-analysis. *Criminal Justice and Behavior, 36*(9), 865–889. https://doi.org/10.1177/0093854809338545

Heilbrun, K., Pietruszka, V., Thornewill, A., Phillips, S., & Schiedel, R. (2017). Diversion at re-entry using criminogenic CBT: Review and prototypical program development. *Behavioral Sciences & the Law, 35*(5–6), 562–572. https://doi.org/10.1002/bsl.2311

Heilbrun, K., Schwartz, J., Wiltsie, K., Lankford, C., Fishel, S., Swenson, A., & Charles, D. (2023). Interventions with individuals exonerated from criminal convictions: Toward development of evidence-based practices in a psychology training clinic. *Practice Innovations, 8*(3), 164–172. https://doi.org/10.1007/s11292-005-3541-7

Hofmann, S. G., Asnaani, A., Vonk, I. J., Sawyer, A. T., & Fang, A. (2012). The efficacy of cognitive behavioral therapy: A review of meta-analyses. *Cognitive Therapy and Research, 36*(5), 427–440. https://doi.org/10.1007/s10608-012-9476-1

Hollin, C. R. (2019). What is cognitive behavioral therapy (CBT) with offenders? In D. L. L. Polaschek, A. Day, & C. R. Hollin (Eds.), *The Wiley international handbook of correctional psychology* (pp. 623–636). Wiley Blackwell.

Landenberger, N. A., & Lipsey, M. W. (2005). The positive effects of cognitive–behavioral programs for offenders: A meta-analysis of factors associated with effective treatment. *Journal of Experimental Criminology*, *1*(4), 451–476. https://doi.org/10.1007/s11292-005-3541-7

Lipsey, M., Landenberger, N., & Wilson, S. (2007). Effects of cognitive-behavioral programs for criminal offenders. *Campbell Systematic Reviews*. http://dx.doi.org/10.15496/publikation-6061

Looman, J., & Abracen, J. (2013). The risk need responsivity model of offender rehabilitation: Is there really a need for a paradigm shift?. *International Journal of Behavioral Consultation and Therapy*, *8*(3–4), 30. https://doi.org/10.1037/h0100980

McGuire, T. G., & Miranda, J. (2008). New evidence regarding racial and ethnic disparities in mental health: Policy implications. *Health Affairs*, *27*(2), 393–403. https://doi.org/10.1377/hlthaff.27.2.393

Nagy, G. A., Wandrey, R. L., Vargas, S., & Cahill, S. (2019). Multiculturalism in clinical psychology journals: A 20-year content and trend analysis. *The Behavior Therapist*, *42*(3), 66–78.

National Institute of Corrections (NIC) (1996). *Cognitive interventions program: Think.* National Institute of Corrections Information Center, U.S. Department of Justice.

Olver, M. E., Stockdale, K. C., & Wormith, J. S. (2011). A meta-analysis of predictors of offender treatment attrition and its relationship to recidivism. *Journal of Consulting and Clinical Psychology*, *79*(1), 6–21. https://doi.org/10.1037/a0022200

Ross, R. R., & Fabiano, E. (1985). *Time to think: A cognitive model of delinquency prevention and offender rehabilitation.* Institute of Social Sciences & Arts, Incorporated.

Ross, R., Hilborn, J., & Liddle, P. (2021). Reasoning and Rehabilitation 2: Program Overview, University of Ottawa.

Schnittker, J., Massoglia, M., & Uggen, C. (2012). Out and down: Incarceration and psychiatric disorders. *Journal of Health and Social Behavior*, *53*(4), 448–464. https://doi.org/10.1177/0022146512453928

Siennick, S. E., Staff, J., Osgood, D. W., Schulenberg, J. E., Bachman, J. G., & VanEseltine, M. (2014). Partnership transitions and antisocial behavior in young adulthood: A within-person, multi-cohort analysis. *Journal of Research in Crime and Delinquency*, *51*(6), 735–758. https://doi.org/10.1177/0022427814529977

Ward, T., & Stewart, C. A. (2003). The treatment of sex offenders: Risk management and good lives. *Professional Psychology: Research and Practice*, *34*(4), 353–360. https://doi.org/10.1037/0735-7028.34.4.353

Wilson, D. B., Bouffard, L. A., & MacKenzie, D. L. (2005). A quantitative review of structured, group-oriented, cognitive-behavioral programs for offenders. *Criminal Justice and Behavior*, *32*(2), 172–204. https://doi.org/10.1177/0093854804272889

Zapotocky, H., Fishel, S., Moore, C., Charles, D., Swenson, A., Jackson, C., Wiltsie, K., & Heilbrun, K. (March, 2022). *The Drexel Reentry Project: Client characteristics and predictions of program engagement.* Presented at the Annual Conference of the American Psychology-Law Society, Denver, CO.

Zapotocky, H., Wiltsie, K., Grisamore, S., Swenson, A., Charles, D., Jackson, C., & Heilbrun, K. (March, 2023). *The Drexel Reentry Project: Prioritizing dynamic risk factors to inform treatment needs.* Presented at the Annual Conference of the American Psychology-Law Society, Philadelphia, PA.

Zarling, A., Scheffert, R., & Russell, D. (2022). Predictors of retention and recidivism of justice-involved women in a community-based gender-responsive CBT program. *Criminal Justice and Behavior*, *49*(3), 291–310. https://doi.org/10.1177/00938548211040850

9

An Intervention for Community Reentry Informed by Dialectical Behavior Therapy

Christopher M. King, Sana Vora, Savannah Cuellar, Jay Gonzales, and Barry Rosenfeld

Services rendered by mental health professionals are an increasingly important component of multisystemic interventions for individuals involved with the criminal legal system. Given the high rate of criminogenic and non-criminogenic treatment needs among this population, it is perhaps surprising that psychotherapy services are not becoming more widely available at the point of reentry. Mental health services for such persons have typically focused on stabilization of those diagnosed with a serious mental disorder or substance use disorder, or in-prison group treatment programming focused on criminogenic needs. These services can be contrasted with individual psychotherapy for persons with no or mild mental disorders, addressing broad-based concerns (both criminogenic and non-criminogenic) to facilitate a successful life in the community following reentry from incarceration, and they are rendered around the time that this transition occurs. The potential benefits of the latter type of service arise in a wide range of legal system settings, including pretrial release and probation, diversion programs, and community reentry for those who have experienced longer terms of incarceration. This chapter describes an example of such a service. Specifically, we describe the application of a brief, community-based, and individually tailored intervention informed by principles of Dialectical Behavior Therapy (DBT; Linehan, 1993) and the Risk-Need-Responsivity (RNR) model (Bonta & Andrews, 2024) that was designed to help fill this gap in services.

Community-Based Reentry Programs

Roughly half a million individuals are released from state and federal prisons annually in the United States, many of whom have been incarcerated for lengthy periods of time (Carson, 2021; Carson & Kluckow, 2023). The challenges facing this population are well known, including difficulty reintegrating into their families and communities,

Christopher M. King et al., *An Intervention for Community Reentry Informed by Dialectical Behavior Therapy*.
In: *The Path Forward*. Edited by: Kirk Heilbrun and David DeMatteo, Oxford University Press.
 DOI: 10.1093/9780197773031.003.0009

finding housing and employment, and avoiding or countering criminogenic risk factors that may have contributed to their index offense(s) (e.g., substance abuse, reliance on criminal behavior or antisocial peers as a means of support). These challenges are exacerbated by pre-existing deficits (e.g., limited education and vocational histories), societal inequities and limited availability of services, and the stigma associated with incarceration and visiting a mental health professional. Given this range of stressors and challenges, it is perhaps not surprising that nearly half of those released from prison are reincarcerated within the first year of release and the vast majority are reincarcerated within five to ten years of release (Berghuis, 2018).

An increasingly common strategy for addressing these challenges is reentry programs. These programs have grown in popularity over the past quarter-century. They may be implemented in the community or in institutional settings, and may serve individuals on pretrial release or following periods of incarceration in jail, prison, or a forensic mental health facility post-adjudication. Some reentry programs may emphasize a single criminogenic need, such as employment or substance abuse, while others may arrange for a suite of services to target numerous criminogenic risk factors. Mental health interventions are also a common element of reentry programs. However, these services are usually limited to pharmacological interventions for serious mental illness or certain forms of substance abuse (e.g., medication-assisted treatment for opioids), or services rendered by psychologists, counselors, and social workers that are similarly targeted toward specific disorders. Reentry interventions meant to generally bolster or develop strengths, toward assuaging transitional stressors and challenges rather than addressing glaring "diagnostic" treatment needs, are rarely incorporated into reentry programs, let alone integrated as a standard element of reentry programming.

This relative neglect of individually tailored strengths-building interventions may explain the limited success that has been demonstrated by reentry programs. For instance, randomized controlled trials (RCTs) of reentry programs have generally failed to demonstrate statistically or clinically significant reductions in rearrest rates (Berghuis, 2018). Our application of a DBT-informed intervention, delivered using a telehealth format, was designed to help fill this void. It seeks to do so by targeting personally-indicated behaviors and helping develop skills to address some of the key challenges that may interfere with the successful readjustment of clients who are living in the community after a term of federal imprisonment.

Foundations and Support for Project Services

DBT was originally developed for clients presenting with chronic suicidal behavior, many of whom were diagnosed with Borderline Personality Disorder (BPD). DBT is an integrative psychotherapy that brings together techniques from cognitive-behavioral therapy, client-centered therapy and Eastern (mindfulness) traditions. DBT has shown utility for a wide range of clinical populations, including those with BPD, substance use disorders, and eating disorders (Behavioral Tech Institute, n.d.). While still preliminary, there is also growing evidence that DBT may be useful for persons involved with the criminal legal system (Tomlinson, 2018).

Much of Linehan's (1993) original biosocial theory and DBT approach is typically carried over for applications to those involved with the criminal legal system. In addition, DBT's traditional focus on attending to life-threatening (Carter et al., 2022; Favril et al., 2020, 2022; Skinner & Farrington, 2020) and therapy-interfering behaviors (a class of responsivity factors) remains relevant for this population. However, for contextual reasons, there have often been efforts to specifically adapt DBT in various ways to correctional and forensic mental health settings (see Ivanoff & Marotta, 2019; Mills et al., 2019; Tomlinson, 2018). These include adjustments to the four core elements (modalities) of DBT (i.e., individual therapy, group skills training, phone coaching, and consultation team) for different criminal legal system settings. They also include simplification of instructional resources (e.g., handouts and worksheets) and efforts to conceptualize common issues, such as antisocial personality traits, in line with DBT's biosocial theory. DBT is also commonly believed to fit well with the RNR model (Bonta & Andrews, 2024), which provides an overarching framework for interventions in the criminal legal system. The RNR model triages services based on criminogenic risk level, prioritizing the targeting of relevant criminogenic needs with therapeutic services and tailoring interventions to fit the strengths and limitations of an individual client that impact their response to services.

Despite the intuitive appeal of DBT for individuals involved with the criminal legal system, much of the research examining adapted forms of DBT for such persons has consisted of small-scale pilot studies, typically conducted in institutional settings (e.g., prisons, forensic psychiatric hospitals). Although some of these studies have yielded promising results with respect to changes in treatment targets, researchers have typically focused on idiosyncratic samples and relied heavily on self-report inventories to assess treatment-related changes. A few examples help to illustrate this. Bianchini and colleagues (2019) found significant decreases in impulsivity and emotional dysregulation in men diagnosed with BPD who were hospitalized in an Italian forensic psychiatric facility. Moulden et al. (2020), in their study of fourteen men hospitalized in a Canadian forensic hospital (most of whom were diagnosed with a psychotic disorder), found that the addition of DBT to standard treatment resulted in increased insight and decreased risk of violence. While participants' ratings of anger actually increased, that may have reflected increased insight or willingness to acknowledge negative emotions. A study of fourteen women incarcerated in the United Kingdom found positive changes in self-esteem and impulsivity following a year-long DBT intervention, but no difference in a range of other self-report variables (Nee & Farman, 2005).

In contrast, very few studies of DBT have focused on reducing criminal recidivism among those involved with the criminal legal system, particularly in community settings. A recent study examined a 16-week adapted DBT and case management program with 20 veterans who had been involved with the criminal legal system within the preceding 2 years (Edwards et al., 2023). While the authors eschewed statistical significance testing in light of the small sample size, effect sizes following treatment and at 1-month follow-up were indicative of decreases in overall evaluator ratings of the Central Eight risk factors from the RNR model, in addition to reductions in psychological distress, substance use, and case management needs, and increased quality of life. A larger study used an RCT design to compare a 12-week DBT intervention to a health promotion intervention in 130 unhoused women who had recently been released from incarceration (Nyamathi et al., 2018). Those assigned to DBT exhibited increased rates of abstinence from substance abuse and decreased criminal recidivism relative to those assigned to the health promotion program.

Prior research by one of the chapter authors (BR), applying an adaptation of DBT for individuals involved with the criminal legal system, also found lower rates of criminal recidivism in a sample of adults charged with stalking (Rosenfeld et al., 2007, 2019). Adults who had been court ordered to participate in mental health treatment as a condition of probation were randomly assigned to either 24 individual and group sessions of DBT or an 18-week individual CBT intervention (Rosenfeld et al., 2019). Although no significant differences in recidivism or self-reported changes were observed between the two treatment groups, rearrest rates were considerably lower than observed in prior studies of comparable, untreated individuals. This experience guided many of the changes implemented in the application of DBT described below, which applies a DBT-informed intervention to community-based clients participating in a voluntary court-based reentry program.

Like prior studies of DBT for individuals involved in the criminal legal system, our intervention includes a focus on key criminogenic risk factors, including what we term "freedom-interfering behaviors." We conceptualize such behaviors as those that increase the risk of reoffending or benefitting from a reduction in community supervision duration, which are prioritized treatment targets. As is also common, treatment materials are tailored to our population, which consists predominantly of men who often present with antisocial traits, rather than DBT's original focus on predominantly women who often presented with BPD traits. In addition, many individuals involved with the criminal legal system have limited reading levels and many have lower levels of cognitive functioning, calling for simplification of written materials and skills instruction. However, other elements of our intervention are notably different, including the elimination of a strict, standardized sequence of skills taught in a group format, as is typical of standard DBT. These and other adjustments, some based on practical considerations, were otherwise informed by our past experience with DBT, correctional and forensic interventions, the published literature (about DBT, RNR, telehealth, and sociocultural tailoring), and experience training clinical psychology students. We describe this in more detail in the next two sections.

The RISE Program

In 2018, the United States District Court for the Southern District of New York developed the Reentry through Intensive Supervision and Employment (RISE) program (Office of the District Court Executive, 2018). The court-based program was launched in 2019 at the initiative of district court judges (primarily District Judge Denise Cote) who were impressed by reentry programs that had emerged in other jurisdictions. Adults released from federal prison under a period (typically 3 years) of supervised release, and who reside in the greater New York City area, are eligible for selection to participate in the RISE program. Enrollment is prioritized for those who have served lengthy prison sentences (or lengthy sentences relative to their chronological age), as these individuals are typically considered to pose the highest risk of criminal recidivism. While the RISE program is entirely voluntary, participation is incentivized by offering a 1-year reduction in the probation term upon successful completion of the 1-year RISE program. Participants are formed into cohorts of approximately fifteen persons and each cohort is assigned to a RISE court judge and probation officer. At present, three to four cohorts typically begin each year and participation involves biweekly meetings with the RISE court judge, probation officer(s), and other court program volunteers. For example, *pro bono* attorneys from private law firms and public agencies attend most biweekly meetings to help participants with legal issues that are unrelated or peripherally related to their underlying index offense(s) or probation (e.g., assisting with family court matters such as child support payments, reactivating a suspended driver's license, setting up a small business structure such as a limited liability company).

Beginning in 2020, the requirements for completion of the RISE program were modified to include mandatory completion of a 12-session therapy service. The decision to mandate therapy, rather than either making it a voluntary service available to those interested in it or attempting to triage those who might benefit most from therapy, was based on several considerations. Most important among these considerations was the desire to destigmatize therapy. Offering therapy as a voluntary element of the RISE program risked failing to provide therapeutic services to those who might need it most, as many individuals involved with the criminal legal system have a negative view of therapy and those who utilize it. Moreover, targeting a subset of individuals exacerbates this problem, creating the appearance that those who engage in therapy are somehow different or "mentally ill." Hence, we recommended a mandatory course of therapy to ensure that those who might otherwise be reluctant or lack insight would also have the opportunity to potentially benefit from therapy. Thus, therapists have the opportunity over the first few sessions to attempt to develop a therapeutic alliance with some clients with whom that opportunity might not otherwise be possible, while respecting the fact that clients retain the autonomy to discontinue services from the RISE program if they choose.

A second key element of our intervention, aside from our integration of DBT and RNR principles into a brief, individualized therapy service, is our reliance on a telehealth format. This decision was pragmatic. The first of our now two parallel university-based clinics began to screen the first referred RISE cohort in February of 2020 and had not yet begun therapy when the onset of the COVID-19 pandemic forced a complete closure of the clinic. RISE court meetings were also placed on indefinite hold. Following the resumption of the RISE program, for a time via virtual court meetings, therapy began using telehealth technology.

Having previously operated a more traditional DBT program for individuals on probation in New York State for stalking or interpersonal violence offenses (Rosenfeld et al., 2019), one of us (BR) was acutely aware of the logistical challenges involved with in-person services for this population. For example, missed or late sessions are far more challenging to reschedule. Reasons for this include the need for clients and therapists to travel to and from a centralized clinic location, potential limitations in the availability of clinic staff, and added security concerns around staff and client safety (often necessitating provisions such as screening for weapons, ensuring adequate staff are present, etc.). Similarly, our clients' busy and often conflicting schedules favored individualized sessions rather than a group format. However, individual telehealth sessions also require a number of special provisions, such as the need for clients to have videoconferencing capability and privacy during sessions. The first of these has been easily addressed given the near-universal availability of cellphones with such capability and the availability of free Wi-Fi routers throughout New York City. The requirement that clients be in a private space for sessions (e.g., not riding a public bus or sitting in a coffee shop) has proven more challenging, as many RISE participants have unstable or shared housing and often fail to perceive the reason for this requirement (e.g., "there's nothing I can't talk about in front of my . . . ."). Additional considerations for therapist privacy also required attention, including the use of Google phone numbers and email addresses for a layer of masking.

There are, of course, many other challenges to providing mandated therapy for our population, including the common failure among clients to appreciate that sessions begin at a precise time and that last-minute cancelations are not acceptable. Many of our participants are unaccustomed to scheduled appointments that begin and end at a specific time, having received most of their medical care in clinic-based settings (either in the community or while incarcerated) where one arrives whenever the clinic is open and simply waits for a doctor to become available. Hence, "socialization" is a key part of our introduction to the intervention. Likewise, firm rules have been implemented regarding late arrivals (e.g., more than 15 minutes late is considered a "missed" session in one of our clinics) and missed sessions (e.g., more than 3 missed sessions result in termination from the therapy in one of our clinics). On occasion, when judges or probation officers request a "second chance" for a client who has exhibited notable attendance problems, we may implement DBT's "vacation" concept for a temporary pause and later resumption of therapy, or alternatively agree to restart therapy with a different therapist (beginning from session one). These "vacations" and "restarts" carry the expectation of significantly improved attendance thereafter, and they have varied in their success.

Our therapy providers are clinical psychology graduate students from two universities in the metropolitan New York City area. Supervision is provided by faculty in the respective training programs (full-time or adjunct), all of whom are licensed psychologists. Supervision is primarily rendered in a group format (complemented by as-needed individual supervision), using DBT's Consultation Team model as the primary vehicle to discuss forensic case formulations, challenges with clients (e.g., therapy-interfering behaviors), successful intervention efforts, and any other issues that arise in the course of therapy. This model also enables student therapists to learn from and support one another, share effective approaches to teach skills and tailor the therapy, and brainstorm ways to resolve the challenges that inevitably arise. While the skills utilized in our intervention are drawn from the extensive repertoire of DBT skills (normally taught in a fixed sequence through weekly group sessions), decisions about which ones will be emphasized are personalized to meet the needs of individual clients and their unique treatment targets, rather than necessarily presenting all skills to all clients, as is typical in standard DBT. In light of all the foregoing, we characterize our intervention as "DBT-informed" rather than an application of standard DBT to a novel set of circumstances (i.e., our intervention is not an adapted form of full-model DBT).

As previously mentioned, commitment and environmental challenges abound for clients involved with the criminal legal system. For instance, clients often express concerns about, or their own biases regarding, the stigma surrounding therapy, and may express doubts about its utility (both of which may be culturally rooted). They may be slow, or frankly unwilling, to develop rapport and a therapeutic alliance with student therapists. Such may be exacerbated by the virtual modality (which lacks some interpersonal qualities of in-person interactions) or demographic differences. Therapists are typically much younger and rarely share the same racial or ethnic background, let alone experiential background, as the clients. Some clients are also resentful and distrustful of mandated therapy and express concerns about privacy. Furthermore, they may be stressed by having to shoehorn therapy into their already hectic schedules, a frequently-cited explanation for lateness and no-shows.

Nevertheless, these and other challenges are counterbalanced by the benefits offered by the therapy to the overall court-based programming effort, the community, and the student trainees. Moreover, RISE graduates often express strong support for the therapy component of the RISE program, as do RISE judges. Over the past several years, the RISE program has expanded to include more judges and participant cohorts. Furthermore, another nearby jurisdiction, with both a preexisting diversion program similar to the RISE program and a new reentry program patterned after the RISE program, has expressed a desire to incorporate our therapy component. We have thus far sought to meet all these expansions. However, the demand for therapy represents a critical stress point, given the *pro bono* nature of both therapists and supervisors.

Generalizability of this Work

The collaboration between university-based training clinics and court-based services presents many unique opportunities, but also many challenges. While the treatment resources available through university-based training clinics are typically limited, the opportunity for graduate student trainees to obtain novel clinical experience with a unique and diverse population is highly appealing. Moreover, our intervention appears to be greatly appreciated by both court personnel and many clients who perceive benefits from the therapy—though some inevitably perceive the required therapy as burdensome. The appeal of the intervention has been evident through consistently increased requests to accommodate more referrals, as the RISE program has expanded and other nearby court programs have sought to include our intervention as a component. Graduate student trainees have also benefited from the opportunity to hone their skills in working with DBT- and RNR-based principles, as well as with a challenging and traditionally underserved client population. Furthermore, university-based clinics are well-suited to facilitate research, despite the likelihood that adequate sample sizes for certain types of research will accrue relatively slowly. Detailed session-by-session "process" research represents one appealing opportunity as sample sizes grow.

However, long-term sustainability is challenging, particularly when relying on voluntary, uncompensated therapy providers and supervisory staff (e.g., faculty members) who are primarily motivated by the opportunity to enhance student training and the potential for research opportunities. While short-term sustainability might be enhanced by securing research funding, grants are inherently time-limited and often require substantial data collection (which further increases time demands). Nevertheless, there are multiple potential solutions for long-term sustainability that are only now being explored.

For example, many community-based clinics bill (albeit nominally) for services, which is feasible for some individuals involved with the criminal legal system (e.g., those with some form of health insurance). However, reliance on reimbursement would be challenging for a therapy service that is mandated for all clients involved in an overarching court-based program regardless of status (e.g., regardless of whether one has health insurance or is a U.S. citizen). Likewise, the opportunity for supervised clinical hours is appealing to students in a wide range of training programs, ranging from doctoral programs in clinical psychology (which is our background) to terminal master's degree programs in clinical psychology and allied disciplines. We have found our intervention to be appropriate for delivery by students relatively early in their training, given the low frequency of very high-risk behaviors among clients, if adequate training is provided in advance. Our student therapists typically first complete either a graduate course on DBT or an online DBT training program.

Training clinics also have the opportunity to plan services and supervision to meet student training needs, such as providing training opportunities, allowing for flexibility in scheduling of sessions and supervision, arranging for opportunities to write assessment reports that can inform intervention, conducting live observation of sessions (or recordings of those sessions), and exposing students to systematic therapy adherence measures. The RISE program also benefits from the support of local law firms, some of which have been willing to provide modest contributions to support external supervision costs, potentially reducing the reliance on faculty volunteers. Creative solutions can also be explored with university administrators for alternative forms of compensation for the demands on faculty supervisors, such as classifying the therapy service as an elective course, applied in nature, for which a faculty supervisor might receive instructional credit.

Ultimately, while our model is not a panacea, particularly considering the large number of persons being released by the criminal legal system and their vast unmet need for therapeutic services, it is one that can be implemented by professionals elsewhere. This is especially true for those working in universities who are involved in student training. Moreover, we have generally found the telehealth modality, while also not a panacea, to be very useful in overcoming barriers represented by a pandemic, state lines, and clients who present with limited finances and transportation needs, and generally busy lives who must also strive to meet other court requirements.

Considerations of Diversity, Equity, and Inclusiveness

The fact that almost all our male-identifying clients also identify as racial and ethnic minorities is unsurprising considering the longstanding problem of racial and ethnic disparities in the criminal legal system (Kovera, 2019; National Conference of State Legislatures, 2022). DBT has shown conceptual and empirical promise across a wide range of demographic groups (Behavioral Tech, n.d.; Fuchs et al., 2013), and several culturally-specific adaptations and recommendations have been presented in the literature for tailoring the treatment to members of different racial and ethnic groups (Haft et al., 2022; Pierson et al., 2022). As for the utility of interventions in the criminal legal system more generally, and particularly for those who identify as racial and ethnic minorities, the research literature is mixed (Spiropoulos et al., 2014) and far less developed than one would hope (Beaudry et al., 2021). Nevertheless, there is evidence to suggest that treatment programs in general can reduce the risk of criminal recidivism among members of historically marginalized groups (Usher & Stewart, 2014).

Accordingly, the fact that our intervention almost exclusively serves persons from marginalized backgrounds is emphasized when recruiting and training new therapists, who rarely reflect the sociocultural backgrounds of their clients. The psychosocial history elicited from clients as part of our intakes is helpful for starting to appreciate some of these issues, followed by ongoing attention during consultation team meetings and discussions with supervisors. That is, our intervention aims to identify and discuss historical and structural inequities relevant to our clients, and to support one another in remaining mindful about how our clients' disadvantaged backgrounds may impact their therapy.

This includes the dialectic of technology both facilitating access to services (e.g., enabling a university-based clinic in one state to serve those located in another; see Hyland et al., 2022) and introducing a range of unique challenges. Some of our clients have never used videoconferencing before and have only rarely used other electronic tools. They may have unreliable Internet connectivity. They often only have access to a smartphone (rather than a personal computer like therapists typically use) and rarely have access to a printer (e.g., for homework assignments that might ideally be printed). Ultimately, therapists are encouraged to acknowledge and explore with their clients their respective sociocultural and telehealth-relevant differences beginning at the point of the intake evaluation, and to employ flexibility to help meet their clients based on "where they have uniquely been" and "where they are currently at." This helps clients reach "where they want to be." Eventually, we intend to incorporate sociocultural factors into any formal evaluation of our service, albeit with appreciation that most of our clients are from historically marginalized groups.

Advice to Others Seeking to Do Similar Work

Establishing and maintaining a *pro bono* treatment clinic is effortful. Accordingly, we offer several recommendations based on experience to date. First, ideal staffing includes having at least two committed supervisors, multiple student therapists, and administrative support (e.g., a non-therapist student), and additional students available to replace those who may "rotate out" of the treatment consultation team each year. Second, supervisors need to consider whether telehealth services will be provided across state lines. If so, they need to be licensed in all involved jurisdictions. Relatedly, for risk management purposes, they need to be knowledgeable about each jurisdiction's requirements for psychological services, and telehealth specifically, and prepared for the possible need to breach confidentiality or make referrals for emergency services, child abuse concerns, or other pressing issues that might arise.

Third, supervisors or clinical directors should have a Memorandum of Understanding or Agreement (MOU or MOA) executed between their university and the court, and they should be prepared with clinic forms and templates that will be needed (e.g., consent for therapy, release of information, note and report templates). They will also need to arrange for secure videoconference and electronic health records platforms, and might consider other potential technological resources (e.g., services such as Google Voice to anonymize student therapist's primary phone numbers, and the use of anonymous client IDs for remote data collection via online survey platforms). If a clinic is a covered entity under the Health Insurance Portability and Accountability Act (e.g., if payment is rendered for services), supervisors will need to ensure compliance with this federal law and similar state laws. All this is made easier, and less costly, when supervisors have access to a previously established university clinic infrastructure. Various university personnel should be consulted to obtain the range of necessary approvals (e.g., department chair, college dean, clinic director, university legal counsel, institutional review board), which will vary depending on institutional demands and goals for the service (e.g., if research is anticipated).

Fourth, supervisors should establish good working relationships with key court personnel, such as judges and probation officers who oversee referral and monitoring processes. Particularly when services are delivered via telehealth, these court personnel can help address a range of client challenges (e.g., access to necessary technology, non-responsiveness to therapist outreach). Importantly, this should include an agreement as to what information will be provided to the court, which could vary from attendance (or non-attendance) to more case-specific information (e.g., renewed or suspected illicit substance use, reports regarding other illegal activity). The frequency of ongoing communication should also be established prior to initiating treatment. While regular (e.g., biweekly) contact is helpful, some clinics and referring agencies may prefer more or less frequent communication. We have found it best for a supervisor (not student therapists) to be the liaison to the court to ensure the exchange of information is appropriate, consistent, and coherent, and that administrative decision-making is proper and authoritative.

Fifth, as part of the consent process and in an ongoing way, common challenges should be anticipated, planned for, and responded to in conjunction with the court. Such issues include limits to confidentiality (e.g., should all disclosures of substance use or criminal activity be reported, or only those deemed "significant" by the therapist or supervisor?); lateness, missed sessions, and termination recommendations; and client resistance to DBT strategies such as diary cards (i.e., forms for daily client tracking of treatment-relevant factors). The underserved and variously burdened nature of persons involved with the criminal legal system should be kept in mind while planning for these and other issues.

Sixth, in the spirit of training and program evaluation, a variety of procedures can help refine training and services, as well as identify gaps and highlight successful strategies. We recommend the use of strategies such as recorded training materials, session recordings (with client consent), and treatment adherence rating forms to ensure satisfactory manifestation and maintenance of DBT principles and strategies. Occasional in-person visits to court sessions are helpful, as well as attendance at court graduation ceremonies (if applicable). While formal outcome assessment may be desirable (e.g., pre–post assessment batteries, tracking of violations of supervision or rearrest), the feasibility of these procedures will vary, and may depend on available resources. Relatedly, we recommend soliciting feedback about the intervention. While therapists and supervisors, as well as clients (e.g., individually or possibly via occasional focus groups), are obvious and valuable sources of feedback, other feedback from an impartial party can also be helpful. For example, in one of our clinics, supervisor and student therapy suggestions have included the implementation of supervisor observation of occasional session recordings, and assessment measures of additional RNR factors (e.g., common responsivity factors such as treatment readiness and verbal cognitive functioning). Furthermore, suggestions from an external reviewer included further solidifying that clinic's phone coaching element (e.g., student therapists inviting brief intersession phone calls from clients to help them with implementing skills "in the moment") and allowing clients to invite their social supports to sessions (considering clients' status as members of a vulnerable group).

Finally, while we benefited from our universities collaborating and sharing resources, others interested in establishing such a clinic may not enjoy the same benefit. One of the chapter authors (CMK) has both selected and created assorted resources to variously focus and manage his clinic's efforts in line with DBT and RNR. In the spirit of support, interested readers can contact the first author for access to any such non-proprietary materials.

Conclusions

DBT has been adapted for various correctional and forensic mental health contexts, with growing (albeit still limited) support for many of these applications. We have described a brief and community-based intervention targeting persons recently released from prison, which is informed by DBT principles and techniques coupled with principles from RNR. In prior applications of DBT to persons involved with the criminal legal system, it has been typical for the treatment to occur in an inpatient setting, and to focus on psychopathology. In contrast, the application we have described in this chapter focuses more on criminogenic needs and non-criminogenic needs (i.e., non-criminogenic needs other than mental disorders) of persons who have already reentered the community following incarceration in prison.

The intervention service was initiated following a request from the administrative judge overseeing a court-based reentry program in the hope that a brief therapeutic intervention would improve overall court-program outcomes. The therapy considers a client's criminogenic risk and is tailored to their individual needs and responsivity factors. It is meant to impart an atmosphere of supportiveness for the stresses and challenges of community reintegration and respect for historical disadvantages and inequities. It also seeks to reduce risk for reoffending by building and strengthening client skills, which may aid them in more effectively navigating their reentry experiences. Anecdotal evidence has provided some support for this intervention, with many RISE graduates (and some who did not graduate) expressing considerable enthusiasm for the therapy experience. However, systematic research is clearly needed to better understand the nature and magnitude of any intervention effects (e.g., reductions in criminogenic risk and recidivism), including to substantiate suspected mechanisms of action (e.g., increased skillfulness), identify elements that may be more or less useful, and guide further adaptations to our and other DBT-based interventions for those involved with the criminal legal system.

Although DBT was originally developed for suicidal and self-injurious behaviors, it has demonstrated effectiveness for treating a variety of difficult-to-treat client characteristics and behaviors, including among some correctional and forensic populations. While some of our adaptations for the community-based reentry context are also common to past applications of DBT in other correctional and forensic mental health settings (e.g., simplification of DBT concepts and materials and incorporating RNR concepts), others are more characteristic of our particular intervention, having been developed for a particular correctional population. For example, the brief duration (12 sessions) and exclusive reliance on individual sessions for the delivery of select DBT skills based on individual client considerations. These latter characteristics of our intervention make the treatment more feasible for, and are more reflective of, our clients, who have a range of other commitments and tend to present with less acute needs than the high-frequency life-threatening behaviors for which traditional full-model DBT was originally developed. Another important characteristic of our intervention, originally driven by necessity during the COVID-19 pandemic, is the exclusive use of a virtual (telehealth) format for therapy. Although a direct comparison of telehealth versus in-person treatment would certainly be beneficial, we have maintained the virtual format for practical reasons, including ease of scheduling and eliminating the costs and time spent traveling. While these modifications to develop a brief, pragmatic intervention may decrease the overall effectiveness of the intervention, our approach allows a more accessible therapy option for a broad range of client circumstances in the community. It has likewise allowed us to meet the demand for our service based on available resources.

Correctional and forensic adaptations of DBT have been evaluated, including for specific types of individuals (e.g., youth, women, those hospitalized in forensic mental health facilities) and types of behavior (e.g., stalking, substance abuse). Whenever DBT is adapted to a new setting, adjustments are made along the way as the intervention is refined. Our DBT- and RNR-informed intervention has been serving the RISE program for the past four years (in addition to more recently beginning to serve two additional court-based programs), and our general approach has been refined to enhance feasibility, effectiveness (hopefully), and sustainability during this period. However, because of these ongoing changes, the relatively modest number of clients our two parallel clinics are able to serve at a time, and the need for long-term outcome data, we have not yet had the opportunity to conduct a systematic evaluation of the effectiveness of our intervention. A strong evaluation of our intervention, with an adequate sample size to detect intended effects, is an important next step.

Further efforts to ensure sustainability will also be critical. For example, fiscal resources are able to compensate supervisory staff and pay for ongoing clinic expenses such as record-keeping software. Such requires continued internal (e.g., a university rolling expenses into its costs for a larger clinic as part of its public interest mission) or new external (e.g., grant or foundation) funding at levels that allow for meeting stable or increased demand. The research literature is replete with examples of innovative therapeutic programs that have been implemented, studied (and published), and then disappear once the motivating outcome has been achieved (e.g., publications or completion of a grant). Long-term sustainability has been a low priority for many in academic settings, but is critical to ensuring that successful community-based interventions for persons involved with the criminal legal system can flourish over the long run.

References

Beaudry, G., Yu, R., Perry, A. E., & Fazel, S. (2021). Effectiveness of psychological interventions in prison to reduce recidivism: A systematic review and meta-analysis of randomised controlled trials. *The Lancet Psychiatry, 8*(9), 759–773. https://doi.org/10.1016/S2215-0366(21)00170-X

Behavioral Tech. (n.d.). *Core evidence & research.* https://behavioraltech.org/research/evidence/

Berghuis, M. (2018). Reentry programs for adult male offender recidivism and reintegration: A systematic review and meta-analysis. *International Journal of Offender Therapy and Comparative Criminology, 62*(14), 4655–4676. https://doi.org/10.1177/0306624X18778448

Bianchini, V., Cofini, V., Curto, M., Lagrotteria, B., Manzi, A., Navari, S., Ortenzi, R., Paoletti, G., Pompili, E., Pompili, P. M., Silvestrini, C., & Nicolò, G. (2019). Dialectical behaviour therapy (DBT) for forensic psychiatric patients: An Italian pilot study. *Criminal Behaviour and Mental Health, 29*(2), 122–130. https://doi.org/10.1002/cbm.2102

Bonta, J., & Andrews, D. A. (2024). *The psychology of criminal conduct* (7th ed.). Routledge. https://doi.org/10.4324/9781003292128

Carson, E. A. (2021). *Prisoners in 2020 – Statistical tables* (NCJ 302776). Bureau of Justice Statistics. https://bjs.ojp.gov/content/pub/pdf/p20st.pdf

Carson, E. A., & Kluckow, R. (2023). *Prisoners in 2022 – Statistical tables* (NCJ 307149). Bureau of Justice Statistics. https://bjs.ojp.gov/document/p22st.pdf

Carter, A., Butler, A., Willoughby, M., Janca, E., Kinner, S. A., Southalan, L., Fazel, S., & Borschmann, R. (2022). Interventions to reduce suicidal thoughts and behaviours among people in contact with the criminal justice system: A global systematic review. *EClinicalMedicine, 44*, Article 101266. https://doi.org/10.1016/j.eclinm.2021.101266

Edwards, E. R., Epshteyn, G., Snyder, S., Gorman, D., Coolidge, B., Marcano, E., Tsai, J., & Goodman, M. (2023). Dialectical behavior therapy for justice-involved veterans: Changes in treatment targets in a small, pre–post design clinical trial. *Psychological Services, 20*(Suppl 2), 98–107. https://doi.org/10.1037/ser0000766

Favril, L., Shaw, J., & Fazel, S. (2022). Prevalence and risk factors for suicide attempts in prison. *Clinical Psychology Review, 97*, Article 102190. https://doi.org/10.1016/j.cpr.2022.102190

Favril, L., Yu, R., Hawton, K., & Fazel, S. (2020). Risk factors for self-harm in prison: A systematic review and meta-analysis. *The Lancet Psychiatry, 7*(8), 682–691. https://doi.org/10.1016/S2215-0366(20)30190-5

Fuchs, C., Lee, J. K., Roemer, L., & Orsillo, S. M. (2013). Using mindfulness- and acceptance-based treatments with clients from nondominant cultural and/or marginalized backgrounds: Clinical considerations, meta-analysis findings, and introduction to the special series. *Cognitive and Behavioral Practice, 20*(1), 1–12. https://doi.org/10.1016/j.cbpra.2011.12.004

Haft, S. L., O'Grady, S. M., Shaller, E. A. L., & Liu, N. H. (2022). Cultural adaptations of dialectical behavior therapy: A systematic review. *Journal of Consulting and Clinical Psychology, 90*(10), 787–801. https://doi.org/10.1037/ccp0000730

Hyland, K. A., McDonald, J. B., Verzijl, C. L., Faraci, D. C., Calixte-Civil, P. F., Gorey, C. M., & Verona, E. (2022). Telehealth for dialectical behavioral therapy: A commentary on the experience of a rapid transition to virtual delivery of DBT. *Cognitive and Behavioral Practice, 29*(2), 367–380. https://doi.org/10.1016/j.cbpra.2021.02.006

Ivanoff, A., & Marotta, P. L. (2019). DBT in forensic settings. In M. A. Swales (Ed.), *The Oxford handbook of dialectical behaviour therapy* (pp. 617–644). Oxford University Press. https://doi.org/10.1093/oxfordhb/9780198758723.013.14

Kovera, M. B. (2019). Racial disparities in the criminal justice system: Prevalence, causes, and a search for solutions. *Journal of Social Issues, 75*(4), 1139–1164. https://doi.org/10.1111/josi.12355

Linehan, M. M. (1993). *Cognitive-behavioral treatment of borderline personality disorder*. Guilford Press.

Mills, L., Murphy, J., Lee, L., & Clarke, C. (2019). Dialectical Behavioural Therapy for forensic service users: A systematic literature review and meta-analysis of the literature. *Journal of Psychiatric Intensive Care, 15*(1), 45–49. https://doi.org/10.20299/jpi.2018.010

Moulden, H. M., Mamak, M., & Chaimowitz, G. (2020). A preliminary evaluation of the effectiveness of dialectical behaviour therapy in a forensic psychiatric setting. *Criminal Behaviour and Mental Health, 30*(2–3), 141–150. https://doi.org/10.1002/cbm.2158

National Conference of State Legislatures. (2022). *Racial and ethnic disparities in the justice system*. https://documents.ncsl.org/wwwncsl/Criminal-Justice/Racial-and-Ethnic-Disparities-in-the-Justice-System_v03.pdf

Nee, C., & Farman, S. (2005). Female prisoners with borderline personality disorder: Some promising treatment developments. *Criminal Behaviour and Mental Health, 15*(1), 2–16. https://doi.org/10.1002/cbm.33

Nyamathi, A., Shin, S. S., Smeltzer, J., Salem, B., Yadav, K., Krogh, D., & Ekstrand, M. (2018). Effectiveness of Dialectical Behavioral Therapy on reduction of recidivism among recently incarcerated homeless women: A pilot study. *International Journal of Offender Therapy and Comparative Criminology*, *62*(15), 4796–4813. https://doi.org/10.1177/0306624X18785516

Office of the District Court Executive. (December 7, 2018). *United States District Court for the Southern District of New York announces a new re-entry court for individuals on supervised release* [Press advisory]. https://www.nysd.uscourts.gov/sites/default/files/pdf/rise-court/Press%20Advisory_RISE%20Court.pdf

Pierson, A. M., Arunagiri, V., & Bond, D. M. (2022). "You didn't cause racism, and you have to solve it anyways": Antiracist adaptations to dialectical behavior therapy for White therapists. *Cognitive and Behavioral Practice*, *29*(4), 796–815. https://doi.org/10.1016/j.cbpra.2021.11.001

Rosenfeld, B., Galietta, M., Foellmi, M., Coupland, S., Turner, Z., Stern, S., Wijetunga, C., Gerbrandij, J., & Ivanoff, A. (2019). Dialectical behavior therapy (DBT) for the treatment of stalking offenders: A randomized controlled study. *Law and Human Behavior*, *43*(4), 319–328. https://doi.org/10.1037/lhb0000336

Rosenfeld, B., Galietta, M., Ivanoff, A., Garcia-Mansilla, A., Martinez, R., Fava, J., Fineran, V., & Green, D. (2007). Dialectical behavior therapy for the treatment of stalking offenders. *The International Journal of Forensic Mental Health*, *6*(2), 95–103. https://doi.org/10.1080/14999013.2007.10471254

Skinner, G. C. M., & Farrington, D. P. (2020). A systematic review and meta-analysis of offending versus suicide in community (non-psychiatric and non-prison) samples. *Aggression and Violent Behavior*, *52*, Article 101421. https://doi.org/10.1016/j.avb.2020.101421

Spiropoulos, G. V., Salisbury, E. J., & Van Voorhis, P. (2014). Moderators of correctional treatment success: An exploratory study of racial differences. *International Journal of Offender Therapy and Comparative Criminology*, *58*(7), 835–860. https://doi.org/10.1177/0306624X13492999

Tomlinson, M. F. (2018). A theoretical and empirical review of dialectical behavior therapy within forensic psychiatric and correctional settings worldwide. *International Journal of Forensic Mental Health*, *17*(1), 72–95. https://doi.org/10.1080/14999013.2017.1416003

Usher, A. M., & Stewart, L. A. (2014). Effectiveness of correctional programs with ethnically diverse offenders: A meta-analytic study. *International Journal of Offender Therapy and Comparative Criminology*, *58*(2), 209–230. https://doi.org/10.1177/0306624X12469507

10

Treating Trauma in Justice-Involved Girls

Apryl A. Alexander and Tracy Moran Vozar

Project Description

In 2020, the Denver FIRST Juvenile Justice Project (Denver FIRST JJP) was created through federal grant funding from the Office of Juvenile Justice and Delinquency Prevention (OJJDP) to provide trauma treatment services to juvenile justice system-involved girls and nonbinary youth. The Denver FIRST JJP is housed within a university-based forensic psychology training clinic, the Denver Forensic Institute for Research, Service, and Training (Denver FIRST), in the Graduate School of Professional Psychology (GSPP) at the University of Denver (DU). The primary aim of the Denver FIRST JJP is to provide gender-sensitive and culturally competent evidence-based intervention and prevention services to juvenile justice-involved girls in the metropolitan Denver area. The implementation of services and care delivery had three phases: (1) screening, intake, and assessment; (2) treatment and recovery supports; and (3) case management and discharge planning. Additionally, per the OJJDP grant requirements, the Denver FIRST JJP provides trauma-informed care training to key community partners who work with juvenile justice-involved girls to increase their knowledge of and engagement in trauma-informed care principles.

The primary intervention used for the program was Trauma-Focused Cognitive Behavioral Therapy (TF-CBT; Cohen et al., 2012, 2017). TF-CBT is a psychosocial model designed to treat posttraumatic stress and related emotional and behavioral problems. The components of the treatment model include psychoeducation and parenting skills, relaxation skills, affect expression and regulation skills, cognitive coping skills and processing, trauma narrative, in vivo exposure (when needed), conjoint parent-child sessions, and enhancing safety and future development. TF-CBT is delivered in twelve to sixteen sessions. TF-CBT is recognized as a Model Program by the Substance Abuse and Mental Health Services Administration (SAMHSA) due to the extensive outcome data from randomized controlled trials that support its effectiveness in reducing posttraumatic stress disorder (PTSD) symptoms and the secondary outcomes of improvement in depressive symptoms for racial and ethnic

Apryl A. Alexander and Tracy Moran Vozar, *Treating Trauma in Justice-Involved Girls*. In: *The Path Forward*.
Edited by: Kirk Heilbrun and David DeMatteo, Oxford University Press. © Oxford University Press (2026).
DOI: 10.1093/9780197773031.003.0010

minorities and LGBTQ subpopulations who have disproportionately higher rates of substance use disorders.

The Denver FIRST JJP partnered with the Caring for You and Baby (CUB) Clinic to provide direct clinical services and provider training because the grant required intervention and *prevention* elements. The CUB Clinic is a perinatal through early school-age clinic for caregivers and their young children within one of the largest psychology training clinics in the country, the University of Denver Professional Psychology Clinic (PPC). CUB Clinic services are patient-centered and evidence-based. All services are offered by training clinicians who are supervised by licensed practitioners, many of whom are also faculty and staff of the GSPP. Utilization of trainees as providers fosters enhanced training of developing professionals as well as no- and low-cost service provision to the community. Further, the CUB Clinic was a clear partner for the JJP as it offers Parent-Child Interaction Therapy (PCIT; see McNeil et al., 2019, for a review). The CUB Clinic utilizes the Integration of Working models of Attachment (IoWA) model of PCIT, an evidence-based approach to training caregivers in effective behavior strategies as well as an effective treatment for child behavioral concerns, emotional dysregulation, and caregiver-child relationship issues (Troutman, 2022). Dr. Troutman developed the IoWA-PCIT model with child welfare and juvenile justice-involved families in mind—a task for which she is well-qualified, given her decades of experience as a provider with these families and systems. The IoWA-PCIT maintains PCIT's effective behavioral foundation while integrating an attachment lens into each session and the planned outcomes of therapy. This attachment lens adds attentiveness to intergenerational trauma, fostering secure attachment and promoting relationship repair between children and safe caregivers, as aligned with the JJP's goals.

Referral and Screening Process

A referral form was created to gather basic information about potential clients and their families. This referral form was made available on the Denver FIRST JJP website and distributed to community partners. Once the referral form was received, a phone screening would be conducted, and additional clinic paperwork would be reviewed. A clinician would be assigned to conduct an initial assessment appointment within a week of the phone screening.

The assessment process consisted of a comprehensive pre-treatment interview and conducting a battery of psychological measures with the client and/or their caregiver. The adolescents completed the following self-report measures: The Youth Self-Report (YSR; Achenbach & Rescorla, 2001), the Trauma Symptom Checklist for Children (TSCC; Briere, 1996), the Adolescent Substance Abuse Subtle Screening Inventory (SASSI-A3; Miller & Lazowski, 1999), and the Juvenile Victimization Questionnaire (JVQ; Hamby et al., 2004). The caregivers completed the Child

Behavior Checklist (CBCL; Achenbach & Rescorla, 2001), the Parenting Stress Index, the Parent Support Questionnaire (PSQ; Mannarino & Cohen, 1996), and the Parent Emotional Reaction Questionnaire (PERQ; Mannarino & Cohen, 1996). For families with younger children and in the Iowa-PCIT program, caregivers completed the Dyadic Parent-Child Interaction Coding System (DPICS; Eyberg et al., 2005). Clinicians also appraised each girl on the Structured Assessment of Violence Risk in Youth (SAVRY; Borum et al., 2002) based on information gathered in the pre-treatment interview and assessment measures.

After the pretreatment interview, the clinician would write up a report and case formulation and present the case in the clinical team meeting for evaluation. The client's fit for services through the Denver FIRST JJP was determined during the clinical team meeting. Common exclusion criteria would be if a client were exhibiting symptoms that would warrant more intensive or inpatient treatment, or if a client did not have a reported history of trauma or trauma symptoms. If the client were to fit, they would be assigned a therapist and begin treatment.

Clients

Local outreach efforts aided in obtaining referrals for the program. Most of the referrals came from established partnerships with juvenile courts. Memoranda of Understanding (MOUs) were created during the grant application process with the local Juvenile Assessment Center (JAC) and Denver Juvenile Probation. The JAC serves juvenile justice-involved youth ages five to seventeen and has two programs: The Community Assessment Program (CAP) and the Law Enforcement Program. The CAP strives to keep youth at home and out of the juvenile justice system by connecting families with supportive services. The Law Enforcement Program attempts to intervene and address factors contributing to concerning behavior and increase positive aspects of a child's life to keep them out of the juvenile justice system. The JAC provides initial screening of at-risk youth who have come into contact with the juvenile justice system for behavior or delinquency matters, and makes recommendations for treatment and care to the court. Their aim is to disrupt a youth's pathway from the municipal and delinquency courts to the district court. They partnered with the Denver FIRST JJP to make court/pre-trial recommendations for our program and refer families for services. The Denver Juvenile Probation Department has been recognized as an innovative local and national leader in juvenile justice and focuses on reducing recidivism and increasing community safety. The Denver Juvenile Probation Department also referred girls on probation and their families to the Denver FIRST JJP for services.

Relatedly, several county juvenile diversion offices referred or mandated girls to the Denver FIRST JJP. Some referrals came from community partners with whom we formed and maintained relationships (e.g., community mental health services, school-based health clinics, and nonprofit organizations). During the outreach efforts, another important partnership developed. The Denver FIRST JJP partnered with a local high school serving pregnant and parenting girls. The girls who attended this high school were identified as frequently having traumatic experiences and being at high risk for juvenile justice system involvement. The Denver FIRST JJP provided onsite assessment and brief trauma treatment services to girls at the school.

Providers and Clinical Training

The Denver FIRST JJP was a program within the Denver Forensic Institute for Research, Service, and Training (Denver FIRST), a university-based forensic psychology training clinic within the GSPP at the University of Denver (DU). Denver FIRST was established in 2014 to provide low-cost, high-quality forensic mental health services, innovative research, and intensive training opportunities to students, academics, and community partners. The clinic offers various forensic psychology services, including evaluating individuals in the criminal, civil, or immigration courts and an outpatient competency restoration program. The primary mission is to train students in evidence-based treatment and assessment.

The Denver FIRST JJP served as a field placement/practicum training site for graduate students in the master's in forensic psychology program or the doctoral program in clinical psychology at GSPP. Potential student clinicians were interviewed to determine whether this field placement site would adequately fit their areas of interest and training needs. Students underwent standard HR hiring through the university as well as background checks and ethics training (e.g., HIPAA). Upon hiring, there was an orientation process, which included an orientation to Denver FIRST JJP as well as to the Professional Psychology Clinic, in which individuals learned about clinic policies such as scheduling, recording sessions, and the electronic medical record system (Titanium). Before service delivery, each clinician completed the online TF-CBT training (https://tfcbt2.musc.edu/) and participated in weekly individual and clinical team meetings.

Community Trainings

As part of the OJJDP grant, the Denver FIRST JJP was required to increase the number of trauma-informed professionals in the Denver community. The Denver FIRST JJP was expected to provide quarterly training and collect data on how staff or professionals integrated the training into their work. Many of the trainings centered on describing trauma-informed care and discussing the literature on the prevalence of trauma among juvenile justice-involved girls and the established treatment models. Trainings were also held for court personnel. For instance, the first author presented workshops on trauma-informed lawyering at the Excellence in Juvenile Defense Conference in Denver, Colorado, and the virtual National Association for Public Defense (NAPD) conference. Community partners also requested presentations, and these included presentations on trauma in adolescents and preventing burnout for staff who work with youth.

Foundations and Support for Project Services

Although there has been a general decline in juvenile arrests, there has been a steady rise in female involvement in the juvenile justice system in the United States. Girls are being arrested more frequently, accounting for thirty percent of all juvenile arrests (OJJDP, 2019). The continued increase in young female offenders has highlighted deficits in gender-specific research and services across the juvenile justice system. Recent research has started examining gendered pathways to offending and appropriate interventions (Jones et al., 2014; Wesely & Dewey, 2018). Though sparse, the existing literature identifies gender-responsive programs as critical to meeting the unique needs of juvenile justice-involved girls.

Research has shown that the trajectory for female juvenile offenders varies in important ways compared to their male counterparts. Specifically, mental health issues and a history of trauma are particularly salient factors for young girls (Kerig, 2018; Marston et al., 2012). Childhood maltreatment and victimization may influence youth's trajectory into the juvenile justice system (Mallet, 2017). Research indicates that approximately ninety percent of juvenile justice-involved youth have experienced one or more types of traumatic events in childhood (Abram et al., 2004; Kerig & Becker, 2012); one study found that two-thirds of detained youth had experienced two or more potentially traumatic events (Ford et al., 2010). Justice-involved girls present with higher rates of victimization than boys, and poly-victimization may be gender-differentiated (Kerig, 2018; Kerig & Modrowski, 2018). Juvenile justice-involved youth often have experienced multiple forms of traumatic events, including victimization across many contexts and interpersonal losses (Abram et al., 2004; Butcher et al., 2016; Ford et al., 2008; Turner et al., 2016). Past traumatic experiences appear to be especially influential for girls, particularly traumatic events involving sexual violence (Espinosa et al., 2013). Saar et al. (2015) described the sexual abuse-to-prison pipeline, which recognizes the high prevalence of sexual abuse among adolescent girls in the juvenile justice system.

Untreated trauma has serious implications for a child's developmental trajectory and can lead to an increased risk of developing serious mental health issues. Justice-involved girls seem to be more susceptible to mental health issues, with higher reported rates of depression, anxiety, and trauma-related diagnoses, such as PTSD (Kerig & Becker, 2012; Moore et al., 2013). The empirical literature demonstrates a connection between trauma and girls' involvement in crime. Experiencing trauma may be an underlying cause of other problematic behaviors directly linked to criminal activity (Belknap & Hoslinger, 2006; Hodge et al., 2015). For instance, females are commonly arrested for crimes related to substance abuse, truancy, running away, and prostitution, all of which may be associated with trauma (Saar et al., 2015). Individuals with unresolved trauma and involvement in the juvenile justice system are less likely to have adequate support and become further susceptible to victimization and involvement in criminal acts (Wolff et al., 2017). An examination of risk for recidivism among justice-involved youth identified sexual abuse as the leading predictor of recidivism for young girls (Conrad et al., 2014). Unfortunately, the system often fails to provide adequate mental health treatment, and conditions of incarceration can exacerbate trauma and other existing mental health issues.

Beginning and Development of Project Services

Girls constitute approximately twenty-five percent of committed or detained youth in Colorado. Of these individuals, 83.9 percent have had two or more out-of-home placements, suggesting the vast majority have experienced child abuse or neglect (Juvenile Justice and Delinquency Prevention Council, 2018). Compared to boys, it is considerably more common for girls to engage in criminal activity through human trafficking. The Division of Youth Services (DYS) in Colorado has identified a significant increase in the number of detained girls victimized through human trafficking (Juvenile Justice and Delinquency Prevention Council, 2018). In line with national findings, a greater proportion of Colorado justice-involved girls also display mental health issues, with nearly ninety percent of newly committed girls demonstrating a need for formal mental health services compared to sixty percent of boys (Colorado Division of Youth Services, 2020). Colorado trends align with national trends and general findings in the empirical literature. The growing number of girls in the juvenile justice system with differential needs elucidates the importance of implementing gender-specific programming. Of additional concern is the limited availability of culturally-responsive services in Colorado.

In Spring 2020, OJJDP released a request for proposals (RFP) for a Reducing Risk for Girls in the Juvenile Justice System grant. The objectives and deliverables were to (1) develop and implement direct service programs for girls involved in the juvenile justice system to reduce reoffending; (2) enhance or expand existing prevention and early intervention programs to meet the specific needs of girls involved in the juvenile justice system; and (3) develop, expand, or enhance targeted curricula for staff (e.g., probation officers, judges) to ensure they have the skills necessary to implement these programs for juvenile justice system-involved girls. Priority was given to applicants providing services in what the OJJDP calls Qualified Opportunity Zones (QOZs) based on zip codes. The Denver metro area had several zip codes that were designated as QOZs. In alignment with the goals of the OJJDP grant program, the objectives of the Denver FIRST JJP were: (1) increase the number of child and adolescent girls (ages six to seventeen) receiving comprehensive treatment for behavioral disorders, adverse childhood experiences, and trauma; (2) increase involvement of parents/caregivers in their child's treatment; (3) improve behavioral and mental health outcomes for participating child and adolescent girls; (4) decrease program participant's involvement in and exposure to crime and violence; and (5) increase the number of trauma-informed community partners (i.e., attorneys, probation officers, case workers, judges).

The grant application was submitted in June 2020, and the notice of award for the Denver FIRST JJP was received in September 2020. After the project was awarded, a Program Coordinator position was developed, and they were hired by February 2021. Training of clinicians began in March 2021. Also, in March, the Director and Program Coordinator held an online kickoff event with our MOU partners to discuss the referral process.

Generalizability

The OJJDP grant allowed the Denver FIRST JJP to hire student clinicians at a rate comparable to their training and experience, and according to standards set forth by the university regarding graduate student pay. Given that the clinicians were graduate students, they were neither full-time employees nor paid at the rate of a full-time employee. Therefore, the number of clinicians on the project would have to be reduced if organizations or clinics hired full-time clinicians to provide the services.

The biggest challenge was creating a program during the COVID-19 pandemic. The grant was submitted two months into the pandemic without consideration for how long stay-at-home orders would last. The Denver FIRST JJP originally planned to have in-person group TF-CBT with girls and their families; however, the stay-at-home orders and university protocols were longer than expected due to the ongoing pandemic. The COVID-19 pandemic allowed us to integrate telehealth services into the university-based clinics that were previously unavailable. The Denver FIRST JJP and PPC quickly navigated how to provide HIPAA-compliant services via Zoom. Even as stay-at-home orders were lifted, youth and their families elected to remain on telehealth, as it alleviated transportation barriers, particularly for those outside the immediate Denver metro area. Current literature suggests telehealth TF-CBT as a promising practice (Martin et al., 2023; Stewart et al., 2017), but there have been concerns regarding treatment completion (Martin et al., 2023).

Diversity, Equity, and Inclusiveness

Most traditional programs and interventions for juvenile offenders are delivered to both boys and girls, although most of these programs have been created to address the needs of males (Chesney-Lind et al., 2008). Several studies have underscored the importance of designing and implementing gender-responsive programming to target the unique needs of justice-involved girls (Chesney-Lind et al., 2008; Day et al., 2015; Hodge et al., 2015; Kerig et al., 2014; Walker et al., 2015). Considering that female development is unique and risk factors and patterns of offending are different for girls, it makes sense that treatment should be different (Day et al., 2015; Walker et al., 2015). Recent research has shown that female-specific programs and services have effectively reduced recidivism and increased positive outcomes (Anderson et al., 2019; Day et al., 2015; Walker et al., 2015). Specifically, programs utilizing culturally responsive, strengths-based, trauma-informed interventions have demonstrated benefits for justice-involved girls (Walker et al., 2015). Another key component of a gender-responsive model is an individualized approach to treatment. Day and colleagues (2015) found that gender-specific programming reduced recidivism when it was applied to girls with gender-specific needs associated with trauma. These findings did not suggest comparable effectiveness with boys, however, further emphasizing the importance of developing interventions guided by both gender variations and gender commonalities. Taken together, the empirical literature highlights that effective gender-specific programming utilizes a risk-need-responsivity (RNR) framework to meet the individual treatment needs of justice-involved girls appropriately.

Despite the garnered support and acceptance of gender-specific programming, there is a significant gap in services and availability (Hodge et al., 2015), with a mere four percent of programs specifically targeting girls (Lipsey, 2009). Preliminary research has demonstrated promising outcomes; however, greater implementation of gender-responsive programming is critical to enhance our understanding of effective practice. A substantial barrier to our knowledge is the limited programming availability in the community. Community-based treatment and supervision have demonstrated effectiveness for youth who have committed various offenses, as resources are more available to promote positive societal contributions (Mulvey, 2011). Best practices for gender-responsive community programs are partly unclear because of the lack of implementation and outcome results. Recommendations include integrating gender-responsive approaches to existing evidence-based treatments emphasizing trauma and interpersonal relationships (Branson et al., 2017; Kerig et al., 2014).

The increase in girls' involvement in the juvenile justice system has disproportionally affected girls of color, with overrepresentation of African American, Latina, and Native American girls in the judicial system compared to the general population (Saar et al., 2015). A similar trend has been observed in Colorado. In 2018, African American and Latina girls represented approximately five percent and twenty-one percent, respectively, of girls in Colorado's general population (Puzzanchera et al., 2019). However, according to DYS report data, 16.4 percent and 33.7 percent of newly detained girls are African American and Hispanic females, respectively. Despite the need for specialized services, there is a significant gap in culturally competent services catering to the unique needs of juvenile justice-involved girls in Colorado (Colorado Division of Youth Services, 2020).

A majority of the clientele at the Denver FIRST JJP consisted of Black and Latina girls, which aligns with data highlighting the overrepresentation of these populations in the juvenile justice system. Therefore, the program needed to engage in culturally responsive practices. The pretreatment interview contained questions about cultural identity to facilitate dialogue regarding culture in treatment. In recent years, cultural adaptations to TF-CBT have been developed, and we have used them as an available resource for our clinicians. For example, Honoring Children, Mending the Circle (HC-MC) serves as an adaptation of TF-CBT for American Indian/Alaska Native (AI/AN) children (BigFoot & Schmidt, 2010; Kelley et al., 2024). The model blends AI/AN cultural teachings with cognitive-behavioral approaches. The TF-CBT adaptation for Black youth and families incorporates racial socialization and addresses cultural trauma (Metzger et al., 2021; Metzger et al., 2023; Phipps & Thorne, 2019). Finally, the TF-CBT implementation manual has been created for LGBTQ youth and their families (Cohen et al., 2018). Clinical supervision and clinical team meetings involved reviewing these practices and discussing how to integrate them into treatment for individual clients.

Advice to Others Seeking to Provide Similar Services

Given the population of girls in the juvenile justice system, the need for trauma-based treatment services and other behavioral health interventions is evident. The Denver FIRST JJP is a model of a university-based treatment program that can be replicated in different community settings, such as community mental health clinics (CMHCs) or outpatient therapy practices. Relationship building with community partners does take time. The Denver FIRST JJP engaged in several outreach efforts to establish community partners for referrals. Once those partnerships were established, the referral base began to grow. As described earlier, the OJJDP required the Denver FIRST JJP to conduct quarterly training within the community. This aided in building our reputation and credibility in the community, and some of our community partners sought us for additional training. For instance, one school we worked with needed a workshop on self-care and vicarious trauma for their clinicians and staff as they returned to in-person schooling after the COVID-19 orders were lifted.

Since the Denver FIRST JJP was a university-based clinic, we had resources from the university to assist with developing our program. First, although most of our services have been via telehealth, the intention was for services to be conducted by our departmental, university-based psychology clinic, the Professional Psychology Clinic (PPC). Second, we were able to have a website for our clinic hosted on the university and Denver FIRST website to describe the program and provide the referral form to community partners. Third, our department and university helped by marketing our program through news articles (Stone, 2021) and podcasts (Graduate School of Professional Psychology, University of Denver, 2021).

Lastly, although the Caring for You and Baby (CUB) Clinic was a partner in this grant and successfully received referrals for their general services, few referrals came in regarding trauma treatment through the Denver FIRST JJP. The referrals for younger children were less frequent. As schools began to reopen during the pandemic, the Denver FIRST JJP engaged with them to build partnerships to bring services to the schools. It would be important to highlight the importance of prevention services for younger children who are at risk for juvenile justice involvement as part of the therapeutic program.

Conclusion

There are many benefits to building a program for justice-involved girls. There is a high need to provide services tailored to the specific population, given the increase in their prevalence in the criminal legal system and the need to provide them with relevant trauma treatment services to aid in their healing and desistance from crime as a secondary outcome. The Denver FIRST JJP is an example of how a university-based psychology clinic could fill the needs of this population in the community. The program benefited from having federal dollars to support the development of the program, which included providing the staff and creating the infrastructure to build community connections. The ability to replicate the program depends on the resources of any agency or clinic providing the services. There are opportunities for federal funding, whether from OJJDP or other agencies such as SAMHSA, to create community-based programs. However, one of the drawbacks may be that these programs might depend on federal funding priorities. Therefore, alternative ways to develop and sustain the services should be explored. For instance, there may be opportunities for local or state-level contracts or partnerships to build the programs or house the programs at sites where costs can be reduced, such as schools. Practitioners would also need to get training and supervision in the models they are using for treatment, such as TF-CBT or Iowa-PCIT.

Acknowledgments

This project was supported by Grant No. 2020-MU-FX-0004, awarded by the Office of Juvenile Justice and Delinquency Prevention, Office of Justice Programs, U.S. Department of Justice. Points of view expressed in this document are those of the author(s) and do not necessarily represent the official position or policies of OJJDP or the U.S. Department of Justice.

References

Abram, K. M., Teplin, L. A., Charles, D. R., Longworth, S. L., McClelland, G. M., & Dulcan, M. K. (2004). Posttraumatic stress disorder and trauma in youth in juvenile detention. *Archives of General Psychiatry*, *61*(4), 403–410. https://doi.org/10.1001/archpsyc.61.4.403

Achenbach, T. M., & Rescorla, L. A. (2001). *Manual for the ASEBA school-age forms & profiles.* University of Vermont, Research Center for Children, Youth, & Families.

Anderson, V. R., Walerych, B. M., Campbell, N. A., Barnes, A. R., Davidson, W. S., Campbell, C. A., . . .Petersen, J. L. (2019). Gender-responsive intervention for female juvenile offenders: A quasi-experimental outcome evaluation. *Feminist Criminology*, *14*(1), 24–44. https://doi.org/10.1177/1557085116677749

Belknap, J., & Holsinger, K. (2006). The gendered nature of risk factors for delinquency. *Feminist Criminology*, *1*(1), 48–71. https://doi.org/10.1177/1557085105282897

Bigfoot, D. S., & Schmidt, S. R. (2010). Honoring children, mending the circle: Cultural adaptation of trauma-focused cognitive-behavioral therapy for American Indian and Alaska Native children. *Journal of Clinical Psychology*, *66*(8), 847–856. https://doi.org/10.1002/jclp.20707

Borum, R., Bartel, P., & Forth, A. (2002). *Manual for the Structured Assessment of Violence Risk in Youth (SAVRY).* Psychological Assessment Resources.

Branson, C. E., Baetz, C. L., Horwitz, S. M., & Hoagwood, K. E. (2017). Traúma-informed juvenile justice systems: A systematic review of definitions and core components. *Psychological Trauma*, *9*(6), 635–646. https://doi.org/10.1037/tra0000255

Briere, J. N. (1996). *Trauma Symptom Checklist for Children: Professional manual.* Psychological Assessment Resources.

Butcher, F., Holmes, M. R., Kretschmar, J. M., & Flannery, D. J. (2016). Polyvictimization across social contexts: Home, school, and neighborhood violence exposure. *Criminal Justice and Behavior*, *43*(12), 1726–1740. https://doi.org/10.1177/0093854816662679

Chesney-Lind, M., Morash, M., & Stevens, T. (2008). Girls' troubles, girls' delinquency, and gender responsive programming: A review. *The Australian and New Zealand Journal of Criminology*, *41*(1), 162–189.

Cohen, J. A., Mannarino, A. P., & Deblinger, E. (Eds). (2012). *Trauma-focused CBT for children and adolescents: Treatment applications.* Guilford Press.

Cohen, J. A., Mannarino, A. P., & Deblinger, E. (Eds.). (2017). *Treating trauma and traumatic grief in children and adolescents* (2nd ed.). Guilford Press.

Cohen, J. A., Mannarino, A. P., Wilson, K., & Zinny, A. (2018). *Trauma-Focused Cognitive Behavioral Therapy LGBTQ implementation manual.* Allegheny Health Network.

Colorado Division of Youth Services. (2020). *2018–2019 Fiscal year management reference manual.* Author.

Conrad, S. M., Tolou-Shams, M., Rizzo, C. J., Placella, N., & Brown, L. K. (2014). Gender differences in recidivism rates for juvenile justice youth: the impact of sexual abuse. *Law and Human Behavior*, *38*(4), 305–314. https://doi.org/10.1037/lhb0000062

Day, J. C., Zahn, M. A., & Tichavsky, L. P. (2015). What works for whom? The effects of gender responsive programming on girls and boys in secure detention. *Journal of Research in Crime and Delinquency, 52*(1), 93–129. https://doi.org/10.1177/0022427814538033

Espinosa, E. M., Sorensen, J. R., & Lopez, M. A. (2013). Youth pathways to placement: The influence of gender, mental health need, and trauma on confinement in the juvenile justice system. *Journal of Youth and Adolescence, 42*(12), 1824–1836. https://doi.org/10.1007/s10964-013-9981-x

Eyberg, S. M., Nelson, M., Duke, M., & Boggs, S. (2005). *Manual for the Dyadic Parent-Child Interaction Coding System*. Author.

Ford, J. D., Elhai, J. D., Connor, D. F., & Frueh, B. C. (2010). Poly-victimization and risk of posttraumatic, depressive, and substance use disorders and involvement in delinquency in a national sample of adolescents. *Journal of Adolescent Health, 46*(6), 545–552. https://doi.org/10.1016/j.jadohealth.2009.11.212

Ford, J. D., Hartman, J. K., Hawke, J., & Chapman, J. C. (2008). Traumatic victimization posttraumatic stress disorder, suicidal ideation, and substance abuse risk among juvenile justice-involved youths. *Journal of Child and Adolescent Trauma, 1*(1), 75–92. https://doi.org/10.1080/19361520801934456

Graduate School of Professional Psychology, University of Denver. (2021, March 5). Denver FIRST Juvenile Justice Project. *Redefining Mental Health* [podcast]. https://rmhatdu.podbean.com/e/denverfirst/

Hamby, S. L., Finkelhor, D., Ormrod, R. K., & Turner, H. A. (2004). *The Juvenile Victimization Questionnaire (JVQ): Administration and scoring manual.* Crimes Against Children Research Center.

Hodge, J. P., Holsinger, K., & Maziarka, K. (2015). Assessing the status of gender-specific programs through the lens of juvenile justice staff. *Women & Criminal Justice, 25*(3), 184–200. https://doi.org/10.1080/08974454.2014.989303

Jones, N. J., Brown, S. L., Wanamaker, K. A., & Greiner, L. E. (2014). A quantitative exploration of gendered pathways to crime in a sample of male and female juvenile offenders. *Feminist Criminology, 9*(2), 113–136. https://doi.org/10.1177/1557085113501850

Juvenile Justice and Delinquency Prevention Council (JJDPC). (2018). *Colorado's Three-Year Juvenile Justice and Delinquency Prevention Plan (2018–2020).* Retrieved from https://dcj.colorado.gov/boards-commissions/oajja-juvenile-justice-and-delinquency-prevention-council-jjdp

Kelley, A., Ertz, D., Witzel, M., Donahue, L., Red Thunder, M., Sipes, A., Posey, S., Campoli, J., Singleton, M., Hartley, C., BigFoot, D., Silovsky, J., & Routzen, J. (2024). *Restoring the Sacred Circle: A toolkit for American Indian and Alaska Native Tribes 2nd Ed.* National Center on the Sexual Behavior of Youth. University of Oklahoma Health Sciences Center.

Kerig, P. K. (2018). Polyvictimization and girls' involvement in the juvenile justice system: Investigating gender-differentiated patterns of risk, recidivism, and resilience. *Journal of Interpersonal Violence, 33*(5), 789–809. https://doi.org/10.1177/0886260517744843

Kerig, P. K., & Becker, S. P. (2012). Trauma and girls' delinquency. In S. Miller, L. Leve, & P. K. Kerig (Eds.), *Delinquent girls: Context, relationships, and adaptation* (pp. 119–143). Springer.

Kerig, P. K., Ford, J. D., & Olafson, E. (2014). *Assessing exposure to psychological trauma and posttraumatic stress in the juvenile justice population.* National Child Traumatic Stress Network. Retrieved from http://www.nctsn.org/sites/default/files/assets/pdfs/assessing_trauma_in_jj_2014.pdf

Kerig, P. K., & Modrowski, C. A. (2018). Testing gender-differentiated models of the mechanisms linking polyvictimization and youth offending: Numbing and callousness versus dissociation and borderline traits. *Journal of Trauma & Dissociation, 19*(3), 347–361. https://doi.org/10.1080/15299732.2018.1441355

Lipsey, M. W. (2009). The primary factors that characterize effective interventions with juvenile offenders: A meta-analytic overview. *Victims & Offenders, 4*(2), 124–147. https://doi.org/10.1080/15564880802612573

Mallet, C. A. (2017). The school-to-prison pipeline: Disproportionate impact on vulnerable children and adolescents. *Education and Urban Society, 49*(6), 563–592. https://doi.org/10.1177/0013124516644053

Mannarino, A., & Cohen, J. A. (1996). Family-related variables and psychological symptom formation in sexually abused girls. *Journal of Child Sexual Abuse, 5*(1), 105–120. https://doi.org/10.1300/J070v05n01_06

Marston, E. G., Russell, M. A., Obsuth, I., & Watson, G. K. (2012). Dealing with double jeopardy: Mental health disorders among girls in the juvenile justice system. In S. Miller, L. D. Leve, & P. K. Kerig (Eds.), *Delinquent girls: Contexts, relationships, and adaptation* (pp. 105–118). Springer.

Martin, A. N., McLeigh, J. D., & Lamminen, L. M. (2023). Examining the feasibility of telehealth Trauma-Focused Cognitive Behavioural Therapy (TF-CBT) with young people in foster care. *Journal of Child & Adolescent Trauma, 16*(4), 1079–1087. https://doi.org/10.1007/s40653-023-00538-w

McNeil, C. B., Robinson, C., Wallace, N. M., Quetsch, L. B., & Highlander, A. (2019). Parent-child interaction therapy. In B. H. Fiese, M. Celano, K. Deater-Deckard, E. N. Jouriles, & M. A. Whisman (Eds.), *APA handbook of contemporary family psychology: Family therapy and training* (pp. 377–391). American Psychological Association. https://doi.org/10.1037/0000101-023

Metzger, I. W., Anderson, R. E., Are, F., & Ritchwood, T. (2021). Healing interpersonal and racial trauma: Integrating racial socialization into trauma-focused cognitive behavioral therapy for African American youth. *Child Maltreatment, 26*(1), 17–27. https://doi.org/10.1177/1077559520921457

Metzger, I., Dandrige, A., Cohen, J. A., & Mannarino, A. P. (2023). *Integrating Trauma-Focused Cognitive Behavioral Therapy (TF-CBT) and racial socialization for Black youth and families: An implementation manual.* Allegheny Health Network.

Miller, F. G., & Lazowski, L. E. (1999). *SASSI-3 manual.* The SASSI Institute.

Moore, E., Gaskin, C., & Indig, D. (2013). Childhood maltreatment and post-traumatic stress disorder among incarcerated young offenders. *Child Abuse & Neglect, 37*(10), 861–870. https://doi.org/10.1016/j.chiabu.2013.07.012

Mulvey, E. P. (2011). *Highlights from Pathways to Desistance: A longitudinal study of serious adolescent offenders* (Juvenile Justice Fact Sheet). Washington, DC: U.S. Department of Justice, Office of Justice Programs, Office of Juvenile Justice and Delinquency Prevention.

Office of Juvenile Justice and Delinquency Prevention (OJJDP). (2019, October 31). *Statistical briefing book.* Online Retrieved from https://www.ojjdp.gov/ojstatbb/crime/qa05104.asp?qaDate=2018.

Phipps, R., & Thorne, S. (2019). Utilizing Trauma-Focused Cognitive Behavioral Therapy as a framework for addressing cultural trauma in African American children and adolescents: A proposal. *Professional Counselor, 9*(1), 35–50. https://doi.org/10.15241/rp.9.1.35

Puzzanchera, C., Sladky, A., & Kang, W. (2019). Easy access to juvenile populations: 1990–2018. Online. Available: https://www.ojjdp.gov/ojstatbb/ezapop/

Saar, M. S., Epstein, R., Rosenthal, L., & Vafa, Y. (2015). The sexual abuse to prison pipeline: The girls' story. Retrieved from: http://rights4girls.org/wp-content/uploads/r4g/2015/02/2015_COP_sexual-abuse_layout_web-1.pdf

Stewart, R. W., Orengo-Aguayo, R. E., Cohen, J. A., Mannarino, A. P., & de Arellano, M. A. (2017). A pilot study of trauma-focused cognitive–behavioral therapy delivered via telehealth technology. *Child Maltreatment, 22*(4), 324–333. https://doi.org/10.1177/1077559517725403

Stone, J. (2021, April 8). University of Denver launches program to help juvenile justice-involved girls. *DU Newsroom.* https://www.du.edu/news/university-denver-launches-program-help-juvenile-justice-involved-girls

Troutman, B. (2022). The IoWA-PCIT Parent Coaching Model. 10.1007/978-3-030-98570-7_2.

Turner, H. A., Shattuck, A., Finkelhor, D., & Hamby, S. (2016). Polyvictimization and youth violence exposure across contexts. *Journal of Adolescent Health, 58*(2), 208–214. https://doi.org/10.1016/j.jadohealth.2015.09.021

Walker, S. C., Muno, A., & Sullivan-Colglazier, C. (2015). Principles in practice: A multistage study of gender-responsive reforms in the juvenile justice system. *Crime & Delinquency, 61*(5), 742–766. https://doi.org/10.1177/0011128712449712

Wesely, J. K., & Dewey, S. C. (2018). Confronting gendered pathways to incarceration. *Social Justice, 45*(1(151)), 57–82.

Wolff, K. T., Baglivio, M. T., & Piquero, A. R. (2017). The relationship between adverse childhood experiences and recidivism in a sample of juvenile offenders in community-based treatment. *International Journal Offender Therapy and Comparative Criminology, 61*(11), 1210–1242. https://doi.org/10.1177/0306624X15613992

11

Interventions among Criminal Justice-Involved Persons with Mental Illness

Implementing *Changing Lives and Changing Outcomes* in Harris County

Daryl G. Kroner and Robert D. Morgan

Overview and Nature of Collaboration

Correctional samples will have between 15 percent and 75 percent with mental illness. With a narrower definition of mental illness, the percentages are lower and with a broader definition the percentages are higher, as we discuss in the next section. This chapter reviews an example of an intervention collaboration that occurred in a sample of criminal justice-involved persons with mental illness.

The collaboration was between the Harris County (Texas) Community Supervision and Corrections Department and Texas Tech University via the second author. The Statement of Work agreement stipulated that the second author would provide training on *Changing Lives and Changing Outcomes* (*CLCO*; Morgan et al., 2018), post-training consultations and assessment reports. The authors were compensated for the training, but there was no fee for the ongoing consultations or assessment reports. The second author retained the rights to publish, in collaboration with the Harris County treatment team, the treatment results as a program evaluation.

The Need: Overlap between Criminogenic Need and Mental Illness

There is substantial overlap between criminogenic need and mental illness among correctional samples. The evidence for this overlap and its pervasiveness comes from rates of mental illness within correctional samples, similarity of criminogenic need and mental illness profiles among varied samples, and from the statistical relationship between criminogenic need and mental illness within these samples. The relatively

Daryl G. Kroner and Robert D. Morgan, *Interventions among Criminal Justice-Involved Persons with Mental Illness*.
In: *The Path Forward*. Edited by: Kirk Heilbrun and David DeMatteo, Oxford University Press.
 DOI: 10.1093/9780197773031.003.0011

higher rates of mental health concerns among correctional samples have been well noted (broadly defined as 55 to 80 percent; Brink, 2005) and have continued to the present (Smith et al., 2022). In fact, the proportion of offenders with mental health concerns has increased, with one jurisdiction noting increases from 61 percent (2009) to 75 percent (2017) (Butler et al., 2022).

In a correctional mental health sample, the criminogenic need areas of antisocial attitudes had a similar profile as with offenders without mental health concerns (Morgan et al., 2010). In a slightly different sample comparison, psychiatric patients with criminal justice involvement presented with the same criminogenic need profile as those incarcerated offenders with mental health concerns (Gross & Morgan, 2013). Furthermore, these two samples had nearly identical psychopathology profiles.

A statistical relationship between criminogenic need/crime-causing factors and mental illness presents evidence of the overlap between these two areas. Such a relationship occurs with mediation models (Matejkowski et al., 2017), logistic regression models (Swartz & Lurigio, 2007), sequential analysis (Peterson et al., 2014), and percentage contrasts (Feder, 1991). Indeed, this overlap between criminogenic need and mental illness is pervasive. With psychiatric samples, this same overlap is found. Across two psychiatric inpatient samples, just over 50 percent of each sample had previous criminal justice involvement (Scanlon et al., 2023). The frequency of past criminal justice involvement among inpatient psychiatric patients is one type of evidence for this overlap. Another is the strength of the relationship between criminogenic need and mental illness. In both of these inpatient samples, the criminogenic need area of antisocial attitudes predicted various indexes of mental illness symptomology.

Not only is there an overlap and a relationship between criminogenic need and mental illness, but there is also an overlap between mental illness symptoms and negative criminal justice outcomes, such as violence. Epidemiological studies provide evidence that psychiatric patients are at a higher risk for violence (Arboleda-Flórez, 1998; Brennan et al., 2000; Elbogen & Johnson, 2009; Kooyman et al., 2007; Swanson et al., 1997). More recent epidemiological and summary studies also note the relationship between mental illness and violent outcomes (Sariaslan et al., 2020; Whiting et al., 2022; Witt et al., 2013). Whereas these epidemiological studies may not demonstrate a causal relationship between mental illness symptoms and outcomes, they do highlight the interconnectedness of mental illness symptoms and violent outcomes. It is this overlap between criminogenic need and mental illness symptoms that the CLCO intervention addresses.

Nature of the Intervention: CLCO

Changing Lives and Changing Outcomes (*CLCO*; Morgan et al., 2018) was developed in response to calls for an intervention that concurrently treats mental illness and criminal risk among criminal justice-involved persons (Draine et al., 2002; Hodgins, 2007; Morgan et al., 2012). CLCO is a treatment approach integrated at multiple levels. First, the intervention approach of CLCO draws upon the best practices in mental illness management and correctional rehabilitation (e.g., targeting known criminal risk factors). Second, cognitive-behavioral theory, social learning paradigms, and psychosocial rehabilitation models are woven into the program. CLCO is based upon the bi-adaptive model, in which individuals' criminalness and mental illness needs are conceptualized as overlapping co-occurring needs. The term *criminalness* captures antisocial behavior and related issues within the treatment context. Criminalness refers to the behavior that breaks laws, social conventions, and/or violates the rights and well-being of others (Morgan et al., 2018). Embedded into this definition is the propensity for these behaviors. These behaviors and propensities may or may not be the immediate antecedent to an arrestable offense. This would include abuse of sick leave, misusing office supplies, blaming others for crimes, misuse of medications, possession of stolen property, and violent crimes. Of note, criminalness is not the same as criminogenic risk factors. Criminalness refers to the continuum of non-productive, non-prosocial behaviors that avoid responsibility, violate the rights of others, and manipulate others. To some degree, all have varying degrees of criminalness. In contrast, criminogenic needs are specific areas that directly contribute to crime. For example, the use of alcohol that did not contribute to an offense would not be considered a criminogenic need. But the use of alcohol by a client to self-medicate would be considered criminalness. Criminalness is related to diagnostic-type labels (i.e., Antisocial Personality Disorder, psychopathy), but differs in that the cut-off nature of the diagnosis may have limited application with an intervention.

The label of criminalness is integrated into the intervention and is directly related to treatment progress along both the mental health and antisocial dimensions. Labeling clients' behaviors and related propensities this way may be at odds with some people-first language approaches, but it does have strong utility in the treatment context. The use of one word to refer to a gamut of behaviors and propensities has a simplicity to which most clients can immediately relate. This compares with terms of antisocial behaviors, Antisocial Personality Disorder, criminogenic need factor, etc., which are more cumbersome with greater definitional requirements. The word criminalness has an intuitiveness that most clients grasp without long, formal definitions. This intuitiveness allows direct application to oneself, but also in defining others' behaviors. In a group context, participants are comfortable (and at times overwilling) in pointing out the criminalness in other participants' behavior.

For a facilitator, there are three aspects of "criminalness" that make it a good fit within an intervention. First, the single word criminalness provides a useful heuristic to discuss all behaviors and propensities that lead to non-prosocial, non-responsible, and dysfunctional outcomes. Once defined, its utility becomes broad. Second, it is a construct that can be present in varied degrees. It is dynamic and changes over time. As a therapeutic tool, it can be used to point out deficiencies among clients, but also to reinforce therapeutic gains. Third, the focus of behaviors and propensities is amenable to being treatment targets (e.g., increasing the number of good days), whereas placing a client's shortcomings within a diagnosis does not easily provide access to resources for therapeutic change.

This bi-adaptive model then guides treatment provision as participants are challenged to develop new attitudes, associates, skills, and responsibilities to foster prosocial change. Both psychoeducational and psychotherapeutic approaches are combined to address not only strategies to effectively manage their criminalness and mental illness needs, but also to develop strategies for effective daily functioning. The central goals of CLCO are mental illness recovery and criminal and antisocial desistance, resulting in a better quality of life and positive life outcomes.

CLCO has nine thematically grouped therapeutic modules delivered across a total of 76 sessions: Preparing for Change (3 sessions); Mental Illness and Criminalness Awareness (8 sessions); Thoughts and Attitudes (13 sessions); Medication Adherence (5 sessions); Coping with Mental Illness and Criminalness (8 sessions); Emotions Management (10 sessions); Associates (10 sessions); Community Skills Development (e.g., general living skills; 9 sessions); and Substance Use (10 sessions). Individual sessions have a basic structure, resulting in a uniform delivery of the intervention materials. Thus, the treatment manual outlines specific learning objectives and exercises for each session. Sessions are structured to include both review and didactic components in individual and group formats. Each session begins with a brief check-in on participants' functioning (approximately 5–7 minutes), followed by a review of prior session material, collection of homework (if applicable), and an opportunity for questions (10–15 minutes). The majority of session time is subsequently devoted to discussion of new material and in-class exercises (75–85 minutes), as well as homework assignment (10–15 minutes). Total session duration thus approximates 1.5–2 hours, with a target length of 1 hour and 50 minutes.

The materials for the program are contained in a treatment manual and a participant workbook. The manual covers the requirements, suggested protocols, theoretical underpinnings, and outlined treatment modules. The workbook includes in-session handouts and worksheets to teach new content and skill development, as well as homework assignments that reinforce learning and retention of session material. Although the manual is available for purchase (https://www.routledge.com/A-Treatment-Manual-for-Justice-Involved-Persons-with Mental Illness-Changing-Lives-and-Changing-Outcomes/Morgan-Kroner-Mills/p/book/9781138700086) the workbook (450+ pages) is at no cost (URL address in the manual). Homework assignments completed outside of session are included in sixty-five of the seventy-six sessions (~86 percent). CLCO was developed for effective implementation across a variety of correctional and forensic settings in both individual and group formats, with a recommended group size of eight to ten participants. Although the program is cumulative in nature (i.e., sessions build upon prior material), open-enrollment groups are feasible, and the program is flexible to accommodate logistical constraints.

The application of CLCO described in this chapter occurs in a group setting in accordance with the program manual. Open enrollment allowed participants to begin classes at any point in the program, with the limitation that participants: (1) could not begin a module after it had already commenced; and (2) were required to complete the first module, Preparing for Change, before entering another module. Not all modules were completed in sequential order. Of the nine total program modules, five were implemented while participants were detained within a Harris County facility, while four were intended to be implemented following release into the community (staff reported inconsistent programming availability at the Dual Diagnosis Residential Program [DDRP] release). Program sessions were mostly conducted Monday through Friday. CLCO was the designated treatment program in the facility between 2015 and 2021.

Clients

Clients in this community-based intervention project were adult male and female individuals sentenced to probation in Harris County, Texas. Clients were mandated as a condition of their probation to a DDRP operated by the Harris County (Texas) Community Supervision and Corrections Department. Clients mandated to the DDRP met mental health, substance abuse, and criminal risk eligibility requirements. First, eligible mental health diagnoses and conditions were defined by the Texas Correctional Office on Offenders with Medical or Mental Impairments (TCOOMMI) to include major depressive disorder (single and recurrent episodes), schizoaffective disorder (bipolar and depressive types), schizophrenia (and other psychotic disorders), anxiety disorders (including posttraumatic stress disorder), delusional disorder, and "any other diagnosed mental health disorder that is severe or persistent in nature" (Texas State Legislature House Bill No. 1908, 2015). Clients eligible for DDRP placement also had a score less than fifty on the Global Assessment of Functioning (GAF) scale (*Diagnostic and Statistical Manual of Mental Disorders*, 4th ed., Text Revision [DSM-IV-TR], American Psychiatric Association [APA], 2000). Second, clients must also have been diagnosed with a substance use disorder. Third, they must have been of moderate to high risk for criminal recidivism as measured by the Texas Risk Assessment System (Texas Department of Criminal Justice, 2015).

Total length of treatment stay in the DDRP averaged between 150 and 180 days, which involved both residential and community supervision components. A solely community-based administration of CLCO may involve a longer completion time with fewer weekly sessions. The DDRP program utilized an open enrollment policy, such that residents entered the program at any module; however, residents could not enter once a module was already underway. Residents were required to complete Module 1 (Preparing for Change) prior to entering a group.

Providers

Treatment providers generally had a terminal master's degree and were licensed as a clinician. They were trained by the authors via multiple full-day workshops and transitioned to a train-the-trainer model halfway through this collaborative project. Treatment providers were trained in the theoretical underpinnings of CLCO, the structure and format of the intervention, implementation and treatment fidelity, and the assessment strategy and process. Following training, treatment providers participated in bi-weekly consultation calls (typically of 30 minutes) with the second author during the first year of program implementation. The purpose of these calls was to address CLCO program questions, implementation and fidelity issues, client issues (e.g., resistance), and treatment barriers.

Assessment Procedure

An assessment battery was implemented as recommended in the CLCO manual as a treatment tool, and to evaluate treatment effectiveness (e.g., client improvement). Measures used in this project included the *Diagnostic and Statistical Manual of Mental Disorders* (5th ed.; American Psychiatric Association, 2013) Self-Rated Level 1 Cross-Cutting Symptom Measure-Adult (Narrow et al., 2013); Medication Adherence Scale (MARS; Thompson et al., 2000), Recovery Assessment Scale (RAS, Giffort et al., 1995), Positive and Negative Affect Schedule (PANAS; Watson et al., 1988), Psychological Inventory of Criminal Thinking Styles-Short Form (PICTS-SF; Walters, 2006), Measure of Criminal Attitudes and Associates (MCAA; Mills & Kroner, 2001), Brief Situational Confidence Questionnaire (BSCQ; Breslin et al., 2000), Working Alliance Inventory (WAI; Horvath & Greenberg, 1989), and the Client Satisfaction Questionnaire (CSQ; Larsen et al., 1979). It is noted that the majority of these measures are in the public domain, but the CSQ and PANAS were purchased for purposes of this collaborative project.

Clients completed the assessment measures during the regular course of treatment as outlined in the CLCO manual following a pre–mid-post treatment paradigm. Clients completed the pre-treatment assessment phase prior to beginning the treatment program, the mid-treatment assessment at approximately two months after the initial assessment, and the post-treatment assessment phase approximately four months following the initial assessment. Residents completed the Self-Rated Level 1 Cross-Cutting Symptom Measure-Adult, MARS, RAS, PANAS, PICTS-SF, MCAA, and the BSCQ at both pre- and post-treatment assessments, whereas the WAI and CSQ-8 were completed only at post-treatment. As this was a real-world treatment implementation project (without research grant funding), assessments were administered by treatment providers. Assessment data were sent to the second author at his academic institution for clinical interpretation. Assessment results were returned to DDRP treatment providers for use in treatment sessions in accordance with the CLCO program.

Keys to an Effective Intervention

Keys to an effective intervention entail both facilitator and administrative efforts. For the facilitator, past person-centered/group training, therapeutic alliance skills, and a balance between criminal justice approaches and mental health are core to the delivery of CLCO. For the administrator, issues include regular consulting/training, adequate facilitator/client ratios, and intervention delivery integrity.

The training of the CLCO facilitator will contribute to an effective intervention. A main premise of the intervention strategy is that the intervention be person-based. Thus, the facilitators need to have training reflecting this CLCO emphasis. For example, a graduate degree in criminal justice will be insufficient for effective delivery. CLCO is therapeutic in nature, and lacks a direct script. The manual and workbook provide a guide for the intervention but do not detail the application of the intervention principles. The facilitator is expected to draw upon their therapeutic expertise in the delivery of the content. For example, in reviewing the homework on changing automatic thoughts, stated goals of the exercise are to teach participants on how to monitor and how to challenge their automatic thoughts. Directions include to "provide feedback to participants ..." and "facilitate a group discussion on ...." To accomplish both tasks well, an understanding of the psychological role of automatic thoughts in behavior is required. In addition, group work and using the group dynamic as a therapeutic tool are essential for completing this aspect of the intervention.

The ability of facilitators to develop a therapeutic alliance is essential for effective delivery of CLCO. Attempting to change with those who have a high level of criminalness and significant mental health issues provides interpersonal challenges in developing a sense of collaboration. Meta-analysis has shown that therapeutic alliance is basic for therapeutic change among those with mental illness and those who have been justice-involved (Flückiger et al., 2018). With CLCO, therapeutic alliance moderates treatment gains (Scanlon et al., 2022). At the low, medium, and high levels of working alliance, significant pre- and post-reductions were found for depression, anxiety, anger, and mania. The highest level of working alliance had the strongest effects. For criminal thinking pre- and post-reductions, therapeutic alliance did moderate the change, but only at medium and high levels of therapeutic alliance. Overall, these results suggest that working alliance is necessary for treatment reductions, with greater importance for the reduction of criminal thinking.

A balance between a criminal justice approach to intervention (i.e., grounded in Risk-Need-Responsivity principles) and a mental health (principles of psychiatric rehabilitation) is necessary for effective delivery of CLCO. Most facilitators will lean one way or the other; thus, for most, some additional training will be helpful in the area in which they have less familiarity.

For the administrator, ensuring regular consultation and training will be central to the effective delivery of CLCO. Providing consultation throughout delivery is important for any intervention, as program drift will occur over time. This is even more pertinent for CLCO, as the facilitators are independent licensed professionals. They are being asked to draw upon their professional experience in the delivery of the intervention. They will naturally want to use their strengths, possibly to the exclusion of other essential aspects of the intervention. In addition to treatment fidelity, there are several other reasons to have ongoing consultation. Consulting will help contribute to an improved case conceptualization and implementation of evidence-based strategies. For example, it can facilitate seeing how to deal with a difficult group situation and how to integrate that experience into therapeutic progress. Furthermore, consultation, to some degree, can assist with the overall training of the facilitators. This is not the primary task, but there will be aspects of the consultation that will contribute to the skill development of the facilitators.

Receiving positive comments on what is going well in the intervention contributes to the morale of the facilitator. Providing intervention to this type of clientele is difficult, especially as therapists typically receive little feedback that things are going well. With these clients, they rarely come back and say that they appreciated your efforts. In fact, there may be legal reasons preventing such a discourse. Nevertheless, receiving feedback regarding what is going well increases one's confidence in conducting future sessions.

Consultation normalizes treatment struggles and failed efforts. When a client (or group) is not making therapeutic gains, facilitators often try a different approach to the issue. Not every effort is going to be successful. Normalizing treatment struggles assists in supporting facilitators for continued involvement in delivering interventions.

Often, assessments are perceived as having little value when the intervention, by itself, is viewed as a full-time endeavor. Assessments have multiple roles in CLCO, including direct feedback for the clients. Consultations can help the facilitator, especially those naïve to the use of assessments as a therapeutic tool, to see how assessment can be integrated into the treatment process. The monitoring of assessment plans through consultations will assist the assessment plan to stay on track.

There are costs to the consultation process. First, it requires time from the facilitators. As a result of this time, the consultation process, even if put in place, may not be utilized. Another drawback to the consultation process is that reliance on consultations may be done in lieu of professional development through accessing scholarly literature for solutions. Third, there is a financial cost to the agency for the consultations.

Foundations and Support for the CLCO Intervention

Theoretical

The basic theoretical foundation for CLCO is the bi-adaptive model. This model focuses on both criminalness and mental illness. As noted above, there is a pervasive overlap between criminalness and mental illness. An overlap, though, does not mean that there is a causal relationship with negative outcomes. The consideration of causation in this relationship involves a complex picture. It appears that psychosis has a small, but robust relationship with criminal justice outcomes, including violence (Douglas et al., 2009). With certain studies, a direct relationship is not observed with recidivism, but an indirect relationship between mental illness and recidivism occurs when the level of criminogenic need is considered (Matejkowski et al., 2017). These direct/indirect results suggest that there are multiple ways that criminalness and mental illness can interact.

Similar to substance abuse co-morbidity, the interaction between crimimalness and mental illness can involve an additive effect (e.g., criminalness and unmedicated psychosis both make behavioral control difficult), a synergistic effect on each other (e.g., taking of street drugs interacts with prescribed psychotropic medications resulting in out of control behaviors), a sequential effect (e.g., leads to a period of destabilization and not going to work, which results in street crime for necessities), or operate in a parallel fashion with minimal crossover effect (e.g., psychosis leads to unstable relationships and antisocial cognitions lead to acting out). A good example of this complexity comes from the results using the National Epidemiologic Survey on Alcohol and Related Conditions study. Grant et al. (2004) reported on the co-occurring substance use disorders, and mood and anxiety disorders. They examined the eleven separate DSM–IV substance use disorders over a twelve-month period. The large sample (N = 43,093) did allow analyses of specific questions related to interactions. For example, researchers considered whether a disorder was substance-induced. Approximately 20 percent of the respondents with any substance use disorder had at least one mood disorder (17.7 percent with anxiety disorder) during the same 12-month period. Respondents with the more severe diagnosis of substance abuse were more likely to have major depression and specific phobia than other anxiety or mood-related disorders. Of note, they found that a small percentage of those who experienced mood (1 percent) or anxiety (1/5 of a percent) disorders were exclusively substance induced (no 12-month substance use disorder). Clearly, there can be multiple interactive effects of substance use on mood and anxiety disorders.

It is this background that provides the impetus for the bi-adaptive model. The bi-adaptive model suggests that there is a synergistic interplay between criminalness and mental illness that increases antisocial/criminal behavior, along with the risk of mental illness relapse. There is a destabilizing effect of each of the areas of criminalness and mental illness. Drawing upon a basic premise from the RNR model (that which causes crime needs to be addressed), it is proposed that for an effective intervention, both criminalness and mental illness need to be addressed.

Evidence

Based upon the bi-adaptive model, a subsequent question is to examine the support for changing both dimensions in the CLCO program. Addressing both areas of criminogenic need and mental health symptoms has shown effectiveness in reducing self-reported criminal thinking and mental health symptoms. With the current Harris County CLCO sample, reductions in depression (larger for females), anger (larger for females), mania, anxiety, somatic illnesses (larger for females), and dissociation (larger for females) occurred (Gaspar et al., 2019). This study also found reductions in antisocial attitudes of entitlement, intent, and violence. Reactive criminal thinking also had similar reductions. With a sample of psychiatric prison and residential treatment participants, pre-post treatment changes were reported for symptom distress, depression, anxiety, hostility, paranoid ideation, and psychoticism (Morgan et al., 2014). As with the Gaspar et al. study, reductions in reactive criminal thinking were also found. Of note, reductions in symptom distress and depression had moderately large effect sizes.

The need for integrating criminalness and mental illness symptoms was highlighted in a process outcome study (Scanlon & Morgan, 2021). This study made a comparison of the treatment gains to the Mental Illness and Criminalness Awareness module and the full treatment pre-post results. In addition to reductions in criminogenic need and mental illness symptoms, increases in overall psychological well-being were noted (Scanlon & Morgan, 2021). The effect size of this change was considered large. Overall, as with the Gaspar results, reductions were noted across criminogenic need and mental illness domains. Of note, the results on the single module only noted reductions in the self-reported mental illness symptoms. The change dynamics are not uniform within the criminalness or mental illness domains, suggesting that a full integration of both areas will result in overall optimal treatment results.

Professional Contributions

The theoretical and scientific foundations, subsequent beta testing, and published evaluations place CLCO in a category of evidence-based practice. Even with the scholarly foundation of CLCO, not all aspects of treatment delivery can be covered by past research. Thus, drawing upon the years of clinical practice of the authors, some practical approaches were adapted into the formulation and delivery of CLCO. One of these professional-based guidelines is highlighted below.

The emphasis on ensuring simplicity in the core CLCO treatment heuristics was informed by professionally-based experience. The intended criminal justice-involved participants of CLCO typically have lower levels of academic cognitive functioning. Thus, to maximize the application of CLCO across these populations, efforts were made to use simplistic heuristics (Morgan et al., 2006). The basic evaluation heuristic used in CLCO is a stoplight. The use of a stoplight is relevant for nearly all treatment participants. Even if they do not drive, red is associated with "stop," and the colors of red, yellow, and green are used in most subway contexts. The stoplight is used to evaluate most decision points in the treatment process. Red is indicative of nonproductive thoughts, emotions, or behaviors, violations of goals, or outright criminalness. Yellow involves caution. In many contexts yellow leads to red. In individualizing the intervention, participants often begin to view the specific contexts or decision points that were previously yellow as turning to red. For example, a life-long friend who has committed a crime in the past, but currently is not participating in criminal activities, is often viewed as a "yellow" associate in the beginning stages of evaluating associates. As the discussion regarding associates moves forward, these associates often become "red."

Simplistic heuristics not only account for participant characteristics, but also assist in maintaining change over time. Some conceptual content areas used in the program are complex (e.g., the role of automatic thoughts in the production of behavior), yet need to be presented in a simple form. This professionally based aspect of the intervention requires considerable skill. We are asking clients to change difficult aspects of their lives (if it were easy, they likely would not be involved in the criminal justice system and would be able to effectively manage their mental illness). Repeatedly utilizing a simple evaluative heuristic throughout the intervention will assist the participant to integrate this into how they view and evaluate future risky thoughts, emotions, and contexts. Thus, there is a change maintenance component to using simplistic heuristics.

Beginning and Development

Original Idea

Preliminary work for CLCO began from the independent efforts of the developers: Morgan on criminogenic treatment and forensic mental health interventions, and Kroner and Mills on criminal risk and program development (e.g., Associates for Success). We met in 2003 at the annual meeting of the American Psychological Association (Toronto, Canada), and began discussions of possible collaborations. The foundational discussions for CLCO then began in 2004 and continued for approximately eight years. During this time, a yearly research retreat (continuing to the present) among the three authors of CLCO was held. The development of CLCO was furthered when the lead author of CLCO obtained an NIMH R34 (treatment development grant) to examine the occurrence of mental illness and criminalness within a prison sample. Drawing upon these data and the clinical experiences of each of the authors led to the foundational ideas in formulating the CLCO program.

The aim of CLCO was to offer a comprehensive and holistic intervention program that targeted the co-occurring needs (criminogenic and mental health) of justice-involved persons with mental illness. The goal was to simultaneously facilitate recovery while reducing criminal risk (with the ultimate goal of increased wellness and public safety). To accomplish this goal, we identified the primary needs from the criminal justice and correctional rehabilitation literature, and the treatment needs of persons with mental illness from the psychiatric rehabilitation literature. We identified eight overlapping needs which included: (1) maladaptive cognitions, (2) unproductive associates, (3) risk (criminal and mental illness relapse) management, (4) symptom awareness, (5) symptom management, (6) treatment compliance, (7) skill development, and (8) managing substance misuse. These overlapping issues formed the basis of the eight treatment modules that were ultimately included in CLCO (of note, CLCO has nine modules as it begins with "Preparing for Change," which is a modification of motivational interviewing).

Program Considerations

The uniqueness of CLCO is that treatment of mental illness and criminalness is integrated into each of the eight treatment modules. For example, teaching clients with mental illness about the etiology, life course, typical symptomology, and treatments for mental illness (e.g., mental illness awareness) is an essential element of psychiatric rehabilitation. It is equally relevant for justice-involved individuals to learn of their criminalness, and especially the antecedents and associated risk for future criminal behavior. Both of these areas are integrated into the "Mental Illness and Criminalness Awareness" module. Thus, for the identified overlapping needs (mental health and criminogenic), we adopted best practices and integrated these practices into the eight therapeutic modules such that each module addressed the co-occurring nature of mental illness and criminalness. Once the multi-level integration was established, we next identified primary intervention strategies to include heuristics and skill development that would be used throughout the program. As noted above, one such strategy is the stoplight mnemonic. The aim was to have universal concepts throughout the program to allow focus on skill development without having to learn complex concepts. We also rooted the intervention in a cognitive-behavioral framework given success of this theoretical model in both correctional rehabilitation and psychiatric rehabilitation efforts. Finally, we developed the bi-adaptive model which emphasized the integration of mental illness and criminalness (bi) and building off strengths to facilitate positive outcomes (adaptive).

Next, each of the authors wrote various modules, with the lead author reviewing all to ensure that there was uniformity throughout. During 2012, implementation began with practicum graduate students delivering the CLCO components. This beta testing resulted in changes to the exercises, session structure, and content of the initial program. For example, a lack of pre-post change for the Thoughts and Attitudes module resulted in this module being increased from ten to thirteen sessions. Also, based on feedback, efforts were made to reduce the needed reading level for program participants. A draft of the workbook was completed in 2015. The manual was completed in the year of publication (2018).

Generalizability

As noted, CLCO was designed to be administered in multiple settings, including forensic hospitals, prisons, and probation/parole settings. In addition, the program can be administered in a group or individual format. With the complexities of the mental health and criminal justice system, two CLCO-derivative programs have been created and implemented. One version is designed for restrictive housing units (*A Mental Health Treatment Program for Inmates in Restrictive Housing: Stepping Up, Stepping Out*, Batastini et al., 2019). The second version is for jail populations (Scanlon et al., 2024).

The restrictive housing version *Stepping Up, Stepping Out* (SUSO) accommodates a typical restrictive housing unit that has higher levels of security and related physical limitations. SUSO was developed for inmates with significant mental health concerns, but inmates with less severe mental illness symptoms will be appropriate candidates for the program. In terms of the instructional components, SUSO has the guide for facilitators and the inmate workbook within one main manual. Accompanying eResources are referenced throughout the book. Like CLCO, SUSO is based on the bi-adaptive model. Integrating intervention for antisocial behaviors and mental illness symptoms, the targeted outcomes focus on issues related to restrictive housing. Thus, the aims of SUSO are to enable inmates to successfully move out of restrictive housing and prevent them from returning to long-term isolation. Similar to CLCO, SUSO is based on psychotherapeutic and psychoeducational approaches. SUSO is conceptualized as a "gateway intervention." Successful program engagement does not have "recovery" as its goal. The intention is to reduce an inmate's risk sufficiently to allow a safe transition into the prison general population. For the facilitator, SUSO accommodates the safety and physical limitations of restrictive housing, while still delivering mental health and correctional-based interventions. The self-directed nature of the program reduces the emphasis on confidential space that is often not available in a restrictive housing context. There is an emphasis on rule compliance and adaptive behaviors, which should facilitate the release back into the general population.

SUSO has nine modules: (1) Understanding Change and Making It Happen: An Introduction; (2) Surviving Solitary: What to Expect and How to Cope; (3) Suicide and Self-Injurious Behavior: Protecting You from You; (4) Understanding My Emotions: Identifying and Dealing with Anger, Fear, and other Frustrating Feelings; (5) Exploring My Mental Illness and Criminalness: Where It Comes From, What It Looks Like, and How to Recognize It; (6) Managing My Mental Illness and Criminalness: Improving Functioning and Preventing Relapse; (7) Seeking Supportive Allies: Finding Helpful Others Among the Crowd; (8) Integrating "Us" and "Them": Improving Inmate-Staff Relations; and (9) Road Map to Recovery: Creating Your Relapse Prevention Plan.

The SUSO format is largely self-directed. Inmates complete the handouts and exercises from each module on their own. Facilitator guidance occurs contingent on how much staff contact is available. Each module addresses a specific problem area and reflects a logical progression. The first addresses basic treatment concepts, then immediate stressors related to segregation, then more global issues within the individual, and finally relapse prevention. The modules are not designed to be standalone; they integrate broader concepts into all nine modules to create a coherent and consistent program for inmates detained in segregated housing units.

An empirical evaluation of SUSO occurred with inmates from the Missouri Department of Corrections (Batastini et al., 2021). The thirty-nine participants with pre-post data were housed in a long-term administrative segregation unit. Pre-post intervention reductions (medium effect sizes) were noted on measures of emotional distress and criminal cognitions, but there were minimal reductions in criminal thinking. As in the beta testing of CLCO's criminal awareness module, particular attention was needed to the criminal thinking component of SUSO. In addition to the overall pre-post measures, each module had a pre-post content quiz. Overall, the average pass rate between pre-post scores across the modules increased from 63.73 percent to 84.52 percent. Regarding working alliance, the post-intervention results suggest that the participants had positive perceptions of the facilitator.

Providing interventions in a jail context has its own challenges, one of which is the short-term stays. To address this concern, CLCO-9 was developed, which involves nine sessions and can be administered within three weeks. Using both qualitative and quantitative approaches, Scanlon et al. (2024) evaluated CLCO-9 among twenty-nine participants and six jail administrators. Three themes related to program feasibility emerged among treatment participants. The first theme was Jail factors, in which treatment participants discussed the difficulties (staff unaware of the program, staff confiscating homework) in treatment participation. The second theme was Individual Contextual factors. These involve limited English proficiency, side-effect issues with medications, and legal problems.

The third theme was The Program, which involved two subthemes. The first subtheme was Treatment Targets as Obstacles. This area highlighted how both criminalness and mental illness make it more difficult to engage in the program and complete the program. The second subtheme involved Finishing the Program. This focuses on participants' difficulties and some ambivalence in completing the program. Even with the difficulties noted, all the treatment participants found the program to be doable. From the administrators' perspective, they found CLCO-9 to be an intervention that was feasible. The overall success of brief jail interventions is reinforced by the effectiveness of continuity of behavioral health care for released offenders (Smith et al., 2022).

Conclusion

Interventions for criminal justice-involved persons with mental illness can be developed and implemented with positive results. Such interventions need to target both criminalness and mental illness. Due to the resources required for such an intervention, collaborations between university-affiliated research teams and service delivery agencies will set the stage for optimal implementation.

Integrating criminalness and mental illness is key for effective interventions among criminal justice-involved persons with mental illness. Turning this endeavor into a practical intervention involved drawing upon the empirical literature (usually meta-analyses), strong psychological theory (e.g., Risk Need Responsivity framework, conceptual model of triadic reciprocal causation [Bandura, 1989]), and past clinical experience. Each of these areas is broad in scope. Guiding what to include was the criterion of considering what would provide treatment results in the most simplistic form. Thus, sessions have the same format, heuristics are simple and repeated, and a simple building block approach is used to develop a relapse plan. Replicating this approach would involve a strong collaboration, planning for multiple stages of development, and understanding multiple approaches to intervention.

References

American Psychiatric Association. (2000). *Diagnostic and statistical manual of mental disorders* (4th ed., text rev.). Author.

American Psychiatric Association. (2013). *Diagnostic and statistical manual of mental disorders* (5th ed.). Author.

Arboleda-Flórez, J. (1998). Mental illness and violence: An epidemiological appraisal of the evidence. *Canadian Journal of Psychiatry. Revue Canadienne de Psychiatrie*, *43*(10), 989–996.

Bandura, A. (1989). Human agency in social cognitive theory. *American Psychologist*, *44*(9), 1175–1184. https://doi.org/10.1037/0003-066X.44.9.1175

Batastini, A. B., Lester, M. E., Morgan, R. D., & Atterberry, E. (2021). Stepping Up, Stepping Out: A program description and preliminary findings. *Psychological Services, 18*(4), 679–688. https://doi.org/10.1037/ser0000430

Batastini, A. B., Morgan, R. D., Kroner, D. G., & Mills, J. F. (2019). *A mental health treatment program for inmates in restrictive housing: Stepping Up, Stepping Out.* Routledge. https://doi.org/10.4324/9781315180755

Brennan, P., Mednick, S., & Hodgins, S. (2000). Major mental disorders and criminal violence in a Danish birth cohort. *Archives of General Psychiatry, 57*(5), 494–500. https://doi.org/10.1001/archpsyc.57.5.494

Breslin, F. C., Sobell, L. C., Sobell, M. B., & Agrawal, S. (2000). A comparison of a brief and long version of the Situational Confidence Questionnaire. *Behaviour Research and Therapy, 38*(12), 1211–1220.

Brink, J. (2005). Epidemiology of mental illness in a correctional system. *Current Opinion in Psychiatry, 18*(5), 536–541.

Butler, A., Nicholls, T., Samji, H., Fabian, S., & Lavergne, M. R. (2022). Prevalence of mental health needs, substance use, and co-occurring disorders among people admitted to prison. *Psychiatric Services, 73*(7), 737–744. https://doi.org/10.1176/appi.ps.202000927

Douglas, K. S., Guy, L. S., & Hart, S. D. (2009). Psychosis as a risk factor for violence to others: A meta-analysis. *Psychological Bulletin, 135*(5), 679–706. https://doi.org/10.1037/a0016311

Draine, J., Salzer, M. S., Culhane, D. P., & Hadley, T. R. (2002). Role of social disadvantage in crime, joblessness, and homelessness among persons with serious mental illness. *Psychiatric Services, 53*(5), 565–573.

Elbogen, E. B., & Johnson, S. C. (2009). The intricate link between violence and mental disorder: Results from the National Epidemiologic Survey on Alcohol and Related Conditions. *Archives of General Psychiatry, 66*(2), 152–161. https://doi.org/10.1001/archgenpsychiatry.2008.537

Feder, L. (1991). A comparison of the community adjustment of mentally ill offenders with those from the general prison population: An 18-month follow-up. *Law and Human Behavior, 15*(5), 477–493. https://doi.org/10.1007/BF01650290

Flückiger, C., Del Re, A. C., Wampold, B. E., & Horvath, A. O. (2018). The alliance in adult psychotherapy: A meta-analytic synthesis. *Psychotherapy, 55*(4), 316–340. https://doi.org/10.1037/pst0000172

Gaspar, M., Brown, L., Ramler, T., Scanlon, F., Gigax, G., Ridley, K., & Morgan, R. D. (2019). Therapeutic outcomes of changing lives and changing outcomes for male and female justice involved persons with mental illness. *Criminal Justice and Behavior, 46*(12), 1678–1699. https://doi.org/10.1177/0093854819879743

Giffort, D., Schmook, A., Woody, C., Vollendorf, C., & Gervain, M. (1995). *Recovery Assessment Scale.* Human Services Research Institute.

Grant, B. F., Stinson, F. S., Dawson, D. A., Chou, P., Dufour, M. C., Compton, W., Pickering, R. P., & Kaplan, K. (2004). Prevalence and co-occurrence of substance use disorders and independent mood and anxiety disorders: Results from the national epidemiologic survey on alcohol and related conditions. *Archives of General Psychiatry, 61*(8), 807–816. https://doi.org/10.1001/archpsyc.61.8.807

Gross, N. R., & Morgan, R. D. (2013). Understanding persons with mental illness who are and are not criminal justice involved: A comparison of criminal thinking and psychiatric symptoms. *Law and Human Behavior, 37*(3), 175–186. https://doi.org/10.1037/lhb0000013

Hodgins, S. (2007). Persistent violent offending: What do we know? *The British Journal of Psychiatry, 190*(49), s12–s14. https://doi.org/10.1192/bjp.190.5.s12

Horvath, A. O., & Greenberg, L. S. (1989). Development and validation of the Working Alliance Inventory. *Journal of Counseling Psychology, 36*(2), 223–233.

Kooyman, I., Dean, K., Harvey, S., & Walsh, E. (2007). Outcomes of public concern in schizophrenia. *The British Journal of Psychiatry, 191*(50), s29–s36. https://doi.org/10.1192/bjp.191.50.s29

Larsen, D. L., Attkisson, C. C., Hargreaves, W. A., & Nguyen, T. D. (1979). Assessment of client/patient satisfaction: Development of a general scale. *Evaluation and Program Planning, 2*(3), 197–207.

Matejkowski, J., Conrad, A., & Ostermann, M. (2017). Does early onset of criminal behavior differentiate for whom serious mental illness has a direct or indirect effect on recidivism? *Law and Human Behavior, 41*(1), 68–79. https://doi.org/10.1037/lhb0000231

Mills, J. F., & Kroner, D. G. (2001). *Measures of Criminal Attitudes and Associates (MCAA).* Unpublished instrument and user guide.

Morgan, R., Fisher, W., Duan, N., Mandracchia, J., & Murray, D. (2010). Prevalence of criminal thinking among state prison inmates with serious mental illness. *Law and Human Behavior, 34*(4), 324–336. https://doi.org/10.1007/s10979-009-9182-z

Morgan, R. D., Flora, D. B., Kroner, D. G., Mills, J. F., Varghese, F., & Steffan, J. S. (2012). Treating offenders with mental illness: A research synthesis. *Law and Human Behavior, 36*(1), 37–50. https://doi.org/10.1037/h0093964

Morgan, R., Kroner, D., & Mills, J. (2006). Group psychotherapy in prison: Facilitating change inside the walls. *Journal of Contemporary Psychotherapy, 36(3)*, 137–144. https://doi.org/10.1007/BF02729057

Morgan, R. D., Kroner, D. G., & Mills, J. F. (2018). *A treatment manual for justice involved persons with mental illness: Changing Lives and Changing Outcomes.* Routledge.

Morgan, R. D., Kroner, D. G., Mills, J. F., Bauer, R. L., & Serna, C. (2014). Treating justice involved persons with mental illness: Preliminary evaluation of a comprehensive treatment program. *Criminal Justice and Behavior, 41*(7), 902–916. https://doi.org/10.1177/0093854813508553

Narrow, W. E., Clarke, D. E., Kuramoto, S. J., Kraemer, H. C., Kupfer, D. J., Greiner, L., & Regier, D. A. (2013). DSM-5 field trials in the United States and Canada, part III:

Development and reliability testing of cross-cutting symptom assessment for DSM-5. *American Journal of Psychiatry, 170*(1), 71–82.

Peterson, J. K., Skeem, J., Kennealy, P., Bray, B., & Zvonkovic, A. (2014). How often and how consistently do symptoms directly precede criminal behavior among offenders with mental illness? *Law and Human Behavior, 38*(5), 439–449. https://doi.org/10.1037/lhb0000075

Sariaslan, A., Arseneault, L., Larsson, H., Lichtenstein, P., & Fazel, S. (2020). Risk of subjection to violence and perpetration of violence in persons with psychiatric disorders in Sweden. *JAMA Psychiatry, 77*(4), 359–367. https://doi.org/10.1001/jamapsychiatry.2019.4275

Scanlon, F., Hirsch, S., & Morgan, R. D. (2022). The relation between the working alliance on mental illness and criminal thinking among justice-involved people with co-occurring mental illness and substance use disorders. *Journal of Consulting and Clinical Psychology, 90*(3), 282–288. https://doi.org/10.1037/ccp0000719

Scanlon, F., & Morgan, R. D. (2021). The active ingredients in a treatment for justice-involved persons with mental illness: The importance of addressing mental illness and criminal risk. *Psychological Services, 18*(4), 474–483. https://doi.org/10.1037/ser0000411

Scanlon, F., Morgan, R. D., & Aceves, D. (2024). Implementing a treatment for people with serious mental illness in jail: A mixed-methods study of stakeholder perspectives on feasibility and acceptability. *Administration and Policy in Mental Health and Mental Health Services Research.* https://doi.org/10.1007/s10488-024-01380-4

Scanlon, F., Morgan, R. D., Mitchell, S. M., Bolaños, A. D., & Bartholomew, N. R. (2023). Criminal risk and mental illness in psychiatric inpatient units: An opportunity to provide psychological services for unmet criminogenic needs. *Psychological Services, 20*(3), 565–575. https://doi.org/10.1037/ser0000612

Smith, J. L., Khatri, U. G., Olubiyi, O., Hadley, T., Lim, S., Mandell, D., & Kang-Yi, C. (2022). Behavioral health service use post-jail release and reduced risk of return to jail. *Journal of Community Psychology, 50*(7), 3044–3053. https://doi.org/10.1002/jcop.22813

Swanson, J., Estroff, S., Swartz, M., Borum, R., Lachicotte, W., Zimmer, C., & Wagner, R. (1997). Violence and severe mental disorder in clinical and community populations: The effects of psychotic symptoms, comorbidity, and lack of treatment. *Psychiatry: Interpersonal and Biological Processes, 60*(1), 1–22.

Swartz, J. A., & Lurigio, A. J. (2007). Serious mental illness and arrest the generalized mediating effect of substance use. *Crime & Delinquency, 53*(4), 581–604. https://doi.org/10.1177/0011128706288054

Texas Department of Criminal Justice [TDCJ]. (2015). The Texas Risk Assessment System: A new direction in supervision planning. *Criminal Justice Connections, 22*(3), 1–2. Retrieved from https://www.tdcj.texas.gov/connections/JanFeb2015/Images/JanFeb2015_agency_TRASS.pdf

Texas State Legislature. (2015). Texas House Bill No. 1908. Retrieved from https://legiscan.com/TX/text/HB1908/2015

Thompson, K., Kulkarni, J., & Sergejew, A. A. (2000). Reliability and validity of a new Medication Adherence Rating Scale (MARS) for the psychoses. *Schizophrenia Research*, *42*(3), 241–247.

Walters, G. D. (2006). *The Psychological Inventory of Criminal Thinking Styles (PICTS): Professional manual.* Center for Lifestyle Studies.

Watson, D., Clark, L. A., & Tellegen, A. (1988). Development and validation of brief measures of positive and negative affect: The PANAS scales. *Journal of Personality and Social Psychology*, *54*(6), 1063–1070.

Whiting, D., Gulati, G., Geddes, J. R., & Fazel, S. (2022). Association of schizophrenia spectrum disorders and violence perpetration in adults and adolescents from 15 countries: A systematic review and meta-analysis. *JAMA Psychiatry*, *79*(2), 120–132. https://doi.org/10.1001/jamapsychiatry.2021.3721

Witt, K., Dorn, R. van, & Fazel, S. (2013). Risk factors for violence in psychosis: Systematic review and meta-regression analysis of 110 studies. *PLOS ONE*, *8*(2), e55942. https://doi.org/10.1371/journal.pone.0055942

12
Forensic Consultation

Joel A. Dvoskin

This chapter will focus on consultation, putting scientific and professional knowledge to work in real-world settings. I will discuss how to become a consultant, and more importantly, my ideas about how to do it well. I will discuss the ethical rules, challenges, and pitfalls of consulting.

Get Over Yourself: Consultants Are Like Bees

I don't know much about bees, but I'm told that they pick up pollen from one flower with pollen to spare, deposit it in another flower that needs it, and everybody profits. A good consultant will see something done well in one place (even if it's not the focus of their visit) and remember it. Soon, they will go someplace else that is failing miserably at the very same task, whereupon they will share the knowledge where it is needed. (You know, like a bee.)

Since you're going to be a bee, be a good one. It is tempting to think of myself as a person with extraordinary knowledge and wisdom, one who will know the answer to every question. This approach is seductive as it feeds my narcissism, and therein lies the danger. Narcissistic consultants never get invited back, and seldom get referrals from past clients. So, this chapter is about humility. (Luckily, I am the world's leading expert on humility, so pay attention.)

More importantly, I don't know enough to be a know-it-all, and neither do you. The world of consulting will present you with a literally endless array of challenges, situations, and kinds of people. Instead of pretending to have an answer for every question, good consultants think of themselves, above all, as problem solvers. And the problems you will be asked to solve are often complex; if they weren't, the client would have solved them already, without paying you.

To solve complex problems, it is almost always necessary to be part of a team (see, e.g., Goltz et al., 2008), and the best teammates are going to be your clients and their employees. The people who know the most about any situation are the people who already work there. Since the problem is unsolved, they obviously need your help, but that doesn't mean you will know more than they do. To the contrary, you will undoubtedly know less. Your goal as their consultant is to be or provide the missing

Joel A. Dvoskin, *Forensic Consultation*. In: *The Path Forward*. Edited by: Kirk Heilbrun and David DeMatteo, Oxford University Press. © Oxford University Press (2026). DOI: 10.1093/9780197773031.003.0012 piece, or better yet the missing link. Ideally, you may help them to realize that they had the answer all along. When you tell them the answer, you solve the problem once. If you can help them discover the answer, you leave them with knowledge and skills that may help them forever.[1] (You know, like "Give a man a fish and he eats for a day, but teach a man to fish and he eats for a lifetime."[2])

The Basics: So you Wanna be a Consultant?

Without question, the most important characteristic of a successful consultant is integrity (see, e.g., Moorman et al., 2018). It can take years to create a reputation for integrity, and it can be destroyed in one weak moment of greed, anger, fear, or laziness. Treat it like you handled your child on the first day of its life. Integrity is not free; it often causes inconvenience or reduces income in the short run. But there is good news: if you play the long game, integrity is lucrative. A reputation for integrity might cost you an opportunity in the moment, but consultants with integrity are more likely to be called a second or a third time, and they are more likely to be referred to similar organizations.

You MUST be willing to turn down cases. That does not mean that you have to be an expert on the topic to accept a job, so long as you are a gifted problem solver (see below). But if specific knowledge or skill is required, do not try to acquire it at a client's expense. Find an expert who is more qualified and offer to refer the case to them and "shadow" them so you can learn.

Integrity is expensive in the short run, but lucrative if you play the long game. If you want a career, play the long game. Example: I was asked to consult with a corporation. At the time, my rate was pretty high. I replied, "I would be pretty good at this situation, but for what I charge, you deserve better than 'pretty good.' Dr. Blank is by far the country's best expert for this particular challenge. I hate to send you elsewhere, but honestly, I'd call her first. If Dr. Blank is not available, I'd be an acceptable second choice, but see what she has to say." Dr. Blank accepted the case, but I received four more consultation requests from the same corporation in the ensuing year.

Integrity, like character, has been defined as our behavior when no one is watching. One strong indicator of integrity is how often we do and say things that are true but contrary to our own personal interests. For example, in one potentially lucrative assignment, I had published an article that contradicted the prospective client's position. When I informed him of the conflict, he thanked me and sent me on my way. A month later, he called me and told me that he had decided to reorganize along the lines I had suggested, and that he needed my help after all.

[1] You may wonder, "Why would I want to do that? Then they won't need me anymore." Do not worry. They will love you because you made them feel smarter and more capable, and they will have other problems in the near future, so they'll need you again. As a bonus, they will sing your praises to everyone they know, except maybe their competitors.

[2] This quote is attributed to the Chinese philosopher Lao Tzu, who was undoubtedly a great consultant.

In another example, I received a call from a company that provides low-cost housing. They were seeking consultation about how to better coordinate their efforts to connect with agencies that serve people with disabilities. At first, I was excited at the prospect of helping this client to connect people in need of low-cost housing with a place to live. But I only spent a day with this client before I discovered its track record of racial discrimination and "quick-trigger" evictions. The homes they provided were badly in need of repair, and they spent almost nothing on maintenance, because "These people never file complaints the right way, so we can ignore them." I learned a good lesson in this instance: Do a little research before agreeing to a gig. I had failed to learn enough about this client; when I did, I wanted nothing to do with them. I called, resigned, and promised not to send them an invoice.[3]

One other characteristic of a successful consultant is the ability to stay calm in a crisis. Frequently, a client will ask for consultation because they are in emotional distress over the problem they are hoping to solve. It is especially useful to have a sense of optimism that allows us to see a successful solution, which helps convince clients to follow the advice.

Knowledge: You Gotta Actually Know Stuff

I once had a case in which a state penitentiary was sued over the use of restrictive housing for people with serious mental illnesses who pose a serious and imminent threat of violence within the prison. Because of severe building limitations, these Incarcerated Persons (IPs) were spending as many as twenty-two hours per day locked in their cells. To avoid litigation, the plaintiff (a civil rights law firm) and the defendant (Department of Corrections) asked me to help craft a solution in the form of a settlement agreement. To make it possible for the IPs to receive at least four hours of programming each day, the Department decided to fast-track a construction project. The result was a building in which IPs with serious mental illnesses could participate safely in group and individual therapy. The lesson learned: to solve this client's problem, it was important to know and understand the laws regarding restrictive housing, best practices for safely treating a challenging population, and how to craft a solution that meets the needs of all parties. It was important to use all of my relevant knowledge, skills, and experiences—in this case, understanding laws regarding restrictive housing and how to work with correctional architects.

In another case in 2008, I was invited to attend a Task Force at the request of the Office of the Vice President of the United States. Our task was to provide advice on how the United States should prepare for and respond to a bioterrorism event. The makeup of the group was intimidating, including the Vice President of one of

[3] Luckily for me, because they were so unapologetically bad, I only lost one billable day. If they had any subtlety at all, I could have lost a lot more time, or even inadvertently contributed to harming people.

the major TV networks, forensic psychologists and psychiatrists, and leaders from several government agencies. The challenge was intellectually stimulating because bioterrorism requires a response that is different from how the United States typically responds to crises and emergencies. In the event of a hurricane or a tornado, the Federal Emergency Management Agency (FEMA) immediately tries to get people to congregate. Congregation allows for a more efficient distribution of essentials like food and water. However, in the event of bioterrorism, the last thing we want is for people to congregate, which would accelerate the spread of the biohazard. Our challenge, therefore, was "How do we get Americans to stay home and do nothing in the event of an attack?" Doing nothing is contradictory to the entire American culture; our heroes never do nothing. They fight back by doing stuff. Relying on my knowledge of psychology, I was able to convince the group of the importance of relabeling inaction as patriotic and courageous if we want people to do nothing. The lesson learned: instead of worrying about what we don't know, focus on the skills, knowledge, and experiences that will help solve the problem.

Nobody likes a know-it-all, but you have to know something. They hired you in part because you're a psychologist, so be a good one. Psychologists are supposed to be competent at evaluating the way people think, feel, and act. One part of that skill set is psychological tests, and it is important to understand their value and limitations. For example, a police chief tells me that he has an excellent police psychologist who has identified the best candidates for hire, then asks, "So why are so many of my officers getting in trouble?" An over-reliance on testing can blind people to other important variables, such as inadequate supervision or poor morale.

Even more important than psychological testing is the art of interviewing. I have consulted with police detectives, attorneys, and salespeople; the successful ones are always good at interviewing. Interviews as part of a consulting assignment have much in common with the interviews we conduct for clinical or forensic purposes, as all require preparation, communication skills, the ability to tolerate silences, and the ability to create a safe space.

Preparing to interview a client includes gaining as much factual information as possible about the organization (e.g., agency, company). What do they do, and how do they do it? Try not to pay attention to opinions about the organization, with one exception. If the organization is experiencing controversy or harsh criticism, it is useful to understand the nature of the controversy. But avoid adopting an opinion on either side, as confirmation bias will limit your ability to devise creative solutions.

Client interviews are of at least two types. The consultant will at times be meeting with the leadership of the organization—the "shot caller." This is the person who will be directing your efforts and deciding whether to accept and implement your suggestions. Other interviews will be with employees, constituents, customers, or clients for the purposes of gathering data (i.e., information that will be essential in forming your recommendations).

Communication skills are important during interviews. Perhaps foremost among them is the ability to listen. During client interviews, the client should do most of the talking, except when the consultant is answering a question. When interviewing to seek information, however, the consultant will likely direct the conversation, mainly with targeted questions. Each question must have a purpose, and it is essential that the questions be clear. That way, when reviewing the gathered data, you will not have to guess about the meaning of each response.

One very effective way to communicate is by telling stories, but there are important cautions. Effective stories are brief, relevant, and have a point, preferably directly related to the problems the consultant has been asked to solve. Self-aggrandizing "war stories" are interesting only to the teller; other people find them boring, arrogant, and off-putting.

A good interviewing technique is heavily dependent on the consultant's ability and willingness to tolerate silences, especially when those silences are awkward. It has been my consistent experience that almost everything of value that is ever learned in an interview comes after an awkward silence. When the consultant fills the silence (often with chatter), it takes the person "off the hook" and an important piece of information is lost.

The final interview skill I want to discuss is the ability to create a safe interview space. By "safe," I mean several things. A safe physical space will allow for audio privacy (i.e., no way the person can be overheard). However, it is also important for the person being interviewed to feel safe from judgment, contradiction, or retribution if their opinion doesn't "toe the party line."

Psychologists are also good at forensic or therapeutic psychological evaluation. It is, of course, a very bad idea to treat your client as if you were their therapist. Still, some clients may want you to use your evaluation skills as one of the tools that will help resolve their problem. The most common example for me has been workplace violence prevention work I have conducted through the Threat Assessment Group. These types of consultation rely heavily on the risk and threat assessment skills that some forensic psychologists have developed.

Later, I will discuss the legal and ethical guardrails that control my consulting career, but for now, it is important to remember state and federal rules about confidentiality, privacy, and informed consent. When a consulting assignment involves interviews, it is important to differentiate between interviews aimed at information gathering on the one hand and psychological evaluations on the other. I recommend taking care to avoid inadvertently violating confidentiality laws that apply to the psychological evaluations. In general, however, one should avoid misrepresenting oneself or tricking the person being interviewed into providing information under misleading premises.

Clinical psychologists, of course, are skilled at providing therapy. As a consultant, it is good to understand the benefits and limitations of psychotherapy; however, one should avoid at all costs providing therapy to a client or their employees. The rare exception is when the consultant is specifically hired to provide such services, and then only after meaningfully informed consent. Simply put, when tempted to "therapize" a client, make a referral.

Often, a client will contact a consultant to address a disruptive or unsettling employee. In many of those cases, the employee in question will have a real or suspected problem with substance abuse, mental illness, or both. As a consultant, your contribution as a problem solver will often result in referrals to clinicians to provide the therapeutic services.

If the consultation is forensic, be good at that as well. For example, one of my clients is a manufacturing company that suspected its truck drivers of breaking federal drug laws. The company leaders were terrified at the damage to the company's reputation if word got out that it was importing drugs. Fortunately, they had a trusting relationship with a consultant who was a forensic psychologist. Initially, I convened a team of leaders, including their Chief Counsel. I convinced them that their fears were based on suspicion, and that the damage of a cover-up would be far greater than the original allegation could cause. I then organized a meeting with the appropriate federal agency, during which the company volunteered complete cooperation, and in turn received a promise of best efforts to keep the whole episode quiet—even if the allegation turned out to be true. The allegation was true, and with the company's help, two employees were arrested. The statements from the agency announcing the arrests included no mention of the company.

Although knowledge of forensic evaluation can be useful to a consultant, it is extremely unlikely that one should conduct such an evaluation as part of a consulting assignment unless that was the purpose of the consultation. Similarly, competence in risk and threat assessment is a useful skill for consultants. It is not unusual for a prospective client to be calling because they are afraid of something. In such cases, a cool-headed ability to think about real versus imagined risk can help to lower the temperature and improve everyone's ability to think clearly. Nowhere is this more evident than when responding to a crisis.

Law and Ethics

To protect yourself and your clients, it is important to know and understand the legal and ethical principles and challenges that will profoundly affect your career. The laws that might apply to a particular consultation will vary tremendously from case to case. You don't need to be a lawyer, but you need to understand how to find out what an applicable law says. Simply put, laws generally tell us what we *must* do, what we *may* do, and what we *must not* do. But laws are jurisdiction-specific, so they may differ across jurisdictions.

In contrast to laws, which change with the jurisdiction, ethical standards for psychologists are more consistent across states, thanks mostly to the American Psychological Association and its Ethical Principles of Psychologists and Code of Conduct (EPPCC). While the EPPCC is a long document with a number of specific standards, for our purposes its core is relatively simple: Psychologists must not misrepresent themselves, they must not perform their duties incompetently, they must keep their promises (e.g., of confidentiality), they must avoid multiple relationships that pose a conflict of interest, and they must avoid unnecessary or gratuitous harm.

The beautiful and simple truth is that operating with integrity covers pretty much the entire EPPCC. If that is too many words for a budding psychologist, try this: Do the right thing. Laws, of course, are a bit more demanding. It is important to understand laws that directly pertain to the client organization, the problem they hope to solve, and the solutions you might recommend. For example, while consulting with a highly regulated aerospace company, I needed to spend a fair amount of time being instructed on the ways in which I would be able to use or share information I obtained during the course of my consultation.

In a different example, I have consulted for many years with a publicly-traded manufacturing company. Impressed with their management team, I considered telling the person who manages my retirement accounts about them. Before doing so, I asked for and received an in-depth explanation of the federal prohibitions against insider trading by the company's Chief Financial Officer to make certain that neither I nor the company would run afoul of the law.

A friend of mine was engaged as a consultant for an insurance company that manages a statewide federal program of mental health benefits for people with serious mental disabilities. His consulting fee was very high, and he was glad to get the gig. It took a few months for him to realize that the system he was working to improve (by increasing efficiency) had a policy of denying every first appeal without reading it. In contrast, every second appeal (i.e., an appeal of the first denial of their appeal) was automatically granted without respect to merit. The reason? According to their data, only two to three percent of people with mental disabilities will file a second appeal. It was a business decision. To preserve his own integrity, he resigned immediately.

It is important to avoid a conflict of interest, where a consultant might be motivated by personal benefit (beyond the agreed-upon consulting fee) rather than benefit to the client. But the longer you do this work and the older you get, the more conflicts you are likely to have. Compared to many of my friends, my organizational skills are not impressive. To protect myself, for many years, I had a part-time administrative assistant, whose most important tasks were keeping track of my clients (to avoid inadvertent conflicts of interest) and remembering to send invoices.

Particularly if your training is in forensic psychology, avoid the temptation to assume you know the law. I routinely see psychologists asking legal questions on a listserv of psychologists, some of whom are all too eager to respond. My simple advice is to disregard any legal advice that did not come from an attorney, preferably one who is knowledgeable about the appropriate area of law in the appropriate jurisdiction. Like psychology and medicine, legal advocacy has become highly specialized. For example, complicated questions regarding intellectual property should be referred to an intellectual property lawyer. Conveniently, if you have professional liability (i.e., malpractice) insurance, you already have access to an attorney, at no additional cost, who is well-versed in most of the common questions psychologists are likely to face and comfortable researching laws in other jurisdictions. Not taking advantage of a free and excellent service is poor practice for a consultant.

As is the case with clinical and forensic psychology, it is always a good practice to strive for objectivity. Since all of us have biases that are impossible to eliminate, remaining as objective as possible requires hard work (see, e.g., Guarnera et al., 2017; Neal & Brodsky, 2016). A list of relevant biases is beyond the scope of this chapter, but one very important and destructive bias is confirmation bias. Occasionally, your first answer might be the best one, but if it is obvious, it is very likely that the client has already tried it. Confirmation bias leads us to systematically ignore or reject other ideas and to selectively attend to evidence that our first answer is the best one.

Overcoming confirmation bias is especially challenging for psychologist consultants. Clients often treat us with more deference than we deserve; among other things, they want to feel they are spending their money wisely. Further, in many cases, I am consulting alone, so there is no co-consultant with whom to test ideas. To account for confirmation bias, I use a technique that has served me well in forensic cases; I am in the habit of cross-examining myself. How do I know this? How would I know if this is wrong? In addition, I try to find the member of the client's team who seems angry and resentful that I'm even there. Often, that anger is borne of a fear that is reasonable, if only I can get them to say it out loud, because they might have a point.

For example, I was once asked to serve as an expert witness in a potential lawsuit against a Department of Youth Services alleging inadequate mental health care and generally unconstitutional conditions of confinement. Class actions of this nature are expensive, can go on for years, and don't always result in the desired reforms. So, I suggested to the potential plaintiff (a civil rights law firm) the following: (1) Ask to let me visit their three facilities; (2) Find some consensus on a group of recommendations; and (3) Use them as the basis of an agreement in lieu of a lawsuit. In this case, the client was less interested in legal fees than better lives for the incarcerated kids, and surprisingly, the Department agreed.

After my visit to the three facilities, I compiled a list of forty-five simple but meaningful recommendations, mainly changes in the behaviors of the staff who supervised the kids, which I presented to the parties.[4] At the end of my presentation, the Director of the Department said, "I agree with every one of those recommendations, but I don't think we have the resources or the know-how to accomplish them."

The two sides relatively quickly negotiated an agreement based on my recommendations. At the Department's request, I was hired as a consultant to spend five full days each quarter for a year (which later expanded to 18 months). In the beginning, it went very poorly. The Director of Security at the largest facility, a former police officer, was the most powerful person in the entire department. Sadly, he appeared to hate my guts. He quite literally scoffed and disagreed in response to everything I said, and glared at me every time we passed in the hallway.

[4] For example, the first recommendation said, "All you do is yell at these kids all day, and it doesn't seem to improve their behavior. Have you tried rewarding them for acting right?"

At the end of my first week, I asked him, "Why do you hate me?" He appeared taken aback by my directness and said, "Do you really want to know?" Inwardly elated that we now had a conversation, I nodded. He said, "I'm afraid you're going to get my staff hurt." This is what I needed to hear. I replied, "I'll tell you what. Are you a handshake guy or should I put this in writing? (Handshake.) I give you my word, if I ever do, say, write, demand, or recommend one change that you truly believe will hurt your staff, I promise to remove it until I convince you otherwise. You have my word."

Almost immediately, my nemesis became my teammate and even my mentor. All of my ideas could be refined or improved upon. Based on his forty years of experience with these kids in these facilities, he gladly did so. Now, instead of falling in love with my own ideas, I could have them tested in real time. Confirmation bias did not disappear, but it had been domesticated. Lesson learned: Seek "pushback" and learn from it.

As a consultant, it is good to have high expectations, but beware of perfection. In a previous article, "Confessions of an Incrementalist" (Dvoskin, 2002), I argued that perfectionism guarantees failure, since perfection is quite literally unattainable. Worse, the false promise of perfection serves to prevent organizations from improving, leading to the adage, "Perfect is the enemy of good."[5] Instead of seeking perfection, I recommend the celebration of incremental improvement. I believe if every person who visited a park would pick up one piece of trash, the park would quickly become spotless. Or, to quote my Mom, "Always leave it just a little better than you found it."

How to Get Your First Consulting Gig

I am going to take a wild guess here. If you have a doctorate, you wrote something like a dissertation, and it was probably your very best work. It is also likely (unless your mentor was asleep at the switch) that at that moment you knew more about the topic of your dissertation than anyone alive. You read and cited everything that had ever been written on the topic, right? So, my friend, for a glorious moment, you are not only an expert, you are *the* expert.

So, before it is too late, write and publish an article about your dissertation. I know it is a lot of work, but do it anyway. When people are looking for help in today's world, they start with a search engine. Somewhere in America, someone is having the same problem you just wrote about, and when they call you, answer the darn phone. (If you're under the age of 50, reply to them however you people communicate.)

In my experience, the first few calls tended to relate to one specific area of expertise, often something I wrote about, during which I always tried to be a good problem solver. Pretty much everything after that came by word of mouth.

[5] According to Google: Voltaire is often credited with saying "the perfect is the enemy of the good," but he stole it from a French proverb. Wikipedia says the French stole it from an Italian proverb. Ah, those quirky Europeans!

Answering the Client's First Call

You publish an excellent article. It might have been your dissertation. A month later, a client calls you with a problem that you just wrote about. How to proceed?

The first step is to give them a chance to introduce themselves and ask a few simple questions. This gives you time for your heart rate to return to normal. You probably will not have to ask them their problem, but just in case, ask them, "How can I help?"

Next, try to make a reasonable decision about the degree to which your knowledge, experience, training, and (most importantly) problem-solving skills seem like a good fit. This may require extra questions, including "What have you already tried and/or considered?" Open-ended questions are best.

If things sound promising, you will next want to know about any guardrails, especially regarding confidentiality and privilege. Until a deal is struck, information shared with you may not be privileged, and many clients, even attorneys, seem to ignore this rule. I therefore ask them to refrain from sharing any secrets until we have an agreement in place.

Next, I try to clarify the potential role I might play in solving the organization's problem. Will the consultation be telephonic, virtual, or in-person? How much time is involved and will my calendar allow it?

It is absolutely essential to clarify your compensation in advance for even a single billable hour. Of course, your hourly or daily rate needs to be decided well in advance of your first call. One problem you are likely to have is how to state your rate with a straight face. Personally, I have never achieved it. Consulting rates seem high to me, and I want to make enough money to retire comfortably, but there is no getting around it—it seems expensive. Of course, you are always free to charge less, but if you don't, practice saying the number, even if you would never pay that much for your services. Be equally clear about the manner of calculating hours or days. Some clients will expect you to travel for free, even if you will be unable to do other work on your travel days. Again, do whatever you want, but make the agreement clear before you start. Also, some consultants "double bill." In other words, they will travel for case A and work on case B during their flight. I have never done that, because it seems wrong, but I know people who do. (That's all I've got on that one.)

Next, make sure that the client's values are adequately aligned with your own. Otherwise, you will likely find yourself in a position of helping your client to more efficiently do something that you find wrong. Alternatively, I might behave in ways that my client finds equally reprehensible for the opposite reason. One clear example of this potential trap is regarding the principles of DEI (diversity, equity, and inclusion) and antiracism. Because I'm hoping to be a better ally, I try to find a way to bring up the topic of racism or cultural bias very early on.

We live in times of a vast cultural divide, where people on either side of serious questions refuse to acknowledge common ground, and disagreement too quickly becomes hatred. It is to your advantage to identify and avoid such differences in essential values long before anyone hates you. Here is an adage for you: If you want a career as a consultant, try not to make *too* many people hate you.

For example, in 2003, I was contacted by the Office of a newly elected Governor. The Governor had appointed a member of his own party as Director of a youth corrections agency. However, this very good person had no relevant experience whatsoever, either in running an agency or working with youth. When I asked about the scope of the consultation, they said, "40 hours per week for a year."[6] I told them that the staff would soon be calling me Geppetto (the carpenter who made Pinocchio), thereby heaping disrespect upon the newly appointed Director. Instead, I agreed to spend a week with him, where I learned the agency was being sued almost every week, and the executive team tended to agree with the plaintiffs. The new Director told me, "We think they're right, but we just don't have the resources (money and staff) to fix the problems." After two days of interviews, I concluded, "Director, I think you have plenty of money and the right amount of staff. You just have way too many kids." My recommendation was to accelerate the parole eligibility dates of every kid by six months, which would still allow the state to make distinctions between the kids who were more culpable and dangerous, while releasing those who were less. Generally following this advice, over the following year, the Director succeeded in lowering his census, thereby easing stress on the organization so they could attend to its problems. My lesson learned: Before committing to a consulting assignment, consider what you can reasonably contribute to solving the organization's problem in a way that enhances the strength of the leadership you will leave behind.

Over the course of my consulting career, I have been retained by a variety of different kinds of organizations. Because of my own work experience, many of them involve the interaction between criminal justice and human services. These include county and municipal jails and sheriff's offices, prisons and departments of corrections, juvenile justice facilities and systems, police departments, state hospitals and departments of mental health, and community mental health systems.

State prisons and departments of corrections will often call a consultant when there is an existing or expected class action alleging unconstitutional conditions of confinement. Similarly, civil rights agencies or law firms will call some of the same consultants for the same reasons. I much prefer the role of consultant as opposed to expert witness. As a consultant for either side, I can focus entirely on improving the system of care, instead of attacking or defending the *status quo*.

Early in my career, I was a correctional psychologist and administrator. My first assignment included serving as the psychologist for death row and administrative segregation (also called restrictive custody by prison administrators, solitary confinement by advocates for its abolition, and "the hole" by inmates). Restrictive custody is an extremely controversial subject and the cause of numerous class actions. At first, I served in a number of cases as an expert witness. Often, these cases, and much of the

[6] I know you don't believe me. I wouldn't either if I was you, but I swear it's the truth.

rhetoric around this topic, presented a falsely dichotomous choice between absolute prohibition and unlimited use of restrictive housing. For departments of corrections, this was a problem, and problems are opportunities for consultants.

I have been able to consult with state forensic and civil psychiatric hospitals in a number of states. These consultations have covered quite a few organizational challenges. One state was primarily interested in how to improve the physical security of its maximum-security hospital. Another was interested in auditing both of its large state hospitals, which allowed me to partner with a psychiatrist and a nurse to conduct a thorough audit of treatment, security, and virtually every aspect of psychiatric hospital care.

Special Issues

Suicide Prevention

One area that has been a frequent topic for consultation has been suicide prevention. For a person who enjoys problem-solving, suicide prevention is both challenging and meaningful. The nature of these consultations has varied tremendously. In one southern state, the plaintiffs and defendants in a statewide prison class action joined together to ask me to identify some of the most egregious physical plant dangers for incarcerated persons in high-risk statuses, such as suicide precaution and restrictive housing. These dangers included sharp objects or places where a ligature can be affixed. Together with a Director of Building and Grounds, we walked through six large prisons, and I watched as suicide hazards were identified and eliminated. Many of them were removed in real time during our visits, while others required capital expenditures that would take some time.

Architectural Design Consultation

During my time as the state director of forensic services in New York, I had the opportunity to work with an incredible group of architects and engineers within our agency's capital operations unit. With each building project under my authority, I learned from our own professionals as well as the architects with whom we contracted. Over time, I started receiving requests to serve as an architectural design consultant for projects to build new or renovate old psychiatric hospital buildings (Dvoskin et al., 2002). To be clear, I am under no illusion that I am an architect. To the contrary, my ignorance of the technical aspects of architecture has become a strength, helping me to ask questions from the perspective of a hospital administrator, and to serve as a liaison between the architects and the patients and staff who will live and work in the building once the project is completed. To date, I have assisted in designing hospitals in Colorado, Washington, D.C., Missouri, Hawaii, and other states. Working on these projects has unquestionably been the most enjoyable and gratifying experience of my career.

There have been, however, a number of consultation opportunities that have arisen with a less obvious connection to my educational background. Among the most rewarding of these has been my work with the United States Secret Service (USSS). For more than a decade, I served on the Research Advisory Board of the USSS, which helped the Service to remain current on the science and scholarship related to risk and threat assessment. In addition to a few case-specific consultations, my work with USSS allowed me to play a small role in the development of processes for investigating various forms of targeted violence (Coggins et al., 1993).

In 1999, the USSS asked me to attend perhaps my weirdest consultative experience. The Service convened a work group to consider ways to assess and prevent harms associated with the turn of the century (i.e., Y2K). For two days, I found myself in a room full of people who were so much smarter and more knowledgeable than me, I was literally terrified. Interestingly, I did not feel as though I had much to add to the highly technical discussion, but I enjoyed a master class in computer forensics. As a consultant, you will find yourself in situations where you learn a great deal more than you contribute.

In 2001, I was asked to join a team to investigate Dylan Klebold and Eric Harris, who committed the shootings at Columbine High School. At the request of the Jefferson County (CO) Attorney, we sought to explore the motivations that led to the shootings and hopefully had implications for preventing similar events in the future (see Cornell & Kerere, this volume, for more extensive discussion of threat assessment in schools). Presenting our findings to the Littleton community, including family and friends of the victims, was one of the most emotionally powerful experiences of my life.

Professional Membership Organizations

I have provided several types of consultative services to the American Psychological Association (APA) over the past four decades. For example, on one occasion, an angry member had written some vaguely threatening communication to the organization. Aware of my experience in threat assessment, APA asked me to review the communications and help them decide whether a response would help to mitigate or even eliminate the threat. In a case like that, a basic principle is almost always useful: if it might help and it won't make things worse, it's OK to try it. In this case, however, the responses under consideration would have failed that test, as they all posed a real possibility of further enraging the member. Because there was no severe and imminent threat, my recommendation was to sit tight and monitor the situation. Eventually, the problem disappeared, as the member had apparently said what he had to say and was satisfied. This case underscores an additional rule: sometimes the smartest thing to do might be nothing. Clients don't always want to hear that, so it is the consultant's job to explain the importance of refraining from making things worse.

Another way in which I have worked with the APA has allowed me to contribute to the development of APA *amicus curiae* briefs for the United States Supreme Court (see, e.g., APA Briefs for *Amicus Curiae* in *Clark v. Arizona, 2006*; *Graham v. Florida*, 2010; *Miller v Alabama*, 2012; *Moore v. Texas*, 2017; *Panetti v. Quarterman*, 2007; and *Roper v. Simmons*, 2005; Gilfoyle & Dvoskin, 2017). While this work has been unpaid, it allows those who work on it to feel a sense of agency in some of the most important questions facing our country, up to and including capital punishment. Working on these briefs with APA's General Counsel has been an incredibly rewarding experience.

Many of the coolest things I have been allowed to do were not lucrative; in fact, they were *pro bono*. For example, the American Psychiatric Association invited Hank Steadman and me to help their Committee on Psychiatry in Jails and Prisons to revise their guidelines on correctional psychiatry. Although we were not paid and our writing was not acknowledged with authorship, the experience was extremely helpful in allowing me to become an expert witness, consultant, mediator, and monitor in correctional class actions all over the country.

In 2003, Kirk Heilbrun, Diane Marsh, and I were invited by APA to join a Task Force on Mental Disability and the Death Penalty for the Individual Rights and Responsibilities Section of the American Bar Association (ABA) to develop a policy to determine how courts should sentence people with mental illnesses in jurisdictions that impose the death penalty. The ABA policy and the APA *amicus* brief were both cited by the Supreme Court in its historic decision in *Panetti v. Quarterman* (2007).

Finally, I have stumbled upon some incredible opportunities to consult in areas that I could have only dreamed of. In the late 1990s, because I had worked as a basketball coach for the U.S. Peace Corps and for twenty-five summers at a college basketball camp, I had an unusual combination of experiences that led me to be invited to serve as one of the mentors for the National Basketball Association (NBA) and the NBA Players' Association (NBPA) in their annual Rookie Transition Program, which is an orientation program for the entire group of drafted rookies entering the league. Subsequently, I was asked by the National Collegiate Athletic Association to help them develop its "First Team Mentoring Program" for elite high school basketball players. Because of my love for basketball and the opportunity to help mentor young men, these experiences were fun and gratifying. Honestly, I did nothing to deserve them, but every time the phone rang, I tried to say yes.

In one case, in 1995, I was stunned to receive a letter from the White House asking me to attend a day-long meeting of the "White House Task Force on the Future of the African American Male." Once I realized it was not a hoax, I agreed to attend, and found myself to be the only White person invited. When I entered the room and sat in the back, a staff person had to tell me to sit at the table. Luckily, I kept myself from asking why. I seriously had no idea why I had been invited to this meeting. I had written nothing about the topic and claimed no special knowledge. So, for once, I kept my mouth shut for the first half of the day. The other members of the group were astonishingly accomplished African American professors of relevant areas, including economics, history, social work, and law. At lunch, one very nice member walked up to me with a sincerely kind smile, and asked, "Are you gonna say anything, White dude?" I was so grateful I wanted to hug him. During the afternoon, I was able to talk about risk assessment, criminal justice, mental health, and other ways that institutional racism has affected young Black men in destructive ways. Once again, I had learned a great deal more than I was able to contribute. My lesson learned: Consultants with a humble attitude often receive a great deal more than they contribute.

My career as a psychologist and consultant has led me to a set of experiences I could only have dreamed of. A number of characteristics and strategies helped me immensely along the way, many of which have been discussed and are summarized here.

Humility

Humility comes easily to some folks; I was not one of them. Like many people, I enjoy being the center of attention. I am by nature a very chatty person who talks more than I listen. Fortunately, I was raised by two remarkable people: my father, a man of unshakeable integrity who solved problems predominantly with his brain; and my mother, an unselfish woman who loved and cared for others and solved problems leading with her heart. Because of the lessons they taught me, I understood the importance of stifling my ego and learning to listen. Successful consultants listen before and more than they speak.

Problem-solving

The best consultants are not the ones who know the most—after all, nobody likes a know-it-all—but they are the very best problem solvers. They work well with others, and skillfully create teams to solve problems.

Integrity

Integrity is important for lots of reasons. It helps you to sleep well at night and convinces others to trust you. However, integrity adds one unexpected benefit: it is lucrative. As a consultant, living and working with integrity increases your value. It helps potential clients to trust that you will serve their interests more than your own.

Conclusion

I hope I have made it very clear that the consulting part of my work has not only been the most interesting and challenging, but also the most fun. So, if you like being stimulated and hate being bored, consider adding consulting to your career path.

Acknowledgements

The author wishes to thank Abigail Tucker, Psy.D. and the editors for their helpful comments on previous drafts of this chapter.

References

Clark v. Arizona, 548 U.S. 735 (2006). Brief for *Amicus Curiae*, American Psychological Association.

Coggins, M. H., Pynchon, M. R., & Dvoskin, J. A. (1993). Integrating research and practice in federal law enforcement: Secret Service applications of behavioral science expertise to protect the President. *Behavioral Sciences & the Law*, *16*(1), 51–70.

Corbin, T. B. (2017). Lessons learned after disaster? Emergency shelter and housing policy after Hurricane Katrina. *Disaster Management and Human Health Risk V: Reducing Risk, Improving Outcomes*, 173.

Dvoskin, J. A. (2002). Knowledge is not power – Knowledge is obligation. *Journal of the American Academy of Psychiatry and the Law*, *30*(4), 533–540.

Dvoskin, J. A., Radomski, S. J., Bennett, C., Olin, J. A., Hawkins, R. L., Dotson, L. A., & Drewnicky, I. N. (2002). Architectural design of a secure forensic state psychiatric hospital. *Behavioral Sciences and the Law*, *20*(5), 481–493.

Goltz, S. M., Hietapelto, A. B., Reinsch, R. W., & Tyrell, S. K. (2008). Teaching teamwork and problem solving concurrently. *Journal of Management Education*, *32*(5), 541–562. https://doi.org/10.1177/1052562907310739

Graham v. Florida, 560 U.S. 48 (2010). Brief for *Amicus Curiae*, American Psychological Association.

Guarnera, L. A., Murrie, D. C., & Boccaccini, M. T. (2017). Why do forensic experts disagree? Sources of unreliability and bias in forensic psychology evaluations. *Translational Issues in Psychological Science*, *3*(2), 143–152.

Miller v. Alabama, 576 U.S. 460 (2012). Brief for *Amicus Curiae*, American Psychological Association.

Moore v. Texas, 137 S. Ct. 1039 (2017). Brief for *Amicus Curiae*, American Psychological Association.

Moorman, R. H., Blakely, G. L., & Darnold, T. C. (2018). Understanding how perceived leader integrity affects follower trust: Lessons from the use of multidimensional measures of integrity and trust. *Journal of Leadership & Organizational Studies*, *25*(3), 277–289. https://doi.org/10.1177/1548051817750544

Neal, T. M. S., & Brodsky, S. L. (2016). Forensic psychologists' perception of bias and potential correction strategies in forensic mental health evaluations. *Psychology, Public Policy, and Law*, *22*(1), 58–76. https://doi.org/10.1037/law0000077

Panetti v. Quarterman, 551 U.S. 930 (2007).

Panetti v. Quarterman, 551 U.S. 930 (2007). Brief for *Amicus Curiae*, American Psychological Association.

Roper v. Simmons, 543 U.S. 551 (2005). Brief for *Amicus Curiae*, American Psychological Association.

13

Cross-Systems Mapping Using the Sequential Intercept Model

Patricia A. Griffin, Kathleen Kemp, and Christy Giallella

Across the United States, communities have long struggled to address the high numbers of people with severe mental illness and often co-occurring substance use disorders (SUDs) involved in their local criminal justice systems. Disproportionately high numbers of arrests, fewer receiving disproportionally low numbers receiving bail, higher numbers in jail, longer lengths of stay in jail, frequent returns to jail, and more frequent revocations of probation (Haneberg et al., 2024; Steadman et al., 2009). All this created significant tension between criminal justice, mental health, and substance abuse systems with much finger-pointing and often rancorous discussion. In the late 1990s, there had been limited efforts nationwide to productively address these problems, and few tools for communities to use in addressing their problems with the high numbers of people with severe mental illness in their criminal justice system.

But what to do about that? In 1997, the first author, a community psychologist with a deep interest in community alternatives to traditional forensic systems, began working with the National GAINS[1] Center for People with Co-Occurring Disorders in the Justice System, housed in Policy Research Associates, Inc., (PRA) in the Center's role providing technical assistance to a number of established jail diversion sites receiving funding through Substance Abuse and Mental Health Services Administration (SAMHSA) (Steadman et al., 1999). The goal of the research project was to study communities in their diversion efforts that served individuals with co-occurring mental health and SUDs, help those communities expand their efforts, evaluate the outcomes of this diversion, and disseminate promising findings. The GAINS Center provided technical assistance for systems integration and program development. Technical assistance efforts evolved over the period of the funding and expanded into other work by the GAINS Center, PRA, and the first author.

Initial formal technical assistance to the nine jail diversion communities used a 2-day substance use and criminal justice curriculum modified to incorporate mental health issues. This was the first time SAMHSA's Center for Substance Abuse Treatment brought severe mental illness into its wide-ranging technical

[1] GAINS is an acronym for Gather, Assess, Integrate, Network, and Stimulate.

Patricia A. Griffin, Kathleen Kemp, and Christy Giallella, *Cross-Systems Mapping Using the Sequential Intercept Model.* In: *The Path Forward.* Edited by: Kirk Heilbrun and David DeMatteo, Oxford University Press. © Oxford University Press (2026). DOI: 10.1093/9780197773031.003.0013

assistance briefs, monographs, and curricula. The GAINS Center hired Griffin as their first senior consultant who, along with other trainers, began to present the "Cross-Training Curriculum for Mental Health/Substance Abuse/Criminal Justice System Professionals Working with Person with Co-Occurring Disorders in Contact with the Justice System" (Addiction Technology Transfer Center, 1996) as part of the GAINS technical assistance. The trainings were generally well received for their substantive work on the issues of screening, assessment, interventions, and community resources for people with co-occurring serious mental illness (SMI) and SUDs in the criminal justice system, yet they did not seem to move the communities to expand their jail diversion activities. More interactive activities and fewer lectures were needed in the training. Fewer prescriptions from "experts" and more opportunities to assess what was happening in their own community were key to building on what was working in their community, improving their processes, and adding services.

The first big opportunity came in Portland, Oregon in 1998, where the cross-training workshop was scheduled to be delivered in the basement of a local church with a number of classrooms available. Each classroom had a whiteboard covering a full wall. The trainers took advantage of those classrooms and, for the first time, divided the participants into three groups—criminal justice, mental health, and substance abuse systems—and asked the groups to use the whiteboards to map out their local system and later explain it to the larger group. We were lucky that the chief assistant district attorney was part of the workshop and enthusiastically led the criminal justice participants in building a map of the local Multnomah County criminal justice system, presenting it to the whole group and fielding many questions from the various presenters. The mental health and substance abuse systems did the same. That first night, the local evaluators for the grant purchased mapping software, and transferred the day's information from the whiteboard maps to paper maps. It was a turning point for the cross-systems workshops. It was clear that local systems could be effective at teaching each other how their systems worked if they were provided a neutral, structured setting that would allow them to closely examine the pathways in which people with severe mental illness and often co-occurring SUDs became involved in their local criminal justice system and moved more deeply into that system. With some help, they could create a map specific to their community and target population. In the process, communities could identify strengths, weaknesses, and opportunities to improve their local processes, services, and systems to develop a plan to move forward. It was also clear that to make real change, the communities had to find multiple ways to collaborate across criminal justice, mental health, and substance abuse systems. Having them explain their systems to each other instead of having outside "experts" explain it to them made all the difference. The cross-systems mapping (CSM) workshops were born.

In the meantime, Summit County (Ohio) was struggling to address their own problems with the behavioral health and criminal justice systems. With significant concerns being raised by their sheriff and other criminal justice system players, the county started to make some progress implementing a Crisis Intervention Team

(CIT) and one of the nation's earliest mental health courts. Mark Munetz, the clinical director for the Summit County Alcohol Drug Abuse and Mental Health Board, recognized these attempts as a beginning in addressing this problem, and started to think about the problems in their community from a broader perspective. He envisioned a series of filters in the flow of the local criminal justice system by which the behavioral health and criminal justice systems would identify people with SMI and work to link them to treatment, attempting to keep them from further involvement in the criminal justice system. Shortly after 9/11, Griffin heard Munetz give a talk at a national conference for state forensic directors in which he described this "sequential filter" model; she realized this provided an organized structure to guide the work of a multidisciplinary forensic task force that was just beginning in Philadelphia and the surrounding four counties. A subcommittee of that task force—the Promising Practices Committee—adopted Munetz's early conceptual model and modified it for use as the five counties considered the overlap of their criminal justice and behavioral health systems. Working with Munetz in consultation with Henry Steadman of the GAINS Center, the task force refined the model and used it to inventory their five counties, identify their strengths and weaknesses, and build plans for improving their collaboration and services. Steadman suggested that "filters" did not quite capture the intent of the model, but "intercepts" more accurately described efforts to identify, screen, assess, divert if possible, and link to the target population to treatment as it moved through every stage of the criminal justice system. The Sequential Intercept Model (SIM) was born (see Figure 13.1).

In 2002, the Southeast Regional Forensic Task Force released their report using the SIM to inventory the five counties making multiple recommendations for each of these counties and the region. About the same time, the Council for State Governments and a number of partner organizations were developing their 600-page report dissecting in detail mental health populations' "events/issues" in the criminal justice system (Council of State Governments et al., 2002).

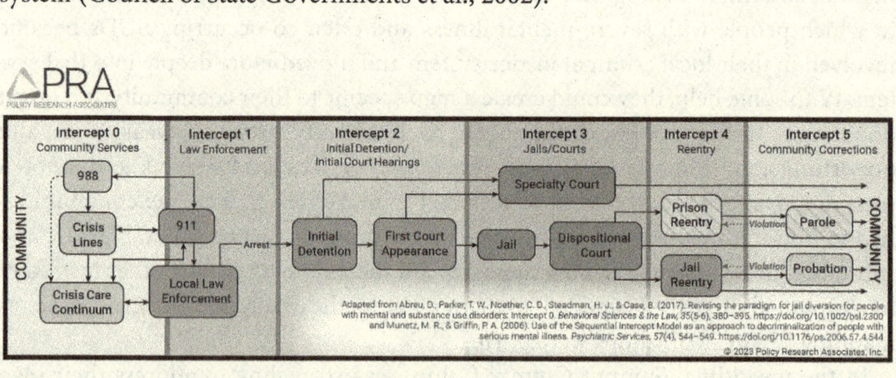

Figure 13.1 The Sequential Intercept Model

Source: Reproduced with permission from Policy Research Associates (https://www.prainc.com/sim/)

We started incorporating the SIM into the GAINS technical assistance workshops, centering the mappings themselves around the model. GAINS and PRA started integrating the model into the rest of their work, resulting in the 2004 brochure "Sequential Intercepts for Change: Developing a Comprehensive State Plan for Mental Health & Criminal Justice Collaboration" (National GAINS Center, 2004). It included a horizontal version of the model with action steps for service and system-level change at each intercept for communities as they planned to improve their continuum of services. This brochure was widely disseminated; it was a turning point for national implementation of the SIM.

Shortly after that, PRA obtained a federal Small Business grant to formalize the GAINS mapping workshops using the SIM as the guiding structure. PRA subsequently hired an experienced training professional to further formalize the workshops. She developed a facilitator's guide and training materials for communities. Since then, PRA has performed over 400 mapping workshops, trained a number of states in how to conduct their own mapping workshops, and modified the workshop to apply to those with SUDs and other challenges. See https://smtc.prainc.com and Desmarais et al., this volume for more information.

Sequential Intercept Model and Cross-Systems Mapping Thinking

Although SIM cross-system mapping workshops were not initially grounded in theoretical underpinnings, the workshops share common foundations with systems mapping frameworks. Systems mapping in healthcare and legal settings began in the early 2000s (Stroh, 2015). Systems mapping frameworks view the world as interconnected and emphasize understanding the relationships and dynamics between components within systems. Future evolution and adaptation of SIM cross-system mapping workshops can benefit from grounding changes in the broader theory and applications of systems mapping.

Systems mapping offers numerous benefits to our field, primarily by helping cross-system partners understand the interconnected relationships within a larger system or across multiple systems (Stroh, 2015; Williams & Hummelbrunner, 2010). Systems mapping synthesizes and connects information by integrating people, data, processes, and insights. Engaging in mapping discussions allows participants to uncover assumptions, examine mental models, and lay out different perspectives, fostering active dialogue and collaboration. Ultimately, systems mapping enhances our ability to navigate complex systems, optimize limited resources, and minimize redundancy.

The application of systems mapping methods varies in focus, ranging from the type of data collected—whether quantitative or qualitative—to the scope, which may emphasize broad systems or specific interventions (see Figure 13.2; Barbrook-Johnson & Penn, 2023). A project's approach to a particular method can

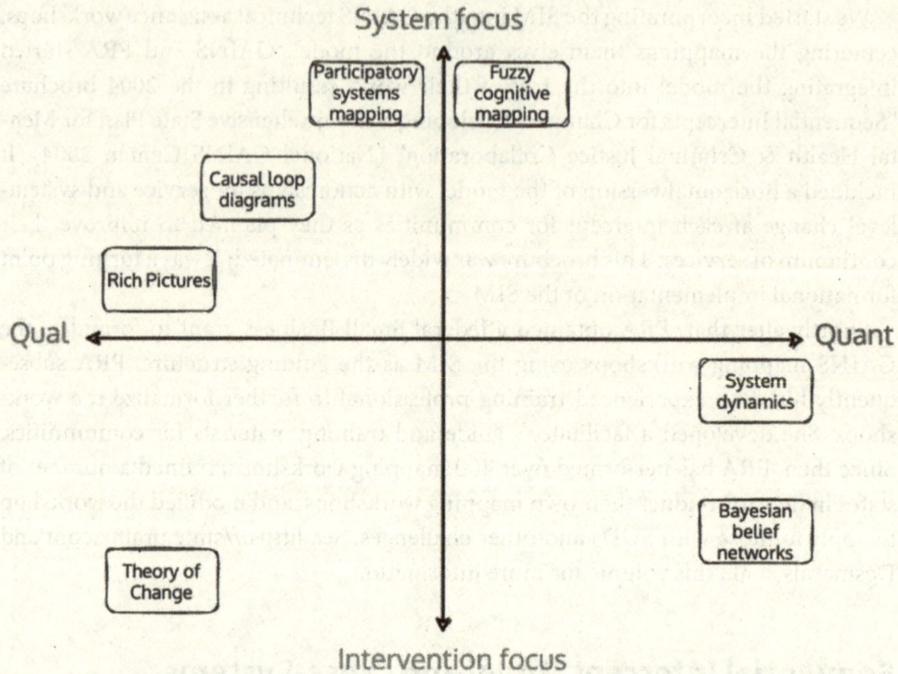

Figure 13.2 System Mapping Methods by Focus and Method

Source: Barbrook-Johnson & Penn (2022), p. 7. Available under a Creative Commons Attribution 4.0 International License (https://creativecommons.org/licenses/by/4.0/)

differ based on two key dimensions: the extent to which the method prioritizes the overall system versus a targeted intervention and the nature of the data used to construct the map (including both qualitative and quantitative). These factors shape how systems mapping is applied and interpreted in different contexts.

Systems mapping has several core steps and considerations important to any CSM adaptation. Here, we review five of the key steps adapted from Barbrook-Johnson and Penn (2022) and Stroh (2015).

- **Define the Problem and Set Goals.** It is important to have a clear idea of the purpose(s) of the mapping workshop—and share that information with participants. What are the topics to be covered and what are the outputs you hope to produce? How will the mapping be of value to partners? What are the immediate and long-term benefits to the partners based on their stated goals? By exploring these questions, the boundaries of the system(s) of interest start to take shape. The boundary is a critical first step in making the analysis more manageable and setting parameters for participants.
- **Select a Diverse Group of Participants.** A diverse set of participants representing different roles, backgrounds, and functions of different parts

within the systems—including administrative and line staff and people with lived experience—is critical to the success of systems mapping. One important goal is to collect data from a diverse group of participants who are working or living within the system(s) of interest. Often, these individuals have never been in the same room together, and some group perspectives may have been marginalized in past efforts at system reform.

- **Structure the Mapping Process.** The success of systems mapping depends on how well the process is organized, managed, monitored, and reported. Facilitation must be carefully employed to move the mapping process toward its goals. One consideration involves designing the process and map to maximize the chance of success. This starts early in the planning process to ensure that you have the right people in the room, asking the right questions, and building a product aligned with your goals and boundaries. It is likely to work best when systems mapping is used in an inclusive and flexible manner, but also with a clear structure and definition of how it will work and be analyzed.
- **Validate the Systems Map.** Validating the systems map does not mean it will ever be perfect. However, checking back with participants or a select subset of participants who can provide feedback on the accuracy of the map helps refine the product for your cross-system partners. Validation will be defined differently depending on the context of your project.
- **Evaluate the Outcomes.** Before initiating the mapping process, it is essential to identify the practical outcomes that local system partners aim to measure or achieve. During the mapping, capturing the complexity that is most relevant to these partners ensures a more meaningful process that maximizes learning. Integrating the desired outcomes into the mapping questions and facilitation process further strengthens the approach. Additionally, it is important to consider how to measure the foundational aspects of the system to ensure comprehensive and actionable results.

Systems mapping focuses on identifying critical points for designing, implementing, and evaluating intervention strategies targeting specific issues within systems. In conjunction with the SIM, systems mapping allows participants to identify key gaps, bottlenecks, service clusters, existing and needed connections, and other data trends within the system to design, implement, and evaluate intervention strategies.

New Adaptations

The use of the SIM for mapping the criminal justice and behavioral health systems within local jurisdictions is well established (Griffin, Heilbrun, et al., 2015). In recent years, the SIM framework has been adapted and applied to different processes and specific interventions. By applying the theoretical foundations of the SIM and the mapping process, the model can be generalized to new areas. When a community is faced with a challenge, they can use the SIM mappings to understand the broader contextual issues and identify gaps, opportunities, and priorities for change. Systems thinking allows communities to understand the interconnections within and across systems to motivate stakeholders, promote collaboration, focus efforts, and stimulate continuous learning.

Adaptation and Application of the SIM to Competency to Stand Trial

One such area faced by communities in recent years centers on the issue of competency to stand trial (CST).[2] The current landscape of the criminal, legal, and behavioral health systems requires a systemic lens to understand and address the problem. The SIM provides a model to apply systems thinking to the specific issue of CST.

CST is the most frequently-raised psycholegal issue in the criminal justice system, and there has been a significant increase in referrals for CST evaluations and restoration across the country. Recent estimates suggest there are 130,000 CST evaluations conducted annually (Kois et al., 2023). Further, there was a 72 percent increase in the number of individuals found incompetent to stand trial (IST) between 1999–2014. Recently, 82 percent of states have seen an increase in CST evaluation referrals and 78 percent of states have seen an increase in restoration referrals (Warburton et al., 2020). The number of individuals found IST is increasing in every state that tracks the data.

While referrals for CST evaluation and restoration are increasing, so are waitlists and wait times for these services. At least 20 states reported a waitlist for evaluations with wait times ranging from 7 to 252 days (Wik et al., 2020). There have been multiple class action lawsuits across the United States with defendants asserting violation of due process rights, in states including Arkansas, California, Colorado, Georgia, Florida, Louisiana, Nevada, Oregon, Pennsylvania, Texas, Utah, and Washington (Locklair, 2016). Outcomes from these class action lawsuits often require states to admit individuals for evaluation or restoration within a specific period ranging from seven to thirty-five days (Locklair, 2016).

The significant increase in referrals for CST evaluation and restoration and resulting litigation in several states have led to concern about a "competency crisis." Relevant issues have been identified that contribute to the crisis, including the significant increase in number of CST referrals; low availability of state hospital beds for restoration; low number and rate of discharges from the hospital, which directly

[2] The term *competency to stand trial (CST)* will be used throughout the chapter. CST has also been referred to as *adjudicative competence* or *competence to proceed.*

affect the number and rate of admissions; the disproportionate and reoccurring arrest for misdemeanors among individuals with SMI; and challenges with access to community-based services (Heilbrun et al., 2019; Murrie et al., 2022; Substance Abuse and Mental Health Services Administration, 2023).

Although it has been termed the "competency crisis," CST is a narrow psycholegal question, and there are wider systemic considerations that provide a more complete picture of the problem. The large number of justice-involved individuals with serious mental illness (SMI) is a well-recognized public health crisis (Haneberg et al., 2024). Individuals with SMI are disproportionately represented in jails across the country, with some jails having 17 percent of their population having a SMI as compared to 6 percent of the general population having a SMI; among individuals with SMI, approximately 76 percent also experience a co-occurring SUD (Steadman et al., 2009). Additionally, individuals with SMI tend to stay longer in jail and re-enter the criminal justice system more quickly than do their counterparts without SMI and co-occurring SUD (Haneberg et al., 2024).

When communities are faced with CST-related challenges, the SIM provides a helpful framework for understanding the systemic factors that contribute to the problem and for identifying creative, forward-thinking solutions. Communities can examine the gaps and opportunities at each intercept that are relevant and related to their local CST-related challenges. The process is similar to a traditional SIM mapping but provides an opportunity for communities to take a "deep dive" into a specific issue.

Similarly, to movement through the system described by the traditional SIM, individuals move through the CST process in a relatively predictable way. By applying the SIM to CST, we can review the common steps in the CST process across the intercepts to identify gaps, opportunities, and priorities for change. The CST process begins when individuals are identified and competency is raised in court by the defense, prosecution, or judge. A referral is processed for a competency evaluation—which is subsequently conducted with a report returned to the court, where the judge makes a CST adjudication. For individuals who are incompetent to stand trial, competency restoration is initiated. Cases are resolved based on legal (e.g., charges, state law) and clinical (e.g., restorability) factors. Relevant issues at each intercept are described below as individuals move through the intercepts throughout the CST process.

- **Intercepts 0 & 1.** At the early stages of contact with the criminal legal system, communities are poised to identify opportunities to deflect and divert individuals from the CST system. Individuals with behavioral health disorders can be effectively treated by the local crisis, mental health, substance use, and other social service systems to prevent criminal justice involvement and entry into the CST process. Communities should prioritize deflection and diversion, because once individuals begin the CST process, it becomes incredibly challenging to get out.

- **Intercept 2.** After an arrest, there are two particularly important considerations. First, communities should continue to consider diversion options, particularly for individuals with misdemeanor charges. Mental health courts, competency dockets, forensic navigator and boundary spanner models, and pre-plea diversion programs are promising practices at this intercept. Second, intercept 2 is a crucial opportunity to identify and triage individuals early in the process. Communities should use reliable, valid, standardized screening and assessment processes to identify individuals with SMI. Once individuals are identified, the information should be used to make determinations about who is referred for diversion programs, CST evaluations, and connections to care.
- **Intercept 3.** At intercept 3, communities should examine the jail-based treatment options that are available. High-quality behavioral health treatment should be provided to individuals with SMI and co-occurring SUDs in jail. Timely access to psychiatric medication should be provided upon admission to jail and throughout incarceration. Psychiatric medication can stabilize mental health symptoms and, in turn, restore individuals to competency, preventing the need for admission to a state hospital for restoration. The use of jail-based competency restoration is growing across states (e.g., California, Georgia, Colorado, Virginia).
- **Intercept 4.** Reentry practices and resources are important in promoting flow through the system so individuals do not spend inordinate amounts of time in institutional settings. When individuals cannot be discharged from the state hospital in a timely way, it creates a gridlock whereby individuals committed to the hospital for restoration cannot be admitted into those beds. The back door affects the front door. Communities should consider the availability and accessibility of community-based resources. Legal practices also affect reentry, and judges, as the ultimate decision-makers when it comes to community release, are in a powerful position to affect change.
- **Intercept 5.** Probation and parole are key stakeholders in the CST system. In some jurisdictions, competency to proceed on a probation violation may be an entry point into the CST process. Also, probation and parole violations are a key driver of local jail populations generally. There are opportunities to promote promising practices at intercept 5 (e.g., specialized probation caseloads) that could affect CST. Further, communities should consider mechanisms for connecting or reconnecting individuals to treatment in lieu of incarceration to prevent additional cycling through the systems.

CST-related challenges are not likely to be "fixed" with a single intervention because the problems are rooted in larger systemic issues. This is why CST is a good example of how to adapt and apply the SIM to new processes and populations. The SIM offers communities a model for applying systems thinking to complex problems to develop practical solutions driven by local priorities.

Diversity, Equity, and Inclusiveness

The SIM and CSMs provide a pivotal opportunity to address issues of racial and ethnic disparities within the criminal justice and behavioral health systems. There is disproportionate representation of Black, Indigenous, and people of color at all phases of the criminal legal system from arrest to pretrial incarceration, higher bail amounts, longer jail stays, and probation violations, among others. In the health care system, there are quantifiable inequities in health insurance coverage, access to services, and culturally responsive treatment.

Communities can use the SIM and CSM to examine local programs, practices, and policies that contribute to inequities in their systems across each intercept. Data are critical to understanding the issues at the local level, and communities should examine what data they currently collect and how to analyze the data to provide relevant information about where change is needed. Individuals from historically marginalized groups should be meaningfully integrated into planning efforts, including leading the work, decision making, data analysis and interpretation, program development, and implementation.

Individuals with lived experience are a particularly vital group to include in the work. They offer a unique perspective by virtue of having experienced mental health and substance use challenges, and for some, personal involvement in the criminal legal system. They should be fully integrated into systemic planning, development, and implementation—and should be included in every SIM mapping workshop. In addition to their role in system reform, individuals with lived experience can work in professional peer support roles. Models of peer support exist across every intercept, and peer specialists can be embedded at each stage. Certifications are offered for Certified Peer Specialists and Certified Recovery Specialists, and there are additional specializations for Forensic Peer Specialists, among others. Communities should examine whether they have the voices of those with lived experience at the table and whether they are embedding peer support specialists across the intercepts and compensating them appropriately for their time and expertise.

Advice to Others Seeking to Provide Similar Services

PRA provides the facilitator training for SIM mapping workshops. PRA offers CSM training focusing on a variety of outcomes. These include behavioral health, criminal justice involvement, homelessness, and veterans' issues (see https://smtc.prainc.com/). Accordingly, the most straightforward way of becoming involved in CSM, or of providing a mapping in a given locale, is through contact with PRA. They can assist individuals and jurisdictions with training of facilitators, and also (if there is interest) in providing CSM on focusing on various outcomes. PRA sometimes seeks out individuals who are interested in serving as facilitators more generally. There may be a formal solicitation or a published notification by PRA that a facilitators' training is planned for a specific state. The less formal avenue is to follow the work done by PRA and the GAINS Center (https://smtc.prainc.com/), become familiar with it through their training, and express interest in opportunities for further involvement that might arise. If a requested mapping will be funded through federal dollars, then relevant financial constraints will apply; there is often more flexibility when communities fund the CSM workshop without federal funds. (For additional details on conducting CSM, see Griffin, LaDuke, et al., 2015).

Key Considerations

There are different "do's" and "don'ts" involved in conceptualizing, planning, conducting, and using CSM workshops. These are sometimes broadly applicable to CSM generally, and other times more specifically to the involvement of a specific person.

Do's

- *Attend a mapping workshop before you pursue facilitators' training.* This will give you an overview of how these CSM workshops operate. It will help you decide whether you might be a good facilitator, and help you experience the workshops from a participant's point of view.
- *Seek advice from more experienced systems mapping facilitators.* There is a growing number of individuals with skills and experience as CSM facilitators. (This includes the three authors of this chapter, each of whom could also provide other names of individuals who might offer helpful advice.) A brief consultation with a number of experienced trainers can be extraordinarily helpful.
- *Carefully define the boundaries of the issue you want to map and avoid trying to model the whole system.* Being focused will be useful, as it leads to the dissemination of knowledge and the generation of potential solutions that are targeted to the particular questions at hand. Overly broad solutions are less likely to be effective, and hence more likely to waste time and resources.
- *Conduct advance planning to define your goals and spend time getting the right cross-system participants.* Advance planning is essential for an effective mapping; do not minimize the time required for the planning process. It is important not only to define the boundaries of the issue(s) that are the focus of a particular mapping, but to do so in advance. This can help attract the necessary participants, who should provide a good representation of cross-system and cross-role perspectives. When potential participants perceive the CSM as a carefully considered and well-planned use of an approach that works, they are more likely

to attend—which in turn means you are more likely to have buy-in and helpful subsequent behavior from key players.

- *Include participants with lived experience.* This is important to represent, to be fair, and to be accurate. CSM without participants with lived experience risks being too abstract. It is important to remind participants constantly that real people will be affected daily by the CSM workshop.
- *Consider the maps a living document that can be iteratively updated as systems change.* You may need a detailed document to help implement some of the solutions generated. There may also be a need in the future for additional mappings. For both reasons, it is valuable to document the CSM carefully in both the map and the summary report which typically contains descriptions of the resources and processes at each local intercept along with identified gaps, opportunities, participants' priorities, and an action plan for moving forward.
- *Make a plan for facilitation of difficult conversations.* There will inevitably be disagreements that stem from differing perspectives and limited resources. Anticipate this.
- *Use experienced facilitators.* In addition to working effectively with participants, they can provide training to new facilitators. It is helpful to include facilitators with differing kinds of expertise—for example, criminal justice, mental health, and substance abuse professionals.
- *Consider involving public health professionals who may have some familiarity with systems mapping frameworks.* Collaboration is a critical component of successful mapping. CSM is also a public health-oriented tool, so the perspective of a public health professional can be quite useful.
- *Anticipate the time needed to administer, document, and coordinate support for CSM workshops.* This is a lot of work.
- *Review how different states, communities, and organizations have used cross-systems mappings.* For example:
  - https://www.mass.gov/massachusetts-community-justice-project
  - https://www.texasjcmh.gov/programs-and-initiatives/sim-mapping-workshop/
  - https://www.ocbhji.org/sim
  - https://www.youtube.com/watch?v=y9PiJBy9e9k&list=PL2Z5F_4X2pTFe0imkZE3gy46pxFH73FEa&index=3

- Also, the National Youth Screening and Assessment Partners (NYSAP) provides systems mappings that guide cross-systems collaborators to improve a community's ability to more effectively serve youth with behavioral health needs involved in the juvenile legal system (see https://www.nysap.us/services/specialized#cim) (See Grisso et al., this volume.).

Don'ts

- Shy away from a healthy discourse among different perspectives. These are a key component of the CSM.
- Let the perfect be the enemy of the good. The map will never be perfect. It is meant to be a living document that evolves and changes over time with collaborator input and system evolution.
- Expect that the results of a single CSM will remain accurate over time and across various changes. Cross-systems mapping is an iterative process; there is a need to build local facilitator expertise for sustainability, and remapping should be considered as systems evolve and change over time.

Future Directions

CSM can be a powerful tool for guiding the effective operation of complex systems with a host of challenges. We have used the example of CST trial in this chapter. But CSM, and the foundational SIM on which it is based, can be applied to a wide range of psycholegal issues and systems. We have a clear conceptual and experiential basis for this conclusion (see, e.g., Griffin, Heilbrun, et al., 2015), although more formal research regarding its effectiveness is needed. In particular, we would like to better understand how to move from initial change to sustained action following the CSM. Retaining the workshop-generated enthusiasm for a longer-term plan is necessary. How can it best be achieved? What are the barriers that might limit implementation and sustainability?

It is also important to consider the question of how to generalize the application of the CSM. We have discussed how this can be done with various psycholegal outcomes. What is the most effective modification process? What are the limits to using the CSM based on the SIM? Answering these questions would help to narrow the gap between theory, experience, and empirically measured outcomes, toward the more effective operation of systems that serve our citizens involved in the justice system.

References

Addiction Technology Transfer Center. (1996). *Cross-training curriculum for mental health/substance abuse/criminal justice system professionals working with person with co-occurring disorders in contact with the justice system.* Virginia, Maryland, North Carolina: Mid-Atlantic Addiction Technology Transfer Center

Barbrook-Johnson, P., & Penn, A. S. (2022). *Systems mapping.* Cham: Palgrave Macmillan. https://doi.org/10.1007/978-3-031-01919-7

Barbrook-Johnson, P., & Penn, A. S. (February 28, 2023). *Seven methods for mapping systems.* Integration and Implementation Insights. https://i2insights.org/2023/02/28/systems-mapping-methods/

Council of State Governments, Police Executive Research Forum, Pretrial Services Resource Center, Association of State Correctional Administrators, Bazelon Center for Mental Health Law, and the Center for Behavioral Health, Justice, and Public Policy. (2002). *Criminal Justice/Mental Health Consensus Project.* Council of State Governments.

Griffin, P., LaDuke, C., Abreu, D., Winckworth-Prejsnar, K., Filone, S., Dorrell, S., & Finello, C. (2015). Using the Sequential Intercept Model in cross-systems mapping. In P. Griffin, K. Heilbrun, E. Mulvey, D. DeMatteo, & C. Schubert (Eds.), *Criminal justice and the Sequential Intercept Model: Promoting community alternatives for people with severe mental illness* (pp. 239–256). Oxford.

Griffin, P., Heilbrun, K., Mulvey, E., DeMatteo, D., & Schubert, C. (Eds.) (2015). *Criminal justice and the Sequential Intercept Model: Promoting community alternatives for people with severe mental illness.* Oxford.

Haneberg, R., Fabelo, T., Osher, F., & Thompson, M. (2024). *Reducing the number of people with mental illnesses in jail: Six questions county leaders need to ask.* The Council of State Governments Justice Center.

Heilbrun, K., Giallella, C., Wright, H. J., DeMatteo, D., Griffin, P. A., Locklair, B., & Desai, A. (2019). Treatment for restoration of competence to stand trial: Critical analysis and policy recommendations. *Psychology, Public Policy, and Law, 25*(4), 266–283. https://doi.org/10.1037/law0000210

Kois, L., Murrie, D., Gowensmith, N., & Packer, I. (2023). A public health perspective to reform the competence to stand trial system, *Psychiatric Services, 74*(12), 1289–1290. https://ps.psychiatryonline.org/doi/10.1176/appi.ps.20230079

Locklair, B. (2016, March). *Due process problems with civil commitment of incompetent defendants: The current round of litigation and the next.* Presented at the Annual Conference of the American Psychology-Law Society, Atlanta, GA.

Murrie, D. C., Gardner, B. O., & Torres, A. N. (2022). The impact of misdemeanor arrests on forensic mental health services: A state-wide review of Virginia competence to stand trial evaluations. *Psychology, Public Policy, and Law, 28*(1), 53–66.

National GAINS Center. (2004). *Sequential intercepts for change: Developing a comprehensive state plan for mental health and criminal justice collaboration.* Author.

Steadman, H. J., Deaner, M. W., Morrissey, J. P., Westcott, M. L., Salasin, S., & Shapiro, S. (1999). A SAMHSA research initiative assessing the effectiveness of jail diversion programs for mentally ill persons. *Psychiatric Services, 50*(12), 1620–1623.

Steadman, H. J., Osher, F. C., Robbins, P. C., Case, B., & Samuels, S. (2009). Prevalence of serious mental illness among jail inmates. *Psychiatric Services, 60*(6), 761–765. https://doi.org/10.1176/appi.ps.60.6.761

Stroh, D. P. (2015). *Systems thinking for social change: A practical guide to solving complex problems, avoiding unintended consequences, and achieving lasting results.* Chelsea Green Publishing.

Substance Abuse and Mental Health Services Administration. (2023). *Foundation work for exploring incompetence to stand trial evaluations and competence restoration for people with serious mental illness/serious emotional disturbance.* HHS Publication No. PEP23-01-00-005. Substance Abuse and Mental Health Services Administration.

Warburton, K., McDermott, B. E., Gale, A., & Stahl, S. M. (2020). A survey of national trends in psychiatric patients found incompetent to stand trial: Reasons for the reinstitutionalization of people with serious mental illness in the United States. *CNS Spectrums, 25*(2), 245–251. https://doi.org/10.1017/S1092852919001585

Wik, A., Hollen, V., & Fisher, W. (2020). Forensic patients in state psychiatric hospitals: 1999–2016. *CNS Spectrums, 25*(2), 196–206. https://doi.org/10.1017/S1092852919001044

Williams, B., & Hummelbrunner, R. (2010). *Systems concepts in action: A practitioner's toolkit.* Stanford University Press. https://doi.org/10.1515/9780804776554

14

Law Enforcement Consultation on Active Bystandership for Law Enforcement (ABLE)

Abigail S. Tucker and Karen Collins Rice

Psychologists working with justice-involved individuals should be aware of and informed about the need for active bystandership in law enforcement regarding the safety and well-being of officers, justice-involved individuals, and the community. This chapter will review specific training promoting Active Bystandership in Law Enforcement (ABLE). ABLE is designed to change views of active bystandership by educating the audience on what it is and what it is not, while creating a strong case for the opportunity for bystandership in law enforcement and the potential consequences of *not* adopting the practice of intervening among law enforcement professionals. It also dedicates considerable time to building the skills necessary to effectively intervene, to reduce mistakes, and prevent misconduct in various commonly experienced scenarios. Critically, it also attends to a growing awareness that the health and wellness of officers is related to officers' responses in communities. This chapter will provide an overview of the development of the ABLE curriculum with law enforcement, teaching the ABLE curriculum with law enforcement, and the ongoing interactive and iterative process in working with law enforcement individuals as well as agencies, to move from training to an active bystandership culture. In addition to reviewing the importance and role of active bystandership training and culture in law enforcement, the present chapter will also highlight the consultation needed to bring expertise from outside fields of knowledge (psychology and curriculum design) to the field of law enforcement.

The focus of this chapter is ABLE. There are alternatives. Law enforcement agencies can adopt an internal policy specific to the affirmative duty to intercede. Those same law enforcement agencies could require the policy to be read aloud at all roll-call shift meetings and document this activity as training. Law enforcement entities could create their own training on the duty to intercede.

Abigail S. Tucker and Karen Collins Rice, *Law Enforcement Consultation on Active Bystandership for Law Enforcement (ABLE)*. In: *The Path Forward*. Edited by: Kirk Heilbrun and David DeMatteo, Oxford University Press.
 DOI: 10.1093/9780197773031.003.0014

We assert that relying solely on policy attestation and self-directed training for a critical subject like the duty to intervene is neither as effective nor prudent as implementing the ABLE[1] program, a nationally recognized and evidence-based model.

Active bystandership is a set of skills grounded in social psychology that reduce harm. These skills can be learned and require practice. Training leverages peer intervention to reduce mistakes, prevent misconduct, and promote health and wellness in law enforcement, and teaches law enforcement professionals to recognize the opportunity for effective intervention when they observe peers engaged in misconduct that risks adversely impacting their health and wellness. The targeted audience is law enforcement professionals and agencies. The intended impact audience includes these professionals, law enforcement agencies, and the communities they serve, including individuals involved in the justice system.

As of 2025, ABLE has partnered with 390 law enforcement agencies, trained 2,729 instructors, is represented in 42 U.S. states and 3 Canadian provinces, estimates 169,000+ officers at ABLE agencies who have received ABLE training, and 181+ million community members served by ABLE agencies. ABLE training is provided in three critical phases: (1) pre-implementation; (2) implementation, including the Train-the-Trainer (T3) portion; and (3) sustainability. Pre-Implementation involves applying to become an ABLE agency. Those agencies wishing to participate in the Train-the-Trainer process must provide three letters of support from organizations in the communities they serve and agree to the ABLE standards. External organization letters of support can and should vary based on the community. Common examples include faith-based organizations embedded in the community, treatment providers (including crisis providers) who often serve those involved in the justice system, public defender officers, and advocacy groups supporting police reform. The agency and external organizations should know the ABLE Standards: reduced unnecessary harm to civilians; reduced unnecessary harm to officers; improved police-community relations; reduced risk of officers losing their jobs; improved officer health and wellness; improved officer job satisfaction; reduced risk of lawsuits against departments, cities, and individual officers; and improved civilian satisfaction with their law enforcement agency. The Implementation Phase includes a three-day Train-the-Trainer during which ABLE National Trainers provide training to individual agency instructors in the ABLE curriculum. The next step in the Implementation Phase is the one-time, 8-hour training of all staff within a department, which must be delivered by two ABLE-approved agency trainers. The third phase—Sustainability—includes an annual 2-hour refresher training. To date, topics for this training have included officer health and wellness and early interventions to prevent harm.

[1] See https://www.law.georgetown.edu/cics/able/.

Role of Psychologists and Other Professionals

ABLE is the intellectual property of Georgetown Law School; however, to promote rapid adoption and open-sourced foundations, Georgetown Law School and its ABLE advisors have maintained their non-profit status and offered the program at either no cost or very low cost for law enforcement agencies in the United States and Canada. ABLE sponsors include the law firm of Sheppard Mullin and the American Arbitration Association. ABLE also leverages supporters who contribute with public endorsement including agencies such as the American Civil Liberties Union (ACLU) of New Hampshire and the Center for Policing Equity. Advisors to ABLE comprise a multidisciplinary team that includes law enforcement professionals, psychologists, attorneys, students, curriculum designers, volunteers, and community advocates. Critical to the success of ABLE are the professionals working in law enforcement agencies and community agencies such as treatment providers, advocacy groups, civil rights-focused law firms, and local and state regulatory bodies. Any individual professional or agency providing services in which public safety (e.g., police, first responders) and justice-involved individuals intersect can potentially benefit from understanding active bystandership training and implementation in law enforcement agencies.

One common way law enforcement and community advocates learn about ABLE is through word of mouth from peers. ABLE has a website and attends law-enforcement conferences (e.g., FBI National Academy, Leadership for Black Law Enforcement, International Association of Chiefs of Police annual conference, and state conferences such as the Colorado State Sheriffs Conference). ABLE has also presented at psychological conferences (e.g., American Psychological Association Convention, N5, Society of Law & Psychology) and engaged strategically with community advocates, including Dedication to Community, to promote awareness and engagement from critical partners. ABLE also leveraged sponsors to support the nonprofit financially and develop that philanthropic perspective to advance the values of ABLE to a broader audience. Sponsors include but are not limited to the American Arbitration Association, Mastercard, PepsiCo, Sheppard Mullin, and Verizon.

There are various training roles for psychologists, students, and other professionals with ABLE and the culture of peer intervention. Those working with an ABLE-engaged police agency should be advised and prepared for a particular role, as ABLE sees tremendous value in engaging internal leaders (formal and informal) with differing credentials. For trainees still involved in predoctoral, internship, or postdoctoral training, this might provide an excellent opportunity to learn about ABLE, take a virtual class at no cost, and potentially become an ABLE Agency Trainer to co-facilitate or support a culture of active bystandership in law enforcement. Psychologists and other behavioral health professionals working in law enforcement agencies, specifically providers who provide clinical services or serve in operational consultation roles with law enforcement, can expand their functional knowledge by learning about active bystandership in policing. Treatment providers working with potentially justice-involved individuals (e.g., Crisis Systems, Co-Responders, alternative response models, shelters for the unhoused, withdrawal management centers) can enhance the police-community partnership by learning whether local agencies are ABLE adoptees, and how to bring ABLE to their community. Forensic psychologists should be aware of active bystandership in policing to supplement their work and consultation with police agencies in a way that elevates both officers and justice-involved individuals. Later in this chapter, we review the expansion of this work into corrections through the Heroes Active Bystandership Training program—particularly relevant for psychologists working in correctional settings.

Other professionals who work alongside psychologists in forensic and police psychology can benefit from enhanced knowledge of active bystandership and play an essential role in expanding this life-saving intervention. Educators and individuals providing training to law enforcement, including Academy trainers; professionals contracted to support law enforcement by providing, evaluating, or revising police training; and professors in higher education who may be teaching future law enforcement providers, will increase their competency and skills through learning about ABLE and the instructional design strategy supporting the ABLE curriculum. Law enforcement leaders who are in positions to model active bystandership may require intervention from their peers or subordinates; these individuals are important in creating the organizational climate and culture that supports and celebrates the practice. City and county officials who collaborate with law enforcement play a crucial role in reforming police-community relationships, as do advocacy groups and law firms focused on civil liberties.

Keys to Effective Service Provision

ABLE was developed and released as a national program in the months following the death of George Floyd. While there was considerable interest from law enforcement agencies around the country in participating in the program, limitations from COVID and the financial cost of broad program dissemination posed significant challenges. When we plan for the service provision of a program such as ABLE, there are two very important considerations: the development of the training and the model for dissemination.

The creation of ABLE began with the Ethical Policing is Courageous (EPIC)[2] program developed years earlier in partnership with the New Orleans Police Department. The challenge with ABLE was to create a program in the face of strong resistance from its target audience because of the climate within the law enforcement profession at the time of its development. The other challenge was to create a

[2] There is not yet a single comprehensive website including guidance for ABLE training. Some relevant information is contained at https://www.heroesintervene.com/heroes-program/ and https://www.law.georgetown.edu/cics/able/apply/.

Train-the-Trainer process that would enable law enforcement professionals to train their peers, rather than having outsiders come into the agency to deliver the program. These requirements were critical to address both the practical barriers (e.g., national accessibility and financial feasibility) and the emotional ones (e.g., feelings of intense scrutiny, blame, and underappreciation by law enforcement officers).

ABLE training asks law enforcement professionals to change how they view loyalty to each other and adopt the practice of intervening to prevent or stop unnecessary harm. For this to occur meaningfully, training must be an *entry point* leading to a larger culture change. Training is a practical component of culture change, and it addresses several aspects of performance. Police professionals must be able to see how the new practice fits within the profession's highest ideals, enabling them to align it with their best identity. Second, they must be able to justify the benefits of the change to be "worth it." The more significant the cultural shift, the stronger the case that is required. ABLE presents this case from three perspectives. The first is linking peer intervention to loyalty, a strength of the current law enforcement culture. By helping the audience understand the difference between blind and constructive loyalty, they can begin to see the practice of active bystandership as one that aligns with their existing values. The second "way in" to building the case for change is to tap into every officer's personal experience when they did not intervene. Even if this experience is outside of the context of policing, every person can relate to and even reconnect with the feelings of moral injury that come from not intervening when needed. Finally, the current statistics on the health and wellness issues in the profession are key to answering the question "What's in it for me?" Beyond the compelling data about substance abuse, depression, health problems, and suicide, almost every agency has a personal experience with at least one colleague who has lost their family, career, or even their life due to the behavioral health impacts of this work. Once the audience buys in, the next requirement is to teach them the skills to intervene effectively. Fifty percent of the ABLE class is spent on these skills, including building the awareness and reflection required for self-intervention.

Ultimately, the most crucial part of the training as it relates to culture change is ensuring that the new behavior—the intervention—will be accepted by the agency without any negative repercussions. There are two aspects to this acceptance: ensuring that every individual trained understands the power of giving permission to their peers to intervene with them when needed, and the leadership of the agency. If people understand and support the need for a change, and they also understand how to execute it—but do not believe their leadership will allow them to practice the change on the job—then little will be accomplished.

Once an effective program is developed, the following service-provisioning phase ensures effective training delivery. The ABLE Train-the-Trainer (T3) process begins with establishing selection criteria for agencies when identifying their internal ABLE instructors. While training experience is preferred, the primary criteria are a strong belief in and support for active bystandership in law enforcement, and perceived legitimacy as an advocate for active bystandership. The program is designed to compensate for having less experience in providing training. The virtual 3-day T3 process begins with agency instructors participating in the 8-hour class as students. This enables them to experience the class as they will subsequently facilitate it for their own participants. Two National ABLE Instructors teach the core curriculum and periodically provide "behind the scenes" commentary during the class to explain and reinforce the program's design. Once agency instructors complete the class, they receive their instructor materials and "teach-back assignments" to prepare to deliver core parts of the program. Day 2 of the T3 process is primarily preparation time for the teach-backs on Day 3. National ABLE Instructors are available for "virtual office hours" to field questions and provide support during the preparation day. The teach-backs are conducted on Day 3. Participants are divided into five small groups, and each group works with a National ABLE Instructor to deliver key parts of the curriculum and receive feedback from the instructor and their peers. To become a certified agency instructor, participants must demonstrate a minimum level of proficiency and commit to ongoing individual preparation and practice.

Legal Considerations and Supporting Foundations

Law enforcement's duty to intervene has been upheld in courts since the 1970s (see, e.g., *Byrd v. Brishke,* 1972). While a law enforcement officer's duty to intervene has been defined differently in case law over the years, one important aspect of these decisions has involved preventing harm to the public and liability for individual officers (*Figueroa v. Mazza,* 2017; *Yang v. Hardin,* 1994). The duty to intervene has been supported by the U.S. Department of Justice (DOJ), Civil Rights Division (n.d.), using the language of duty to intercede when an officer fails to stop harm and describing this as misconduct (U.S. Department of Justice, 2022, § 1–16.400). The DOJ released an Updated Use of Force Policy in 2022 that included Section 1–16.400, Affirmative Duty to Intervene (U.S. Department of Justice, 2022, § 1–16.600). This updated policy explicitly stated that officers must be trained to intervene. Officers and law enforcement agencies should also use legal counsel to review best practice documents (e.g., IACP Best Practices Guide: Internal Affairs: A Strategy for Smaller Departments, 2018) and other sources, such as union organizations or Department of Justice publications.

The tenets of active bystandership within the intervention-related training of ABLE focus on critical issues in law enforcement in responding to and preventing excessive use of force, misconduct, and mistakes that can lead to deviant officer behavior. IACP (2020) emphasized the importance of training officers in peer bystander intervention, calling attention to the importance of going beyond a policy regarding duty to intervention and ensuring that officers are trained in both the inhibitors to active bystandership and the specific skills to prevent harm to both peers and superiors. Many other training courses in law enforcement focus on the impacts of stress and trauma within these professions. As well, many programs train and use a peer-intervention model to support officer wellness. These trainings and programs are critically important. However, specific to this intervention-based training, the connection to active bystandership is grounded in early intervention to prevent harm, including health problems, mistakes, and misconduct (Tucker, 2023).

Research has been emerging on the role of stress, mental health diagnoses, and other stressors in police misconduct (Cubitt & Judges, 2018; Cubitt et al., 2020; Wu & Makin, 2020). We hear accounts from officers about misconduct and mistakes that end careers. In these stories, we often see unmet psychological needs coexisting with financial and occupational stress. These intervention-related trainings are not intended to directly address mental health or occupational stress. Instead, they are designed to enlist the allies of peer officers who are better positioned to identify early signs of stress—and then to intervene and connect their colleagues to the proper agency and community support needed. Officers are well-positioned for successful peer intervention when they are trained to recognize the early signs of stress, including risk factors for suicide, and use that to guide their interventions with their peers (IACP, 2014, 2016). After explaining both acute examples of stress impacts (such as "Amygdala Hijack," first coined by Daniel Goleman in 1995) and chronic examples (such as sleep disturbance and weight gain), the curriculum then uses the elevated awareness and asks: *How does this help you intervene with peer officers to prevent harm?* The responses flood in, including citing when a peer officer may be experiencing sensory exclusion or observing chronic stress indicators in each other. This tactic is grounded in adult learning and pulls from the student's experiences in and knowledge of a learner-centered framework. The learning objective is grounded in empirical and practical knowledge that peer intervention is effective in public safety cultures.

Self-awareness is the first step in behavioral change, but additional action is needed to develop, enhance, and increase the application of skills. The training, therefore, includes role-play affirmed in the science that practice improves performance. Trainees often groan and attempt to avoid the relatable awkwardness of role-play. Instructors are wise to use the knowledge from adult learning to counter those reactions and reassure officers that role-play practice increases their likelihood to intervene and prevent harm. While research dating back to the 1970s substantiates the effectiveness of role-play, more recent research supports its use with complex concepts for adult learners (Rosa, 2012; Sogunro, 2004). The role-plays in ABLE are designed using understandable, realistic scenarios; they each require perspective-taking and intentionally engage trainees in practicing their new skills of active bystandership. This role-play style is often dubbed pedagogy and has shown effectiveness in attending to affective, cognitive, and behavioral learning outcomes (Maier, 2022; Rao & Stupans, 2012). To solidify these learning outcomes as they pertain to active bystandership, instructors ask the class following role-plays about what social inhibitors were at play, what skills of active bystandership were used or could have been used, and what negative consequences were hypothetically avoided in the role-play scenario. Role-play is a unique opportunity in the training to challenge a common misnomer that ABLE is solely focused on police misconduct. ABLE attends to mistakes and officer health as avoidable harms equal to potential misconduct. For example, one of the role-play scenarios includes an avoidable documentation error where bystanders can practice their intervention skills with peers to prevent harm. Another role-play scenario is specific to health and well-being and gives participants the opportunity to practice identifying and taking action when they observe a peer employee in potential emotional distress.

Beginning and Development of Project Services

ABLE's origins date back to the 1990s, following the assault on Rodney King in Los Angeles, California. Dr. Ervin Staub, a preeminent national researcher on active bystandership, provided consultation on how training could be developed to support law enforcement peers intervening when they observe others engaging in wrongdoing. Fast forward two decades, and Staub, among others, supported law enforcement in developing a training model with the New Orleans Police Department (NOPD) in response to their federal consent decree. NOPD leaders, Federal Monitor Jonathan Aronie, psychologist Joel Dvoskin, civil rights advocate Ted Quant, and civil rights attorney Mary Howell were all eager to learn from Dr. Staub about the social psychology of active bystandership. Within months, the collaborators at NOPD, community advocates, and psychologists developed EPIC and launched a cultural shift in law enforcement.

The importance of this work was heightened with the death of George Floyd in May 2020. The NOPD was flooded with requests to share their model and support other agencies in applying the duty to intervene by combining it with an actionable skill in the context of law enforcement. NOPD could not meet this overwhelming demand and decided to partner with a law firm (Sheppard Mullin) and a law school (Georgetown University Law School) to establish ABLE. To share active bystandership with a national audience of police departments, ABLE was created as a non-profit project within the Georgetown University Law Center in January 2020. The resources required to get it to that stage, including the human, financial, and curriculum development, totaled about $50,000, including one instructional designer and about seven subject matter experts.

Expansion into Corrections

None of the requests that ABLE expand into other areas (e.g., corrections, dispatch, and fire and rescue) has resulted in expansion beyond police and the patrol side of sheriff's offices until recently. In 2022, ABLE and Heroes Active Bystandership Training collaborated in signing a Memorandum of Understanding (2022) between

ABLE and Heroes to allow the foundation of the ABLE curriculum to be adapted for cultures outside of law enforcement, including but not limited to corrections. Heroes Active Bystandership Training[3] is an organization providing active bystandership training to corrections, recognizing the important role correctional facilities play in their community. The critical role of correctional officers and staff is to maintain control and safety within the facility. This mission not only ensures that staff go home to their families but also that incarcerated persons safely complete their time and return to society ready to work, stay healthy, and engage with their families and communities. Active bystandership plays a key role in reducing mistakes and preventing misconduct that disrupts the safety of staff, the facility, and incarcerated persons. We find that correctional administrators and other leaders are familiar with the duty to intervene, but regretfully acknowledge that this duty alone does not consistently translate into bystander intervention by correctional staff.

As previously reviewed in this chapter, according to the U.S. Department of Justice (DOJ), officers must act upon the affirmative duty to intervene to prevent or stop excess force and agencies must provide training on the duty to intercede (U.S. Department of Justice, 2022, § 1–16.400 & § 1–16.600). The U.S. DOJ agencies[4] include corrections such as Federal Bureau of Prisons and National Institute of Corrections. Eiser (2023) discusses the importance of the duty to intervene in jails, emphasizing that officers are required to act to prevent or stop misconduct among their peers.

The correctional officer's duty to intervene has been upheld in legal proceedings. In 2022, former Alabama Department of Corrections Lieutenant Willie M. Burks, III was sentenced to imprisonment after being convicted of failure to intervene with former Correctional Sergeant Ulysses Oliver Jr., an officer under his command. Sergeant Oliver was convicted of assaulting two inmates, both with his hands and a collapsible baton, while they were handcuffed and unresisting. Lieutenant Burks observed the beating of the second inmate and did not intervene.

In a different case, the failure to intervene was again raised. In *McGee v. Parsano* (2022), which did not result in a conviction, the United States Court of Appeals for the Seventh Circuit held that correctional officers have a duty to intervene, including when witnessing inadequate care. The court further held that since the medical staff indicated that the care was adequate, the officers were not constitutionally expected to supersede the medical professionals' judgment unless they had reason to know that the care was inadequate. Although the correctional officers were thus granted qualified immunity in this case, the court affirmed the duty to intervene for correctional officers. This is consistent with the legal need for active bystandership to reduce the risk of harm in situations that include correctional health care.

[3] See https://www.heroesintervene.com.
[4] See https://www.justice.gov/agencies/chart/grid.

Ethical Considerations

Ethical considerations associated with active bystandership include overlapping principles in the American Psychological Association (APA) *Ethical Principles of Psychologists and Code of Conduct* (EPPCC, 2017). Generally, the principles of beneficence and nonmaleficence are relevant. Psychologists seek to benefit those with whom they work (in this case, law enforcement) and those whose lives are affected by law enforcement, including the general public and justice-involved persons. Active bystandership training in law enforcement promotes reasoning aligned with ethical values and avoids an "us vs. them" view of the world. For example, the curricula engage officers in a discussion about the potential harm to the public when officers fail to intervene with their peers in the face of wrongdoing. This conversation is designed to engage officers in critical thinking about harm that can occur and shifting their mindset from focusing on the "wrong-doer" to the witness to the wrongdoing. Officers routinely begin by sharing the adverse impacts on their profession, careers, and risk of lawsuits. Reviewing the International Association of Chiefs of Police (1957) Law Enforcement Code of Ethics, the International Corrections and Prison Association's (n.d.) Code of Ethics, and Goodman's (2008) *Enforcing ethics: A scenario-based workbook for police and correctional recruits and officers* (*3rd ed.*), a theme of ethical standards in police and corrections emerges—including commitment to integrity and honesty, respect for rights and dignity, professionalism and service. Psychologists can leverage their professional ethics of nonmaleficence, respect for people's rights and dignity, and responsibility to inquire about adverse impacts on the public and justice-involved persons with police and corrections to elevate collective critical thinking on ethical matters. The goal is to shift the focus from the "wrongdoer" to the bystander, and cultivate compassion through applicable ethical and moral standards presented to officers.

Under both the EPPCC and the American Psychological Association's (2013) *Specialty Guidelines for Forensic Psychology*, psychologists are encouraged to provide *pro bono* services as part of their broader work in delivering psychological services. ABLE provides an opportunity for psychologists to deliver relevant services at a greatly reduced or unbilled rate. Such psychologists (including students, trainees, and early career providers) may provide ABLE training as part of their position, on a fully *pro bono* basis, or at a reduced rate of payment. Similarly, psychologists may contribute to ABLE through curriculum content development, training content review, and educating other ABLE trainers on psychological theory, research, and practice—and their application to active bystandership.

Psychologists will likely find that reimbursement rates for ABLE-related services are closer to government professional services rates than standard private rates. This seems in line with similar training for law enforcement in other areas, such as Crisis

Intervention Team (CIT) training, Peer Support training, and Mental Health First Aid for Public Safety. Services in all these areas are delivered by front-line law enforcement and correctional staff but are often developed, researched, implemented, and supported by non-law enforcement professionals (including psychologists). It is often expected that work in these areas be provided at reduced or fully pro bono rates or as "other duties as assigned." Psychologists and other professionals will probably not find their work in active bystandership training to be financially very profitable. It may have other benefits, however, including expanded contacts with relevant individuals in law enforcement and corrections, greater visibility in the community, an opportunity for consultation in other areas—and the gratifying sense of making a difference in a very important area.

Generalizability of ABLE and Future Directions

Active bystandership training is now being used in school settings to address bullying, on college campuses to address sexual assault, and on in-flight decks to reduce pilot errors that can quickly become tragic. The application of active bystandership to law enforcement is relatively new despite its rapid adoption by ABLE in the last four years. ABLE has been asked to expand into other areas, such as civilians working in law enforcement, corrections, dispatch, and fire and rescue. ABLE has developed a civilian curriculum for professionals in ABLE law enforcement agencies. ABLE has signed a Memorandum of Understanding with Heroes Active Bystandership Training to allow the foundation of the ABLE curriculum to be used in cultures outside of law enforcement, including but not limited to corrections, dispatch, and fire departments. Heroes is working to enhance the impact of its curriculum by building out additional support tools in the pre-implementation and sustainability phases. Heroes has already shared a customizable Communications Kit with ABLE to help corrections and law enforcement agencies ensure organizational readiness with a comprehensive internal and external communication plan before implementing the 8-hour curriculum.

Concerning others in the field doing work that is complementary to active bystandership training in law enforcement, more work is needed. One primary aim of this chapter and these authors is to call for diverse professionals to work in this space—to understand active bystandership training and critically evaluate how their contributions can reduce mistakes and prevent misconduct by promoting health and wellness and adopting an active bystandership culture. However, promoting officer health and wellness and adopting an active bystandership culture takes more than training. It requires a culture shift and commitment from many collaborators, both internal and external, to law enforcement and to corrections. We offer a brief case example in Box 14.1.

Box 14.1 Developing ABLE in Denver

Denver Police Department (DPD) in Colorado became an ABLE agency in September 2020 after seeing the need for their community and employees, including their officers. The department lead for the ABLE project, Program Manager Elisa DiTrolio in the Strategic Initiatives Bureau, carefully considered how best to integrate ABLE philosophy and skills across the department and within their community. Ms. DiTrolio initiated a community board for Denver's ABLE project to double down on their external agency support letters and bring live feedback to the initial months of implementation. Additionally, she partnered with the Training Academy to use instructors from the field vs the academy who met the criteria of ability, understanding, and credibility. Given DPD's roll-out strategy to integrate into the Academy for recruits simultaneously with the agency-wide roll-out, this intentional adjustment strategically places peer intervention at the heart of this crucial mindset change for the department.

The replicability of ABLE requires careful consideration of copyright approvals and ethical considerations. Practically speaking, the implementation and replication of ABLE efforts depend on the activity (e.g., training vs. collaborative consultation) and the competency of each individual professional. See Table 14.1 for a guide designed to support professionals considering joining ABLE efforts.

Finally, more work is needed to research the implementation and impact of active bystandership training for law enforcement. ABLE's current research efforts are funded by Arnold Ventures, which is evaluating New Jersey's statewide initiative of ABLE implementation for law enforcement officers. They are still analyzing findings, and their evaluation includes Integrating Communications Assessment and Tactics (ICAT) and ABLE training. Additionally, Georgetown Law's Center for Innovations in Community Safety (CICS) is working on analyzing 40,000+ pre- and post-training surveys for change in perceptions over time and with respect to training satisfaction. Finally, CICS was funded by the American Institutes for Research to conduct a randomized controlled trial using ABLE data in one municipal police department, which involves a process and impact evaluation to measure change in police performance (e.g., uses of force, complaints) and racial disparities in those outcomes. Dr. Cassandra Ramdath, Director of Research and Evaluation at CICS, was directing the four year study at the time of this publication. Results are anticipated in 2027. We see a future of dissertations and growing social psychology research that incorporates outcomes beyond implementation and includes specific tenets of training and agency culture that may promote active bystandership principles, reduce mistakes, prevent misconduct, and promote the health and wellness of officers and community members alike.

Table 14.1 ABLE-Relevant Skills and Activities

ABLE-RELEVANT SKILLS	WIDELY ACCESSIBLE	MODERATE CHALLENGE TO REPLICATE WITHOUT DIRECT KNOWLEDGE, EXPERIENCE, AND PROFESSIONAL CONSULTATION	DIFFICULT TO REPLICATE WITHOUT DIRECT KNOWLEDGE, EXPERIENCE, AND PROFESSIONAL CONSULTATION
ABLE-RELEVANT ACTIVITY			
RECEIVE ABLE TRAINING	X		
BECOME AN ABLE AGENCY OR NATIONAL INSTRUCTOR		X	
IMPLEMENT ABLE TRAINING AT LAW ENFORCEMENT AGENCIES.		X	
CURRICULUM DESIGN (ABLE IS COPYRIGHTED—THIS "TASK" COMMUNICATES DIFFICULTY LEVEL, NOT ACTUAL CAPACITY)			X
IMPLEMENTATION AND SUSTAINABILITY OF ACTIVE BYSTANDERSHIP CULTURE			X

Diversity, Equity, and Inclusion (DEI) Considerations

ABLE requires that the agency provide this training to all staff, focusing on inclusivity. ABLE provides coaching to agencies when selecting T3 agency instructors to consider DEI and ensure that officers being trained can "see themselves" in their peer trainer. In addition, for the virtual ABLE's T3 events, careful consideration for gender, race, ethnicity, and other diversity factors is used to determine who is placed into which small group for teach-backs. This thoughtfulness seeks to use diversity as a strength in adult learning and create a more inclusive learning environment. The ABLE and Heroes curriculum design accommodates DEI considerations in the following ways: (1) gender, race, and ethnic diversity in program visuals; (2) use of gender-neutral pronouns; and (3) gender, race, and ethnic diversity in the case study and role-play scenarios. The future of ABLE will be strengthened by continued focus on DEI efforts, including the impact of ABLE on agency-wide DEI efforts, the impact of ABLE on responding to DEI interests of the communities they serve, and thoughtful research on the intersection of DEI and ABLE.

Lessons Learned and Recommendations

Any programs aimed at reform with rapid expansion will yield "lessons learned," and ABLE is no different. In reflecting on their noteworthy progress in less than five years, a few key considerations can be identified for agencies and psychologists working with law enforcement agencies. First, start slowly. EPIC started at a moderate pace due to the Consent Decree in NOPD and then moved much more quickly due to police reform. We will discuss the pros and cons of both and the current focus, which is more strategic and intentional. Second, the strength of ABLE was and remains their collaborative consultation with other disciplines and professionals. There is untapped potential to leverage ABLE's success and active bystandership in law enforcement to elevate officer health and wellness (police psychology), justice-involved individuals with behavioral health needs (forensic and correctional psychology), and community safety at large (psychology, criminal justice, law, enforcement, law, advocacy, and education). Finally, marketing is a form of advocacy when approached strategically. The best publicity starts with an authentic understanding and informed knowledge. For individuals who have already become informed about the role of active bystandership training in law enforcement, we would encourage the following measures to further increase awareness of how your knowledge and services can be utilized: face-to-face discussions with law enforcement leaders/agencies; word of mouth; and promoting your role in active bystandership training on your website, social media or other presentations, publications, and conference sessions.

Psychologists working with justice-involved individuals should recognize the importance of active bystandership in law enforcement for the safety and well-being of officers, justice-involved individuals, and the larger community. This chapter reviews specific training designed to promote active bystandership, emphasizing the need to shift mindsets and educate law enforcement on its principles and impacts. The ABLE program highlights the connection between officer wellness and community responses, detailing the development and implementation of the ABLE curriculum and its iterative process with law enforcement agencies. Correctional agencies' integration of active bystandership provides an important model for those in forensic psychology involved in delivering healthcare services to pretrial clients.

In describing the ABLE Program, we hope to underscore the value of external expertise from various fields (including psychology) to enhance law enforcement training. Active bystandership in policing, grounded in social psychology, is vital for reducing misconduct and promoting wellness in law enforcement through peer intervention. The training aims to equip law enforcement professionals with the skills to recognize and intervene in situations involving mistakes, misconduct, or behaviors detrimental to health and wellness, ultimately benefiting law enforcement agencies and their communities. ABLE's website and program staff make it easy to determine if your local law enforcement agency is an ABLE agency. If they are, then we would recommend that you consider providing support and other contributions to active bystandership training using your professional expertise. If the agency is not an ABLE agency, your task may be simpler: asking leaders how they are training their department on duty to intervene. Should the agency wish to become ABLE-certified, they can contact ABLE staff via their website, and local support such as yours will be an important consideration in whether they succeed in becoming an ABLE agency (see Table 14.2).

Research is an underdeveloped area as it pertains to active bystandership in law enforcement. While both ABLE and other law enforcement departments are evaluating their implementation and impact of active bystandership training, more research is needed. Research focusing on the quantitative and qualitative aspects of implementation, outcomes of various kinds (e.g., impact on the use of force data, staff wellness measures, or community complaints), the intersection of active bystandership and DEI efforts, and best practice implementation research will be particularly valuable.

Table 14.2 Do's and Don'ts in Becoming an ABLE Agency

Do's	Don'ts
Learn the history of the duty to intercede and social psychology as it pertains to active bystandership (include research and focus on the role of psychologists)	Confuse your role as a psychologist in support of ABLE (even if co-presenting) with the intent for it to be peer-to-peer.
If training, co-train with law enforcement; provide support by connecting Health & Wellness to ABLE (intentional work with Peer Support, EAP, in-house psychologists, etc.)	Underestimate the need for a mindset shift, knowledge increase, and skills-based learning when advocating for active bystandership in policing.
Support law enforcement agencies that are considering ABLE in connecting with community advocates and individuals who have lived experience through justice involvement.	Miss the opportunity to leverage your professional services and networking opportunities by learning about ABLE (police) and Heroes (corrections)

References

American Psychological Association. (2013). *Specialty guidelines for forensic psychology. American Psychologist, 68*(1), 7–19. https://doi.org/10.1037/a0029889

American Psychological Association. (2017). *Ethical principles of psychologists and code of conduct (2002, amended effective June 1, 2010, and January 1, 2017).* Author.

Byrd v. Brishke, 451 U.S. 935 (1972).

Cubitt, T. I., & Judges, S. J. (2018). Show cause analysis: A qualitative assessment of the factors influencing police misconduct from the perspective of the officers who commit it. *Policing: An International Journal, 41*(6), 782–797.

Cubitt, T. I., Wooden, K. R., Kruger, E., & Kennedy, M. H. (2020). A predictive model for serious police misconduct by variation of the theory of planned behaviour. *The Journal of Forensic Practice, 22*(4), 251–263.

Eiser, D. (May 3, 2023). *Duty to intervene applies in jails.* Lexipol. *https://www.lexipol.com/resources/blog/duty-to-intervene-applies-in-jails/*

Figueroa v. Mazza, No. 11-CV-3160 (ARR)(CLP), (E.D.N.Y. Mar. 30, 2017).

Goleman, D. (1995). *Emotional intelligence: Why it can matter more than IQ.* Bantam Books.

Goodman, D. (2008). *Enforcing ethics: A scenario-based workbook for police and correctional recruits and officers* (3rd ed.). Prentice Hall.

International Association of Chiefs of Police. (1957). *Law enforcement code of ethics.* https://www.theiacp.org/resources/law-enforcement-code-of-ethics

International Association of Chiefs of Police. (2014). *IACP National Symposium on Law Enforcement Officer Suicide and Mental Health: BREAKING THE SILENCE on law enforcement suicides.* Office of Community Oriented Policing Services.

International Association of Chiefs of Police, Police Psychological Services Section. (2016). *Peer support guidelines.* Author.

International Association of Chiefs of Police. (2018). *Best practices guide: Internal affairs: A strategy for smaller departments.* Author.

International Association of Chiefs of Police. (2020). *Peer bystander intervention in law enforcement agencies.* Author.

International Corrections and Prisons Association. (n.d.). *ICPA's code of ethical conduct.* https://icpa.org/icpa-about/icpa-s-code-of-ethical-conduct.html

Maier, H. W. (January, 2002). Role-playing: structures and educational objectives. https://cyc-net.org/cyc-online/cycol-0102-roleplay.html

McGee v. Parsano, No. 20-2414, 58 F.4th 1061 (7th Cir. 2022).

Rao, D., & Stupans, I. (2012). Exploring the potential of role-play in higher education: Development of a typology and teacher guidelines. *Innovations in Education and Teaching International, 49*(4), 427–436.

Rosa, J. A. (2012). Marketing education for the next four billion: Challenges and innovations. *Journal of Marketing Education, 34*(1), 44–54.

Sogunro, O. A. (2004). Efficacy of role-playing pedagogy in training leaders: Some reflections. *Journal of Management Development, 23*(4), 355–371.

Tucker, A. (2023). *Work sample submitted for board certification in police and public safety psychology.* Unpublished manuscript, American Board of Professional Psychology.

U.S. Department of Justice, Civil Rights Division. (n.d.). Law enforcement misconduct. Office of Civil Rights.

U.S. Department of Justice. (2022). *Justice manual: § 1-16.400 affirmative duty to intervene.* https://www.justice.gov/jm/section-1-16-400-affirmative-duty-to-intervene

U.S. Department of Justice. (2022). *Justice manual: § 1-16.600 training.* https://www.justice.gov/jm/section-1-16-600-training

Wu, G., & Makin, D. A. (2020). The differential role of stress on police officers' perceptions of misconduct. *Asian Journal of Criminology, 16*(3), 213–233.

Yang v. Hardin, 37 F.3d 282 (7th Cir. 1994).

15

Consultation on Treatment Court Development and Implementation

Douglas B. Marlowe

Nearly two-thirds of adults who are convicted of a crime in the United States have a moderate to severe substance use disorder (Bronson et al., 2017; Fearn et al., 2016), and approximately 40 percent have a mental health disorder or report distressing mental health or trauma symptoms (Bronson & Berzofsky, 2017). Among persons with substance use disorders in the criminal justice system, continued substance use is one of the most impactful, yet treatable, risk factors for criminal recidivism, increasing the odds of a new offense by two to three times (Kopak et al., 2016). Although most mental health disorders do not increase criminal recidivism directly (Peterson et al., 2014), untreated symptoms can interfere with other rehabilitation services, such as counseling aimed at reducing interactions with antisocial peers and addressing deficient problem-solving skills (Hubbard & Pealer, 2009; Taxman & Caudy, 2015).

Treatment courts were developed beginning in the late 1980s in response to burgeoning criminal court caseloads resulting from a crack cocaine epidemic. The earliest programs were adult drug courts that focused on diverting persons charged with simple drug possession into court-supervised treatment in lieu of prosecution. Subsequent research, however, has determined that these intensive programs exert the greatest effects for *high-risk* and *high-need* participants, defined for present purposes as persons who have a severe and persistent substance use and/or mental health disorder and serious risk factors for treatment attrition or criminal recidivism, such as extensive criminal records, antisocial peers, impulsivity, or antisocial thought processes (Carey et al., 2012; Cissner et al., 2013; Reich et al., 2016). In line with this evidence, best practice standards for treatment courts have evolved toward serving a wider range of higher risk and need populations, including adults or juveniles with serious and persistent substance use, mental health, trauma, or co-occurring disorders who are charged with felony property and theft offenses, serious probation or parole violations, and some violent offenses such as domestic violence (All Rise, 2024). Serving high-risk and high-need populations has required treatment courts to reinforce and expand their delivery of safe, effective, developmentally and age-appropriate, and culturally equitable services. In addition, recent

Douglas B. Marlowe, *Consultation on Treatment Court Development and Implementation*. In: *The Path Forward*. Edited by: Kirk Heilbrun and David DeMatteo, Oxford University Press. © Oxford University Press (2026).
DOI: 10.1093/9780197773031.003.0015

exigencies, including the opioid epidemic and infiltration of highly toxic and addictive substances into the illegal drug supply (e.g., fentanyl, xylazine), have placed greater demands on treatment courts to confidently protect public health and safety. This chapter focuses on the critical roles and responsibilities of psychologists and other treatment professionals in ensuring that treatment courts deliver evidence-based and culturally proficient treatments, match services to clients' validly assessed treatment needs and desired goals, and carefully avoid practices that interfere with treatment aims and client welfare.

Program Description

Treatment courts are specialized court dockets that operate within the criminal justice, juvenile justice, or family dependency court systems. As mentioned previously, the first treatment courts were developed to serve adults charged with drug-related crimes. Eligible clients for these adult drug courts have a moderate to severe substance use disorder and are charged with a substance-related offense, such as possession or sale of a controlled substance or another offense caused or influenced by drug use, such as theft or forgery to support a drug use disorder. The defining ingredients of these programs are described in a founding document that is colloquially referred to as the *Ten Key Components*, which was developed by All Rise, formerly the National Association of Drug Court Professionals (NADCP, 1997). The positive results reported from adult drug courts (reviewed below) have spawned a wide variety of other types of treatment courts, including but not limited to DWI courts serving persons charged with repeated or aggravated instances of driving while intoxicated, mental health courts serving persons charged with crimes influenced by a mental health or co-occurring disorder, juvenile treatment courts for teens in juvenile court proceedings, family treatment courts for parents or guardians facing founded allegations of child abuse or neglect, reentry treatment courts for persons released conditionally from jail or prison, and veterans treatment courts serving military veterans or active-duty personnel whose justice system involvement is related to a service-connected injury or trauma. Key components have been published for several of these models, which incorporate the original *Ten Key Components* while adding other elements required to serve the specific needs of each population. As of mid-year 2023, there were approximately 4,000 treatment courts in the United States, including nearly 1,700 adult drug courts (DeVall et al., 2023).

The treatment court judge serves as the leader of a multidisciplinary team that brings together the diverse expertise, legal authority, and resources required to rehabilitate high-risk and high-need persons. Significantly better effectiveness, cost-effectiveness, and cultural equity have been reported when the team included, at a minimum, a program coordinator, treatment professionals, prosecutor or other state's attorney, defense or legal aid attorney, community supervision officer (e.g., probation, parole, or child welfare services officer), law enforcement officer (e.g., police officer or sheriff's deputy), and program evaluator (Carey et al., 2012; Ho et al., 2018). Depending on client needs and developmental levels, other rehabilitation, child welfare, school, or social service professionals may also serve on the team and have been shown to improve outcomes (Center for Children and Family Futures [CCFF] & All Rise, 2019; Korchmaros et al., 2016; Office of Juvenile Justice and Delinquency Prevention [OJJDP], 2016).

Clients attend frequent status hearings in court, during which the judge encourages their commitment to recovery, reviews their progress, and may impose a range of consequences contingent on their performance. These consequences may include desired incentives (e.g., verbal praise, reduced supervision requirements, or inexpensive prizes), service adjustments (e.g., supporting treatment recommendations for the provision of psychiatric medication or medication for addiction treatment [MAT]), or punitive sanctions (e.g., verbal warnings, community service, or brief jail detention commonly ranging from 1 to 7 days). The judge typically administers these consequences in open court after the treatment court team has met in a confidential collaborative setting to review each case and reach a tentative determination about the appropriate course of action. Team members contribute information about client progress and offer recommendations for suitable consequences to deliver; however, the judge is legally and ethically required to make the final decision concerning imposing sanctions after giving due consideration to all relevant information and discussing the matter with the client or the client's legal representative in court.

Treatment plans vary according to clients' assessed needs. In addition to substance use, mental health, and/or trauma treatment, services may include family counseling, vocational training, educational assistance, housing assistance, or help with obtaining medical or dental care. In addition, case managers or social workers assist clients to access health care coverage, financial benefits, and other needed public resources like subsidized housing. Most programs employ a brokerage model for treatment, in which treatment representatives or clinical case managers on the team assess clients' needs, refer them to community providers for needed and desired services, receive progress reports, and explain treatment progress information and the implications of that information to other team members for effective team decision-making.

Most treatment court curriculums are scheduled to be twelve to twenty-four months in duration; however, some clients may require more time to satisfy the criteria for successful discharge. To be discharged successfully, clients must complete a regimen of substance use, mental health, and/or trauma treatment and other indicated services such as vocational training; achieve at least ninety days of continuous abstinence from illegal drugs and alcohol (if relevant in the case); avoid criminal activity or new arrests; obey court conditions such as curfews or travel restrictions; obtain employment or engage in other prosocial activities like education or household management; and complete community service or victim restitution.

Entry into treatment court is the product of a negotiated legal agreement between the client or client's attorney and the prosecutor or state's attorney. In most programs, clients plead guilty or no contest to the underlying charge(s) as a condition of entry, or they stipulate to (acknowledge the truth of) the factual basis for the allegations. This requirement is intended to keep clients engaged in treatment because the case ordinarily proceeds to final disposition or sentencing in the event of treatment attrition or other repetitive rule infractions. Clients also waive several, but not all, of their adversarial trial rights as a condition of entry, including their right to a speedy trial and to be free from self-incrimination and suspicionless searches, such as random drug testing or probation home visits. With limited exceptions (e.g., reports of child abuse or an imminent threat to another individual), information obtained via in-program procedures can be used only to gauge a client's compliance with the program's conditions and cannot be used to bring or substantiate a new charge. In exchange for relinquishing these rights, clients have their charges reduced or avoid prosecution, incarceration, or other negative legal repercussions (e.g., termination of parental rights) for completing the program. In some criminal treatment courts, the arrest or charge may also be expunged from the client's legal record, which helps to avoid some of the negative collateral consequences of a criminal record, such as a loss of voting rights or access to subsidized housing. Other programs are ordered after a conviction as a condition of probation, parole, or another criminal sentence. Graduates avoid or shorten their period of incarceration and may reduce the length or conditions of their probation or parole.

Potential candidates for treatment court are typically informed about the program by their defense counsel, the prosecutor, a bail magistrate, or outreach caseworkers who may approach them in pretrial detention or at a preliminary hearing or arraignment. Candidates are evaluated for admission using validated risk and need tools to ensure they meet treatment court criteria for being high-risk and high-need, reside or were arrested in the program's catchment area, and do not have disqualifying charges or convictions, such as for sex offenses or aggravated assault. Unfortunately, focus groups have determined that many defendants, especially Black or African American defendants, first learned about treatment court after they had already served several weeks or months in pretrial detention (Janku, 2017). At that point, many of these individuals were likely to be sentenced to time served if convicted and were therefore uninterested in further involvement with the criminal justice system. Focus groups have also found that many defendants learned about treatment court from a source they did not trust (often the prosecutor), emphasis was placed on the program's rules and the punitive consequences that ensue for infractions, and stigmatizing language was often used in describing the program, such as "addicts" or "dirty urines" (Gallagher, 2013; Janku, 2017; Witkin & Hays, 2019). Such practices might explain why many eligible individuals decline referral offers.

Clinically trained professionals, such as psychologists, counselors, social workers, or certified peer recovery specialists, are most likely to use nonstigmatizing language, to be viewed by candidates as a reliable source of information about the pros and cons of participation, and to be competent in counseling strategies that enhance motivation for change. In some treatment courts, trained clinicians or peer specialists confidentially screen all persons who are eligible for a community sentence and offer them needed voluntary pre-plea services as soon as possible after arrest, booking, or entry into custody. Participating in the program is a possible mitigating factor in plea offers and sentencing, and no information obtained from the program can be used to substantiate the current charge(s), bring new charges, or increase the person's sentence upon conviction. Studies of these pre-plea programs are preliminary, but early evidence suggests they may increase entry rates, hasten access to MAT and other needed treatment, and reduce overdose rates, without increasing criminal recidivism (Carey et al., 2022). Several technical assistance organizations offer practitioner training and toolkits describing these and other outreach strategies to help treatment courts increase their entry rates and enhance sociocultural equity in their recruitment practices (see Appendix) at the end of this chapter.

Foundations of and Support for Treatment Courts

Meta-analyses and multisite studies have determined that adult drug courts significantly reduced criminal recidivism—typically measured by rearrest rates over two to three years—by an average of approximately twelve to thirty-five percent, with the most effective drug courts reducing recidivism by fifty to eighty-five percent (Carey et al., 2012; Mitchell et al., 2012; Rossman et al., 2011; Trood et al., 2021). Reductions in recidivism have been shown to last for at least three years after entry (Mitchell et al., 2012) and for as long as fifteen years (Kearley & Gottfredson, 2019). A national study in the United States found that adult drug courts also significantly reduced illegal drug and alcohol use, improved clients' family relationships, and increased their access to needed financial and social services (Rossman et al., 2011). Finally, cost-effectiveness evaluations have concluded that adult drug courts produced an average of approximately $2 to $4 in cost savings for every $1 invested (Downey & Roman, 2010; Washington State Institute of Public Policy, 2019).

Significant reductions in recidivism or improvements in child welfare outcomes have also been reported in meta-analyses of studies involving DWI courts (Mitchell et al., 2012), family treatment courts (Zhang et al., 2019), and mental health courts (Jalain et al., 2024). Juvenile treatment courts, in contrast, have produced small average effects on recidivism (Tanner-Smith et al., 2024). This disappointing finding may stem from the fact that many juvenile treatment courts are not focusing on serving teens with a high risk for recidivism and high need for substance use or mental health treatment (Long & Sullivan, 2016). Low-risk or low-need teens are likely to perform as well or better in less burdensome and less costly programs. Significant improvements have been reported when juvenile treatment courts were trained carefully to serve high-risk and high-need youth and deliver proven, developmentally appropriate practices (Dennis et al., 2022).

Scholars have dedicated considerable effort to understanding how and why treatment courts work. As noted earlier, these programs were created out of necessity by local criminal justice practitioners in response to burgeoning court dockets.

The earliest programs were developed based on the experiences and intuitions of these practitioners, and were not predicated on an identified psychological, criminological, or other a priori theory or body of evidence. Early efforts to explain their effects under the broad rubric of therapeutic jurisprudence have provided a sense of legitimacy (Hora et al., 1999) but are unsatisfying because they do not propose testable hypotheses about the programs' mechanisms of action. A jurisprudential philosophy that seeks to achieve healthy psychological effects from legal processes is laudable but does not explain why some programs are successful and others are not, nor does it offer guidance for enhancing program operations or developing new programs to address other underserved populations or unmet needs.

Although many theories have been proffered to explain the mechanisms of action of treatment courts, the proposed theoretical constructs (e.g., reintegrative shaming, structural ritualization) have often been vaguely defined and poorly measured (e.g., by administering unvalidated self-report instruments), leading to mixed or lackluster findings. Two theories, however, have received substantial empirical support in experimental and quasi-experimental studies. Risk-need-responsivity (RNR) theory posits that the most effective and cost-efficient outcomes are achieved when the intensity of criminal justice supervision is matched to clients' risk for recidivism or serious technical violations, and services focus on the specific disorders or conditions that are responsible for their crimes (Bonta & Andrews, 2017). Consistent with RNR principles, outcomes are significantly better when treatment courts serve high-risk and high-need individuals, but they can produce ineffective or harmful outcomes if they imprudently deliver the full complement of services for low-risk or low-need persons (Cissner et al., 2013; Long & Sullivan, 2016; Reich et al., 2016). Ineffective outcomes for low-risk and low-need individuals may result from increased interactions with high-risk peers in the programs, or excessive treatment or supervision requirements may interfere with productive activities like work or childcare. Controlled studies have also reported better outcomes when adult drug courts and DWI courts assigned clients to different frequencies of court hearings and/or treatment sessions based on a risk and need assessment (Carey, 2021; Carey et al., 2018; Marlowe et al., 2006), and when they increased the frequency of court hearings or treatment sessions in response to inadequate performance in the program (Carey et al., 2015; Marlowe et al., 2012). These findings confirm that treatment courts improve outcomes, at least in part, by titrating the amount of supervision and treatment that are delivered based on clients' assessed risk and need levels.

Behavior modification principles of contingency management or operant conditioning have also been well-validated in treatment courts. Examples of contingency management practices include delivering incentives to enhance involvement in beneficial activities like counseling, and delivering sanctions to deter avoidable behaviors that interfere with recovery goals or threaten public safety, such as associating with substance-using peers or violating curfew restrictions. Longitudinal studies have determined that outcomes in treatment courts were significantly mediated by the careful monitoring of client progress and delivery of swift, certain, and procedurally fair responses for their performance (Cissner et al., 2013; Gottfredson et al., 2007; Roman et al., 2020; Shaffer, 2010). Reliable delivery of these contingency management practices was required and largely responsible for favorable results.

Importantly, effective contingency management requires an understanding of the critical distinction between proximal and distal behavioral goals. Some infractions, such as not attending counseling sessions or delivering tampered drug test specimens, are avoidable by many clients and often reflect inattention to one's responsibilities or willful misconduct. Such *proximal* infractions require relatively higher-magnitude sanctions to ensure that clients take their responsibilities seriously in the program, and to avoid habituation in which persons can become accustomed (and thus less responsive) to being sanctioned (Marlowe, 2017). Providing weak or no sanctions in response to avoidable infractions may encourage clients to test the limits of the program's tolerance, leading to more of the same or worse behavior and reducing the likelihood that indicated sanctions will work in the future, even if they are applied correctly. Other infractions, such as illegal substance use, are often a symptom of a client's illness or reflect deficient problem-solving skills. For such *distal* infractions, treatment, not punishment, is required to address relevant symptoms (e.g., depression or withdrawal), remediate skill deficits, and help them to avoid repeating such infractions in the future. Delivering high-magnitude sanctions for distal infractions worsens outcomes by precipitating learned helplessness, in which persons become despondent or resentful because they are unable to avoid punishment, leading to higher rates of treatment attrition, substance use, emotional distress, and crime (Seligman, 1975).

Studies have confirmed that outcomes were less effective in treatment courts that delivered high-magnitude sanctions, especially jail detention, for distal infractions like substance use before clients were clinically stable, were no longer experiencing distressing symptoms such as withdrawal or drug cravings, and could avoid substance use (Brown et al., 2011; McRee & Drapela, 2012; Vaske, 2019). However, in the later phases of treatment court, when clients were likely to be clinically stable and could satisfy more demanding expectations (i.e., when the demands had become proximal), high-magnitude sanctions including jail detention for substance use and other avoidable infractions have been associated with improved outcomes (Brown et al., 2011; Shannon et al., 2022).

These findings underscore a critical role for treatment professionals in treatment courts. Expert treatment guidance is essential for informing the team when clients have attained sufficient clinical stability for abstinence or other conditions to be considered achievable goals for them and, if applicable, for warning the team if symptom recurrence may have temporarily returned some conditions to being distal goals, thus requiring treatment adjustments, not sanctions, to reestablish clinical stability. If treatment professionals do not attend pre-court team meetings and court hearings routinely, and participate proactively in team decision-making, they may undermine treatment effectiveness by allowing ill-informed actions to interfere with treatment objectives and the therapeutic process.

Development of Program Services and Generalizability

Decades of research and practical experience have led to a substantial evolution in treatment court practices. Studies have identified dozens of best practices that are associated with fifty to one hundred percent greater improvements in successful completion rates, recidivism, cost-effectiveness, illegal substance use, and cultural equity (Carey et al., 2012; Ho et al., 2018; Rossman et al., 2011; Shaffer, 2010). These practices are described objectively in best practice standards promulgated by All Rise (2024) and other organizations (CCFF & All Rise, 2019; OJJDP, 2016). Notably, research suggests that two overarching practice domains—team training and team functioning—may be primarily responsible for effective outcomes. Treatment courts that adhere to best practices in these domains are likely to apply other best practices as well. Ensuring that all team members remain abreast of current information on best practices and apply that knowledge during team decision-making is essential for achieving success and for generalizing the potential benefits of treatment courts across different programs and client populations.

Three training components in treatment courts—pre-implementation training, new staff orientation, and annual continuing education—are associated with more than two times greater cost-effectiveness and fifty percent larger reductions in criminal recidivism (Carey et al., 2012; Shaffer, 2010; Van Wormer, 2010). In pre-implementation training, the team meets as a group for several days before starting the program to learn from expert faculty about the key components and best practices in treatment courts, create their mission statement and goals and objectives for the program, and develop effective policies and procedures to govern their operations. In the event of team member turnover, orientation for new team members is also required to avoid a downward drift in service quality. Typically, orientation provides an overview of the key components and best practices in treatment courts, with the goal of avoiding acute disruption in services and degradation of outcomes. To sustain efficacy, new staff should receive formal training as soon as practicable after assuming their position. Ideally, new hires should also attend pre-court team meetings and court status hearings before the transition to learn how the program operates, observe their predecessor's actions, and receive advice and direction from an experienced colleague. Finally, studies have determined that knowledge retention and delivery of best practices decline within six to twelve months of an initial training, thus requiring annual booster training to sustain efficacy and ensure that practitioners stay abreast of new information (Chadwick et al., 2015). Multisite studies have reported that annual team booster training was the greatest predictor of program effectiveness and adherence to the treatment court model (Shaffer, 2010; Van Wormer, 2010).

Team functioning is the second major factor impacting treatment court outcomes. Studies have revealed that the reliable involvement of all team members in the program's daily operations, especially pre-court staff meetings and court status hearings, significantly enhanced effectiveness, cost-effectiveness, and sociocultural equity

(Carey et al., 2012; Cissner et al., 2013; Ho et al., 2018; Rossman et al., 2011; Shaffer, 2010). Staff and clients consistently rate effective team functioning as being among the most important elements for success (Korchmaros et al., 2016; Van Wormer et al., 2020). How well team members coordinate their responsibilities, avoid role confusion, share pertinent and appropriate information, and function in accordance with evidence-based practices and ethical standards has an outsized influence on outcomes.

Studies have identified effective communication strategies that enhance team functioning in treatment courts. One example is the Network for the Improvement of Addiction Treatment (NIATx) Organizational Improvement Model. The NIATx model is derived from research in organizational and industrial psychology on effective and collaborative team communication and decision-making skills. It seeks to create a climate of "psychological safety" by teaching team members how to articulate divergent views in a manner that is likely to be heard and heeded by fellow team members. Studies in more than ten adult drug courts found that training on the NIATx model significantly increased staff job satisfaction (Melnick et al., 2014a), enhanced team communication skills (Melnick et al., 2014b), and improved program efficiency, leading to higher admission rates, shorter wait times for treatment, and reduced no-show rates at scheduled appointments (Wexler et al., 2012). Psychologists and other treatment professionals can provide critical consultation using NIATx or other evidence-based strategies to enhance rational team decision-making and avoid "groupthink" and other communication barriers.

These findings indicate that although team members must acquire and apply new skills to be successful in treatment courts, the knowledge sets can be taught and sustained through a firm commitment to professional education and skill acquisition. No evidence suggests that success requires unusually committed, charismatic, or exceptional "believers." Numerous organizations offer free or low-cost training, resources, and technical assistance to enhance and sustain effective team functioning and delivery of other best practices (see Appendix).

Diversity, Equity, and Inclusion

Treatment courts were created to improve justice system outcomes, including by making service access and provision more culturally equitable and inclusive. Yet cultural disparities in referral, admission, and completion rates are reported in many programs. A study of more than 20,000 clients in 142 adult drug courts, DWI courts, and reentry courts reported an average successful completion rate of 38 percent for Black or African American clients and 49 percent for Hispanic or Latino/a clients, compared with 55 percent for non-Hispanic White clients (Ho et al., 2018). Another study in ten geographically diverse communities in the United States found that Black persons who were arrested for drug offenses were approximately half as likely as White persons to be referred to drug court; of those referred, Black persons were less likely to be admitted in seven of the eight jurisdictions for which admission data were available; and of those admitted, Black persons were less likely to graduate in six of the ten jurisdictions (Cheesman et al., 2023). These findings suggest that cascading impacts at successive stages in the treatment court entry and completion process may contribute additively or multiplicatively to higher justice system involvement for Black and Hispanic persons, lesser access to needed treatment and social services, and poorer criminal justice and health outcomes. Comparable research has not, to date, been conducted with members of other sociocultural groups, such as Native American persons or LGBTQIA+ persons, raising concern that inequities might be broader than currently recognized.

Best practice standards require treatment courts to monitor their operations for evidence of sociocultural disparities in access, service provision, and outcomes, review the findings as a team at least annually, take achievable corrective measures to eliminate identified disparities, and evaluate the effects of their corrective measures (All Rise, 2024). Resources are available to help treatment courts define and measure key performance indicators of sociocultural equity, examine disparities in practice delivery, and enhance equitable access and outcomes (see Appendix).

Studies in treatment courts have also reported better outcomes for Black and Hispanic clients when same-race, same-ethnicity, and/or same-gender clinicians delivered culturally proficient treatments that incorporated clients' cultural backgrounds and experiences as core components of the intervention and addressed culturally related stress and social determinants of health (Beckerman & Fontana, 2001; Marlowe et al., 2018; Vito & Tewksbury, 1998; Waters et al., 2018). Expertise from treatment professionals is required to help programs adopt evidence-based, culturally proficient curricula, ensure that facilitators deliver the interventions reliably and respectfully, and gauge client reactions.

Advice to Treatment Professionals in Treatment Courts

Several opportunities have been discussed for psychologists and other treatment professionals to enhance treatment court recruitment, effectiveness, and sociocultural equity. Additional cautions and advice are required, however, to help these professionals navigate practical challenges and ethical quandaries that are commonly confronted in the programs.

Treatment courts are characterized as nonadversarial programs because clients waive many of their trial rights, the judge receives ex parte (out of court) information about them from the team and other direct service providers, and the judge speaks directly to clients in court rather than primarily through their legal counsel. This process does not, however, imply that team members relinquish their professional responsibilities. Prosecutors and supervision officers must continue to advocate on behalf of public safety and client accountability, defense counsel must advocate for clients' legal rights and preferred interests, and treatment providers must advocate for effective, equitable, and humane treatment. The principal difference in treatment courts is that advocacy occurs primarily in pre-court team meetings as opposed to court hearings, thus reserving the greater share of court time for intervening with clients rather than gathering background information and arbitrating uncontested facts or legal issues. Treatment professionals must understand that they retain their traditional professional, ethical, and legal responsibilities to deliver effective and equitable services, safeguard client welfare, adhere to all laws governing client privacy and confidentiality, and interact with other professionals in a collegial and respectful manner. One can advocate effectively for best practices without being adversarial.

Many justice professionals are insufficiently informed about evidence-based treatments and may hold unwarranted views opposing certain safe and proven interventions, such as agonist medications like methadone or buprenorphine that have attenuated opioid properties, and health-risk prevention measures like naloxone that can reverse an opioid overdose, fentanyl or xylazine test strips, and syringe services programs (Grella et al., 2020). Despite compelling evidence that these interventions save lives and reduce nonprescribed opioid use without increasing the use of other illegal substances or criminal activity, they are underutilized in many treatment courts (Marlowe et al., 2022). Treatment professionals should not defer to invalid team beliefs when client welfare is at stake, but rather should make every effort to alter those beliefs by marshaling and explaining the available research evidence for fellow team members and clients.

Maintaining appropriate and ethical professional boundaries can also be challenging in these multidisciplinary programs. Treatment professionals are responsible, first and foremost, for helping clients to stay healthy and reach their recovery goals, and they should not be responsible for enforcing court orders or imposing sanctions for noncompliance. These latter duties are performed by other team members, including the judge, the supervision officer, and the prosecutor. For public safety reasons and to preserve the integrity of the justice system, some team members may insist routinely on abstinence from all nonprescribed drugs and alcohol, adherence to prescribed medications, and achievement of other goals like obtaining employment or earning a GED. Yet despite these mandates, treatment is most effective when therapists work collaboratively with their clients to set treatment goals and avoid insisting on or enforcing such conditions unless they are required to protect a client from serious and imminent harm and are consistent with the person's individualized needs (Friedmann et al., 2009). Nevertheless, it is well within a treatment professional's role to help clients appraise their situation realistically, navigate their mandates, and take the necessary steps to avoid punitive consequences and reap the benefits of program completion. By working collaboratively with clients to help them meet program requirements, treatment providers can assist them to advance their legal and welfare interests without disturbing the therapeutic alliance or substituting the therapist's values for those of the client.

Treatment professionals also walk a fine line in deciding what information to share with the team. Clients may be reluctant to trust their treatment provider or to acknowledge concerns or infractions if they fear the information will be shared with the court and might result in a punitive sanction. Careful policies and procedures should be agreed upon in advance by all team members that protect the treatment alliance while ensuring that clients do not elude responsibility for their actions by providing inconsistent information to different team members.

Treatment staff must, of course, comply with HIPAA provisions governing medical and mental health information, with 42 C.F.R. Part 2 governing substance use treatment information, and with other applicable state laws. HIPAA and 42 C.F.R. Part 2 permit treatment professionals to share specified elements of health information pursuant to a voluntary, informed, and competent waiver of a clients' confidentiality and privacy rights, or pursuant to a valid court order. Although consent is not required and cannot be revoked if disclosure is required by a court order, treatment professionals should nonetheless ensure that clients are clearly informed and competent to understand the program's confidentiality policies and procedures, including knowing what information will be released, who can receive the information, what steps the client should take to revoke consent (if revocation is permissible), and when the consent expires.

Pursuant to HIPAA and 42 C.F.R. Part 2, disclosures must be limited to the minimum information that is necessary for authorized recipients to monitor client progress, support treatment objectives, and ensure that treatment is being delivered safely. Health information should be shared only as necessary to inform other team members whether clients are progressing adequately in treatment, complying with treatment-related court-ordered conditions (e.g., attending counseling sessions), and avoiding interference with other clients' treatment. For example, treatment providers should report proximal (avoidable) infractions that reflect noncompliance or interference with treatment, such as willfully missing counseling sessions, disrupting counseling groups, or threatening treatment staff or other clients. To preserve client trust and openness, however, greater caution is required concerning distal infractions that reflect a client's clinical symptoms, such as compulsive substance use, which can be ascertained by other team members through drug testing, home visits, or other routine surveillance. Treatment professionals should not report such distal infractions without a client's consent unless doing so is necessary to avoid serious and imminent harm. Instead, they should encourage clients to self-disclose the information, and they should keep the team apprised of whether clients have achieved adequate clinical stability for abstinence or other conditions to be considered proximal goals for them, and should offer evidence-based recommendations for suitable treatment responses. For example, a treatment provider might caution the team that a client is not yet clinically stable without disclosing specific instances of substance use, and advocate for treatment adjustments rather than sanctions for positive drug tests obtained by a probation officer. Similarly, a treatment provider might advise the team that a client would benefit from health-risk prevention measures, such as training on how to use fentanyl test strips, without disclosing recent opioid use. Such balanced practices enable treatment professionals to serve client welfare without disturbing the therapeutic alliance, interfering with other team members' core responsibilities, or becoming an inadvertent agent of the justice system.

Conclusion

More than thirty-five years of research has demonstrated the potential benefits of treatment courts for enhancing client welfare, protecting public safety, and conserving public resources. Studies have identified the most effective client populations for these programs and have uncovered dozens of best practices that optimize results. Treatment professionals serve critical roles in these programs, including applying their clinical skills to increase entry rates, delivering or overseeing the delivery of evidence-based and culturally proficient treatments, cautioning other team members to avoid ineffective and potentially harmful sanctioning practices, and assisting the team to make rational and informed decisions. Resources, training, and technical assistance are available to help treatment professionals fulfill these critical responsibilities, conduct themselves in an ethical and appropriate manner, and enhance public health and safety.

Author Note

The views expressed in this chapter are those of the author and do not necessarily reflect the positions or policies of any organization with which he is affiliated.

Appendix: Treatment Court Technical Assistance Organizations

All Rise, the National Association of Treatment Court Professionals*
https://allrise.org/about/treatment-courts/

Bureau of Justice Assistance (BJA), Adult Treatment Court Program
https://bja.ojp.gov/program/adult-treatment-court-program/overview

Center for Children and Family Futures (CCFF)
https://www.cffutures.org/family-treatment-courts-focus/

Center for Justice Innovation (CJI)
https://www.innovatingjustice.org/areas-of-focus/treatment-courts

* *Note.* This list is not exhaustive but includes technical assistance providers that focus substantially or exclusively on treatment courts.

National Center for State Courts (NCSC)
https://www.ncsc.org/consulting-and-research/areas-of-expertise/behavioral-health/treatment-courts

National Council of Juvenile and Family Court Judges (NCJFCJ), Juvenile Drug Treatment Court Information Center
https://progdev.ncjfcj.org/child-welfare-and-juvenile-law/substance-abuse-and-opioids/jdtc/

National Treatment Court Resource Center (NTCRC)
https://ntcrc.org

References

All Rise. (2024). *Adult treatment court best practice standards* (2nd ed.). https://allrise.org/wp-content/uploads/2024/05/Adult-Treatment-Court-Best-Practice-Standards-I-VI_VIII_X-final.pdf

Beckerman, A., & Fontana, L. (2001). Issues of race and gender in court-ordered substance abuse treatment. *Journal of Offender Rehabilitation*, *33*(4), 45–61. https://doi.org/10.1300/J076v33n04_03

Bonta, J., & Andrews, D. A. (2017). *The psychology of criminal conduct* (6th ed.). Routledge.

Bronson, J., & Berzofsky, M. (2017). *Indicators of mental health problems reported by prisoners and jail inmates, 2011-12* (NCJ 250612). Bureau of Justice Statistics, U.S. Dept. of Justice. https://bjs.ojp.gov/content/pub/pdf/imhprpji1112.pdf

Bronson, J., Stroop, J., Zimmer, S., & Berzofsky, M. (2017). *Drug use, dependence, and abuse among state prisoners and jail inmates, 2007-2009* (NCJ 250546). Bureau of Justice Statistics, U.S. Dept. of Justice. https://bjs.ojp.gov/content/pub/pdf/dudaspji0709.pdf

Brown, R. T., Allison, P. A., & Nieto, J. (2011). Impact of jail sanctions during drug court participation upon substance abuse treatment completion. *Addiction*, *106*(1), 135–142. https://doi.org/10.1111/j.1360-0443.2010.03102.x

Carey, S. M. (2021). *San Joaquin DUI Monitoring Court: Evaluation key findings report*. NPC Research. https://npcresearch.com/wp-content/uploads/SJDMC-Outcome-and-Cost-Evaluation-Key-Findings-Report-2021.pdf

Carey, S. M., Allen, T. H., Einspruch, E. L., Mackin, J. R., & Marlowe, D. (2015). Using behavioral triage in court-supervised treatment of DUI offenders. *Alcoholism Treatment Quarterly*, *33*(1), 44–63. https://doi.org/10.1080/07347324.2015.982455

Carey, S. M., Ho, T., Johnson, A. J., Rodi, M., Waller, M., & Zil, C. E. (2018). *Missouri treatment courts: Implementing RNR in a drug court setting: The 4-track model in practice. Outcome and cost study summary.* NPC Research. https://npcresearch.com/wp-content/uploads/MO-4-Track-Outcome-and-Cost-Summary.pdf

Carey, S. M., Mackin, J. R., & Finigan, M. W. (2012). What works? The ten key components of drug court: Research-based best practices. *Drug Court Review, 8*(1), 6–42. https://npcresearch.com/publication/what-works-the-ten-key-components-of-drug-court-research-based-best-practices-3/

Carey, S. M., Van Wormer, J., & Johnson, A. (2022). Responding to a state of emergency: The creation of a new triage to treatment court model to address the opioid crisis. *Journal for Advancing Justice, 4*, 5–21. https://allrise.org/resources/the-journal-for-advancing-justice/

Center for Children and Family Futures, & All Rise. (2019). *Family treatment court best practice standards.* https://www.wicourts.gov/courts/programs/problemsolving/docs/ftcstandards.pdf

Chadwick, N., DeWolf, A., & Serin, R. (2015). Effectively training community supervision officers: A meta-analytic review of the impact on offender outcome. *Criminal Justice and Behavior, 42*(10), 977–989. https://doi.org/10.1177/0093854815595661

Cheesman, F. L., Marlowe, D. B., & Genthon, K. (2023). Racial differences in drug court referral, admission, and graduation rates: Findings from two states and eight counties. *Journal of Ethnicity in Criminal Justice, 21*(1), 80–102. https://doi.org/10.1080/15377938.2023.2193952

Cissner, A. B., Rempel, M., Franklin, A. W., Roman, J. K., Bieler, S., Cohen, R., & Cadoret, C. R. (2013). *A statewide evaluation of New York's adult drug courts: Identifying which policies work best.* Center for Court Innovation. https://www.innovatingjustice.org/publications/statewide-evaluation-new-yorks-adult-drug-courts-identifying-which-policies-work-best

Dennis, M. L., Estrada, B., Modisette K. A., Belenko, S., Hiller, M., Weiland, D., Cain, C., Kagan, R., Pappacena, L., Ostlie, E., Carnevale, J., Mackin, J., & Carey, S. (2022). *Final report of the cross-site evaluation of the Juvenile Drug Treatment Court (JDTC) Guidelines.* https://www.ojp.gov/library/publications/final-report-cross-site-evaluation-juvenile-drug-treatment-court-jdtc

DeVall, K., Lanier, C., & Baker, L. J. (2023). *Painting the current picture: A national report on treatment courts in the United States.* National Treatment Court Resource Center. https://issuu.com/ndcrc/docs/pcp_nationalreport_combined_content_2022_5_22_23_d

Downey, P. M., & Roman, J. K. (2010). *A Bayesian meta-analysis of drug court cost-effectiveness.* Urban Institute. https://ntcrc.org/wp-content/uploads/2021/11/A_Bayesian_Meta-Analysis_of_Drug_Court_Cost_Effectiveness.pdf

Fearn, N. E., Vaughn, M. G., Nelson, E. J., Salas-Wright, C. P., DeLisi, M., & Qian, Z. (2016). Trends and correlates of substance use disorders among probationers and parolees in the United States, 2002-2014. *Drug and Alcohol Dependence, 167*, 128–139. https://doi.org/10.1016/j.drugalcdep.2016.08.003

Friedmann, P. D., Rhodes, A. G., & Taxman, F. S. (2009). Collaborative behavioral management: Integration and intensification of parole and outpatient addiction treatment services in the Step'n Out study. *Journal of Experimental Criminology, 5*(3), 227–243. https://doi.org/10.1007/s11292-009-9079-3

Gallagher, J. R. (2013). African American participants' views on racial disparities in drug court outcomes. *Journal of Social Work Practice in the Addictions, 13*(2), 143–162. https://doi.org/10.1080/1533256X.2013.784689

Gottfredson, D. C., Kearley, B. W., Najaka, S. S., & Rocha, C. M. (2007). How drug treatment courts work: An analysis of mediators. *Journal of Research on Crime & Delinquency, 44*(1), 3–35. https://doi.org/10.1177/0022427806291271

Grella, C. E., Ostlie, E., Scott, C. K., Dennis, M., & Carnevale, J. (2020). A scoping review of barriers and facilitators to implementation of medications for treatment of opioid use disorder within the criminal justice system. *International Journal of Drug Policy, 81*, Article 102768. https://doi.org/10.1016/j.drugpo.2020.102768

Ho, T., Carey, S. M., & Malsch, A. M. (2018). Racial and gender disparities in treatment courts: Do they exist and is there anything we can do to change them? *Journal for Advancing Justice, 1*, 5–34. https://www.ncjrs.gov/App/Publications/abstract.aspx?ID=275429

Hora, P. F., Schma, W. G., & Rosenthal, J. T. A. (1999). Therapeutic jurisprudence and the drug treatment court movement: Revolutionizing the criminal justice system's response to drug abuse and crime in America. *Notre Dame Law Review, 74*(2), 439–537. https://scholarship.law.nd.edu/cgi/viewcontent.cgi?article=1629&context=ndlr

Hubbard, D. J., & Pealer, J. (2009). The importance of responsivity factors in predicting reductions in antisocial attitudes and cognitive distortions among adult male offenders. *Prison Journal, 89*(1), 79–98. https://doi.org/10.1177/0032885508329987

Jalain, C. I., Lucas, P. A., & Higgins, G. E. (2024). Assessing the effectiveness of mental health courts in reducing recidivism: A systematic review with meta-analysis. *Justice Evaluation Journal, 55*(7), 1073–1098. https://doi.org/10.1080/24751979.2024.2373245

Janku, A. D. (2017, October). *Equity and inclusion in treatment courts* (conference presentation). Illinois Association of Problem-Solving Courts 5th Annual Conference, Normal, IL.

Kearley, B. W., & Gottfredson, D. (2019). Long term effects of drug court participation: Evidence from a 15-year follow-up of a randomized controlled trial. *Journal of Experimental Criminology, 16*(3), 27–47. https://doi.org/10.1007/s11292-019-09382-1

Kopak, A. M., Hoffmann, N. G., & Proctor, S. L. (2016). Key risk factors for relapse and rearrest among substance use treatment patients involved in the criminal justice system. *Criminal Justice and Behavior, 41*(1), 14–30. https://doi.org/10.1007/s12103-015-9330-6

Korchmaros, J. D., Baumer, P. C., & Valdez, E. S. (2016). Critical components of adolescent substance use treatment programs: The impact of *Juvenile Drug Court: Strategies in Practice* and elements of Reclaiming Futures. *Drug Court Review, 10*(1), 80–115. https://ndcrc.org/drug-court-review/dcr-archive/

Long, J., & Sullivan, C. J. (2016). Learning more from evaluation of justice interventions: Further consideration of theoretical mechanisms in juvenile drug courts. *Crime & Delinquency, 63*(9), 1091–1115. https://doi.org/10.1177/0011128716629757

Marlowe, D. B. (2017). Applying incentives and sanctions. In D. B. Marlowe & W. G. Meyer (Eds.), *The drug court judicial benchbook* (text rev., pp. 139–157). National Drug Court Institute. https://allrise.org/publications/the-drug-court-judicial-benchbook/

Marlowe, D. B., Festinger, D. S., Dugosh, K. L., Benasutti, K. M., Fox, G. & Croft, J. R. (2012). Adaptive programming improves outcomes in drug court: An experimental trial. *Criminal Justice and Behavior, 39*(4), 514–532. https://doi.org/10.1177/0093854811432525

Marlowe, D. B., Festinger, D. S., Lee, P. A., Dugosh, K. L., & Benasutti, K. M. (2006). Matching judicial supervision to clients' risk status in drug court. *Crime & Delinquency, 52*(1), 52–76. https://doi.org/10.1177/0011128705281746

Marlowe, D. B., Shannon, L. M., Ray, B., Turpin, D. P., Wheeler, G. A., Newell, J., & Lawson, S. G. (2018). Developing a culturally proficient intervention for young African American men in drug court: Examining feasibility and estimating an effect size for Habilitation Empowerment Accountability Therapy (HEAT). *Journal for Advancing Justice, 1*, 109–130. https://advancejustice.org/wp-content/uploads/2018/06/AJ-Journal.pdf

Marlowe, D. B., Theiss, D. S., Ostlie, E. M., & Carnevale, J. (2022). Drug court utilization of medications for opioid use disorder in high opioid mortality communities. *Journal of Substance Abuse Treatment, 141*, Article 108850. https://doi.org/10.1016/j.jsat.2022.108850

McRee, N., & Drapela, L. A. (2012). The timing and accumulation of judicial sanctions among drug court clients. *Crime & Delinquency, 58*(6), 911–931. https://doi.org/10.1177/0011128708330761

Melnick, G., Wexler, H. K., & Rajan, S. (2014a). Measuring team members' satisfaction in drug courts: An instrument to gauge the component disciplines in drug court. *Drug Court Review, 9*(1), 56–73. https://ndcrc.org/drug-court-review/dcr-archive/

Melnick, G., Wexler, H. K., & Zehner, M. (2014b). Communication in drug courts: The consensus-building enhancement. *Drug Court Review, 9*(1), 99–116. https://ndcrc.org/drug-court-review/dcr-archive/

Mitchell, O., Wilson, D. B., Eggers, A., & MacKenzie, D. L. (2012). Assessing the effectiveness of drug courts on recidivism: A meta-analytic review of traditional and nontraditional drug courts. *Journal of Criminal Justice, 40*(1), 60–71. https://doi.org/10.1016/j.jcrimjus.2011.11.009

National Association of Drug Court Professionals. (1997). *Defining drug courts: The key components.* Office of Justice Programs, U.S. Department of Justice. https://www.ncjrs.gov/pdffiles1/bja/205621.pdf

Office of Juvenile Justice and Delinquency Prevention. (2016). *Juvenile drug treatment court guidelines* (NCJ 250368). https://ojjdp.ojp.gov/sites/g/files/xyckuh176/files/pubs/250368.pdf

Peterson, J. K., Skeem, J., Kennealy, P., Bray, B., & Zvonkovic, A. (2014). How often and how consistently do symptoms directly precede criminal behavior among offenders with mental illness? *Law and Human Behavior, 38*(5), 439–449. https://doi.org/10.1037/lhb0000075

Reich, W. A., Picard-Fritsche, S., Rempel, M., & Farley, E. J. (2016). Treatment modality, failure, and re-arrest: A test of the risk principle with substance-abusing criminal defendants. *Journal of Drug Issues, 46*(3), 234–246. https://doi.org/10.1177/0022042616638490

Roman, J. K., Yahner, J., & Zweig, J. (2020). How do drug courts work? *Journal of Experimental Criminology, 16*, 1–25. https://doi.org/10.1007/s11292-020-09421-2

Rossman, S. B., Rempel, M., Roman, J. K., Zweig, J. M., Lindquist, C. H., Green, M., Downey, P. M., Yahner, J., Bhati, A. S., & Farole, D. J. (2011). *The multisite adult drug court evaluation: The impact of drug courts* (Vol. 4). Urban Institute. https://www.urban.org/research/publication/multi-site-adult-drug-court-evaluation-impact-drug-courts

Seligman, M. E. P. (1975). *Helplessness: On depression, development, and death.* W. H. Freeman.

Shaffer, D. K. (2010). Looking inside the black box of drug courts: A meta-analytic review. *Justice Quarterly, 28*(3), 493–521. https://doi.org/10.1080/07418825.2010.525222

Shannon, L. M., Jones, A. J., Perkins, E., Newell, J., & Nichols, E. (2022). Examining the impact and timing of jail sanctions on drug court completion. *Journal for Advancing Justice, 4*, 65–84. https://allrise.org/resources/the-journal-for-advancing-justice/

Tanner-Smith, E. E., Mojekwu, F., & Frankel, L. (2024). Examining the effects of juvenile drug treatment courts: A systematic review and meta-analysis. *Criminal Justice and Behavior, 51*(1), 148–170. https://doi.org/10.1177/00938548231208208

Taxman, F. S., & Caudy, M. S. (2015). Risk tells us who, but not what or how: Empirical assessment of the complexity of criminogenic needs to inform correctional programming. *Criminology & Public Policy, 14*(1), 71–103. https://doi.org/10.1111/1745-9133.12116

Trood, M. D., Spivak, B. L., & Ogloff, J. R. P. (2021). A systematic review and meta-analysis of the effects of judicial supervision on recidivism and well-being factors of criminal offenders. *Journal of Criminal Justice, 74*, Article 101796. https://doi.org/10.1016/j.jcrimjus.2021.101796

Van Wormer, J. G. (2010). *Understanding the operational dynamics of drug courts* (doctoral dissertation). University of Washington. https://rex.libraries.wsu.edu/esploro/outputs/99900581662001842

Van Wormer, J., Holbrook, M. A., Lu, R., Lutze, F., & Mei, X. (2020). Collaboration within drug courts: A national survey of drug court professionals. *Justice Evaluation Journal, 3*(2), 178–199. https://doi.org/10.1080/24751979.2020.1744470

Vaske, J. C. (2019). The effect of disproportionate sanctioning on client noncompliance. *Drug Court Review, 3*, 8–25. https://ndcrc.org/drug-court-review/dcr-archive/

Vito, G., & Tewksbury, R. (1998). The impact of treatment: The Jefferson County (Kentucky) drug court program. *Federal Probation, 62*(2), 46–51. https://www.uscourts.gov/sites/default/files/62_2_7_0.pdf

Washington State Institute of Public Policy. (2019). *Benefit-cost results.* https://www.wsipp.wa.gov/BenefitCost

Waters, N. L., Lee, C. G., Cochran, N., & Holt, K. (2018). Trauma treatment for men in recovery for substance use disorders: A randomized design within the Miami-Dade County Adult Drug Court. *Journal for Advancing Justice, 1*, 131–157. https://allrise.org/resources/the-journal-for-advancing-justice/

Wexler, H. K., Zehner, M., & Melnick, G. (2012). Improving drug court operations: NIATx organizational improvement model. *Drug Court Review, 8*(1), 80–95. https://ndcrc.org/drug-court-review/dcr-archive/

Witkin, S. H., & Hays, S. P. (2019). Drug court through the eyes of participants. *Criminal Justice Policy Review, 30*(7), 971–989. https://doi.org/10.1177/0887403417731802

Zhang, S., Huang, H., Wu, Q., Li, Y., & Liu, M. (2019). The impacts of family treatment drug court on child welfare core outcomes: A meta-analysis. *Child Abuse & Neglect, 88*, 1–14. https://doi.org/10.1016/j.chiabu.2018.10.014

16

Consultation and Program Development

Juvenile Probation

Amanda NeMoyer, Jeanne McPhee, Ilsa Papunen, Rena Kreimer, and Naomi Goldstein

Although juvenile legal system reform has often focused on preventing youth confinement (i.e., detention and commitment), approximately half of youth with cases petitioned in court experience community-based supervision (i.e., probation) at some point in their case processing (Hockenberry, 2023). Extant research has identified problems with the use of traditional probation processes—which prioritize surveillance and control as a strategy to compel compliance—with young people, leading to recent calls for a nationwide transformation of juvenile probation (e.g., Annie E. Casey Foundation, 2018; National Council of Juvenile and Family Court Judges [NCJFCJ], 2017). Specifically, experts, practitioners, and advocates have highlighted the benefits of approaches that account for youth development and leverage established understanding of how best to motivate youth to change their behaviors (e.g., Fabelo et al., 2011; Goldstein et al., 2016; Schwartz, 2018).

Psychologists—given their training and expertise in youth development and behavior change—can serve in a consulting role for probation departments seeking to transform their approaches to youth probation to align with best practices. In this position, intervention efforts would focus on changing the practices of *system actors*, rather than the behaviors of individual youth directly, as such consultants work directly with probation officers and leadership to modify how they structure and engage in youth supervision. In particular, psychologists can apply their knowledge of relevant participatory and implementation research methodologies to foster partnerships with probation departments, leadership, and officers and educate probation personnel on the relevant behavioral principles underlying recommended juvenile probation policy and practice and support their implementation. Similar collaborative efforts between probation departments and professionals trained in psychology and related disciplines have demonstrated important successes (e.g., Cunningham et al., 2023; Farrell et al., 2020; Goldstein et al., 2019) and offer continued promise for juvenile probation transformation on a national scale.

Amanda NeMoyer et al., *Consultation and Program Development*. In: *The Path Forward*. Edited by: Kirk Heilbrun and David DeMatteo, Oxford University Press. © Oxford University Press (2026). DOI: 10.1093/9780197773031.003.0016

Strategies for Partnering with Probation Departments

Psychologists might partner with probation departments by taking several steps (see Goldstein et al., 2019, for more details about identified steps). First, either the psychologist or a juvenile probation department leader initiates the partnership, with the goal of transforming existing policy and practices in line with current empirical understanding of adolescent development and youth behavior change. Second, the partnership expands to include other probation staff (e.g., supervisors, officers)—and, when possible, youth and families with relevant lived expertise—and then all groups work together to develop new probation policies and practices for the department. Third, partners should establish a plan for implementing the reforms, and fourth, stakeholders should evaluate the effectiveness of both the reformed policies and practices *and* their implementation. Continuing support from the psychologist (e.g., in the form of ongoing technical assistance or support in developing a peer mentorship model) might benefit and support reform sustainability (e.g., Ingel et al., 2022).

Carrying out these steps and successfully developing and maintaining partnerships with probation departments relies upon many of the principles underlying community-based participatory action research, co-design, and implementation science frameworks. As a result, psychologists with exposure to, training in, and/or experience implementing these frameworks—and who have knowledge and experience with the juvenile legal system—will be well positioned to conduct this work. Below, we describe some of the foundational principles of these frameworks and discuss how they can be applied by psychologists working in a consultation role with juvenile probation departments.

Foundational Principles

Community-based participatory action research (CBPAR) frameworks—developed in response to concerns that traditional researcher-community dynamics do not adequately consider the expertise and input of the community of interest (Wallerstein et al., 2017)—emphasize equitable, non-hierarchical *partnerships* between research professionals and community members aiming to execute an intervention to drive change (Collins et al., 2018). Specifically, equal contribution from stakeholders serves as a central component of this form of research, which emphasizes the importance of building and maintaining relationships based on mutual trust and respect (Wallerstein et al., 2017). In this way, CBPAR is conducted "*with* the community, rather than *on* or *in* the community" (Rodriguez Espinosa & Verney, 2021, p. 314) and in ways that leverage and add to the strengths and resources of community members (Clinical and Translational Science Awards Consortium et al., 2011). Co-design, an element of CBPAR, emphasizes shared power and decision making during the planning phase of an intervention (Vargas et al., 2022); however, these and other CBPAR principles should apply throughout the ongoing planning, implementation, evaluation, and adjustment phases of intervention development (Collins et al., 2018).

When used together, CBPAR and co-design principles can aid in promoting the *implementation of evidence-based practices in community settings*, a major goal of the discipline of implementation science (Haynes et al., 2019). Recommended implementation strategies often include elements of CBPAR to improve the speed and quality with which agencies adopt evidence-based practices (Cook et al., 2019). As an example, implementation science research has often emphasized the importance of generating *buy-in*, or personal investment in an intervention, among individuals at all levels of an implementing agency—from top leadership to those front-line staff who will be putting a novel program or policy into practice (McCrae et al., 2014). Importantly, the use of CBPAR techniques—such as having these relevant stakeholders involved throughout the planning and implementation processes and developing trusting and respectful relationships between community and researcher partners throughout that process—has been linked to increased buy-in among practitioners (Ivankova, 2017). Therefore, when establishing partnerships with practitioners and other community members, psychologists should rely upon their own expertise but also recognize and elicit expertise from partners at all levels of existing hierarchies.

Psychologist consultants might encounter resistance or distrust when first meeting with practitioners, as a result of practitioners' existing attitudes or beliefs regarding their institution, the individuals they serve, their current roles and ability to carry out their roles, psychology or psychological research as a field, the feasibility of enacting meaningful change within their agency (Debus-Sherrill et al., 2023; Kang Balzarini & Eno Louden, 2024), and negative experiences with previous consultants. As a result, implementation science research has emphasized the need to both explain the underlying empirical support for an evidence-based practice *and* work in collaboration with practitioners from the same field who can offer anecdotal evidence about how similar efforts have been successful in other locations (Young et al., 2006). In this way, building staff competencies involves helping them increase knowledge about evidence-based practices in general and the specific reforms most relevant to their work—together, these methods can help make staff more open to implementing novel ideas (Ingel et al., 2022). Further, psychologists should recognize the many competing demands on practitioners and ensure that, whenever possible, novel initiatives and plans for their implementation can be incorporated into existing systems to reduce the additional burden on staff, thereby increasing the likelihood of implementation success (Swain-Bradway et al., 2013).

In sum, partnerships between psychologists and practitioners should be approached as a continual, reciprocal process that adapts and changes based on ongoing feedback from community partners. Ideally, such relationships serve as learning opportunities for all involved parties, as opposed to an unequal or hierarchical arrangement in which expertise and knowledge flows only from one side to the other. These partnerships, when constructed thoughtfully and with CBPAR and implementation science principles in mind, are well-positioned to create lasting, sustainable reform.

Applying Foundational Principles to Work with Juvenile Probation Departments

In line with CBPAR and implementation science, psychologists can most impactfully engage with probation departments by approaching partnerships intentionally and ensuring that probation department leaders and staff feel empowered throughout the reform process. As a result, psychologists aiming to work with local probation departments to transform existing structures should approach department leadership with the proposal in a respectful, collaborative manner, recognizing and appreciating practitioners' expertise from working directly with youth, and make it clear from the beginning that equal contributions from all involved parties will be imperative for success. Additionally, psychologists must center the needs and priorities of the probation department in question and emphasize how the project will directly benefit their department, their staff, and the youth and communities they serve. Psychologists should create open lines of communication from the beginning of the project, ensuring that probation department staff feel willing and comfortable sharing their perspectives, feedback, and questions throughout the project, and maintaining ongoing communication throughout the partnership via regular updates, informal conversations, and formal meetings, communications, and discussions.

Establishing common goals and priorities among those involved with the project will help lay the foundation for collaborative work. Psychologists can find common ground with probation leaders and staff by discussing goals (e.g., youth well-being, community safety) early in the collaborative process and continually referencing these common goals and shared values throughout the subsequent steps of reform development. Specifically, psychologists and psychology researchers can actively identify and engage various legal system stakeholders (i.e., outside of probation), share information and provide context so that all partners are on the same page. Psychologists may also help facilitate conversations to ensure that stakeholders agree upon shared definitions of relevant concepts. They might next gather baseline data about current practices and work in close partnership with probation departments to develop research-informed policies and procedures for youth on probation. Finally, psychologists and researchers can evaluate the effectiveness of reform efforts, informing probation departments about the outcomes and impacts of reformed policies and practices.

As an example, in Philadelphia, a partnership between a psychology researcher (the last author of this chapter) and the city's juvenile probation department centered the goals and priorities of probation leaders and staff (i.e., reducing frequency of technical violations of probation and decreasing unnecessary use of secure detention) and, ultimately, facilitated the incorporation of research-informed, evidence-based techniques (e.g., emphasizing youth effort toward short term, incremental goals, providing incentives for positive behavior) into departmental policy and practice related to youth probation supervision (Goldstein et al., 2019). This work led to another partnership between the same psychology researcher and *state*-level probation leadership in Pennsylvania. Specifically, this researcher and her team leveraged their expertise in adolescent development to embed research-informed principles in state-level policy regarding youth probation.

In addition to the partnership with state-level probation leadership, the psychology researchers engaged with local probation departments around Pennsylvania to develop a model facilitating peer-to-peer mentorship for juvenile probation officers from jurisdictions that have implemented evidence-based reforms to assist probation officers in other jurisdictions seeking to implement similar initiatives (DeYoung et al., 2024). Through this model, psychology researchers serve as expert consultants and technical assistance providers, helping probation departments build research-informed principles into their policies and practices while *also* helping to build the capacity of probation staff around the state to support their peers in new locations develop and implement research-informed probation practices in their own departments. Importantly, Pennsylvania's statewide probation leadership demonstrated an organizational commitment to aligning their policies and practices with research around adolescent development and behavior change, and they actively sought out the continued involvement of the consulting psychology research team. This organizational commitment and investment helped demonstrate that respected leaders in the probation field valued insights and feedback from the consulting psychology research team; in turn, the research team embraced the principles of CBPAR and co-design by prioritizing elements most important to probation leadership and staff, while ensuring equal and active voice from all parties in the policy and practice design process.

Applying Behavioral Principles to Probation

As discussed in detail above, psychologists can use knowledge of participatory action research and implementation science principles to establish partnerships with one or more probation departments to transform the way they approach youth probation. Subsequently, psychologists can leverage their knowledge of foundational behavioral principles of psychology to help probation leaders and staff better understand youth behavior and more effectively promote positive behavior change. Below, we discuss these principles and how they might be applied to youth probation policy and practice.

Operant Conditioning Principles

Many effective behavior change programs are grounded in operant conditioning, which suggests learning occurs when people associate specific behaviors with particular responses from others, themselves, or the world around them (Bellack et al., 1982). According to the theory, *responses* to a behavior can increase or decrease the chance that the behavior will be repeated. Specifically, *reinforcing* the behavior—whether by adding something pleasant (positive reinforcement) or taking away something unpleasant (negative reinforcement)—will increase the likelihood of a repeated behavior. In contrast, providing an unwanted *consequence* or targeted intervention in response to a behavior—for example, adding something unpleasant (positive punishment) or taking away something pleasant (negative punishment)—will decrease the likelihood of a repeated behavior. Research from the past several decades has demonstrated effective behavior shaping as a result of operant conditioning, even when conducted with a variety of groups, including school-aged students, children with behavioral or attention deficits, and adults on probation (e.g., Corepal et al., 2018; Flick, 2010; Sloas et al., 2019).

Given the rapid and uneven development of the adolescent brain (e.g., Casey et al., 2008; Cauffman et al., 2010), youth are particularly motivated by rewards that offer a surge of dopamine to the parts of their brains involved in reward processing (van Duijvenvoorde et al., 2016). Although rewards and incentives often involve tangible items, experiencing success by achieving goals and receiving praise from authority figures can also be motivating for youth (Fefer et al., 2016). Thus, probation officers can capitalize on the developing and reward-seeking parts of adolescents' brains through operant conditioning by providing reinforcement and incentives in response to desired behaviors. Furthermore, though the landscape of juvenile probation has been shifting away from punitive responses (Goldstein et al., 2019; Schwartz, 2018; Walker et al., 2019), responding to undesired or problematic behavior with realistic and commensurate consequences—and that, ideally, specifically target reasons for unwanted behaviors—can also lead to youths' learning and reduce the reoccurrence of these behaviors moving forward.

In probation settings, positive and negative reinforcement can be reframed as *rewards* or *incentives*, provided as responses when youth demonstrate desired behaviors.[1] Incorporating rewards or incentives in this way contrasts with traditional probation strategies that often overly rely on *sanctions* (i.e., positive and negative punishment as the psychological analog) as the primary tool to address youth misbehavior. Probation-related rewards and incentives can take many forms, including praise (e.g., from a probation officer), reduced restrictions (e.g., later court-ordered curfew), tangible incentives (e.g., a new phone case, gift card), and support for desired positive youth development activities (e.g., paying enrollment fees for community-based activities). In addition to enhancing youths' learning, utilizing incentives can help kickstart new behaviors or prosocial activities that replace risky behaviors; for example, if a legally involved youth is provided an incentive of new sneakers with which to play on a community sports team, they may be motivated to reach their target goal to participate in an activity of interest. Engaging in this prosocial activity, in turn, leaves the youth with less free time in which to engage in substance use or delinquent behaviors. Further, such opportunities can provide

[1] To clarify, an incentive is a specific type of reward or reinforcement that has been clearly established in advance. For instance, if a child is told that they will get to have ice cream for dessert if they eat all their vegetables, that ice cream serves as an *incentive* that can help motivate the child to perform the desired behavior (i.e., eating vegetables). Rewards include incentives but also include surprise forms of reinforcement that the individual did not know they would receive in exchange for performing the desired activity or behavior.

new contexts in which youth can learn to problem solve, make better decisions, and engage with new groups of peers.

Of note, incentives and other forms of reinforcement work best when they are particularly meaningful to a given young person. As a result, probation departments should consider developing procedures for identifying which types of incentives would be most motivating to the youth they supervise—for instance, some departments have developed a menu of incentive options from which youth can choose (e.g., Ingel et al., 2023). However, many probation departments have restrictions on what probation officers can use as incentives—for instance, in some counties, court conditions cannot be altered without a court order. Therefore, psychologists working in a consultant role with probation departments should engage in collaborative problem solving—including with youth, parents, and other agencies (e.g., juvenile courts)—to develop incentive options that align with existing restrictions (or change policies to allow broader categories of incentives) and provide meaningful motivation to the young people they serve. Psychologists might also relay research findings suggesting that, though more tangible incentives (e.g., something physical, like art supplies) can jumpstart behavior change in the short term, natural reinforcements (e.g., positive internal feelings) can be most effective in helping youth continue new behaviors in the long term (Cottle et al., 2001). Such information might help probation staff structure the order of provided incentives, encourage them to build natural reinforcement into their check ins with youth as much as possible, and emphasize the value of connecting youth with enjoyable community-based services or positive youth development activities that produce natural reinforcement to increase the probability that youth will continue to engage with them and sustain positive behavioral changes beyond their involvement with probation.

Goal Setting

To capitalize on the learning opportunities presented in adolescence and to increase the likelihood of positive behavior change while a youth is on probation, psychological principles related to goal setting can be applied to case planning with legally involved youth. When youth receive their probation dispositions, they may be placed on probation for a long period of time (e.g., several months to several years; Gozani et al., 2021) or they may receive an indeterminate period of probation (Development Services Group, Inc. 2017; Westat & National Center for Juvenile Justice, 2013) that can continue to age 18 or 21, depending on the state. Although these long periods under court and probation supervision can have negative impacts on youth (Dir et al., 2021; Gupta-Kagan, 2021; The Pew Charitable Trusts, 2023), they may also offer extended opportunities for learning; probation officers can introduce evidence-based goal setting strategies to youth and support them in developing related skills so they can generalize and incorporate these practices into their daily lives.

Probation case planning and supervision typically requires setting specific targets for youth to meet before they can be successfully discharged from court supervision. Identifying individualized goals that seem most relevant to a particular youth on probation, to the probation officer, and to the court can be challenging. Psychologists might introduce principles of motivational interviewing or emphasize the use of those familiar strategies to probation departments as a way to help officers work collaboratively with youth to set individualized and meaningful goals and increase youth buy-in about working toward those goals (Naar & Suarez, 2021). In particular, juvenile probation officers can benefit from using open-ended questions and reflective listening in their discussions about goals and future directions with youth on their caseloads. Open-ended questions offer an opportunity for youth to share their thinking without leading them in a specific direction. In addition, reflective listening—repeating back what was said while also reflecting the emotion or underlying meaning—can help strengthen the relationship between probation officers and youth, as it demonstrates that what the youth says to their probation officer has been heard and understood. Providing training in the spirit of motivational interviewing and encouraging use of this strategy—namely collaborative partnership, having compassion, and expressing the belief that youth have good ideas for themselves and their lives—can be transformational to the culture of juvenile probation departments (Schwartz et al., 2017).

In addition to identifying goals that youth find meaningful, psychological consultants should help juvenile probation officers understand the importance of establishing goals that youth can successfully achieve with support from probation, family, and other community resources. In particular, psychologists should advocate that officers help youth adopt "SMART" goals—goals that are specific, measurable, achievable, relevant, and time-oriented—as an effective way to help adolescents change their behavior (e.g., Grimsley, 2017). Theoretical models of goal achievement (e.g., goal-setting theory) assert that the *specificity* of set goals can significantly impact the likelihood and frequency of the goal setter's task-focused behavior (Locke & Latham, 2006). In practice, setting specific goals might focus on changing just one or two behaviors at a time—in line with empirical literature on how best to shape child and adolescent behavior (e.g., Flick, 2010; Manassis, 2008). Thus, when case planning with youth, probation officers might decide to focus on the one or two most important goals to address in a given period (e.g., the time until the next meeting with the probation officer) to increase the likelihood of success.

Given the importance of reinforcement when encouraging behavior change, goals and related targets must be *measurable* so that youth and probation officers can monitor progress, understand when youth are successful, and provide appropriate responses (e.g., reinforcement or intervention). In addition to external reinforcement (e.g., praise, tangible incentives, targeted interventions) provided by a probation officer, observing one's own progress toward a goal can provide a sense of self-efficacy and, therefore, is also reinforcing (Fujita & MacGregor, 2012). Take, for example, a common expectation for youth on probation: to do well at school. Although a worthy goal in sentiment, it is too broad and immeasurable to demonstrate specific progress. Instead, probation officers may reframe this goal to be measurable: attend school for two weeks while remaining free from formal school sanction (e.g., detention). If a youth and officer meet during this time, the officer can check in on the progress toward the goal (e.g., has the youth attended school for one week without receiving detention?) and offer praise and, potentially, external reinforcement to encourage the youth's continuing positive behavior toward the specified two-week goal and attainment of a pre-set reinforcing incentive.

Organizational psychology research has demonstrated that goals that individuals believe are *achievable* and attainable improve performance toward that goal (Miller & Weiss, 2015). Although a goal's difficulty has a positive relationship with performance generally (Kleingeld et al., 2011), when a goal becomes so challenging that it is seen as unachievable, goal-oriented behavior ceases. Research suggests, too, that success can be a powerful reinforcer for youth to continue the behaviors that helped them succeed (Martin & Dowson, 2009; Van Hasselt & Hersen, 1998), even as goals become more challenging. Together, these findings bolster the importance of setting achievable goals with youth on probation: as youth complete initial action steps and short-term goals, they are encouraged by their incremental successes to continue their positive behavior and to be able to report on this progress during court appearances and probation officer check-in meetings.

Commitment to a goal is also central to the success of behavior change (Miller & Weiss, 2015), highlighting the importance of identifying *relevant* goals for each individual youth during case planning. Often, for youth on probation, completing probation may be the most important goal they can identify. However, this goal may not be specific enough to establish a path to success; therefore, probation officers should help youth break this overarching goal into smaller goals that will help them reach the discharge stage and will feel personally important to them as well. Similarly, ensuring that goals are *time-limited* can bolster legally involved youths' goal-oriented behaviors. Given their still-developing prefrontal cortices (Casey et al., 2008), adolescents experience more difficulty considering the long-term outcomes of their actions than do adults—instead, adolescents often focus on what may occur more immediately. Therefore, psychologists can help probation staff consider how to best support youth on their caseloads by breaking long-term goals (e.g., graduate from high school) into related short-term goals that can be achieved within a couple of days (e.g., attend 3 days of school this week). However, short-term goals themselves may require significant behavior change (e.g., if an adolescent has not been to school in 6 months); thus, these goals can be further broken down into action steps (e.g., plan the best way to get to school, pack school bag the night before) that will allow the young person to practice their problem-solving skills with support and positive reinforcement from their probation officer. These action steps can also be rewarded or reinforced by probation officers using incentives identified by the youth and probation staff during the goal-setting process.

Functional Behavior Analysis

In addition to setting effective goals and reinforcing positive behavior through operant conditioning practices, functional behavior analysis can be a crucial strategy to effectively intervene and change problematic or unlawful behavior for legally involved adolescents. Probation officers are often trained to address misbehavior through sanctions to deter continued negative or problematic behaviors. However, training in functional behavior analysis can help probation staff better understand and target their responses to misbehavior by using appropriate *interventions* tailored to address the specific causes of the misbehavior. Functional analyses include two central questions: (1) what is causing the behavior? and (2) what is maintaining it? By examining these questions, legally involved youths' behaviors are not considered in isolation but, rather, in their ecodevelopmental contexts (e.g., educational, social, familial, individual; see Hoskins et al., 2020). After holistic consideration of the causes and maintainers of a certain behavior, the probation officer—ideally in collaboration with the youth and, potentially, the family—can identify a targeted intervention to modify the antecedents so that the problem behavior does not continue or can be replaced with a more adaptive behavior (Yoman, 2008).

An idiographic behavioral approach also provides opportunities for adolescents to learn the associations between antecedents (e.g., events, experiences, stimuli) and their behavior, as results of the functional analysis are identified and explained to them. Importantly, results of such an analysis may indicate additional needs for a given youth and their family. For example, a functional analysis might reveal that an individual youth on probation has been continuously missing their first period of school because they must take a younger sibling to pre-school while their parent is working. In response, probation officers can work with the youth's family and other community-based resources (e.g., the pre-school) to identify how to support the family with childcare while allowing the youth to attend school; for instance, the probation officer and parent may be able to arrange no-cost early care at the pre-school, so the youth can arrive at school on time after dropping off the sibling. Alternatively, the functional analysis might reveal that the youth is struggling to understand the concepts taught in their first period class and would benefit from additional tutoring.

Additionally, given the high rates of mental health concerns among legally involved youth (Wasserman et al., 2010), functional analyses also consider the potential interactions of mental health symptoms with environmental stressors or antecedents that an adolescent experiences. For example, if the underlying cause of a young person's alcohol use is that they drink to reduce social anxiety when around peers, helping this youth engage in mental health treatment to address social anxiety would best target the concerning behavior. In this way, functional analysis offers unique opportunities for probation officers to help youth enhance their insight to better understand their behaviors in ways that will help them successfully comport themselves with the expectations of community supervision—and that, hopefully, will benefit them long beyond their court involvement.

Conclusion

As illustrated in this chapter, psychologists—especially those well versed in CBPAR frameworks and behavioral principles—can provide meaningful support to juvenile probation departments seeking to transform their approaches to working with youth in a consulting role. We have focused here on how psychologists might leverage psychological principles to inform how probation officers interact with the youth they serve. However, professionals in the psychology field should also consider additional avenues where specialized psychological knowledge and related skillsets could be a benefit, such as thinking about how to meaningfully integrate family members and other professionals (e.g., school personnel, mental health providers) into case planning and intervention strategies, recognizing the need for additional consultation regarding privacy laws and concerns for the sharing of sensitive information. Ultimately, consulting psychologists working with juvenile probation departments should aim to support agency leaders and staff to make changes grounded in research and to accomplish goals related to better-serving youth, families, and their larger communities.

References

Annie E. Casey Foundation. (2018). *Transforming juvenile probation: A vision for getting it right.* https://assets.aecf.org/m/resourcedoc/aecf-transformingjuvenileprobation-2018.pdf

Bellack, A. S., Hersen, M., & Kazdin, A. E. (Eds.). (1982). *International handbook of behavior modification and therapy.* Springer US. https://doi.org/10.1007/978-1-4615-7275-6

Casey, B. J., Jones, R. M., & Hare, T. A. (2008). The adolescent brain. *Annals of the New York Academy of Sciences, 1124*(1), 111–126. https://doi.org/10.1196/annals.1440.010

Cauffman, E., Shulman, E. P., Steinberg, L., Claus, E., Banich, M. T., Graham, S., & Woolard, J. (2010). Age differences in affective decision making as indexed by performance on the Iowa Gambling Task. *Developmental Psychology, 46*(1), 193–207. https://doi.org/10.1037/a0016128

Clinical and Translational Science Awards Consortium, United States, National Institutes of Health (U.S.), Centers for Disease Control and Prevention (U.S.), & United States (Eds.). (2011). *Principles of community engagement* (2nd ed.). Department of Health and Human Services, National Institutes of Health, Centers for Disease Control and Prevention, Agency for Toxic Substances and Disease Registry, Clinical and Translational Science Awards.

Collins, S. E., Clifasefi, S. L., Stanton, J., Straits, K. J. E., Espinosa, P. R., Andrasik, M. P., Miller, K. A., Orfaly, V. E., Gil-Kashiwabara, E., Nicasio, A. V., Hawes, S. M., Nelson, L. A., Duran, B. M., & Wallerstein, N. (2018). Community-based participatory research (CBPR): Towards equitable involvement of community in psychology research. *American Psychologist, 73*(7), 884–898. https://doi.org/10.1037/amp0000167

Cook, C. R., Lyon, A. R., Locke, J., Waltz, T., & Powell, B. J. (2019). Adapting a compilation of implementation strategies to advance school-based implementation research and practice. *Prevention Science, 20*(6), 914–935. https://doi.org/10.1007/s11121-019-01017-1

Corepal, R., Tully, M. A., Kee, F., Miller, S. J., & Hunter, R. F. (2018). Behavioural incentive interventions for health behaviour change in young people (5–18 years old): A systematic review and meta-analysis. *Preventive Medicine, 110*, 55–66. https://doi.org/10.1016/j.ypmed.2018.02.004

Cottle, C. C., Lee, R. J., & Heilbrun, K. (2001). The prediction of criminal recidivism in juveniles: A meta-analysis. *Criminal Justice and Behavior, 28*(3), 367–394.

Cunningham, K. A., Gubner, N. R., Vick, K., Herting, J. R., & Walker, S. C. (2023). Redesigning juvenile probation to align with behavioral health and positive development principles: A quasi-experimental study. *Criminal Justice and Behavior, 50*(1), 6–21. https://doi.org/10.1177/00938548221082997

Debus-Sherrill, S., Breno, A., & Taxman, F. S. (2023). What makes or breaks evidence-based supervision? Staff and organizational predictors of evidence-based practice in probation. *International Journal of Offender Therapy and Comparative Criminology, 67*(6–7), 662–686. https://doi.org/10.1177/0306624X211049182

Development Services Group, Inc. (2017). *Formal, post-adjudication juvenile probation services: Literature review.* Office of Juvenile Justice and Delinquency Prevention. https://www.ojjdp.gov/mpg/litreviews/Probation_Services.pdf

DeYoung, L., Kreimer, R., NeMoyer, A., Brogan, L., & Goldstein, N. E. (March, 2024). A model for exponential growth: Peer-to-peer mentorship for dissemination of new probation practices. In N. E. Goldstein & L. Parker (Chairs), *Beyond the grant: Strategies for sustaining community-based interventions.* Symposium paper presented at the annual conference of the American Psychology-Law Society, Los Angeles, CA.

Dir, A. L., Magee, L. A., Clifton, R. L., Ouyang, F., Tu, W., Wiehe, S. E., & Aalsma, M. C. (2021). The point of diminishing returns in juvenile probation: Probation requirements and risk of technical probation violations among first-time probation-involved youth. *Psychology, Public Policy, and Law, 72*(2), 283–291. https://doi.org/10.1037/law0000282

Fabelo, T., Nagy, G., & Prins, S. (2011). *A ten-step guide to transforming probation departments to reduce recidivism.* Council of State Governments Justice Center. https://csgjusticecenter.org/wp-content/uploads/2020/01/CSG_10Step_Guide_Probation.pdf

Farrell, J. L., Betsinger, S. A., Flath, N., & Irvine, J. (2020). *Assessing the impact of a graduated response approach for youth in the Maryland juvenile justice system.* The Institute for Innovation & Implementation, University of Maryland School of Social Work. https://www.ojp.gov/pdffiles1/ojjdp/grants/254601.pdf

Fefer, S., DeMagistris, J., & Shuttleton, C. (2016). Assessing adolescent praise and reward preferences for academic behavior. *Translational Issues in Psychological Science, 2*(2), 153–162. https://doi.org/10.1037/tps0000072

Flick, G. L. (2010). *Managing ADHD in the K-8 classroom: A teacher's guide.* Corwin Press.

Fujita, K., & MacGregor, K. E. (2012). Basic goal distinctions. In H. Aarts, & A. Elliot (Eds.), *Goal-directed behavior* (pp. 85–114). Psychology Press.

Goldstein, N. E. S., Gale-Bentz, E., McPhee, J., NeMoyer, A., Walker, S., Bishop, S., Soler, M., Szanyi, J., Schwartz, R. G. (2019). Applying the National Council of Juvenile and Family Court Judges' resolution to juvenile probation reform. *Translational Issues in Psychological Science, 5*(2), 170–181. https://doi.org/10.1037/tps0000192

Goldstein, N. E. S., NeMoyer, A., Gale-Bentz, E., Levick, M., & Feierman, J. (2016). "You're on the right track!" Using graduated response systems to address immaturity of judgment and enhance youths' capacities to successfully complete probation. *Temple Law Review, 88*(4), 803–836.

Gozani, D., Ridolfi, L., & Wong, A. (2021). *Ending endless probation.* National Center for Youth Law and W. Haywood Burns Institute. https://youthlaw.org/sites/default/files/attachments/2022-03/2021.03.02-End-Endless-Probation-v2.pdf

Grimsley, P. D. (2017). *The effects of a goal-setting intervention on delinquent adolescent group treatment outcomes.* University of Denver.

Gupta-Kagan, J. (2021). Beyond "children are different": The revolution in juvenile intake and sentencing. *Washington Law Review, 96*(2), 425–492.

Haynes, E., Marawili, M., Marika, B. M., Mitchell, A. G., Phillips, J., Bessarab, D., Walker, R., Cook, J., & Ralph, A. P. (2019). Community-based participatory action research on rheumatic heart disease in an Australian Aboriginal homeland: Evaluation of the 'On track watch' project. *Evaluation and Program Planning, 74*, 38–53. https://doi.org/10.1016/j.evalprogplan.2019.02.010

Hockenberry, S. (2023). *Delinquency cases in juvenile court, 2020.* U.S. Department of Justice Office of Justice Programs. http://www.ncjj.org/pdf/Juvenile%20Justice%20Bulletin/DelCasesinJuvCt20.pdf

Hoskins, D., Tahir, P., Del Cid, M., Perez-Gualdron, L., Tolou-Shams, M. (2020). Ecological systems in relation to Latinx youth in the juvenile justice system: A narrative literature review. *Children and Youth Services Review, 117*, 104669.

Ingel, S. N., Davis, L. R., Rudes, D. S., Hartwell, T. N., Drazdowski, T. K., McCart, M. R., Chapman, J. E., Taxman, F. S., & Sheidow, A. J. (2022). Misunderstanding and sensemaking among juvenile probation officers working with evidence-based practices. *Victims & Offenders, 17*(7), 975–993. https://doi.org/10.1080/15564886.2021.1985670

Ingel, S. N., Davis, L. R., Rudes, D. S., Taxman, F. S., Hartwell, T. N., Drazdowski, T. K., Mccart, M. R., Chapman, J. E., & Sheidow, A. J. (2023). Juvenile probation officer perceptions of parental involvement in juvenile probation and with contingency management. *Criminal Justice and Behavior, 50*(1), 40–55. https://doi.org/10.1177/00938548221106468

Ivankova, N. V. (2017). Applying mixed methods in community-based participatory action research: A framework for engaging stakeholders with research as a means for promoting patient-centredness. *Journal of Research in Nursing, 22*(4), 282–294. https://doi.org/10.1177/1744987117699655

Kang Balzarini, T., & Eno Louden, J. (2024). What factors contribute to differential perceptions toward evidence-based practices? An examination of officer role orientation, job satisfaction, confidence, and skill proficiency. *Criminal Justice and Behavior, 51*(5), 687–706. https://doi.org/10.1177/00938548241230085

Kleingeld, A., van Mierlo, H., & Arends, L. (2011). The effects of goal setting on group performance: A meta-analysis. *Journal of Applied Psychology, 96*(6), 1289–1304. https://doi.org/10.1037/a0024315

Locke, E. A., & Latham, G. P. (2006). New directions in goal-setting theory. *Current Directions in Psychological Science, 15*(5), 265–268. https://doi.org/10.1111/j.1467-8721.2006.00449.x

Manassis, K. (2008). *Keys to parenting your anxious child.* Barron's Educational Series.

Martin, A. J., & Dowson, M. (2009). Interpersonal relationships, motivation, engagement, and achievement: Yields for theory, current issues, and educational practice. *Review of Educational Research, 79*(1), 327–365. https://doi.org/10.3102/0034654308325583

McCrae, J. S., Scannapieco, M., Leake, R., Potter, C. C., & Menefee, D. (2014). Who's on board? Child welfare worker reports of buy-in and readiness for organizational change. *Children and Youth Services Review,* 37, 28–35. https://doi.org/10.1016/j.childyouth.2013.12.001

Miller, L. E., & Weiss, R. M. (2015). Setting goals in different roles: Applying key results from the goal-setting literature. *Organizational Management Journal, 12*(1), 14–22.

Naar, S., & Suarez, M. (2021). *Motivational interviewing with adolescents and young adults.* Guilford Publications.

National Council of Juvenile and Family Court Judges. (2017). *Resolution regarding juvenile probation and adolescent development.* https://www.ncjfcj.org/wp-content/uploads/2019/08/regarding-juvenile-probation-and-adolescent-development.pdf

The Pew Charitable Trusts. (2023). *Many youth kept on probation despite being at low risk for rearrest.* https://pew.org/43ogDdr

Rodriguez Espinosa, P., & Verney, S. P. (2021). The underutilization of community-based participatory research in psychology: A systematic review. *American Journal of Community Psychology, 67*(3-4), 312–326. https://doi.org/10.1002/ajcp.12469

Schwartz, R. G. (2018). A 21st century developmentally appropriate juvenile probation approach. *Juvenile and Family Court Journal, 69*(1), 41–54.

Schwartz, K., Alexander, A. O., Lau, K. S., Holloway, E. D., & Aalsma, M. C. (2017). Motivating compliance: Juvenile probation officer strategies and skills. *Journal of Offender Rehabilitation, 56*(1), 20–37.

Sloas, L., Murphy, A., Wooditch, A., & Taxman, F. S. (2019). Assessing the use and impact of points and rewards across four federal probation districts: A contingency management approach. *Victims & Offenders, 14*(7), 811–831. https://doi.org/10.1080/15564886.2019.1656691

Swain-Bradway, J., Swoszowski, N. C., Boden, L. J., & Sprague, J. R. (2013). Voices from the field: Stakeholder perspectives on PBIS implementation in alternative educational settings. *Education & Treatment of Children*, 36(3), 31–46. https://www.proquest.com/docview/1445136603/abstract/45F93AC9E85B406EPQ/1

van Duijvenvoorde, A. C. K., Peters, S., Braams, B. R., & Crone, E. A. (2016). What motivates adolescents? Neural responses to rewards and their influence on adolescents' risk taking, learning, and cognitive control. *Neuroscience & Biobehavioral Reviews*, 70, 135–147. https://doi.org/10.1016/j.neubiorev.2016.06.037

Van Hasselt, V. B., & Hersen, M. (1998). *Handbook of psychological treatment protocols for children and adolescents*. Routledge.

Vargas, C., Whelan, J., Brimblecombe, J., & Allender, S. (2022). Co-creation, co-design, co-production for public health – A perspective on definition and distinctions. *Public Health Research & Practice, 32*(2). https://doi.org/10.17061/phrp3222211

Walker, S. C., Valencia, E., Miller, S., Pearson, K., Jewell, C., Tran, J., & Thompson, A. (2019). Developmentally-grounded approaches to juvenile probation practice: A case study. *Federal Probation, 83*(3), 33–41.

Wallerstein, N., Duran, B., Oetzel, J. G., & Minkler, M. (Eds.). (2017). *Community-based participatory research for health: Advancing social and health equity*. John Wiley & Sons.

Wasserman, G. A., McReynolds, L. S., Schwalbe, C. S., Keating, J. M., & Jones, S. A. (2010). Psychiatric disorder, comorbidity, and suicidal behavior in juvenile justice youth. *Criminal Justice and Behavior, 37*(12), 1361–1376. https://doi.org/10.1177/0093854810382751

Westat & National Center for Juvenile Justice. (2013). *Redesigning the Census of Juvenile Probation Supervising Offices (CJPSO)*. Office of Juvenile Justice and Delinquency Prevention.

Yoman, J. (2008). A primer on functional analysis. *Cognitive and Behavioral Practice, 15*, 325–340. https://doi.org/10.1016/j.cbpra.2008.01.002

Young, D., Moline, K., Farrell, J., & Bierie, D. (2006). Best implementation practices: Disseminating new assessment technologies in a juvenile justice agency. *Crime & Delinquency, 52*(1), 135–158. https://doi.org/10.1177/0011128705281752

17

Doctoral Training in Forensic Psychology

David DeMatteo, Haleh Kanani, Simone P. Grisamore, and Avery Chard

Introduction

Forensic psychology has grown tremendously over the past few decades. Indicators of the field's growth include national and international professional organizations devoted to forensic psychology (or psychology-law more broadly), numerous scientific journals that publish forensic psychology research, and hundreds of books (and some targeted book series) that focus on forensic psychology (see DeMatteo & Scherr, 2023). As forensic psychology has become more accepted by the legal profession (e.g., *Jenkins v. United States, 1962*), the field has continued to grow, with forensic psychologists assuming more varied roles (e.g., clinicians, researchers, consultants) (DeMatteo et al., 2020).

The growing interest in forensic psychology, combined with the increasing demand for forensic psychological services, has led to a recent proliferation in forensic psychology training programs. There are a growing number of colleges and universities that offer undergraduate psychology courses in various forensic psychology topic areas. Those interested in advanced education/training in forensic psychology can choose from among several graduate programs that provide specialized forensic psychology training (research, clinical, or both). For those interested in practicing forensic psychology independently, either as a clinician or researcher, it is typically necessary to have a doctoral degree, and there are several doctoral programs that provide relevant training.

This chapter focuses on doctoral training in forensic psychology (for a discussion of training opportunities at the internship and postdoctoral levels, see Anumba et al., this volume). After a brief discussion of doctoral training in psychology more generally, we focus on forensic-specific doctoral training. The chapter then takes an in-depth look at basic competencies and essential components of doctoral-level training in forensic psychology. The chapter concludes with some thoughts about the future of doctoral training in forensic psychology.

David DeMatteo et al., *Doctoral Training in Forensic Psychology*. In: *The Path Forward*. Edited by: Kirk Heilbrun and David DeMatteo, Oxford University Press. © Oxford University Press (2026). DOI: 10.1093/9780197773031.003.0017

Doctoral Training in Psychology

The growth of psychology as a profession over the past 50+ years has resulted in many options for those interested in graduate training in psychology. Given the different degree programs, training opportunities, and mentorship models, differentiating among graduate programs can be challenging. This section describes the different types of doctoral programs, what those differences mean for students, and the career paths associated with the different types of doctoral programs.

Types of Doctoral Degrees in Psychology

Several seminal events shaped graduate training in psychology in the United States. In 1949, the Conference on Graduate Education in Clinical Psychology was held at the University of Colorado at Boulder to discuss standards for doctoral training in psychology (Benjamin & Baker, 2000). This two-week meeting was the first national meeting to discuss doctoral training in psychology. The most notable outcome was recognition that doctoral training in clinical psychology should provide extensive training in both research and practice, which gave rise to the scientist-practitioner model adopted by many PhD programs (Norcross & Castle, 2002).

In 1973, the Conference on Levels and Patterns of Training, which was sponsored by the American Psychological Association (APA), concluded that the breadth of the field of psychology had grown sufficiently to justify creating separate educational paths for students primarily interested in clinical practice (Merced et al., 2015). Conference members concluded that because the educational and training curriculum for those interested in practice differs from the curriculum for those interested in research, a new degree—Doctor of Psychology (PsyD)—should be developed to reflect a primarily clinical focus. The conference members decided that the PsyD was the appropriate training program for those pursuing a clinical path, while the PhD was more appropriate for students seeking training in research (Merced et al., 2015). The content of the degree paths varies among schools, and most graduate programs include some training in both practice and research, but PsyD programs place a heavier emphasis on clinical practice.

Other differences between PhD and PsyD programs include the length of the degree program and the average size of financial aid packages. PhD programs have a longer time to degree completion than PsyD programs, with a difference of approximately one year (Norcross et al., 2010). Further, PhD programs are more likely to offer financial support to students; only one to ten percent of PsyD programs include both a tuition waiver and assistantship stipend, compared to eighty-nine percent of PhD programs (Doran et al., 2016).

Beyond the choice between a PhD or a PsyD for those interested in clinical practice, there is a distinction between a counseling degree and a clinical degree. The programs often differ in theoretical orientation, with clinical programs leaning more toward a cognitive-behavioral approach and counseling degrees being more likely to endorse a humanistic approach (Karazsia & Smith, 2016). Despite this and other differences, graduates from both programs often end up with similar jobs and experiences (Norcross et al., 1998).

Several schools also offer joint-degree programs, which are a less common and more specialized psychology degree path. There are several iterations of joint-degree programs, but the model typically permits students to be part of two graduate-training programs simultaneously, which provides a unique interdisciplinary education. The most common example of a joint-degree program is in the specialty area of forensic psychology (Perry & Boccaccini, 2009), with a JD/PhD option and a PhD/Master's in Legal Studies (MLS) option. Other examples of joint-degree programs include combining a clinical psychology doctorate (PhD or PsyD) with a Master's in Public Health (MPH), Master's in Business Administration (MBA), or even a Doctor of Medicine (MD). Although joint-degree programs provide a specialized and distinctive education, they are offered by a very small number of APA-accredited doctoral programs.

Nature of Degree Training Programs

In the United States, there are three training models commonly used in graduate psychology programs: scientist-practitioner, scholar-practitioner, and clinical scientist (Routh, 2015). The *scientist-practitioner model* is the most common training model among psychology graduate programs. In a survey of 231 APA-accredited programs, 57 percent reported using this model (Perry & Boccaccini, 2009). The scientist-practitioner model, which is also known as the "Boulder model" in recognition of its development at the 1949 conference at the University of Colorado at Boulder, places emphasis on both research skills (science) and clinical skills (practice). Although the scientist-practitioner model is the most prevalent training model in the United States, it has been criticized for being too idealistic in assuming that students will be interested in both research and practice; there is also a concern that it is unrealistic to adequately train students in both science and practice during the relatively short span of a doctoral program (Frank, 1984). Most graduate programs that have adopted the scientist-practitioner model award PhDs.

The *scholar-practitioner model* places emphasis on the student based on the belief that a student cannot be an effective participant in their field without an understanding of their interests and motivations. This model is also called the Vail model, named after the location of the conference where the distinction between a PsyD and PhD was initially articulated. Similar to the scientist-practitioner model, the scholar-practitioner model emphasizes both research and practice, but it places a heavier emphasis on clinical training. This model also has an added element related to the self, encouraging self-reflection and self-improvement to ensure the student is growing and changing as psychology does (Hebert, 2010). Most programs that have adopted the scholar-practitioner model award a PsyD.

If the scholar-practitioner model is heavy on clinical practice, the *clinical scientist model* is its research counterpart. Though clinical practice may be addressed in part with the clinical scientist model, its main tenet is the importance of focusing on science and further developing our understanding of psychology. This model emerged in the mid-1990s in response to the growing scholar-practitioner movement and adoption of PsyDs, with the primary impetus being the concern that the scientific/research aspect of psychology was being neglected (McFall et al., 2015). Clinical scientist model programs typically award PhDs due to the emphasis on research.

Forensic-Specific Doctoral Training

Undergraduate Education/Training

Although the majority of training in forensic psychology occurs at the doctoral and post-doctoral levels, there are some opportunities for forensic training at the undergraduate level (Burl et al., 2012; DeMatteo et al., 2009; Hall et al., 2010). Educational/training opportunities may include relevant coursework, research involvement, and some level of clinical exposure. The growth in forensic psychology training at the undergraduate level is reflected by the growing number of forensic psychology textbooks (e.g., Costanzo & Krauss, 2020; Greene & Heilbrun, 2019; Huss, 2025). A few schools offer specialized undergraduate degrees or concentrations in forensic psychology, such as a BA in Forensic Psychology (e.g., John Jay College of Criminal Justice) and the concentration in forensic psychology within the BA in psychology program at the University of New Haven. Institutions with graduate training in forensic psychology may be ripe with undergraduate training opportunities because there is an established faculty to teach forensic courses, supervise research, and mentor students. These undergraduate opportunities are often viewed as preparatory steps for further education because employment opportunities in forensic psychology typically require an advanced degree (DeMatteo et al., 2009).

Master's Programs

Opportunities for forensic psychology training at the master's level have expanded considerably in recent years, with approximately twenty-five programs offering a master's degree (MA or MS) or concentration in forensic psychology (American Psychology-Law Society, 2025), compared to approximately fifteen programs a little more than a decade ago (Burl et al., 2012). These programs, which are typically completed in two years, offer two broad models of training, with some focusing on clinical practice and others emphasizing research (Zaitchik et al., 2007). Requirements vary substantially across programs, but may include coursework in psychology and law, comprehensive examinations, theses, research projects, and clinical practicum. Graduates of master's programs may obtain employment in a number of government, private, non-profit, or academic settings, although several programs focus primarily on preparing graduates for further study in a doctoral program (American Psychology-Law Society, 2025).

Doctoral Training

Doctoral training in forensic psychology can be categorized by degree type (PsyD, PhD, or joint-degree) and training model (e.g., clinical or non-clinical). The American Psychology-Law Society (Division 41 of the American Psychological Association) maintains a guide to forensic and legal psychology graduate programs that includes master's programs, doctoral programs, and joint-degree programs. As of late 2025, among institutions offering doctoral training in forensic psychology, approximately twenty-five programs offer PhDs, eleven offer PsyDs, and seven are joint-degree programs (see American Psychology-Law Society, 2025, for a comprehensive list of programs). As will be discussed later in this chapter, doctoral training in forensic psychology includes both clinical (applied) and non-clinical (experimental) programs. These programs generally ensure broad competence in psychology, with specialized forensic training tailored to the program's focus. The curriculum often includes a combination of coursework, comprehensive examinations, forensic psychological research, clinical (and clinical-forensic) practice, and occasionally some legal training (Burl et al., 2012).

Some graduate programs that lack a formal forensic track (major area of study) or degree provide ways for students to gain experience in forensic psychology. Students can take relevant coursework and collaborate with faculty members to gain training in forensic psychology (e.g., assessment, consultation). However, opportunities to gain forensic experience may be more prevalent for doctoral students in clinical programs, which provide external training via clinical practica and a clinical internship. For example, a survey of correctional training opportunities among clinical doctoral programs found that more than half of the programs reported offering a practicum in a criminal justice setting, although only 19 percent had faculty with a reported interest in corrections and even fewer programs offered correctional coursework (Magaletta et al., 2013). Further, as noted, most clinical programs require that students complete a one-year internship, which provides an opportunity for students to receive forensic-specific training. Internship sites include forensic settings (e.g., assessment clinic, group practice), correctional settings (e.g., jails, prisons), or rotations providing experience in forensic assessment or treatment with forensic populations (DeMatteo et al., 2009) (see Anumba et al., this volume, for an overview of internship training).

PsyD Programs

PsyD programs focus on professional and clinical practice. Most programs that offer forensic training offer a PsyD in clinical psychology, although at least one program offers a PsyD specifically in clinical forensic psychology. Median completion of these programs ranges from four to six years. Forensic courses offered at these programs tend to focus on clinical topic areas, with the majority offering forensic assessment, treatment, and juvenile offending courses (Burl et al., 2012). Clinical training via practicum and internship is critical in preparing students for licensure as a psychologist. Although research expectations are generally lower in PsyD programs, PsyD programs almost always require the completion of a dissertation or capstone research project. Graduates from PsyD programs with forensic training find employment in correctional settings, psychiatric hospitals, private forensic evaluation practices, government agencies, treatment/counseling positions, and academia (if there is not a heavy research focus) (American Psychology-Law Society, 2025).

Clinical PhD Programs

PhD programs with forensic training can be clinical or non-clinical, with clinical programs alternately referred to as applied programs and non-clinical programs broadly called experimental programs. Clinical programs typically award PhDs in clinical psychology with specialized forensic psychology training, while non-clinical programs offer either forensic-specific PhDs or PhDs in a non-clinical area (e.g., social, cognitive, developmental). Of the approximately twenty-five schools that offer forensic training culminating in a PhD, a little more than half of the programs are clinical (American Psychology-Law Society, 2025).

Clinical psychology PhD programs include a focus on both research and clinical practice. Consequently, these programs tend to take longer to complete, with a median duration of five to six years. Students in these programs typically engage in clinical rotations and internships, which may or may not include a focus on forensic populations, depending on student preference, the program's focus, and available opportunities. Clinical psychology PhD programs are more likely to offer clinical courses in forensic assessment and treatment than non-clinical PhD programs (Burl et al., 2012). Notably, the percentage of programs offering these courses is higher among PsyD programs and master's programs than among PhD programs. Upon completion, graduates are equipped with the necessary training for licensure eligibility in most states. Graduates of clinical psychology PhD programs with forensic training are prepared for diverse employment opportunities spanning settings that include academia, government, policy, non-profit organizations, research institutes/organizations, think tanks, treatment/counseling, and specialized forensic practice (American Psychology-Law Society, 2025).

Non-Clinical PhD Programs

Non-clinical psychology PhD programs prioritize research, generally require a master's thesis and doctoral dissertation, and typically take four to six years for completion. The curriculum varies across programs, with courses offered on a wide range of topics. Because of the varied experimental areas that can form the basis of study, there is more variability among these programs than among the clinical programs. As non-clinical programs, they are not preparing students for licensure as a psychologist. Graduates of non-clinical programs can work in academia, government agencies, private industry, and research institutes/organizations (American Psychology-Law Society, 2025). Forensic psychologists with a non-clinical degree can serve as expert witnesses and consultants in cases that involve a variety of topic areas (e.g., eyewitness identification, credibility of child witnesses).

Joint-Degree Programs

Joint-degree programs offer concurrent degrees in psychology (PhD, PsyD, or Master's) and law (JD or Master's of Legal Studies). JD/PhD programs require completion of both law school and a PhD program (clinical or experimental), and they take 6+ years to complete, while programs that combine a doctoral degree in psychology with a master's degree in law (MLS) take slightly less time to complete (approximately 5 years). The clinical requirements depend highly on the specific degrees, although they typically emphasize research and legal knowledge. Graduates of joint-degree programs pursue diverse careers spanning both psychology and the legal field, with settings ranging from research, clinical, clinical-forensic, nonprofit, industry, policy, and legal practice (American Psychology-Law Society, 2025).

Basic Competencies and Essential Components of Doctoral-Level Training in Forensic Psychology

APA Requirements

The APA Committee on Accreditation (CoA) (2008) has provided guidelines and principles for doctoral programs in psychology regarding curricula, practicum training, diversity, and other domains. However, the CoA provides programs with broad latitude in deciding how to fulfill these requirements. As long as a program's training model, mission, and methods satisfy the basic requirements and are accepted as appropriate to the profession, there is room for variation (APA CoA, 2008). APA's CoA (2008) reviews doctoral programs in psychology that provide "broad and general training in scientific psychology and in the foundations of practice," which includes clinical, counseling, school, and some other developed practice areas (p. 2).

In terms of basic requirements, the CoA requires that a program's curriculum enables students to develop competence in a number of areas integral to the practice of psychology: the history, research methods, and range of applications of psychological science; the foundations of practice in the program's substantive area of emphasis; the assessment and treatment of psychological problems; issues of diversity as they are relevant to all areas of practice; and "attitudes essential for life-long learning, scholarly inquiry, and professional problem-solving" (APA CoA, 2008, p. 7). The focus on generalist training ensures that future forensic psychologists first develop sufficient knowledge in the basic competencies of clinical psychology before pursuing more specialized training in forensic psychology.

Curricula, Experiential Components, & Graduate Student Research

Efforts to reach a consensus on appropriate training models and core competencies in forensic psychology stretch back several decades (e.g., Bersoff, 1999; Bersoff et al., 1997; DeMatteo et al., 2009; Heilbrun & Brooks, 2010; Otto et al., 1990; Poythress, 1979). This task is particularly difficult because forensic psychology allows for practice in a wide range of areas, both clinical and non-clinical. For example, the knowledge and skills required to provide risk-reduction therapy to individuals convicted of violent offenses are quite different from the skills required to evaluate an individual's competence to stand trial. Additionally, as a relatively young sub-specialty, the field of forensic psychology is continuing to evolve. What was considered competence in forensic practice a few years ago may not be considered competence currently. As Krauss and Sales (2013) stated, "The key is for forensic training programs to instill in their graduates the necessary intellectual rigor that they will regularly ask themselves this question: Is what I am about to do what ought to be done or am I simply repeating past practices?" (p. 128).

There is a lack of empirical research evaluating forensic psychology training programs at the doctoral level, making it difficult to identify which training model is best suited to prepare students to work in the field (Najdowski et al., 2015). However, several scholars have synthesized the available descriptive data and offered informed suggestions. DeMatteo et al. (2009) proposed that model forensic psychology training programs should be designed to provide doctoral students with training and experience in at least the following areas:

1. Core knowledge relevant to the program's substantive area of focus (e.g., clinical, cognitive, experimental).
2. Research design, methodology, and statistics.
3. Conducting empirical research (not applicable to PsyD programs).
4. Legal knowledge, including relevant case law, substantive law in relevant areas (e.g., competence to stand trial), and legal rules related to expert testimony.
5. Integrative law-psychology knowledge, including foundational courses on forensic psychology and courses on psycho-legal areas such as forensic assessment and treatment of justice-involved populations.

6. Ethical and professional issues in general psychology and forensic psychology.
7. Clinical forensic training (specific to clinical psychology programs).

The first three elements cover generalist competencies that align with requirements for program curricula as defined by APA's CoA, while the last four elements represent specialty-specific competencies in forensic psychology (DeMatteo et al., 2009).

The status of doctoral-level forensic psychology programs in addressing these specialty competencies is mixed. Nearly all of the programs included in a 2009 survey reported providing the opportunity for clinical experience in forensic psychology, but less than half offered coursework focused on legal knowledge (DeMatteo et al., 2009). All of the programs reported offering coursework on integrated law-psychology knowledge, but most of these offerings were introductory courses. Only three programs reported offering a course on ethics and professional issues specific to forensic psychology. By other estimates, one-third of forensic psychology clinical PhD and joint-degree programs offer courses in mental health law, while just ten percent of PsyD programs and zero percent of non-clinical PhD programs do the same (Burl et al., 2012). Across degree types, less than fifteen percent of doctoral programs offer coursework on ethics in forensic psychology (Burl et al., 2012). Of note, these articles were published more than a decade ago, so it is possible that some doctoral programs have evolved and improved their offerings. However, based on the available data from DeMatteo et al (2009) and Burl et al. (2012), integrated law-psychology knowledge and training on forensic ethics appear to be two areas in which many programs have gaps in their training. We address these areas in the next sections.

Legal and Integrative Psychology-Law Knowledge

Practicing forensic psychology requires the skills to identify and understand the relevant law. Students should be trained on the relevant legal standard in a specific jurisdiction, but also in the skills necessary to identify the legal standard in any jurisdiction in which they may work and to understand the implications of that standard for forensic practice. Krauss and Sales (2013) propose that there are five skills, at a minimum, that are necessary to perform any type of forensic mental health assessment:

1. Identify and read the key case law on the evaluation question in the relevant jurisdiction.
2. Use that case law to ensure the evaluation the legal standard that controls the forensic issue in the case.
3. Stay up-to-date on changes in the law and their impact on evaluation practices.
4. Be aware of case law in other jurisdictions that may have implications for work on the case at hand.
5. Be aware of legal developments closely related to the success of forensic work more generally (e.g., changes in what types of psychological evidence or testimony the court will find acceptable).

At first glance, this list may appear to set lofty goals for students who may never be in a law school classroom, but any psychologist who claims to specialize in forensic work should be expected to meet a higher standard than a generalist (DeMatteo et al., 2013). Indeed, Section 2.04 of the APA *Specialty Guidelines for Forensic Psychology* underscores the necessity for forensic clinicians to obtain a "fundamental and reasonable level of knowledge and understanding of the legal and professional standards, laws, rules, and precedents that govern their participation in legal proceedings and that guide the impact of their services on service recipients" (American Psychological Association, 2013, p. 9). Though they are not "expected to be legal scholars," forensic psychologists are "required to have a reasonable knowledge of legal concepts that are relevant to their areas of forensic practice" (Packer, 2008, p. 246). This requirement is particularly salient when learning to conduct forensic mental health assessments because the evaluator must understand the psycho-legal concepts that form the basis for the referral question and be cognizant of the legal context during the evaluation (e.g., limited confidentiality, right to avoid self-incrimination, potential use of records in court proceedings) (Varela & Conroy, 2012). Skills like these are what distinguish forensic psychologists from other types of practitioners who may be hired to conduct psycho-legal evaluations.

Forensic Ethics and Professional Issues

Forensic psychologists are also likely to face ethical issues that require highly specific ethical training. They work frequently with vulnerable populations and with legal actors or institutions whose goals and responsibilities may conflict with theirs. For example, a psychologist retained to evaluate a defendant in a criminal case must understand that, unlike in almost any other evaluation setting, their client is not the person they are evaluating but rather the attorney who retained them. A psychologist working at a Bureau of Prisons facility is considered a corrections officer first and a mental health professional second—is it ethical for them to take part in cell searches and look through the personal belongings of a person they may see the next day in a treatment group? If a psychologist evaluates a death row inmate for competency to be executed and the evaluation plays a central role in allowing the execution to move forward, have they violated their duty to do no harm? These questions do not have easy answers. All psychologists are likely to face complicated ethical dilemmas over the course of their career, but forensic psychologists will almost certainly face dilemmas that differ in type, and perhaps also in degree, from those faced by their non-forensic colleagues. The APA *Specialty Guidelines for Forensic Psychology* (2013) provide assistance in navigating these types of issues, but if students are exposed to them only in passing, they are unlikely to be prepared to handle the complex ethical situations common to forensic practice. As such, doctoral programs that provide forensic training should include education on ethical standards and guidelines applicable to psychological practice generally and forensic psychology in particular.

Working with justice-involved populations necessarily involves interacting with the effects of many decades of policymaking that have disproportionately impacted people of color. Yet, according to early data, courses dealing with socio-cultural issues in forensic psychology are offered by just 13 percent of forensic psychology graduate training programs (Burl et al., 2012). Given the increased focus on diversity and equity in recent years, it is likely that some programs have enhanced their focus on these topics in terms of coursework and training. Further, forensic practitioners must be familiar with and sensitive to socio-cultural issues common in forensic settings (Varela & Conroy, 2012), including considerations related to criminal subcultures (e.g., prison culture, gang culture), victims of violence, and law enforcement. Ethics training for aspiring forensic psychologists must prepare them to navigate these and related areas.

Addressing Specialty Competencies

Forensic-specific specialty competencies can be addressed through coursework, but classes are not the only way to impart necessary training to students. Competencies based on substantive knowledge, such as legal knowledge and integrative law-psychology knowledge, may be best addressed in a classroom setting, while competencies related to ethics and clinical skills may be better addressed through a combination of coursework and experiential learning. It is important not to overlook the role of practicum experiences in clinical doctoral training, including forensic training. According to the APA CoA (2008), students should receive "adequate and appropriate" practicum experiences that include supervision and training in the application of evidence-based interventions (p. 7). Practicum experiences would ideally be integrated into other elements of the program and be consistent with the program's training objectives. Similarly, programs should not overlook the role of research experience in a student's forensic training trajectory. Theses and dissertations provide opportunities for students to refine and apply their knowledge of research design/methodology and data analysis to forensic issues.

Conclusion

Doctoral training is a necessary prerequisite to practice as a forensic psychologist in both clinical and research settings. The opportunities for doctoral training in forensic psychology have increased in recent years, but more work needs to be done. Along those lines, we offer two conclusions. First, given the low admission rates to doctoral programs that provide forensic training, it is safe to conclude that the demand for forensic training is far outpacing the supply. Second, we lack up-to-date data on the educational/training curricula used in doctoral programs. Several of the surveys that documented doctoral training in forensic psychology were conducted more than a decade ago. As a result, it is unclear, for example, whether doctoral programs are providing sufficient training on key areas of forensic practice, such as legal and integrative psychology-law knowledge, forensic-specific ethics, diversity-related considerations, and forensic-specific competencies. A broad survey of forensic training opportunities in doctoral programs would provide informative data on the current state of doctoral training.

References

American Psychological Association Committee on Accreditation. (2008). *Guidelines and principles for accreditation of programs in professional psychology*. APA Office on Program Consultation and Accreditation. https://www.apa.org/about/policy/accreditation-archived.pdf

American Psychological Association. (2013). Specialty guidelines for forensic psychology. *American Psychologist, 68*(1), 7–19. doi: 10.1037/a0029889.

American Psychology-Law Society. (2025). *Guide to graduate programs in forensic and legal psychology* (7th ed.). https://ap-ls.org/resources/training/graduate

Benjamin, L. T., & Baker, D. B. (2000). Bolder at 50: Introduction to the section. *American Psychologist, 55*(2), 233–236. https://doi.org/10.1037/h0087859

Bersoff, D. N. (1999). Preparing for two cultures: Education and training in law and psychology. In R. Roesch, S. D. Hart, & J. R. P. Ogloff (Eds.), *Psychology and law: The state of the discipline* (pp. 375–401). Kluwer Academic/Plenum.

Bersoff, D. N., Goodman-Delahunty, J., Grisso, J. T., Hans, V. P., Poythress, N. G., & Roesch, R. G. (1997). Training in law and psychology: Models from the Villanova Conference. *American Psychologist, 52*(12), 1301–1310. https://psycnet.apa.org/doi/10.1037/0003-066X.52.12.1301

Burl, J., Shah, S., Filone, S., Foster, E., & DeMatteo, D. (2012). A survey of graduate training programs and coursework in forensic psychology. *Teaching of Psychology, 39*(1), 48–53. https://doi.org/10.1177/0098628311430313

Costanzo, M., & Krauss, D. (2020). *Forensic and legal psychology: Psychological science applied to law* (4th ed.). Worth Publishers.

DeMatteo, D., Fairfax-Columbo, J., & Desai, A. (2020). *Becoming a forensic psychologist*. Routledge/Taylor & Francis Group.

DeMatteo, D., Keesler, M. E., & Strohmaier, H. (2013). Accessing the law and legal literature. In I. B. Weiner & R. K. Otto (Eds.), *The handbook of forensic psychology* (4th ed., pp. 57–83). Wiley.

DeMatteo, D., Marczyk, G., Krauss, D. A., & Burl, J. (2009). Educational and training models in forensic psychology. *Training and Education in Professional Psychology, 3*(3), 184–191. https://doi.org/10.1037/a0014582

DeMatteo, D., & Scherr, K. C. (2023). Training for careers in psychology-law. In D. DeMatteo & K. C. Scherr (Eds.), *The Oxford handbook of psychology and law* (pp. 3–17). Oxford University Press.

Doran, J. M., Kraha, A., Marks, L. R., Ameen, E. J., & El-Ghoroury, N. H. (2016). Graduate debt in psychology: A quantitative analysis. *Training and Education in Professional Psychology, 10*(1), 3–13. http://dx.doi.org/10.1037/tep0000112

Frank, G. (1984). The boulder model: History, rationale, and critique. *Professional Psychology: Research and Practice, 15*(3), 417–435. https://doi.org/10.1037/0735-7028.15.3.417

Greene, E., & Heilbrun, K. (2019). *Wrightsman's psychology and the legal system* (9th ed.). Wadsworth.

Hall, T. A., Cook, N. E., & Berman, G. L. (2010). Navigating the expanding field of law and psychology: A comprehensive guide to graduate education. *Journal of Forensic Psychology Practice, 10*(2), 69–90. https://doi.org/10.1080/15228930903446690

Hebert, T. R. (2010). The scholar-practitioner concept and its implications for self-renewal: A doctoral student's perspective. *Scholar-Practitioner Quarterly, 4*(1), 33–41. https://files.eric.ed.gov/fulltext/EJ942495.pdf

Heilbrun, K., & Brooks, S. (2010). Forensic psychology and forensic science: A proposed agenda for the next decade. *Psychology, Public Policy, and Law, 16*(3), 219–253. https://psycnet.apa.org/doi/10.1037/a0019138

Huss, M. T. (2025). *Forensic psychology: Research, clinical practice, and applications* (3rd ed.). John Wiley & Sons.

Jenkins v. United States, 307 F.2d 637 (D.C. Cir. 1962).

Karazsia, B. T., & Smith, L. (2016). Preparing for graduate-level training in professional psychology: Comparisons across clinical PhD, counseling PhD, and clinical PsyD programs. *Teaching of Psychology, 43*(4), 305–313. https://doi.org/10.1177/0098628316662760

Krauss, D. A., & Sales, B. D. (2013). Training in forensic psychology. In I. B. Weiner & R. K. Otto (Eds.), *The handbook of forensic psychology* (4th ed., pp. 111–134). Wiley.

Magaletta, P. R., Patry, M. W., Patterson, K. L., Gross, N. R., Morgan, R. D., & Norcross, J. C. (2013). Training opportunities for corrections practice: A national survey of doctoral psychology programs. *Training and Education in Professional Psychology, 7*(4), 291–299. https://psycnet.apa.org/doi/10.1037/a0033218

McFall, R. M., Treat, T. A., & Simons, R. F. (2015). Clinical science model. In R. L. Cautin & S. O. Lilienfeld (Eds.), *The encyclopedia of clinical psychology* (pp. 606–614). Wiley-Blackwell. DOI: 10.1002/9781118625392.wbecp458

Merced, M., Stutman, Z. E., & Mann, S. T. (2015). A developmental lag in the evolution of doctor of psychology programs. *Training and Education in Professional Psychology, 9*(3), 248–257. http://dx.doi.org/10.1037/tep0000096

Najdowski, C. J., Bottoms, B. L., Stevenson, M. C., & Veilleux, J. C. (2015). A historical review and resource guide to the scholarship of teaching and training in psychology and law and forensic psychology. *Training and Education in Professional Psychology, 9*(3), 217–228. https://doi.org/10.1037/tep0000095

Norcross, J. C., & Castle, P. H. (2002). Appreciating the PsyD: The facts. *Eye on Psi Chi, 7*(1), 22–26. https://doi.org/10.24839/1092-0803.Eye7.1.22

Norcross, J. C., Evans, K. L., & Ellis, J. L. (2010). The model does matter II: Admissions and training in APA-accredited counseling psychology programs. *The Counseling Psychologist, 38*(2), 257–268. https://psycnet.apa.org/doi/10.1177/0011000009339342

Norcross, J. C., Sayette, M. A., Mayne, T. J., Karg, R. S., & Turkson, M. A. (1998). Selecting a doctoral program in professional psychology: Some comparisons among PhD counseling, PhD clinical, and PsyD clinical psychology programs. *Professional Psychology: Research and Practice, 29*(6), 609–614. https://doi.org/10.1037/0735-7028.29.6.609

Otto, R. K., Heilbrun, K., & Grisso, T. (1990). Training and credentialing in forensic psychology. *Behavioral Sciences & the Law, 8*(3), 217–231. https://doi.org/10.1002/bsl.2370080305

Packer, I. K. (2008). Specialized practice in forensic psychology: Opportunities and obstacles. *Professional Psychology: Research and Practice, 39*(2), 245–249. https://doi.org/10.1037/0735-7028.39.2.245

Perry, K. M., & Boccaccini, M. T. (2009). Specialized training in APA-accredited clinical psychology doctoral programs: Findings from a review of program websites. *Clinical Psychology Science and Practice, 16*(3), 348–359. https://doi.org/10.1111/j.1468-2850.2009.01173.x

Poythress, N. G. (1979). A proposal for training in forensic psychology. *American Psychologist, 34*(7), 612–621. http://dx.doi.org/10.1037/0003-066X.34.7.612

Routh, D. K. (2015). Training models in clinical psychology. In R. L. Cautin & S. O. Lilienfeld (Eds.), *The encyclopedia of clinical psychology* (pp. 3060–3067). Wiley–Blackwell. https://doi.org/10.1002/9781118625392.wbecp061

Varela, J. G., & Conroy, M. A. (2012). Professional competencies in forensic psychology. *Professional Psychology: Research and Practice, 43*(5), 410–421. https://doi.org/10.1037/a0026776

Zaitchik, M. C., Berman, G. L., Whitworth, D., & Platania, J. (2007). The time is now: The emerging need for master's-level training in forensic psychology. *Journal of Forensic Psychology Practice, 7*(2), 65–71. https://psycnet.apa.org/doi/10.1300/J158v07n02_05

18

Internship and Postdoctoral Training in Forensic Psychology

Natalie M. Anumba, Heidi Putney, Jeffrey Burl, and Ashley Murray

As the field of forensic psychology has grown, training in this field has expanded in recent decades, leading to increased opportunities for training at the undergraduate, graduate, internship, and postdoctoral levels (Grisso, 2018; Otto & Heilbrun, 2002). Graduate and internship training in psychology may now include exposure, track, or major emphasis in forensic psychology (DeMatteo et al., 2009). Similarly, review of evolving literature on forensic psychology education (see, e.g., Bersoff et al., 1997; Malesky & Proctor, 2012) and resources available to students (American Psychology-Law Society Student Committee, 2024) demonstrate clear growth in the number of postdoctoral programs providing specialty training in forensic psychology.

This chapter will focus on forensic training at the internship and postdoctoral levels at the University of Massachusetts (UMass) Chan Medical School Department of Psychiatry, with the former training stage consisting of a forensic track and the latter stage entirely forensic in focus. These two training programs are separately funded. Leadership is also separate, with some co-authors (HP, JB) directing the internship and another (AM) leading the postdoctoral residency. Nevertheless, the two training programs are closely connected, given their common setting in a public psychiatric hospital, administration by faculty within the Law & Psychiatry program of UMass Chan's Department of Psychiatry, and professional and physical proximity of program leadership. We will describe the respective development and theoretical foundations of these programs, and relevant practical considerations to their operation. Considering the training programs together, we also discuss the generalizability of the training models; describe implications for diversity, equity, and inclusion; and provide advice for those contemplating similar training programs.

Natalie M. Anumba et al., *Internship and Postdoctoral Training in Forensic Psychology*. In: *The Path Forward*.
Edited by: Kirk Heilbrun and David DeMatteo, Oxford University Press.
DOI: 10.1093/9780197773031.003.0018

The UMass Chan Medical School/Worcester Recovery Center and Hospital Doctoral Internship

Project Description

The American Psychological Association requires all students in clinical, counseling, and school psychology doctoral programs to obtain the equivalent of a one-year full-time doctoral internship[1] prior to graduation (American Psychological Association [APA], 2019). Training at the internship level is typically generalist in nature, but students with specialty interests are often able to obtain introductory to intermediate experiences on internship. The UMass Chan Medical School/Worcester Recovery Center and Hospital Doctoral Internship in Clinical Psychology is an APA-accredited training program based in Worcester, Massachusetts. It is run by Massachusetts's only public academic medical center, with its primary training site at a state psychiatric treatment center. In line with its housing in public mental health services facilities, this program trains students completing their doctorates in psychology and prepares them for public-sector mental health practice. This program provides two training tracks for interns: General Inpatient/Severe Mental Illness, and Forensic Evaluation. The number of interns in each training year varies with funding, but it is generally between three and five.

For the purposes of this chapter, we will focus our attention on the forensic track. Interns in this track regularly conduct various forensic mental health evaluations (primarily assessments of competence to stand trial and need for civil commitment; criminal responsibility evaluations may also occur if the intern has demonstrated sufficient skills in the initial assessment domains) and other risk assessments (e.g., for violence, fire setting, and problematic sexual behavior). While some rotations may offer work with outpatient populations and adolescent psychiatric inpatients, persons receiving clinical services at this internship are largely adults of all genders, involved with the justice system and hospitalized at the state psychiatric hospital Worcester Recovery Center and Hospital (WRCH). Forensic track interns come into the program with varied levels of preparation, but all work toward the goal of completing a certain number of full evaluation reports (ideally coauthoring with their supervisor but potentially also on a "shadow" basis depending on their need for training). Interns could potentially be called to testify in hearings on some forensic issues, and all participate in a Mock Hearing at the conclusion of their rotation. Regarding intervention, forensic interns lead competency restoration groups and engage in other relevant activities (e.g., treatment based on the Good Lives Model, individual therapy). Research opportunities are available in several rotations. All forensic interns are

[1] Consistent with the policy of the Association of Psychology Postdoctoral and Internship Centers (APPIC) that internship programs are to avoid referencing themselves as "pre-doctoral," this chapter uses the term "doctoral internships."

required to attend a weekly caselaw seminar and a biweekly Psychiatry & Law seminar, and to present a research project (often their dissertation) to a wider hospital audience.

We also wish to highlight several training initiatives that have traditionally received less attention in the forensic training literature but which are relevant when training psychologists who will be delivering services to justice-involved individuals, and also reflect emerging areas of need in our field. These support our interns' general and forensic-tailored experience.

Social Justice Advocacy Project

Using the framework pioneered by the University of Tennessee, Knoxville (the first graduate program in the United States to be accredited by APA with a Scientist-Practitioner-Advocacy model; Miles & Fassinger, 2021), the UMass Chan/WRCH clinical psychology internship has implemented an action-learning social justice advocacy project. Working collaboratively with a local nonprofit agency, interns conduct a needs assessment and present the results to the executive board of directors over the course of the internship year. Additionally, they engage in a monthly journal club didactic series facilitated by a postdoctoral fellow to critically consider the role of psychologists in advocacy.

Professional Development Seminar Series

Monthly virtual Professional Development Seminar Panels were created to target different pathways to the workplace while highlighting barriers individualized to specific relevant issues (e.g., issues of diversity/discrimination, CV development, starting a private practice in forensic evaluation, self-care). Each panel is composed of three professionals (primarily doctoral-level psychologists) from across the nation representing diverse demographics. Co-facilitated by a postdoctoral fellow, panelists engage in an informal, discussion-based seminar highlighting their journey to their current professions and answer questions meant to assist each intern in developing their professional identity as a psychologist.

Theoretically Grounded Didactic Series

For our forensic track interns, profession-wide competency didactic training experiences involve having interns present their dissertations to the department. They also present two cases to practice these communication skills and further develop their conceptualization of forensic cases. They are also invited to attend a number of other educational events:

- forensic postdoctoral resident presentations;
- weekly didactics in case law (national and state) and in ethical considerations specific to a forensic, inpatient environment;
- a monthly cultural humility practice and process group,
- weekly supervision from an external cultural consultant, and didactics specific to diversity;

- assessment didactics focused on general assessment competencies, forensic evaluations (e.g., competency to stand trial, criminal responsibility, malingering), and risk assessment (e.g., structured professional judgment and other violence risk assessment, stalking, fire setting risk, and sexual violence risk);
- interventions with specific attention to forensic issues (e.g., competency restoration groups, addictions-related therapy, and risk reduction therapy) and specific populations (i.e., first episode psychosis, eating disorders, deaf/hard of hearing);
- supervision of an assessment and therapy case by a forensic postdoctoral resident, as well as "supervision of supervision" didactics both internally and externally with another program in the state; and
- didactics given by a wide array of professionals they will encounter at a forensic inpatient hospital (e.g., social work, peer support specialists, interpreter services, rehabilitation, psychiatry).

Foundations and Support for Project Services

The first psychology internships were developed in the early 1900s and ranged from ad-hoc initiatives to more coordinated efforts by different clinics, hospitals, and institutions (Morrow, 1946). A consensus grew through the 1920s and 1930s not only about the necessity of this period of practical training but also the need for more consistent standards, and through a series of meetings and reports undertaken in the 1940s. This culminated with the 1949 Boulder Conference, and a training model for professional psychology emerged (Baker & Benjamin, 2000; Routh, 2000). The latter half of the twentieth century witnessed further significant developments in internship training, such as proposed adaptations to internship training models (e.g., Hoch et al., 1966; Korman, 1974) and the development of a national organization to bring structure and regulation to the internship application process (Erickson Cornish & Baker, 2023).

The history of internship training reflects an ongoing interest in equipping psychologists to study and work in juvenile and criminal justice systems. Some of the earliest psychology internships included programs established at a state penitentiary and at an institute researching causes of antisocial conduct in juveniles (Morrow, 1946). Other programs with justice-involved individuals were developed in the following years, and when apparently the first study of such opportunities was conducted in the 1970s, researchers found that over half of the responding internships endorsed having some relevant training rotations or experiences (Levine et al., 1980). In the twenty-five years since the publication of that study, the fields of correctional and forensic psychology have experienced significant expansion and emerged as distinct practice areas (see DeMatteo et al., this volume), and internships offering training in areas at the intersection of psychology and the law have similarly grown (Otto et al., 1990; Packer, 2008; Potts & Kois, 2023).

One of the benchmarks during this period of progress was the National Invitational Conference on Education and Training in Law and Psychology (Bersoff et al., 1997). At this summit, commonly known as the Villanova Conference, leaders in the field gathered to evaluate the state of professional training in forensic psychology at that time (including the application of psychology to correctional and other legal systems). The Villanova Conference proposed models across the continuum of law and psychology training but recommended further discussion and contributions, especially given the understanding that the training opportunities at any given site would be affected by available resources. More than a decade later, DeMatteo and colleagues (2009) identified a need for greater clarity about the substantive components of training programs and presented a model of forensic training at the doctoral level. Their model did not address training during internship per se but contained guidance applicable to this level of training. Specifically, they proposed that students seeking eventual forensic specialization should obtain relevant foundational clinical training during their graduate program, including on forensically based assessments and interventions, which could occur on predoctoral practicum rotations as well as during the doctoral internship year. (Specialization in forensic psychology is generally expected to occur at the postdoctoral level, as discussed further in this chapter; see also Neal, 2018, for a discussion about some differences in the field of correctional psychology.) Given the differences in foci across training sites and the recognition that a doctoral student is striving for a foundational level of competence instead of specialization, it is a "foregone conclusion" (Krauss & Sales, 2014, p. 126) that a student will not be competent in all areas relevant to psychological practice in forensic and other related areas upon completion of internship. It is therefore important for psychology internships to thoughtfully design their training, including the elements directly relevant to applied practice in psychology and the law as well as others pertinent to general professional competence.

The Social Justice Advocacy Project implemented by this program reflects a broader evolution in professional competencies. The APPIC has incorporated understanding research and developing consultative skills when engaging in social service into their core competencies; some specialties have encouraged psychologists to use their experience to serve those persons/institutions who cannot afford our services (APA, 2013). However, clinical psychology has been somewhat slow in its efforts to directly address systemic oppression and economic injustice (Alexander & Allo, 2021). Building social justice advocacy into psychologists' training is an important goal to increase their understanding of the context of social problems, allow them to demonstrate skills in social action research methods, implement and evaluate interventions targeted at influencing public policy decisions, and learn to work with clients to help them make informed choices about engaging in advocacy for themselves.

Professional development has been a longstanding topic of interest in the field of psychology. Over the last forty years, there has been limited consensus on the meaning of professional development and the appropriate training methods seen in the literature on the topic (Elman et al., 2005). In 2002, APPIC initiated a conference aimed at establishing competencies essential in professional psychology practice (Kaslow et al., 2004). This ultimately led to a recommendation that training faculty provide regular professional development seminars (APPIC, 2002). The UMass Chan/WRCH internship has aimed to develop one possible model of a year-long professional development program for doctoral psychology interns.

The theoretically grounded didactic series was developed to address each of the profession-wide competencies identified by APA as foundational to the practice of health service psychology (see APA, 2019): Research; Ethical and Legal Standards; Individual and Cultural Diversity; Professional Values, Attitudes, and Behaviors; Communication and Interpersonal Skills; Assessment; Intervention; Supervision; and Consultation and Interprofessional/Interdisciplinary Skills.

Beginning and Development of Project Services

Dr. Grace Kent introduced an internship program at what was then Worcester State Hospital (WSH) in 1922, and this program was expanded under the leadership of Dr. David Shakow beginning in 1928. As he built the internship program, Shakow (1946) focused on three foundational pillars that he believed were essential to the professional psychologist: therapy, assessment, and research. Shakow developed the scientist-practitioner training model while directing the internship program, and his internship prototype was adopted by the Boulder Conference in the 1940s (Baker & Benjamin, 2000; Cautin, 2008). The University of Massachusetts Medical School (now UMass Chan Medical School) was founded in the 1970s and soon became affiliated with WSH, including through sponsorship of the internship program. Dr. Jack Terry took leadership in 2002 and helmed the program for twenty years. During this time, the internship continued refining its program offerings (with Dr. Ira Packer developing its forensic track in 2000), moved into the facility now known as the Worcester Recovery Center and Hospital (WRCH), and maintained its APA accreditation. While grounded in theoretical models, the program was also practical, with its design based on hospital resources, administrative needs, funding, and staff competency. Generally, little to no protected professional time has been available to support internship training efforts; as such, program development occurred in addition to full-time clinical duties.

Following Dr. Terry's retirement in 2022, Dr. Jeffrey Burl took over direction of the internship, with Drs. Heidi Putney and Meredith Ronan serving as Co-Assistant Directors. During this time, Burl, Putney, and Ronan applied for a training grant from the Department of Mental Health (DMH) for additional resources to support the internship and better meet intern training needs. In 2024, Putney moved from the Co-Assistant Director to the Director of the internship. In line with state efforts to increase the mental health workforce in Massachusetts, the training program was awarded a training grant, which expanded the internship to a Comprehensive

Psychology Training Program offering predoctoral advanced practicum training, the doctoral internship, and a postdoctoral fellowship for specialization in working with individuals with severe mental illness. This grant also provides additional funds to increase the number of trainees and trainee stipends. Grant proceeds have provided professional allowances for trainees, funding for external speakers, a salary for a half-time administrative assistant, and funds for a graduation ceremony; however, the resources for these non-stipend expenses fluctuate by fiscal year. Notably, the grant also provides financial coverage for program leadership, specifically 0.4 FTE for the training director and 0.2 FTE for an assistant director.

UMass Chan Medical School Forensic Psychology Residency Program

Project Description

The Forensic Psychology Postdoctoral Residency Program at UMass Medical School recruits and trains individuals who have completed their doctorates in psychology and wish to further their specialized expertise in public-sector forensic mental health assessment.[2] An added goal of the program is to attract more trained forensic psychologists to Massachusetts to work within the public-sector mental health system to complete court-ordered evaluations.

The fellowship program was designed to provide one year of specialty training in criminal forensic mental health evaluations for psychology trainees, who train alongside one psychiatry trainee completing the Department of Psychiatry's Fellowship in Forensic Psychiatry. Like the doctoral internship, the program is based in Worcester, developed and operated by UMass Chan Medical School faculty, and financially supported by funding from DMH. Much of the training experience takes place at WRCH, as it is a major provider of court-ordered, hospital-based evaluations of individuals involved in criminal proceedings across the Commonwealth. In addition to completing their doctorate by the start of the training year, residents are expected to have had some training and preparation in forensic psychology through graduate coursework, forensic clinical experience (practica and/or internship), and/or exposure to psychological testing a clinician may utilize in forensic mental health assessment.

The postdoctoral residency emphasizes the development of in-depth knowledge of law, clinical and psycholegal concepts, and mental health systems. The typical postdoctoral residency cohort consists of three psychology trainees who engage in training activities with one forensic psychiatry fellow. One major focus of postdoctoral training is the completion of court-ordered mental health evaluations, under supervision and with gradually increasing levels of independence. Forensic evaluation

[2] This program is called a "Residency," both to make clear the clinician's stage of training in a medical school context and to distinguish forensic psychology trainees from individuals completing multiyear postdoctoral research training programs offered by other departments at the Medical School.

work consists of psychological assessments of individuals involved in criminal legal proceedings. These evaluations address a range of legal questions, including competence to stand trial, criminal responsibility, aid in sentencing, whether a prisoner/detainee is in need of mental health treatment, and/or whether an individual requires psychiatric commitment. This applied clinical experience extends to violence risk assessment and consultation to state hospital treatment teams making clinical decisions regarding increased privileges or discharge for patients identified as high-risk, as required by state policy. Residents are expected to conduct such evaluations at WRCH as the program's home base, but there are additional opportunities for a training rotation at a Department of Corrections Psychiatric Hospital, which is designated for men requiring higher security. There are additional minor rotations conducting outpatient forensic mental health assessments at Court Clinics (located at courthouses across the Commonwealth), as well as placement with the statewide program providing specialized assessment and treatment of individuals with mental illness combined with histories of sexually problematic behaviors. Given the centrality of forensic mental health evaluations to the training year, program clients are generally courts throughout Massachusetts. In the instances of violence risk consultations, the identified clients are state hospital treatment providers. All clients refer justice-involved adults (men and women) for evaluation, with many of these persons presenting with some combination of histories of serious mental illness, alcohol/substance use disorders, personality disorders, and/or traumatic experiences.

The training year also includes multiple seminars, including weekly topics in forensic psychology and forensic psychiatry. In addition, there is weekly analysis of national and state-level landmark legal cases relevant to the field, bi-weekly empirical and theoretical presentations covering various topics related to mental health and the law (as part of the larger Law & Psychiatry Program in the Department of Psychiatry), a quarterly diversity and culture brownbag series (described further below), and yearly Foundations trainings offered by the Department of Mental Health to train new forensic mental health professionals across the state.

Scholarship is another component of the training year, particularly a supervised research project concerning a topic of the resident's choosing in the broad field of psychology and law. This project culminates in a seminar presentation on the research topic, and the resident is encouraged to prepare and submit a paper for publication as the first author. Authorship of a legal case summary is an additional avenue for publication, as is submission of a conference presentation or joining program faculty in other writing as opportunity arises.

Other training activities include expert testimony, in the form of two mock trial experiences, one hosted by a law school in the state and the other developed internally. Both exercises involve the provision of feedback from mental health professionals and legal professionals. In addition, at times, forensic evaluations completed by trainees require expert testimony; as the primary evaluator, the resident is expected to serve as the expert under the observation of a supervisor. Residents also have opportunities to develop their supervision and clinical teaching experience, through the facilitation of the internship's Professional Development series (described above) and supervision of intern assessment and therapy cases.

Foundations and Support for Project Services

Forensic psychology postdoctoral fellowships have been an evolving and growing opportunity for doctoral graduates who seek the additional specialized training the field requires (beyond graduate school curriculum and internship-level experience). There are currently at least sixty-three forensic psychology fellowship programs across the country; of these, thirty-seven programs (as of June 2024) have qualified for the American Board of Forensic Psychology (ABFP) five-year waiver for application (American Board of Forensic Psychology, 2024). Forensic psychology fellowship programs have continued to sub-specialize, to provide more in-depth training in specific areas. This includes focus on juveniles, individuals who have committed sexual offenses, private practice, corrections, academia, and public sector hospitals. Directors of these programs in recent years have collaboratively worked to improve the quality and consistency of training being provided. Additionally, professional organizations such as APPIC, the Council of Specialties in Professional Psychology, the APA Commission on Accreditation, and the American Board of Professional Psychology seek to ensure that training provided across sites is consistent, evidence-based, and in accordance with best practices and relevant specialty guidelines. The residency also follows expectations identified for forensic mental health evaluators in Massachusetts, in that its elements are designed to meet the training requirements for state certification as a Designated Forensic Professional (DFP) of public-sector forensic psychologists and psychiatrists conducting evaluations in correctional facilities, courthouses, and state hospitals (Commonwealth of Massachusetts, 2018).

The weekly seminars focus on the broad empirical and theoretical literature undergirding specialty practice in forensic psychology and forensic psychiatry. The sessions span a broad range of topics, including ethical practice, criminal and civil procedures, and specific types of evaluations (e.g., competence to stand trial, disability), populations (sexual offenders, juveniles), and practice considerations (e.g., feigning, functioning as an expert witness, fiscal health). The Case Law Seminars involve an in-depth review of landmark federal and state cases relevant to forensic mental health practice. These seminars were structured to comport with training guidelines promulgated by ABFP (2024) and to prepare trainees for the written examination required for state certification as a public-sector forensic evaluator.

Clinical supervision is integral to the development of a psychologist. In addition to direct training of the clinician learning to practice, supervision also protects those served by psychologists, and ensures that those who enter the field are sufficiently prepared for practice (Falender et al., 2004; O'Donovan et al., 2011). As such, supervision is considered a distinct professional practice within clinical psychology (APA, 2014) and is generally integrated into psychology training requirements (APA, 2019). In the postdoctoral residency program, supervision is provided with the goals of enhancing the professional competence and science-informed practice of the supervisee, monitoring the quality of services provided, protecting the public, and providing a gatekeeping function for entry into the profession. This program also operates under the premise that supervision is integral to the practice of forensic psychology; it meets requirements and guides skill development in areas that are distinctive to the specialty (Varela & Conroy, 2012), as well as mentorship. While literature concerning forensic assessment supervision is relatively scarce, supervision in this program is consistent with emerging ideas that specialty practice within psychology requires supervision that is highly attuned to foundational differences between forensic and therapeutic assessment (Hunt et al., 2024). Additionally, in this jurisdiction, forensic assessment supervisors must attain another state credential beyond DFP; for this credential, the Forensic Mental Health (FMH) Supervisor must have at least five years of forensic experience, be actively engaged in public sector forensic work, provide letters of recommendation, and pass statewide committee review of the FMH Supervisor candidate's work samples. Given that the residency involves supervision of doctoral-level clinicians who are expected to seek DFP certification, all clinical supervisors must have both DFP and FMH Supervisor credentials.

Beginning and Development of Project Services

In the context of the relatively short period of time that forensic psychology has existed as a specialty field, the first forensic psychology postdoctoral program was developed in the late 1980s, primarily by Dr. Thomas Grisso. This program arose secondary to a collaboration between the University of Massachusetts Medical School and the public behavioral health system, the Massachusetts DMH. This collaboration was prompted by the increasing number of criminal defendants with mental illnesses requiring competency to stand trial and/or criminal responsibility evaluations, and the small number of forensically trained psychologists and psychiatrists in the state capable of doing the work well. At the time, forensic mental health evaluations were poorly done, and the availability of evaluators was limited. The collaboration provided two parallel training avenues for psychologists to specialize in forensic evaluation work: the development of the formalized DFP credentialing process and the development of the medical school's formalized forensic psychology postdoctoral training program.

The program began in 1988, and it expanded in 1992 to include a Forensic Psychiatry Fellowship for individuals who have completed medical degrees and residency training as psychiatrists. After the Forensic Psychiatry Fellowship was established, psychology and psychiatry trainees were trained together. Over time, increased funding allowed three fellows yearly in the forensic psychology program. Fellows could receive training in state inpatient psychiatric hospitals, and also in the courts, conducting screening evaluations of defendants to appraise their need for further evaluation within inpatient settings. In 1999, Dr. Ira Packer joined the faculty of what was then the UMass Medical School and assumed the leadership of the forensic psychology postdoctoral program. In that role, he oversaw the ongoing development of the seminars and the application for ABFP waiver. In 2021, Dr. Ashley Murray, who served as the Assistant Director, took on the role of Director. She continued the program's development by maintaining existing relationships, and forming new ones, with external sites. She also expanded training activities available to residents, arranged for training and mentoring more specifically focused on professional development, and developed with the Comprehensive Psychology Training Program opportunities for residents to become involved with supervision. Program funding, provided by DMH, included protected time for the Director (.15 FTE); funded the half-time administrative assistant; and provided fee-for-service compensation for the attorney co-facilitator, research supervisors, and trainee mentor.

Generalizability

This training program is intended to provide high-quality and specialized training for new psychologists, with emphasis on preparation for practice in the public sector. There are presently shortages in the mental health professional workforce across the United States, with access to care being further disparate by race/ethnicity, socioeconomic status, and geographic location (see Adams et al., 2022; Belz et al., 2024; Covino, 2019; Olfson, 2016). Efforts to increase access to care have led to modified training, recruitment, and retention; utilization of technology; system reform; and using the example of low- and middle-income nations (Adams et al., 2022; Belz et al., 2024). It is therefore reasonable to conclude that the field needs similar internships to train psychologists. Mental health workforce shortages are also apparent in larger systemic patterns, such as the "competence crisis" delaying criminal legal proceedings and causing long waits for forensic evaluations and/or inpatient hospitalizations (Kois et al., 2024). Given that forensic psychology is recognized as a specialty with distinctive training and practice components (APA, 2013), forensic training at the internship and postdoctoral levels is particularly important—particularly if there is ongoing, unmet demand for psychologists and forensic psychologists.

That said, despite high levels of public need and the efforts by state systems to create or expand training, there are also associated challenges. For instance, the new comprehensive program that incorporates the internship provides some protected time for leadership (the Director and Assistant Director). Similarly, the director of the postdoctoral residency in forensic psychology also has protected time dedicated to program leadership. However, the faculty serving in these leadership roles do so in addition to maintaining active caseloads as clinicians; directing a clinical training program is not considered a full-time role. As such, directing these programs requires work beyond that covered by available FTE, such as during application and candidate selection seasons; this work is therefore essentially performed by leadership and faculty *pro bono* in addition to other professional duties. Beyond program leadership, the internship relies on approximately twenty supervisors for the entire program and the forensic postdoc relies on three forensic supervisors who possess supervision certification required by the state. For the residency, in addition to the Director (AM) and three primary clinical supervisors (including NA), there are two research supervisors, two co-facilitators of the Landmark Case Law Seminars (a forensic psychiatrist and an external attorney), and a professor emeritus mentor at UMass Chan. There are also credentialed supervisors at the external training sites. Supervisors provide supervision and training on a voluntary basis, as they receive no FTE coverage for supervision. Some program faculty also serve in separate administrative roles in addition to their clinical caseloads and education of trainees. As such, leadership must be thoughtful in demands placed on busy clinicians who are volunteering their time and expertise. Another consideration, due to the program's funding by a state agency grant, is fluctuations in financial support in accordance with an annual state budget. This means that even with state commitment to training, a budget shortfall one year may lead to reductions in funding that require difficult decisions regarding resources.

At the postdoctoral level, despite growth in forensic psychology training and the strong need for specialized practitioners, we have informally observed a decrease in applicants to forensic psychology postdoctoral programs across the nation in recent years. Whether this change in application numbers reflects the beginning of an ongoing trend versus a time-limited fluctuation remains unclear. It should be noted that while an internship is required for completion of the doctorate and licensure as a psychologist, a postdoctoral residency is not. It is certainly possible that immediate needs associated with the "trial competency" crisis have prompted direct hiring of staff evaluators who receive on-the-job training, rather than the slower and longer-term process of formally training specialists. It is also likely that the relatively low stipends of one-year postdoctoral training programs are less competitive with the salary and benefits of full-time positions, particularly if the postdoctoral training program requires a trainee to relocate. Although answers to these questions will not be forthcoming without more time and further research, they are certainly relevant to the development of additional postdoctoral training programs in forensic psychology (even when there is a clear demonstrated need).

Replicating this program would require a number of considerations. First, as mentioned above, high levels of mental health needs and demand for qualified psychologists may improve buy-in from the government agencies that might support the program. Despite yearly changes in funding, these needs in Massachusetts have led to a long-term state commitment to education and training. It is also important to note that creating, developing, and maintaining public-sector training programs in forensic psychology requires an array of other skills—something we have come to appreciate more over time. First, unsurprisingly, is a high level of foundational knowledge and competency needed for specialization in forensic psychology, from generalized clinical foundations to the specialized competencies specific to forensic psychology (Varela & Conroy, 2012). Also necessary are knowledge, skills, and abilities related to supervision and training in clinical psychology and in forensic psychology (Hunt et al., 2024). Also important are the knowledge and skills that may not have been developed during psychology training; these involve personnel management, human resources, and employment law, among other areas. A combination of learned skills and personal qualities appear additionally necessary for the success of a training program, particularly with regard to funding, operational support, and development of training rotations both internal and external. These skills include a deep knowledge of the specific public-sector agencies, systems, and institutions that would be involved in such a training program; knowledge of and relationships with the persons within them, specifically those in positions of authority and responsibility; the ability to create and foster good relationships between multiple stakeholders with intersecting interests; the ability to juggle multiple responsibilities and tasks while providing timely products; and assertiveness in advocating for and protecting the program, particularly as changes occur in personnel, resources, and stakeholder priorities.

Diversity, Equity, and Inclusiveness

Given the high demand for forensic mental health services, a substantial portion of individuals at WRCH are justice involved at the time of their stay, whether they are admitted to Court Evaluation Units for time-limited evaluations or committed for continuing inpatient care. As such, trainees are exposed to a broad range of persons involved with the criminal legal system who are referred for mental health evaluation. The programs' placement in a state hospital setting also means that many individuals receiving services or undergoing evaluations have histories of serious mental illness. However, there are also disparities in the individuals who are involved with Commonwealth criminal proceedings and who are referred for services. A 2020 analysis of the Massachusetts Criminal System (Tsai Bishop et al., 2020) revealed racial and ethnic disparities in initial charging decisions, adjudication, and incarceration. Prior analysis of defendants evaluated at Massachusetts court clinics had revealed similar disparities in subsequent referrals for inpatient evaluations and in security decisions associated with such referrals, and raised questions regarding differential access to mental health treatment prior to involvement with the criminal legal system (Pinals et al., 2004).

Despite the growth in research on racism in psychology (Neville et al., 2024), the existence of multiple divisions of APA dedicated to the study of diverse and minoritized populations, and empirical evidence of inequity and bias in the legal system (see, e.g., Avery & Cooper, 2020), there has historically been relatively limited attention to this in forensic psychology research (Nijdam-Jones et al., 2023; Wylie et al., 2018) or training (Cantone et al., 2019). This area of relative neglect became salient in the early 2020s (see Hunt & Shepherd, 2023). Regardless, there is emerging guidance (e.g., Heilbrun et al., 2021; Ratkalkar et al., 2023; Riggs Romaine & Kavanaugh, 2019) that our programs have moved to integrate into training more meaningfully in recent years.

Psychology trainees are preparing to serve an increasingly diverse public, and we strive to recruit diverse trainees while also retaining and expanding the pipeline for these trainees into the professional workforce (e.g., see Cullinan et al., 2024). The internship is fortunate to have faculty willing to lead the internship's Diversity, Equity, Inclusion, and Belonging (DEIB) efforts and to have received a small amount of funding to hire a diversity consultant; however, interns have reported the non-clinical activities developed through these initiatives have been difficult to integrate into their already-full schedules. Similarly, mentoring can be an impactful component of a training program and an important avenue for career advancement (e.g., see Johnson et al., 2023), but interns have reported that their availability to see mentors is limited by time or by the difficulty in finding a mentor. To address these concerns, internship leadership has attempted to build a culture in which mentoring opportunities are available in multiple areas of the interns' experience. We have found that this remains an ongoing challenge.

The postdoctoral residency includes a two-part didactic series focusing on Race, Ethnicity, and Culture (REC) early in the training year. These seminars focus on the development and structural impacts of racism in the United States, exploring racial identity during a forensic evaluation, and integrating REC into the psychological and forensic conceptualization. The postdoc has also implemented an REC Brownbag Series, in which clinicians present a case in which identity context was relevant, discuss available literature, consider how to address it in the evaluation and report, and consider means of improving future practice. During supervision with trainees, we discuss identities (our own and the examinees'), identity context in specific cases, and consider how we may incorporate them into the evaluation and report. In this, we consider the limits of our knowledge and engage in as-needed consultation with clinicians with relevant expertise, whether they are program faculty, affiliated faculty, or fully external to the program. However, challenges associated with these efforts include attempts to prevent or mitigate trainee feelings of added work to the already long list of requirements of the residency, ensuring consistency of REC integration across supervisors, and managing inevitable (and normative) feelings of discomfort that come with explicit consideration of REC in forensic evaluation reports.

Over the next decade, it is likely that guidance around meaningful incorporation of REC into forensic mental health will further coalesce and evolve. As such, it is important to follow the literature and incorporate it into training. Important priorities to be addressed in this domain over the following, in addition to the considerations identified above, are continuing efforts to contribute to a diverse psychology workforce pipeline. Other considerations center around the demographic and clinical needs of the populations with which trainees work, specifically equitable linguistic access for individuals with limited English proficiency, evaluations of aggrieved groups (such as white supremacist groups, Sovereign Citizens, and Moorish Americans), and differentiating between extreme beliefs and delusions.

Advice to Others Seeking to Provide Similar Services

Gauging the Market

In creating and developing training programs in forensic psychology, one should involve awareness of overall training needs in the discipline of psychology. As noted previously, there is strong demand for trained mental health professionals and for forensic mental health professionals, and expansion of training opportunities should be expected to increase the number of professionals. With regard to internship training, although the longtime imbalance involving far fewer internship training positions than applicants has changed since 2012, the growth of internship positions has also slowed or stopped entirely in recent years. Additionally, national training needs involve not only the number of slots but also the availability of internships that are accredited by APA (Keilin et al., 2022). Internships that offer high-quality training and provide specific opportunities for mock trials, didactics in case law, conducting (rather than observing) forensic evaluations, and experience in risk assessment are particularly likely to be high in demand.

The market for postdoctoral training programs is likely to be different, as noted above. However, training programs offering opportunities to engage in multiple types of foundational forensic mental health assessments (e.g., competence to stand trial, criminal responsibility), courtroom testimony, exposure to multiple settings, formal didactic training, and preparation for board certification (that is, programs accepted for the ABFP waiver) are likely to be more competitive. Training programs that can offer relatively high stipends compared with other programs are likely to be particularly competitive, which may be a challenge for jurisdictions with more limited resources. Regardless of the stage of training, even if the applicant pool is national (or international), local/regional needs are likely to shape the development of the program, allocation of resources to and within the program, and training emphasis.

Getting Started

In both the internship and postdoctoral programs, their foundation in a psychiatric hospital setting that is one of few identified locations for court-ordered evaluations within the Commonwealth means that there is an immediate pool of individuals to evaluate, limited competition by other service providers, and the availability of on-site clinicians to serve as faculty and leadership. These have eliminated the typical practical concerns related to creating and spooling up a training program. Gradual development of a training program is preferable, as it is quite difficult to develop a program while it is actively training psychologists. Gradually starting and then making changes in a long-running program allows for establishing the procedures that work, making incremental improvements and adjustments, and slowly building a reputation. However, while developing a strong theoretical foundation for the program is important, aspects of program development require piloting with trainees. Such piloting provides direct translation from theory to practice, highlights logistics that may not have been evident at first, and it allows for adjustment in response to direct feedback from trainees to ensure the training is meeting its objectives. Additionally, rapid growth and development may make a program more agile and responsive to change and evolving training needs.

Specialization

In our jurisdiction, both psychologists who conduct forensic mental health assessments and psychologists supervising forensic clinicians in training are required to obtain specialized state credentials. Thus, program faculty and leadership are necessarily specialized in their professional practice. The benefit of this requirement is that faculty are thus qualified and experienced in forensic practice, have an in-depth knowledge base to provide specialty training, and develop a national reputation for strong training. That being said, in addition to professional specialization, those involved in creating and maintaining a training program must also have the interest, energy, and non-clinical professional skills (as detailed above) to engage in this time- and labor-intensive endeavor.

Publicity

Our programs (both internship and postdoctoral) are listed in the APPIC Directory, with important keywords included to describe populations, service modalities, and training experiences. Each training program also has its own website (with links to both found on the UMass Chan Department of Psychiatry website), each describing the program and training experiences, and providing the respective director's contact information. The Doctoral Internship also maintains a downloadable Brochure detailing the rotations, compensation and benefits, leadership, and faculty. The Postdoctoral Residency publishes this information directly on its website, rather than in a separate brochure.

Due to their longevity, the programs also benefit extensively from word-of-mouth. That is, these long-running programs have an extensive list of alumni who are dispersed throughout the country and engaged in various professional activities. It is not uncommon for program alums, particularly those involved in teaching students preparing for internship and/or postdoctoral training, to inform and encourage students to apply. Also assisting the development of a reputation is the relatively small number of programs offering forensic training, even though training opportunities are expanding. More indirectly, faculty in both training programs maintain academic productivity by publishing and regularly presenting at conferences. As many faculty have a particular interest in clinical and/or forensic training, a number of publications and presentations tend to focus upon this topic and thereby introduce audiences to faculty and the psychology training opportunities at UMass Chan. Finally, faculty involvement in academic service (e.g., committees, leadership) also contribute to ongoing visibility even when program leadership changes.

Despite the ongoing pursuit of program improvement, our programs have not joined the twenty-first century in one substantial way: our training programs do not have a major presence on social media. We instead rely on UMass Chan communications personnel for online publication of program news.

Do's and Don'ts

Based upon our experience, we can offer some recommendations. Do set up a strong leadership team; one or two directors cannot prepare for every eventuality, and a group can assist with decision making, program development, and implementation. Do establish strong lines of communication with supervisors, as they are the bedrock of the program. Do solicit feedback (including anonymized feedback) from trainees and program alums to inform ongoing program development. Do establish networks of other educational leaders, such as the email listserv for directors of forensic psychology postdoctoral programs across the United States. Do seek out opportunities for networking and connections, in part for identifying new training opportunities, and for the purpose of word-of-mouth advertising. Finally, dedicate funding for administrative support, as this becomes crucial as the training program grows.

Don't assume that funding will remain the same. While public funding is secure in some respects, it is also subject to larger state budgetary shifts, shortfalls, surpluses, and changes in legislative and/or executive goals. As such, seeking outside grants can provide supplemental funding during lean years. Don't take for granted established training rotations or faculty, as individual circumstances, program priorities, and availability may change year to year (or even within a year). Finally, don't assume that cohort values and training needs will remain the same from training year to training year; cultural and generational shifts are normal and to be expected.

Conclusions

Our internship and postdoctoral training programs, while separate in some ways, are also deeply interconnected parts of a larger whole that together help represent the discipline of psychology in the psychiatry department of a large medical school. These two long-running programs provide some examples of the incorporation of clinical forensic training into practice with justice-involved persons. Beyond building the foundational professional and specialty competencies, the setting, available resources, and the skillsets of program leadership can illustrate ways to develop unique training opportunities. These programs require extensive time and labor, at times beyond what immediate financial resources may fully support, but are a deeply rewarding aspect of psychological practice that serves regional mental health needs by training more specialized psychologists for competent practice in needed areas.

References

Adams, E., Watanabe-Galloway, S., Baerentzen, M. B., Grennan, A., Obermeier Schneider, E., & Doyle, M. (2022). The Behavioral Health Education Center of Nebraska: A creative solution to a persistent behavioral health workforce shortage. *Psychiatric Clinics of North America, 45*(2), 259–270. https://doi.org/10.1016/j.psc.2022.03.004

Alexander, A., & Allo, H. (2021). Building a climate for advocacy training in professional psychology. *The Counseling Psychologist, 49*(7), 1070–1089. https://doi.org/10.1177/00110000211027973

American Board of Forensic Psychology. (2024). *Postdoctoral training programs in forensic psychology accepted for experience waiver.* https://abpp.org/wp-content/uploads/2025/08/ABFP-Postdoc-Programs-Accepted-Experience-Waiver-8.12.25.pdf

American Psychological Association. (2014). *Guidelines for clinical supervision in health service psychology.* Retrieved from http://apa.org/about/policy/guidelines-supervision.pdf

American Psychological Association. (2013). Specialty guidelines for forensic psychology. *American Psychologist, 68*(1) 7–19. https://doi.org/10.1037/a0029889

American Psychological Association. (2019). *Standards of accreditation for health service psychology and accreditation operating procedures.* Retrieved from https://www.apa.org/ed/accreditation/about/policies/standards-of-accreditation.pdf

American Psychology-Law Society Student Committee. (December 3, 2024). *Clinical postdoctoral positions in forensic psychology.* http://www.apls-students.org/clinical.html

Association of Psychology Postdoctoral and Internship Centers. (2002). *2002 competencies: Future directions in education and credentialing in professional psychology.* https://www.appic.org/Portals/0/downloads/CompetenciesCombinedWorkgroupSummaries.pdf

Avery, J., & Cooper, J. (Eds.). (2020). *Bias in the law: A definitive look at racial prejudice in the U.S. criminal justice system.* Lexington.

Baker, D. B., & Benjamin, L. T., Jr. (2000). The affirmation of the scientist-practitioner: A look back at Boulder. *American Psychologist, 55*(2), 241–247. https://doi.org/10.1037/0003-066X.55.2.241

Belz, F. F., Vega Potler, N. J., Johnson, I. N. S., & Wolthusen, R. P. F. (2024). Lessons from low-and middle-income countries: Alleviating the behavioral health workforce shortage in the United States. *Psychiatric Services, 75*(7), 699–702. https://doi.org/10.1176/appi.ps.20230348

Bersoff, D. N., Goodman-Delahunty, J., Grisso, J. T., Hans, V. P., Poythress, N. G., & Roesch, R. G. (1997). Training in law and psychology: Models from the Villanova Conference. *American Psychologist, 52*(12), 1301–1310. https://doi.org/10.1037/0003-066X.52.12.1301

Cantone, J. A., Clomax, T. D., Woolard, J., & Kemp, K. (November, 2019). Early career professionals in law and psychology: The state of training and areas of needed support. *American Psychology-Law Society (AP-LS) Newsletter.* Retrieved from https://ap-ls.org/resources/reports/#early-career-professionals-survey

Cautin, R. (2008). David Shakow and schizophrenia research at Worcester State Hospital: The roots of the scientist-practitioner model. *Journal of the History of the Behavioral Sciences, 44*(3), 219–237. https://doi.org/10.1002/jhbs.20312

Commonwealth of Massachusetts Department of Mental Health. (2018). *Designated forensic professional procedures manual.* https://www.mass.gov/doc/designated-forensic-professional-procedures-manual/download

Cullinan, C. C., Harrison, R. R., & Hughes-Reid, C. (2024). Meeting the moment: Centering cultural humility and antiracism in health service psychology internship training. *Training and Education in Professional Psychology, 18*(3), 213–220. https://doi.org/10.1037/tep0000473

Covino, N. A. (2019). Developing the behavioral health workforce: Lessons from the States. *Administration and Policy in Mental Health and Mental Health Services Research, 46*(6), 689–695. https://doi.org/10.1007/s10488-019-00963-w

DeMatteo, D., Marczyk, G., Krauss, D. A., & Burl, J. (2009). Educational and training models in forensic psychology. *Training and Education in Professional Psychology, 3*(3), 184–191. https://doi.org/10.1037/a0014582

Elman, N., Illfelder-Kaye, J., & Robiner, W. (2005). Professional development: Training for professionalism as a foundation for competent practice in psychology. *Professional Psychology: Research and Practice, 36*(4), 367–375. https://doi.org/10.1037/0735-7028.36.4.367

Erickson Cornish, J. A., & Baker, J. (2023). A brief history of the association of psychology postdoctoral and internship centers: Trends and directions for the education and training of health service psychologists. *Training and Education in Professional Psychology, 17*(2), 115–125. https://doi.org/10.1037/tep0000401

Falender, C. A., Cornish, J. A. E., Goodyear, R., Hatcher, R., Kaslow, N. J., Leventhal, G., Shafranske, E., Sigmon, S. T., Stoltenberg, C., & Grus, C. (2004). Defining competencies in psychology supervision: A consensus statement. *Journal of Clinical Psychology*, 60(7), 771–785. https://doi.org/10.1002/jclp.20013

Grisso, T. (2018). The evolution of psychology and law. In T. Grisso & S. Brodsky (Eds.), *The roots of modern psychology and law: A narrative history* (pp. 1–27). Oxford.

Heilbrun, K., Kavanaugh, A., Grisso, T., Anumba, N., Dvoskin, J., & Golding, S. (2021). The importance of racial identity in forensic mental health assessment. *Journal of the American Academy of Psychiatry and Law*, *49*(4), 478–487. DOI: 10.29158/JAAPL.210099-21

Hoch, E. L., Ross, A. O., & Winder, C. L. (Eds.). (1966). *Professional preparation of clinical psychologists.* American Psychological Association. https://doi.org/10.1037/10537-000

Hunt, E., Hodges, H. J., Armstrong, N. E., Anumba, N. M., DeMier, R. L., & Holden, C. E. (2024). Forensic psychology is different: Supervision approaches in forensic assessment. *Journal of Forensic Psychology Research and Practice. Published online September 24, 2024.* https://doi.org/10.1080/24732850.2024.2407347

Hunt, J. S., & Shepherd, S. M. (2023). Racial justice in psycholegal research and forensic psychology practice: Current advances and a framework for future progress. *Law and Human Behavior, 47*(1), 1–11. https://doi.org/10.1037/lhb0000526

Johnson, W. B., Long, S., Smith, D. G., & Griffin, K. A. (2023). Creating a mentoring culture in graduate training programs. *Training and Education in Professional Psychology, 17*(1), 63–70. https://doi.org/10.1037/tep0000404

Kaslow, N. J., Borden, K. A., Collins Jr., F. L., Forrest, L., Illfelder-Kaye, J., Nelson, P. D., Rallo, J. S., Vasquez, M. J. T., & Willmuth, M. E. (2004). Competencies conference: Future directions in education and credentialing in professional psychology. *Journal of Clinical Psychology, 60*(7), 699–712. https://doi.org/10.1002/jclp.20016

Keilin, W. G., Aosved, A. C., Ponce, A. N., & Self, M. M. (2022). Balancing the imbalance: An examination of recent changes in psychology doctoral internship supply and demand. *Training and Education in Professional Psychology, 16*(1), 1–9. https://doi.org/10.1037/tep0000357

Kois, L. E., Potts, H., Cox, J., & Zapf, P. (2024). Court-reported competence to proceed data across the United States. *Law and Human Behavior, 48*(3), 182–202. https://doi.org/10.1037/lhb0000565

Korman, M. (1974). National conference on levels and patterns of professional training in psychology: The major themes. *American Psychologist, 29*(6), 441–449. https://doi.org/10.1037/h0036469

Krauss, D. A., & Sales, B. D. (2014). Training in forensic psychology. In I. B. Weiner & R. K. Otto (Eds.), *The handbook of forensic psychology* (4th ed., pp. 111–134). John Wiley & Sons.

Levine, D., Wilson, K., & Sales, D. (1980). An exploratory assessment of APA internships with legal/forensic experiences. *Professional Psychology*, *11*(1), 64–71. https://doi.org/10.1037/0735-7028.11.1.64

Malesky, L. A., & Proctor, S. L. (2012). Training experiences essential for obtaining a forensic psychology postdoctoral fellowship. *Journal of Forensic Psychology Practice*, *12*(2), 163–172. https://doi.org/10.1080/15228932.2012.650146

Miles, J. R., & Fassinger, R. E. (2021). Creating a public psychology through a scientist-practitioner-advocate model. *American Psychologist*, *76*(8), 1232–1247. https://doi.org/10.1037/amp0000855

Morrow, W. R. (1946). The development of psychological internship training. *Journal of Consulting Psychology*, *10*(4), 165–183. https://doi.org/10.1037/h0053807

Neal, T. M. S. (2018). Forensic psychology and correctional psychology: Distinct but related subfields of psychological science and practice. *American Psychologist*, *73*(5), 651–662. https://doi.org/10.1037/amp0000227

Neville, H. A., Monette, M., Lewis, J. T., & Safir, S. (2024). Shifting the gaze from racism to healing from racism: A systematic review of selected psychology journals from 1992 to 2022. *American Psychologist*, *79*(5), 706–724. https://doi.org/10.1037/amp0001317

Nijdam-Jones, A., Cortvriendt, J., & Daffern, M. (2023). Diversity in the International Journal of Forensic Mental Health. *International Journal of Forensic Mental Health*, *22*(4), 354–365. https://doi.org/10.1080/14999013.2023.2243853

O'Donovan, A., Halford, W. K., & Walters, B. (2011). Towards best practice supervision of clinical psychology trainees. *Australian Psychologist*, *46*(2), 101–112. https://doi.org/10.1111/j.1742-9544.2011.00033.x

Olfson, M. (2016). Building the mental health workforce capacity needed to treat adults with serious mental illness. *Health Affairs*, *35*(6), 983–990. https://doi.org/10.1377/hlthaff.2015.1619

Otto, R. K., & Heilbrun, K. (2002). The practice of forensic psychology: A look toward the future in light of the past. *American Psychologist*, *57*(1), 5–18. https://psycnet.apa.org/doi/10.1037/0003-066X.57.1.5

Otto, R. K., Heilbrun, K., & Grisso, T. (1990). Training and credentialing in forensic psychology. *Behavioral Sciences and the Law*, *8*(3), 217–231. https://doi.org/10.1002/bsl.2370080305

Packer, I. K. (2008). Specialized practice in forensic psychology: Opportunities and obstacles. *Professional Psychology: Research and Practice*, *39*(2), 245–249. https://doi.org/10.1037/0735-7028.39.2.245

Pinals, D. A., Packer, I. K., Fisher, W., & Roy-Bujnowski, K. (2004). Relationship between race and ethnicity and forensic clinical triage dispositions. *Psychiatric Services*, *55*(8), 873–878. https://doi.org/10.1176/appi.ps.55.8.873

Potts, H., & Kois, L. E. (2023). Survey of doctoral internships in psychology offering experience in forensics and corrections. *Training and Education in Professional Psychology*, *17*(1), 106–113. https://doi.org/10.1037/tep0000375

Ratkalkar, M., Jackson, C., & Heilbrun, K. (2023). Race-informed forensic mental health assessment: A principles-based analysis. *International Journal of Forensic Mental Health, 22*(4), 314–325. https://doi.org/10.1080/14999013.2023.2178556

Riggs Romaine, C. L., & Kavanaugh, A. (2019). Risks, benefits, and complexities: Reporting race and ethnicity in forensic mental health reports. *International Journal of Forensic Mental Health, 18*(2), 138–152. https://doi.org/10.1080/14999013.2018.1531094

Routh, D. K. (2000). Clinical psychology training: A history of ideas and practices prior to 1946. *American Psychologist, 55*(2), 236–241. https://doi.org/10.1037/0003-066X.55.2.236

Shakow, D. (1946). The Worcester internship program. *Journal of Consulting Psychology, 10*(4), 191–200. https://doi.org/10.1037/h0059797

Tsai Bishop, E., Hopkins, B., Obiofuma, C., & Owusu, F. (2020). *Racial disparities in the Massachusetts Criminal System.* Harvard Law School Criminal Justice Policy Program. https://hls.harvard.edu/wp-content/uploads/2022/08/Massachusetts-Racial-Disparity-Report-FINAL.pdf

Varela, J. G., & Conroy, M. A. (2012). Professional competencies in forensic psychology. *Professional Psychology: Research and Practice, 43*(5), 410–421. https://doi.org/10.1037/a0026776

Wylie, L. E., Hazen, K. P., Hoetger, L. A., Haby, J. A., & Brank, E. M. (2018). Four decades of the journal *Law and Human Behavior*: A content analysis. *Scientometrics, 115*(2), 655–693. https://doi.org/10.1007/s11192-018-2685-y

19

Policy Research and Education Services

The Policy Research Associates (PRA) Approach

Sarah L. Desmarais, Elan C. Hope, Holley Davis, and Shannon M. Bader

Project Description

Introduction

Policy research and education play a critical role in shaping effective community-based services for justice-involved individuals. In this chapter, we describe the Policy Research Associates (PRA) approach to delivering policy research and education services to improve outcomes for justice-involved individuals. Founded in 1987, PRA is a women-owned firm headquartered in Troy, New York. PRA's first grant was from the National Institute of Mental Health to assess the impact of insanity defense reforms. PRA quickly added policy education to its services with the award of the Substance Abuse and Mental Health Services Administration's (SAMHSA) National Resource Center on Homelessness and Mental Illness a year later. Since then, PRA has maintained a balance of policy research and education services (see Figure 19.1).

Services

PRA's **research and evaluation** services are focused on analyzing policy implementation and impact, typically within the fields of behavioral health, youth development, and the criminal legal system. Activities include designing research protocols and gathering, integrating, and analyzing quantitative and qualitative data toward the dual goals of advancing science and providing recommendations for policy and practice (Policy Research Associates, 2024). Recent efforts include the *Understanding the Population of People with Frequent Jail Contact* project funded by the MacArthur Foundation Safety and Justice Challenge Research Consortium to examine the flow of people through the criminal legal system in three counties, and to evaluate the success of strategies to reduce frequent jail contact—especially among people of color and those with behavioral health conditions. Another example is the California

Sarah L. Desmarais et al., *Policy Research and Education Services.* In: *The Path Forward.* Edited by: Kirk Heilbrun and David DeMatteo, Oxford University Press. © Oxford University Press (2026). DOI: 10.1093/9780197773031.003.0019

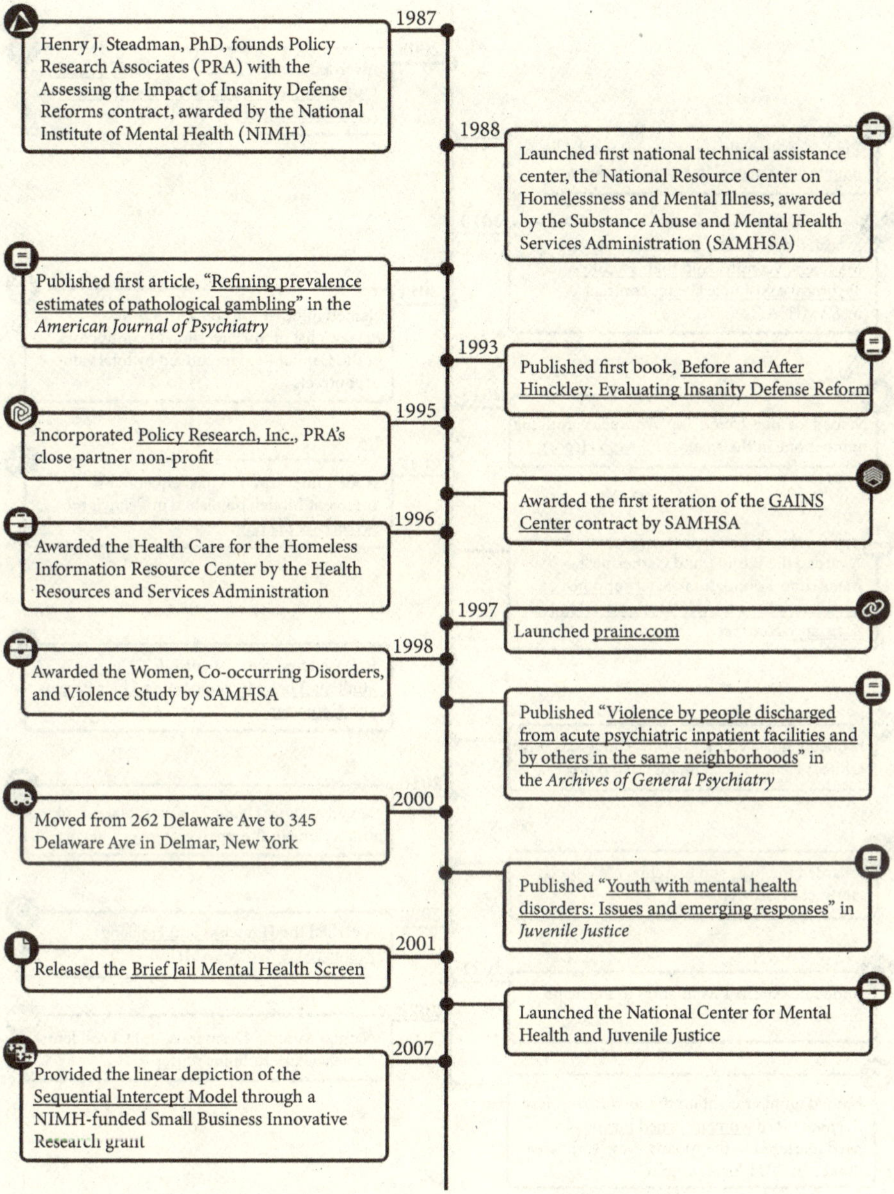

Figure 19.1 The Evolution of Policy Research Associates over Thirty-Five Years

Department of State Hospitals Felony Incompetent to Stand Trial (IST) Continuum of Care project, through which we are evaluating the implementation and impact of programs for people with serious mental illness who face felony charges and could be determined to be IST.

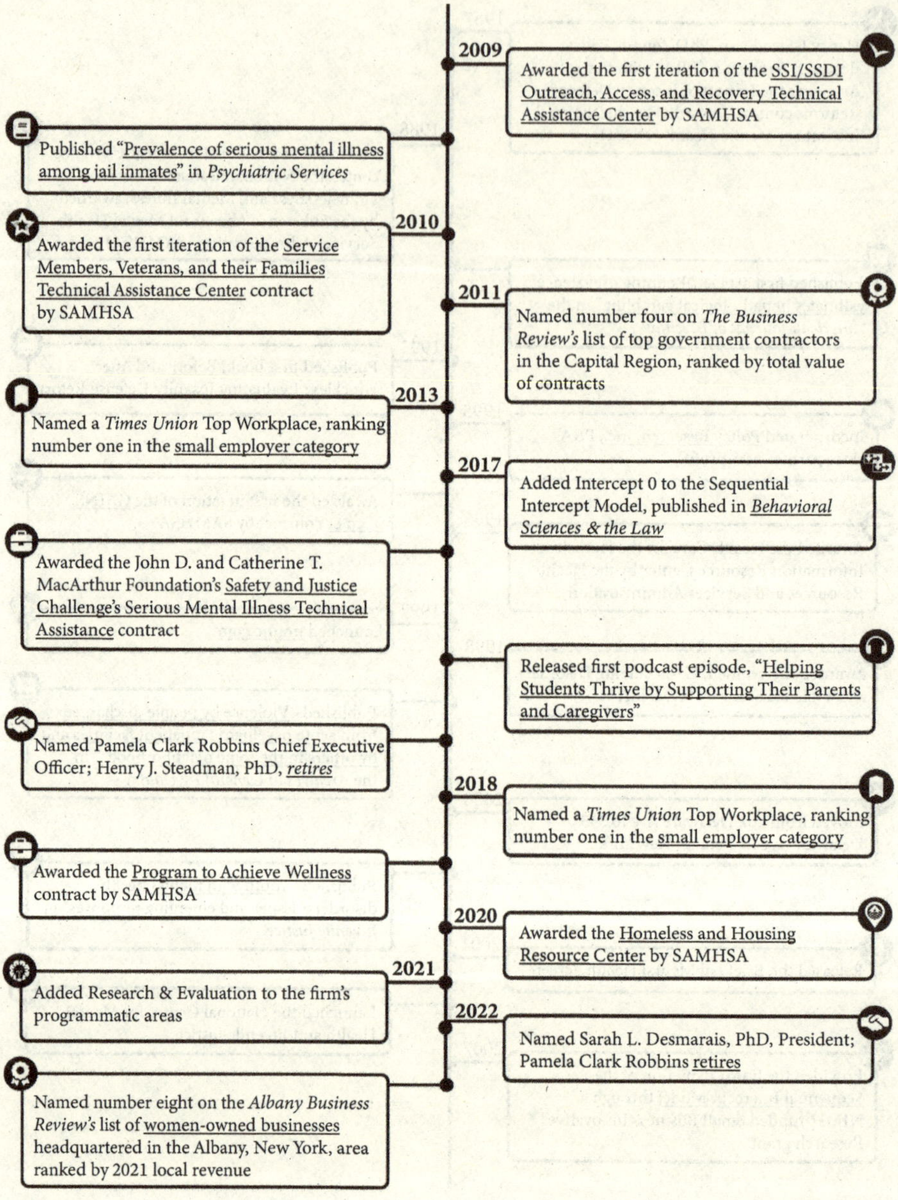

Figure 19.1 continued

PRA's **policy education services** are comprised of ***technical assistance*** and ***training***. ***Technical assistance*** involves planning, developing, and delivering services to enhance knowledge, support the implementation of innovative practices, and enhance collaboration. These activities include needs assessments, environmental scans, strategic planning sessions, connections with subject-matter experts for intensive support, and peer-to-peer learning exchanges. They can be offered as a one-off for a community or agency seeking assistance with a particular issue, or as part of a broad, coordinated multi-year strategy, where communities are provided step-by-step coaching to design and implement a strategic plan. PRA offers both through contracted fee-for-service events or, more frequently, as part of national Technical Assistance (TA) centers. TA centers provide training and technical assistance through various activities to a defined audience to enhance knowledge and capacity on a particular topic. One notable example is SAMHSA's GAINS (Gather, Assess, Integrate, Network, and Stimulate) Center for Behavioral Health and Justice Transformation, operated by PRA since 1995.

PRA's TA centers typically provide intensive, long-term, peer-supported services. One example is a policy academy, where interagency teams engage in strategic planning on broad topics (e.g., providing medications for opioid use disorder in prisons). Before the policy academy begins, invited teams are guided through an initial strategic planning process. Post-academy support includes phone calls or site visits to finalize and implement the plan. Teams receive peer feedback, work with subject-matter experts, and collaborate with technical assistance staff to meet milestones. Some policy academies lead to implementation academies, where teams continue to receive guidance on implementing their strategic plans. Another example is learning collaboratives, which focus on creating and implementing strategies on specific issues. For instance, PRA has operated the Competence to Stand Trial/Competence Restoration Learning Collaborative within SAMHSA's GAINS Center since 2019. Teams receive targeted training through these collaboratives, participate in peer-to-peer exchanges, and learn best practices.

Training involves delivering a curriculum designed to support knowledge development or the acquisition of a specific set of skills. Trainings are delivered as self-paced online courses, in-person or virtual training deliveries, or in-person or virtual Train-the-Trainer (TTT) models. One example of a self-paced online course is the SSI/SSDI Outreach, Access, and Recovery (SOAR) Online Course: Adult Curriculum offered through the SOAR Technical Assistance (TA) Center, operated by PRA since 2009. The SOAR model aims to improve access to Social Security Administration disability income benefits for adults and children who are homeless or at risk of homelessness and have a serious mental illness, medical condition, or co-occurring substance use disorder (Dennis et al., 2011). A different example of a curriculum offered as both a training and TTT event is *How Being Trauma-Informed Improves Criminal Justice System Responses*, which helps criminal legal professionals understand trauma, recognize its impact on behavior, and develop trauma-informed responses (Krider et al., 2024). The training lasts four hours, while the TTT event is sixteen hours. Since December 2022, over 5,000 people have completed the training.

Clients

PRA's clients include government agencies at the federal, state, and local levels as well as non-governmental organizations. PRA is soft-funded, meaning we rely on external, time-bound funding. Continuous efforts are required to secure new grants and contracts to sustain ongoing work and, more broadly, to maintain the organization's financial well-being. When a grant or contract ends, typically, the work will end, and staffing levels will be reassessed to meet the needs of the current work portfolio. PRA most often engages in a competitive bidding process to work with these clients. Clients may release funding to prequalified bidders or to the field more generally. In our policy research and education services, we must balance the priorities and directives of the funders with the needs and priorities of communities in which we work.

Providers

PRA staff members and consultants provide policy research and education services. PRA's staff has professional and lived experience, as well as training in the systems we work in. Our staff includes psychologists and social workers; licensed mental health clinicians; ex-law enforcement, parole, and probation officers; managed care executives; homelessness service providers; research scientists; data scientists; and people with lived experience.

Role and Type of Training

PRA staff backgrounds and professional expertise vary considerably. Formal education is common but not necessary, depending on the specific role, team, or service. The highest level of educational attainment among staff members ranges from high school and associate degrees to doctorates and postdoctoral training. Current staff members have degrees from fields including (but not limited to) psychology, sociology, criminology, data science, social work, public health, and public administration. Many PRA staff have experience providing direct services, directing programs in service systems, or lived experience. All staff members participate in professional development opportunities through conferences, training, and observations of project work.

Size and Scope

While PRA is classified as a small business by the U.S. federal government, our work has national reach and influence. For example, research products such as the Brief Jail

Mental Health Screen (Steadman et al., 2005) have been implemented nationwide and internationally (Callahan & Noether, 2018). We also have provided technical assistance and training to every state and all U.S. territories. Between 2019 and 2023, PRA's criminal legal system area staff delivered technical assistance and training services that engaged over 78,000 people nationwide through more than 500 meetings, nearly 300 trainings, and over 200 site visits. We delivered more than 60 conference presentations and published over 100 resources on topics at the intersection of behavioral health and criminal legal systems. Communities reported that at least fourteen policies and practices changed as a result of our work.

Time Spent

Policy research and education services are typically time-intensive, requiring considerable planning, preparation, coordination, delivery, and follow-up. The time spent varies across services and specific projects, ranging from one week to five years to a decade or more. Research services often require multi-year engagements to implement policies and evaluate their impact. For example, the IST Continuum of Care evaluation is a five-year project involving site visits, interviews, surveys, analyses, and regular meetings with internal partners, external partners, and funders to evaluate and make recommendations across various phases of policy and program implementations. Other multi-year projects may represent shorter consecutive contracts for phases of research that build on the previous one. For example, PRA recently completed a multi-year effort to gain insights into programs across the United States that provide court navigation and support services for people with behavioral health issues involved in the criminal legal system (Zottola, Morrissey, et al., 2024). The State Justice Institute funded this work through three separate twelve-month contracts, each with a distinct scope and set of activities. PRA occasionally engages in shorter-term, time-sensitive efforts; however, we prioritize those representing long-term collaborations that afford iterative feedback opportunities.

TA centers operate in multi-year (typically 5-year) funding cycles. If a funding agency has determined that a technical assistance project will continue in a new contract cycle (anywhere from 2 to 5 years), the agency will release a request for proposals for which all qualified and interested bidders can apply. A TA center may be run for one funding cycle, be awarded to a competitor for another cycle, or be re-awarded to the original bidder multiple times, as has been our experience operating SAMHSA's GAINS Center for Behavioral Health and Justice Transformation. TA centers are assigned a set of activities that must be completed in a specified period, typically one year, and the time spent on activities can vary greatly. A policy academy, for example, could be a 1.5-to-2.5-day event, but the preparation and post-event work takes several months. Learning collaboratives typically last for six months but sometimes go on for years.

Prospective Client Awareness

PRA builds relationships with prospective clients by joining and networking with relevant professional associations, participating in conferences, serving as subject matter experts, developing partnerships with organizations doing similar work, and releasing publications and other products to the field. We also share our work through presentations, reports, newsletters, social media, podcasts, and joint releases with partners. Through these dissemination efforts, clients are made aware of the scope and impact of services that PRA offers.

Keys to Effective Delivery of Services

PRA has been a national leader in behavioral health research and education for more than thirty-five years. Here we highlight some strategies that have been key to the effectiveness of our services and, thus, our success. First, we anchor our services in our values and guiding principles. For instance, our value of inclusion is reflected in opportunities for staff to collaborate within and outside their teams to gain fresh perspectives and a deeper understanding of the work. As another example, ensuring our recommendations are data-driven is one of our guiding principles, and we prioritize using our research findings to inform our policy education services, and vice versa. Second, we are on the ground in communities across the country. By being present where change is needed, we develop local knowledge, build relationships that foster trust, and ensure our efforts are responsive to community needs. For example, we have conducted over 150 Sequential Intercept Model (SIM) mapping workshops across the United States in nearly 100 communities (Systems Mapping and Training Center at Policy Research. (n.d.). We return to the SIM later.

Third, we emphasize authentic and meaningful community engagement and partnership. Our TA centers cultivate long-standing partnerships with local initiative leaders to maintain initiative momentum, troubleshoot challenges, and improve outcomes at the state and local levels. For example, the SAMHSA SOAR Technical Assistance Center, operated by PRA, works with state-appointed team leaders to grow and sustain statewide SOAR implementation, facilitate the state's steering committee, liaise with local SOAR leaders and providers, and maintain relationships with Social Security and Disability Determination Services, among other activities. These relationships are strengthened through individual calls and emails, regional meetings, in-person academies, and regular appearances by SOAR Technical Assistance Center staff at state-level meetings. Fourth, we integrate principles of science communication into our efforts to disseminate research findings, project news, and accomplishments. We tailor our messaging to reach and engage diverse audiences by leveraging multiple platforms and approaches.

Foundations and Support for Services

Policymakers and Processes

A basic understanding of policies, how they are made, and by whom is foundational for policy research and education. However, these topics are not often covered in traditional psychology training at either the undergraduate or graduate level. As a result, psychology research and writing on issues that may have significant policy implications for community-based services with justice-involved individuals have been overlooked, missed, or even ignored because they do not ask policy-relevant questions or do not clearly articulate actionable policy recommendations (Greenhalgh & Russell, 2009). While an in-depth discussion is beyond the scope of this chapter, we provide a very basic and high-level overview of policies and policymaking. Those aspiring toward policy research and education work should do more reading and learning (see, for example, Howlett & Giest, 2012; McKnight et al., 2005).

Policies are laws, regulations, administrative actions, incentives, or expectations of governments and other institutions that guide decision making. Policies can be formal (i.e., written) or informal (i.e., unwritten but still understood within a group) sets of guidelines that direct actions that are designed to achieve a broader strategy. In this way, policies can play a key role in setting goals, defining requirements and regulations, and determining resource and funding allocations. In the context of community-based services with justice-involved individuals, policies often serve as a framework for developing programs to guide interventions that improve individual, community, or system outcomes. There is no such thing as a value-neutral policy. The issues and population of focus, as well as the desired outcomes, will be determined by some majority or authority within a group and reflect their interests, preferences, or values (Ruggeri, 2017). One critical aspect of our strategic planning involves determining how best to engage in policy research and education services on issues consistent with our professional and organizational values and guiding principles.

Policies can be made and changed in numerous ways, but the process generally includes four steps: (1) agenda setting, (2) policy formulation, (3) policy implementation, and (4) policy evaluation and revision. Agenda setting involves identifying and prioritizing issues that require a new (or revised) policy. The next phase, policy formulation, involves developing potential solutions and policy proposals. Psychologists can play a significant role in this phase (Sunstein, 2015). Once a policy proposal has been adopted, it must be implemented. The final phase, policy evaluation and revision, involves assessing effectiveness and sustainability and adjusting as necessary. The process is cyclical and iterative, involving engagement, input, and revision from various actors, including elected officials, government agencies, interest groups, researchers, media, justice-involved individuals, their families, and the public.

In the United States, policy guiding community-based services for justice-involved individuals reflects various levels of governance, each with distinct roles and responsibilities (see Table 19.1). At the national level, policymakers include federal government agencies, national organizations, and legislative bodies. Policies at this level shape the overarching framework for community-based services for justice-involved individuals through federal laws and national standards. For example, the Second Chance Act, enacted in 2008 and reauthorized in 2018, authorizes federal grants to state and local governments, tribal authorities, and nonprofits for programs that offer essential reentry services such as job training, housing assistance, substance abuse treatment, and mentoring (Office of Justice Programs, 2024). At the state level, state legislatures, mental health and correctional departments, and forensic directors, among others, develop statewide laws and regulations, which are often accompanied by funding and program mandates. One example is statutory law governing IST and competence restoration criteria and procedures (for a review, see SAMHSA, 2023). At the institutional level, policymakers, including administrators and governing bodies, establish guidelines and procedures that govern the provision of community-based services for justice-involved individuals. One example includes reentry planning protocols. At the local level, policies are typically crafted by local government authorities, community boards, and law enforcement agencies. They often focus on law enforcement and community-based supervision, but may also guide service delivery. Some examples include local citation-in-lieu-of-arrest policies (Desmarais, McKinsey, et al., 2023) and mental health screening and referral protocols in local jails (Callahan & Noether, 2018).

Theoretical Frameworks and Models

Our policy research and education services are informed by theoretical frameworks and models not only from the field of psychology but also from the social, behavioral, and health sciences more broadly. We determine the specific frameworks and models on a project-by-project basis, considering the issue, population, or policy of interest, as well as the phase of the work in relation to the policy-making process. That said, there are two models we consistently apply across the vast majority of our policy research and education work: the Sequential Intercept Model (SIM) and the Risk-Need-Responsivity (RNR) model.

The **SIM** is the overarching framework for our policy research and education services. Discussed elsewhere in this book (Griffin et al., this volume), the SIM was developed as a conceptual model to inform community-based responses to the involvement of people with mental and substance use disorders in the criminal legal system (Munetz & Griffin, 2006). Each intercept represents a pathway in and out of

Table 19.1 Example Policies and Policymakers across Various Levels of Governance

Level	Description	Potential Policymaker(s)	Policy Examples
Local	• Regulations and ordinances at the local/municipal level • Often focus on law enforcement and community-based supervision • Guide the delivery of community-based services	• Local government authorities • Community boards • Law enforcement agencies	• Trauma-informed care training mandates for law enforcement • Local citation-in-lieu-of-arrest policies • Mental health screening and referral protocols in local jails • Intake and assessment protocols to inform case management and treatment plans for probationers
Institutional	• Guidelines and procedures that govern the treatment and management of individuals	• Administrators • Governing bodies	• Use of restraints • Assessment protocols
State	• Statewide laws and regulations • Include funding and program mandates	• State legislatures • State mental health departments • State correctional/public safety agencies • State forensic directors	• Incompetent to Stand Trial (IST) criteria and competence restoration procedures in state statutes • Statutory statewide diversion initiatives
National	• Federal laws and national standards • Shape framework for community-based services for justice-involved individuals	• Federal government agencies • National organizations • Legislative bodies	• Second Chance Act • Medicaid expansion

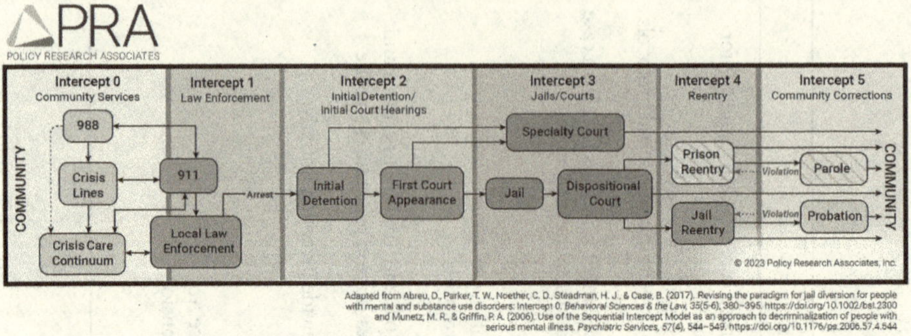

Figure 19.2 Policy Research Associate's Application of the Sequential Intercept Model

Source: Reproduced with permission from Policy Research Associates (https://www.prainc.com/sim/).

the system. PRA adapted the SIM to include intercept 0, representing community-based services for people with behavioral health issues (see Figure 19.2, Abreu et al., 2017). This expanded SIM emphasizes early intervention for individuals with behavioral health issues and helps us to identify, implement, and evaluate strategies, such as the 988 Suicide & Crisis lifeline, crisis lines, and services within the crisis care continuum, that may prevent individuals in crisis from entering the criminal legal system altogether. In our policy education services, work with a new jurisdiction often begins with a SIM mapping workshop. During mapping, we identify and bring together community partners at key intercepts to identify current practices and gaps, which inform a local strategic plan that reflects local priorities. In our preparation for research projects, the SIM helps us identify potential partners and informants. We also use the intercepts to organize the presentation of information, findings, and recommendations.

We also routinely apply the **RNR model** (Andrews & Bonta, 2010) in our policy research and education services. The RNR model informs policy by providing a strategic approach to resource allocation, prioritization of target populations, and operationalizing community-based services. Specifically, the Risk principle informs decisions on how to allocate resources across an agency or system, supporting scalable policies that optimize resource use, reduce unnecessary burdens, and focus on areas where the greatest impact on public safety can be achieved. The Need principle guides policy by emphasizing interventions to address dynamic factors in legislative and funding priorities and supporting the use of validated assessment tools. The Responsivity principle shapes policy by promoting adaptable, inclusive strategies that mandate specialized training, like trauma-informed practices, and establish standards for personalized care for justice-involved individuals. Education on the RNR model can support the effective implementation of policies, improve fidelity, and contribute to better outcomes for justice-involved individuals. In our research, the RNR model guides methods and interpretation of findings that speak to why a policy is achieving (or not) the intended outcomes and supports the translation of findings into recommendations.

Scientific Evidence

A central purpose of our services is to improve policy effectiveness by applying scientific evidence and methods. Research findings may inform criminal legal policies, but they are also shaped by budgetary constraints, political and industry interests, and societal views on crime and punishment (Carter & Ward, 2022). Our approach is aligned with **evidence-*informed* policymaking**, which acknowledges the complex interplay between scientific knowledge and the myriad influences on policy formation and implementation (Jabali et al., 2024). Readers may be more familiar with evidence-based policymaking, which is the process of developing and implementing policies that are grounded in the best available empirical evidence, with emphasis on randomized controlled trials (RCTs; Doleac, 2019). While RCTs represent a very rigorous research design, they also can be limited in the policy research context because they do not reflect real-world conditions, are time-consuming, and can be very resource-intensive (Cartwright, 2011). Evidence-informed policymaking values multi-method research, integrating qualitative and quantitative approaches. In our experience, evidence-informed policies are more likely to be successful because they speak to the needs, resources, and challenges of the local community, and foster community engagement and buy-in.

Regarding the application of scientific evidence in our work, we use two general strategies that mirror our two core services. First, we use what we already know from our policy research or extant evidence in our policy education services. For instance, we may draw from studies or program evaluations on interventions, mental health services, and behavioral outcomes in our provision of policy education services to help communities develop policies. This approach is often best suited to inform policy built around well-established strategies and interventions. Second, we build more knowledge to inform future policy by conducting our own research and program evaluations. This approach involves generating new evidence to inform policies addressing emerging issues or new interventions. The COVID-19 pandemic, for example, drastically altered practices almost overnight, necessitating new research on the implementation and effectiveness of policies (Miller & Blumstein, 2020).

Research and Education Practices

We use established practices from many fields, including psychological research methods, adult education strategies, and behavior change interventions, just to name a few. In the sections that follow, we describe specific research and education practices in more detail.

Beginning and Development of Project Services

This section describes how individual projects may begin and be developed. For our policy research services, we will use our Frequent Jail Contact project as a case example. For policy education services, we will use a hypothetical example of a community mental health clinic seeking to reduce wait times for justice-involved individuals.

Initiation

Projects at PRA are initiated in several different ways. Our research services may be initiated by submitting a research grant proposal or via an evaluation request from a community partner or agency. For instance, we submitted a research proposal for a grant award that initiated the Frequent Jail Contact project. The funding opportunity reflected a policy need identified by three vested parties: community and criminal legal system practitioners, social science researchers, and philanthropic funders dedicated to reducing the population of people in jail in the United States. The need for technical assistance or training services may emerge internally at an agency through a self-identified desire to improve policies, practices, and outcomes or externally following a lawsuit, threat of litigation, or other pressures. For example, a community mental health clinic may seek to reduce the wait time for justice-involved individuals due to public scrutiny and pressure from local agencies or court systems due to rising recidivism rates or funding contingent on meeting service delivery timelines. An agency representative may respond to a solicitation open through one of our TA centers or contact us directly.

Preparation

We prepare for a project using multiple strategies, many of which are shared across our research and education services. We often thoroughly review the pertinent state and federal laws, written policies, and procedures. We also may conduct brief, preliminary surveys or interviews with staff members, service recipients, collaborators, or others. We completed these steps in the preparatory phase of the Frequent Jail Contact project. We may look for service gaps, workforce issues, or discrepancies between policy and procedures. These assessments allow us to prioritize factors that reflect the impetus for the project, the focus of the specific funding, and local priorities. In the community mental health clinic example, a workforce shortage may be identified by agency staff, but our preparatory work may reveal additional challenges stemming from internal leadership, compensation, and employee burnout. Furthermore, we may find that certain referral sources send many people to the clinic because they are unaware of other local providers. An effective solution to reducing wait times may include improving recruitment policies and procedures, increasing employee satisfaction, and distributing referrals across agencies.

System Mapping

We conduct a SIM mapping workshop in the early stages of a project to identify and bring together community partners to identify current practices, gaps, and, critically, local priorities. If a jurisdiction has been mapped recently, we will review the SIM report and action plan during our preparation work. For example, in the Frequent Jail Contact project, all three partner sites had recently been or were in the process of being mapped; we reviewed the reports during our preparatory work. In the community clinic example, a SIM mapping workshop would be a key strategy for identifying and connecting with possible alternative provider agencies.

Plan

With a team in place and priorities set, we will develop a plan. A research plan may resemble a typical proposal detailing research questions, design, and planned analyses. However, it may also be at a much higher level, focusing instead on the timeline, activities, and deliverables. Typically, our plans for community-initiated evaluation efforts look more like the latter, while plans for internally initiated efforts funded by grants may look more like the former. As described earlier, our research approach is typically multi-method, multi-site, and multi-phase. To the extent possible, we employ Community-Based Participatory Research (CBPR) methods, including collaboration, shared-decision making, co-creation, and principles, including emphasizing local issues, balancing research and action, and centering people with lived experience (Corrigan & Oppenheim, 2024). In the Frequent Jail Contact project, for example, partners at each site determined the policies and outcomes we evaluated. We also engaged in an iterative data analysis and interpretation process. Site partners had multiple opportunities to review the findings, offer recommendations for the data analysis plan, provide insights about the local landscape to guide the interpretation of findings, and participate in dissemination. Through this process, PRA was able to provide trends and recommendations for reducing the jail population across the sites, along with recommendations for each site.

For policy education services, we develop plans that include multiple activities to enhance knowledge, inform policy creation or refinement, support the implementation of innovative practices, and foster collaboration. In our experience, training alone does not create system-wide change, so our plans are typically multimodal. We combine formal training to address knowledge gaps with services like consultations, resource sharing, and coaching. Individual consultations provide space for agencies to discuss specific needs, while peer-to-peer consultations allow administrators to share successes and challenges privately. We also bridge resource gaps by sharing guides, publications, and best practices. Coaching offers support for innovation, connects agencies to additional resources, and provides accountability for continued progress on system change. In the community mental health clinic example, the TA plan might include group trainings for supervisors on staff morale and retention, consultations with local experts on compensation, targeted reviews of agency policies affecting retention, and frequent coaching to improve workplace culture. We may additionally help develop a strategic plan to distribute referrals across agencies, including facilitated meetings with referral sources, site tours to build trust, and a comprehensive list of community providers with locations and contacts.

Time and Resources

Rather than providing short-term services, we seek to build lasting relationships with communities, foster collaboration, and support sustainable change. Our services, then, are inherently resource- and time-intensive, often spanning multiple years. For instance, our partnership with one of our Frequent Jail Contact project sites continues more than a year after the study concluded, as we engage in efforts to support the implementation of policy recommendations stemming from that work as well as new research (e.g., Zottola, Stewart, et al., 2024). The most successful recipients of our services dedicate the time, commit the financial and human resources, and often make upgrades to technology and data management systems.

Generalizability

Need for Similar Work

There is a growing demand for policy research and education services in the context of criminal justice reform (Blomberg et al., 2024). Psychologists are well-positioned to fill a critical gap in these areas, leveraging their expertise in human behavior, behavioral health, and intervention strategies to inform policy through research and education services. But they must be ready to contribute as one of many voices, acknowledging the strengths and limitations of their expertise and appreciating the insights brought by others. We recommend familiarity with and drawing from CBPR to guide engagement with policymakers, communities, and others (Oliver & Cairney, 2019). Doing so should help foster mutual respect, partner meaningfully, and contribute more effectively to policymaking.

Pro Bono or Reduced-Rate Services

Our provision of *pro bono* or reduced-rate services is restricted by our soft funding. Because PRA depends on external grants and contracts, which typically have strict charging and spending guidelines, our ability to offer subsidized or PRA-funded services is limited. As such, we rarely provide services *pro bono* or at reduced rates. As these opportunities arise, our considerations may include the project's significance and impact on the field, resource implications and timelines, adherence to our strategic plan, and alignment with our values and guiding principles. Balancing our mission-driven work with a sustainable business model is an ongoing challenge.

Replicability

The replicability of our work is a central consideration in policy research and education, but it is not straightforward. In our research, for example, we aim to develop and employ replicable methodologies, but full replication of results across different communities is not necessarily the goal. Local context, culture, resources, and priorities mean that outcomes will inevitably vary. For example, we recently conducted a local validation of a well-known and commonly used pretrial risk assessment instrument, the Public Safety Assessment (PSA; Advancing Pretrial Policy and Research, n.d.), in a largely rural jurisdiction with a high proportion of Indigenous people (Zottola, Stewart, et al., 2024). Although the instrument was well-validated in other communities, rural areas face unique barriers (e.g., limited transportation, few services, lack of cellular coverage), as do Indigenous people (e.g., distrust of public institutions, reluctance to engage with services), which may affect the accuracy of pretrial risk assessments, particularly in predicting court appearance. We found poor validity in predicting failure to appear, especially among Indigenous people, and are working with partners in this community to implement strategies to address issues identified in our evaluation.

Instead of focusing on replicability, we emphasize **transferability** in our work. Transferability involves applying core insights across different settings, while replicability aims to duplicate outcomes. We highlight essential elements that can inform policy in diverse contexts, even as implementation adjusts to local needs. To support transferability, we provide detailed descriptions so others can understand the project's context and boundaries (Merriam & Tisdell, 2016). Local investigators then determine how the research and policy components can apply to their situations. This approach allows our work to be broadly applicable while remaining responsive to local contexts, balancing research rigor with real-world flexibility. For example, in our Frequent Jail Contact project, we identified nine policy recommendations to reduce system involvement for people frequently in jail while addressing their behavioral health and social service needs. These recommendations are flexible for jurisdictions at different stages of policy reform (Desmarais,

Morrissey, et al., 2023). We also developed a resource to help communities operationalize and identify those with frequent jail contact (Policy Research Associates, 2023).

Closely related to replicability, **open science** promotes transparency, accessibility, and replicability by encouraging the sharing of data, methods, and findings. These principles foster collaboration, build trust, and advance knowledge across disciplines; however, they can be difficult to apply in this policy research and education context. Privacy, confidentiality, and informed consent are paramount in research involving justice-involved individuals with behavioral health issues (Stiles et al., 2011). In our work, we often analyze archival, system-level data collected without individual consent through routine clinical and legal processes, including a mix of information potentially covered by HIPAA and Title 42 CFR Part 2, and those in public records like court documents. While these issues do not preclude data sharing, they can raise concerns with community partners and their legal teams. As a result, our data-sharing agreements typically include narrow guidelines on use, storage, and dissemination, and strict adherence to open science principles could violate these agreements. Moreover, some community partners and research participants distrust researchers as a result of past exploitative practices in marginalized communities. Justice-involved individuals may fear that data sharing could have legal or stigmatizing consequences, while court, law enforcement, and community partners may worry that data could be misused, misinterpreted, or publicly disclosed, undermining their work or harming those they serve. These concerns underscore the need to balance open science goals with protecting marginalized populations and respecting community partners.

Diversity, Equity, and Inclusion

The problems that we work on do not exist in a vacuum and were not created outside of the context of oppression that has existed throughout U.S. history. We cannot improve services and outcomes for justice-involved individuals without recognizing the ways that racism and classism impact who is in contact with the criminal legal system and why (Fix et al., 2023). We also must address racism and classism in our own field and their roles in upholding systemic inequities (Anderson & Jones, 2024). In our view, Diversity, Equity, and Inclusion (DEI) is a minimum requirement in policy research and education services. With this recognition, psychologists can shift focus from changing individuals to changing institutions (Grzanka & Cole, 2021). At PRA, our commitment to DEI shows up in the work that we do and how we do it (Paley, 2024). We have embedded DEI into the values and guiding principles that steer our work. DEI-related goals are operationalized in our annual strategic plan, and we monitor our progress through ongoing evaluation informed by a DEI-specific logic model.

In our research services, our commitment to DEI shows up in the questions we ask, the process through which we develop and conduct the research, and the partners with whom we collaborate. For example, in the Frequent Jail Contact project, we worked with each jurisdiction to identify the racial and ethnic groups most disproportionally impacted by the criminal legal and behavioral health systems in their community. In the first community, this was Black and African American individuals; in the second, this was Indigenous and Native American people; and in the third, this was Hispanic and Latino people. We found that experiences of frequent jail contact differed with respect to the demographic makeup of each community. Considering these differences, we were able to provide broad policy recommendations that applied across jurisdictions, and specific recommendations that supported equity and justice locally.

In our policy education services, our commitment to DEI shows up in our efforts to promote inclusive, community-informed solutions that address systemic inequities. For example, we recently expanded the scope and reach of the SIM through the *Centering Racial and Ethnic Diversity, Equity, and Inclusion: Sequential Intercept Model Mapping* workshop. This workshop focuses on the behavioral health experiences of Black, Indigenous, and other people of color disproportionately involved in or at risk of involvement in the criminal legal system. Through this DEI SIM workshop, we educate participants about racial and ethnic disparities across the intercepts, document culturally responsive services in their community, and help create a DEI-responsive action plan. By centering on racial and ethnic disparities, communities can address the systemic issues driving the overrepresentation of people of color in the criminal legal system and their underrepresentation in culturally relevant behavioral health services.

Advice to Others

Gauging the Market

Given the urgent need for policy research and education to improve community-based services for justice-involved individuals, it is crucial that we all do not focus on the same issues or work in the same communities. To maximize policy effectiveness and impact, there should be an awareness of what work is currently underway and by whom; for instance, competence to stand trial is at the center of much policy research and education work, and various individuals and organizations are supporting efforts to reform the Competence to Stand Trial (CST) and competence restoration system (Callahan & Pinals, 2020). These efforts share common goals but they use different mechanisms. For example, some of our work involves providing services to jurisdictions that are developing and implementing diversion programs (e.g., Van Dorn et al., 2024), while other efforts focus on expanding outpatient restoration services (e.g., Krider & Huerter, 2024). Rather than having multiple efforts addressing one issue, delivering complementary policy research and education services will benefit a wider range of individuals, have a more significant impact, and contribute to broader reform goals.

Strategic Development and Partnership

Various strategies may inform the development of complementary (rather than competing) policy research and education services, such as needs assessments, listening sessions, environmental scans, policy reviews, and system mapping. One or more of these strategies may be appropriate. We briefly describe environmental scans since they may be less familiar to psychologists. Environmental scans identify existing programs, policies, and interventions relevant to the topic, and highlight trends and gaps, determining where innovations are needed while ensuring that new efforts build on existing knowledge and avoid duplication. They also can identify commonalities that we can use for benchmarking and comparative analysis. Environmental scans are conducted using a combination of methods, including reviewing existing literature, analyzing policy documents, and conducting interviews or surveys. To demonstrate, our court navigation and support services project began with an environmental scan that compiled information about program funding, core components, and implementation (Zottola et al., 2023). As another example, we completed an environmental scan of federal and state competence to stand trial-related statutes and processes to identify emerging issues as part of our SAMHSA's GAINS Center activities (SAMHSA, 2023).

With this type of information in hand, psychologists can engage with community partners and established policy research and education service providers, such as PRA, to foster collaboration and develop strategic partnerships. Given the scope and complexity of policymaking as it relates to community-based services for justice-involved individuals, there are ample opportunities for contribution, and building cooperative relationships allows for more efficient use of resources, knowledge, and expertise (Desmarais, 2024). Accordingly, partnering with other organizations and universities is a key feature of our PRA business model. Doing so allows us to round out our expertise and conduct a substantial volume of work without necessitating growth within our organization. Moreover, the transformation of our criminal legal system will require collaboration and multiple integrated solutions (Desmarais et al., 2022).

Interdisciplinary Approach

The interdisciplinary approach in our policy research and education services is central to our work. As discussed earlier in this chapter, the diversity of our staff's disciplinary backgrounds provides a strong foundation for high-quality research and education services. One key advantage of this approach is leveraging cross-disciplinary expertise to create comprehensive and effective solutions to complex issues. For example, integrating psychological principles of behavior change with sociological theories of social structures enables us to develop more holistic services tailored to specific populations or challenges. Additionally, the flexibility of an interdisciplinary approach allows us to adapt to the needs of each project. Working across disciplines fosters innovation, as integrating diverse frameworks and practices often leads to new methodologies or approaches. This collaboration enhances the quality of our services while also enriching our team's professional development by expanding their knowledge and expertise.

Publicity Strategies

We recommend prioritizing efforts to build your reputation through robust, multipronged communications. PRA's communications strategy emphasizes sharing practical resources at little or no cost in ways that will promote uptake in the field. We distill complex topics into short, digestible formats to reach audiences and achieve different goals using the following platforms:

- **Social media**. We use social media platforms like LinkedIn to announce events, highlight key products or resources, share job opportunities, and update PRA's work. Content includes project updates, field events, new research, and organizational news. Posts, released daily, are concise, focus on one or two topics, and include links for more details.
- **Blogs.** Blog posts provide background and an entry-level approach to our work, and extend the information provided in a one-off event (e.g., webinar). We write blogs to target artificial intelligence (AI) search results that will bring users key facts on substantive topics.
- **Video shorts.** Video shorts published on YouTube provide a visual and aural representation of one part of a more complex idea. They provide a high-level overview with encouragement to access the complete publication.
- **Podcasts.** We produce multiple podcast series, including *Data Points* and *Conversations on Leadership*. Episodes are conversational and translate research and key company decisions for a general audience. These episodes are typically 30 minutes long and emphasize transferable and actionable findings or policies.
- **eNewsletter.** PRA's monthly newsletter describes new resources, research, news, and upcoming events. It summarizes key project information and previews full content, serving as a one-stop shop for news and updates from PRA.

Those new to policy research and education services may find it useful to develop an initial advertising strategy for building visibility in the field. Even so, much of our policy research and education work is secured through contract and grant awards, particularly in the early years.

Recommendations

For over thirty years, PRA has delivered policy research and education services to support community-based services for justice-involved individuals. In writing this chapter, we asked some senior staff to share some lessons learned, focusing on policy education services that are likely to be less familiar to psychologists. Below are their recommendations.

- **Preparation and team building.** Using systematic tools such as questionnaires and inventories, gather detailed information about the community or agency, including data, key partners, and readiness for change. Thoughtfully build your team, considering expertise, training styles, demographic diversity, and alignment with the target audience.
- **Engage key partners.** Involve partners at multiple levels, including leadership, frontline workers, and individuals with lived experience, to ensure a comprehensive perspective on changes or improvements. Identify and collaborate with key allies who can champion the work and sustain results. Frontline workers and those with lived experience are essential to developing practical solutions that will be implemented and used locally as intended.
- **Facilitation and delivery.** Tailor services to engage participants through diverse methods, accommodating different levels of knowledge. Incorporate adult learning principles to foster engagement and retention, including using interactive formats. Be intentional about the roles you take (e.g., educator, facilitator, collaborator), adjusting as needed. Foster a collaborative, diverse working group and elevate lived experience, particularly when addressing issues affecting marginalized communities.
- **Evidence-based or promising practices**. Emphasize evidence-based or promising practices, providing research and supporting resources to build buy-in and understanding. Educate participants on how to maintain fidelity and provide them with resources that can guide the appropriate use of assessments and interventions. Do not assume they will correctly apply strategies without ongoing education and evaluation of fidelity.
- **Sustainability**. Facilitate local ownership by ensuring that participants develop clear expectations, next steps, timelines, and responsibilities before services conclude. Without clear post-service plans, the long-term impact may be lost. Use local evidence to foster collaboration and reduce blame, especially on sensitive

topics. Establish and maintain a local cross-systems workgroup that takes ownership of the initiative, serving as a central hub for coordination and ensuring accountability after services conclude.

- **Evaluation.** Evaluate the impact of services on knowledge acquisition, attitudes, and behavior changes over time. Incorporate equity impact assessments to ensure that program or policy changes do not negatively affect marginalized populations. Continuously refine and update training content based on evaluation results and feedback, considering cultural diversity and evolving needs.

Finally, we offer actionable recommendations for prioritizing DEI in this work.

- **Educate and train for DEI.** Training should encompass staff background preparation and ongoing professional development, including DEI training at undergraduate, graduate, and postgraduate levels (e.g., Volpe et al., 2023). Policy education services should also incorporate DEI content into training and technical assistance.
- **Move beyond implicit bias.** Examine local and national histories of racism and other forms of oppression and how these histories shape the present (Grzanka & Cole, 2021). Implicit bias focuses on how individuals quickly and unconsciously associate negative constructs and ideas with minoritized groups (Baron & Banaji, 2006), emphasizing the need for DEI work at the individual level. However, the root causes of oppression are systemic and institutional, which are upheld consciously and intentionally by individuals.
- **Promote equity through policy.** Racism is systemic, historically developed through cultural norms, and reinforced through policies (Bonilla-Silva, 2022). Challenge the assumption of neutrality and consider the unintended consequences of policies for disenfranchised groups. Further, consider whether and how policies intentionally address and remediate racism and oppression for marginalized communities.
- **Co-create and share decision making.** Policy research and education should involve partners from marginalized racial/ethnic groups, lower socioeconomic backgrounds, and those with lived experience. Community engagement does not ensure equity but is a crucial step toward achieving it (see Haapanen & Christens, 2021).
- **Describe the demographic makeup of participants.** Highlighting who was included and excluded (Volpe et al., 2022) provides context for interpreting the findings and helps communities determine how to best apply policy recommendations.
- **Examine if and how construct measurement, associations, and processes vary within and between groups.** Whole-group analyses can mask differences

between groups. Analyses should account for broad demographic categories (e.g., race/ethnicity, gender) and subgroups (e.g., race/ethnicity by gender) to challenge the assumption of group homogeneity and determine how policies impact subgroups within a population.

Conclusion

In this chapter, we describe PRA's approach to providing policy research and education services. We employ interdisciplinary teams that elevate lived experience, apply established frameworks and models (particularly the SIM and the RNR model), and engage authentically with communities to ensure that policies are responsive to local needs, fostering both short-term and long-term success. We emphasize building long-term partnerships and are committed to addressing the systemic inequities affecting marginalized populations in the criminal legal system. We also emphasize a reciprocal relationship between research and education, integrating diverse research methods with practical, community-centered approaches. By sharing the PRA approach, we hope to encourage psychologists and others to join us in the policy research and education space so we can collectively contribute to meaningful and lasting improvements in community-based services with justice-involved individuals.

References

Abreu, D., Parker, T. W., Noether, C. D., Steadman, H. J., & Case, B. (2017). Revising the paradigm for jail diversion for people with mental and substance use disorders: Intercept 0. *Behavioral Sciences & the Law*, *35*(5-6), 380–395. https://doi.org/10.1002/bsl.2300

Anderson, R. E., & Jones, S. C. T. (2024). Reflections from the wading pool: Detoxifying racist psychological waters while submerged in their waves. *American Psychologist*, *79*(4), 606–617. https://doi.org/10.1037/amp0001248

Andrews, D. A., & Bonta, J. (2010). Rehabilitating criminal justice policy and practice. *Psychology, Public Policy, and Law*, *16*(1), 39–55. https://doi.org/10.1037/a0018362

Advancing Pretrial Policy and Research. (n.d.). *About the Public Safety Assessment.* https://advancingpretrial.org/psa/about/

Baron, A. S., & Banaji, M. R. (2006). The development of implicit attitudes: Evidence of race evaluations from ages 6 and 10 and adulthood. *Psychological Science*, *17*(1), 53–58. https://doi.org/10.1111/j.1467-9280.2005.01664.x

Blomberg, T. G., Copp, J. E., & Turanovic, J. J. (2024). Challenges and prospects for evidence-informed policy in criminology. *Annual Review of Criminology*, *7*, 143–162. https://doi.org/10.1146/annurev-criminol-022422-124116

Bonilla-Silva, E. (2022). *Racism without racists: Color-blind racism and the persistence of racial inequality in America* (6th ed.). Rowman & Littlefield.

Callahan, L. A. & Noether, C. D. (2018). Brief Jail Mental Health Screen utilization in U.S. jails. *Journal of Forensic Medicine Forecast, 1*(1), 1006. https://scienceforecastoa.com/Articles/JFMF-V1-E1-1006.pdf

Callahan, L., & Pinals, D. A. (2020). Challenges to reforming the competence to stand trial and competence restoration system. *Psychiatric Services, 71*(7), 691–697. https://doi.org/10.1176/appi.ps.201900483

Carter, E., & Ward, T. (2022). The correctional classification hub: A framework for classificatory pluralism. *Aggression and Violent Behavior, 62*, 101679. https://doi.org/10.1016/j.avb.2021.101679

Cartwright, N. (2011). Predicting "it will work for us": (Way) beyond statistics. In P. Illari, F. Russo, & J. Williamson (Eds.), *Causality in the sciences* (pp. 750–768). Oxford University Press. https://doi.org/10.1093/acprof%3Aoso/9780199574131.001.0001

Corrigan, P. W., & Oppenheim, M. (2024). The power of community-based participatory research (CBPR). *Psychiatric Rehabilitation Journal, 47*(1), 2–8. https://doi.org/10.1037/prj0000568

Dennis, D., Lassiter, M., Connelly, W. H., & Lupfer, K. S. (2011). Helping adults who are homeless gain disability benefits: The SSI/SSDI outreach, access, and recovery (SOAR) program. *Psychiatric Services, 62*(11), 1373–1376. https://doi.org/10.1176/ps.62.11.pss6211_1373

Desmarais, S. L. (June, 2024). *Enhancing forensic mental health service outcomes through policy: Potential, challenges, and call to action* [Keynote lecture]. San Francisco, CA: International Association of Forensic Mental Health Services Annual Conference.

Desmarais, S. L., McKinsey, E., Rex, E., & Smith, J. (February, 2023). *The Citation Project: Final stakeholder report.* UNC School of Government, Criminal Justice Innovation Lab. https://cjil.sog.unc.edu/wp-content/uploads/2023/07/Citation-Project-Final-Report-2023.02.28.pdf

Desmarais, S. L., Monahan, J., & Austin, J. (2022). The empirical case for pretrial risk assessment instruments. *Criminal Justice and Behavior, 49*(6), 807–816. https://doi.org/10.1177/00938548211041651

Desmarais, S. L., Morrissey, B., Callahan, L., Zottola, S., Elder, J., Lupfer, K., Hope, E. C., & Van Dorn, R. A. (May, 2023). *Recommendations to reduce frequent jail contact.* Policy Research Associates. https://www.prainc.com/wp-content/uploads/2023/07/FJC-Policy-Brief.pdf

Doleac, J. (2019). "Evidence-based policy" should reflect a hierarchy of evidence. *Journal of Policy Analysis and Management, 38*(2), 517–519. https://doi.org/10.1002/pam.22118

Fix, R. L., Thurston, I. B., Johnson, R. M., & Andrisse, S. (2023). Promoting anti-racism in the legal system: An application of the STYLE framework. *Frontiers in Psychology, 14*, 1061637. https://doi.org/10.3389/fpsyg.2023.1061637

Greenhalgh, T., & Russell, J. (2009). Evidence-based policymaking: A critique. *Perspectives in Biology and Medicine, 52*(2), 304–318. https://doi.org/10.1353/pbm.0.0085

Grzanka, P. R., & Cole, E. R. (2021). An argument for bad psychology: Disciplinary disruption, public engagement, and social transformation. *American Psychologist, 76*(8), 1334–1345. https://doi.org/10.1037/amp0000853

Haapanen, K. A., & Christens, B. D. (2021). Community-engaged research approaches: Multiple pathways to health equity. *American Journal of Community Psychology, 67*(3-4), 331–337. https://doi.org/10.1002/ajcp.12529

Howlett, M., & Giest, S. (2012). The policy-making process. In Araral, E., Fritzen, S., Howlett, M., Ramesh, M., & Wu, X. (Eds.), *Routledge handbook of public policy* (pp. 17–28). Routledge. https://doi.org/10.4324/9780203097571

Jabali, S. H., Yazdani, S., Pourasghari, H., & Maleki, M. (2024). From bench to policy: A critical analysis of models for evidence-informed policymaking in healthcare. *Frontiers in Public Health, 12*, 1264315. https://doi.org/10.3389/fpubh.2024.1264315

Krider, A. & Huerter, R. (2024). *Mapping your competence to stand trial process: Key questions to decrease waitlists and length of stay.* Policy Research Associates. https://www.prainc.com/resources/mapping-cst-process

Krider, A. E., Ihara, E., Hope, E. C., Noether, C. D., Parker, T. W., & Desmarais, S. L. (2024). A mixed-methods evaluation of a program for promoting trauma-informed responses among criminal legal system professionals. *International Journal of Forensic Mental Health, 23*(4), 390–402. Advance online publication. https://doi.org/10.1080/14999013.2024.2311409

McKnight, K. M., Sechrest, L., & McKnight, P. E. (2005). Psychology, psychologists, and public policy. *Annual Review of Clinical Psychology, 1*, 557–576. https://doi.org/10.1146/annurev.clinpsy.1.102803.144130

Merriam, S. B., & Tisdell, E. J. (2016). *Qualitative research: A guide to design and implementation.* Jossey-Bass.

Miller, J. M., & Blumstein, A. (2020). Crime, justice & the COVID-19 pandemic: Toward a national research agenda. *American Journal of Criminal Justice, 45*(4), 515–524. https://doi.org/10.1007/s12103-020-09555-z

Munetz, M. R., & Griffin, P. A. (2006). Use of the Sequential Intercept Model as an approach to decriminalization of people with serious mental illness. *Psychiatric Services, 57*(4), 544–549. https://doi.org/10.1176/ps.2006.57.4.544

Office of Justice Programs. (April 30, 2024). *Impacts of the Second Chance Act.* https://www.ojp.gov/safe-communities/from-the-vault/impacts-second-chance-act

Oliver, K., & Cairney, P. (2019). The do's and don'ts of influencing policy: A systematic review of advice to academics. *Palgrave Communications, 5*, 21. https://doi.org/10.1057/s41599-019-0232-y

Paley, E. (Host). (2024). Steering toward equity: A conversation with Sarah Desmarais & Elan Hope [Audio podcast episode]. In *Conversations on leadership*. Policy Research Associates. https://soundcloud.com/policyresearch/col-steering-toward-equity

Policy Research Associates. (2023). *Defining the population of people with frequent jail contact* [Infographic]. https://www.prainc.com/resources/population-people-frequent-jail-contact/

Policy Research Associates. (2024). *Overview and corporate capabilities*. https://www.prainc.com/about-us/

Ruggeri, K. (2017). Editorial: Psychology and policy. *Frontiers in Psychology*, *8*, 497. https://doi.org/10.3389/fpsyg.2017.00497

Steadman, H. J., Scott, J. E., Osher, F., Agnese, T. K., & Robbins, P. C. (2005). Validation of the Brief Jail Mental Health Screen. *Psychiatric Services*, *56*(7), 816–822. https://doi.org/10.1176/appi.ps.56.7.816

Stiles, P. G., Epstein, M., Poythress, N. G., & Edens, J. F. (2011). Formal assessment of voluntariness with a three-part consent process. *Psychiatric Services*, *62*(1), 87–89. https://doi.org/10.1176/ps.62.1.pss6201_0087

SAMHSA. (2023). *Foundation work for exploring incompetence to stand trial evaluations and competence restoration for people with serious mental illness/serious emotional disturbance*. https://library.samhsa.gov/sites/default/files/pep23-01-00-005.pdf

Sunstein, C. R. (2015). On interesting policymakers. *Perspectives on Psychological Science*, *10*(6), 764–767. https://doi.org/10.1177/1745691615614257

Systems Mapping and Training Center at Policy Research. (n.d.). *Systems mapping*. Policy Research Associates. https://www.prainc.com/expertise/systems-mapping/

Van Dorn, R. A., Chen, L., Weber, A., Morrissey, B., Adams, S., Burnette, E., Callahan, L., Zottola, S. A., Massey, I., Hope, E., & Desmarais, S. L. (October, 2024). *California's pretrial felony IST mental health diversion: Category 1 services & program outcomes (Q3 2019–Q4 2023)*. Policy Research Associates.

Volpe, V. V., Hope, E. C., Mosley, D. V., Javidi, H., Sosoo, E. E., & Benson, G. P. (2023). How we get free: Graduate Training as an opportunity for equitable participation and liberation. *Perspectives on Psychological Science*, *18*(2), 428–444. https://doi.org/10.1177/17456916221096086

Volpe, V. V., Smith, N. A., Skinner, O. D., Lozada, F. T., Hope, E. C., & Del Toro, J. (2022). Centering the heterogeneity of Black adolescents' experiences: Guidance for within-group designs among African diasporic communities. *Journal of Research on Adolescence*, *32*(4), 1298–1311. https://doi.org/10.1111/jora.12742

Zottola, S. A., Morrissey, B., Massey, I., & Desmarais, S. L. (2024). *A resource guide on court navigator programs: Providing connections and support across the legal and behavioral health systems*. Policy Research Associates. https://www.prainc.com/resources/court-navigation-programs/

Zottola, S. A., Morrissey, B., Massey, I., Hope, E. C., & Desmarais, S. L. (2023). *A national compendium of court navigation and support services.* Policy Research Associates. https://www.prainc.com/wp-content/uploads/2023/05/CourtNavigatorCompendium-508.pdf

Zottola, S. A., Stewart, D. K., Cloud, V., Hassett, L., & Desmarais, S. L. (2024). Predictive bias in pretrial risk assessment: Application of the Public Safety Assessment in a Native American population. *Law and Human Behavior 48*(5–6):398–414. https://doi.org/10.1037/lhb0000562

20

Trauma-Informed Training for Correctional Officers

Robin Timme

This chapter presents an approach to training professionals who work in correctional settings. The chapter begins by describing the uniquely toxic stressors found in jails and prisons and presents a combination of factors leading to an occupational health crisis. The chapter then explores the critical importance of training for those who work in these settings, while acknowledging the tremendous challenges inherent to training practices, and provides guidance on content, process, and the role of experiential practices to effectively convey information. The chapter includes an actual training case describing the delivery of educational sessions on developmental disabilities to the entire workforce of correctional officers in a small rural jail. It includes the impetus for the training, the methods employed, and feedback from the correctional professionals who completed the training series.

Introduction

The United States Bureau of Labor Statistics (2021) estimates that more than 400,000 people work as correctional officers in the United States, and they are responsible for the safety, security, rehabilitation, and supervision of justice-involved individuals. They are posted inside jails and prisons, or outside facilities on perimeter posts, transportation details, courthouse security, or otherwise supervising and securing individuals in the custody of city, county, state, or federal agencies. While this group of professionals includes both sworn and unsworn, civilian and non-civilian positions, most correctional professionals are uniformed officers responsible for the safe and secure day-to-day operations of jails and prisons. Although the term "guard" was used for many years, the term "officer" is far more appropriate given the responsibilities of today's correctional professionals, as they do much more than *guard* inmates. This evolution in terminology involves more than a job title—it reflects a genuine effort to professionalize the field of corrections. Such change includes newly defined identities as law enforcement officers, increased expectations, roles and responsibilities, public scrutiny, and an intensive focus on required training to

Robin Timme, *Trauma-Informed Training for Correctional Officers*. In: *The Path Forward*. Edited by: Kirk Heilbrun and David DeMatteo, Oxford University Press. © Oxford University Press (2026). DOI: 10.1093/9780197773031.003.0020 prepare individuals to do much more than stand guard. The professional training and education of correctional officers requires an appreciation of job responsibilities, existing training requirements, and the uniquely toxic occupational stressors to which correctional professionals are exposed.

The defined role of correctional professionals varies slightly among jurisdictions, but it always includes working directly with incarcerated individuals. According to the current job posting for the Corrections Officer job series with the Pennsylvania Department of Corrections,[1] the series is defined as "work involving the care, custody, control, and non-professional counseling of inmates (Pennsylvania Job Code 47210)." The officer "directs inmate activities in cellblocks, housing units, work areas, dining areas, and recreation areas and observes inmates from various locations throughout the facility to ensure security is maintained and facility rules are adhered to (Commonwealth of Pennsylvania, 2024)." The description also notes, "Work also includes providing advice and guidance to inmates in their adjustment to and participation in the correctional process." Specific duties include inspection of living areas "for cleanliness, contraband, stolen goods, and signs of escape plans or procedures (Commonwealth of Pennsylvania, 2024);" searches of incarcerated individuals and visitors; and observation of behavior with a note that the officer "reports anything unusual to a higher-level officer (Commonwealth of Pennsylvania, 2024)." Additionally, officers control access and egress from cellblocks and housing units, "quell disturbances," and the officer "assists other officers in emergency situations." Officers are also expected to administer first aid to incarcerated individuals and staff as needed (Commonwealth of Pennsylvania, 2024).

Although there is some variability across the country, the Pennsylvania Department of Corrections' job description is representative of the core duties and responsibilities for these professionals. It may even be an outlier insofar as the description explicitly articulates a role in counseling the incarcerated population and supporting adjustment to the prison setting. Carrying out those responsibilities requires substantial training, both prior to and during employment, to maintain adequate and current knowledge. According to the Pennsylvania Department of Corrections, Trainees to become Correctional Officers in Pennsylvania receive a 4-week basic training program with 158.5 hours of instruction in topics ranging from ethics and sexual harassment to use of force, Mental Health First Aid, legal aspects of corrections, and basic first aid. In total, the curriculum comprises approximately 50 courses ranging from 0.5 hours to 35.5 hours, reflecting the depth and value of training placed upon each course. For example, the Firearms course requires 35.5 hours of training across the 4-week curriculum, the most intensive of courses listed, while the Assault Management Applications in Corrections (AMAC) Course comes in second at 22.5 hours across a series of six modules. The next most intensive training

[1] The Pennsylvania Department of Corrections was selected as an exemplar agency due to the author's familiarity with the organization, its reputation as a respected department across the country, and the transparency of the department by way of publicly available reference material.

program, according to the 2024 syllabus, is Dayroom Scenarios at 11.0 hours. From there, course length and intensity diminish. Of the least intensive requirements, the syllabus includes 0.5 hours of training in courses titled, "Leadership Team Intro," "Orientation," "Naloxone," "Leadership and Mentoring," "Uniform Presentation," and most germane to this discussion, "Staff Wellness."

The fact that staff wellness comprises thirty minutes of a four-week curriculum is not surprising, and many jurisdictions do not include it at all. The training requirements for officers are simply too extensive to cover every topic, and it should be reassuring that so much time is spent on firearms training and assault management for a group of trainees where no prior experience in either area is required, and where it is reasonably expected that officers will need to manage assaults and will carry and even discharge firearms in the line of duty. Yet more must be done to adequately prepare and support officers for the breadth and depth of the work they do every day. In Norway, which has become an exemplary model for correctional best practices and which describes itself and its correctional practices as the "most humane" in the world, trainees complete a two-year curriculum of classroom and in vivo instruction before working independently (Hoidal & Hanssen, 2023). Coursework is organized in semesters, with intensive focus on areas similar to those taught in correctional training academies in the United States—but with far more time and resources devoted to topics.

Becoming Trauma-Informed

Long before I was board-certified by the American Board of Forensic Psychology with the American Board of Professional Psychology, or specialized in the operations of secure facilities, I found myself drawn to the impact that psychological trauma and suffering had on subsequent human behavior. As a psychologist-in-training, I carefully studied the impact of traumatic experiences, including post-traumatic stress and the constellation of symptomatology and psychopathology that can emerge as a result. I learned about concepts of subclinical syndromes and vicarious trauma. I had even discovered that Posttraumatic Stress Disorder (PTSD) was not the only clinical diagnosis correlated with early experiences of trauma, as trauma in childhood and adolescence is associated with subsequent development of an array of affective or psychotic mental disorders in adulthood (McKay et al., 2021). I had spent practicum rotations in a federal prison and two psychiatric hospitals, one community-based with a forensic unit and the other a private psychiatric facility serving patients of all ages. I had carefully attended to my academic teachings and observed as they manifested in the clinical populations I was serving as a trainee, and I would bring those experiences back to the classroom in what I found to be a profoundly iterative feedback loop. In my training settings, emotions and behaviors that many other clinicians were inclined to pathologize or criminalize—anger, hostility, irritability, substance use, even violence—could instead be seen through a trauma-informed lens that considered what the person had survived, and treating professionals could incorporate that knowledge into how we interpreted the affect and behaviors today. Rather than simply seeing behavior as irrational and abnormal—which of course it was—those behaviors also became logical and understandable when interpreted through a lens of *what happened* to the individual, instead of *what is wrong* with the individual. As a young trainee, I found this new conceptualization to be empowering, invigorating, and like a superpower for a trainee desperate to contribute and to see a pathway forward in treatment, especially when so many cases were interpreted as intractable, treatment-resistant, help-rejecting, refractory, or in one particularly challenging case, "medically futile." To become curious about human behavior, rather than to stop at a checklist of symptoms and simply categorizing the behavior, created the possibility of a pathway to recovery that the treatment team could see, and a newfound sense of optimism in a sea of despair.

Although I had worked in jails and prisons as a trainee, my first post as a staff psychologist exposed me to levels of trauma I had never seen in any other population. Indeed, researchers have long identified elevated rates of trauma in populations of individuals experiencing incarceration, consistently reflecting over-representation of PTSD diagnoses and symptoms associated with trauma, relative to the general population. These findings are consistent across research studies that span genders (Baranyl et al., 2018) and even in international samples (Almuneef et al., 2014; Kazeem, 2015). Theoretically, these findings comport with what we know about childhood adversity, social determinants of health, and the subsequent physical and behavioral health correlates. Positive and Adverse Childhood Experiences (PACEs) (Baglivio & Wolff, 2021; Lee et al., 2022), originally discussed as Adverse Childhood Experiences (ACEs) (Felitti, 2002; Felitti et al., 1998), have been shown to predict a series of maladies in adulthood, including domestic violence, intravenous drug use, substance use disorders, mental illness, and incarceration.

These observations hold true in professional literature. According to the *Diagnostic and Statistical Manual of Mental Disorders—Fifth Edition—Text Revision (DSM-5-TR)*, using the same data that were published in the Fifth Edition (*DSM-5)*, 8.7 percent of individuals in the United States will meet the full diagnostic criteria for PTSD at some point across the lifespan (American Psychiatric Association, 2022). The *DSM-5-TR* notes that the twelve-month prevalence rate for PTSD, also known as the current or cross-sectional rate, is 3.5 percent. Meanwhile, in populations of incarcerated individuals, rates of traumatic experiences are often found to be ubiquitous in samples, meaning that nearly 100 percent of those sampled were found to have experienced, directly or vicariously, a life-threatening event, sexual assault, or other potentially traumatizing experience prior to incarceration. Furthermore, although producing a wide range of results due to methodological differences, researchers consistently find extremely elevated rates of PTSD among incarcerated populations, with lifetime prevalence rates estimated around 60 percent for males, and with a current or cross-sectional prevalence rate hovering around 30 percent (Sindicich et al., 2014; Wolff et al., 2014). In samples of incarcerated women, the numbers are even higher, with lifetime prevalence rates of PTSD estimated around 68 percent, while more than half of incarcerated women are estimated to meet criteria for PTSD at any given point (DeHart et al., 2014; Ruzich et al., 2014; Zlotnick, 1997).

Beyond the focus on trauma specifically, psychopathology is particularly prevalent behind the walls of jails and prisons. Cloud (2023) and his colleagues make a strong and logical argument for public health approaches for the treatment of incarcerated populations. Synthesizing the peer-reviewed literature, they described rates of serious mental illness (SMI) two-to-four times higher than in community settings. They cited suicide as the leading cause of mortality in prisons in the United States, with an 85 percent increase in death by suicide between 2001 and 2018. They also described elevated rates of non-suicidal self-directed violence (i.e., swallowing, head-banging, cutting) reflecting five to eighteen percent of men and twenty-four percent of women engaging in these behaviors during their imprisonment. In addition, 58 percent of people in state prisons met criteria for a substance use disorder, with overdose as a leading cause of death among incarcerated individuals and a 600 percent increase in deaths of prisoners by "drug or alcohol intoxication" between 2001 and 2018. Finally, they noted that people re-entering the community were 12.7 times more likely than others to die from an overdose during the first two weeks following release (Cloud et al., 2023).

Meanwhile, most jails and prisons were not architecturally designed to provide treatment for a population with this level of physical and mental illness, although in certain areas of the country that is starting to change. Until recently, clinical services have been shoehorned into jails and prisons that were designed to incapacitate and to punish, rather than to stabilize, rehabilitate, and connect community-based services. Jails and prisons are often under-resourced with respect to clinical staff, and rarely is there adequate space, technology, or systemic infrastructure to provide appropriate care for this level of clinical need. Beyond clinical staffing and access to care, correctional officers who spend the most time with the incarcerated population have historically received little training in the recognition, triage, or crisis intervention for individuals with SMI. Not surprisingly, therefore, they apply the tools of their training to behaviors that may be manifestations of behavioral health disorders, interpreting those symptoms of behavioral health conditions as threats, aggression, violence, and disorderly conduct requiring increased containment, control, or use of force (recall the Pennsylvania Department of Corrections' training curricula for AMAC, Dayroom Scenarios, and Firearms training).

In stark contrast, Norway uses what is called an *import model*, whereby local municipalities are responsible for the oversight and delivery of healthcare services inside prisons through community-based providers (Kriminalomsorgen, 2024). The model focuses on continuity of care, provides for medical autonomy and clinical independence, reduces the bureaucracy of requiring employment by a separate healthcare provider or the correctional agency, and reflects the commitment to the core Norwegian principle of normality in corrections (Kriminalomsorgen): that life for individuals who are incarcerated will resemble life outside of incarceration as much as possible (Norwegian Correctional Service, 2024). This model is predicated on an entirely different sociopolitical, economic, and cultural foundation than is found in the United States, but it affords a far more robust opportunity to provide adequate levels of care for a population with particularly pronounced needs.

Through my work in jails and prisons, it became clear to me that the day-to-day operations of correctional facilities were in many ways dominated by the behavioral correlates of trauma. Knowing the rates of traumatic experiences in populations of incarcerated individuals, we could extrapolate the behaviors one might expect—elevated autonomic arousal, poor sleep, irritability, impulsivity, depression, reexperiencing traumatic events, in addition to elevated rates of violence and suicide. None of these are prosocial or adaptive in a rigid paramilitary environment such as jail or prison. These signs of trauma played out in formative ways for me early in my career, as I witnessed tremendous human suffering. I found myself pulled desperately to help in myriad ways. As a young psychologist, I believed that by providing screening, assessment, diagnosis, treatment, and clinical supervision—the tools of my trade—I would have the greatest impact, reduce harm inflicted by the criminal legal system, and influence healing and desistence from crime. Unfortunately, in a sea of trauma and suffering, my tools were woefully inadequate.

A Traumatized System

In 2013, I was promoted to oversee statewide mental health services within a state correctional agency. As part of that role, I served as a liaison to other agencies, including the state health department. I worked with an interagency team to develop a two-day training for forty staff employed at the women's prison, entitled "Trauma-informed correctional environments." Each two-day cohort would include twenty correctional officers. As an early career psychologist at the time, I diligently studied peer-reviewed literature, consulted with colleagues, and developed training materials that dived deeply into the experience of the incarcerated individual. Our team prepared and rehearsed, eager to educate correctional officers on the elevated rates of physical and behavioral health conditions in correctional populations, the implications of exposure to trauma, and basic techniques for referral and brief intervention.

The first day began with introductions and an icebreaker, proceeding into an exploration of the basics of trauma (Trauma 101). The afternoon session described the unique aspects of the incarcerated population, along with facets of the correctional setting that create risk for traumatization or re-traumatization. The second day continued to explore these concepts of trauma-informed approaches, summarized by the Substance Abuse and Mental Health Services Administration (SAMHSA) (2014) using *The Four "R"s:*

> A program, organization, or system that is trauma informed **realizes** the widespread impact of trauma and understands potential paths for recover; **recognizes** the signs and symptoms of trauma in clients, families, staff, and others involved with the system; **responds** by fully integrating knowledge about trauma into policies, procedures, and practices; and seeks to actively **resist** retraumatization (p. 9).

It was after the lunch break on the second day that everything I thought I knew about trauma in corrections was challenged to its core. The plan was to move into techniques for brief interventions, including basic concepts drawn from Miller and Rollnick's (1992) Motivational Interviewing and specific behavioral techniques like *grounding.* An officer raised his hand. He said, "This has all been interesting, but I thought I was coming here to learn about *my own* trauma." He continued, "I'm just being honest; I don't really care about the inmates traumas. I thought I was coming here to learn about how I can avoid putting my hand through my wall at home when I'm upset, or how I can stop needing to drink a six-pack in order to go to sleep at night. I thought I was coming here for *me,* not for the inmates." Immediately, I shifted from teacher to student and became curious about the experiences of other officers in the room. Other officers began to share similar feelings of anger, fear, worry, isolation, sadness, and a deep sense of disconnection from others in their lives. More importantly, officers began to empathize with one another about their struggles, coping mechanisms, and shared experiences that took on a healing quality in the room. Feedback at the end of the day was extremely positive and officers reported feeling more connected to one another than they had previously. But I learned a lesson I would never forget: trauma-informed training for correctional professionals must focus as much on officers as on the incarcerated population.

Despite the ubiquitous impact of trauma on daily operations in jails and prisons, research and public education on the issue have lagged. Discussions of trauma in correctional samples have been a relatively recent development when compared with the United States' decades-long reliance on jails and prisons for managing individuals with mental illness. A framework for trauma-informed care had existed in hospital settings for many years, and despite the systematic sociopolitical process of emptying state hospitals and exponentially increasing the numbers of individuals with serious mental illnesses in jails and prisons known as *transinstitutionalization* (Harcourt, 2011; Primeau et al., 2013), the concept of trauma-informed care in correctional settings is fairly new. To the extent the concept has been applied to incarcerated populations, until even more recently, the discussion has basically ignored the implications of the people who work in these institutions.

Levels of stress in correctional settings are known to be some of the highest of any occupation (American Correctional Association, 2021). Most correctional officers report violent incidents as a regular occurrence in the workplace, with one study reporting that 80 percent of officers had personally responded to violence in the previous six months (Bierie, 2012). The same study indicated that serious injuries were common, nearly half of officers feared they would be injured, and nearly three-quarters of respondents reported having seen someone seriously hurt or killed in their place of work. Only about half of all correctional officers surveyed reported feeling safe at work.

Furthermore, the correctional setting's requirements for vigilance, emergency responses, rehabilitative services, and frequency of crises within settings where the incarcerated population outnumbers the employees can create the immense pressures that lead to high turnover rates, mandated overtime, and a national staffing crisis among officers (Finn, 2000; Finney et al., 2013; Sawyer & Wagner, 2024; U.S. Senate Committee on the Judiciary, 2024). These rates of stress exceed nearly every other occupation, with exposure to violence surpassed only by policing, and rates of exposure to serious injury and death comparable to those reported by military veterans (Bierie, 2012).

In 2012, a group of researchers surveyed nearly 4,000 correctional professionals and found that 27 percent met the full diagnostic criteria for PTSD in a self-report study (Spinaris et al., 2012). Those findings described extremely high levels of memory impairment, depression, obesity, sleep problems, and rates of substance misuse, among other physical and behavioral ailments. Moreover, the physiological and behavioral correlates of trauma have been observed in staff as well, with evidence showing that correctional officers use sick leave to cope with the stress of their work environments, and that correctional officers as a group have significantly elevated levels of heart disease, diabetes, cholesterol, and hypertension. One large survey study in 2010, for example, found that 31 percent of correctional officers self-reported serious psychological distress, twice the rate found in the general public (Morse et al., 2010). Particularly concerning, the rate of suicide among correctional officers has been as much as 39 percent higher than that of others (Stack & Tsoudis, 1997). As a consultant to justice systems across the country, my colleagues and I have supported several systems where the rate of suicide among correctional officers is higher than it is among the incarcerated population.

This level of exposure to toxic stress and trauma rivals that found in the population for whom correctional officers are responsible. However, the impact and meaning of this chronic exposure to trauma and stress have not received enough attention, and they certainly have not been incorporated into training and wellness programs for correctional officers. Although Cheek's (1984) landmark work which identified the life expectancy of correctional officers at age 59 (the average American lived to age 75 at the time) is frequently cited, discussing the health and wellness of the correctional workforce was simply not done until more recently. In fact, I was once admonished by a prominent professional society to discuss this topic *less,* after I presented a workshop on trauma and correctional professionals in 2014, arguing that nobody will want to work in corrections, and staffing is hard enough. Ironically, I received overwhelmingly positive correspondence from workshop attendees who told me they felt heard for the first time, and as if they were more connected to a supportive community of professionals.

Making Meaning of the Trauma

As a psychologist who was committed to improving the lives of those who are justice-involved, I realized that each incarcerated individual exists within a system that is fundamentally traumatized. Whether an individual is incarcerated in a jail or prison, or whether the person is employed there, we must act on an assumption of trauma for every individual, and act in accordance with that understanding. For me, as a psychologist and a professional responsible for the training of staff, this meant synthesizing this information into core principles that I could then apply to training correctional officers:

1. *Correctional officers serve a critical function in the operation of jails and prisons.* In recent years, the role of the correctional officer has evolved to include a complex interplay of safety, security, care, and custody, implicating a skill set involving a wide array of administrative, operational, and psychological functions. These professionals require and deserve enhanced levels of support, education, and training.
2. *As a group, people experiencing incarceration have extremely elevated rates of physical and behavioral health conditions.* People entering our jails and prisons are among the most vulnerable in society, reflecting greatly elevated rates of chronic medical conditions, SMI, and substance use disorders, and as a group, they are far less likely to have been adherent with treatment prior to incarceration, less likely to be insured, less likely to have primary care physicians, and require intensive assessment and treatment while incarcerated.
3. *Correctional officers must be provided with education and training on relevant topics including healthcare in correctional settings, identification of physical and psychiatric emergencies, suicide prevention, and other healthcare-related topics.* Correctional officers are generally the first line of defense against healthcare emergencies and adverse events. Recognizing that candidates for employment as correctional officers are not required to have formal training in any healthcare-related fields, and recognizing that pre-employment training in these arenas competes for time and resources with a wide array of other critical topics (i.e., firearms, assault management, and many others), regular training on healthcare-related topics is critical to instill and reinforce care while in custody.
4. *Like their incarcerated counterparts, correctional officers as a group reflect extremely elevated rates of physical and behavioral health conditions.* Depression, anxiety, posttraumatic stress disorder, substance use disorders, chronic medical conditions, suicide, and even shortened lifespan are all significantly elevated in populations of correctional officers. These findings implicate a critical need for education and intervention to address this occupational health crisis.

5. *Initial and routine training for correctional officers must prioritize staff wellness and care despite many competing interests.* Wellness and care of staff must be infused throughout training curricula, including educating staff and supervisors about the risks of toxic stress and potentially traumatic experiences, as well as providing opportunities for staff to practice self-care in real time to capitalize on opportunities provided through training experiences.

Case Study: Smith County Detention Center

Background and Context

I delivered and supervised mental health care at the Smith County Detention Center (SCDC)[2] for more than five years, overseeing all clinical services within this small county jail. SCDC became a pilot site for these tenets of trauma-informed training for correctional officers due to its small size, dedicated workforce, training requirements for correctional officers, and the request of the Warden to provide training specifically on trauma and mental health. Smith County is located in a notably rural area, and when I was on-site each week, I was the only licensed psychologist in Smith County. The jail's population hovered around 75–100 individuals, nearly all of them awaiting trial rather than sentenced, and on a day shift there were seven or eight correctional officers working in the building. Although I have delivered or supervised services in more than 100 jails and prisons, ranging from 50 beds to 3,000 beds, there has always been something alluring and particularly rewarding about working in small rural jails. Not only are you apt to find locally grown, dedicated officers committed to community improvement, but the speed with which new policies and practices can be implemented in small facilities makes them fertile ground for innovation.

Like many jails across the country, SCDC's healthcare was partially funded through a longstanding grant administered by the state's health department. One of the requirements of the grant was the provision of initial and refresher training, specifically with a focus on suicide prevention, again typical of the critical risk management functions associated with correctional healthcare broadly. However, this requirement to conduct suicide prevention training created an opportunity to seat that content within training materials focused on broader workshops targeting healthcare of incarcerated individuals, including the role of trauma, mental health, and substance use disorders in the justice system. With the support of the Warden and the health department, my team and I created a series of trainings for correctional officers, entitled "Special Topics in Correctional Healthcare."

[2] Smith County Detention Center (SCDC) is a fictional name, and all facts in this case study have been altered to de-identify individuals and the jurisdiction.

We began by establishing a content threshold we believed that every officer should meet and exceed: the basics of correctional healthcare, including prevalence rates of chronic medical conditions, SMI, substance use disorders, and a basic understanding of the intersectionality between healthcare and justice-involvement. The curriculum was designed by starting with the state's (minimal) statutes on required training for officers; we then used the current *Standards for Mental Health Services in Correctional Facilities* from the National Commission on Correctional Health Care (NCCHC) (2015) to construct the framework for what would become a required initial and refresher training.

In addition to an opportunity to educate correctional staff, this basic training served as an opportunity to assess the correctional officer workforce at SCDC, specifically evaluating the officers' familiarity with these topics, as well as their interest in and tolerance for perspective-taking and consideration of the incarcerated population as survivors of trauma rather than fundamentally flawed humans (i.e., *What happened to you?* versus *What is wrong with you?*). As I often find in smaller communities across the country, the group was extremely interested in the topics presented, quickly engaged with questions and anecdotes, interjected to challenge me at times, and otherwise demonstrated interest and engagement throughout several cohorts of officers who systematically completed the training.

It is important to note that as in any paramilitary organization, especially one so prone to trauma, crisis, and general adversity, relationships among peers are of critical importance. Building credibility as a messenger, one of the most fundamental aspects of effectiveness as a trainer, is grounded in relationships. This group of correctional officers had seen me show up at the jail every week for years, recognizing the relative scarcity of mental health professionals in this very rural community. They had seen me respond to emergencies inside the jail, de-escalate potentially violent or suicidal incarcerated individuals, volunteer my time on local homelessness and addiction committees, and even provide emergency services to a handful of officers who had witnessed a horrific motor vehicle accident on the way to work one morning. I personally connected more than one officer with the Employee Assistance Program (EAP) after personal losses in their families, and I had become a frequent sounding board for many of the officers when issues of mental health arose in their personal lives. I am certain that my relationships with so many of the officers at SCDC created the foundation of credibility on which my training was built and delivered.

With the first workshop series under our belt, we turned to the development of the Special Topics curriculum. The general approach was to select topics from within the basic training to explore more deeply in targeted workshops. I began to interview and survey jail leadership and correctional officers, including the Warden and command staff, as well as line officers I would approach on the cell blocks during their shifts. I would ask what topics were most interesting or germane to their jobs or their lives more broadly, and the responses were powerfully informative. The Warden was particularly interested in personality disorders, while another member of the command staff was curious about the impact of addiction on the brain. The jail's own training director was aware of legislation that would potentially mandate medications for treatment of opioid use disorder (MOUD) in all county jails in the state, and she requested training on that topic. One officer was particularly interested in forensic psychology, specifically the concepts of competency to stand trial, mental state at the time of an offense, and the role of state hospitals in those legal processes. The topics generated were excellent and fueled my desire to provide an expanded series of trainings, and to incorporate the health and wellness of *officers* into the topics wherever I could. SCDC quickly developed a culture of training and curiosity, with officers frequently asking me when the next training would be held.

And then the culture of training was hijacked by a tragic incident, for which there is no shortage in jails and prisons. A 19-year-old male had been admitted to the jail, alleged to have engaged in inappropriate sexual behaviors with a child several years his junior. The defendant was unknown to the jail, experiencing his first incarceration, but he had a long history of involvement with the state agency responsible for services provided to individuals with developmental disabilities. Over several days, we obtained records that painted a picture of a young man with significantly sub-average intellectual functioning, extreme deficits in adaptive functioning, and longstanding diagnoses of intellectual disability and autism spectrum disorder. He presented in a childlike manner, demonstrating little capacity for social reciprocity and obvious limitations in his cognitive abilities.

Like most small jails across the country, SCDC was ill-prepared to receive an individual with this profile, and conflicts emerged immediately. For starters, the built environment at SCDC was comprised of linear cell blocks with an indirect supervision style, leaving cell blocks to operate as small communities supported by correctional officers, rather than having correctional officers on the cell blocks and part of the community as with direct supervision approaches. Recognizing the risks inherent in exposing this young man to those communities, he was held indefinitely in the booking area of SCDC, immediately adjacent to the medical office, directly across from the booking desk, which was the only post other than central control that was staffed 24/7. This left the young man in a single cell with vertical bars and no sound protection, no more than ten feet from the booking desk and from the medical office, which meant constant stimulation and opportunities for verbal engagement. Clinical staff tried to engage the young man multiple times per shift, to consult with correctional officers regularly throughout the day, and create opportunities for the young man to engage in prosocial activities that would occupy his attention and his time.

It was not a surprise when my phone rang, and the Warden informed me that there had been an incident involving the use of force. The details were murky as they often are, but what was clear was that the young man had "refused to follow a directive," was "insubordinate and verbally aggressive," and was "disrupting the orderly operation of the jail." The result was a physical altercation resulting in officers deploying Oleoresin

Capsicum (OC)—often referred to as pepper spray—and the young man being transported to the emergency department where he received seven stitches (and caught the attention of the office overseeing services for developmental disabilities, along with the public defender's office).

Inquiries began almost immediately, and SCDC was shrouded in controversy and turmoil. Officers were disciplined, and the Warden referred one officer for criminal prosecution. Emotions and tensions ran high as factions emerged supporting or attacking the officers in question, and leading many to question the protections they believed they were afforded in discharging their duties as correctional officers. As the initial intensity of the incident subsided, the Warden came to me and asked me to provide a full-day workshop for all correctional staff on developmental disabilities in the justice-involved population.

Developmental Disabilities in Correctional Settings: A Workshop for Correctional Staff

Recognizing that these officers had recently experienced a trauma—not only the use of force incident, but also the resulting disciplinary action against their colleagues—we decided to hold the training outside of the jail. The local fire department invited us to use their hall, which had surprisingly decent technological capabilities and comfortable seating. The officers were all instructed to wear plain clothes and not to arrive in uniform, prepared to spend a full day engaged in training activities.

Learning objectives were included in the lesson plan, and were articulated in the opening slides as follow:

1. Describe features of developmental disabilities.
2. Examine how people with developmental disabilities come into contact with law enforcement.
3. Explore ways of working with individuals with developmental disabilities, focused on the following:
   a. Recognizing unique needs.
   b. Managing risk to staff, the incarcerated individual, and the institution.
   c. Safely move the individual through the criminal justice system.
4. Practice mindfulness throughout today's workshop.

After discussing the agenda for the day, the audience completed a seven-question pre-test on the very basic elements for the day's instruction. Question included: *When are developmental disabilities usually identified? What are the three domains of impairment for people with developmental disabilities?* and *Why might it be important to speak clearly with simple language to someone with a known developmental disability?*

Following the pre-test, the group revisited the concept of mindfulness, which was not entirely new to the audience from previous trainings. We reviewed definitions of mindfulness and spent some time discussing why mindfulness is important in this line of work. I reminded the audience of their exposure to chronic traumas and put words to the more recent trauma the institution had collectively experienced. I also reminded the group that mindfulness is a *practice,* and it should always be seen as a work-in-progress. I often self-disclose that mindfulness practice has never come naturally to me, and although I still find it awkward at first, I always feel better afterward.

We then moved into the first mindfulness exercise, which was an adaptation of *The Five Senses* activity. As with most exercises, the audience were asked to relax and ground themselves, drawing attention to their breathing. I then asked the group to bring their attention to one thing they can *hear,* followed by one thing they can *see,* followed by one thing they can *smell,* and then *feel or touch,* and finally, *taste.* Allowing for ample silence to fill the room, I then called attention back to their breathing and invited everyone to focus back on the group. The room was quiet, almost still, and the officers appeared relaxed in their chairs for the moments just prior to one officer joking that another was asleep. The group laughed together briefly, and then the silence returned. People took turns sharing their experiences—what they had heard, touched, smelled, and even where their minds took them during the activity. In all, this exercise took just over 4 minutes, and the impact in that moment was palpable.

The workshop then dove into the didactic components, defining developmental disabilities, identifying preconceived notions and biases, and presenting definitions and conceptualizations from authoritative sources like the Centers for Disease Control and Prevention (CDC) and the *Diagnostic and Statistical Manual of Mental Disorders.* Content included diagnosis in the earliest stages of life, with me sharing personal photographs of my children at various developmental stages, showing examples of smiling, eye contact, waving "bye-bye," crawling, walking, talking, and toileting. Causes of developmental disabilities, as well as diagnostic labels, were then presented, followed by adaptive deficits in *conceptual, social,* and *practical* domains. Each domain of adaptive functioning was expounded upon with examples of mild, moderate, severe, and profound impairment, which was followed by a short break.

As the group filed back into the hall, I had set up another mindfulness activity with more of a cognitive component to it, called *Mental Tic-Tac-Toe.* In this exercise, officers are asked to visualize a tic-tac-toe board and to number the squares left to right, top to bottom, arriving at a total of nine squares on the game board. A tic-tac-toe board, fully numbered, is provided in early stages of game play, eventually replaced with an unnumbered game board, and eventually the game board is entirely removed, and the players must visualize the game of tic-tac-toe, declaring the number of the space selected for their Xs and Os. Three in a row is a winner. If an individual forgets the gameboard layout or otherwise becomes distracted, he or she loses. However, audience members very quickly come to the aid of their peers in this game, and camaraderie always wins the day. While not a traditional mindfulness exercise, I find this particular activity to be more accessible than others that might include deep breathing or other silent meditations. The game requires complete and continuous attention, an unwavering effort at visualization, and an inability to allow distraction of any sort. Participants report feeling centered, focused, and enjoying the friendly competition and fellowship that can emerge around this activity. In this training, inclusive of game instructions, the entire activity took less than 6 minutes and included four different players. It was a welcome infusion of energy after the break.

The didactic component of the training pivoted to justice-involvement for people with developmental disabilities, articulating far greater risk for victimization than for perpetrating crimes, describing rates of physical and sexual abuse in the population, and identifying the overrepresentation of developmental disabilities in correctional settings. We unpacked the reasons for elevated rates of victimization and the link between being a victim and subsequently becoming a perpetrator. The group was able to identify how certain types of crimes could be related to deficits in adaptive functioning within *conceptual, social,* and *practical* domains. Through the use of vignettes, the officers were able to describe how social immaturity, misinterpretation of social cues, or inability to read emotional expressions on others could lead to criminal behaviors. Images of facial expressions and participation from the audience as to the emotions the person was expressing led to an experiential understanding of these issues, as well as several humorous moments.

The content of the training then shifted to the justice-involvement of suspects with developmental disabilities, specifically how they may behave relative to other arrestees. Concepts like *masking,* limited verbal abilities, becoming easily overwhelmed by police presence, potential for false confessions, and poor emotional regulation all resonated with the audience of officers, given their recent experiences with the young man in their jail. The group was then dismissed for their lunch break.

After returning from lunch, we engaged in another exercise, this one focused more on physical movement combined with cognitive engagement. Called *Toss*, the audience and facilitator stand in a large circle. The first person states the name of another participant and tosses a soft ball to that individual. The second person states the name of another participant and tosses the ball again. This continues until every person has received and thrown the ball to another participant without anyone receiving the ball twice. The group repeats the activity in exactly the same order several times before the facilitator introduces a second softball into the same rotation. A third ball in the rotation is usually the pinnacle of the operation, but with larger groups, four or even five balls can be swiftly moving through the air in the same order for several minutes. The officers are required to focus intently on the ball that may be headed their way, recalling the person who will be tossing it, and transferring the ball to the next participant each time. This requires intense focus and concentration, fine motor coordination, and a collectivist engagement among a group of like-minded peers. On this occasion, *Toss* lasted approximately 7 minutes, and the activity finished with laughter, joking, and positive energy infused into the training space for the afternoon.

Content of the workshop then shifted from arrestees and detainees to an overview of developmental disabilities in the incarcerated population in prisons. Research was presented around the likelihood for receiving penalties for misconduct, declining programming due to fear of being identified, risk for victimization, acquisition of violent or antisocial behaviors, and being more likely to "max out" their sentences. The importance of interdisciplinary collaboration and case management was stressed, and participants began to tie the research back to the specific case of the young man in their jail, describing gaps in information-sharing, lapses in communication, and recognizing the need to develop a best practice model to address these issues in the future.

Following another short break, the group returned for the final section of the day's training, which presented a series of scenarios and asked participants to identify concerns, describe what information would be helpful, and then to choose from various decisions or dispositions. Provided with information about the individual, officers were asked to consider various aspects of the case, including inviting them into discussion beyond legal or professional considerations, and into the moral and ethical. For example, *should* the fact that someone has an intellectual disability have an impact on what happens when she enters the justice system?

Here is one example from that section:

- 23-year-old White male committed to the facility on charges of Rape Fourth Degree.
- According to the newspaper, he sexually assaulted his 4-year-old stepsister on at least seven occasions.
- An outside agency contacts the jail and states that he has an intellectual disability.
- He enters the booking area and immediately becomes non-compliant with directions.
- When told to change out of his clothes and into a uniform, he begins arguing, pointing at the deputies, "These people here aren't listening to me! I didn't do nothing. You have to let me go. I'm going home."
- The young man begins walking toward the door.

Questions for consideration included:

- What would you do?
- What information are you considering?
- Would you do something different if he did not have an intellectual disability?

Before completing the post-test for the training, we engaged in one final mindfulness exercise, this one more traditional in that it focused on deep breathing. I find correctional officers to be somewhat reluctant to engage in deep breathing if it is earlier in the day's exercises. In this example, the officers had already completed three different exercises, although they required more experiential, cognitive, and physical aspects. I prefer to use breathing exercises that are more structured, again likely due to my own discomfort with deep breathing and general desire for structure in my life. *Balanced Breathing* is an exercise that takes just a few minutes but can have a tremendous impact on levels of arousal. The group is asked to breathe in for 1 second, and then out for 1 second; in for 2 seconds, and then out for 2 seconds; in for 3 seconds, and then out for 3 seconds, and so on. When the facilitator reaches a six-count inhale and six-count exhale, the count goes down, inhaling for 5 seconds and exhaling for 5 seconds, until the group inhales for 1 second and exhales for 1 second.

A quick review of take-home points, followed by the post-test (matched to the pre-test), concluded the day's training. Discussions with participants in the days and weeks that followed indicated that the experiential components of the training were the most valuable, with many officers telling me that they would never practice those skills or engage in those exercises outside of the training, but they felt safe enough in that space to play along, and many reported feelings at least temporary relief from the stress of their jobs.

Conclusion

Today's correctional officers are tasked with matters of care and custody that were never contemplated in traditional models. Expectations of officers have evolved from working as *guards* to serving as helping professionals, capable of maintaining order and institutional control while also being able to identify, triage, and respond to serious medical and behavioral health needs of the incarcerated population. Individuals who experience incarceration present with greatly elevated rates of serious medical, psychiatric, and substance use disorders, relative to those who are not incarcerated, and experiences of trauma in this population are ubiquitous. In recent years, the same has been discovered about those who work inside correctional facilities. Correctional officers present with many of the same physical and mental health conditions as their incarcerated counterparts, creating an occupational health crisis and contributing to an environment that is fraught with trauma. Those who work in jails and prisons must be seen as survivors of trauma, met with compassion and empathy, and provided with a new set of tools to accomplish their critical mission. Those tools need to include expanded training on trauma within their own ranks, delivered in a way that incorporates actual experiences of wellness and connection among our greatest assets in corrections today.

References

American Correctional Association. (2021). *Correctional employee wellness: Improving the health of our greatest asset.* Alexandria, VA: ACA. Retrieved August 22, 2024 from: https://www.aca.org/ACA/ACA_Member/Staff_Wellness_Prep.aspx

American Psychiatric Association. (2022). *Diagnostic and statistical manual of mental disorders – fifth edition – text revision* (DSM–5–TR). Author.

Almuneef, M., Qayad, M., Aleissa, M., & Albuhairan, F. (2014). Adverse childhood experiences, chronic diseases, and risky behaviors in Saudi Arabian adults: A pilot study. *Child Abuse & Neglect, 38*(11), 1787–1793.

Baglivio, M., & Wolff, K. (2021). Positive Childhood Experiences (PCE): Cumulative resiliency in the face of Adverse Childhood Experiences. *Youth Violence and Juvenile Justice, 19*(2), 139–162.

Baranyl, G., Cassidy, M., Fazel, S., Priebe, S., & Mundt, A. (2018). Prevalence of Posttraumatic Stress Disorder in prisoners. *Epidemiological Review, 40*(1), 134–145.

Bierie, D. (2012). The impact of prison conditions on staff well-being. *International Journal of Offender Therapy and Comparative Criminology, 56*(1), 81–95.

Cheek, F. E. (1984). *Stress management for correctional officers and their families.* American Correctional Association.

Cloud, D., Garcia-Grossman, I., Armstrong, A., & Williams, B. (2023). Public health and prisons: Priorities in the age of mass incarceration. *Annual Review of Public Health, 44*, 407–428.

Commonwealth of Pennsylvania. (2024). *Commonwealth Careers: Expanded Job Info for: Corrections Officer 1.* Retrieved September 11, 2024 from: https://careers.employment.pa.gov/Home/GetJobNameInfo?jobCode=47210

DeHart, D., Lynch, S., Dass-Brailsford, P., & Green, B. (2014). Life history models of female offending: The roles of serious mental illness and trauma in women's pathways to jail. *Psychology of Women Quarterly, 38*(1), 138–151.

Felitti, V., Anda, R., Nordenberg, D., Williamson, D., Spitz, A., Edwards, V., Koss, M., & Marks, J. (1998). Relationship of childhood abuse and household dysfunction to many of the leading causes of death in adults. *American Journal of Preventive Medicine, 14*(4), 245–258.

Felitti, V. (2002). The relationship between Adverse Childhood Experience and adult health: *Turning gold into lead. The Permanente Journal, 6*(1), 44–47.

Finn, P. (2000). Addressing correctional officer stress: Programs and strategies. *National Institute of Justice.* Retrieved August 28, 2024 from: https://www.ojp.gov/pdffiles1/nij/183474.pdf

Finney, C., Stergiopoulos, E., Hensel, J., Bonato, S., & Dewa, C. (2013). Organizational stressors associated with job stress and burnout in correctional officers: A systematic review. *BMC Public Health, 13*, Article 82.

Hoidal, A., & Hanssen, N. (2023). *The Norwegian prison system: Halden prison and beyond.* Routledge.

Harcourt, B. (2011). Reducing mass incarceration: Lessons from the deinstitutionalization of mental hospitals in the 1960s. *John M. Olin Law and Economics Working Paper No. 542.* Retrieved September 11, 2024 from: https://chicagounbound.uchicago.edu/cgi/viewcontent.cgi?article=1411&context=law_and_economics

Kazeem, O. (2015). A validation of the Adverse Childhood Experiences Scale in Nigeria. *Research on Humanities and Social Sciences, 5*(11), 18–23.

Kriminalomsorgen (Norwegian Correctional Service). (2024). *About the Norwegian Correctional Service.* Retrieved August 26, 2024 from: https://www.kriminalomsorgen.no/informasjon-paa-engelsk.536003.no.html.

Lee, H., Boyd, R., Slack, K., Mather, R., & Murray, R. (2022). Adverse childhood experiences, positive childhood experiences, and adult health. *Journal of the Society for Social Work and Research, 13*(3), 441–461.

McKay, M., Cannon, M., Chambers, D., Conroy, R., Coughlan, H., Dodd, P., Healy, C., O'Donnell, L., & Clarke, M. (2021). Childhood trauma and adult mental disorder: A systematic review and meta-analysis of longitudinal cohort studies. *Acta Psychiatrica Scandinavica, 143*, 189–205

Miller, W., & Rollnick, S. (1992). *Motivational interviewing: Preparing people to change addictive behavior.* Guilford Press.

Morse, T., Dussetschleger, J., Warren, N., & Cherniack, M. (2010). Talking about health: Correction employees' assessments of obstacles to healthy living. *Journal of Occupational and Environmental Medicine, 53*(9), 1037–1045.

National Commission on Correctional Health Care (NCCHC). (2015). *Standards for mental health services in correctional facilities.* Author.

Primeau, A., Bowers, T. G., Harrison, M. A., & XuXu. (2013). Deinstitutionalization of the mentally ill: Evidence for transinstitutionalization from psychiatric hospitals to penal institutions. *Comprehensive Psychology, 2*, Article 2.

Ruzich, D., Rechert, J., & Lurigio, A. (2014). Probable posttraumatic stress disorder in a sample of urban jail detainees. *International Journal of Law and Psychiatry, 47*(5), 455–463.

Sawyer, W., & Wagner, P. (2024). Mass incarceration: The whole pie 2024. *Prison Policy Initiative.* Retrieved August 29, 2024 from: https://www.prisonpolicy.org/reports/pie2024.html

Sindicich, N., Mills, K., Barrett, E. & Indig, D. (2014). Offenders as victims: Post-traumatic stress disorder and substance use disorder among male prisoners. *Journal of Forensic Psychiatry and Psychology, 25*(1), 44–60.

Spinaris, C., Denhof, M., & Kellaway, J. (2012). *Posttraumatic Stress Disorder in United States corrections professionals: Prevalence and impact on health and functioning.* Desert Waters Correctional Outreach.

Stack, S. J., & Tsoudis, O. (1997). Suicide risk among corrections officers: A logistical regression analysis. *Archives of Suicide Research, 3*, 183–186.

Substance Abuse and Mental Health Services Administration. (2014). *SAMHSA's concept of trauma and guidance for a trauma-informed approach.* HHS Publication No. (SMA) 14-4884. Author.

United States Bureau of Labor Statistics. (March 31, 2021). *Occupational employment and wages, May 2020, 33–3012 Correctional Officers and Jailers.* https://www.bls.gov/ooh/preotective-service/correctiona-officers.htm.

United States Senate Committee on the Judiciary. (2024). *The nation's correctional staffing crisis: Assessing the toll on correctional officers and incarcerated persons.* Retrieved August 28, 2024 from: https://www.judiciary.senate.gov/committee-activity/hearings/the-nations-correctional-staffing-crisis-assessing-the-toll-on-correctional-officers-and-incarcerated-persons

Wolff, N., Huening, J., Shi, J., & Frueh, B. C. (2014). Trauma exposure and posttraumatic stress disorder among incarcerated men. *Journal of Urban Health: Bulletin of the New York Academy of Medicine, 91*(4), 707–719.

Zlotnick, C. (1997). Posttraumatic stress disorder (PTSD), PTSD comorbidity, and childhood abuse among incarcerated women. *The Journal of Nervous and Mental Disease, 185*(12), 761–763.

21

Expert Witness Training

Stanley L. Brodsky

Mental health expert testimony has been prominent in many of the publicized and contentious trials in American history. In the trial of Charles J. Giteau, who had assassinated President James Garfield in 1881 just a few months after his inauguration, forensic experts testified about Giteau's lack of mental fitness to be responsible for the criminal act (Rosenberg, 1968). Their reasonable testimony, at least from a present perspective, was disregarded and Giteau was convicted and executed.

Other presidential assassinations or attempts have also been associated with psychological or psychiatric testimony. The trial of Jack Ruby for shooting the alleged assassin Lee Harvey Oswald after the John F. Kennedy assassination in 1963 included expert testimony opining about organic brain damage and transient psychotic states, all of which was followed by a conviction (Belli & McCarroll, 1964). In contrast, the expert testimony about John Hinckley Jr's severely impaired mental state at the time of offense during his attempted assassination of President Reagan in 1981 led to an atypical acquittal on not guilty by reason of insanity (NGRI) grounds (Simon, 1983).

Even with forensic mental health testimony in such important trials, professional and scholarly attention has typically been paid more to the content of the testimony rather than the specific testifying skills and training the experts have received. This chapter is directed at identifying the sources and models of such expert witness training. It draws on different approaches to training as well as some of my work in this area. The early literature in this field was seated in the work of attorneys who sought to prepare their experts to testify effectively. One of the long-term providers of this training has been the Cape Cod-based company SEAK.

SEAK

Since 1980, a series of workshops, training resources, and other programs have been offered by SEAK, an acronym for **S**kills **E**ducation **A**bilities and **K**nowledge. They have offered mentoring as well as direct training, testifying textbooks, support, and

Stanley L. Brodsky, *Expert Witness Training*. In: *The Path Forward*. Edited by: Kirk Heilbrun and David DeMatteo, Oxford University Press. © Oxford University Press (2026). DOI: 10.1093/9780197773031.003.0021 marketing services for expert witnesses. Attorneys Steven Babitsky and James Mangraviti Jr. provided such training to forensic nurses (2005a), engineers (2001), and physicians (2011). Their self-published books include one with the intriguing title of *How to Become a Dangerous Expert Witness* (Babitsky & Mangraviti, 2005b), as well as a guide for experts about cross-examination (Babitsky & Mangraviti, 2003).

Reviewers have noted that much of their content is aimed at attorneys (Ginsburg, 2001). Indeed, no publications by Babitsky or Mangraviti have appeared in the PsycInfo database. They describe themselves as The Expert Witness Training Company, and have marketed themselves especially to corporations and to government agencies. Other attorneys have gone in-depth into the best ways to offer excellent expert testimony (for example, Lubet & Boals, 2020).

Thomas Gutheil

Harvard psychiatrist Thomas Gutheil has been one of the prominent figures in conceptualizing and offering expert witness advice for psychiatrists in court. His books (Brodsky & Gutheil, 2016; Gutheil, 1998, 2009; Gutheil & Datillio, 2008) have offered practical advice to psychiatric experts for dealing with common problems and challenges on the stand. One of the unique contributions from the Gutheil books has been applying psychodynamic concepts to understanding and improving expert testimony. Thus, his writings include chapters on narcissistic obstacles to effective testimony, such as narcissistic rage and narcissistic excitement. He often addresses countertransference issues in working with attorneys and in court testimony. In a recent article, Goldenson and Gutheil (2023) discussed how emotional bias can seep into forensic assessments. They then expanded on and defended the use of constructs such as transference and countertransference in professional forensic work.

Psychologists in Expert Witness Training

Within the literature in psychology on expert witness training, two approaches will be described here. Otto et al. (2014) presented an integrated discussion of expert psychological reports related to the hazards and methods of offering credible testimony. Postal (2019, 2021) interviewed judges, attorneys, clinical psychologists, and neuropsychologists about important aspects of effective testimony. Postal addressed what she called person-centered credibility on the stand, as well as what she termed testimony that sticks. My own work falls within this general literature. What follows is a descriptive report of my developmental processes to move toward the concepts, practical approaches, and research in expert witness training that has occupied much of my career.

Beginnings

When I attended the organizing meeting and then the first real gathering of the American Psychology-Law Society in 1968 and 1969 (Grisso, 1991), I had no clue that court testimony would be a major focus in my career. Shortly afterwards, largely because of the mentorship of Saleem Shah, I found myself considering the whole range of psychologists' activities within the criminal justice system (Brodsky, 1973).

Because my background to that point had been mostly in correctional psychology and teaching, I took off for a summer to be at the Center for Forensic Psychiatry in Ann Arbor, Michigan. I met and worked with Norman Poythress, David Shapiro, and the Director, psychiatrist Ames Robey, whom I watched testify in court. He and I subsequently wrote an article about effective court testimony (Brodsky & Robey, 1972). We included this teaching lesson when experts are asked about fees compromising their objectivity.

> "Would you tell the court," the attorney asked, "if there is any chance, because the defendant has paid your fee, that your testimony might be biased?" Instead of denying possible bias, the witness replied, "Certainly. It's impossible not to be biased in some way about most things. It has been written 'whose bread I eat, his songs I sing.' Being very much aware of this, I try to be even more cautious than usual and do my best to be sure that my bias is not interfering with my clinical judgment."
>
> **(Brodksy & Robey, 1972, p. 176)**

The same year that the article came out, I shifted to working at The University of Alabama. The initial emphasis there on correctional psychology soon segued into a broad psychology-law focus, and so did I. Before long, I was conducting forensic assessments and evaluating jails, prisons, and mental hospitals as part of class action suits that had become widespread in the United States (Miller et al., 1976). Some class action suits in Alabama in which I was involved stretched over decades, ending with mixed results (Yackle, 1989). I joined many others in writing about these efforts, both in Alabama (Brodsky, 1977) and elsewhere. Those evaluations led frequently to testifying in court. And I started talking about court testimony at meetings and workshops.

Jay Ziskin

During this time, something happened that galvanized the attention of clinical and forensic psychologists. Jay Ziskin wrote his fiercely critical book for attorneys about the scientific gaps and problems in the testimony of mental health professionals (Ziskin, 1970). His criticisms were so piercing in content and devastating for mental health expert witnesses that eventually the President and

President-Elect of the American Psychological Association wrote a rebuttal in *Science* (Fowler & Matarazzo, 1988).

Part of my entry to contentious issues of court testimony took the form of Jay Ziskin and me presenting opposing sides at panels in professional meetings. Jay was a sweet and thoughtful man, and a friend, as well as being the co-founder of the American Psychology-Law Society. The acidic reception of his writings struck me as overdone and unbecoming. Full disclosure: I also joined in some of the criticisms, describing some of the Ziskin (and later of his co-author David Faust) criticisms as overly seated in an adversarial process (Brodsky, 1989).

This give-and-take at repeated professional meetings with Ziskin shaped many of my ways of thinking about court testimony and training expert witnesses. Indeed, many of the Ziskin criticisms were right on target. It is hard in the current day to appreciate that many forensic psychology assessments then included use of House-Tree-Person or Draw-A-Person tests, the Bender-Gestalt test, the Rorschach, and the Thematic Apperception Test. Our group at the Center for Forensic Psychiatry covertly snuck made-up Draw-a-Mushroom and Draw-a-Bicycle tests into assessments as an ironic commentary about the use of such projective tests in forensic assessments.

Testifying and Writing About Testifying

Court testimony increasingly interested me, as I found myself conducting evaluations and testifying in criminal cases and class action suits about solitary confinement, prison overcrowding, and other toxic sequelae of harmful institutional conditions (Brodsky & Miller, 1981). This work continued through the turn of the century, at which time class action suits became more difficult. And I began writing about testifying in court and leading workshops at state and national meetings of psychologists.

The demand for these workshops was accelerated by the perception—and perhaps the reality—that mental health professionals were being sued more often than before. Many mental health professionals felt vulnerable and frightened about being dragged into court, and they sought out consultation and help. The least popular talk I gave during this time was surely a lapse from common sense; in a grand rounds talk at a prestigious medical school, I asserted that psychiatrists were not being sued enough for the egregious errors they were making. I concluded with the closing line from the E.E. Cummings (1920) poem *Buffalo Bill's Defunct*: "What I want to know is how do you like your blueeyed boy Mister Death?" I do not know what got into me.

Expert Witness Workshops

Personal transitions often influence our professional lives. When I got divorced in 1981, against the advice of counsel, I directed my money and possessions to my wife. I found myself without much money. It unsettled me. An entrepreneur who had heard me talk encouraged me to pool my remaining resources into underwriting marketing and arrangement costs (and his substantial fee) for a few nationwide testifying workshops. If they drew 200 people each, I would make a lot from my investment. They did not, and I lost all of the money I put into it. But the advertisements, the regional publicity, and word of mouth from the workshops had the positive effect of groups inviting me to lead testifying workshops for their members. And the ball was rolling.

Specialized Training Services from San Diego had organized workshops around the country, and I joined Phil Resnick, Reid Meloy, Les Morey, and Marsha Linehan, among others, in the stable of presenters. For my workshops, I spent two full seven-hour days in a combination of lectures, demonstrations, and behavior rehearsals and role plays. In these workshops, I learned to mimic both the content and demeanor of aggressive and knowledgeable cross-examining attorneys. With teeth bared and fangs dripping, so to speak, I pushed, criticized, and professionally challenged the participants, while at the same time offering techniques for handling successfully just such nuclear attacks (please forgive this mixing of werewolf and atom bomb metaphors). The basic philosophy was that if participants could manage these worst-case scenarios, they could easily manage the more routine and lower-intensity examinations of most depositions and courtroom testimony. The fourteen hours in the workshops allowed time to do just that—to get past participants' fears and anxiety enough to be calm, in control of themselves, and poised, to give reasonable and appropriate answers.

101 Maxims and Other Testifying Books

Although I had been writing articles about court testimony, the time seemed right to put together a book on court testimony. The problem was that I had many examples and lessons, but I had no way of organizing them into a coherent and meaningful flow. I had already written six books, so I knew what it took to write a book, but I was flummoxed here. Everything I knew about testimony seemed so fragmented that I could not hang it together. Then Norman Poythress came to the rescue.

Norm was then the Director of Clinical Services at the Taylor Hardin Forensic Hospital, the main forensic mental health facility in Alabama, as well as being on the psychology faculty at The University of Alabama. He and his wife Kim were avid duplicate bridge players, and I occasionally joined them in informal bridge games. When I bemoaned my inability to synthesize my disparate pieces of expert training knowledge, Norm gave me a copy of the book *101 Bridge Maxims* (Kelsey, 1986). Although the Kelsey book on bridge maxims was mostly too advanced for me, the concept lit a light bulb above my head. Many brief chapters each with a maxim in a book sounded excellent, with no need to integrate them.

I struggled with the title; 101 Testifying Maxims did not work, although I did copy the Kelsey (1986) concept of finishing each chapter with a maxim. I searched the titles of published books to get ideas. I found a little-read book that had content very different from mine titled *Testifying in Court*. Titles of books cannot be copyrighted, so I made this also my title, with the subtitle *Guidelines and Maxims for the Expert Witness* (Brodsky, 1991). And it caught on.

Two more editions, each substantially different from its predecessor, followed (Brodsky, 2014, 2022). Because catchy titles have always entertained me, in my own writings and reading others' work, I wrote two related books titled *The Expert Expert Witness* (Brodsky, 1999), the second edition with psychiatrist Tom Gutheil who had been writing for psychiatrists the same genre of advice I had been writing for psychologists (Brodsky & Gutheil, 2016).

The model of teaching in these books was similar to my expert witness training workshops. Brief lessons about specific questions, problems, and challenges were followed by advice and examples of how to deal with such problems. The books had the added lagniappe of the maxims serving to summarize the essence of the lesson in such a brief form that remembering was usually easy.

My one testifying book that did not follow the very brief chapters plus maxims model was *Coping with Cross Examinations* (Brodsky, 2004). While the other books had a wide and receptive audience, *Coping* did not do as well (even though APA Books did ask me to explore with them the possibility of a second edition). *Coping* had the same catchy cartoon cover and engaging artwork within, but it had longer chapters and a more leisurely exposition of testifying principles. Readers of the other books had written to me about the value of going over the brief chapters from the other books the night before trial or deposition testimony. No such emails ever came regarding *Coping*.

Part of my professional career has included teaching, supervising, and practicing psychotherapy, and I have had involuntary clients referred to me. These clients included attorneys mandated to seek therapy by their ethics disciplinary boards, employees pushed to get help by supervisors, and spouses nudged into treatment by their partners. As I worked with them, some of the same methods for managing aggressive, challenging attorneys on the stand appeared to apply as well to working with reluctant, truculent, and belligerent therapy clients. Or maybe the law of the hammer was in effect. It was Abraham Maslow (1966) who wrote that if a hammer is your only tool, you then proceed to treat everything as if it were a nail. My techniques similar to dealing with aggressive attorneys came out in a book about therapy with coerced clients (Brodsky, 2011), which reached further than these ideas for managing cross-examining lawyers.

The Witness Research Lab

When Marc Boccaccini joined me as a graduate student in Clinical Psychology-Law at The University of Alabama, among our various projects was the development of a lab to study the actual components of behaviors associated with the believability of expert and lay witnesses. We started with a lab in an unused closet-like office in which we recorded testimony sometimes drawn from actual cases and sometimes constructed to permit manipulation and study of specific variables. After a while, a faculty member left who had a huge but equally windowless office on the floor of the psychology building that had at one time been used for comparative and physiological research with rats, mice, pigeons, and the occasional Siamese fighting fish. With the help of Michael Griffin and other graduate students, I constructed a realistic witness stand, with expensive wood paneling behind it, an American flag to the side, and cameras, microphones, and the equivalent of a teleprompter, a large monitor scrolling displays of stimulus materials for the experts. Our expert witnesses in the research were either actual testifying experts, faculty members who were available, or our own graduate students. A number of published studies came from the lab, starting with Boccaccini and Brodsky (2002), Boccaccini et al. (2004), Barnett et al. (2004), Boccaccini et al. (2005), and Brodsky and Cannon (2006). Particular attention early on was directed to aspects of expert testimony in capital trial sentencing mitigation that might make a difference (Barnett & Brodsky, 2007; Tetterton & Brodsky, 2007).

Witness Credibility

Before long, the question arose of what components of expert witness testimony actually made a difference. That is, when experts testified in court, what was it about their presentation, interpersonal style, manner, content, or other factors that served to promote believability? The process began, as such things do, with diving into the literature and surfacing with the characteristics that experienced experts, attorneys, researchers, and scholars identified as enhancing or diminishing credibility. Not surprisingly, more simple assertions of various factors appeared than did meaningful research. The pathway for the Witness Research Lab seemed clear.

Part of the impetus for one variable had come after Marc Boccaccini and I watched a murder trial in our local county courthouse in which a knowledgeable medical expert from New York had testified about how problematic the physical evidence was. We were impressed by his detailed, scientific, in-depth knowledge. When the jury came back with a guilty verdict disregarding his findings, we figuratively scratched our heads and talked with other observers. They agreed that the physician came across as distant, scientifically preachy, and hard to relate to. That segued right into a study of likability in experts.

A subsequent study of likability (Brodsky et al., 2010) in experts used trained actors as tall, bearded, male professors who were either likable or unlikable—in retrospect, an inappropriately gendered choice—in videorecorded testimony. Likeability was operationally defined, after a series of prior steps, as degree of smiling, use of *we* or *us* in reference to groups, absence of arrogant responses, and maintenance of good eye contact. A key finding was that likability was significantly associated with being seen as credible and as trustworthy. Later, additional studies investigated the components of likability, such as smiling.

That study and others used the Witness Credibility Scale (WCS) we had developed in the lab and that was published about the same time (Brodsky et al., 2010). Development of the WCS followed the conventional course of time, with successive pooled iterations of items followed by a factor analysis. The process eventually led to a 20-item credibility scale with five items each allocated to subscale ratings of likeability, knowledge, trustworthiness, and confidence. With the working understanding that these items overlapped with other conceptualizations of closely related variables, the scale served as a regular measure of expert witness credibility in a series of studies, most of which used controlled variables in different testimony conditions. The subscales themselves were also the subject of studies, with only the knowledge variable not yielding consistent and useful results.

Among other topics studied, a particular focus was on gender and credibility of testimony, which arose in part from repeated reports by women in testifying workshops. These reports included highly intrusive questions by attorneys during cross-examinations or depositions. For example, women, but rarely men, were asked about medicines they were taking, about their use of discipline with their children, about marital status, about car-pooling, about having been abused, and other unwelcome, difficult, and inappropriate inquiries.

Bridget Larson and I conducted two studies investigating how women should respond to such intrusive questions. In the first study (Larson & Brodsky, 2010), women experts were rated lower than men experts on all four of the WCS subscales—likeability, knowledge, trustworthiness, and confidence. However, when confronted with aggressive and intrusive questions, women and men alike were rated as more trustworthy and credible, and the attorney was viewed less favorably. In a follow-up study (Larson & Brodsky, 2014) of defensive versus assertive expert responses to gender intrusive questions, assertive replies were associated with higher witness credibility. Perhaps surprisingly, the participants' own sexism scores were unrelated to any of their judgments about the experts. In a related study, Nagle et al. (2014) reported different findings. We found that men expert witnesses were rated as more trustworthy than women experts, and that smiling women expert witnesses were rated as more likable than both smiling men experts and non-smiling women experts.

A further study in our lab looked at ways in which expert knowledge was associated with expert witness likeability (Parrott et al., 2015). High knowledge in experts was not associated with credibility or with mock jurors' agreement with the experts' opinions. However, low knowledge experts were reported to be more likable than their high knowledge counterparts. In an overview article, Brodsky et al. (2017) cautioned against the risks for expert witnesses of argumentativeness, emotionality, narcissism, and stubbornness on the stand.

Not Exactly a Model of Expert Witness Training

It would be an overstatement to describe what I have done and still do in expert witness training as representing a model, in either of the two possible meanings of that word in this context. It is neither a desirable example nor an organized and clearly defined structure. So, I ask the reader to bear with me calling this training format a model because that word seems to be the closest meaningful term to encompass these methods and steps. The following components outline the parts of this expert witness training.

High Levels of Participation

Experts can locate on their own much of the published research, the means of effective delivery of testimony, and the management of aggressive and skilled cross-examinations. A yawning gap separates reading about expert testimony from being able to perform better. By itself, participation is the antidote to the oppressive lecture format about almost anything. In addition, the following elements have special applications to expert witness participatory training.

Multiple Options

When experts are faced with unexpected, difficult, or challenging questions, it is not unusual for them to come up with only one option for responding. I see a goal of individuals having many options at any one moment, and the training helps expert witnesses produce at least a half dozen reasonable responses. When participants cannot do it on their own, I shift roles, I ask volunteers to play the attorney role and I offer multiple desirable witness replies. Then I toss the ball (usually figuratively) back to them, pose the same attorney questions, asking them to reply. And repeat.

Pairing Off

With more than twenty or thirty participants, individualized behavior rehearsals between trainer and trainees are not possible. In those instances, participants are paired off, and take turns being attorney and expert, typically with a single scenario that has been presented to the group. As trainer, I meander through the room, listen to the back and forth, may intensify the cross questions, or demonstrate additional response options.

Raise a Little Anxiety

It sounds paradoxical that in training about anxiety-arousing situations, the trainer should promote some anxiety. Still, I typically start off with a half dozen generic but tough questions, asking people at random to answer them. Examples of such questions are, "Like everyone else, you psychologists make mistakes, don't you?" and "Isn't it true that you psychologists still have a huge amount to learn about predicting human behavior?"

Why ask such questions? They galvanize attention. They offer the promise of help. Most participants are on the edge of their seats.

Overstated Attorney Mannerisms and Questions

With the objective of portraying a reasonable simulation of actual examinations, I sometimes overdo it. I may roar like the Incredible Hulk, slam my fist on the table, and mix sarcasm, intimidation, and disdain. I like doing this. Why? Well, I have to refer you to my psychotherapist for the best answers. In contrast, the alternative attorney ploy is offered as well—the bright, sweet, interested, likable attorney asking questions that can lead some experts to go much further with their interpretations, reservations, and conclusions than they normally would. In the hands of such positive energy attorneys, many experts let go of some of their cautions they usually maintain and slip into problematic testimony.

The Basic Techniques

The expert training focuses on about ten useful and credible ways of thinking about replies. It is beyond the reach of this chapter to repeat the details of what I have described elsewhere many times (e.g., Brodsky, 2022). However, the categories include the push-pull, the admit-deny, the use of silence, the negative assertion, responses to yes-no questions, eye contact, personal space, posture and gestures, and tone of voice.

What They Want

In training professional groups, such as forensic mental health professionals employed by individual states, I ask them to submit a list of what most concerns them about testimony or to describe their worst experiences on the stand. Then the training addresses these topics.

The Impromptu

Can one plan for impromptu elements of expert training? I don't know. But I sometimes sing or tell testimony stories I had not planned on describing. Occasionally, I will link a topic to the Jabberwocky poem (Twas Brillig and The Slithy Toves . . .) or other Lewis Carroll lines (why the sea is boiling hot and whether pigs have wings). Why do it? It breaks fixed expectations of structured training. It is usually playful. Maybe it is worthwhile.

The Unexpected

I do promote and seek to roll with unexpected training events. It may run in the family. My brother Howard Brodsky authored an entertaining and clever book about creative business practices called *The Unexpected* (H. Brodsky, 2013). Especially with already skilled practitioners, I invite one or two people in the audience to volunteer and to allow them to work with me on a real case they have coming up. I don't know what people will say. It might be productive. A friend who will be in the audience of a forthcoming training workshop said that open-endedness would petrify her. Me, I am curious.

In the same sense of the unexpected, Joel Dvoskin and I were once well into leading a testifying workshop when a non-psychologist stormed into the room and scathingly criticized all of us for being responsible for her loss of custody of her child. Joel and I offered to talk with her privately afterwards. She ignored us and continued ranting for about 15 minutes until hotel security took her away. Was it unexpected and unpredictable? Oh, yes. Did it offer a useful learning lesson for appreciating the anger of parties to legal proceedings? Perhaps. Was it memorable? Oh, yes!

Cartoons

Of the 189 slides I will show at my next testifying workshop, about 60 are cartoons, selected for the overlap of testifying principles and good humor. My favorite cartoon shows someone advising a performer about to go on stage, "Dance like they are all looking at their cellphones."

Positive Outcomes

Given the preexisting anxiety of many participants, and my fang-baring attacks as a pretend attorney, an important aspect is to ensure that every behavior rehearsal and testimony simulation ends with a demonstration of a positive and successful way of handling the questioning. From the start, I ask that participants demand a positive and constructive outcome of every role-play and never allow bad feelings and struggling responses to hang on like undercooked brussels sprouts.

Consultation

In contrast to the more common group training for expert testing, forensic consultation is a one-on-one process, usually conducted by Zoom or another medium. Forensic professionals who have read my books or articles or attended my workshops contact me. Sometimes their concern has been a singularly awful testifying experience. Other issues have been when their reports often have had major weaknesses revealed during cross, or a rebuttal expert has offered a harshly critical analysis of their reports. Additional concerns have included major anxiety during testimony, or an attorney with a notorious reputation who will be deposing or examining them, or specific repeated problems, such as English as a second language. For professionals with anxiety issues the consultations almost leak over into therapeutic work.

The Finish

I aspire to wrap up every training experience with a positive, encouraging finish that ties together some of the content. I also invite participants to contact me about their continuing issues. A few people take me up on this invitation, and we email or talk about various testifying topics.

Replication Issues

The editors requested that contributors discuss whether our work could be replicated and how much of what we do was a function of knowledge and experience versus a product of our distinctive style. In the words of Borat Sagdiyev, my favorite mock journalist, "Wa Wa Wee Wa," that is, my goodness! It is a challenge to try to think of one's distinctive professional career in a totally humility-free way! I am reminded of how the Winnie the Pooh character Tigger in the animated Disney movies sings about himself. After describing Tiggers in grandly energetic ways, he concludes that "The most wonderful thing about Tiggers is that I'm the only one."

I am far from being Tigger-like. It would be a galling mixture of hubris and narcissism to think I am the only one to be able to do my kind of work, training experts to testify in court. The obvious start for generalizability is in development and writing. Existing bases and practices can be the foundation for the efforts of others. Furthermore, the anecdotes, principles, and maxims in my six testifying books came in part from stories other forensic professionals told me.

Can other professionals replicate in general the workshops, talks, and training, as well as the consultations? Sure. I am not unique in being able to do it. My style of leading workshops, when the workshops go right, can be entertaining, playful, and full of dramatized teaching and role plays of court testimony. But everyone brings personal styles to instruction and training, and nobody would expect to do precisely what I do.

A second question posed by the editors was, can this work and style be acquired? A reasonable answer would be yes, not by everybody. But surely some people can do almost the same thing, and sometimes better. I count the testifying talks by Joel Dvoskin as falling in that category of better, and especially in terms of his ways of engaging the participants through a mix of song and music, and empathy and humility. When a friend was interviewing for a job for which she was clearly overqualified, she was asked by the interviewer if she would be able to meet the requirements of the position and adequately do the work. She replied, "Oh yes, and much much better." That same perspective applies to other forensic professionals interested in expert witness training. Some certainly can do it, and some, indeed, much much better.

The Future of Expert Witness Training

Considerable written information about effective court testimony is already set in the books on forensic mental health evaluations by Melton et al. (2018), Otto, et al. (2014) and many similar resources. Although no definitive information is available about how much time and effort in predoctoral training is devoted to training in testifying, Najdowski, et al. (2015) reported that psychology-law Ph.D. programs devote much time to related active learning techniques. Mock trials are common demonstrations of forensic work that include illustrations of effective testimony. As a frequent participant, I would characterize these mock trials as informative and useful, but they nevertheless do not provide sufficient in-depth preparation of graduate students for court testimony. Little time is available in most forensic psychology graduate programs for much training in testifying. More opportunities appear in internships, post-doctoral placements, and subsequent professional conferences and continuing education talks.

When I began my private pilot training, the instructor put me in a power-off situation for an emergency landing as well as in controlled stalls at altitude. This scenario-based training is designed to promote good decisions and judgment in flight emergencies. In the same sense, it should go into expert witness training for felt crises. Serious threats to the effective presentation of professional knowledge and self on the witness stand can come about unexpectedly if infrequently. Simply being competent at most expert testimony work will be adequate a high percentage of the time. But many mental health experts worry about the occasionally well-prepared, very challenging cross-examining attorney.

It is just for the testimony equivalent of pilot emergencies that extensive testifying training is needed, with much role-playing, practice, and scenario-based training. Lectures and reading are good. But for broad-ranging preparation, nothing else takes the place of high involvement, high participation, small-group, or individual training.

References

Babitsky, S. (2001). Becoming an expert witness. *Civil Engineering, 71*(4), 54–55.

Babitsky, S., & Mangraviti, J. (2003). *Cross-examination: The comprehensive guide for experts.* SEAK, Incorporated.

Babitsky, S., & Mangraviti, J. (2005a). How to start a lucrative expert witness practice. *Journal of Nursing Law, 10*(2), 77–78.

Babitsky, S., & Mangraviti, J. (2011). *Understanding the AMA guides in workers' compensation.* Wolters Kluwer.

Babitsky, S. B., & Mangraviti, J. (2005b). *How to become a dangerous expert witness: Advanced techniques and strategies.* SEAK. *Inc.*

Barnett, M. E., Brodsky, S. L., & Davis, C. (2004). When mitigation evidence makes a difference: Effects of psychological mitigating evidence on sentencing decisions in capital trials. *Behavioral Sciences & the Law, 22*(6), 751–770.

Barnett, M. E., & Brodsky, S. L. (2007). Differential impact of mitigating evidence in capital case sentencing. *Journal of Forensic Psychology Practice. 7*(1), 39–45.

Belli, M. M., & Carroll, M. C. (1964). *Dallas justice: The real story of Jack Ruby and his trial.* McKay.

Boccaccini, M. T., Boothby, J. L., & Brodsky, S. L. (2004). Development and effects of client trust in criminal defense attorneys: Preliminary examination of the congruence model of trust development. *Behavioral Sciences & the Law, 22*(2), 197–214. https://doi.org/10.1002/bsl.584

Boccaccini, M. T., & Brodsky, S. L. (2002). Believability of expert and lay witnesses trial consultation. *Professional Psychology: Research and Practice, 33*(4), 384–388. https://doi.org/10.1037/0735-7028.33.4.384

Boccaccini, M. T., Gordon, T., & Brodsky, S. L. (2005). Effects of witness preparation on witness confidence and nervousness. *Journal of Forensic Psychology Practice, 3*(4), 39–51.

Brodsky, H. B. (2013). *The unexpected: Breakthrough strategies to supercharge your business and earn loyal customers for life.* Smart Business Network.

Brodsky, S. L. (1973). *Psychologists in the criminal justice system.* University of Illinois Press.

Brodsky, S. L. (1977). Psychology at the interface of law and corrections: The Alabama correctional psychology experience. *Law and Psychology Review, 3*, 1–13.

Brodsky, S. L. (1989). Advocacy in the guise of scientific objectivity: An examination of Faust and Ziskin. *Computers in Human Behavior, 5*(4), 261–264.

Brodsky, S. L. (1991). *Testifying in court: Guidelines and maxims for the expert witness.* American Psychological Association Books.

Brodsky, S. L. (1999). *The expert expert witness: More maxims and guidelines for testifying in court.* American Psychological Association Books.

Brodsky, S. L. (2004). *Coping with cross-examination and other pathways to effective testimony.* American Psychological Association Books.

Brodsky, S. L. (2011). *Therapy with coerced and reluctant clients.* American Psychological Association Books.

Brodsky, S. L. (2014). *Testifying in court* (2nd ed.). American Psychological Association Books.

Brodsky, S. L. (2022). *Testifying in court* (3rd ed.). American Psychological Association.

Brodsky, S. L., & Cannon, D. E. (2006). Ingratiation in the courtroom and in the voir dire process: When more is not better. *Law and Psychology Review, 30,* 103–117.

Brodsky, S. L., Dvoskin, J. A., & Neal, T. M. S. (2017). Temptations for the expert witness. *Journal of the American Academy of Psychiatry and Law, 45*(4), 460–463.

Brodsky, S. L., Griffin, M. P., & Cramer, R. J. (2010). The Witness Credibility Scale. *Behavioral Sciences & the Law, 28*(6), 892–907. doi: 10.1002/bsl.917

Brodsky, S. L., & Gutheil, T. G. (2016). *The expert expert witness* (2nd ed.). American Psychological Association Books.

Brodsky, S. L., & Miller, K. S. (1981). Coercing change in prisons and mental hospitals: The social scientist and class action suit. In J. M. Joffe & G. W. Albee (Eds.), *Prevention through political action and social change* (pp. 208–227). University Press of New England.

Brodsky, S. L., & Robey, A. (1972). On becoming an expert witness: Issues of orientation and effectiveness. *Professional Psychology, 3*(2), 173–176.

Cummings, E. E. (1920, January). Buffalo Bill's Defunct. In *Seven Poems, Dial, 68*(1), 22.

Fowler, R. D., & Matarazzo, J. D. (1988). Psychologists and psychiatrists as expert witnesses. *Science, 241*(4870), 1143–1143.

Ginsburg, W. H. (2001). Review of the comprehensive forensic services manual: The essential resources for all experts. *Journal of Legal Medicine, 22,* 299–306.

Goldenson, J., & Gutheil, T. (2023). Forensic mental health evaluators' unprocessed emotions as an often-overlooked form of bias. *Journal of the American Academy of Psychiatry and the Law, 51*(4), 551–557. DOI: https://doi.org/10.29158/JAAPL.230077-23

Grisso, T. (1991). A developmental history of the American Psychology-Law Society. *Law and Human Behavior, 15*(3), 213–231.

Gutheil, T. G. (1998). *The psychiatrist in court: A survival guide.* American Psychiatric Press.

Gutheil, T. G. (2009). *The psychiatrist as expert witness.* American Psychiatric Publications.

Gutheil, T. G., Dattilio, F. D., & Dattilio, F. M. (2008). *Practical approaches to forensic mental health testimony.* Lippincott Williams & Wilkins.

Kelsey, H. M. (1986). *101 bridge maxims.* Devyn Press.

Larson, B. A., & Brodsky, S. L. (2010). When cross-examination offends: How men and women assess intrusive questioning of male and female expert witnesses. *Journal of Applied Social Psychology, 40*(4), 811–830. https://doi.org/10.1111/j.1559-1816.2010.00599

Larson, B. A., & Brodsky, S. L. (2014). Assertive women as expert witnesses: A study of assertive and defensive responses in male and female experts. *Behavioral Sciences & the Law, 32*(2), 149–163. https://doi.org/10.1002/bsl.2116

Lubet, S., & Boals, E. I. (2020). *Expert testimony: A guide for expert witnesses and the lawyers who examine them.* Aspen Publishing.

Maslow, A. H. (1966). *The psychology of science: A reconnaissance.* HarperCollins.

Melton, G. B., Petrila, J., Poythress, N. G., Slobogin, C., Otto, R. K., Mossman, D., & Condie, L. O. (2018). *Psychological evaluations for the courts: A handbook for mental health professionals and lawyers* (4th ed.). Guilford Publications.

Miller, H. L., Brodsky, S. L., & Bleechmore, J. R. (1976). Patients' rights: Who's wrong? The changing role of the mental health professional. *Professional Psychology, 7*(3), 274–279.

Nagle, J. E., Brodsky, S. L., & Weeter, K. (2014). Gender, smiling, and witness credibility in actual trials. *Behavioral Sciences & the Law, 32*(2), 195–206. doi: 10.1002.bsl.2112

Najdowski, C. J., Bottoms, B. L., Stevenson, M. C., & Veilleux, J. C. (2015). A historical review and resource guide to the scholarship of teaching and training in psychology and law and forensic psychology. *Training and Education in Professional Psychology, 9*(3), 217.

Otto, R. K., DeMier, R. L., & Boccaccini, M. T. (2014). *Forensic reports and testimony: A guide to effective communication for psychologists and psychiatrists.* John Wiley & Sons.

Parrott, C. T., Neal, T., Wilson, J. K., & Brodsky, S. L. (2015). Differences in expert witness knowledge: Do mock jurors notice and does it matter? *Journal of the American Academy of Psychiatry and Law, 43*(1), 69–81.

Postal, K. (2019). *Testimony that sticks: the art of communicating psychology and neuropsychology to juries.* Oxford University Press.

Postal, K. (2021). *The art and science of expert witness testimony: A multidisciplinary guide for professionals.* Routledge.

Rosenberg, C. E. (1968). *The trial of the assassin Guiteau: Psychiatry and the law in the gilded age.* University of Chicago Press.

Simon, R. J. (1983). The defense of insanity. *The Journal of Psychiatry & Law*, *11*(2), 183–201.

Tetterton, V. S., & Brodsky, S. L. (2007). More is sometimes better: Increased mitigating evidence and sentencing leniency. *Journal of Forensic Psychology Practice*, *7*(3), 79–85.

Yackle, L. W. (1989). *Reform and regret: The story of federal judicial involvement in the Alabama prison system*. Oxford University Press.

Ziskin, J. (1970). *Coping with psychiatric and psychological testimony*. Law and Psychology Press.

22

Protect International

A Company Focused on Violence and Other Adverse Behavior in Organizational Contexts

Stephen D. Hart

It is typical, expected, and even in the common good for academic psychologists to be involved in practice. This was true for me after I was hired as a faculty member in the Department of Psychology at Simon Fraser University (SFU). My practice was directly related to my research and, in particular, my work on violence risk assessment and management. Very quickly, however, I encountered challenges engaging in practice within the traditional administrative and bureaucratic structure of the university. My colleagues and I, all associated with SFU, had developed the Structured Professional Judgment (SPJ) approach to decision making (for a brief review, see Hart et al., 2016) and several sets of SPJ guidelines for violence risk assessment and management, including the development of the SPJ approach to decision making (for a brief review, see Hart et al., 2016) and various SPJ guidelines for violence risk assessment, such as the Guidelines for Spousal Assault Risk Assessment (Kropp et al., 1994), Version 2 of the Historical-Clinical-Risk Management-20 (Webster et al., 1997), the Sexual Violence Risk-20 (Boer et al., 1997), and the Risk for Sexual Violence Protocol (Hart et al., 2003). We were also consulting with agencies around the world on implementation. However, our efforts to commodify this work at the university were unsuccessful. The university was unwilling or unable to find a way to publish, sell, and distribute resource materials or negotiate and manage a large number of service contracts, most of which were relatively small (several thousands of dollars) and involved clients who were unwilling or unable to pay the university's standard overhead rate, which could be as high as 65 percent.

It did not make sense to me to resign from my position at the university to commodify the work I had started and wanted to continue there. I discussed options with others, and eventually, I decided to start a business. After twenty-five years, what started as the division of another company and was later established as an independent company, Protect International Risk and Safety Services Inc.

Stephen D. Hart, *Protect International*. In: *The Path Forward*. Edited by: Kirk Heilbrun and David DeMatteo, Oxford University Press. © Oxford University Press (2026). DOI: 10.1093/9780197773031.003.0022

(Protect International), is healthy and growing.[1] If you are a psychologist—academic or non-academic, clinical or non-clinical, forensic or non-forensic—considering the possibility of building something more than a conventional private practice, something that provides more and bigger opportunities for growth, then read on. What follows may help you plan your future or, at the very least, how to avoid or overcome some of the challenges you may encounter.

Project Description

Nature of Services

Protect International's mission is to assist organizations in reducing the harmful effects of violence and related adverse behavior through effective prevention and intervention. The related adverse behavior includes self-injury and suicide, harassment and discrimination, damage to privacy and reputation, insider threats, and serious misconduct. With respect to all its services, Protect International works on behalf of (i.e., as an agent of) its clients, trains its clients to do such work for themselves, or supports its clients to do such work themselves. The prevention services include the development or review of relevant organizational policies and procedures, as well as assisting with policy implementation through the education, training, and support of organizational staff. The intervention services include investigations, remediation, and organizational support. The investigations focus on allegations or suspicions of past adverse behavior, risk for future adverse behavior (triage and assessment of risk, also known as threat assessment), and readiness for duty (fitness for work or studies, return to work or studies, and reasonable accommodation). Finally, the remediation involves risk management (also known as threat management), fear management, and safety planning, as well as consultation with human resources and legal professionals dealing with such litigation support and expert witness services. Protect International considers all of its services to be forensic in nature, as they concern either laws or policies that have contractual force. But by no means do these matters all involve criminal law; indeed, most involve occupational health and safety, mental health, employment and education, immigration, child protection, human rights, tort, or privacy law instead of or in addition to criminal law.

In addition to services, Protect International develops, publishes, and distributes products (i.e., resource materials) in print and digital formats. Most of the print products are SPJ guidelines for various forms of violence, including updated versions of older guidelines (e.g., Boer et al., 2017; Douglas et al., 2003; Hart et al., 2022;

[1] Protect International is a trademark of Protect International Risk and Safety Services Inc. in countries including but not limited to Canada, the United States, the United Kingdom, and Australia, and a common law trademark in other countries where it is used.

Kropp et al., 2020; Kropp & Hart, 2015; Kropp et al., 2024) and brand-new guidelines (e.g., Storey et al., 2021; Watt et al., 2023). Protect International sells and ships these guidelines in print form internationally and manages the intellectual property rights associated with them on behalf of the authors in relation to such things as licensing and translation. The digital products include SPJ guidelines in the form of e-publications and bespoke software to facilitate the use of guidelines in organizations. Over the past five years, Protect International has spent considerable effort on the development of software applications. One application provides users, from individuals to small teams to large organizations, with online and desktop access to SPJ guidelines in digital form, thus avoiding costs associated with printing and shipping. Another application supports the administration of SPJ guidelines, with features that include the ability to work on cases individually or as part of a team, securely complete and store worksheets and related documents, and generate editable reports from completed worksheets.

Clients

Protect International operates on a business-to-business model. Its clients in the government sector include a wide range of ministries, departments, and agencies. At the national (federal) and subnational (state, province, territory) levels, most clients are super-ministries or the departments thereof responsible for internal, domestic, or home affairs, such as national security, law enforcement, and corrections; health, including somatic health, mental health (both civil and forensic), and occupational health and safety; social services, including protection of children and vulnerable adults and support for victims of crime; and education, including primary (elementary school), secondary (i.e., high school, gymnasium, or college), and tertiary (i.e., post-secondary, higher education, continuing education). At the local (county, regional, district, municipal) level, most are specific agencies responsible for law enforcement or emergency services, such as a police or fire and rescue service; corrections, such as a courthouse, jail or prison, or probation or parole office; health care, such as a hospital, community clinic, or ambulance service; education, such as a university, high school, or elementary school; transportation, such as a public transit service.

Clients at the non-governmental level include non-profit or charitable organizations and civil society organizations. Most of them deal with specific social issues, such as support services for victims of domestic violence and sheltered housing for people with serious mental health difficulties.

Clients in the private sector include publicly and privately owned companies. They have ranged in size from small (10 or fewer employees operating in a single location) to national (tens of thousands of employees spread across the country) to multinational (100,000 or more employees spread across 100 or more countries). Many national or multinational companies have internal resources to handle much or all of the work Protect International does, such as departments responsible for investigation, threat assessment and management, fitness for work and accommodation, and so forth; but they still may request outside assistance for tasks such as policy review, staff training, or help with specific issues that are sensitive (e.g., concern about risk posed by or to a senior executive, concerns about risk for extremist violence posed by a regular employee) or outside their area of expertise.

Providers

The primary activities of service providers at Protect International involve consulting (broadly defined) with respect to prevention and intervention regarding matters of security, health, and safety. With only rare exceptions, service providers act in the capacity of business management consultants, not as licensed professionals in fields such as psychology or law.

At present, five of the seven service providers have degrees in clinical psychology, with concentrations in either clinical-forensic or clinical-community psychology; one has a degree in law; and one has degrees in both psychology and law. Yet, their employment agreements do not identify them as psychologists or lawyers, do not require them to be registered or licensed as psychologists or lawyers (or even to have a degree in psychology or law), and their job duties do not include activities related to the assessment or diagnosis of behavioral, emotional, or cognitive disorders in clients; the provision of counseling or therapy to clients; or the practice of law.[2] It is only in a minority of cases, primarily involving readiness for duty investigations, that Protect International provides psychological services related to the assessment and diagnosis of mental disorder; in such cases, the contract with the client makes clear that the service provider is a licensed psychologist practicing in that capacity.

In Canada, when a legal matter requires assessment and diagnosis of a mental disorder, it is usual that these services are provided by an independent mental health evaluation (rather than one working on behalf of one of the parties) to mitigate actual, potential, or perceived conflict of interest. As a general rule, then, Protect International avoids situations in which one of the company's employees conducts an investigation of a person and another employee conducts a mental health evaluation of the same person. For example, if, in the course of conducting a violence risk assessment, a service provider uncovers reasonable grounds to suspect that the evaluee suffers from mental health problems, Protect International will assist clients in retaining an independent mental health evaluator professional. The exception to this general rule arises when a client requires an urgent mental health evaluation but is unable to find an independent professional who is available to work or willing to travel for work. In such a case, Protect International may agree to provide

[2] Protect International does not provide legal consultation services. In British Columbia, only a law firm can hire members of the legal profession to provide legal advice and representation to external clients.

psychological services at the request of the client, but only under a contract that sets out the nature of the services to be provided, the urgent nature of the request, assurance that the services will be delivered by a duly qualified and licensed professional, and the steps that will be taken to mitigate any conflict of interest. Those steps will include ensuring the licensed psychologist was not involved in and has no access to information about Protect International's other involvement with the evaluee.

Psychologists sometimes express confusion or concern that Protect International's service providers may be practicing psychology without a license, thereby exposing the public to the risk of unethical or unprofessional practice. This is not the case. First, activities such as policy review, training, conducting investigations, and so forth are activities that are not restricted to the practice or profession of psychology. Indeed, the vast majority of people who engage in them are not psychologists—most have backgrounds in law enforcement, private security, corrections, social work, human resources, and so forth, and many of them are not licensed professionals of any sort. Second, as all the service providers at Protect International belong to associations that have their ethical codes or practice standards, such as the Canadian Association of Threat Assessment Professionals or the American Psychology-Law Society, everyone who believes they have been harmed as a result of services provided by Protect International can file a formal ethics complaint with the relevant body. Of course, they can also seek redress before courts (e.g., in relation to complaints of negligence) or tribunals (e.g., in relation to complaints of breach of privacy or human rights). Third, Protect International maintains full business insurance in the event that some person or organization is harmed due to errors or omissions on its part.

Size and Scope

In terms of personnel, Protect International may be considered a micro-business, one with ten or fewer full-time employees. At the time of writing, it employs three full-time, one part-time, and three contract service providers; job searches for a further two full-time service providers are in progress. The service providers are supported by two full-time administrative staff. Working closely with service providers, they handle communications with clients, contracts, marketing, and sales. Finally, the service providers and administrative staff are supported by about a dozen external contractors who provide assistance with finances (bookkeeping, accounting, taxes, auditing), information technology (network, servers, individual computers), software engineering (app development), publishing and distribution, and legal matters (employment, contract, and intellectual property law).

In terms of geographic scope, Protect International's office is located in Vancouver, British Columbia, Canada. It has a subsidiary company in the United States with a virtual office in Delaware, but operations in the United States are serviced through the Vancouver office. In its current and previous incarnations, Protect International has provided services to organizations located in more than fifty countries on five continents. This means service providers are required to travel both domestically and internationally as part of their work. Its resource materials are sold and distributed even more widely. As shipping resource materials in print form is expensive, Protect International has a contract with a company in the United Kingdom to expedite the distribution of materials in print form to locations in Europe, Africa, and Southwest Asia.

Time Allocation

With respect to time spent on the provision of services to clients, this depends entirely on the nature of those services. Services related to consultation about the development, review, or evaluation of policy, training, and so forth may require anywhere between a few days (a day being defined internally as 8 hours of billable time) to 100 days or more over multiple years. Services related to education, training, and support may require anywhere between a few hours to five days for a single event, or twenty days or more over a year or longer for a long-term contract involving multiple events spread over months or years. Case-related services (investigation, risk assessment and management, victim safety planning, fear management, litigation support, expert witness services, etc.) may require anywhere between one or two days to ten or more days.

With respect to the time spent by service providers on different tasks, about twenty to twenty-five percent of their available days will be allocated for billable work, and another twenty to twenty-five percent of available days will be allocated for non-billable work involving preparation, travel, and follow-up for service provision. The remaining time is projected to be divided among four other areas of activity, with about ten to fifteen percent allocated for each of the following: administration, including correspondence, documentation, and record-keeping in relation to services delivered; sales support, such as responding to requests for information about services, preparing proposals or quotations for potential clients, and finalizing contracts with potential clients; marketing support, such as presentations at conferences, non-profit agencies, and public fora and publications for books, periodicals, and academic journals; and research and development, including business development, professional development, and development of new services and resource materials.

With respect to the time spent by administrative staff on different tasks, about forty percent of available days are allocated for administration, including correspondence, documentation, and record-keeping, as well as preparation, follow-up, and invoicing for service delivery. Another forty percent of available days are allocated for marketing and sales support, including maintenance of the content of the company's website, preparing marketing materials such as brochures and emails, managing inventory, and handling orders for resource materials. The final twenty percent of available days are allocated for development, including business development and professional development.

Attracting Prospective Clients

Attracting prospective clients is also known as marketing. Most psychologists instinctively hate business terms such as "marketing" and "sales." This knee-jerk reaction is unfortunate. Marketing is simply letting people know what products and services you provide and where to find you. Sales is simply helping people make an informed decision about purchasing your products and services—that is, making sure your products and services fit their needs.

As noted above, Protect International allots considerable time for marketing-related activities. Protect International's marketing focuses on three things: the company itself, the products and services provided by the company, and the company's employees. The overarching objective is to increase the extent to which clients, both potential and actual, become familiar with all three. With respect to the company, the goal is to convey that it offers specialized (focused) services related to violence and other adverse behavior and is established (stable, reliable, trustworthy) and international (wide-reaching). With respect to the products and services, the goal is to convey that they are standardized (structured yet flexible), evidence-based (valid, justifiable, well-founded), and authoritative (respected, influential). With respect to the employees, the goal is to convey that they are highly knowledgeable (educated, expert) and professional (experienced, qualified, talented). All Protect International's marketing efforts, from branding to website design to email blasts to the design of resource materials, are developed and evaluated according to these goals.

Training

The scope of services provided by Protect International is narrow in its focus on harm due to violence and other adverse behavior, yet the underlying legal issues are broad and complex. Most forensic psychologists acquire experience working in forensic mental health and corrections agencies as trainees, but the proportion of those who work with police, courts, or national security is relatively small. The proportion of those who work outside the criminal justice system—for example, in the civil justice system dealing with mental health, child protection, family, or immigration law issues, or in organizational settings dealing with employment and education, human rights, or privacy law—is very small indeed, in my experience. The work at Protect International, however, requires some familiarity with all these issues; at a minimum, service providers must know what they do not know and be able to recognize when a matter is complex and requires assistance from others.

Employees hired at Protect International spend about a year being trained on the job. This involves frequent discussions with senior colleagues (acting as supervisors), reading and researching different areas of the law, watching and practicing the delivery of training with the assistance of scripts and video recordings, and assisting with investigations and risk assessments. The learning curve over this year is really more like a straight line increasing at 45°. New staff steadily take on additional responsibility: more modules of training programs, then co-leading training programs with a senior colleague; primary responsibility for collateral interviews, then co-leading interviews of evaluees; drafting sections of investigation or risk assessment reports, then preparing the first draft of an entire report.

After a year, the training slows down, but it never really ends. Everyone keeps learning new material and sharing it with others, developing and practicing revised training curricula, or trying to improve templates for oral and written communications. One feature of the work at Protect International is that, whenever feasible, two or more providers are involved in the delivery of services. Indeed, there have been as many as three service providers involved in an investigation or risk assessment, which at times may involve a dozen or more collateral interviews or the review of many thousands of pages of documentary evidence; and in large, multi-day trainings, several of which last five days, there have been as many as three trainers per day and as many as five trainers in total. This is something that service providers really like. One of the worst things about operating a private practice is that it can be so, well, private.

Protect International supports the work of trainees at universities in Canada and abroad. It provides students with a fifty percent discount on training. It has provided some students interested in program evaluation with access to data collected by the company for internal purposes. It has even supported the thesis or dissertation research of several students through a grant program that matches funding from the private sector dollar-for-dollar. Finally, aside from two service providers who have regular faculty positions at SFU, three other service providers have adjunct faculty positions at SFU, where they serve on the supervisory committees of graduate students, lecture, and teach graduate seminars.

Keys to Effective Service Provision

When contacted by potential clients, Protect International's employees take care to understand their needs in terms of the problems clients want to address, any special constraints with respect to time or budget, and their unique characteristics. If the employees determine that Protect International's products or services are not a good fit for the needs of clients, the employees explain why and suggest where more appropriate products or services are available. If the employees determine that Protect International's products or services are, in fact, a good fit for the needs of clients, then clients are provided with a clear description and justification of the recommended products or services, including an estimate of the timelines and cost for completion. Some clients request and are provided with the opportunity to review samples of Protect International's work product or the opportunity to speak with its past clients. In most cases, the clients request written proposals or quotations. If the clients decide to proceed, the proposals form the basis for subsequent contracts.

This stage of service provision is critical for expectation management—it helps to prevent misunderstandings that might lead to unhappy clients.

Delivering good products or services is the easy part. Protect International strives to ensure that the products and services clients receive are consistently excellent: standardized, evidence-based, and authoritative; and developed and provided by employees who are highly knowledgeable and professional. Employees follow up with clients to evaluate their satisfaction with the products and services they receive and address any dissatisfaction.

Foundations and Support for Project Services

Theoretical

Protect International's services and products are not based on a specific or named theory, but rather on the general decision making or rational model of voluntary, purposive behavior that underlies virtually all contemporary theories of human behavior in psychology, cognitive neuroscience, criminology, microeconomics, and legal philosophy.

Scientific

Protect International's approach is evidence-based. All its products and services are informed by research, experience, and theory related to violence and other adverse behavior. The products and services are updated regularly to reflect developments in the evidence base. Protect International also contributes to the evidence base by supporting its employees to supervise, conduct, and publish or present research and supporting research conducted by external researchers.

Professional

The products and services developed and provided by Protect International are based on the SPJ approach to decision making. This approach is intended to ensure decisions are based on information that is comprehensive, individualized, and contextualized, as well as informed by the relevant legal, scientific, and professional literature. With respect to the latter, Protect International's service providers not only read and contribute to the professional literature, but are also active in relevant professional associations. They belong to relevant professional associations, attend and present at the meetings of professional associations, and serve on the boards and executive committees of professional associations.

Beginning and Development of Project Services

Conception

As noted already, Protect International was originally established as a division of another company, ProActive ReSolutions Inc., which was incorporated in Canada as a privately owned business in 2000. After fifteen years, when the principals discussed possible options for restructuring, I decided to spin off the division for which I was responsible as an independent concern. Protect International was incorporated in Canada as a privately owned business and began operations on January 1, 2016.

Resources Required to Start Operations

Protect International did not require much in the way of resources to begin operations. As part of the spin-off from ProActive ReSolutions, Protect International existed with staff (service providers and administrators), office equipment, and cash reserves. The up-front costs were relatively minor: legal expenses related to incorporation, drafting employment agreements, and purchasing a business license; office expenses related to moving, a new lease deposit, and lease or purchase of equipment; and IT costs related to purchasing desktop and laptop computers and a server and then setting up a network. The cash reserves and the cash flow from work already booked and in progress meant that all the up-front and continuing operational costs were covered; there was no need for a loan.

Within a year of starting operations in Canada, Protect International incorporated a wholly owned subsidiary in the United States. The purpose of this office is primarily to facilitate work for governmental (federal, state, and county) agencies. It is much easier for governmental agencies in the U.S. to hire domestic than foreign entities. Also, establishing a U.S. company means that taxes in relation to products and services provided by Protect International are paid in the United States rather than in Canada.

Generalizability

Does the Field Need Others Doing Similar Work?

Yes. The field needs more people doing work of the sort done by Protect International, but it needs people to do so in a way that is reliable and organized. There are lots of competitors in the marketplace, but most are private practices or sole proprietorships rather than businesses. This means virtually everything depends on a single person. It is difficult to run a business with one service provider. The pressure is on a single service provider to be everything to everyone, responsible for and good at all aspects of running a business. Also, all it takes is one sick dog, one snow day, or one delayed flight to wreak havoc. Do consider starting your own company, sharing the risk and the reward with a group of people whom you like and respect.

What Proportion of This Work Should Other Providers Expect to be Pro Bono or at a Significantly Reduced Rate?

As a trainee, I had a wise supervisor who said good consultants should charge as much as the market will bear for their services. This prevents them from undervaluing their services, he said; and when I asked about providing services to those who cannot afford them, he responded that it is only by charging a fair market rate for your services that they will be able to offer services at a discount rate or *pro bono*.

Protect International offers discounted rates for certain groups. As noted previously, a discount of fifty percent is offered to full-time students in graduate programs at accredited educational institutions who attend its "open" (i.e., open to all comers) trainings. In addition, it routinely offers a discount of fifty percent on products and services to charitable organizations staffed by volunteers or in countries with developing economies. Finally, it offers discounted or *pro bono* products and services on a case-by-case basis. For example, Protect International has provided investigation and risk assessment services well below its standard rate or *pro bono* in relation to matters of urgency or public interest or when funding for such services is simply unavailable.

Can Your Work Be Replicated?

Yes. The philosophy underlying Protect International's work is that, with appropriate structure and good training, any reasonably competent professional should be able to replicate the services Protect International provides.

That said, it is difficult for most psychologists to think about business except in terms of private practice. As I frequently say, many psychologists are cats, happy to work alone and unhappy to change their way of doing things to fit the needs or preferences of a group. Establishing a business in the form of a group-based practice or a company is only appropriate for people who love interacting and collaborating with others, are willing to accommodate to become a part of something bigger than themselves, and can admit to themselves that they are not the best at everything.

Diversity, Equity, and Inclusiveness (DEI)

Incorporating DEI

DEI considerations are part of daily life at Protect International. Of six regular employees, three were born outside of Canada, including two who did not speak English as a first language; five of the six identify as female. The office is located in Metro Vancouver, where more than forty-five percent of the citizens were born outside of Canada and speak a first language other than English or French. Protect International also delivers services around the world. When delivering services, many of the people it works with are diverse with respect to gender, gender identity, or sexual preference; race, nationality, culture, ethnicity, language; age or developmental status; and physical or mental health. Finally, Protect International's work sometimes is directly related to diversity. For example, employees have consulted with agencies and provided expert evidence internationally related to risk assessment and management of people from racial and ethnic minorities and transgender people and provided education and training related to respecting diversity when conducting investigations and risk assessments.

Changes in DEI Considerations

Protect International's work has not really changed over the last decade with respect to DEI. Perhaps the sole exception is that the popularity of its products has required it to make them available in a modified format to better serve people with visual impairments.

Access to Services by Minority Group Individuals

Protect International's products and services are not difficult for minority group individuals to access, as we operate on a business-to-business basis and are willing to provide products and services at a discounted rate or *pro bono*.

Important Priorities

Protect International will continue its work in this area, particularly in relation to education and training related to respecting diversity when conducting investigations and risk assessments.

Advice to Others Seeking to Provide Similar Services

Gauging the Market

If you are active in your field, I do not know if it is necessary to do any complicated market research. Your market research is your own service delivery, as well as your interaction with other service providers and potential clients at events such as trainings, seminars, and conferences. You should be aware already of what clients need, what is available, and, therefore, what and where opportunities exist. Of course, talking to people—especially potential clients—never hurts!

Protect International was established with the intention of doing business internationally to provide opportunities for growth. Even if you want to stay in your home country, try to minimize reliance on a single, smaller market that may be vulnerable to local pressures, such as economic or budgetary downturns or changes in law or policy. Make sure your services are not parochial, that is, not hyper-optimized for delivery in a particular jurisdiction.

Starting Up

As is true for almost everything in life, preparation is key. Once you have some good ideas about available opportunities for service delivery, research the best ways to do that work. Get the training, materials, and experience you need to do a good job.

If you are thinking about establishing a company, think about various options. What services will you deliver, in which markets, and using how many people for service provision and administration? Who will own the business? Who will manage day-to-day operations? What will be required to get things up and running—an office, a business license, bank accounts, insurance, and a loan?[3] What would a budget look like in terms of anticipated revenues and expenditures? And one critical thing you should consider from the outset: What is your end game or exit plan? Is your dream to run a services company where you pay yourself and your partners, shareholders, and employees as much as possible until you retire? Do you want to pay people slightly less and build up cash reserves to fund business development? Or do you want to establish something that accrues value over time in terms of real or intellectual property, which can be passed on or sold when you retire? At what age do you hope to retire?

When you are ready to start working on plans, meet with a lawyer to figure out the best kind of company to establish (there are different types of corporations in different jurisdictions), what kind of ownership structure would be ideal,

[3] My advice, for what it is worth: If at all possible, avoid borrowing money from the bank for expenses related to start-up, operations, or business development. If you want to borrow money, the best reason is to purchase real estate for an office. This way, instead of paying rent, the business makes mortgage payments and acquires an asset that will increase its value when it comes time for you to exit.

what a partnership or shareholder agreement should look like, and where the best places to incorporate would be. Then start looking for potential partners, investors, and employees. Remember that business partners or investors are like life partners. You will need to work hard to keep your relationships with them healthy, as things may get rocky at times; and they may even end, despite your wishes or best efforts. Make sure your plans anticipate potential problems and are flexible enough to accommodate other people's needs and wishes. Do not get too involved or wrapped up with people unless and until you are aware of their strengths and limitations, as well as your own, and know you can work with them even when things get stressful.

Next, start working on operations. Read some books about running human services and other small businesses. Read some more books and watch some videos about budgeting and reading a profit and loss statement. Consult with an accountant about setting up procedures for invoicing, bookkeeping, and taxes. Find an experienced businessperson to recruit as a mentor—it does not matter what kind of business they are in!—with whom you can discuss everything from strategy to troubleshooting minor problems.

Lastly, once you are approaching the launch date, you need to finalize a name and branding. Do not cheap out here; pay someone to help you develop a name, logo, website, and communications template you will be able to live with for at least 5 years or so. Read even more books about marketing and sales.

Specialization

Should you specialize in the services you deliver? Yes! Within reason, of course. There should be some clear theme that ties together the products and services your company will provide. This will be captured in your branding and reinforced through your marketing. If you do not have a clear theme, then everything will lack coherence and you will give the impression that you do not really know what you are doing or, perhaps worse, you do not recognize your own expertise (or limitations) and are willing to do anything for money.

Publicity

Your work should speak for itself. There is nothing wrong with telling people at professional meetings or in professional publications about the work your company does and has done. But Protect International has never spent money on public relations or broadcast advertising. Also, its employees are cautious when speaking to the media or posting online. Our clients value their privacy and our good judgment; they do not want us to promote ourselves by identifying them as our clients or seeking publicity for its own sake. I recommend spending more time speaking with clients and potential clients face-to-face and less time posting on LinkedIn or appearing as a talking head for 15 seconds on the national news.

Concluding Comments

I am happy to have established a company. It is immensely satisfying to have increased the implementation and public impact of the research I have done over the past forty years. It is just as satisfying to have used the social capital I built up in my position as an academic to help support the livelihood of more than a dozen other people. If you are not a cat, maybe it is for you, too.

References

Boer, D. P., Hart, S. D., Kropp, P. R., & Webster, C. D. (1997). *Manual for the Sexual Violence Risk – 20: Professional guidelines for assessing risk of sexual violence.* Mental Health, Law, & Policy Institute, Simon Fraser University.

Boer, D. P., Hart, S. D., Kropp, P. R., & Webster, C. D. (2017). *Manual for the Sexual Violence Risk – 20, Version 2: Professional guidelines for assessing risk of sexual violence.* Protect International.

Douglas, K. S., Ogloff, J. R. P., & Hard, S. D. (2003). Evaluation of a model of violence risk assessment among forensic psychiatric patients. *Psychiatric Services, 54*(10), 1372–1379. https://doi.org/10.1176/appi.ps.54.10.1372

Hart, S. D., Douglas, K. S., & Guy, L. S. (2016). The structured professional judgment approach to violence risk assessment: Origins, nature, and advances. In L. Craig & M. Rettenberger (Volume Eds.) and D. Boer (Series Ed.), *The Wiley handbook on the theories, assessment, treatment of sexual offending: Volume II. Assessment* (pp. 643–666). Wiley.

Hart, S. D., Kropp, P. R., Laws, D. R., Klaver, J., Logan, C., & Watt, K. A. (2003). *The Risk for Sexual Violence Protocol (RSVP): Structured professional guidelines for assessing risk of sexual violence.* Mental Health, Law, and Policy Institute, Simon Fraser University.

Hart, S. D., Kropp, P. R., Watt, K. A., Darjee, R., Davis, M. R., Klaver, J. A., Laws, D. R., Logan, C. (2022). *RSVP-V2: Version 2 of the Risk for Sexual Violence Protocol.* Protect International.

Kropp, P. R., Belfrage, H., & Hart, S. D. (2020). *Assessment of risk for honour based violence (PATRIARCH), Version 2: User manual.* Protect International.

Kropp, P. R., & Hart, S. D. (2015). *SARA-V3: Manual for Version 3 of the Spousal Assault Risk Assessment Guide.* Protect International.

Kropp, P. R., Hart, S. D., & Lyon, D. (2024). *Guidelines for Stalking Assessment and Management, Version 2 (SAM-V2): User guide.* Protect International.

Kropp, P. R., Hart, S. D., Webster, C. D., & Eaves, D. (1994). *Manual for the Spousal Assault Risk Assessment Guide*. British Columbia Institute Against Family Violence.

Storey, J. E., Hart, S. D., & Kropp, P. R. (2021). *HOPE: User Manual for the Harm to Older Persons Evaluation*. Countering and Ending Abuse via Structured Evaluation (CEASE) International and Protect International.

Watt, K. A., Hart, S. D., Rypdal, K., & Hoff, H. A. (2023). *Aid for Violence Risk Triage (AVRT): User guide*. Protect International.

Webster, C. D., Douglas, K. S., Eaves, D., & Hart, S. D. (1997). *HCR-20: Assessing risk for violence* (Version 2). Mental Health, Law, & Policy Institute, Simon Fraser University.

23

Psychological Services in the Community with Justice-Involved Individuals and to Forensic Systems

Why We Are Optimistic

David DeMatteo and Kirk Heilbrun

Throughout this book, we have attempted to capture some of the most distinctive, necessary, and relevant services provided by psychologists to individuals and systems in the contexts of juvenile and criminal justice. We did not set out to be comprehensive in covering the range of topics and services that are provided by psychologists with justice-involved individuals and systems. Instead, we focused on important services provided in a specialized fashion, with particular emphasis on established projects that reflect "best practices," or projects that have the potential for growth and widespread adoption in the coming years as the empirical base continues to develop.

This succeeded far beyond our expectations. The credit for this goes almost entirely to the individuals and organizations described by these chapter contributors. Across these chapters, you will see how the early beginnings of forensic psychology have evolved, how this specialty has become better integrated with other areas within psychology while maintaining a strong connection with law, how intervention *and* assessment are now both viable components, how we provide research and training in specialized areas, and how specialized tools have become vital in the areas of assessment, intervention, policy research, and consultation. You can also appraise the remarkable successes of these particular projects, and judge the combination of personal characteristics and substance that will be needed to continue and refine them—and to develop similar, cutting-edge work as our society evolves.

In this final chapter, we distill the highlights, lessons, and themes from the previous chapters. First, we discuss what these chapters can teach us about the provision of community-based psychological services with justice-involved individuals. In the aggregate, these chapters effectively illustrate key points about providing psychological services in the community, whether with individuals or to systems. Second, we

David DeMatteo and Kirk Heilbrun, *Psychological Services in the Community with Justice-Involved Individuals and to Forensic Systems.* In: *The Path Forward.* Edited by: Kirk Heilbrun and David DeMatteo, Oxford University Press.
 DOI: 10.1093/9780197773031.003.0023

identify the common elements of the projects described in the chapters. Focusing on lessons learned and common elements in these chapters provides a blueprint for the field, hopefully contributing to the improvement of existing services, the retention of high priorities, and the development of new services.

Lessons Learned

The wide variety of projects and initiatives described in this book makes it challenging—although exciting—to identify the key take-home points. The book's chapters address a range of topics in several distinct domains, including assessment, intervention, consultation, and education, so distilling these chapters to a few key points could be reductionistic or overly simplistic. But we believe there is value in identifying and summarizing what we can learn from the chapters. As such, we focus on three key points.

First, when viewed in the aggregate, the clearest take-home message is that the field has developed a number of important and needed projects and initiatives that are making valuable contributions to the delivery of community-based psychological services with justice-involved individuals. Although there has often been a focus on "best practices" in the provision of psychological services to justice-involved individuals in carceral settings, this book illustrates the exceptional efforts that are being made to provide *community-based* psychological services. Given continued efforts to reduce the number of incarcerated individuals in the United States, particularly among individuals with behavioral health needs, the provision of community-based psychological services with justice-involved individuals will hopefully become more important. As such, the chapters included in this book should be viewed as models for practitioners, clinical administrators, and policymakers whose work is relevant to justice-involved individuals.

Second, the chapters illustrate that important services with justice-involved individuals and to forensic systems are being provided in different domains: (1) forensic mental health assessment, (2) interventions, (3) consultation and program development, and (4) education. These four domains, which encompass an impressive range of community-based services, illustrate two things. First, the projects described in the chapters provide a snapshot of our field's current focus on community-based psychological services in these areas. That snapshot reveals a number of ways in which psychologists are focusing on community-based forensic services. Second, the projects described in this book provide an exciting preview of how the field might develop. This focus on forward-thinking and novel initiatives highlights the potential for continued growth in the nature, range, and quality of community-based services that are relevant for justice-involved individuals. When viewed through this lens, this book helps to inform planning for the field's continued development.

Accordingly, we hope readers will be inspired to develop, implement, evaluate, and refine community-based services with justice-involved individuals and systems.

Although these chapters describe a range of projects that span multiple domains, there is clearly room for continued growth beyond the areas that have been highlighted in this book. For example, as some services shift from carceral to community settings, there will be an increasing need to expand existing services, improve those services, and develop and implement new services based on existing or emerging needs. The "competency crisis" (see Murrie et al., this volume), for instance, highlights the need for additional services to meet the higher demand, for improvement in existing services, and for the development of new community-based services to address the growing number of justice-involved individuals who present with trial competency challenges. We encourage readers to think broadly and creatively. Some of the novel services described in this book were probably viewed with skepticism when they were initially proposed, but they have subsequently made valuable contributions to our collective work with justice-involved individuals.

Third, the chapters included in this book illustrate the importance of training and continuing education for those involved in developing, implementing, and evaluating these community-based services. When discussing service provision, particularly with justice-involved individuals, some resources provide limited coverage of training and education; we included a section on those topics because we believe they are foundational to effective service development, provision, and evaluation. Professionals with proper training in clinical assessment, intervention, research design/methodology, and data analysis, among other areas, are well-positioned to develop, implement, empirically examine, and refine community-based programs relevant to justice-involved individuals. Those efforts are further enhanced when working collaboratively with individuals from other professional disciplines who have complementary expertise. This book also provided several examples of specific training for those involved in providing community-based services with justice-involved individuals, including trauma-informed training for correctional staff (see Timme, this volume) and expert testimony training (see Brodsky, this volume). There is also a chapter addressing continuing education and consultation related to broader policy (see Desmarais et al., this volume), which includes valuable information about translating research into policy. All of these efforts, at both the predoctoral and post-doctoral stages, provide an effective foundation for the provision of relevant community-based services.

Comment Elements

The chapters in this book describe a range of projects, initiatives, and services. While some focus on assessment and intervention, which are the more traditional components of psychological practice, others focus on consultation, program development, and education/training. Despite the wide range of these projects, it is apparent that they (and the individuals involved in them) share some common elements, which we discuss in this section.

Identified Need and Relevant Expertise

The projects described in this book often began with the identification of a particular need (or market), combined with the professional interests and expertise of motivated individuals. For example, recognition of the importance of intersectionality among justice-involved individuals led Ratkalkar (this volume) to outline an approach that thoughtfully considers an examinee's intersectional identity in the context of forensic mental health assessment. A second example: the high rates of mental illness among justice-involved individuals in correctional settings led Morgan and colleagues (2018) to develop *Changing Lives and Changing Outcomes* (*CLCO*), an intervention designed to address mental illness and criminal risk among individuals involved in the criminal justice system (see Kroner & Morgan, this volume). In both of these examples (and many others from different chapters), the project work began because a recognized need was not being sufficiently addressed through existing services. Further, in both examples, psychologists were motivated by their professional interests to apply their particular expertise toward developing an approach or program to meet the identified need.

Developing new initiatives is rarely easy or straightforward. It takes time, effort, and often persistence. It can be challenging to convince stakeholders to adopt a new way of doing things, particularly when some services have been used for many years. However, rather than accepting the status quo, or deciding to work within existing structures that were not sufficient, many of the chapter authors sought to greatly improve existing services or develop new ones. These chapters reflect the work of many who have undertaken these efforts with dedication, vigor, and passion. The desire for attention, renown, and financial compensation does not appear to be a primary motivating factor for these chapter authors (although these sometimes accrue). In short, the powerful combination of identified need, subject matter expertise, and motivation has been effective in refining or developing community-based services with justice-involved individuals and systems in a remarkably successful fashion.

Adaptation of Existing Structures

Many of the projects described in this book are adaptations or extensions of well-established approaches based on a specific identified need or context. For example, recognition of the prevalence and role of trauma among justice-involved adolescents led Zelechoski and colleagues (this volume) to develop and refine a trauma-informed approach for conducting forensic mental health assessments with youth. Their approach is based on established principles of forensic mental health assessment (see Heilbrun, 2001; Heilbrun et al., 2009), which they adapted based on the specific needs of the population for which their approach is intended. As another example, recovery-oriented cognitive therapy (CT-R; Beck et al., 2021), a cognitive-behavioral approach for working with individuals involved with the criminal justice system, is based on the foundational principles and strategies of cognitive therapy (see Arnold et al., this volume). For a third example, King et al. (this volume) describe a brief intervention for community reentry that was largely informed by the principles of Dialectical Behavior Therapy (DBT; Linehan, 1993) and the Risk-Need-Responsivity (RNR) model (Bonta & Andrews, 2024). Relying on existing and established structures provides a solid empirical and theoretical foundation for many of the adapted approaches and initiatives described in the chapters.

Forensic Psychology, Correctional Psychology, and Police Psychology

There are important differences among the specialty areas of forensic psychology (American Psychological Association, 2013), correctional psychology (see Neal, 2018), and police psychology (American Psychological Association, 2023). We noted earlier in Chapter 1 that traditional professional boundaries would describe forensic psychology as applicable to legal decisions made prior to conviction, correctional psychology as applicable to post-conviction classification and rehabilitation of offenders, and police and public safety psychology as related to officer selection and promotion of effective performance.

Some of the services and initiatives described in this book cannot be understood using only these traditional boundaries, however. For example, some projects would not be considered clearly forensic or clearly correctional, because they contain elements of both. Evaluations of risk for violence are a good example: they can be conducted pretrial, which would place them within the realm of forensic psychology, or at the beginning of an individual's incarceration to determine classification and placement, which would put them within the correctional psychology domain. Rather than adhering to strict boundaries, the projects described in this book often demonstrate overlap across these traditional specialty areas. Nowhere is this better illustrated than in the application of the Sequential Intercept Model to systems mapping (Griffin et al., this volume), which is used to modify systems and policy toward the more effective treatment of multiple justice-involved individuals. Understanding these boundaries, and acquiring the tools to work within (and beyond) them, is greatly facilitated by specialized training at the predoctoral level (DeMatteo et al., this volume), postdoctoral level (Anumba et al., this volume), and continuing professional level (Brodsky, this volume; Dvoskin, this volume).

Applied Science

The assessment and intervention approaches described throughout this book focus on the provision of clinical services with justice-involved individuals. Both assessment and intervention play important and distinctive roles for the individuals to whom the services are provided, the criminal justice system, and society more broadly. For example, forensic mental health assessments assist legal decision-makers to make better-informed decisions about a variety of legal issues, ranging from competence to stand trial and the appropriateness of pretrial release to criminal responsibility and capital sentencing. Interventions with justice-involved individuals are often a key component in a treatment plan intended to reduce the risk of recidivism and/or address behavioral health needs (e.g., substance use) that increase the likelihood of future contact with the criminal justice system.

Given the central importance of assessment and intervention services and the various contexts in which those services are provided, these clinical services should be supported by applied research. Relying on such methodologically sound research provides a defensible empirical basis and foundational effectiveness guidance for the provision of those services. For instance, the Denver FIRST Juvenile Justice Project described by Alexander and Vozar (this volume) provides trauma treatment services to juvenile justice system-involved girls and nonbinary youth. The primary intervention used in the Denver First program was Trauma-Focused Cognitive Behavioral Therapy (TF-CBT; see Ramirez de Arellano et al., 2014), which is recognized as a Model Program by the Substance Abuse and Mental Health Services Administration (SAMHSA); there are extensive outcome data from randomized controlled trials that support TF-CBT's effectiveness in reducing posttraumatic stress disorder (PTSD) symptoms and depressive symptoms for racial and ethnic minorities and LGBTQ subpopulations, who have disproportionately higher rates of substance use disorders. As another example, *National Youth Screening and Assessment Partners*, LLC, (see Grisso et al., this volume) relies on research in implementation science to identify strategies essential for fidelity to and sustainability of evidence-based assessment practices in juvenile justice contexts. As a third example, the systematic multi-disciplinary process of school-based threat assessment, with effectiveness supported by substantial research, has made schools safer while reducing the harm to individuals who make threats (Cornell & Kerere, this volume). Such empirically grounded initiatives. Empirically grounded initiatives demonstrate the value of relying on applied science in the development and provision of services.

Collaboration

Another common element across many of the projects and initiatives described in this book is collaboration. These chapters demonstrate that collaboration can take several different forms and involve a range of entities. Some of the collaborations are between universities and government entities; others are between two private entities or between individual psychologists and governmental entities. For example, Kroner and Morgan (this volume) described the implementation of *Changing Lives and Changing Outcomes* in a sample of criminal justice-involved persons with mental illness involving a collaboration between the Harris County (Texas) Community Supervision and Corrections Department and Texas Tech University. Desmarais et al. (this volume) described how Policy Research Associates operated the Competence to Stand Trial/Competence Restoration Learning Collaborative within SAMHSA's GAINS Center. Treatment courts, as described by Marlowe (this volume), rely on a collaborative and non-adversarial team approach among the prosecutors, defense attorneys, case managers, and treatment providers. NeMoyer et al. (this volume) highlight the importance of collaborative problem-solving when psychologists are working with probation departments, as do Tucker and Rice (this volume) in working with police. These efforts highlight the increasingly important role of collaboration in providing services to justice-involved individuals.

There are several benefits to the types of collaboration described throughout this book. Among other benefits, collaboration combines the knowledge and experience of varied stakeholders, reduces groupthink, provides a voice to individuals with diverse expertise, and leverages the resources of multiple entities. Justice-involved individuals may be involved with various entities and systems, both overlapping and independent. A justice-involved individual, for instance, may be under the supervision of the correctional system (e.g., probation, parole) and also receiving mental health and related services from a city-contracted treatment agency. For those individuals, a collaborative approach involving experts and stakeholders from both systems would likely be most effective. The types of collaborations described in this book effectively enhance the services that are provided.

Dissemination and Implementation

Many of the projects and initiatives described in this book demonstrate the value of focusing on both dissemination and implementation. Ideally, a new initiative would have demonstrated empirical support before being disseminated more broadly. For example, an intervention designed to address criminogenic needs should be supported by research indicating that it does so before wider adoption of the intervention. Such research may involve, among other things, demonstrating the relationship between criminogenic needs and risk-relevant outcomes in a particular population, experimentally examining whether the new intervention reduces criminogenic needs and relevant outcomes, and using a dismantling research design to identify the effective components of the intervention. This type of outcome-focused research provides an empirical foundation to support the wider dissemination of the intervention.

In addition to addressing an intervention's relationship to relevant outcomes and identifying the effective components of an intervention, it is important to address considerations related to the implementation of an intervention. An intervention that is demonstrated to be effective under controlled research conditions has limited real-world value if it cannot be integrated into practice. If there are barriers that would prevent or limit the implementation of the intervention, those barriers must first be identified. Toward this end, the field of implementation science can be instructive (see Viljoen & Vincent, 2024). Implementation science is broadly defined as the study of methods and strategies that facilitate the systematic uptake of evidence-based research and practice into use by practitioners and policymakers (see Eccles & Mittman, 2006). Implementation science is also an attempt to close the gap between what we *know* and what we *do*, which has been called the "know-do gap" (e.g., Donohue et al., 2023; Skolarus & Williams, 2024), by identifying the structural barriers that limit effective implementation of empirically supported practices. Several of the chapters in this book highlight the importance of the implementation of what we know. For example, as described by Desmarais et al. (this volume), Policy Research Associates' research and evaluation services focus on analyzing policy implementation and impact in several related fields, including behavioral health, youth development, and the criminal justice system. The dissemination and implementation of evidence-based services has benefits for the individual clients who receive those services, the broader systems in which those services are provided (e.g., criminal justice, juvenile justice, behavioral healthcare), and our larger society.

Integration with Established and Emerging Priorities of Contemporary Society

A final important consideration involves the effort by many of the chapter authors to offer services that are consistent with both established and emerging societal priorities. Many stakeholders in the criminal justice and mental health fields believe that the number of incarcerated individuals in the United States should be reduced, particularly those individuals with certain behavioral health needs (e.g., substance use, mental illness). There is also recognition that many of these individuals would benefit from receiving services in the community to address their criminogenic and mental health needs, which will hopefully reduce the likelihood that they will have further involvement with the criminal justice system. As such, this book's focus on community-based psychological services underscores the priority of reducing the carceral population in the United States while also protecting public safety. Organization consultation and the development and dissemination of specialized risk appraisal measures (see Hart, this volume) provide an excellent example of applying science to a societal priority of reducing antisocial conduct in various community contexts.

Additionally, diversity considerations among justice-involved individuals have received increasing attention in recent years. Justice-involved individuals present with a range of diverse demographic characteristics and cultural backgrounds, and there is increasing recognition that diversity, broadly defined, should be considered when developing, providing, and evaluating psychological services. There is also agreement among many within the criminal justice and mental health fields that a one-size-fits-all approach should no longer be the default expectation, and that diversity must be considered in assessment, intervention, and education. Many of the services described in the chapters reflect that focus.

Finally, many of the programs and initiatives described in these chapters reflect a focus on rehabilitative efforts. The criminal justice system is largely based on a punitive model that prioritizes incapacitation, deterrence, and retribution. Many would argue that rehabilitation is not a primary focus of the criminal justice system (in contrast with the juvenile justice system, which prioritizes rehabilitation). However, in recent decades, there has been growing recognition that the legal system can improve the psychological and emotional health of justice-involved individuals while still addressing accountability and public safety. This idea is an important aspect of therapeutic jurisprudence (see Wexler & Winick, 1991, 1996; Winick & Wexler, 2003). The increased focus on rehabilitation among justice-involved individuals is perhaps seen mostly clearly in problem-solving courts (see DeMatteo et al., 2019; Marlowe, this volume; Winick, 2003), which use a non-adversarial team approach to address the criminogenic and mental health needs of justice-involved individuals. A focus on rehabilitation is also seen among some of the more traditional clinical interventions discussed in this book, including both cognitive-behavioral interventions (Heilbrun et al., this volume) and recovery-oriented cognitive therapy (Arnold et al., this volume) with justice-involved individuals.

Conclusion

We are pleased to highlight the impressive work, seen throughout this book, being done by mental health professionals with justice-involved individuals and systems in the community. Over the past few decades, numerous efforts have been made to refine or develop various services in assessment, intervention, and consultative contexts. As always, there is more work to do. Existing services can be (further) evaluated and refined, new initiatives can be developed and tested, and dissemination of research findings can be enhanced. An increased focus on implementation science would add benefits by expanding our knowledge of how well these services work. But the need for further work should not detract from the impressive efforts of many individuals who have focused on providing and improving the community-based services described throughout this book. They have made this area stronger, and they offer reasons to believe that it will grow stronger yet—toward improving the lives of justice-involved individuals while promoting public safety in our communities.

References

Alexander, A. A., & Vozar, T. M. (xxxx). Treating trauma in justice-involved girls. In K. Heilbrun & D. DeMatteo (Eds.), *The path forward: Psychological services in the community with justice-involved individuals and to forensic systems* (pp. xx–xx). Oxford University Press.

American Psychological Association. (2013). Specialty guidelines for forensic psychology. *American Psychologist*, *68*(1), 7–19. http://dx.doi.org/10.1037/a0029889

American Psychological Association. (2023). *Specialties and subspecialties: Police and public safety psychology*. https://www.apa.org/ed/graduate/specialize/police.

Anumba, N., Putney, H., Burl, J., & Murray, A. (xxxx). Internship and postdoctoral training in forensic psychology. In K. Heilbrun & D. DeMatteo (Eds.), *The path forward: Psychological services in the community with justice-involved individuals and to forensic systems* (pp. xx–xx). Oxford University Press.

Arnold, S., Pinto, L., & Grant, P. M. (xxxx). Recovery-Oriented Cognitive Therapy for justice-involved individuals. In K. Heilbrun & D. DeMatteo (Eds.), *The path forward: Psychological services in the community with justice-involved individuals and to forensic systems* (pp. xx–xx). Oxford University Press.

Beck, A. T., Grant, P. M., Inverso, E., Brinen, A. P., & Perivoliotis, D. (2021). *Recovery-Oriented Cognitive Therapy for serious mental health conditions.* Guilford Press.

Bonta, J., & Andrews, D. A. (2024). *The psychology of criminal conduct* (7th ed.). Routledge.

Brodsky, S. L. (xxxx). Expert witness training. In K. Heilbrun & D. DeMatteo (Eds.), *The path forward: Psychological services in the community with justice-involved individuals and to forensic systems* (pp. xx–xx). Oxford University Press.

Cornell, D., & Kerere, J. (xxxx). Behavioral threat assessment in schools. In K. Heilbrun & D. DeMatteo (Eds.), *The path forward: Community-based psychological services with justice-involved individuals* (pp. xx–xx). Oxford University Press.

DeMatteo, D., Heilbrun, K., Thornewill, A., & Arnold, S. (2019). *Problem-solving courts and the criminal justice system.* Oxford University Press.

DeMatteo, D., Kanani, H., Grisamore, S., & Chard, A. (xxxx). Doctoral training in forensic psychology. In K. Heilbrun & D. DeMatteo (Eds.), *The path forward: Psychological services in the community with justice-involved individuals and to forensic systems* (pp. xx–xx). Oxford University Press.

Desmarais, S. L., Hope, E. C., Davis, H., & Bader, S. M. (xxxx). Policy research and education services: The Policy Research Associates (PRA) approach. In K. Heilbrun & D. DeMatteo (Eds.), *The path forward: Psychological services in the community with justice-involved individuals and to forensic systems* (pp. xx–xx). Oxford University Press.

Donohue, J. F., Elborn, J. S., Lansberg, P., Javed, A., Tesfaye, S., Rugo, H., ... Chan, J. C. (2023). Bridging the "know-do" gaps in five non-communicable diseases using a common framework driven by implementation science. *Journal of Healthcare Leadership, 15*, 103–119. https://doi.org/10.2147/JHL.S394088

Dvoskin, J. (xxxx). Forensic consultation. In K. Heilbrun & D. DeMatteo (Eds.), *The path forward: Psychological services in the community with justice-involved individuals and to forensic systems* (pp. xx–xx). Oxford University Press.

Eccles, M. P., & Mittman, B. S. (2006). Welcome to *Implementation Science. Implementation Science, 1*, 1. https://doi.org/10.1186/1748-5908-1-1

Griffin, P. A., Kemp, K., & Giallella, C. (xxxx). Cross-systems mapping using the Sequential Intercept Model. y. In K. Heilbrun & D. DeMatteo (Eds.), *The path forward:*

Psychological services in the community with justice-involved individuals and to forensic systems (pp. xx–xx). Oxford University Press.

Grisso, T., Vincent, G., & Kruk, I. (xxxx). NYSAP, LLC: Implementing evidence-based screening and assessment in juvenile justice. In K. Heilbrun & D. DeMatteo (Eds.), *The path forward: Psychological services in the community with justice-involved individuals and to forensic systems* (pp. xx–xx). Oxford University Press.

Heilbrun, K. (2001). *Principles of forensic mental health assessment*. Kluwer Academic/Plenum Press.

Heilbrun, K., Fasone, H., Wiltsie, K., Zapotocky, H., Jackson, C., & Huppert, T. (xxxx). Cognitive behavioral therapy and interventions with justice-involved individuals. In K. Heilbrun & D. DeMatteo (Eds.), *The path forward: Psychological services in the community with justice-involved individuals and to forensic systems* (pp. xx–xx). Oxford University Press.

Heilbrun, K., Grisso, T., & Goldstein, A. M. (2009). *Foundations of forensic mental health assessment*. Oxford University Press.

King, C. M., Vora, S., Cuellar, S., Gonzales, J., & Rosenfeld, B. (xxxx). An intervention for community reentry informed by dialectical behavior therapy. In K. Heilbrun & D. DeMatteo (Eds.), *The path forward: Psychological services in the community with justice-involved individuals and to forensic systems* (pp. xx–xx). Oxford University Press.

Kroner, D. G., & Morgan, R. D. (xxxx). Interventions among criminal justice involved persons with mental illness: Implementing Changing Lives and Changing Outcomes in Harris County. In K. Heilbrun & D. DeMatteo (Eds.), *The path forward: Psychological services in the community with justice-involved individuals and to forensic systems* (pp. xx–xx). Oxford University Press.

Linehan, M. M. (1993). *Cognitive-behavioral treatment of borderline personality disorder*. Guilford Press.

Marlowe, D. B. (xxxx). Consultation on treatment court development and implementation. In K. Heilbrun & D. DeMatteo (Eds.), *The path forward: Psychological services in the community with justice-involved individuals and to forensic systems* (pp. xx–xx). Oxford University Press.

Morgan, R. D., Kroner, D. G., & Mills, J. F. (2018). *A treatment manual for justice involved persons with mental illness: Changing Lives and Changing Outcomes*. Routledge.

Murrie, D. C., Agee, E., & Kelley, S. (xxxx). University clinic-based forensic mental health assessment. In K. Heilbrun & D. DeMatteo (Eds.), *The path forward: Psychological services in the community with justice-involved individuals and to forensic systems* (pp. xx–xx). Oxford University Press.

Neal, T. M. S. (2018). Forensic psychology and correctional psychology: Distinct but related subfields of psychological science and practice. *American Psychologist*, *73*(5), 651–662. http://dx.doi.org/10.1037/amp0000227

NeMoyer, A., McPhee, J., Papumen, I., Kreimer, R., & Goldstein, N. (xxxx). Consultation and program development: juvenile probation. In K. Heilbrun & D. DeMatteo

(Eds.), *The path forward: Psychological services in the community with justice-involved individuals and to forensic systems* (pp. xx–xx). Oxford University Press.

Ramirez de Arellano, M. A., Lyman, R., Jobe-Shields, L., George, P., Dougherty, R. H., Daniels, A. S., Ghose, S. S., Huang, L., & Delphin-Rittmon, M. E. (2014). Trauma-Focused Cognitive-Behavioral Therapy for children and adolescents: Assessing the evidence. *Psychiatric Services, 65*(5), 591–602. https://doi.org/10.1176/appi.ps.201300255

Ratkalkar, M. (xxxx). Considering intersectional identity in forensic mental health assessment. In K. Heilbrun & D. DeMatteo (Eds.), *The path forward: Psychological services in the community with justice-involved individuals and to forensic systems* (pp. xx–xx). Oxford University Press.

Skolarus, L. E., & Williams, L. S. (2024). Implementation research: An approach to overcoming the know-do gap. *The Lancet Neurology, 23*(7), 656–658. https://doi.org/10.1016/S1474-4422(24)00219-9

Timme, R. (xxxx). Trauma-informed training for correctional officers. In K. Heilbrun & D. DeMatteo (Eds.), *The path forward: Psychological services in the community with justice-involved individuals and to forensic systems* (pp. xx–xx). Oxford University Press.

Tucker, A., & Rice, K. Law enforcement consultation on Active Bystandership for Law Enforcement (ABLE). In K. Heilbrun & D. DeMatteo (Eds.), *The path forward: Psychological services in the community with justice-involved individuals and to forensic systems* (pp. xx–xx). Oxford University Press.

Viljoen, J. L., & Vincent, G. M. (2024). Risk assessments for violence and reoffending: Implementation and impact on risk management. *Clinical Psychology: Science and Practice, 31*(2), 119–131. https://doi.org/10.1111/cpsp.12378

Wexler, D. B., & Winick, B. J. (1991). *Essays in therapeutic jurisprudence*. Carolina Academic Press.

Wexler, D. B., & Winick, B. J. (1996). *Law in a therapeutic key: Developments in therapeutic jurisprudence*. Carolina Academic Press.

Winick, B. J. (2003). Therapeutic jurisprudence and problem solving courts. *Fordham Urban Law Journal, 30*(3), 1055–1090.

Winick, B. J., & Wexler, D. B. (Eds.). (2003). *Judging in a therapeutic key: Therapeutic jurisprudence and the courts*. Carolina Academic Press.

Zelechoski, A. D., Baetz, C. L., Thompson, K., Roberts, E., & Cenzon, E. (xxxx). Conducting forensic mental health assessments with youth: A trauma-informed approach. In K. Heilbrun & D. DeMatteo (Eds.), *The path forward: Psychological services in the community with justice-involved individuals and to forensic systems* (pp. xx–xx). Oxford University Press.

Index

For the benefit of digital users, indexed terms that span two pages (e.g., 52–53) may, on occasion, appear on only one of those pages.

Tables and figures are indicated by an italic *t* and *f* following the page number.